Constitutional Moments

History of European Political and Constitutional Thought

VOLUME 11

The titles published in this series are listed at *brill.com/hepct*

Constitutional Moments

Founding Myths, Charters and Constitutions through History

Edited by

Xavier Gil

BRILL

LEIDEN | BOSTON

Francisco Vázquez de Mendieta, *The Oath of the Laws of the Seignoiry of Biscay by Ferdinand the Catholic* (c. 1609), House of the Assembly of Gernika (Biscay). Reproduced with permission.

Library of Congress Cataloging-in-Publication Data

Names: Gil Pujol, Javier, editor.
Title: Constitutional moments : founding myths, charters and constitutions through history / edited by Xavier Gil.
Description: Leiden ; Boston : Brill, 2024. | Series: History of European political and constitutional thought, 2589-5966 ; volume 11 | Includes index.
Identifiers: LCCN 2023045814 (print) | LCCN 2023045815 (ebook) | ISBN 9789004549135 (hardcover) | ISBN 9789004549159 (ebook)
Subjects: LCSH: Constitutional history. | Constitutional law. | Constitutional law–Political aspects. | Constitutional law–Philosophy. | Constitutions. | Charters.
Classification: LCC K3161 .C6665 2024 (print) | LCC K3161 (ebook) | DDC 342–dc23/eng/20231002
LC record available at https://lccn.loc.gov/2023045814
LC ebook record available at https://lccn.loc.gov/2023045815

Typeface for the Latin, Greek, and Cyrillic scripts: "Brill". See and download: brill.com/brill-typeface.

ISSN 2589-5966
ISBN 978-90-04-54913-5 (hardback)
ISBN 978-90-04-54915-9 (e-book)
DOI 10.1163/9789004549159

Contents

Illustrations

Notes on Contributors

Jon Arrieta
is full professor of History of Law at the University of the Basque Country. He is specialist on public institutions of the kingdoms of the Crown of Aragon during the Early Modern period, with special attention to the War of Spanish Succession, the so called Austracists and the Decrees of Nueva Planta. More recently he studies the forms of union in the making of large monarchies, particularly the Spanish case, from a comparative point of view. Another research field is Basque law and institutions, on which he has published studies on legal treatises of lawyers such as Martín de Azpilcueta, Andrés de Poza and Pedro de Fontecha y Salazar.

Niall Bond
Ph.D. Freiburg im Breisgau 1991, habilitation 2010 EHESS Paris, is a historian of political, social and economic thought and has worked extensively as a translator and conference interpreter in political, economic, sociological and other academic contexts. He has authored an intellectual biography (*Understanding Ferdinand Tönnies' Community and Society:* Volume 1: *Political philosophy and sociological theory between enlightened liberal individualism and transfigured community*, Lit Verlag, 2013), translated Tönnies' *Community and Society* into French (PUF, 2010), edited volumes in German and English and published more than 60 articles and chapters. He at present works at the research centre IHRIM at University Lyon 2 and as a research associate at the Department of Sociology, Faculty of Humanities at the University of Johannesburg.

Luc Brisson
is Director of Research (Emeritus) at the National Center for Scientific Research (Paris [Villejuif], France; Centre Jean Pépin, UMR 8230 CNRS-ENS, PSL). He is known for his works on both Plato and Plotinus, including bibliographies, translations, and commentaries. He has also published numerous works on the history of philosophy and religions in Antiquity. Among his publications are *Platon, les mots et les mythes* (Maspero, 1982), *Orphée et l'Orphisme dans l'Antiquité gréco-romaine* (Variorum, 1995), *Vocabulaire de Platon*, with Jean-François Pradeau (Ellipses, 1998), reprinted as *Le Vocabulaire des Philosophes. De l'Antiquité à la Renaissance* (Ellipses, 2002), and "Plato's style and argument", in *The Routledge Handbook of Neoplatonism*, edited by Paulina Remes and Svetla Slaveva-Griffin (Routledge, 2014).

Petar Cholakov
is Associate Professor of Sociology at the Institute of Philosophy and Sociology of the Bulgarian Academy of Sciences (BAS) in Sofia. He is the author of the monograph *Punishment for Tyrants: The Protestant and the Liberal Doctrines of Resistance against Power* (Sofia: BAS Press). His latest book is *Ethnic Entrepreneurs Unmasked: Political Institutions and Ethnic Conflicts in Contemporary Bulgaria* (Ibidem Press, distributed by Columbia University Press). He also works as a journalist and writes on contemporary Bulgarian politics for Deutsche Welle.

Nóra Chronowski
JD., Ph.D., Habil., Professor of Constitutional Law, is a Senior Research Fellow at Centre of Social Sciences Institute for Legal Studies and at National University of Public Service Faculty of Law Enforcement in Budapest. She was former Jean Monnet Chair (2007–2010) at the University of Pécs Faculty of Law, she has authored several books and over 190 articles. She participated in half a dozen international research projects supported by the ERC and European Commission and gave over 30 presentations at international academic conferences. Her research interests include comparative-, EU- and constitutional law, human rights, and minority rights.

Angela De Benedictis
is a retired Professor of Early Modern History at the University of Bologna. She is the author of *Repubblica per contratto: Bologna, una città europea nello Stato della Chiesa* (Il Mulino, 1995); *Politica, governo e istituzioni nell'Europa moderna* (Il Mulino, 2001); *Tumulti: Moltitudini ribelli in età moderna* (Il Mulino, 2013; English translation: *Neither Disobedient nor Rebels: Lawful Resistance in Early Modern Italy*, Viella, 2018); *Revolts and Political Crime from the 12th to the 19th Century: Legal Responses and Juridical-political Discourses* (Klostermann, 2013), co-edited with Karl Härter. Among her latest essays, "Prefacio. Resistere alla polizia che agisce ingiustamente: Comportamenti collettivi e letteratura politico-giuridica in età moderna", in T.A. Mantecón Movellán, M. Torres Arce and S. Truchuelo García, *Dimensiones del conflicto: Resistencia, violencia y policía en el mundo urbano* (Universidad de Cantabria, 2020).

Fatma Sinem Eryilmaz
is a cultural historian of the early modern period specialized in Ottoman history. Since receiving her Ph.D. from the University of Chicago, her work has focused on the relationship between knowledge and political power in the Eastern Mediterranean. Previously she has published on sixteenth century

Ottoman dynastic literature and its significance for the political and cultural history of the period. Currently, she is working on the enigmatic Imperial Scroll prepared in the Ottoman court in the sixteenth century. Among her publications are: "The *Sulaiman-nama* (*Süleymanname*) as an Historical Source", in Ch. Melville and G. van den Berg, eds., *Shahnama Studies III: The Reception of Firdausi's Shahnama* (Brill, 2017); and "From Adam to Süleyman: Visual Representations of Authority and Leadership in 'Ārif's *Şāhnāme-yiĀl-i 'Os̱mān*", in H. E. Çıpa and E. Fetvacı, eds., *Writing History at the Ottoman Court* (Indiana University Press, 2013). She teaches at the Universitat Autònoma de Barcelona.

Håkon Evju

Ph.D. (2014) in History, University of Oslo, is Associate Professor of Intellectual History at that university. He has published *Ancient Constitutions and Modern Monarchy: Historical Writing and Enlightened Reform in Denmark-Norway 1730–1814* (Brill, 2019) and numerous articles on different aspects of the Enlightenment in Denmark-Norway. His research interests include history of historiography, history of economic and political thought as well as the history of censorship and freedom of the press.

Pablo Fernández Albaladejo

is Emeritus Professor at the Universidad Autónoma de Madrid, where he held the chair on Early Modern History of Europe. Since 1992, when he published *Fragmentos de Monarquía: Trabajos de historia política*, his main research field has been political and constitutional history. In adition to his collected volume *Materia de España: Cultura política e identidad en la España moderna* (Marcial Pons, 2007), he has publisehd "Rethinking Identity: Crisis of Rule and Reconstruction of Identity in the Monarchy of Spain", in *The Transatlantic Hispanic Baroque*, H. E. Braun and J. Pérez Magallón eds. (Ashgate, 2014); and "Spanish Atlanteans: Rewriting the Origins of the Spanish Monarchy, 1672–1740", *Culture & History. Digital Journal*, 4.2 (2015). He has edited two volumes: *Los Borbones: Dinastía y memoria de nación en la España del siglo XVIII* (Madrid: Marcial Pons, 2002), and *Fénix de España: Modernidad y cultura propia en la España del siglo XVIII, 1737–1766* (Marcial Pons, 2006), and has published *La crisis de la Monarquía*, vol. 4 of the *Historia de España*, eds. J. Fontana and R. Villares (Crítica and Marcial Pons, 2009).

Javier Fernández-Sebastián

is Professor of History of Political Thought at the University of the Basque Country (Bilbao). He has published extensively on modern intellectual and conceptual history, in particular focused on Spain and the Ibero-American world. He has recentely published the book *Historia conceptual en el Atlántico ibérico: Lenguajes, tiempos, revoluciones* (Fondo de Cultura Económica, 2020), and co-edited the volumes *Conceptual History in the European Space*, with W. Steinmetz and M. Freeden (Berghahn, 2018), and *In Search of European Liberalisms: Concepts, Languages, Ideologies*, with M. Freeden y J. Leonhard (Berghahn, 2019). He is currently preparing the book *Key Metaphors for History* (Routlegde).

Mareike Gebhardt
Ph.D., works at the Department of Political Science at Münster University. She studied Political Science, Sociology, and Philosophy at the universities of Trier, Wuerzburg, and Regensburg and wrote her dissertation on Hannah Arendt's and Jürgen Habermas's concepts of the political public and their implications for political action in late capitalism. In her teaching and research, she focuses on political theory, theories of radical democracy, and post-structuralism. Currently, she is working on a project on "democratic closure" to analyse constructions of otherness in Europe's contemporary migration dicourse. Among her recent publications are "Flüchtige Präsenz. Umkämpfte Solidaritäten des EU-Migrationsregimes", *Femina Politica*, 28.2 (2019), 54–67; and "The Populist Moment: Affective Orders, Protest, and Politics of Belonging", *Distinktion: Journal for Social Theory*, (2019): https://www.tandfonline.com/doi/abs/10.1080/1600910X.2019.1653346.

Xavier Gil
is Professor of Early Modern History at the University of Barcelona, fellow of the Real Academia de la Historia and of the Reial Acadèmia de Bones Lletres de Barcelona. He was co-founder of the European Society for the History of Political Thought and served as its president in 2014–2016. He also edits *Pedralbes: Revista d'Història Moderna*. He studies politics and political thought and culture in the Early Modern Iberian world. He has contributed to the volumes *Republicanism*, eds. M. Van Gelderen and Q. Skinner (Cambridge, 2002); *European Political Thought, 1450–1700*, eds. H.A. Lloyd, G. Burgess and S. Hodson (New Haven, 2007); *Athenian legacies: European debates on citizenship*, ed. P. Kitromilides (Florence, 2014); and *The Iberian World, 1450–1820*, eds. F. Bouza, P. Cardim and A. Feros (London, 2020). He is the author of *La fábrica de la Monarquía: Traza y conservación de la Monarquía de España de los Reyes Católicos y los Austrias* (Madrid, 2016) and of a number of articles on historical writing and the origins of international law.

Mark J. Hill
has a background in intellectual historian and digital humanities. He completed a DPhil at the University of Oxford, writing on Rousseau's political thought, and post-docs at the London School of Economics and the University of Helsinki (where he applied digital methods to early modern political and social history). He is currently lecturer in Computational Social Science at the University of Kent.

Ferenc Hörcher
is a political thinker and historian of political thought. He studied in Budapest, Oxford and Brussels. He is research professor and head of the Research Institute of Politics and Government of the University of Public Service, and a senior fellow and former director of the Institute of Philosophy of the Research Centre for the Humanities, both in Budapest. He was a visiting researcher in Cambridge, Göttingen, Wassenaar, Edinburgh and the University of Notre Dame in the US. His last two books are: *A Political Philosophy of Conservatism* (Bloomsbury, 2020), and *The Political Philosophy of the European City* (Lexington Books, 2021).

Jaska Kainulainen
is a docent of history of ideas at the University of Helsinki. He has published the monograph *Paolo Sarpi: A Servant of God and State* (Brill, 2014) and several shorter pieces on religious and political ideas in early modern Europe, including two articles on the Jesuits: "Isocrates's *phronesis* and the early Jesuits", *Journal of Early Modern History,* 22.6 (2018); and "Virtue and civic life in early-modern Jesuit education", *Journal of Jesuit Studies*, 5.4 (2018). He is currently finalizing a monograph on the early Jesuits and the rhetorical tradition.

Thomas Lorman
is a historian of Central Europe. Since 2010 he has taught at UCL's School of Slavonic and East European Studies. He has published widely on Hungarian and Slovak history and also serves as editor of the journal *Central Europe*. His last two books are *The Making of the Slovak People's Party: Religion, Nationalism and the Culture War in Early 20th-Century Europe* (Bloomsbury, 2019) and A *History of the Hungarian Constitution: Law, Government and Political Culture in Central Europe*, which he co-edited with Ferenc Hörcher (Bloomsbury, 2020).

Adriana Luna-Fabritius
is an Academy of Finland Researcher to the Department of History at the University of Helsinki. She has published on early modern languages of

republicanism, natural law and political economy in the Spanish monarchy, especially Naples, Catalonia, Milan and New Spain. Her research expands to the transformation of imperialism and colonialism through legal, scientific, and political practices and ideas in the communicating networks of the Spanish monarchy in early modern time. Before arriving the to the University of Helsinki she was appointed in the History Department at the Centre for Economic Research and Education (CIDE) in Mexico (2009). Luna-Fabritius was the President of the European Society for the History of Political Thought in 2018–2022 and Associate Editor of its book series on the *History of European Political and Constitutional Thought* (Brill). She is affiliated with the research groups: "Cameralism as a European Political Science: A Reassessment"; Società Italiana per la Storia dell'Età Moderna; "International Research Network: Natural Law 1625–1850"; and the Helsinki Centre for Intellectual History.

Ere Nokkala

Ph.D. 2010 European University Institute, Florence, is University Researcher at the University of Helsinki. He is a member of the Helsinki Centre for Intellectual History with a focus on eighteenth-century Germany, Scandinavia and Finland. His publications include *From Natural Law to Political Economy: JHG von Justi on State, Commerce and International Order* (LIT Verlag, 2019) and the edited volume *Cameralism and the Enlightenment: Happiness, Governance and Reform in Transnational Perspective* (Routledge, 2020), co-edited with Nicholas B Miller. He has published widely in aspects of cameralism and early modern republicanism, including in *History of European Ideas*, *European Review of History*, and *Contributions to the History of Concepts*. Nokkala is co-director of the International Research Network on Cameralism across the World of Enlightenment.

Brian Kjær Olesen

is a historian of early modern and Enlightenment political thought, who specialises in Scandinavia and Northern Europe. His research includes theories of monarchism, religious toleration and rival interpretations of freedom in monarchical and republican political discourses. He defended his PhD dissertation, "Monarchism, Religion, and Moral Philosophy: Ludvig Holberg and the Early Northern Enlightenment", at the European University Institute in Florence (2016), and, since then, he has been a fellow at IZEA – Interdisziplinäres Zentrum für die Erforschung der Europäischen Aufklärung, Martin-Luther-Universität Halle-Wittenberg, a postdoctoral fellow at the SAXO-Institute, University of Copenhagen and, most recently, a visiting fellow at Pompeu Fabra University.

András L. Pap
is Research Chair and Head of Department for the Study of Constitutionalism and the Rule of Law at the (formerly Hungarian Academy of Sciences) Institute Centre for Social Sciences Institute for Legal Studies. He is also Professor of Law at the Institute of Business Economics at Eötvös University (ELTE) and at the Law Enforcement Faculty of the National University of Public Service, and Adjunct (Recurrent Visiting) Professor in the Nationalism Studies Program at the Central European University in Budapest and Vienna. His research interest includes comparative constitutional law, human rights, law enforcement, hate crimes, discrimination and the conceptualization of race and ethnicity. In 2018 he founded the International Association of Constitutional Law (IACL) Research Group on identity, race and ethnicity in constitutional law. Among his recent publications are *Democratic Decline in Hungary: Law and Society in an Illiberal Democracy* (Routledge, 2018) and two articles in *Nationalities Papers: The Journal of Nationalism and Ethnicity*, 49.2 (2021), special issue on "Conceptualizing and Operationalizing Identity, Race, Ethnicity, and Nationality by Law".

Nikola Regent
is Professor at the Australian National University, he has published on various topics in the history of political and economic thought, history of philosophy, and political theory. A significant part of his research deals with the influence of ancient writers, and ancient history more generally, on ideas and politics, from the sixteenth to the nineteenth century. His peer-reviewed articles have appeared in various venues, including *History of Political Thought*, *History of Political Economy*, *Journal of the History of Economic Thought*, *European Journal of the History of Economic Thought*, *History of European Ideas*, *Global Intellectual History*, *English Historical Review* and *History of the Human Sciences*.

José Reis Santos
Ph.D. in Contemporary History at the Faculty of Social Sciences and Humanities at the New University of Lisbon. He published *Salazar e as Eleições: Um estudo sobre as eleições gerais de 1942* (Assambleia da República, 2011), and "Self-fashioning of a conservative revolutionary: Salazar's integral corporatism and the international networks of the 1930's" in *Authoritarianism and Corporatism in Europe and Latin America: Crossing Borders*, A.C. Pinto and F. Finchelstein, eds. (Routledge, 2019). He has also been a consultant for (historical) media productions, and a frequent writer in printed and online media for more than a decade, namely in *Visão*, *Jornal Económico*, *Expresso*, *Eurozine*, and other outlets.

Alberto Mariano Rodríguez Martínez
is a PhD candidate at Universidad Pablo de Olavide (Seville, Spain). His research interests focus on the political and diplomatic connectors between the Dutch Republic and the Spanish Monarchy in the first decades of the seventeenth century. Special attention goes to local authorities and their role in the rapprochement of both systems. He has published some works on the Twelve Years Truce and is currently completing his dissertation 'Negotiation, power and sovereignty in the Low Countries (1598–1621)'.

Pablo Sánchez León
is currently a researcher at the Centro de Humanidades CHAM in Universidade Nova de Lisboa. His dissertation was in the field of historical sociology, comparing the social and institutional dynamics of urban Castile between the late medieval and early modern periods. He has published amply on conceptual history, history of economic and political thought and the history of citizenship in Spain between the Old Regime and Liberalism. His latest book is *Popular Political Participation and the Democratic Imagination, in Spain. From Crowd to People, 1766–1868* (Palgrave, 2020).

Ersin Yildiz
has been a scholar at the Frankfurt Institute of Social Research. He received his MA studies in Political Science and Philosophy at Goethe University in Frankfurt. After research studies at the New School for Social Research as a visiting scholar, he completed his dissertation on the socialist constitutional theories of the Weimar Republic at the Goethe University in Frankfurt. His research interests are political theory and history of ideas, especially in the German tradition. He is currently working on the changing relationship between public sphere and political consciousness. He has published essays on critical political thought including "Marx' verfassungstheoretische Schriften und die Entwicklung der materialistischen Rechtstheorie" (2015); "Max Horkheimer" (2015); "Lefort und Kantorowicz: Repräsentation und die politische Form der modernen Gesellschaft" (2013); "Kritik und politische Aufklärung in der Tradition der Kritischen Theorie" (2012).

FIGURE 0.1 Francisco Vázquez de Mendieta, *The Oath of the Laws of the Seignoiry of Biscay by Ferdinand the Catholic* (c. 1609), House of the Assembly of Gernika (Biscay). Reproduced with permission

Introduction

Xavier Gil

In a well-known passage of *Don Quixote*, Sancho Panza is appointed governor of a territory, the Ínsula Barataria. Despite being illiterate, he turns out to have a keen natural sense of justice. In fact, he is so adept at resolving litigation that he is compared to the legendary lawgiver Lycurgus of Sparta. At the end of his term Sancho issues ordinances concerning good government, principally devoted to social reform and poor relief, and the laws are "so good that to this day they are obeyed in that village and are called *The Constitution of the Great Governor Sancho Panza*".[1]

Sancho thus was not only a surprisingly expert governor, but his laws were also so good they survived intact for many years. Longevity was an unfailing criterion of quality when it came to assessing the worth of laws and rules. There are other examples of this: the founder of Utopia, Utopos, designed his community so well that physically, politically, and religiously it remained constant for centuries.[2] Moses was a lawgiver, especially in the eyes of the Roman historian Flavius Josephus, and that image was common as well among Renaissance writers, most notably Machiavelli. Indeed, Josephus regarded Moses's laws as an immutable constitution, the *politeia biblica*, which was the focus of later writers including Benito Arias Montano, Petrus Cunaeus, and Johannes Althusius, the patriarch himself drawing less attention from them than his creation.[3]

Longevity was all the more desirable in the face of evidence that societies' laws lost their quality and deteriorated with the passing of the years so that the initial legislative act had to be repaired through subsequent acts. Aristotle, thinking about political crisis, or *stasis*, argued in favour of returning to the constitution of previous generations, the *patrios politeia* that Solon

1 Miguel de Cervantes, *Don Quixote* [1605–1615], trans. Edith Grossman (New York: Harper Collins, 2003), Book II, ch. 51, 797.

2 Thomas More, *Utopia* [1516], ed. George M. Logan, trans. Robert M. Adams (Cambridge: Cambridge University Press, 1989), 42, 46, 94–5.

3 Lea Campos Boralevi, "Mosè legislatore", *Il Pensiero Politico*, 40 (May-August 2007), 269–81, esp. 268, 274–77; *Eadem*, "Classical Foundation Myths of European Republicanism: The Jewish Commonwealth", in Martin Van Gelderen and Quentin Skinner, eds., *Republicanism: A Shared European Heritage* (Cambridge: Cambridge University Press, 2002), vol. 1, ch. 12; Miguel A. Granada, "Maquiavelo y Moisés", *Res Publica: Revista de Historia de las Ideas Políticas*, 20 (2017), 141–56.

 | DOI:10.1163/9789004549159_002

had handed down to the Athenians. Polybius described the cyclical decline of the three good regimes (monarchy, aristocracy, and democracy) into their antithetical opposites and the subsequent need for returning to the original ones. Machiavelli believed that in order for a republic to last, it was necessary to return periodically to its initial form, adding that the occasional intervention of a dictator might prove beneficial. Later on, in a very different political and cultural context, Thomas Jefferson in 1789 famously argued that a constitution, like every law, should expire after just nineteen years so that the next generation was not bound by the decisions of their parents; but James Madison clearly disagreed, pointing to what would become a crucial constitutional debate.[4]

In the realm of political practice, years of confrontation between crown and estates led to a succession of medieval charters that generally limited the crown's capacities. This was the origin of kingdoms' parliamentary life; examples are the Cortes of Leon (1188), the English *Magna Charta* (1215), the Hungarian Golden Bull (1222), the Aragonese Privileges of the Union (1287), and the *Joyeuse Entrée*, or charter of liberties, in the Duchy of Brabant (1356). Legendary accounts, both believable and convincing, of these political agreements appeared either when the agreements were enacted or later on as a response to the rise of absolutism, situating their origins in a more or less distant past. These were foundational myths, such as the liberties enjoyed in the Netherlands by the Batavians before the Romans arrived or the medieval laws (*fueros*) of Sobrarbe in Aragon. In some cases, true documents were subject to different readings and interpretations according to the historical context or political concerns; one such example is the Scottish Declaration of Arbroath (1320). There were myths on the monarchical side as well, of course, tales of ancient genealogies that went back for ages and ages, being that a dynasty's ancestry was one of the principal sources of its legitimacy and authority: Aeneas provided this for the Habsburgs, while Brutus did the same for the Britons.

Regardless of the particularities, the passage of certain laws, their subsequent amendment, the establishment of charters, and the crystallization of foundational myths all signify constitutional moments. These are moments

4 Aristotle, "The Athenian Constitution", chs. v-xi, in *The Athenian Constitution, the Eudemian Ethics, On Virtues and Vices*, bilingual ed., transl. H. Rackham, Loeb Classical Library (Cambridge, Mass.: Harvard University Press, 1971), 21–35; Niccoló Machiavelli, *Discorsi sopra la prima deca di Tito Livio*, ed. Francesco Bausi (Rome: Salerno, 2001), vol. 2, book 3, ch. 1, 523–35; Thomas Jefferson, *Writings*, ed. Merrill Peterson (New York: The Library of America, 1984), 959–64; James Madison, *Writings*, ed. Jack N. Rakove (New York: The Library of America, 1999), 473–5.

found in literary fiction, legislative and gubernatorial practice, juridical thinking, and accounts of times past. This is the subject addressed in this volume, which emerges from the Fourth International Conference of the European Society for the History of Political Thought, held at the University of Barcelona in October 2016.

The expression "constitutional moments" of course makes one think of J. G. A. Pocock's *The Machiavellian Moment* (1975). There, "moment" has a dual significance, referring to both historical and conceptual time. Pocock uses this duality to examine the circulation of texts over a 300-year period through discourses, the idea being that all discourse contains its opposites.[5] The expression also reminds us, though not as explicitly, of the work of Reinhart Koselleck, who writes about the temporality of concepts and historical figures' awareness of temporality as they deploy these concepts, semantic innovation and obsolescence, and, especially, the genesis of the historical semantics of modern times.[6] That said, this book does not seek express inspiration in either of these important writers. But it does share with them an appreciation for the linguistic, cultural, and conceptual contexts where these constitutional moments took place, an appreciation one finds in many historical studies today. Thus, the meaning of "moments" in this book is both simpler and broader, referring to diverse episodes or manifestations of the subject under analysis. That is why the chapters range from classical Greece to the twenty-first century, albeit with no pretension of comprehensiveness.

The word "moment" has become rather frequent in recent works of political theory. Sometimes it is in the plural, spanning long periods; for example the series "Textual Moments in the History of Political Thought" (Bloomsbury) includes books on patriarchal, revolutionary, and utopian moments, among others, and "Malthusian moments" refer to developments ranging from Malthus's own times up to the rise of neo-Malthusianism in the mid-twentieth century.[7] Or, sometimes it is used in the singular to illuminate a particular

---

5 J. G. A. Pocock, *The Machiavellian Moment: Florentine Political Thought and the Atlantic Republican Tradition* (Princeton: Princeton University Press, 2003) [1975], with his postscript, XXIII-XXIV, 554, 577, 579.

6 Javier Fernández Sebastián, introduction to his edited volume, *Political Concepts and Time: New Approaches to Conceptual History* (Santander: Cantabria University Press, 2011).

7 Cesare Cuttica and Gaby Mahlberg, eds., *Patriarchal Moments: Reading Patriarchal Texts* (Basingstoke: Bloomsbury, 2015), and other titles in the same series; Alison Bashford, Duncan Kelly, and Shailaja Fennell, eds., *Malthusian Moments*, special issue of *The Historical Journal* 63.1 (February 2020), 1–13.

theme: the Lockean moment (which Pocock said did not exist), the Cadiz moment, the Polybian moment, or the Weimar moment.[8]

This book explores constitutional moments, with the terms "constitution" and "constitutional" being understood in a broad sense. Rather than following the widely-used criterion of thinking of them solely with regard to the so-called modern constitutions – the United States in 1787 and France in 1791 – they are understood here to have a broader definition, both thematically and chronologically, a criterion equally commonly used. Thus, Old Testament covenants, the Greek *politeia*, the Roman *constitutio*, medieval charters, foundational myths, *leges fundamentales*, historical constitutions, nineteenth century *chartres octroyées*, and modern and contemporary constitutions can all be accommodated. Not only are the authority and development of the state not excluded from this notion of constitution, but the term "constitution" itself is not limited to contractualism. In that regard, ancient constitution, medieval constitution, and modern constitution are expressions referring to a time prior to constitutional texts as such that were linked to the above-mentioned revolutions.[9] Constitutional moments therefore can have markedly different durations and natures: the passage of eras, such as the case of the Roman *res publica*, which, according to Cicero, was *constituta saeculis et aetatis*; the passage of generations that brought about England's ancient constitution; or a particular date when a constitutional text or code was promulgated during the liberal period.

Understood broadly to apply to diverse principles of governance, constitutional moments can also include coups d'état (which in the pre-modern era were often carried out by established powers) and emergency governments (in accordance with a drastically executive conception of politics based on

---

8 T. H. Breen, *The Lockean Moment: The Language of Rights on the Eve of the American Revolution* (Oxford: Oxford University Press, 2001); for Pocock's opposing vision see his postscript to *The Machiavellian Moment*, 574; Marta Lorente and José M. Portillo, eds., *El momento gaditano: La Constitución en el orbe hispánico, 1808–1826* (Madrid: Congreso de los Diputados, 2011); Cary J. Nederman and Mary Elizabeth Sullivan, "The Polybian Moment: The Transformation of Republican Thought from Ptolomy of Lucca to Machiavelli", *The European Legacy*, 17 (2012), 867–81; Eloy García, editorial note, in Walter Jellinek, *et al.*, *La Constitución de Weimar: La Constitución alemana de 11 de agosto de 1919* (Madrid: Tecnos, 2019), 11.

9 Francisco Tomás y Valiente, "Constitución", in his *Constitución: Escritos de introducción histórica* (Madrid: Marcial Pons, 1996), ch. 1; Graham Maddox, "Constitution", in Terence Ball, James Farr and Russell L. Hanson, eds., *Political Innovation and Conceptual Change* (Cambridge: Cambridge University Press, 1989), ch. 3; Maurizio Fioravanti, *Costituzione* (Bologna: Il Mulino, 1999); António M. Hespanha, "Qu'est-ce que la 'constitution' dans les monarchies ibériques de l'époque moderne?", *Themis*, 1 (2000), 5–18.

absolute rule).[10] They can also include other sorts of "moments" such as descriptions of cities' and countries' political systems, especially in the pre-modern era, which could help define a system and make it intelligible, overcoming the lack of legislative systematism. Relevant cases are the above-mentioned piece of Aristotle on the constitution of the Athenians, Leonardo Bruni's panegyric to Florence (c. 1403), and a succession of treatises. Some of them were realistic though laudatory: Claude de Seyssel on France (1519), Thomas Smith on England (1565, published in 1583), and João Salgado de Araujo on Portugal (1627); others were quite critical, including Samuel von Pufendorf (alias Mozambano) on the Empire (1667); and still others were scholarly, such as Jean-Louis De Lolme (1771) and Walter Bagehot (1867) on England. Other such treatises were idealistic, such as Donato Giannotti's on Venice (1540), and still other works sketched out ideal regimes, meaning they were imaginary, a genre that adopted different literary styles, notably Utopian descriptions up to contemporary times.[11]

"Constitutional" has a broad and neutral connotation, while "constitutionalist" conveys more doctrinal and chronological meaning. Constitutionalism, based on the rule of law and separation of powers, has been dated differently depending on how it is understood. There are a multitude of studies on the matter, but it will suffice to refer to just two interpretations: First, it appeared by the mid- and late-seventeenth century as an accentuation of certain characteristics of the prior constitutional tradition in opposition to modern theories of the prince's absolute sovereignty, with particular attention to the limits of government, subjects' participation, and judicial guarantees; or, second, it appeared only with the 1776 Constitution of Virginia and developed with the mentioned American and French constitutions, which distinguished between the title and exercise of sovereignty, identified constituent power, and conceptualized law as the expression of the general will. This second interpretation, which has been labeled "modern constitutionalism", went hand in hand with new notions of citizenship, based on individual liberties and civil rights, as expressed in the 1789 Declaration of the Rights of Man and of the Citizen.[12]

10 Jean-Philippe Genet and José Manuel Nieto Soria, eds., *Coups d'état à la fin du Moyen Age? Aux fondements du pouvoir politique en Europe occidentale* (Madrid: Casa de Velázquez, 2005); Francesco Benigno and Luca Scuccimarra, eds., *Il governo dell'emergenza: Poteri straordinari e di guerra in Europa tra XVI e XX secolo* (Rome: Viella, 2007).

11 Vittor Ivo Comparato, *Utopia* (Bologna: Il Mulino, 2005). See also Heinrich C. Kuhn and Diana Stanciu, eds., *Ideal Constitutions in the Renaissance* (Frankfurt: Peter Lang, 2009).

12 Shannon C. Stimson, "Constitutionalism and the rule of law", in John S. Dryzek, Bonnie Honig, and Anne Philips, eds., *The Oxford Handbook of Political Theory* (Oxford: Oxford University Press, 2006), ch. 17. On the two notions and dates: Fioravanti, *Costituzione,*

Charles McIlwain's *Constitutionalism, Ancient and Modern* (1940; rev. ed., 1947) established an influential framework in this regard.[13] The binomial "ancient and modern" – not unrelated to Benjamin Constant's famous 1819 speech, "The Liberty of the Ancients Compared to that of the Moderns" – has become a common way of identifying and addressing one of the leading issues in the history of political ideas. There are several recent examples of this: Pocock says that the debate between ancient and modern liberty is one of the fundamental issues in his *Machiavellian Moment*; Quentin Skinner acknowledges his renewed interest in the contrasts between past and present systems of thought; Javier Fernández Sebastián examines the nuances between ancient and modern politics in around 1800; Ioannis D. Evrigenis looks at it in terms of approaches to liberty and law; and László Kontler and Mark Somos focus on premodern and modern notions of trust and happiness. In a more general vein, Richard Whatmore points out that the relations between ancients and moderns constitute a central question of intellectual history.[14]

A book such as this cannot ignore these reference points, even if it addresses them only tacitly. Therefore, it seems right that this Introduction offer an overview of the question. After Otto Hintze's and Otto Brunner's work, Gerhard Oestreich addressed the evolution from medieval charters to modern constitutions, and from ruling contracts to constitutional instruments. With the repeated caveat that this evolution was neither direct nor simple, and pointing to the difficulty of analyzing the connection between constitutions and the

85–6, 92, on the one hand; and Horst Dippel, "Modern constitutionalism. An introduction to a history in need of writing", *Legal History Review*, 73 (2005), 153–69, and his multi-volume edition of sources *Constitutions of the World from the late 18th Century to the middle of the 19th Century* (Munich: K.G. Sauer, started in 2005), and Roberto Blanco Valdés, *La construcción de la libertad: Apuntes para una historia del constitucionalismo europeo* (Madrid: Alianza, 2020), 35, on the other. See also Paschalis Kitromilides, "Redeeming European Political Thought", in his edited volume *Athenian Legacies: European Debates on Citizenship* (Florence: Leo S. Olschki, 2014), 11–2.

13 Maddox, "Constitution", 56–7; Angela de Benedictis, *Politica, governo e istituzioni nell'Europa moderna* (Bologna: Il Mulino, 2001), 374–5.

14 Pocock, postscript to *Machiavellian Moment*, 573, 577, 582; Quentin Skinner, "Surveying the *Foundations*: a retrospect and reassessment", in Annabel Brett, James Tully and Holly Hamilton-Bleakley, eds., *Rethinking the Foundations of Modern Political Thought* (Cambridge: Cambridge University Press, 2006), 237; Javier Fernández Sebastián, "Política antigua, política moderna. Una perspectiva histórico-conceptual", *Mélanges de la Casa de Velázquez*, 35 (2005), 165–81; Ionnas D. Evrigenis, "Liberty and Law", in Richard Whatmore and Brian Young, eds., *Companion to Intellectual History* (Chichester: Wiley Blackwell, 2015), ch. 15; László Kontler and Mark Somos, "Introduction" to their edited volume, *Trust and Happiness in the History of European Political Thought* (Leiden: Brill, 2018), 8–9, 11–12; Richard Whatmore, *What is Intellectual History?* (Cambridge: Polity, 2015), 85.

organization of government, Oestreich noted that during the central decades of the seventeenth century there was a notable proliferation of written "forms of government" with a variety of political meanings: popular sovereignty in the Levellers' "Heads of Proposals" and "An Agreement of the People" (1647–49), aristocratic power in Sweden's 1634 *Regeringsform* and Prussia's "Constitution" of 1661, mixed monarchy in the Pomeranian *Regierungsform* of 1634, the concentration of personal powers in Cromwell's Instrument of Government of 1653, monarchical absolutism in Denmark's *Lex Regia* of 1665, and various constitutional provisions in the Peace of Westphalia.[15]

Though Oestreich focuses on the seventeenth century, his work is especially relevant to the aims of this volume because he describes the great variety of political perspectives in these constitutional texts and does not turn them into direct predecessors of modern constitutions simply because they are written down and contain a greater or lesser collection of themes. Similarly, a study of medieval and modern constitutional thought (mostly concerned with the limits of princely powers and the relevance of canon law) raised the delicate issue of the influence of past writers on more modern ones, and the latter' use of quotations and adaptations that ended up defining or molding ways of thinking in a sort of Whiggish teleology.[16] More recently, an edited volume addressed the constitutional nature of charters in medieval urban communes and kingdoms as well as of similar later documents concerning both government and doctrine, with similar warnings regarding anachronism.[17]

So constitutional historians are mindful of the dynamics of continuity and change, which is true as well in other historical fields. In this regard, António M. Hespanha wrote that the lasting validity of Roman canon *ius commune* in much of Western Europe was a crucial element of long-term continuity. According to his careful analysis, that juridical culture held that the principal creative force of law lay in nature, rather than in human will. This means that the constitution of society was above all a natural phenomenon. A higher body of laws was thus unavailable to specific, subsequent political actors. By way of contrast, the doctrine of natural law enabled legislative voluntarism, through

15 Gerhard Oestreich, "From contractual monarchy to constitutionalism", in his *Neostoicism and the Early Modern State* (Cambridge: Cambridge University Press, 1982), ch. 10. A further case is that of the revolt of Naples in 1647–48: Vittorio Conti, *Le leggi di una rivoluzione: I bandi della repubblica napoletana dall'ottobre 1647 all'abrile 1648* (Naples: Jovene, 1983).

16 Brian Tierney, *Religion, Law and the growth of constitutional thought, 1150–1650* (Cambridge: Cambridge University Press, 1982), viii-x, 103–108 on his analytical caveats.

17 Jean-Philippe Genet and François Foronda, eds., *Des chartes aux constitutions: Autour de l'idée constitutionelle en Europe (XIIe XVIIe siècles)* (Paris: Éditions de la Sorbonne, 2019).

which the constitution and the law could become available, a process consolidated in 1750–1850 through liberal individualism.[18]

This voluntarism acquired its full force in the key notion of constituent power and its realization through revolution. But before that point, during the Enlightenment, "contract" and "constitution" became main terms. While some princes, such as Pietro Leopoldo I, duke of Tuscany (later Emperor Leopold II), Catherine II of Russia, and Friedrich II of Prussia encouraged the writing of constitutions, and Jean-Jacques Rousseau was asked to prepare constitutional texts for Poland and Corsica, in other countries, including the British colonies in America, there were debates over the existence (or not) of a traditional or historical constitution and its possible utility for the new demands of the day. If Thomas Paine demanded a written text proclaiming clear principles, the doctrines of his fellow Commonwealthmen were in fact an amalgam of intellectual and religious traditions, including Aristotle, ancient republican theories, common and natural law, Whig constitutionalism, rationalism and others. In France the debate regarding whether the constitution should be restored or newly written from scratch was especially intense and decisively resolved in 1789 in favour of the latter. In England, Edmund Burke rejected such voluntarism; defending the historical constitution, he argued that it was unavailable to political actors. In Spain, meanwhile, building on a tradition – in the metropolis and also in her American dominions – of contractualism, the common good and natural law, the 1812 Constitution of Cadiz was an amalgam also, made of neoscholasticism, rationalist contractualism, and the historical constitution, together with direct influences from current French and English debates.[19]

In Philadelphia and Paris, it was thought that a revolution would generate a constitution, a true constitution in accordance with the word's new meaning. This was a creatively constitutional moment, though in Philadelphia it

18 António M. Hespanha, *Cultura jurídica europea: Síntesis de un milenio* (Madrid: Tecnos, 2002), 62, 70–72, 173; see also Jacques Revel, "Monarchie absolue", in François Furet and Mona Ozouf, eds., *Dictionnaire critique de la Révolution Française* (Paris: Flammarion, 2017), vol. 4, 300 (or. ed., 1988) [partial Eng. trans.: *A Critical Dictionary of the French Revolution*, trans. Arthur Goldhammer (Cambridge, MA: Harvard University Press, 1989)].

19 Keith M. Baker, "Constitution", in Furet and Ozouf, eds., *Dictionnaire critique*, vol. 3, 179–205, esp. 179–81, 86–87, 190; Maddox, "Constitution", 59–61; Fioravanti, *Costituzione*, 100, 102, 118–20; J.H. Elliott, *Empires of the Atlantic World: Britain and Spain in America, 1492–1830* (New Haven and London: Yale University Press, 2006), 323, 329, 334–5, 348–50, 376; Tomás y Valiente, "Constitución", 30; Fernández Sebastián, "Política antigua", 5–6; Ignacio Fernández Sarasola, "Constitution projects during the Spanish Enlightenment", in Jesús Astigarraga, ed., *The Spanish Enlightenment Revisited* (Oxford: Voltaire Foundation, 2015), 129–47.

was more a matter of restoration while in Paris it meant a radical rupture. The moment in Philadelphia lasted about two years, from 1787 to 1789, after which the U.S. Constitution underwent a series of amendments with the Bill of Rights; while in Paris the process was long and hypothetically endless, as each new phase of the revolution inspired a new constitution.[20] The new stage of constitutional history was marked by tension between the democratic principle of the primacy of constituent will, on the one hand, and aspirations for juridical stability according to the principles of social order, on the other.[21]

The French Revolution immediately took upon itself the meaning of absolute inauguration, making a *tabula rasa* of the past. It was the dawn of new times, an event that could radiate over the world, and with it political modernity constructed its powerful foundational myth.[22] Nevertheless, political modernity preserved certain premodern elements, and modern constitutions contained an underlying text, like a palimpsest. Indeed, the historical constitution was still present in political and historical debates in the nineteenth century, especially through an idea adapted to changing circumstances, that of tracing a tradition of liberty from the pre-absolutist stage, a way of underplaying the recent revolutionary rupture. Conservatives, some French liberals, cultural and political movements inspired by Romanticism and the new regional nationalisms all did this, endowing medieval charters and *fueros* with new relevance for their own aspirations.[23]

New times brought with them both the idea of progress and a new medievalism, and visions of the future and the past influenced political-constitutional debates, not unlike what had happened in previous times. In medieval and early modern times, historical writing had been more concerned with rhetoric and ideological truth than with actual facts, and humanist historiography's innovations did not really change the view that history should mainly be something exemplary. This was due above all to reigning cultural categories regarding memory and the capacity to reconstruct past events as history or

20 Mona Ozouf, "Révolution", in Furet and Ozouf, eds., *Dictionnaire critique*, vol. 4, 415–35, esp. 420, 424, 432–33.

21 Hespanha, *Cultura jurídica europea*, 175.

22 Ozouf, "Révolution", 419–22; Pietro Costa, *Cittadinanza* (Bologna: Il Mulino, 2005), 51; Javier Fernández Sebastián, *Historia conceptual en el Atlántico ibérico. Lenguajes, tiempos, revoluciones* (Madrid and Ciudad de México: Fondo de Cultura Económica, 2021), 282, 286.

23 Diego Quaglioni, "Constitution et constitutionalisme (XVI-XVIIIe siècle)", in Genet and Foronda, eds., *Des chartes*, 442–45, 450; François Furet, "Ancien Régime", in Furet and Ozouf, eds., *Dictionnaire critique*, vol. 4, 38–40; Tomás y Valiente, "Constitución", 31; Fernández Sebastián, *Historia conceptual*, 297, 313.

as memory; in other words, past events were valid only insofar as they were intelligible and meaningful for the present. In the end, history consisted of a constructed narrative reminiscence, and foundational narratives were as frequent as they were efficient. Thus legends created to confirm the origins of corporative privilege or royal legitimacy were part of that historical culture, and they were more complex than mere fabrications openly designed for political purposes.[24] However there were such fabrication cases, probably because they came late; one example is that of the Portuguese Cortes which supposedly met in Lamego in around 1140 to establish the juridical bases for electing the monarch, a falsehood firstly aired in 1632 and subsequently developed as an argument to bolster the cause of the Portuguese revolt against the Spanish monarchy.[25]

Now the nineteenth century was a time of important advances in the profession of history and historical research, but it was not immune to foundational myths or, better put, to retrospective genealogies of nation states and of smaller entities. Along with the myth of the revolution looking to the future (e.g., liberals, socialists), these genealogies – be they ethnic, cultural, or linguistic – and retellings of the past played an important role in nation-building. They provided a sense of continuity throughout the centuries at a time when people were increasingly aware of the acceleration of time and change. They provided also arguments for political and constitutional struggles, the contemporary narratives about the Battle of Kosovo (1389) during the expansion of the Ottoman Empire being a good example.[26]

In the twentieth century there were constitutional moments as well, expressly linked to constitutions, whether brief or longer lasting. Three such moments can be drawn. The first was the Weimar Constitution, already mentioned, a landmark in that it included social rights, together with new juridical

24 Janet Coleman, *Ancient and Medieval Memories: Studies in the Reconstruction of the Past* (Cambridge: Cambridge University Press, 1992), 558–61, 564–65, 599; Gabrielle Spiegel, "Historical thought in Medieval Europe", in Lloyd Kramer and Sarah Maza, eds., *A Companion to Western Historical Thought* (Oxford: Blackwell, 2002), 92, 94.

25 Pedro Cardim, *Portugal unido, Portugal separado: Felipe II, la unión de territorios y el debate sobre la condición política del reino de Portugal* (Valladolid: Universidad de Valladolid, 2014), 209, 215, 227–8.

26 Patrick J. Geary, *The Myth of Nations: The Medieval Origins of Europe* (Princeton: Princeton University Press, 2002); R. J. W. Evans and Guy P. Marchal, eds., *The Uses of the Middle Ages in Modern European States: History, Nationhood, and the Search for Origins* (Basingstoke: Palgrave, 2011); Javier Fernández Sebastián, "'Riding the devil's steed'. Politics and historical acceleration in an age of revolution", in his edited volume *Political Concepts and Time*, ch. 13.

requirements. The second moment, which took much longer to develop and also lasted longer was that of the post-World War II constitutions, specifically Italy (1947), the German Basic Law (*Grundgesetz*) (1949), Portugal (1976), and Spain (1978), all of which brought a clear end to dictatorships. Sensitive to their respective historical circumstances, framers offered a nuanced vision of constituent power and encouraged and consolidated another key element, that of the principle of the constitutionality of laws by means of judicial review. This was the moment of constitutional democracies, which developed further in Eastern Europe after 1989.[27] Along the way, the debate on the so called eternity or entrenchment clauses concerning the old debate on the durability of constitutions underwent new developments.[28] And third, at the turn of the century, the articulation of the European Union is yet another moment developed in phases from the Treaty on European Union (Maastricht, 1992) to the Treaty of Lisbon (2007).

•••

This collection of articles on constitutional moments is not a history of the genesis and evolution of constitutions. Nor does it provide a history of political thought about constitutions. Rather, the book's aim is, on the one hand, to offer a selection of moments, episodes, and instructive cases throughout history, most of them situated at the intersection of reflection and action, and, on the other, to understand them in their proper historical and conceptual context.

The essays are in chronological order, starting with classical Greece and ending with the twenty-first century, followed by a closing part in a more theoretical vein. This order is not only logical, it illustrates the individuality of each case and at the same time situates it in its proper temporal sequence so as to facilitate an understanding of the antecedents and consequences that might be relevant without forcing matters into a linear progression. Thanks to the authors' sensitivity to context and concept, the volume does not "discover"

---

27 Tomás y Valiente, "Constitución", 37–9; Fioravanti, *Costituzione*, 146–47, 157–62; Jan-Werner Müller, "Political Thought in Twentieth Century Europe: A Framework for Analysis", in Janet Coleman and Paschalis Kitromilides, eds., *In the Footsteps of Herodotus: Towards European Political Thought* (Florence: Leo S. Olschki, 2012), 191–3; R. Gherardi, et al., "La Repubblica di Weimar come esperanza, come laboratorio e come paradigma", *Il Pensiero Politico*, 52 (May-August 2019).

28 Michael Hein, "Entrenchment clauses in the history of modern constitutions", *Tijdschrift voor Rechtsgeschiedenis – Revue d'Histoire du Droit – Legal History Review*, 86 (2018), 434–81.

anachronic harbingers or assume a teleological vision linking one moment with the next.

The section on the Renaissance and the early modern period has more chapters than the other ones because that was the programme of the conference that gave rise to the volume and, more importantly, that is the period that has recently most drawn the attention of constitutional scholars. We thus provide a balance to the existing bibliography, which has tended to favour contemporary history.

As for the spatial coverage, the volume offers a likewise wide sampler of European places, from Bulgaria to Portugal, from Naples to Sweden, while including also the Ottoman world, and the newly independent United States of America, and Hispano-American countries. Thus, a variety of issues in a variety of places through a long-time span: a fertile ground for the interplay of shared heritages and local particularities, tradition and innovation, creativity and diffusion, for the interaction among past, present, and future, experiences, actions, and expectations, all of them showing different forms, meanings and moments of constitution.

"Constitutional moments" means, then, a novel topic and a fruitful approach to constitutional history and, more broadly, to the history of political thought and action as it widens the issues under study while keeping the current concern for a careful assessment of historical and conceptual timing. In their variety of manifestations through time, these moments successfully test the thesis that conceptual change is a species of political innovation.[29] They offer rich substance for analysis, just like "crisis" do, that is, those critical events (as both empirical reality and diagnosis) that, mostly in the modern times, prompted action for renewal and new responses in political thought.[30]

Therefore, the book finds a most fitting place in the collection "History of European Political and Constitutional Thought", published by Brill, a series that also includes Francesco Biagi, Justin O. Frosini, and Mason Mazzone, eds., *Comparative Constitutional History*, vol. 1: *Principles, Developments, Challenges* (2020). This is currently a widening field, as seen in other important volumes.[31]

29 Ball, Farr and Hanson, "Introduction", in their edited volume *Political Innovation and Conceptual Change*, 2.

30 Cesare Cuttica, László Kontler and Clara Maier, "Introduction", in their edited volume *Crisis and Renewal in the History of European Political Thought* (Leiden and Boston: Brill, 2021), 1, 16–8.

31 Xenophon Contiades and Alkmene Fotiadou, eds., *The Routledge Handbook of Comparative Constitutional Change* (Abingdon-New York: Routledge, 2021).

Constitutional Moments makes thus a peculiar addition to an old and yet renewed and expanding field.

This volume took longer to appear than expected. As editor, I wish to warmly thank the fellow authors for their fine collaboration in the preparation thereof. Thanks also to the anonymous reviewer who offered thoughtful comments on its contents.

PART 1

Ancient and Medieval Times

CHAPTER 1

The Critic of the Family (*oikos*) at the Foundations of Plato's Political Doctrine

Myth and Reality

Luc Brisson

In our day and age, politics can be defined as the management of conflicts within a society or between countries. For Plato, by contrast, politics must be defined as the prevention of conflicts. With this goal in mind, he attacks what seems to him to be the source of all conflicts, the *oikos*, that is, the family: not the nuclear family, as it came to be constituted in the 19th century, but the family in the broad sense, as an instrument of power. For Plato, the goal of politics is thus to abolish or neutralize the *oikos* as a community intermediary between the citizen and the city.[1]

1 The Context

The first thirty years of Plato's life took place in a tragic context, marked by two catastrophes: the fall of the Athenian empire[2] and the death sentence imposed upon Socrates. As a result of its victories on the Persians in the course of the "Medic" wars (490 and 479 BC),[3] Athens became the dominant power in Greece during the 5th century. The Delian League, a military alliance founded to keep the Persians at a distance, became the center for the coordination of armed forces under the command of Athens, which demanded tribute from its allies. This imperialist policy worried Sparta and was the cause of the "Peloponnesian" wars. At the beginning of the conflict in 431, Athens had 60,000 citizens, that is, exclusively adult males, for neither women, children, foreign residents (metics) nor slaves could be citizens. One year later, in 430/429, just before Plato's birth, plague broke out in the city, causing the deaths of

1 On this question, see Carlo Natali, "L'élision de l'*oikos* dans la *République* de Platon", in Monique Dixsaut and Annie Larivée, eds., *Études sur la* République *de Platon*, 1. *De la justice* (Paris: Vrin, 2005), 199–223.

2 As told by Thucydides.

3 As told by Herodotus.

 | DOI:10.1163/9789004549159_003

20,000 citizens, including Pericles, an exceptional personality who was *strategos*, the highest authority in the city. In 412, battles, particularly those leading up to the disastrous Sicilian expedition which Alcibiades had supported, were responsible for the deaths of 17,000 citizens. Finally, Sparta and its allies laid siege to Athens in 404; 3,000 of its inhabitants died, and the city finally capitulated. Sparta then imposed an oligarchic system, giving power to a group of Athenians who supported it, the "Thirty Tyrants", who maintained power in the city though terror, ordering many executions. This dictatorship fell in 403, after fierce fighting; 1,500 citizens perished in the course of this civil war. By the time peace and democracy were re-established, Athens had fewer than 30,000 citizens, taking account of the birth rate during this quarter of a century. In thirty years, the number of citizens had been cut in half.

This is the context in which we must replace the trial of Socrates, who was relatively close to the "Thirty Tyrants", since his circle included not only Alcibiades, the main instigator of the Sicilian campaign who had fled to the enemies of Athens, but also Critias, and Plato's uncle Charmides, two of the Thirty Tyrants. The charges against Socrates, as reported by Plato in the *Apology of Socrates*, read as follows: "Socrates is guilty of corrupting the young people and of not believing in the gods in whom the city believes, but in other new divine beings" (*Apology* 24b-c). In the course of his trial, Socrates has no difficulty in showing that the last two elements of the charge are invalid. There remains the accusation of corrupting the youth, already raised against him by Aristophanes in his comedy *The Clouds*, produced in 423. But everything leads us to believe that the reason for this charge against Socrates in 399 was political and referred implicitly to his links with Alcibiades, and with Critias and Charmides, the Tyrants. However, since the amnesty law of 403 made any prosecution for political reasons impossible at Athens, an indictment vague enough to be acceptable was completely fabricated. The political aspect of this trial was, moreover, pointed out by Xenophon, who replied in his *Memorabilia* to the accusations made by a certain Polycrates in a pamphlet entitled *Accusation of Socrates* (see Isocrates, *Busiris*, 4), which was published only a few years after Socrates' death. In this pamphlet, Socrates was accused of having been the instigator of the crimes of Critias and Alcibiades, and of having incited the members of his circle to despise democratic institutions, particularly the choice of magistrates by lot (see Xenophon, *Memorabilia*, 1, 2, 9), and of taking sides with tyranny (see Xenophon, *Memorabilia* I, 2, 56). Finally, the orator Aeschines accused Socrates of having inspired Critias (*Against Timarchus* 173).

The Athens in which Plato lived was a divided city, on both an economic and a political level, and these cleavages had their origin in the family in the broad sense (*oikos*), which was based on marriage. The *oikos* was a family community made up of human beings, free or slaves, animals, and moveable and immoveable assets. Its management is described in the *Economics* of Xenophon, Aristotle, and Theophrastus, among others. The orators Isaeus, Demosthenes, and Aeschines explain, moreover, that a good administrator must try to increase his patrimony regularly. In the first book of the *Republic*, Cephalus, a metic from Syracuse, son of Lysanias and father of the orator Lysias and of Polemarchus, who made a fortune through his shield factory[4] in the Piraeus, gives a good example of this ideal:

> *SOCRATES* Did you inherit most of your wealth, Cephalus, or did you make it for yourself?
>
> *CEPHALUS* What did I make for myself, Socrates, you ask. As a money-maker I'm a sort of mean between my grandfather and my father. My grandfather and namesake inherited about the same amount of wealth as I possess but multiplied it many times. My father Lysianias, however, diminished that amount to even less than I have now. As for me, I'm satisfied to leave my sons here not less but a little more than I inherited.
>
> *Republic* I 330a–b, transl. G.M.A. GRUBE, REV. C.D.C. REEVE here and after

Families constantly sought to increase their patrimony, which was the source of their political power. But this competition was a direct source of war, both civil and external, as Plato explains quite clearly in books VIII and IX of the *Republic*. In a democratic city like Athens, the gap between the rich, who hold real political power, and the poor, leads the latter to rebel and give power to a single man who does not obey any law, the tyrant. Even if it does not provoke a civil war, the competition between families leads the city to seek riches abroad by taking control of new territories, and therefore, by waging more and more frequent wars.[5] Competition between *oikoi* to acquire wealth is thus at the origin of war, both civil and external.

4 See Debra Nails, *The People of Plato: A Prosopography of Plato and Other Socratics* (Indianapolis and Cambridge: Hackett, 2002).

5 Victor D. Hanson, *The Western Way of War: Infantry Battle in Classical Greece* (Berkeley-Los Angeles-London: University of California Press, 1989).

2 Plato's Political Thought

Yet how can one conceive of a city in which the *oikos* no longer plays a dominant role? Plato will propose two solutions, one in the *Republic* and the other in the *Laws*, while the *Statesman* suggests another viewpoint.[6]

2.1 The *Republic*

In Book 5 of the *Republic*, Plato defines as follows the greatest evil and the greatest good in the city:

> *SOCRATES* Is there any greater evil we can mention for a city than that which tears it apart and makes it many instead of one? Or any greater good than that which binds it together and makes it one?
>
> *GLAUCON* There isn't.
>
> *SOCRATES* And when, as far as possible, all the citizens rejoice and are pained by the same successes and failures, doesn't this sharing of pleasures and pains bind the city together?
>
> *GLAUCON* It most certainly does.
>
> *Republic* V 462a–b

The perfect city will thus be the one in which emotions, and the possession of goods from which they derive their origin, are no longer causes of division. This is why Socrates asks "Then, is the best-governed city the one in which most people say 'mine' and 'not mine', about the same things in the same way?" (*Republic* V 462c). Hence the desire to realize the maxim attributed to the Pythagoreans: "all is in common among friends". How, then, can this ideal be achieved?

Plato will first try to conceive of a city in which the leaders, who possess nothing, will be separated from the producers, who will see to their upkeep. Those who hold power are, moreover, divided into two groups: 1) that of the guardians, warriors who defend the city against external dangers by limiting them to defensive wars and who maintain order within by making civil war impossible, and 2) that of the philosophers, who come from the ranks of the guardians, and who wield power. Quite naturally, power goes to those who, because they can contemplate the Good, are best able to know what virtues

6 Luc Brisson, "Plato's View on Greek Government", in Hans Beck, ed., *A Companion to Ancient Greek Government* (Oxford: Wiley-Blackwell, 2012), 93–104; Jean-François Pradeau, *Plato and the City* [1997], transl. by Janet Lloyd (Exeter: University of Exeter Press, 2002).

stand for, which are intelligible realities. For Plato, the definition of a virtue cannot be obtained from the observation of virtuous acts, for it belongs to a world that can be perceived only by the intellect. The task of the philosopher-kings will therefore be to educate the rest of the citizens by directing their inner gaze toward these virtues. This leadership will be imposed upon them, for all competition between them will have disappeared, since they will have no relation to wealth.

Plato knew that this political model would unleash three waves of protest, in which contempt would be mixed with ridicule. The third wave is the one raised by the proposition of placing philosophers in power (*Republic* v 471c–480a). Yet the first – women, like men, can be guardians and philosophers (*Republic* v 455e–457b) and especially the second: the community of women and children (*Republic* v 457b–467d) are no less formidable.

In the *Republic*, Plato calls into question two essential presuppositions in the Athenian political system. A citizen by birth was a male who had rights, political, namely voting and being elected as a magistrate and economical, namely access to land ownership; and a duty, to be a soldier. Thus the prohibition of possession and the sharing of the military task with women were considered as challenging the status of a citizen.

And more fundamentally Plato implies a radically new conception of the human being. For Plato, what defines a human being is not his body but his soul (*Alcibiades* 132b-135b). The consequences of this position are decisive, particularly for women,[7] whose fate is no longer determined by their body. In the Athens where Plato lived, as in most traditional societies, the social role of women is determined by the fact that they conceive children, bear them, and raise them. This task keeps them confined inside the house, making all outside activity impossible for them. In short, the social role of women is dictated by their body, which imposes their fate upon them. Plato, in contrast, wished to define beings by their soul. For him, human beings, whatever their gender, are living beings,[8] made up of a body and a soul which has come to inhabit this body for a limited time, and which will survive it. Yet it is by the soul that a human being's identity is defined,[9] and the soul has no sex. This supposition

7 Natalie H. Bluestone, *Women and the Ideal Society: Plato's* Republic *and the Modern Myths of the Gender* (Amherst: University of Massachusetts Press, 1987).

8 Luc Brisson, "Le corps animal comme signe de la valeur d'une âme chez Platon", in Barbara Cassin and Jean-Louis Labarrière, eds., Gilbert Romeyer Dherbey, general ed., *L'Animal dans l'Antiquité* (Paris: Vrin, 1997), 227–45.

9 Luc Brisson, "L'intériorité chez Platon", in Gwenaëlle Aubry and Frédérique Ildefonse, eds., *Le moi et l'intériorité* (Paris: Vrin, 2008), 269–76.

has fundamental consequences as far as the distribution of roles in society is concerned, and particularly for women, as one might have expected. The tasks assigned to men and women must consequently be the same. A woman can therefore be a guardian, which must in itself have been scandalous at a time when being a soldier was the prerogative of men.[10] Consequently, women will therefore be subject to the same education as men, not only the education which implies culture (*mousiké*), but also that which involves physical exercises (*gumnastiké*) and hence nudity (*Republic* V 457a–b, cf. 452a–b).[11] And if they can be guardians, women can become philosophers, and lead the city.

At this point, a problem arises. If the *oikos*, the family in the broad sense, is eliminated, marriage disappeared at the same time. How, then, can one ensure the survival of the group of leaders, guardians and philosophers, which implies sexual relations between men and women, and how can one ensure the education of the children born from these unions? The survival of the species presupposes procreation and implies a certain stability in the first years of a child's life. Hence the idea of the community of women, which also implies that of children among the male and female guardians (*Republic* V 457c–d).

Since the male and female guardians must share everything – activities, meals, lodging etc. – they are naturally inclined to have sex with one another (*Republic* V, 458c–d).

However, these unions will not be left up to chance. Taking the example of animal husbandry, Plato suggests selecting, by means of rigged drawing of lots, men and women whose moral and physical excellence is established, so that they can unite on specific occasions (*Republic* V 460a–b). By law, the age of procreation begins at age 25 for a man, and at age 20 for a woman. Healthy children born from these unions will be confided to nursemaids, the others being eliminated (*Republic* V 460c). This law has not ceased to cause the greatest perplexity over the years, for two points seem to be intolerable: children do not know their parents, and above all, those who are malformed are exposed, as was the custom at the time.[12]

Incest – the union of a father or mother with their daughter or son, or with brothers and sisters – remains to be avoided as far as is possible. Strict rules are established to avoid it: boys and girls born after the gestation period following each union are considered brothers and sisters and cannot unite with one another or with those who can be considered as their parents. There is one

10 Example of the Amazons and the Sarmatians (*Laws* VIII 806a-b).

11 There is a similar requirement in the *Laws* (V 814c–d).

12 Pierre Brulé, "Infanticide et abandon d'enfants: pratiques grecques et comparaisons anthropologiques", *Dialogue d'Histoire Ancienne*, 18 (1992), 53–90.

exception, however: "But the law will allow brothers and sisters to have sex with one another if the lottery works out that way and the Pythia approves" (*Republic* v 461e). It should be noted, therefore, that even in Plato, incest is not condemned in all cases, although every effort is made to avoid it.

The same holds true for homosexuality, which is only condemned when it prevents procreation and violates the rules of *paederastía* (*Republic* III 403a-c).[13] In principle, the relations between lover and beloved in the context of *paederastía* should be chaste. Yet Socrates' words allow us to suppose that what counts in the last analysis is discretion.[14] Nevertheless, from the age of 40 for women and 55 for men, heterosexual activity becomes free, on two conditions: incest and procreation must be avoided (*Republic* v 461b–c). Thus, beginning with a specific age, male and female citizens rediscover considerable sexual freedom.[15] In short, for Plato the community of women and children takes its place within a very precise metaphysical context, in which human beings are defined by their soul and not by their body, and within a precise revolutionary project: to overthrow an existing constitution, democracy, in order to replace it by another one, an intellectual aristocracy.

Philosophers, who possess nothing, will have to be forced to lead the city, and the guardians will refrain from using their strength to appropriate the possessions of the producers. Thus, there will be no more families (*oikoi*) among the leaders of the Platonic city, competing to accede to political power.

How, then, can the unity of a city based on community, be ensured, in a city where the leaders are radically separated from those who must provide them with food and services? In practice, nothing can ensure the realization of this ideal. This is why Plato has recourse to myth in this dialogue:

SOCRATES How, then, could we devise one of those useful falsehoods we were talking about a while ago (II 383a ff.), one noble falsehood that would, in the best case, persuade even the rulers, but if that's not possible, then the others in the city?

GLAUCON What sort of falsehood?

13 On this, see Luc Brisson, "Eros éducateur: entre *paiderastia* et *philosophia*", in M. Tulli and M. Erler, eds., *Plato in Symposium*, Selected papers from the Tenth Symposium Platonicum [Pisa, July 2013] (Sankt Augustin: Academia Verlag, 2016), 24–35.

14 The same requirement is found at *Laws* VIII 840e.

15 Even though a law stipulates that the relations between a lover and his beloved must remain chaste (*Republic* III 402d-403c).

S. Nothing new, but a Phoenician story[16] which describes something that has happened in many places. At least, that's what the poets say, and they've persuaded many people to believe it too. It hasn't happened among us, and I don't even know if it could. It would certainly take a lot of persuasion to get people to believe it.

G. You seem hesitant to tell the story.

S. When you hear it, then, you realize that I have every reason to hesitate.

G. Speak, and don't be afraid.

S. I'll tell it, them, though I don't know where I'll get the audacity or even what words I'll use. I'll first try to persuade the rulers and the soldiers and the rest of the city that the upbringing and the education we gave them, and the experiences that went with them, were a sort of dream, that in fact they themselves, their weapons, and the other craftsmen's tools were at that time really being fashioned and nurtured inside the earth, and that when the work was completed, the earth, who is their mother delivered all of them up in to the world. Therefore, if anyone attacks the land in which they live, they must plan on its behalf and defend it as their mother and nurse and think of the other citizens as their earthborn brothers.

G. It isn't for nothing that you were so shy about telling your falsehood.

S. Appropriately so. Nevertheless, listen to the rest of the story. "All of you in the city are brothers", we'll say to them in telling our story, "but the god who made you mixed some gold into those who are adequately equipped to rule, because they are most valuable. He put silver in those who are auxiliaries and iron and bronze in the farmers and other craftsmen.

For the most part you will produce children like yourselves, but, because you are all related, a silver child will occasionally be born from a golden parent, and vice versa, and all the others from each other. So, the first and most important command from the god to the rulers is that there is nothing that they must guard better or watch more carefully than the mixture of metals in the souls of the

16 An allusion to the legend of the foundation of Thebes by the Phoenician Cadmos (see *Laws* II, 663d-e). Having killed a dragon, the guardian of a source, Cadmos, instructed by Athena, sowed the teeth of the dragon. Warriors sprang up from the earth; some of them survived and were the ancestors of the Thebans.

next generations. If an offspring of theirs should be found to have a mixture of iron or bronze, they must not pity him in any way, but give him the rank appropriate to his nature and drive him out to joint the craftsmen and farmers. But if an offspring of these people is found to have a mixture of gold or silver, they will honor him and take him up to join the guardians or the auxiliaries, for there is an oracle which says that the city will be ruined if it ever has an iron or bronze guardian". So, do you have any device that will make our citizens believe this story?

G. I can't see any way to make them believe it themselves, but perhaps there is one in the case of their sons and later generations and all the other people who come after them.

S. I understand pretty much what you mean, but even that would help to make them care more for the city and each other

Republic III 414b–415d

According to these myths, the city, in which families have been eliminated, henceforth constitutes a single family born of the same mother, the territory, but in which irremovable distinctions are established. We therefore find ourselves in a paradoxical situation: in the city of the *Republic*, the leaders, that is, the guardians and the philosophers, cannot have a family, but all the citizens are supposed to be part of the same family. This myth is explicitly considered to be a lie.

Even during Plato's life, criticisms must have rained down on military obligations extended to women, the community of women and children, and the prohibition against all possessions imposed on the guardians and the philosophers, who, moreover, are obliged to govern.

2.2 The *Laws*

Some forty years later, at the end of his life, Plato remodelled his political project in the *Laws*, still trying to neutralize the *oikos*, which is a divisive factor (*Laws* III 681a7-b7), and source of all other conflicts within the city[17] Plato adopts another strategy: he subordinates the family in the broad sense (*oikos*) to the share or domain (*kleros*).

17 See Luc Brisson, "Ethics and Politics in Plato's *Laws*", *Oxford Studies in Ancient Philosophy*, 28 (2005), 93–121.

The fundamental economic unit of the city of the *Laws* is the share or domain (*kleros*), which is not only to feed the owner and his family, but also to produce what is necessary for the upkeep of the slaves and resident aliens (*metics*), and the various contributions demanded by the city, which must live in a closed circuit, for commerce is forbidden. Thus, the basic social cell of the city (*oikos* or *hestia*) is defined; its number is fixed at 5,040 shares divided among twelve sectors, with the population being divided into twelve tribes. Each share consists of two parcels, one of which is situated near to the city center, and the other near the borders. Each family will therefore possess two houses, one in town and the other in a village.

In the share (*kleros*)- family (*oikos*) couple, it is not the human element that predominates. The originality of Platonic legislation, particularly with regard to inheritance law, resides in the will to harmonize the number of the population with that of the shares of land. The family is the means for preserving the share (*kleros*), and not *vice versa*. This is equivalent to the neutralization of the family (*oikos*) from an economic and human viewpoint.

The population is divided into four census classes. At first, the shares are identical from the viewpoint of their fertility, and each is attributed to a citizen farmer. Then, according to the revenue the colonists possess when they arrive, they are distributed into one of the four classes: in the first, which is the poorest, the farmer possesses his share and the value of this share as inalienable property. At the other extreme, the citizen-farmers of the fourth class will possess the equivalent of the value of five shares (*Laws* V 744a–d). Steps are taken to keep this distribution unchanged. All paid labour is forbidden to the citizens (V 742e, 743d–e, VIII 846d), and is reserved for non-citizens, whether resident aliens (*metics*) or slaves (VII 806d-e). Citizens cannot, moreover, engage in commerce (XI 919d-e, see also VIII 847d-e). The produce of the land is distributed among the citizens outside of any market; only non-citizens will have the right to buy food and other products at market (VIII 847e-848c). When products must be imported from abroad, certain magistrates (the guardians of the laws) will take charge of these transactions, once again outside of any market (VIII 847b-c). In any case, the currency used in the city will be worthless outside of it (V 741e–742b).

Men and women, who are equal in everything, including in education and military obligations, are obliged to marry at an age established by law: for a male, between 25 and 35 (IV 721a-b; VI 772b), and for a woman between 15 and 20 (VI 785b; VIII 833d). Expenditures are fixed in proportion to the class to which the families belong (VI 774e-775b). The goal of marriage is to ensure the permanence of the number of shares; this is why a childless marriage is dissolved after ten years (VI 775e-776a). Between the age of one and three, children are in the care of nursemaids, supervised by female magistrates (the marriage inspectors) (VII 793d-794c) who also regulate spouses and take charge of the re-marriage of widows (XI 926d-932d). The nuclear family is not annulled, as in the *Republic*, but it has limited room for manoeuvre.

Education is considered as the civic moulding of the body and the soul. From the age of six, it is universal and compulsory (VII 804c-d) for boys and girls, who, although they are separated from boys, receive a similar education. In addition to gymnastics, the study plan is detailed: reading and writing, general culture (poetry, music, dance, comic and tragic theater), mathematics, astronomy. In addition, the life of the citizen, who does not work, is a continuation of his education. Religious festivals and celebrations take place daily, and each time there is a festival that includes musical or sports competitions.

In this context, the functional tripartism described in the *Republic* recedes onto the background but subsists.[18] The leaders are magistrates chosen among all the citizens: the "Country Wardens" (*agronomoi*) fulfill the function of the guardians, and the members of the "Watch Committee" (*nukterinos sullogos*) play a role equivalent to that of the philosophers, while the remaining part replaces the producers. The unity of the city is maintained by means of the myth of *autochthony*; this time considered to be a lie:

ATHENIAN VISITOR But just suppose that the truth had been different from which the argument has now shown it to be, and that a lawgiver, even a mediocre one, had been sufficiently bold, in the interests of the young, to tell them a lie. Could he have told a more useful lie than this, or one more effective in making everyone practice justice in everything they do, willingly and without pressure?

CLINIAS Truth is a fine thing, and it is sure to prevail, but to persuade men of it certainly seems no easy task.

A.V. Yes, but what about that myth about the Sidonian. That was well-nigh incredible, but it was easy enough to convince men of it, and of thousands of other similar stories.

C. What sort of stories?

---

18 Luc Brisson, "Soul and State in Plato's *Laws*", in Rachel Barney, Tad Brennan and Charles Brittain, eds., *Plato and the divided self* (Cambridge: Cambridge University Press, 2012), 281–307.

A.V. The sowing of the teeth and the birth or armed men from them. This remarkable example shows the legislator that the souls of the young can be persuaded of anything; he has only to try. The only think he must consider and discover is that conviction would do the state most good; in that connection, he must think up every possible device to ensure that as far as possible the entire community preserves in its songs and myths and speeches an absolute and lifelong unanimity. But if you see the matter in any other light, have no hesitation in disputing my view

Laws II 663d-664a, transl. TREVOR J. SAUNDERS here and after

A city which is, in theory, without conflict is thus achieved. Yet at what a price! This is a city closed upon itself, highly hierarchical, in which authority, which comes from above, is not limited by any intermediary institution, since the family is either non-existent or else muzzled.

3 Assessment

Certain features seem intolerable to us today. Nevertheless, Plato was a man of his time.

1) The exposure of excess or malformed children constitutes the worst scandal, in our view. Yet it was a rather frequent practice at the time, as is shown by the story of Oedipus. To avoid the fulfillment of the oracle that had predicted that his son would kill him, Laios exposed the newborn, after having pierced his ankles to tie them with a strap, and the swelling caused by this wound explains the name of Oedipus ("swollen-footed"). The child was saved and raised in a royal family. As an adult, he killed his father Laios and married his mother Jocasta, before blinding himself.
2) Slavery is considered as an inevitable reality, for in the absence of technology and industry, enslaved human beings represented an indispensable labour force. Ancient Greece did not live in a market economy, dominated by exchange, as is the case today, but in a use economy. In this context, producers are subject to consumers, who assign them concrete tasks. It is the flutist who describes and judges the work of the flute-maker, for instance. This is why manual labour is held in low esteem and left to slaves. We can therefore understand why, except for purely defensive campaigns, the goal of military expeditions was almost always to seize slaves, who, along with metics, constitute the only labour force in

the *Laws*, and seem indispensable in the *Republic*, especially for transporting the warriors' heavy equipment.

A collateral consequence should be noted, moreover, of this attitude toward work, which is left to the slaves, and commerce, left up to the resident aliens or *metics*, in the society. These prejudices contributed to establish the idea that only the administration of an agricultural domain is appropriate for the status of a gentleman.

In contrast, Plato is positively innovative in at least two areas.

1) He proposes to give power to knowledge, as represented by the philosophers (*Republic* V 473c–e). Yet this desire to place philosophers in power, in one way or another, has never been realized. Plato's involvement in the affairs of Syracuse was marked by a resounding defeat, which, moreover, was to be continually repeated throughout history: Seneca with Nero, Descartes with Christina of Sweden, Voltaire with Frederick II of Prussia and Diderot with Catherine II of Russia, and Marx, who inspired so many revolutionaries. Philosophers and heads of state cannot smoothly collaborate. A philosopher is a man of the necessity sought by science, implied by moral imperatives, whereas a head of state is a man of the possible, in which strength and wealth predominate. The former is situated in the domain of the rational, whereas the latter must deal with human passions, which are, if not rebellious, then at least indifferent to reason. Whereas philosophers project over the long term, heads of state are assailed by the short- and middle-term. The production and exchange of wealth require to be realized in a specific period of time, and a military action must be undertaken at the right moment. Nevertheless, even if a head of state cannot conduct himself like a philosopher, some balance can be sought between political action and lofty principles.

However, modern societies have a strong tendency toward the rationalization of politics. Scientists from every background play an ever more important role in the management of society, and Plato, who sought to take power away from the wealthy and the violent, seems to have played a part in this process.

2) The most important innovation may well have been the position of women in society. By defining human beings not by their bodies, but by their souls, Plato liberated women. In the *Republic* and the *Laws*, women, who have the right to the same type of education, can be part of the armed forces, and although this is not stated explicitly, she can rise to the highest positions of responsibility. This revolution constitutes one of the three waves of mockery Socrates must confront in the *Republic* (V 473b–c). It is, however, difficult if not impossible to make Plato a feminist in the modern sense of the term, because the social context is not at all the same. He is nevertheless a precursor,

by insisting on the equality of men and women, whose destiny is no longer attached exclusively to their bodies.

If one leaves aside these intolerable features and these innovations, one can wonder, following Karl Popper, whether Plato did not, directly or indirectly, inspire Stalin or even Hitler. Yet is this really the case? This question cannot be answered directly, because of the chronological distance between Plato and his critics, but here is what can be said.

National Socialism and the Dictatorship of the Proletariat made their appearance within open, more or less democratic societies, in which elections were possible. A troubling analysis of this phenomenon is found in book IX of the *Republic* (565a- 571c) which describes how tyranny is born from democracy. The tyrant is desired by a population that wants to be protected. At first pleasant to all those he encounters, the tyrant is soon constrained to provoke wars to get rid of his enemies, to whom he hands over those who do not obey him. He seizes wealth and obtains absolute power. We see, then, that an open democratic society is not protected from totalitarianism.

As we have seen, Plato was reacting to a similar situation, which had brought about the destruction of a considerable part of the citizen population of Athens. In his view, this situation was the result of external conflicts and of internal conflicts caused by the incessant quest for wealth. This sociological analysis was not mistaken, but it was partial, for one can wonder whether the lure of wealth is the only cause of conflict, and whether strict control of wealth is enough to make all conflict impossible. All indications are that this is not the case.

One can, moreover, wonder whether it is possible for a society closed upon itself to last over time. Books VIII and IX of the *Republic* describe the decline of the excellent city that has just been described, and Plato is obsessed by the safeguarding of the city, particularly in the *Laws*.

There remains the question of myth considered as a lie. It is indeed myth that constitutes the cement of the societies of the *Republic* and the *Laws*. In both cases, the family in the broad sense is abolished or diminished, and it is replaced by the myth of autochthony. The city thus constitutes a single family, born of the same mother – the territory – but in which unshakeable distinctions are inevitable. We are thus in a paradoxical situation: in the city of the *Republic*, the leaders, that is, the guardians and the philosophers, cannot have a family, but all the citizens are supposed to be part of the same family. This myth is explicitly considered as a lie. Nevertheless, it must be admitted that Rousseau's social contract, on which our democracies are based, insofar as it intends to transcend the opposition between the people and political power, is a fiction. Never in the history of humanity has such an agreement been made among individuals. In short, no regime can lay claim to a real foundation: it is always based on a mythical tale.

Bibliography

Main Sources

Aeschines, *Against Timarchus* 173
Apology 24b-c
Herodotus
Isocrates, *Busiris*, 4
Laws II 663e-664a, transl. Trevor J. Saunders
Plato
Republic I 330a-b, transl. G.M.A. Grube, rev. C.D.C. Reeve
Republic III 414b-415d
Republic V 462a–b
Thucydides
Xenophon, *Memorabilia* I, 2, 56

Main Bibliographical References

Brisson, Luc, "Ethics and Politics in Plato's *Laws*", *Oxford Studies in Ancient Philosophy*, 28 (2005), 93–121.

Brisson, Luc, "Plato's View on Greek Government", in Hans Beck, ed., *A Companion to Ancient Greek Government* (Oxford: Wiley Blackwell, 2012), 93–104.

Brisson, Luc, "Soul and State in Plato's *Laws*", in Rachel Barney, Tad Brennan and Charles Brittain, eds., *Plato and the Divided Self* (Cambridge: Cambridge University Press, 2012), 281–307.

Natali, Carlo, "L'élision de l'*oikos* dans la *République* de Platon", in Monique Dixsaut et Annie Larivée, eds., *Études sur la* République *de Platon*, 1. *De la justice* (Paris: Vrin, 2005), 199–223.

Pradeau, Jean-François, *Plato and the City* [1997], transl. by Janet Lloyd (Exeter: University of Exeter Press, 2002).

CHAPTER 2

The Influence of Roman Law on Medieval Bulgarian Legislation

Sources and Developments of the Main Constitutional Issues

Petar Cholakov

This work studies the impact of Roman law on the institutions, statutes and legal proceedings during the First (680–1018) and the Second Bulgarian Tsardom or Empire (1185–1396). Mediaeval Bulgaria was characterized by legal dualism, a combination between customs (mostly of Slavs and Bulgars) and written laws which were, to a large extent, based on the Byzantine jurisprudence. The influence of the latter increased tremendously after the pagan state adopted Christianity from Constantinople in 864.[1] During the Middle Ages and the Renaissance the term 'Roman law' has been primarily used to denote the greatest achievement of Byzantine legal and political thought—*Corpus Iuris Civilis*, issued by order of Emperor Justinian I (527–565). The Byzantine statutes which were translated and adopted in Bulgaria elaborated on the text of *Corpus Iuris*.

In the first part of the chapter, I explain how the Byzantine *Ecloga* and Farmer's Law shaped the Slavic *Ecloga* and *Zakon Sudnyi Liudem*. I examine the connections between the *Nomocanon* (the first *Νομοκανών* was based on the *Novellae*, one of the four parts of the *Corpus Iuris Civilis*) and *Kormchaia Kniga*. The second part addresses the impact of Roman law on governance and institutions, an impact which is not easy to assess, as will be seen below. The position of the Bulgarian ruler towards the Church was even stronger than that of the Byzantine Emperor. I reveal that although the power of the tsar (khan, knyaz) had a divine origin, the Council of the Great Boyars was often instrumental in his selection, legitimation and even deposition. The third part explores the projections of Byzantine jurisprudence on the criminal law in Bulgaria. I juxtapose and analyze the vast catalogues of offences and punishments in the two countries.

1 One should remember, however, that the modern understanding of the term 'state' emerged much later: Quentin Skinner, *The Foundations of Modern Political Thought* (Cambridge: Cambridge University Press, 1978), vol.1, x.

 | DOI:10.1163/9789004549159_004

1 Legislation in the First and the Second Bulgarian Tsardom

There are several main historical sources regarding the jurisprudence and institutions of Mediaeval Bulgaria.[2] The most important are: statutes and collections of laws and regulations; endowment charters; peace treaties, as well as other sources (for example: the Name List of Bulgarian Khans; the *Reponsa Nicolai I Papae ad consulta Bulgarorum*; the *Boril's Synodic*; the *Sermon against the Heretics* of Cosmas the Priest, and others). The First Bulgarian Tsardom or Empire (State) was established in the autumn of 680 after a successful war with Byzantium. The only legislative acts from the pagan period, for which we have information, are Krum's (803–814) laws, which date from the beginning of the ninth century.[3] The development of the feudal society and economics were profound changes in Mediaeval Bulgaria. They lead to the adoption of Christianity during the rule of Boris I (852–889). However, this did not happen without problems. In 866 (or 865), the boils,[4] who opposed Christianity, rebelled against Boris I. Because the new religion was 'imported' from the Byzantine Empire the influence of the latter increased tremendously. The Bulgarian jurisprudence borrowed heavily from Byzantine legal writings and laws. Some of the latter were adopted in their entirety while others were modified and supplemented *ad hoc*.

The Byzantine *Ecloga* (or "selection") was adopted most likely in 726 by Leo III the Isaurian. The *Farmer's Law* (*Nomos Georgikos*, from the eight century) was used for the application of the *Ecloga*. The compilation included texts from both the civil and criminal law and its purpose was, as it was declared in the title, a rectification (of the Justinian legislation) towards a more philanthropic version.[5] On the one hand the *Ecloga* was based on *Corpus Iuris Civilis*, which however was a monument of the chattel slavery system, while the *Ecloga* mirrored the interest of the early feudalism. On the other hand, it

2 For an encompassing list of the sources, see Galabina Petrova, *History of the Bulgarian State and Law (680–1878)* (Sofia: Sibi, 2009) [in Bulgarian], 21–55; Dimitar Tokushev, *A History of Mediaeval Bulgarian State and Law* (Sofia: Sibi, 2009) [in Bulgarian], 27–89.

3 The main source for Krum's laws is the Byzantine *Suidae* lexicon—*Σουΐδας*, also known as the *Sudaor Souda*, a large tenth century Byzantine encyclopedia of the ancient Mediterranean world, formerly attributed to an author called Suidas.

4 The old Bulgar title '*boila*' (pl. '*boils*') denoted a high aristocratic status among the Bulgars. The oldest Slavic form of the word '*boyar*' (pl. '*boyars*'; similar to sg. '*bolyarin*', pl. '*bolyari* '(in Bulgarian: '*болярин*', pl. '*боляри*')) dates from the tenth century Bulgaria, where it may have stemmed from the old title '*boila*'.

5 The emperor issued the *Ecloga* in Greek instead of the traditional Latin, so that it could be understood by more people and utilized by judges as a practical legal manual.

also incorporated the customary law (the customs of the Slavs included) which was applied in the Eastern Roman Empire between the sixth and the eighth centuries. This is the reason why the *Ecloga* was introduced in Bulgaria immediately after the Christianization. It was translated into Bulgarian most likely during the reign of Tsar Simeon (893–927).

The analysis of the Bulgarian version reveals that is contains deviations from the original text. While the latter had a vast introduction and eighteen chapters (headlines), the Bulgarian version consisted of sixteen chapters. Because the economic relations had been less developed there than in Byzantium, chapter XII, which discussed long term rentals of real estate, was omitted. For the same reason, the crime "counterfeit of coins" went also unmentioned. Chapter XVII, which dealt with "sharing the profit", was merged with chapter XVIII on "punishment of crimes" (*ibidem*). Furthermore, the Slavic version of the famous compilation did not distinguish between civil and criminal lawsuits. The *Ecloga* regulated matters such as: betrothal (chapter I); marriage (chapter II); dowry (chapter III); donations (chapter IV); inheritance (chapter V), etc. The Slavic *Ecloga* introduced a more lenient treatment of slaves as well as a special right of inheritance to the poor.[6] The *Farmer's Law* was also translated into Bulgarian after the Christianization. It was very important, because the economy was primarily based on agriculture and stock breeding. Thus, the need to protect private property was great.[7]

The *Nomocanon* (*Νομοκανών*) is a collection combining elements from both the civil law (such as the *Ecloga*) and the canon law. It was also translated into Bulgarian after the Christianization. The first *Nomocanon* in Byzantium was created by Patriarch John Scholasticus in the sixth century and consisted of fifty titles; the second was created in the seventh century and had fourteen chapters. This second *Nomocanon* was edited in the ninth century by the Patriarch of Constantinople Photios. The Bulgarian name used at the time for this book was *Kormchaia kniga*—Helmsman's or Pilot's Book. The title stems from the Biblical comparison of the Church of Christ with a ship, steered by the Holy Scripture and the Canons, in the way a vessel is guided by its helmsman.

Zakon Sudnyi Liudem (*Законъ соудьныи людьмъ* in Old Church Slavonic, from now on abbreviated *ZSL*), sometimes referred to as "the Legal Code of Tsar Constantine", is also based on the Byzantine law, more particularly on Title XVII of the *Ecloga*—"On Crimes and Punishments". The prevailing

6 According to it, half of the property of the deceased husband belonged to his wife, the other half to the Church and the poor.

7 Petrova, *History of the Bulgarian State and Law*, 29–33.

understanding is that the code has a Bulgarian origin.[8] It was written in Old Church Slavonic. The original is not preserved, only the text from the Russian *Kormchaia kniga*. The ZSL was most likely promulgated during the rule of Boris I. The *ZSL* consists of thirty-two articles. Article 1 is dedicated to the heathens; arts. 2 and 7a are on testimonials; art. 3 discusses spoils of war; arts. 4 to 13 deal with crimes against sexual morality (fornication; seduction; rape; incest; bigamy); arts. 14 and 15 are on arson; art. 16 discusses the right of asylum; art. 17 is on arbitrariness; art. 18 is on testimonies; art. 19 is on liberation of slaves; art. 20 deals with "testimony based on rumours"; art. 21 is on apostasy; art. 22 is on loans. Articles 23 to 30 deal with different types of thefts (e.g., a theft during the time of war, a theft by a slave, by a freeman, etc.). Article 30a describes the grounds for dissolution of marriage.[9]

The analysis of the historical context reveals that ZSL responded to the urgent imperatives of the epoch. In 865, malcontents from all ten administrative regions (*komitats*) revolted against Boris I and accused him of giving them "a bad law". The ruler ordered the execution of fifty-two boyars—the leaders of the revolt, "along with their whole families". Later, Boris's son Knyaz Vladimir Rasate (889–893) attempted to eradicate Christianity. Boris blinded him and installed his third son Simeon on the throne. Therefore, it is not at all surprising that the sanctions for the heathens which the ZSL envisages are the most severe. The heathens posed the main threat for the authorities and institutions of the young Christian state at the time. However, the sanctions for those who deviated from the "Christian morality" were lenient in comparison with Byzantine law. The latter postulated corporal punishments while the Bulgarian lawgivers envisaged spiritual ones (fasting, excommunication, anathema, etc.).

Zakon Sudnyi Liudem reiterates some of the Byzantine legal provisions, departs from or modifies others and introduces new ones. The Bulgarian law does not mention the crimes and punishments described in the original, such as: treason, forming a party against the emperor, conspiracy, murder (murder by poisoning, premeditated murder, involuntary murder, inflicting body injuries with a sword), libel, etc. Of course, these crimes existed, and they were punished by death but on the basis of the old customary law, as it was apparent

8 Petrova, *History*, 35; Gustav Andreevich Rosenkampf, *A review of the Pilot's book in its historical form* (Moscow: Imperial University, 1829) [in Russian]; M. Andreev, "Regarding the Question about the Origin and the Essence of *Zakon Sudnyi Liudem*" (Sofia: University of Sofia, Yearbook of the Faculty of Law, 1957), vol. 4 [in Bulgarian]; Venelin Ganev, '*Zakon Sudnyi Liudem*': *Legal-historical and legal-analytical research* (Sofia: Bulgarian Academy of Sciences Press, 1959) [in Bulgarian]; Tokushev, *A History*.

9 Petrova, *History*, 35; Tokushev, *A History*, 69–70.

from the answers of Pope Nicholas I. The text of ZSL also contains original provisions. For example, art. 1 states that one who practices pagan rituals and spells must be punished severely. No such text existed in the Byzantine *Ecloga* because paganism had long been eradicated in the Byzantine Empire.

Between 1018–1185 Bulgaria was under Byzantine rule. During this period the Byzantine laws were enforced in the Bulgarian lands. The most important ones were the *Basilicae* (*repurgatio veterum legum*) or *Basilics* of Leo the Philosopher (called also "the Wise"), which by the eleventh century had replaced Justinian's laws as the primary source of Roman law;[10] the *Prochiron* (c. 870 or 872) of Basil the Macedonian, which invalidated parts of the *Ecloga* and restored Justinian's Laws; and last but not least the *Epanagoge* or *Eisagoge*[11] (*repetita pro electio legis*), also of Basil the Macedonian, which was completed by his son Leo VI the Wise. As indicated by the title, *Eisagoge* was intended to be an introduction to the *Basilicae*. The latter consisted of sixty books. The *Basilics* did not abrogate the *Corpus Iuris Civilis* but gave some ordering to its (at times) chaotic nature; they supplemented and expanded the creation of Justinian and his lawyers. The *Basilics* included the *Prochiron* (a handbook of civil laws and customs which excluded those that were no longer in use), the *Epanagoge*, as well as numerous decrees of the Iconoclast Emperors. Importantly, the Code still followed the tradition set by the *Corpus Iuris*. It began with ecclesiastical law, followed by sources of law, procedure, private law, administrative law, and criminal law.

After the successful uprising of Asen and Petar in 1185, Bulgaria became independent again. There are very few sources regarding the legislation during the Second Bulgarian Empire. The historians have only indirect evidence of the main pieces of legislation which existed in that epoch. Kormchaia, Zakon, *Ecloga* and *Farmer's law* were used and applied (for example a version of Kormchaia-Zonara, was sent to Russia in 1265 by despot Svetoslav). Of some importance were also other legal collections, such as the *Syntagma Canonum* of Matthew Blastares (1290–1360), the *Hexabiblos* of Constantine Harmenopoulos (1320-c. 1385) and the Dušan's Code.

10 An abridged version, the *Synopsis Basilicorum*, was also prepared in the tenth century. By the ninth century the knowledge of Latin was more and more obsolete which made the *Corpus Iuris Civilis* virtually unusable for most of the Greek speaking subjects of the Byzantine Empire. Furthermore, the development of social relations demanded new and unambiguous legislation.

11 An introduction (to the law)—*εἰσαγωγή* (*τοῦ νόμου*).

2 Governance and Institutions

2.1 *On the Byzantine Sources*

In order to fully assess the impact that the Byzantine legislation had on Mediaeval Bulgaria, we have to turn to the political ideas and institutions of the (Eastern) Roman Empire. The political thought of Byzantium was very conservative. It was based on the philosophy of Ancient Greece. This is most apparent in the idea of *basileia* as *mimesis* of the celestial order. The Greek element was but one of the building blocks of the Byzantine civilization, the other two were of Roman and Christian origin.[12] The first historian of the Christian Church, Eusebius of Cesarea (263–339), was able to adapt the ideas of Ancient Greece to the notion of a Christian Empire led by a Christian Emperor. Unlike the pagan rulers before him, Constantine the Great (c. 272–337) was not *dominus et deus* but a *lord* who received his power from God. The emperor was a friend of God, guided by the *logos*. After his death Constantine was canonized as Saint Constantine (*Άγιος Κωνσταντίνος*), but he was 'elevated' to only an equal of the apostles (*isapostolos*).

The Byzantines did not have a written constitution. Therefore, if one wanted to understand how the institutions of the Empire operated one had to explore essential pieces of legislation, such as *Corpus Iuris Civilis*, to consider the political ideas outlined above, as well as the historical traditions and practices. *Corpus Iuris Civilis* of Emperor Justinian I was perhaps the greatest monument of the jurisprudence of the Byzantine Empire.[13] Through *Corpus Iuris* the ideas of Roman and Byzantine jurists reached the European West in the twelve century. The impact of the reception was enormous and long-lasting. It developed as *ius commune*, a combination of cannon law and Roman law (after *Corpus Iuris* was 'rediscovered' in the twelfth century), which formed the basis of a common system of legal thought in Western Europe, with the important exception of England. The latter had its own distinct legal tradition,

12 D.M. Nicol, "Byzantine Political Thought", in J.H. Burns, ed., *The Cambridge History of Medieval Political Thought, c.350–c.1450* (Cambridge: Cambridge University Press, 1997), 53. For more information on Byzantine political thought and institutions, see as well: Ernst Barker, *Social and Political Thought in Byzantium from Justinian I to the Last Palaeologus* (Oxford: Clarendon Press, 1957); John Procopé, "Greek and Roman Political Theory", in Burns, ed., *The Cambridge History of Medieval Political Thought*, 21–37.

13 For a thorough introduction to Roman law see David Johnston, *"The Jurists", in Christopher Rowe and Malcolm Schofield, eds., The Cambridge History of Greek and Roman Political Thought (Cambridge: Cambridge University Press, 2005), pp. 616–34.*

which was separate from the rest of Europe, because it was based on its own common law.[14]

The ambiguous nature of *Corpus* Iuris had been thoroughly examined in the scientific literature.[15] On the one hand, this remarkable compendium was used in the West during the Middle Ages, Renaissance and Reformation in order to support the aspirations of absolutism (e.g., "*quod principi placuit legis habet vigorem*", "*νόμος ἔμψυχος*"). On the other hand, it 'helped' the attempts to justify the ideas of limited government and even resistance against tyranny ("*vim vi repellere licet*", "*quod omnes tangit ab omnibus approbari debet*",[16] etc.). But first and foremost, the ambivalent character of the Roman law had applications for the political practice in the Byzantine Empire itself. According to *Corpus Iuris*, the emperor was the embodiment of justice ("*lex animata, nomos empsychos*") and above the law ("*princeps legibus solutus*"). However, in theory, the Byzantine monarchy *was also elective*—by the senate, the army, and the people. The choice revealed the will of God. The emperor could, therefore, be removed by his electors. The patriarch could even excommunicate the *βασιλεύς Ῥωμαίων*. Forty-three of the Byzantine emperors were violently removed or forced to abdicate. Thus, *Corpus Iuris* was probably employed as a political weapon by those who wanted to *legitimize* the abrupt shifts in the corridors of power.[17]

The term 'caesaropapism' which has been used to describe the relationship between the Emperor and the Church is not apt.[18] Perhaps this notion most closely mirrored the reality during the reign of Justinian the Great. Contrary to

---

14 Ennio Cortese, *La norma giuridica: Spunti teorici nel diritto commune classico* (Milan: Giuffrè, 1962–1964), 2 vols; António M. Hespanha, *Cultura jurídica europeia: Síntese de um milénio* (Coimbra: Almeida, 2012).

15 Alexander Passerin d'Entrèves, *Natural Law: An Introduction to Legal Philosophy* (London: Hutchinson, 1967); Skinner, *Foundations*.

16 Of course, the original meaning of the latter principle ("what concerns all must be approved by all") had nothing to do with limited government or popular sovereignty. It arranged the legal relationship between a guardian and a ward, see *Corpus Iuris Civilis* (1922), 14 ed. stereotyp., vol.1, *Institutiones*, recognivit P. Krueger; *Digesta*, recognivit Th. Mommsen (Beidinum, Weidman, 1922); P. Stein, "Roman Law", in Burns, ed., *The Cambridge History of Medieval Political Thought*, 47. This postulate, as well as many others were taken out of their context and used in the political struggles; see Skinner, *Foundations*; Petar Cholakov, "Roman Law as Political Weapon", *Political Studies*, 1 (2008), 99–113 [in Bulgarian]; *Idem*, *Punishment of Tyrants: the Protestant and the Liberal Doctrines of Resistance* (Sofia: Bulgarian Academy of Sciences, 'Marin Drinov' Press, 2013) [in Bulgarian].

17 Nicol, "Byzantine Political Thought", 64; Cholakov, "Roman Law as Political Weapon".

18 Nicol, *ibidem*, 67.

his own statements,[19] he disrupted the sacred accord (συμφωνία) between the two institutions. During his rule the 'symphony' was broken and, as a contemporary remarked, one could hear only the voice of the 'State' while the Church was silent. In my opinion, the balance of power between the two institutions was not a constant. It shifted through the centuries.[20] Firstly, the Romans (the Byzantines) did not make a specific, firm difference between 'state' and 'church'. The empire (*basileia*) was the church on earth. The emperor was its visible head and the arbiter of its councils. He could not only revise but create new laws (*novelae*). The canon laws, the laws of the church, were also laws of the land. The emperor presided the church councils as princeps presided the *senatus.*[21] He signed the decrees of these assemblies—otherwise they could not become laws. Theodosius the Great (347–395) coined the term 'orthodoxy'; heterodoxy was a crime.[22] Justinian declared laws the decisions of the first four councils (Nicaea, Constantinople, Ephesus and Chalcedon). There were as well the *nomocanones*, also established by the emperors. The true boundary between *imperium* and *sacerdotium* was in the fact that the emperor was not a priest. He was holy but not *hiereus kai basileus.*

Secondly, from the fifth century on, the emperor was crowned by the patriarch. This was a new element which was not present in the pagan Roman tradition. At first this ritual did not signify the supremacy of the church over the state. But inevitably this act "became one of consecration of the duly elected ruler and the patriarch required a profession of faith from the emperor before he would perform it". And in the thirteenth century, when the authority of the church clearly dominated over that of the emperor, to the ceremony of anointment with oil was added that of Chrismation, in which the patriarch "set the seal of holy Spirit" on the ruler. During the periods of iconoclasm[23]

19 Justinian claimed that there is a clear distinction between *regnum* and *sacerdotium*. He professed the need of harmony between church and state. "The imperial authority is concerned with human affairs and the priesthood with things divine; the two are regarded as closely interdependent, but, at least in theory, neither is subordinated to the other", see F.L. Cross and E.A. Livingstone, eds., *The Oxford Dictionary of the Christian Church* (New York: Oxford University Press, 1985), 2nd edition, revised 771.

20 My thesis here ("Roman Law as Political Weapon") is close to this in George Ostrogorsky, *History of the Byzantine State* (New Brunswick: Rutgers University Press, 1986), revised edition.

21 In the Roman Republic, the *princeps senatus* summoned and adjourned the senate, decided its agenda, etc. After the fall of the Republic, the Roman Emperor became *princeps senatus*.

22 Nicol, 'Byzantine Political Thought', 67.

23 The Byzantine Iconoclasm has been subdivided into two periods. The "First Iconoclasm" lasted between about 726 and 787. The "Second Iconoclasm" was between 814 and 842.

scholars like John of Damascus (c.674/5–749) and Theodore the Studite (759–826) were not afraid to remind emperors that their authority must be exercised within certain limits. According to them the *basileus* could not make laws for the church. Ultimately, the latter emerged stronger and victorious out of the *Εἰκονομαχία*.[24]

2.2 *Institutions of the First and the Second Bulgarian Empire*

The Bulgarian state ruled over several main ethnicities: Bulgars, Slavs and Thracians. According to Theophanes the Confessor (c. 758/760–817/818) it was based upon a pact (*to koinon*) between Bulgars and Slavs. The name 'Bulgaria' was used for the whole state from the ninth century onwards.[25] Initially the Bulgarian ruler bore the title 'Great Khan';[26] the first 'kniaz' was Boris I (852–889), and the first 'tsar'—Simeon (he was crowned as "Caesar" / "Emperor of the Bulgarians" by the Byzantine Patriarch Nicolas Mystikos in 913).[27] Simeon the Great, however, dared to call himself "Basileus of Bulgarians and Romans". The title 'tsar' was officially recognized by the Romans (the Byzantines) in 927 to Simeon's son Petar I of Bulgaria (927–969).[28]

The political power had a divine origin during both the pagan period and in the Christian era. The ruler was placed on the throne by God. The state was seen as patrimony or a private property of the ruler. The first born or, as an exception a younger son(s),[29] inherited the throne. The cases of violent seizure

---

24 Nicol, "Byzantine Political Thought", 63–4; Galabina Petrova, *Church and Church Law in Mediaeval Bulgaria* (Sofia: Sibi, 2008) [in Bulgarian], 274.

25 In the Malamirovo or Hambarli inscription (a Bulgarian Greek inscription of around 813, commemorating Bulgarian victories of Khan Krum over the Byzantines) the name of the territory of the Bulgars was described with the Bulgar word *'sacart'* ('state'). It is possible that, at that time, the perception distinguished between two states, Bulgars and Slavs, joined in a union. Petrova, *Church and Church Law*, 72–73.

26 However, the Byzantine sources, until at least 927, used a chaotic multitude of titles to describe his status: *'arhon'*; *'kurios'*, *'hegemon'*, *'protos'*, etc.; the situation with the Western sources is similar, the titles used included but were not limited to; *'princeps'*, *'rex'*, *'dominus'*, etc. The Bulgarian sources called the ruler *'arhon'* (before 907, when the title *'kniaz'* is used for Boris I).

27 There are other interpretations of this ceremony, but this is the prevailing theory. See George *Ostrogorsky, "Avtokrator i samodržac", Glas Srpske kraljevske akademije, 164 (1935), 95–187 [in Serbian];* cf. Vasil Zlatarski, *History of Bulgarian State during the Middle Ages* (Sofia: Bulgarian Academy of Sciences, 'Marin Drinov' Press, 1994), 3 vols.

28 For more information, see the now classic analysis of S. Runciman, *"Emperor of the Bulgars and the Romans", A History of the First Bulgarian Empire (London: George Bell and Sons, 1930).*

29 For example, Simeon I is the third son of Boris I, Petar is the son of Simeon from his second marriage.

of power were not rare. For example, the dynasty Vokil has been violently deposed by Ugain. The ruler was supreme governor of the country. The treasury was his. He was the supreme military commander, legislator (Krum, Boris, Simeon) and judge. During the pagan period he was also the high priest.

The power of the *khan* was, however, not unlimited. In order to understand the role of the "people" and of the popular assembly (council) we could take a look at the following telling example. In 766 Sabin was removed from the throne because he did not take advantage of the defeat of the Byzantines at sea and, instead, wanted to make peace with them. The angry boils convened a council (*conventus*) and elected a new great khan. Therefore, the popular assembly could legitimise or revoke particularly important decisions/policies. Another essential institution was the Council of the Great Boyars[30] (or Bolyars). It could be seen as a 'predecessor' to the council of ministers. It was much more than a consultative body and had an important role, especially when taking crucial decisions. The most powerful figure in the Council was the *kavkhan*. He was the second most important person in the state after the Bulgarian ruler. The *kavkhan* was a commander-in-chief of the Bulgarian army and one of the primary diplomats in the state; the *kavkhan* was sometimes a regent or co-ruler. The *ichirgu-boila*or *chargobilya* was the commander of the garrison of the capital and was the third most important person in the state after the ruler and the *kavkhan*.

In 1185 Bulgaria gained its independence after 167 years of Byzantine rule. The pinnacle of the Second Bulgarian Tsardom was during the reign of Ivan Asen II (1218–1241) when it bordered on three seas (Black, Aegean, and Adriatic). The Second Bulgarian Empire was a hereditary monarchy ruled by a tsar. The monarchs of Bulgaria styled themselves "In Christ the Lord Faithful Emperor and Autocrat of all Bulgarians" or variations of this formula, sometimes including "and Romans, Greeks, or Vlachs".[31] The Bulgarian ruler, the tsar, was a complete master of the country. He had the treasury at his disposal; appointed the governors of the provinces, senior dignitaries; distributed property and titles; he was the supreme commander and judge; declared war and concluded international treaties; he presided church councils. His power came from God. In the Chronicle of Manassas Ivan Alexander was painted next to Jesus Christ, with a crown and a gold halo on his head. The power of the queen

30 I use the terms 'Boyars' and 'Bolyars' (as well as 'Boyar' and 'Bolyar') interchangeably.

31 P. Petrov and V. Gyuzlev, *Reader on the History of Bulgaria, volume 2: High Middle Ages (XII–XIV centuries) (Sofia: Nauka i Izkustvo, 1978) [in Bulgarian], 608.*

(*tsaritsa*) came also from God. She was depicted on coins; she participated in the regency, she was a *ktitor* (a donator) of churches, monasteries, etc.[32]

The crown was passed by custom and by law. In general, power was passed from father to his eldest son, from brother to brother, and then on to the next of kin. When there was no legitimate heir or as a result of a *coup d'état*, the boyars *elected* a new tsar (for example, Mihail Shishman).[33] Not surprisingly, the Council of the Great Boyars was an institution of great importance and standing. It could not only choose, but, at certain circumstances, even depose the ruler. The Boyar Council included the greater boyars and the patriarch. It discussed issues about external and internal policies, such as declarations of war, formations of alliances, or the signing of peace treaties. The highest-ranking administrative officials were the *great logothete*, who had the functions of a first minister, and the *protovestiarios*, who was responsible for the treasury and finance. High court titles such as *despot* and *sebastokrator* were awarded to the emperor's relatives but were not strictly concerned with administrative functions. Nonetheless they were even more important than the officials mentioned above. Most *despots* were close relatives of the tsar. They were his 'first assistants' in the government of the country. Despots and *sebastokrators* had substantial administrative, military, and financial power.[34]

Unlike what happened in the First Empire, the administration during the Second Bulgarian Empire was heavily influenced by the Byzantine system of administration. Most of the titles of the nobility, the court, and the administration were directly adopted from their Byzantine counterparts in Byzantine Greek or were translated into Bulgarian. There were still some differences in the ranking systems between the two countries.[35] The capital of the Second Bulgarian Empire was Tarnovo. Bulgaria was divided into provinces, the numbers of which varied with the territorial changes of the country. In surviving primary sources, the provinces were named with the Byzantine term '*hora*' or the Bulgarian terms '*zemya*', '*strana*' and '*oblast*'. The provincial governors were titled 'duke' or '*kefalia*' (both from Byzantine '*dux*' and '*kephale*') and were directly appointed by the tsar. During the Second Empire, the Bulgarian society was divided into three social classes: clergy, nobility, and peasantry. The

32 Petrova, *History*, 89. Powerful women exercised important influence on government. For example, Irina, the second wife of Ivan Asen II, participated in the plot against underaged Kaliman I; after his murder she was a regent of her son Mihail II Asen.

33 Petrova, *History*, 92–3.

34 When there were two brothers, one became a *despot*, the other a *sebastokrator*.

35 There are few surviving sources about the precise obligations, insignia, or ceremonial affairs of the mediaeval Bulgarian administration.

nobility included the aristocracy: the bolyars, the judges, and, according to the tradition, the "whole army".

The question regarding the balance of power between state and church (between tsar and patriarch) was decided in favour of the secular authorities in Mediaeval Bulgaria. There were several reasons for that. In the first place, for almost two centuries, during the pagan period, the Bulgarian ruler was also the supreme priest of the pagan religion. As we saw above, according to the official *theocratic* doctrine, the khan's power was from God. This tradition became embedded in the Bulgarian political culture and had an impact during the latter Christian period. Secondly, the Christianity was adopted from the Byzantine Empire where the state, at least in that particular period (ninth century), often dominated the Church. Thirdly, the initiative for Christianization belonged to the Bulgarian *khan*. The adoption of the new religion was carried through Byzantine priests, however, in order to limit their impact (and the influence of the Byzantine court), their work was closely monitored by the ruler. Boris I was not only the one who was able to establish but also to defend the Bulgarian church. The ruler crushed mercilessly the pagan rebellion which followed immediately after the adoption of Christianity. During Boris's rule, in 870 the Church of Bulgaria became autonomous from Byzantium. As mentioned above, Knyaz Boris deposed his own firstborn son Vladimir in 893, after the latter tried to restore paganism. Boris then chaired the council (*subor*) of Preslav (893) on which Simeon was elected knyaz of the Bulgars. The Byzantine clergy was expelled, and the Ancient Bulgarian alphabet became the official language of state and church. Finally, Boris moved the political and administrative centre from the old pagan capital Pliska to Preslav—a symbol of the new beginning. For all these reasons, it was natural that the archbishop will be selected by the *knyaz*. Still, it is important to emphasize the fact, that there is insufficient historical evidence regarding the precise role of the *knyaz* in hierarchy and appointments in the church. In 927 the Byzantine Empire officially acknowledged the title 'tsar' of the Bulgarian ruler as well as the title 'patriarch' of the head of Bulgarian church. The Bulgarian ruler continued to protect the Church. The Bulgarian Tsar Petar I waged a war against the Bogomils.[36] The

---

36 He asked the Byzantine Patriarch Theophylactos for advice. The latter stated that according to the civil laws the heretics must be punished by death. Based on these recommendations, state and church both waged a war against the heretics, Cosma the Priest, for example, wrote his famous *Sermon against the Heretics*. See *J. Sampimon and S. van Halsema, "Cosmas Presbyter. Homily Against the Bogumils. Operational Edition"* (*Columbus: Ohio State University, 2005*), *full text available from: https://www.webcitation.org* (*webpage retrieved on October 22, 2017*).

leading role of the state in the matters of faith was apparent in the communion with Rome (1204) as well as the Second council against the Bogomils in 1211 (chaired by Boril); in the restoration of the Bulgarian Patriarchy in 1235 and in the councils in 1355 and 1360 against the heretics.[37]

3 The Law in Mediaeval Bulgaria—Revisited

The analysis of the impact of the Byzantine law paints thus far a rather broad, non-detailed picture. The purpose of this section is to go deeper into the matter. More particularly, I examine the way the reception of Roman law affected the criminal jurisprudence in Mediaeval Bulgaria. Certainly, the influence of the Byzantine legal genius was much broader, profound, and encompassing; it affected all branches of law, and society. Let us take the institution of 'marriage' for example. In the pagan period, women had virtually no rights. The power of the man over the family was almost unlimited. Polygamy was allowed. After the Christianization of Bulgaria, the status of woman was elevated, she became almost an equal to man. For instance, her agreement was necessary for concluding engagement and marriage; she could ask for divorce; after her husband's death she managed his property and was guardian of his children; the dowry remained wife's property during the marriage, etc.[38]

3.1 *Criminal Law—General Characteristics and Types of Crime*

In ancient times the personal (private) revenge,[39] the talion, was widespread. In order to avoid the severe and uncontrollable consequences of *ius talionis* the wealthier members of society started to use a ransom (paid in kind or later in money to the family of the victim which would otherwise seek revenge)—*compositio*. Before the adoption of Christianity, the state prosecuted only the crimes against institutions of government or those offences which endangered the interest of the ruling classes. The crimes against personal freedom, morality (such as rape, etc.) and bodily harm were considered of private

37 Petrova, *History*, 288–309.

38 Still, the legal requirements for a divorce were not strictly observed regarding the tsar and the higher aristocracy. The personal lives of Gavril Radomir and Ivan Asen II are telling examples, see Petrova, *History*, 124–8, 140.

39 This institution of *lex talionis* was well-known in ancient times. For example, it existed in the code of Hammurabi and the Talmud. The rule 'an eye for an eye' however was seen as incompatible with the 'turn the other cheek' principle, enshrined in the words of Jesus in the Sermon on the Mount.

nature (excluding libel, however). It was the family or the clan that revenged for them. After the Christianisation, the Bulgarian *Zakon Sudnyi* Liudem incorporated from the Byzantine *Ecloga* the law of asylum. Furthermore, art. 18 of the ZSL explicitly prohibited the use of *ius talionis* in a property dispute and art. 17 listed the sanctions for those who do not observe the right of asylum. Nonetheless, the old pagan tradition of 'taking the law in one's own hands' was preserved in certain cases. For example, in the ZSL, in the chapter "On Murder", remained the old custom of blood revenge and blood money or *compositio* together. The modern-day principle of the rule of law was not established in the legislation—the rich received a lesser, lighter punishment for the same offence, as exemplified in the *Ecloga* and in the ZSL.[40]

A crucial question in any judgement of a court of law is this of the guilt of the perpetrator. In other words, to use the modern-day legal lingo, it is essential to determine if the crime is premeditated, is it an accident or a result of negligence. In ancient times such differences were not made. But during the Middle Ages these aspects started to be taken into consideration. This is evident in historical sources such as Reponsa Nicolai I Papae, which reveal that Bulgarians asked the Roman Pontiff what should be done if a man accidently ("involuntary") murders another.[41] The concept of 'guilt' was considered in *Nomos georgikos* and in *Zakon Sudnyi Liudem*. However, mediaeval legislators did not use the concepts of self-defense and exigency.[42] The mediaeval Bulgarian law distinguished between several main types of crimes: against state and faith, bodily integrity, honour and personal freedom, morality, and property.

3.1.1 Crimes against State and Faith

The Mediaeval Bulgarian state was based on a very strict military organization, service and discipline. Unsurprisingly, the oldest crimes against state were those in which the offender did not fulfill his obligations towards the army. It is known how these crimes were dealt with before the Christianization from sources such as Pope Nicholas's Responses.[43] For instance, in the latter, Knyaz Boris I asked the Bishop of Rome what is to be done, according to the Christian faith, with the deserters. Although in pagan times such offences were punished

40 Petrova, *History*, 168–9, 171.

41 See P. Petrov and G. Petrova, eds., *History of the Bulgarian State and Law-Sources, 680–1944*, (Sofia: Albatross, 2010) [in Bulgarian], 31. The Responses of Pope Nicholas I: chapter XXX.

42 The notion of the 'right of the sword' or *'ius gladii'*, which was known during the Middle Ages in Western Europe, can be seen as a predecessor of the right of self-defense. See Petrova, *History*, 179; Cholakov, *Punishment of Tyrants*.

43 Petrov and Petrova, *History*, 31.

by death, Pope Nicolas's counsel to the legislator was, if possible, to be more lenient. The death penalty was also applied to soldiers who were not properly equipped for the battlefield, or to those who rode military horses during the time of peace.[44]

The offences against the ruler such as *lèse-majesté* were punished severely. A telling fact, which revealed that the power struggles in Mediaeval Bulgaria were ferocious, was that many rulers were murdered.[45] Title XVII of the *Ecloga*, which followed the norms of the Justinian's law, postulated that "whoever forms a party against the tsar, conspires, or creates a plot against him or against the Christian state, he must be killed on the spot". This legislation was also used to suppress and eradicate any form of resistance[46] or even disapproval of government. The Church fully supported the legitimate rulers. For example, in *Boril's* Synodic there was a special "triple anathema" to "those who want to harm the tsar".[47]

In pagan times, Christians were subjected to merciless persecutions. After the adoption of the 'new' religion, Bulgarian lawgivers strived to eradicate the crimes against Christianity.[48] Heresy was a criminal offence which was typically punished by death as Title XVII of the *Ecloga* testifies. Apart from Bogomilism[49] which was widespread in Bulgaria, other important sects were the Manichaens, the Paulicians, the followers of Barlaam of Seminara (Barlaam of Calabria) and Gregory Akindynos who opposed Hesychasm of Gregory Palamas. Apostasy was also a dangerous offence, punished not only by the canons, but by the statutes—*nomoi*. Another group of crimes were those against Christian norms, customs and rules. To this group belonged paganism, divination, witchcraft, etc. The pagan nobles were punished more severely than the rest of the population. The authorities realised that with their influence the members of the aristocracy could undermine the stability of the state itself. The properties of pagan nobles were sold and the funds which were obtained were given to the poor. Furthermore, as we saw above, the pagan boyars who revolted against Boris I were sentenced to death.[50] Perjury was also offence

44 Petrov and Petrova, *History*, 31; Petrova, *History*, 181–2.

45 For example, the brothers Asen, Petar and Kaloyan, Kaliman I Asen, Mihail II Asen, etc.

46 For instance, Tsar Boril was a usurper who used the council in 1211, convened against the Bogomils, also to get rid of the boyars who were against him.

47 Petrov and Petrova, *History*, 111.

48 St. Kliment of Ohridski mentioned as such crimes "idolatry, slander, theft, robbery, drunkenness, fornication" and many other "sinful deeds". See Petrova, *History*, 185.

49 Bogomilism was Christian neo-Gnostic or dualist religious sect founded in the First Bulgarian Empire by the priest Bogomil in the tenth century.

50 As art. 1 of *Zakon Sudnyi Liudem* postulates.

against Christianity. Ancient peoples had the custom to swear on a sword—a pagan custom. After the Christianisation of Bulgaria, during a trial the witnesses swore in the Gospel that they will tell only the truth. If it was established that this was not the case, their tongues were cut from their mouths.[51]

3.1.2 Crimes against Bodily Integrity, Honour and Personal Freedom

Only after the Christianisation, under the influence of the Roman law, Bulgars started to distinguish between premeditated murder and manslaughter (in the case of the latter, one intended bodily harm but instead killed the victim). The Slavic *Ecloga* followed Byzantine legislation in stating that premeditated murder was a public crime punishable by death by state institutions (Title XVII). There were lesser punishments for involuntary manslaughter. Abortion was a specific case. The mother who committed this act was punished with flogging and sent into exile. The Church stated that this was an immoral act, but it was punished by death only if it had led to the death of the mother (*Ecloga*). According to *ZSL* and the *Ecloga*, libel was punished in the following manner—he who accused unjustly received the penalty imposed for the offence in which he had incriminated another person. I am not going to examine in detail the two other main groups of crimes—the ones against morality (rape, incest, fornication, etc.) and property (robbery, theft). In general, the Bulgarian law followed the Byzantine legal norms, however there were also, as a rule, specific additions and/or alterations of them.[52]

3.2 *Courts of Law, Trial, Forensic Evidence, and Types of Punishment*

The ruler was the supreme judge. He decided the cases with the help of the supreme boyars and the patriarch. There were other lower courts as well. Perhaps the boyars were involved in them. After the Christianization there were also ecclesiastical courts: episcopal, metropolitan and patriarchal. As far as serfs were concerned the local feudal (secular or ecclesiastical) was the judge except regarding the gravest crimes—those against state and religion. As far as prosecution, forensic evidence and court proceedings were concerned, an important instrument of establishing if the accused was guilty or not was the trial by ordeal. For example, the accused was submerged in cold, hot (boiling) water, hot iron, etc.[53] The verdict was based on her reactions. The oath

---

51 Petrova, *History*, 191.

52 Petrova, *History*, 193, 199–221.

53 There is evidence that these practices continued even during the thirteenth century. See Petrova, *History*, 241.

was considered evidence before and after the adoption of Christianity.[54] The confession was also essential evidence. Pope Nicholas advised that the confession should be based on the free will of the suspect. With regards to the question who is eligible to be a witness, the Byzantine *Ecloga* listed as witnesses "who are generally acceptable" the ones with "a high rank or profession, or who are rich". In the Slavic *Ecloga*, however, this text was completely altered and replaced with a possession of "military rank" and/or "trade". Parents and children could not testify against each other.[55] The ZSL followed the *Ecloga* in the principle that one witness is not a witness (*unus testis nullus testis*). Torture was used extensively as part of the trial. In his Responses, Pope Nicolas stated that "the custom of torturing the accused was considered contrary to divine as well as to human law".[56] Nontheless, the practice of torture continued.[57]

Mediaeval lawgivers distinguished between secular and spiritual punishments. As far as the first group was concerned, the death penalty (beheading/decapitation with a sword; hanging, stoning, etc.) was applied for various offences listed in the Laws of Krum and other statues, including "telling lies and slander".[58] This punishment was used mostly in cases of crimes against state and faith (e.g., forming a conspiracy against the ruler, 'espionage', the profession of heretical beliefs, etc.), but also in cases of murder, arson, crimes against morality and etc. Corporal punishments (or mutilation—cutting the nose and/or hands of the offender, breaking his shinbones—for example for theft, etc. in the Krum's laws) were widespread. They usually affected the part of the body which was 'used for' committing the offence. These punishments were rare in the legal system of ancient Rome but were frequent in the Byzantine *Ecloga* and the *Farmers Law*. In Bulgaria they existed in the pagan period and, under the impact of the Roman law, remained after the Christianization. According to some scholars the corporal punishments were introduced in Byzantium under the influence of Arabs and Persians. The Byzantines had strong ties with them in the seventh and eighth centuries. In the ZSL the punishments for the corresponding offences in generally were more lenient than in the Byzantine statutes. Another subgroup of secular punishments included those which intended the disgrace of the offender: branding, flogging (for theft, fornication,

54 Naturally, after the new religion was adopted, one took an oath not in a sword (as during the paganism) but in God, the cross or the Gospel.

55 Petrov and Petrova, *History*; Petrova, *History*, 243–8.

56 See *The Responses of Pope Nicholas I to the Questions of the Bulgars*.

57 Torture was a freely accepted form of punishment in the Middle Ages. It was only abolished in England in 1640.

58 Petrova, *History*, 223.

procuring, usually combined with fines, banishment or exile, etc.). Finally, there were other punishments such as: banishing (in cases of abortion, for attacking a priest, theft, manslaughter, etc.), confiscation; imprisonment in a dungeon; fines (e.g., for crimes against morality when the offender is wealthy) and others.

The spiritual punishments were imposed by the Church. They were mentioned in the *ZSL* as well: condemnation (for instance, each side in the trial had to present their witnesses, if not—they were condemned), excommunication (the purpose of which is the penance of the offender), anathema (the most severe ecclesiastical punishment used, for example, for heretics); and for the gravest offences against church and state was reserved the "triple anathema".

In conclusion, the legislation in the First and the Second Bulgarian Empire heavily borrowed from the Roman heritage but often did not follow them verbatim. It was common for Bulgarian jurists to omit passages, add, alter, or completely modify the original texts. These changes were required by the specifics of the economy, social relations, and traditions in Bulgaria.

A modified version of the Byzantine *Ecloga* was introduced in the First Bulgarian Tsardom almost immediately after the Christianization (864). The new provisions in the Slavic Ecloga stemmed mainly from the less developed economic relations. *Kormchaia kniga* was based on the Second Byzantine *Nomocanon* and *Zakon Sudnyi Liudem* was 'inspired' by the Byzantine *Ecloga*. However, ZSL also included original provisions, because of urgent political imperatives, such as the need to suppress the heathens' revolt. Byzantine laws, such as Basilicae, *Eisagoge* and *Prochiron*, were enforced in Bulgaria, while the country was under Byzantine rule (1018–1185). There are only indirect sources regarding the legislation during the Second Bulgarian Empire. It consisted, perhaps, once again, of *Kormchaia Kniga*, ZSL, *Ecloga*, *Farmer's Law*, but also of collections such as *Syntagma Canonum, Hexabiblos*, and the Dušan's Code.

In *Corpus Iuris*, the emperor was the embodiment of justice. The Byzantine monarchy, according to the tradition, was also elective (by the senate, the army and the people) and the emperor could be removed by his electors. In comparison, the position of the Bulgarian ruler was somewhat stronger, *vis-à-vis* the patriarch and the church. In Mediaeval Bulgaria the ruler was placed on the throne by God, and the 'state' was his patrimony. In practice, however, tsar's power was restrained by institutions such as the Council of the Great Boyars. He could be resisted and deposed by the aristocracy if he violated the written and unwritten norms and rules of the land.

Bulgarian ruler was the supreme judge. The cases were decided with the help of the boyars and the patriarch. After the adoption of Christianity, the application of *ius talionis* persisted, although it was reduced substantially.

Mediaeval Bulgarian lawyers distinguished between crimes against state and faith, bodily integrity, honour and personal freedom, morality and property. Under the influence of the Roman law, Bulgars started to distinguish between premeditated murder and manslaughter. One of the groundbreaking principles, which ZSL adopted from the *Ecloga*, was *unus testis nullus testis*. However, trial by ordeal and torture, against which Pope Nicholas advised, were still used extensively.

The legislation of the Second Bulgarian Empire was abrogated during the Ottoman Rule (1396–1878). The customary laws, which existed side by side with the state laws during the previous epoch, however continued to exist.

Bibliography

Main Sources

Blastares, Matthew, *The Alphabetic Syntagma of Mathew Blastares* (Moscow, 1996) [in Russian].

Petrov, Petar; Vassil Gyuzlev, *Reader on the History of Bulgaria, vol. 2: High Middle Ages (XII–XIV centuries)* (Sofia: Nauka i Izkustvo, 1978) [in Bulgarian].

Petrov, Petar; Galabina Petrova, eds., *History of the Bulgarian State and Law-Sources, 680–1944*, (Sofia: Albatross, 2010) [in Bulgarian].

Sampimon, Janette; Sara van Halsema, *Cosmas Presbyter: Homily Against the Bogumils, Operational Edition* (Columbus: Ohio State University, 2005).

Main Bibliographical References

Andreev, Mihail, "Regarding the Question about the Origin and the Essence of *Zakon Sudnyi Liudem*" (Sofia: University of Sofia, Yearbook of the Faculty of Law, 1957), vol. 4.

Cholakov, Petar, "Roman Law as Political Weapon", *Political Studies* (Sofia), 1 (2008), 99–113 [in Bulgarian].

Ganev, Vanelin, *'Zakon Sudnyi Liudem': Legal-historical and legal-analytical research* (Sofia: Bulgarian Academy of Sciences Press, 1959).

Petrova, Gabina, *History of the Bulgarian State and Law (680–1878)* (Sofia: Sibi, 2009) [in Bulgarian].

Tokushev, Dimitar, *A History of Mediaeval Bulgarian State and Law* (Sofia: Sibi, 2009) [in Bulgarian].

Zlatarski, Vasil, *History of Bulgarian State during the Middle Ages*, 3 vols. (Sofia: Bulgarian Academy of Sciences, 'Marin Drinov' Press, 1994).

PART 2

Renaissance and Early Modern Era

SECTION 1

Myths and Politics

CHAPTER 3

Biscay in the Spanish Monarchy

Myth, History, and Law in the Making of Its Constitutional Regime (14th to 17th Centuries)

Jon Arrieta

1 Introduction: Oath and Allegiance in Francisco Vázquez de Mendieta's Painting*

The painting featured on the programme of the Conference on Constitutional Moments, painted by Francisco Vázquez de Mendieta in Bilbao (Biscay) around 1609 and now hanging in the House of the Assembly in Guernica, depicts local noblemen as they kiss the king's hand (*juramento de los fueros*) after he has sworn to honour the *fueros* of the province, since he is also Lord of Biscay, a scene that took place back in 1475. The monarch in question was Ferdinand V, known as Ferdinand the Catholic. The painting depicts him swearing to respect the ancient laws of the territory, thus confirming them anew as all the previous Lords of Biscay had customarily done. At the same time Ferdinand is receiving the allegiance of those local noblemen.

Biscay is in the Western part of the Spanish Basque Country, currently named Euskadi, and traditionally comprises three provinces: Bizkaia, Gipuzkoa and Araba (or Álava) according to the current official denominations.

The principal distinguishing feature of the Basque people is their language. One of the dialects of the language was, and is still, the one spoken in Biscay. This was sufficient to make Biscay a part of the Basque Region, although during the times this paper is dealing with, "Biscay" was often used to refer to all the Basque territories (for instance, the Gulf of Biscay). The lower part of Mendieta's painting contains a text under the image of the king (see the caption of Figure 3.1; translated from the original Basque dialect of Biscay).

An initially large area, "Biscay" gradually shrank until it reached its current size, which includes the present Basque Autonomous Community (Biscay,

* This article belongs to the work of the Research Group PID2021–128509NB-C21, of the Spanish Ministerio de Economía y Conocimiento. The traditional English word "Biscay" and the adjective "Biscayen" will be used, instead of other names such as Bizkaia (in Basque) or Vizcaya (in Spanish).

 | DOI:10.1163/9789004549159_005

FIGURE 3.1 Detail of Vázquez de Mendieta's painting, *The Oath of the Laws of the Seignoiry of Biscay by Ferdinand the Catholic* (c. 1609). "This is how King Ferdinand the Fifth confirmed laws of Biscay to its people and how, in turn, they confirmed him as their lord in the year one thousand and four hundred and seventy-six beneath the tree of Guernica."

Gipuzkoa and Alava), a part of Navarre and the French Basque Region (*Le Pays Basque Français*). The dialects were studied by Louis Lucien Bonaparte, nephew of Napoleon, who completed a highly accurate map in 1866, like the one appearing on the next page.

The Northern area, including parts of France and Navarre, had a high proportion of Basque speakers until the 18th century. Following a decline in numbers during the 19th century and an even greater one in the 20th, knowledge and practice of the Basque language is increasing and the proportion of bilinguals is rapidly growing. I will be concentrating here on Biscay, historically known as the Lordship or Seigneurie (*Señorío*) of Biscay.

Mendieta's painting gives us another interesting piece of information on our subject: besides being a skilful and professional painter, he was also an historian and maybe a lawyer too, who wrote a chronicle of Biscay entitled *Annales de Vizcaya*. Mendieta requested a grant from the Government of Biscay to publish the manuscript in January of 1596, but he does not seem to have received any reply.[1] These *Annales* were lost, except for the fourth book, eventually published by Juan Carlos Guerra in 1914.

1 Andrés de Mañaricua, *Historiografía de Vizcaya* (*Desde Lope García de Salazar a Labayru*), second ed. (Bilbao: Gran Enciclopedia Vasca, 1973), 91.

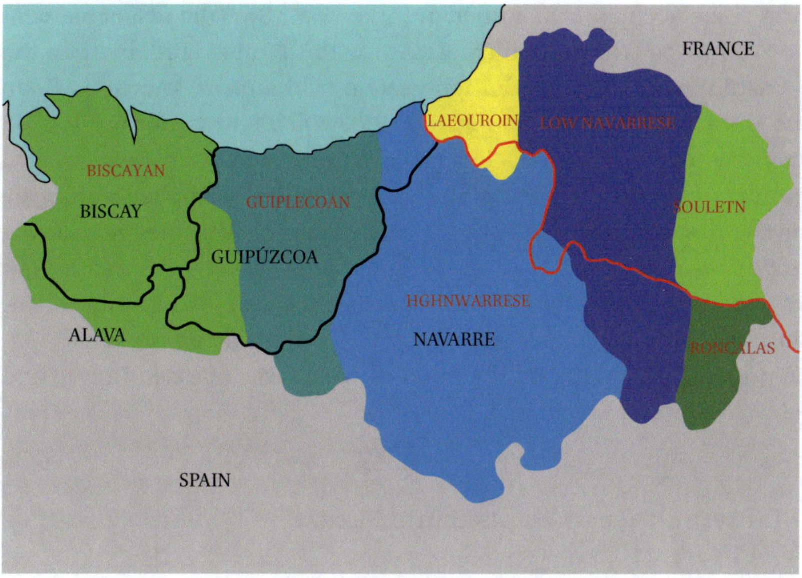

FIGURE 3.2 Map of dialects spoken in Biscay by the mid-19th century

The book describes conditions in Biscay between the years 1399 and 1456, a time of pain, sorrow, and conflict within the local society. King Ferdinand brought peace to Biscay and an end to the period of conflict. This is what Mendieta wanted to celebrate with his painting, which shows the two rival factions of noblemen from Biscay as they kiss the king's hand; the "oiñacinos" are on his left hand and the "gamboinos" on his right hand. This factionalism continued in Biscay and the rest of the Basque area until the end of the fifteenth century.[2]

This paper deals with the aspects of the ceremony described in Mendieta's painting: the king's oath to honour the Old Law and the confirmation of the rights of the people of Biscay. The event is thus related with the terms of this volume: foundational myths, charters, agreements, and constitutions.

The Seigneurie of Biscay offers us a very complete model indeed. On one hand, the history of the king's oath of the ancestral law of Biscay, including the founding legend, was very well structured and narrated. On the other hand, the establishment of an historical justification and its legal basis, the *Capitulaciones* or charter, was quite well drafted. Several "constitutional

2 Julio Caro Baroja, "Linajes y bandos", *Vasconiana* (San Sebastián: Txertoa, 1974); and *Los Vascos* (Madrid: Itsmo, 1949; I use its fourth ed., 6th printing, 1980).

landmarks" were accurately identified over the years: 870 (the first agreement with the Lord); 1379 (the second agreement with the new Lord, by then the king of Castile); 1452 (the first written version of the *fuero*, known as *Fuero Viejo*, the Old Law of Biscay), and 1526 (the new *fuero*, in vigour until 1959). The 1526 *fuero* was in force for a long time: its most important section, civil law governing relationships between private persons, was applied until 1959, when these rules were adapted to the legal Civil Law code as the *Compilación del Derecho Civil de Vizcaya*.

There were two important points in the defence and justification of this constitution: Andrés de Poza's legal report (1589) and the *Escudo de la más constante fe y lealtad*, the first partial edition of which was released in 1749 and followed by a complete one in 1762.

2 The Jurisdictional Composition of Biscay

2.1 *Biscay, a Small Member of the Spanish Monarchy*

A review of the different examples of constitutional creation considered in the present book (a glance at the list of contributions will suffice) reveals the wide range of areas dealt with. One of those areas comprises some of the territories that used to belong to the Spanish Monarchy: Castile, Aragon, Catalonia, Flanders, Naples, and Biscay. This approach, which focuses on the Monarchy as a whole, is necessary since Biscay belonged to Castile in the Middle Ages. Castile, including Biscay, as a part of the Spanish Monarchy, was subsequently inherited by Charles V in 1516.

The development of the history, law and legal justification of the existence and place of Biscay within the Spanish Monarchy must be considered jointly with all the above-mentioned Hispanic territories, since the two processes took place simultaneously.[3]

When discussing the process of law making, there are three factors that must be taken into account for each polity: the territory and its organization; the institutions; and the law, particularly the written texts that defined those institutions and their functions. These three elements were very well defined in the case of Biscay.

3 J.H. Elliott, "A Europe of Composite Monarchies" [1992], in his *Spain, Europe and the Wider World, 1500–1800* (New Haven: Yale University Press, 2009), ch. 1.

FIGURE 3.3 Map of towns (*villas*) in Biscay

2.2 *The Land: the Duality between the Open Land (Tierra Llana) and the Burghs (Villas)*

In the early Middle Ages Biscay was an open or flat ground (*Tierra Llana*) containing lots of small towns, called *anteiglesias* because they were built around their parishes. The *Fuero* of Biscay placed the *Tierra Llana* under customary law until it was written down and promulgated in 1452–1454. From the 13th century onwards, as in the rest of Europe, the Land of Biscay saw the establishment of new towns or burghs (*villas*), each of them under the jurisdiction of its own particular law. Each *villa* had its own charter or *fuero*. These towns (shown in blue on the map below, Image Number 3.3) were founded according to their *carta puebla*.

They ran from Valmaseda, constituted in 1199, to Rigoitia, constituted in 1376. The city (*ciudad*) of Orduña, located outside the territory, completed the picture. The most remarkable foundation, however, was that of the Villa of Bilbao (1300), which in a few years became the central point of the economy of Biscay. These charters were a kind of foundational document and formed the basis for the law in each settlement. Each of these burghs grew thanks to the concession of new privileges. The development of new townships changed and completed the "habitat" and way of life: they offered better living conditions, increased safety, brighter prospects, and greater opportunities to participate in manufacture and commerce in general.

The rest of Biscay, that is, the open ground or *Tierra Llana*, with 72 *anteiglesias*, was subject to traditional law, first recorded in 1452 (with some 225 laws or articles), and replaced by the new version of 1526, known as *Fuero Nuevo.*[4] The previously mentioned distinction between cities or *villas* and the rest of the countryside, the *Tierra Llana*, was maintained and it still exists today in Biscay, although applying only to private law (family, inheritances, and propriety).

2.3 *The Three Jurisdictional Areas of Biscay and the Rest of the Basque Country*

The territory of Biscay was divided into three jurisdictional areas: the first one was central Biscay (shown in brown on the above map); it gave its name to the whole province; the second one, in the Southeast, was known as the Duranguesado (in green) and centred around the town of Durango; the third one, in the West, was known as the Encartaciones (in red). Each of these three areas had its own assembly, a sort of small parliament, but all of them, following their incorporation, formed part of the general territorial organization of Biscay and were part of its administrative structure. Each of the three areas had its own seats in the General Assembly in Guernica. This central assembly (*Junta General*) was instrumental in preserving the balance among the three areas (Biscay, Durango and the Encartaciones). It should be added that today's Biscay has its own parliament, still called the Juntas of Bizkaia, and still located in Guernica, where Mendieta's painting hangs.

The focus here will be on Biscay, but to have an overview of the Basque region, some brief attention will be given to the other territories that comprised it. These had long-term relationships with both the kingdoms of Navarre and Castile which disputed the area until 1200 when the king of Castile, Alphonse VIII, conquered a part of Gipuzkoa and Alava which had belonged to Navarre until then.

The distinctive character of Biscay was its status as a Seigneurie, a county belonging to Castile but having jurisdiction over its own affairs. Gipuzkoa had been under royal jurisdiction since its beginnings: it depended on the kingdom of Navarre until 1200 and then continued to be a royal territory (*realengo*) after its integration into the kingdom of Castile. Royal jurisdiction facilitated uniform provincial organization: there were around twenty-five *villas* founded

---

4 The first printed edition of the Fuero of 1452 was published again in 1958 and then in 2016, the latter as a better edition, and translated into English in 2007: *The Old Law of Bizkaia (1452)*, introduction and ed. by Gregorio Monreal Zia; transl. by William A. Douglass and Linda White, preface by William A. Douglass (Reno: Center for Basque Studies, University of Nevada, 2005).

by royal largesse and each one included the hamlets and farmhouses around it; there was no legal distinction between burghs and open land. In Álava, or Araba, the rather atypical seigneurie, the Guild or *Cofradía de Arriaga*, covered about half the territory. In 1332, however, the entire area came under direct royal jurisdiction. According to the royal concession (the so-called *Privilegio del Contrato*), which specified the new conditions, the nobles ceded their jurisdiction over the land and renounced their right to hold meetings and engage in political activities.

Having looked at the territorial organization, now the administrative structure requires analysis. It should be born in mind that the Assemblies or *Juntas* of each Basque provinces (Biscay, Gipuzkoa and Alava) were attended by the representatives of the burghs and *anteiglesias* mentioned above. But these representatives were not chosen along the same class lines as the parliaments of Castile, Crown of Aragon, or Navarre. The Basque assemblies were not organized according to social or estate lines and were not divided into the usual groupings of Church, nobility and cities or royal burghs. The executive branches were made up of groups that formed regional councils called *Diputaciones*.

The Northern Basque region, located in France, comprised three different areas: Labourd (Lapurdi), Lower Navarre and Soule (Zuberoa), and was organized along the same lines: it comprised burghs such as Bayonne, Saint-Jean-de-Pied-de-Port and Mauleon and open land, where the population was scattered into numerous hamlets and farmhouses. The small region of Labourd (zone number 5 in the above map) formed part of the Duchy of Aquitaine. When Eleanor of Aquitaine contracted matrimony with Henry II, in 1152, the former became Duke of Aquitaine. The new subjects of the English king, inhabitants of Vasconia (the Basque-speaking part of the territory), refused to recognize the authority of an English ruler at the times of Henry III (1216–1272) and demanded that the king took up residence in their territory (Vasconia). The case was studied by the greatest legal expert and teacher of the times, Francesco de Accursius, an Italian *glosatore*, who was the author of a comprehensive commentary of the entire *Corpus Iuris Civilis*, in other words, the entire body of Roman law.[5] In his gloss on the fragment of the *Digesta Iustiniani* dealing with the "*praeses provintiae*" (governors of provinces), this outstanding Bolognese legal expert argued that the king could appoint a delegate to act on his behalf in Vasconia. However, such a delegate would be obliged to observe

5 Jon Arrieta, "Laburdi y Ustaritz en la *Magna Glossa* de Accursio", in *Eugène Goyeneche: Omenaldia, Hommage* (Donostia-San Sebastián: Ikaskuntza, Lankidetzan, n. 20. 2001), 85–105.

the laws and traditions of the land, the *"mores maiorum"*, when governing and administering justice.

3 The Law

A balanced relationship between monarchies and these regions, as proposed in Accursius's commentary and conclusion, was an essential condition for the formulation of written legal codes, approved or acknowledged by the monarchs. Navarre presented its general charter or *Fuero* to the king of the new Champagne dynasty around the year 1237; Biscay, ruled by the kings of Castile since 1379, presented its charter or *Fuero* in 1452; Gipuzkoa finally gave shape to its provincial entity in 1397, and Alava formulated a written legal code, the Ordinances, in 1463. Thus, all their provinces had their own legal system by the end of the 15th century.

The dynastic union of the Crown of Castile and the Crown of Aragon through the marriage of Isabella of Castile and Ferdinand of Aragon in 1469, created new political conditions for all the constituent members of the new Spanish Monarchy. And then, the advent of Charles of Ghent in 1516 as heir to his grandfathers and grandmothers, meant a more pronounced change: not only was Charles ruler of all the Spanish dominions (including the Indies) and of Austria and the Low Countries, but was also elected Holy Roman Emperor three years later.

Once again, small territories such as the provinces of Biscay, Gipuzkoa and Alava and the kingdom of Navarre, which was in turn incorporated into Castile in 1515 after its conquest in 1512, had to try to keep their status and find their rightful place within such a large structure. Their efforts met with complete success. The Basques also managed to obtain important positions in government as secretaries and counsellors to the kings and queens of Spain. In this way they succeeded in protecting not just the laws and institutions in their home regions but also its industry; they also ensured a place for themselves in the New World.

In Biscay, the *Fuero Viejo* of 1452 was the written formulation of the *franquezas, libertades, privilegios* (franchises, liberties, and privileges) enjoyed by the people of Biscay. In fact, each clause, called a "ley" in the *Fuero*, begins with the formula: "*Tenían por*", which means that what was written and recognized as law by the Lord was not something new but instead a confirmation of what was already considered as law. Biscay presented a revised version of the *Fuero* in 1526 during the reign of Charles I. This document detailed the territory's legal system and thus Biscay demonstrated its sophistication and capacity to hold a place of its own within the Monarchy.[6]

These new versions and editions of the legislative framework were aimed at achieving a competitive position amongst the more powerful members of the Spanish Monarchy. These were the territories that had their own Council (*Consejo*) at the court in Madrid and thus enjoyed direct representation before the king. All the kingdoms, large and small, strived for an equal position within the monarchy but accepted the monitoring and supervision of the supreme courts (*Consejos Supremos*). Once again, we see how important it was for each kingdom to find its own position or space as a visible part of the whole. Myths and stories about "first" moments and foundations played a crucial role to this effect.

4 The Role of Myths and Legends in the Status of Biscay in the Spanish Monarchy

Biscay is rich in myths of origin and foundation. The most important text was written by a Portuguese genealogist, Pedro de Barcelos, who appeared as the author of the *Livro de Linhagens*, in the middle of the 14th century. Barcelos was a son of the king of Portugal, Don Dionis. His book (the 1980 edition by José Mattoso is considered the best) was written as a universal genealogical history and included the Biblical period and the genealogical traditions of Troy, Rome, Great Britain, and Persia. The book deals with the origin and genealogy of several dynasties or houses of the Iberian nobility. One of them is the House of Haro and Lara[7]which spanned nineteen generations in Biscay from Froom to Juan Núñez de Lara (1340), Lord of Biscay during Barcelos' times. Barcelos attributed the foundation of the Haro dynasty to a certain Froom, supposedly the brother of the king of England, elected Lord of Biscay and said to have defeated Count Don Munio of Asturias in the Battle of Arguriega (Arrigorriaga). His son, Furtam Froez, managed to marry a local nobleman's daughter, named Doña Elvira.

---

6 Jon Arrieta, "Ubicación de los ordenamientos de los reinos de la Corona de Aragón en la Monarquía Hispánica: concepciones y supuestos varios (siglos XVI–XVIII)", in Italo Birocchi and Antonello Mattone, eds., *Il diritto patrio tra diritto comune e codificazione* (*secoli XVI-XIX*) (Rome: Viella, 2006), 127–71.

7 Maria do Rosário Ferreira, "D. Pedro de Barcelos e a representação do pasado ibérico", *Cuadernos de Literatura Medieval. O contexto hispànico de historiografia portuguesa nos séculos XIII e XIV* (Coimbra: Centro de Literatura Portuguesa, 2010), 81–106.

One hundred years later, in the middle of the 15th century, Lope García de Salazar wrote a *Crónica de los Señores de Bizkaya,* the annals of the Lords of Biscay.[8] Salazar changed the origin of the newcomer. According to his version, the Haro dynasty started with the Biscay-born son of a granddaughter of the king of Scotland. Salazar did not take the *Livro de Linhagens* as a source in recreating the succession of Lords of Biscay. According to Salazar, a legitimate daughter of the king of Scotland was shipwrecked on the coast of Biscay. She became pregnant although nobody knew exactly how or to whom. According to her vague explanation, she was asleep when a kind of elf (*culebro*) visited her. She concealed the name of the father and gave birth to a son with blonde hair and fair skin, known as the *White Lord, Jaun Zuria* in Basque. He became the leader of Biscay's troops in the abovementioned battle of Arrigorriaga (870) against the king of Leon. The troops of Biscay won, and the new Lord broke his links with the king. That date of 870 opened a new era which gave rise to a series of Lords of Biscay. This event marked the beginning of a new historical and constitutional era.

The third lord was Iñigo Ezkerra (Ezkerra means "left-handed" in Basque). His mother allegedly had goat's feet. The story of "Lady Goat foot" and the Scottish Princess who became pregnant to a mysterious snake could be said to form part of the so-called "Melusinian" tradition. This tradition comes from the tale written by the count of Arras in 1392–1393, the *Roman de Melusine,*[9] a fairy who would take human form every Saturday to attract men. The Lord of Lusignan was born out, according to the mentioned tale, from one of these sexual encounters. In the opinion of the specialists on the subject, "Melusinian" explanations of the remote origins of dynasties and peoples were quite widespread in Europe, particularly among genealogists searching for family origins in the universal repository of foundation myths.[10] This is, without a doubt, the case of the House of Haro, included in the "Melusinian" story of the origin of the first Lord of Biscay who signed an agreement with the people of Biscay.

---

8 *Crónica de las siete casas de Vizcaya y Castilla. Escrita por Lope García de Salazar, año 1454,* introd. Juan Carlos Guerra (Madrid: Sucesores de Rivadeneyra, 1914).

9 Jean d'Arras, *Melusina o la Noble Historia de Lusignan,* ed. and translation Carlos Alvar, Biblioteca Medieval, 29 (Madrid: Siruela, 2008).

10 I follow José Ramón Prieto Lasa, *Las leyendas de los Señores de Vizcaya y la tradición melusiniana* (Madrid: Universidad Autónoma de Madrid and Universidad del País Vasco, 1995). See also Jon Juaristi, "Los mitos de origen en la génesis de las identidades nacionales: La batalla de Arrigorriaga y el surgimiento del particularismo vasco (ss. XIV-XV)", *Studia Historica: Historia Contemporánea,* 12 (1994), 191–228.

5 *The Role of Historians, Lawyers, Advisors and* Consultores*: the* Capitulaciones *as the Constitutional Body of Biscay*

Having looked at the law, institutions, myths, and legends, it is time to devote some attention to other additional, very important players, in order to understand how the system worked: the lawyers, advisors, and *consultores* (councellors). These experts helped in the process of law-making and shaping institutions. In particular, they worked on preparing and developing the law, and after its implementation, the defence of the entire legal system.

The legends and myths created by Barcelos and García de Salazar were recounted time and time again by historians and lawyers of Biscay. One of them was the painter and historian Mendieta while another one was Martín de Coscojales.[11] But more was to come, this time from historians and lawyers at the beginning of the modern era (16th-18th centuries). As has already been stated, in the matters that concern us here the case of Biscay shows how the narrative, or storyline, was created when it was necessary to explain and justify a change in the 225 or so articles of traditional law written in 1452, to turn them into the new Fuero of 1526.

On one hand the community was presented as a cohesive group, the "Vizcaínos", with a highly developed legal system. As a political aphorism of Biscay goes: "el Señor no entró dando sino recibiendo" (the Lord didn't lay down the law, but it was laid down on him). The political principle evoked in Navarre was similar: "Antes fueron leyes que reyes" (laws before kings). In consequence, when a new Lord of Biscay took power, he received and recognized a constitutional inheritance as if it were a will. This was the remarkable case of Ferdinand the Catholic, depicted in Mendieta's painting.

The integration of Biscay in the Spanish Monarchy marked the beginning of a period of important advances towards social equality. In fact, in 1526 the "Vizcaínos" were presented as an egalitarian group of people, all sharing the same rights and duties.[12] This becomes clear when comparing the *Fuero* of 1452 with that of 1526. The latter contains a very strong statement on the egalitarian social status of the people of Biscay, the so-called universal nobility.[13] This uniformity probably helped to improve the political and constitutional situation. Anyway, the constitutional value of the *Fuero* of 1526 should again

11 Mañaricua, *Historiografía*, 164–5.

12 Lourdes Soria Sesé, "La hidalguía universal", *Iura Vasconiae*, 3 (2006), 283–316; at 291–2.

13 Jon Arrieta, "Claroscuros de una realidad debatida: la hidalguía universal de los vascos", in F. Borja de Aguinagalde, ed., *El País Vasco, tierra de hidalgos y nobles: Momentos singulares de su historia* (Madrid: Fundación Banco Santander, 2016), 89–124.

be stressed: several *capitulaciones* were included in its text. The Biscayens succeeded in obtaining a formal written record of all the benefits to be enjoyed by them as the *capitulations* contained the privileges that the king swore to enforce and respect. The Biscayen people responded with their commitment of loyalty and military support for the defence of the territory. In its first chapters, the *Fuero* is a kind of contract. Andrés de Poza wrote the first complete commentary on these regulations in 1589.[14] He gave special importance to a list of ten rights which came immediately after the first articles (called "leyes") of the *Fuero*: election of the Lord by the Biscayen community (I, 1); the Lord's oath (I, 1); foundation of *villas* with the approval of Biscayens (I, 8); exemption from taxes, especially several precisely defined ones (I, 4); the inviolable nature of an individual's dwelling (XVI, 4); prohibition of the confiscation of property (XI, 25); exemption from the most important Castilian tax, the *alcabala* (I, 4); the creation of the court (*Sala de Bizkaia*) of the Chief Judge (*Juez Mayor*) of Biscay in Valladolid as a special court of appeal within the Seigneurie, with special jurisdiction in case of criminal arrest (I, 19); and a guarantee that any new law affecting the whole of Biscay had to be passed by the Assembly of Guernica.

These privileges, initially enjoyed only by noblemen, were extended to the whole Bicayen population. There were changes between the Fuero of 1452, that still separated noblemen and peasants (*labradores*), and the Fuero of 1526, where this distinction had disappeared, were very relevant. This paved the way for the abovementioned list.[15]

6 The Legend Revisited: Esteban de Garibay and Andrés de Poza (End of the Sixteenth Century)

The versions by Barcelos and Lope García de Salazar were amended in the last years of the 16th century. Esteban de Garibay, historian and official chronicler of Philip II, was born in Mondragón, Gipuzkoa, very close to Biscay. He found it difficult to endorse mythical explanations and turned the mysterious and supernatural lady into a distant king's daughter who became the wife of a

14 Andrés de Poza, *Fuero de hidalguía: Ad Pragmaticas de Toro et Tordesillas*, ed. Carmen Muñoz de Bustillo, transl. María de los Ángeles Durán Ramos (Bilbao: Servicio Editorial de la Universidad del País Vasco, 1997), 254–6.

15 Privilege, in the sense of corrections of the general law, corrections turned in this case into general law. See Angela de Benedictis, *Politica, governo e istituzioni nell'Europa moderna* (Bologna: Il Mulino, 2001), 279–85.

local knight.[16] Their son, Lope, who inherited the blonde hair and fair skin of his mother, was able to lead the Biscayen people to victory against the king of Leon. The story was adapted by Andrés de Poza, who introduced a new speech in his version. He stressed the right to resort to violent rebellion as an act of resistance against abusive power.[17] Thanks to his success, the leader gained enough credibility to be elected as new Lord. But the collective nature of the electors should be pointed out: the "vizcaínos", all the people of Biscay. They chose the new Lord, who was obliged to swear to respect the law, which he received rather than laid down.

In this way, Poza was able to offer a new, complete, and coherent general explanation of the political and legal conditions. First, the Biscayens were noble men. In consequence, they were equals as members of an egalitarian community, as was defined in the *Fuero*: the law forbade the confiscation of property, imprisonment for defaulting on a debt, torture, or unauthorized invasion of private premises.

In 1527 this general status of "hidalguía" was granted to the entire population of Biscay and Gipuzkoa.[18] But, as Poza insisted in his report, this change was possible because "hidalguía" did not enjoy the same status as aristocracy, which would be impossible to confer on the whole population[19] But if all members of the industrious society of Biscay worked and co-operated for the common good, they likewise all deserved the right to enjoy an equal status. Following the doctrine of André Tiraqueau on this matter, Poza added the main argument in support of his thesis: the general status of nobility had been recognized by the prince.[20] The rights were defined in a charter, the *Fuero* of 1526. The new king, and new Lord of Biscay, Charles V, ratified the charter and

16 Julio Caro Baroja, *Los vascos y la historia a través de Garibay* (San Sebastián: Txertoa, 1973; reed., Madrid: Caro Raggio, 2002, introduction by Guadalupe Rubio de Urquía).

17 Poza, *Ad Pragmaticas*, 252–4.

18 Soria, "La hidalguía", 291–2. See a previous reference to the general status of *hidalguía* in Francisco Elías de Tejada, *La provincia de Guipúzcoa* (Madrid: Minotauro, 1965), 42; and in two recent ones: Alfonso de Otazu, and José Ramón Díaz de Durana, *El espíritu emprendedor de los vascos* (Madrid: Sílex, 2008), 93; and Borja de Aguinagalde, "La sociedad vasca y sus élites (s. XI-1500) y la formulación de la hidalguía universal en 1527. Distinción, jerarquía y prácticas sociales (con particular referencia a Guipúzcoa)", in his edited volume *El País Vasco, tierra de hidalgos y nobles*, 25–88.

19 Poza, *Ad Pragmaticas*, 16–8.

20 André Tiraqueau, *Commentarii de Nobilitate et Iure Primigeniorum* (1549).

committed himself to respecting it one year after it was drafted. And in the following year, 1528, the *Fuero* was printed and ready for widespread circulation.[21]

7 The Biscayen Story Inside the Spanish Larger Narrative

This narrative of Biscay, including myths and legendary stories, is not an isolated invention. On the contrary, the story of the Biscayen *Fuero* forms part of Spanish historiography.[22] The myth was kept alive both in Biscay and in Spain, but the former depended on the latter. This inclusion is reflected in the wider account of Spanish history which attributed a Biblical origin to the Spanish people. Many Spanish historians and writers believed that the first settlers in the Iberian Peninsula were descended from a grandson of Noah, named Tubal. This story established the Biblical origin of Spanish people. Moreover, Tubal provided not only a rich heritage of religion, law and customs but language as well. The religious legacy was founded on the worship of a single God and was imparted to and deeply embedded in Spanish society. But what language did Tubal and his followers speak? Historians and lawyers from Biscay and the rest of the Basque region had a ready response to this question: Tubal's language was Basque.[23] When the Romans and other peoples coming from outside the peninsula brought their languages with them, the original Iberian language disappeared almost completely and the only place where the language spoken by Tubal survived was the Basque speaking area.

This interpretation—so-called "Tubalism"— circulated widely in Spain but it was particularly current in the Basque region where local historians strove to achieve a position of privilege, authenticity, and primacy for the Basque population in establishing the antiquity of their ancestors. Consequently, Basques were considered the most genuine Spaniards.

In their re-creation of historical events, both Basque and Spanish historians pointed out that the rebellion of 870 was not the first instance of resistance by the Basques. In the battle of Arrigorriaga, the Biscayens had demonstrated the same attitude they had previously shown against the Romans and Visigoths. There was friction with both Romans and Visigoths, but in the end

21 Imanol Merino, "'Ayunos de fuero'. La distribución de ejemplares del Fuero Nuevo de Vizcaya por las instituciones provinciales vizcaínas (c. 1575–1700). Una aproximación", *e-Legal HistoryReview*, 26 (2018), 1–43.

22 Caro Baroja, *Los vascos y la historia a través de Garibay*.

23 Andrés de Poza, *De la antigua lengua, poblaciones y comarcas de las Españas,* (Bilbao: Mathias Mares, 1587), ff. 9 v., 12 v.

the Biscayens signed agreements with them. According to accounts of their dealings with the Visigoths, the first king who was accepted by the Basques was Suintila in 621. Subsequently, the attitude of the Basque people towards the Romans and Visigoths was not a demonstration of perpetual resistance and refusal but rather the confirmation of their capacity to reach a confederal relationship. Following the same trend, the 870 capitulation was explained as an agreement between two parts, later to be renewed in 1379 and in 1527. The latter, however, was signed between the king and an egalitarian community recognized as such by the law.

8 The Attack against the Fuero and the Victory of Biscay (1588–1590)

In 1588 Juan García Saavedra, prosecutor at the High Court (*Chancillería*) of Valladolid, wrote a book about the nobility in which he severely criticized the tax exemptions enjoyed by the Biscayen people even when outside their province.[24] The Council of Government (*Diputación*) of Biscay reacted swiftly and commissioned a legal expert, the aforementioned Andrés de Poza, better known as Licenciado Poza, to draft a reply to the prosecutor's claims.

The roots of Poza's family were in the Biscayen city of Orduña, but he was probably born in Antwerp, where he spent his childhood and youth.[25] He later excelled at humanities in Leuven and at law in Salamanca, where he finally obtained his degree in Laws in 1570.[26] He made a name for himself with his book on the Basque language, *La antigua lengua de las Españas* (The Ancient Language of Spain), published in 1587 (facsimile ed., 1959), and widely quoted during his lifetime and thereafter. He was a polyglot and dedicated scholar well informed on a variety of topics.

In addition, he was a highly capable legal expert and subsequently drafted the report requested by the *Diputación*. Thanks to this tract, Biscay won the lawsuit against the mentioned prosecutor, Saavedra. However, the *Diputación* of Biscay decided to publish the work under another name, that of Juan Gutiérrez, a prestigious Castilian legal expert. Consequently, Poza received no

24 Juan García de Saavedra, *Tractatus de Hispanorum Nobilitate et Exemptione, sive ad Pragmaticam Cordubensem, quaeest l. 8. Tit. 11. Lib. 2 Novae Recopilationis, in ultima editione Madriti edita* (Köln: Sumptibus Societatis,1737) (first ed., Valladolid: 1588).

25 Nadine Aernouts, "Presencia vasca en Bravante en el siglo XVI: ¿Licenciado Poza Antwerpiensis?", in *El licenciado Poza en Flandes* (Bilbao: Diputación Foral de Vizcaya, 1996), 67–86.

26 Muñoz de Bustillo, ed., *Ad Pragmaticas* … (1997), p. VI.

credit for the work. To add insult to injury, Juan Gutiérrez incorporated Poza's text into his complete commentary on Castilian Law: his famous *Practicarum Quaestionum Civilium* (first ed., 1593). In passing off Poza's ideas and text as their own, Gutiérrez transformed them into official Castilian legal doctrine. This was precisely what the governors of Biscay wanted.

Beyond his defence of the universal nobility of Biscayens, some excerpts of Poza's tract are of especial interest. In one of these Poza claimed that Biscay had the same political status as Flanders, Aragon, and Portugal, as it had been incorporated into Castile as a federated territory. According to him, Biscay retained its original structure and legal system, acknowledged, and guaranteed by the king. Poza thus asserted a relationship of equality, *aeque et principaliter*, with the main territories of the Spanish monarchy by the late sixteenth century.

It should be borne in mind that Poza was writing his report, which amounted to a full treatise, from the point of view of a Northern European lawyer. He belonged to a country that had its own high court, the Council of Flanders, at the court in Madrid, just like Castile, Portugal, the Crown of Aragon, and the Italian territories (Sicily, Milan, and Naples). In this way, Poza cited the example of Brabant as an autonomous duchy which belonged to the Holy Roman Empire and asked: why not confer the same status to Biscay as a member of the Spanish Monarchy?

The importance of Poza's ideas was acknowledged through the work of Gutiérrez and, as already stated, they passed into Castilian law. Poza was forgotten as the author of the report. Unlike Gutiérrez, the career of Poza as a lawyer subsequently came to an abrupt end. He tried to continue his career, but it seems that the *Diputación* of Biscay gave him no further opportunities and he had to earn his living as a teacher of cosmography, a job where he was successful enough as to write a book on hydrography and cosmography, published in 1585.

9 Biscayen Legal Doctrine in the 18th Century: the 'Escudo de la más constante fe y lealtad'

The most important book on the legal doctrine of Biscay is the *Escudo de la más constante fe y lealtad* (*The shield of the most constant faith and loyalty*), published by the mid-18th century.[27] The *Escudo* was a general work designed

27 Pedro de Fontecha y Salazar (attributed), *Escudo de la más constante fe y lealtad del Muy Noble y Muy Leal Señorío de Vizcaya*, edited with an introductory study by Jon Arrieta

to shed light on the history, laws, and institutions of Biscay. The book's author is unknown, and it seems that there was an attempt to hide his identity, although it has been attributed to Pedro de Fontecha y Salazar, a counsellor of the Seigneurie from 1718 until his death in 1753. The work was censored and banned but finally appeared in several editions together with the charter or *Fuero* of Biscay. It deals with a range of topics: the origins of Biscay; the history of the land in general and of its laws and customs in particular; the language of the inhabitants of Biscay, originally brought to Spain by Tubal and still spoken in some areas; the religion practised by the inhabitants of Biscay, monotheists even before converting to Christianity.

However, the most important part is devoted to the idea that Biscay's relationship with the monarchy was one of equality vis-à-vis the other Spanish kingdoms and dominions. The *Escudo* stressed that this relationship was a union *aeque et* principaliter and supported its arguments with quotations from the *Practicarum Quaestionum Civilium* by Juan Gutiérrez, who, as previously stated, copied Poza's text. Almost all quotations were taken from the 17th *quaestio* in the third volume.

The *Escudo* devoted its first two chapters to the history of Biscay. The author of these chapters is, according to our research, the Jesuit historian Gabriel de Henao. He is very emphatic in repeating the thesis detailed above: Biscay was an independent and separate county, whose inhabitants had chosen a local nobleman as its first ruler in 870. This first ruler had agreed to comply with a number of conditions or clauses. When a Castilian king, Juan I, became Lord of Biscay in 1379, the inhabitants of Biscay accepted him as king with the following condition: they were prepared to fulfil all their obligations as long as the king and his successors fulfilled theirs.

The legal basis of the *Escudo* is, without doubt, the *Fuero* of Biscay, frequently cited in the text, especially when dealing with the ten mentioned *capitulaciones*. This is because they accurately specified the conditions accepted by the rulers of Biscay in their relationship with its population, whose legal status, in turn, was related to their quality as *vecinos* or residents.

On the other hand, this long tract on Biscayen law took the legal and political texts written by prestigious Spanish and European legal experts as its essential basis. In fact, legal doctrines (doctrinal jurisprudence) or commentaries on law were highly important, almost as important, or even more so, than laws

(Bilbao: Universidad del País Vasco / EuskalHerriko Unibertsitatea, Argitalpen Zerbitzua – Servicio editorial, 2015).

themselves. This was the very aim of the *Escudo*: to consolidate a line of constitutional continuity.

No wonder Gutiérrez – and thus, Poza as well-- was quoted so frequently. Other important authors were likewise mentioned, always with the same purpose in mind: justifying the union *aeque principaliter* between Biscay and the Crown. The most celebrated among them was Cristóbal Crespí de Valldaura, a great legal expert and an important magistrate and politician in the Spain of the second half of the seventeenth century. A native of Valencia, he was President (*Vicecanciller*) of the Council of the Crownof Aragon for twenty years (1652–1671). Several other authors from each of the various parts of the Crown of Aragon were also mentioned. The reason for such a long list was clear: the territories of the Crown of Aragon comprised a composite monarchy in themselves from the thirteenth century onwards on the basis of an *aeque principaliter* union of them under one king, the sort of union duly advocated by these authors. Therefore, such historical and legal precedents were extremely valuable for a similar claim in Biscay.

10 The Reception of Biscayen Theories in Catalonia and in Europe

One of the most significant books on the topic in Catalonia was the *Summari dels títols de honor de Catalunya* (*A summary of the titles of honour in Catalonia*) by Andreu Bosch.[28] A lawyer and expert in canon law, born in Perpignan, he wrote a complete treatise on Catalan history, its laws, and institutions. His principal purpose was to explain and defend the status of the Northern counties of Rousillon and Cerdagne within Catalonia (France eventually annexed the former and part of the latter through the Treaty of the Pyrenees in 1659).

Bosch focused on the initial resistance of the Catalans against the Muslims. He was concerned to show that this resistance took place on both the Northern and the Southern sides of the Pyrenees when some Catalans took refuge from the Muslim invasion high in the mountains. Bosch thought these individuals to be all noblemen. To prove their noble quality, he looked straight to Biscay and took it as a model for the Catalan case: "We could follow the same reasoning that has been used by Biscayen writers". Even though he talked of writers in plural, he mentioned only one, the *licenciado* Poza, as could be expected.[29]

28 Andreu Bosch, *Summari, index o epítome dels admirables y nobilissims títols de honor de Cathalunya, Rosselló i Cerdanya* (Perpignan: Pere Lacavelleria, 1628; facsimile ed., Barcelona-Sueca, 1978).

29 Bosch, *Summari*, 73.

What were the reasons put forward by Bosch to equate Biscay and Catalonia in terms of nobility? According to him, Catalans and Biscayens shared an important basic condition: they were not conquered by the invading Muslims and consequently retained the ability to recover the lands which they had lost. Moreover, he pointed out another similarity by arguing that the Catalan and the Biscayen peoples were equals (*iguals*) because they had both elected their respective lords or "first heads" according to the limits and conditions established by the electors, which the respective ruler had to respect. It was, in fact, a version of the *lex regia* invoked in Biscay through Poza's legal and historical text. Although Bosch could not read Poza's treatise, the latter had summarized the main political argument in his book on the ancient language of Spain (the mentioned *La Antigua Lengua de las Españas*), which Bosch did use as a guide on this issue. Bosch was unaware of Poza's report *Ad Pragmaticas de Toro et Tordesillas* [see note 15], but he used the same doctrinal basis as Poza did: the book on nobility by the French lawyer, expert on this issue, André Tiraqueau.[30]

Bosch's borrowing of the established Biscay thesis could not be more apparent. When he wanted to explain the foundations of the Catalan nobility, he mentioned blood, antiquity, and lineage, adding that it was just like the case of the nobility in Biscay. Thanks to the Biscay model, he did not feel the need to develop the argument any further. One of the most important reasons for taking this standpoint had to do with fiscal exemptions and the procedures for making law: both the Lord of Biscay and the Count of Barcelona, as princes (*principes*), were obliged to summon their general assemblies to pass any law related to the political conditions or the fiscal status of their subjects. In both cases, the original pact was the basis for a contractual procedure in law making.

Here was another sign of the way these two authors, one Basque-Flemish and the other Catalan, had begun to adopt increasingly similar positions in their approach to forms of political union in a composite monarchy such as the Spanish one. Bosch, rather than Poza, was the outstanding authority in this area of forms of political unions. He devoted a great deal of attention to the subject in his *Summari*.[31] He could adress all areas of the issue from both the broader Spanish perspective and the narrower Catalan one. But it should be pointed out that Bosch, the Catalan, had no doubts when choosing the

30 André Tiraqueau, *Commentarii de Nobilitate et Iure Primigeniorum* (1549) profusely quoted by Bosch in *Summari*, 65–77.

31 Jon Arrieta, "Formas de unión de reinos: tipología y casuística en perspectiva jurídico-política (siglos XVI-XVIII)", in Alfredo Floristán, ed., *1512. Conquista e incorporación de Navarra: Historiografía, Derecho y otros procesos de integración en la Europa renacentista* (Barcelona: Gobierno de Navarra and Ariel, 2012), 89–125, at 119.

political and legal bases for the birth of a society: he opted for the ones already put forward in Biscay. His choice is surprising as he could very well have used the arguments already established in Catalonia: Jesús Villanueva has explained them adequately.[32] Thus there is absolutely no doubt about Bosch's certainty that adhering to the Biscay "model" would be enough.

How much external repercussion could the Biscayans' claim to universal nobility, their origins and relationship with Tubalism have had? A work that made amajor contribution in addressing this issue was Arthur Duck's *De usu et authoritate Ius Romanorum in dominiis Príncipum Christianorum.*[33] Duck leaves little doubt as to his ideas on the subject in the chapter on Spanish kingdoms (book II, chapter VI). He regarded the Navarrese and Cantabrians (the latter included the Biscayens) as the most remarkable among the Iberian Christian polities in their reactions to the Roman and Muslim occupations. On one hand, Duck draws on Martín de Azpilcueta (known as Martín Navarro because of his Navarrese origin) and his views on the Roman occupation which he believed was based on force and armed conquest. Azpilcueta, a distinguished authority on cannon law and a Basque-speaking Navarrese, strongly defended this standpoint and Duck commented on it, fully aware that it was an original and sound theory. In addition to this, Duck repeated the idea that there were "the Navarrese and the Cantabrians", in Northern Iberia, those who resisted to the Romans and then to the Muslims. Duck uses the term "*Cantabri*" as an equivalent for "Basque" or even "Biscayan", as is confirmed by numerous other texts and authors. Thus, there is no doubt that the arguments dealt with in this chapter enjoyed wide circulation in Europe. It is also clear that they originated in Biscay and were further developed in other passages of Duck's book. It is important to read these ideas in their original form (allow me to translate directly from the original Latin):

> Martín Navarro is the only author who does not acknowledge that the Spanish were Roman subjects (*subditos Romanis*): they were submitted by the use of unjustified force and without any legal basis; there were also a number of Spanish peoples such as the Navarrese and the Cantabrians that never really bowed to Roman domination.[34]

32 Jesús Villanueva, *Política y discurso histórico en la España del siglo XVII: Las polémicas sobre los orígenes medievales de Cataluña* (Alicante: Publicaciones de la Universidad de Alicante, 2004).

33 *De usu et authoritate Ius Romanorum in dominies Príncipum Christianorum.* I use editions of London, 1653; and London, 1689: the text is exactly the same in both.

34 *Solus Martinus Navarrus* [Navarr. ad d. c. novit. de Judic. not. 3. n. 160.] negat hispanos fuisse subditos Romanis, sive quod vi injusta et sine titulo idoneo devictisunt, sive quod

Duck then adds some comments on their resistance to the Muslims. He regards it as a merit of

> those who remained in the mountains of Asturias and Cantabria. They are now considered to be the noblest amongst the peoples of the peninsula: the Spanish regard the Biscayens as the authentic aboriginals of Hispania, a people that has never mixed with others and speakers of a language that was one of the seventy-two that God imposed on human beings during the confusion of tongues at the Tower of Babel. And this is the reason that the native Biscayens regard themselves as noblemen.[35]

There is a further fact that gives final confirmation to the virtues attributed to the Biscayens: Arthur Duck, the English civil lawyer who was so well informed on the legal system and history of Europe including that insignificant corner, the Lordship of Biscay, had no hesitation in quoting Juan Gutiérrez to support his statement. Juan Gutiérrez himself, as we have seen and demonstrated, had literally copied the work of the Flemish-Biscayan lawyer Andrés de Poza, the real creator of this hypothesis. Arthur Duck was completely unaware of this fact and indeed it was impossible for him to have known it. We, however, do know and it is relevant to uncover it and to draw a complete picture of how the narrative of the political birth of a community was created and, what is more important, how such narrative was incorporated into law and real and effective public institutions.

---

aliqui Hispaniae populi praesertim Navarraei et Cantabri in eorum Dominationem nunquam consenserunt (London edition, 1689, 230–1; London edition, 1653, fol. 106r).

35 *Ibidem*, paragraph. v (1689 edition, p. 232; 1653 edition, fol. 106v): "qui in Asturorum et Cantabrorum montibus ex eo tempore remanserunt, a quibus praecipua hodie inter Hispanos nobilitas originem suam repetit, ideoque Biscaynos Hispani tradunt [Navarr. d. Notab. 3.n.160; Gutierr. d. lib. 1 qu. 17, n. 160;] esse originarios Hispaniae populos cum aliis populis numquam commixtos, eorumque idioma fuisse unum ex iis septuagesima duabus Linguis, quae Deus in confusione Turris Babylonicae gentibus inspiravit, eademque de Causa Biscaynos originarios omnes Hidalgos et Nobiles esse praedicant". Duck quotes Azpilcueta's lecture on the decretal *Novit. de Judiciis* [Navarr. d. Notab. 3.n.160], that I study in "Martín de Azpilcueta como fuente doctrinal y testimonio personal para el análisis y valoración de la integración de Navarra en la Monarquía de los Austrias", in Jon Arrieta, Xavier Gil and Jesús Morales, eds., *La diadema del rey: Vizcaya, Navarra, Aragón y Cerdeña en la Monarquía de España (siglos XVI-XVIII)* (Bilbao: Publicaciones Universidad del País Vasco, 2017), 383–446. Then he quotes Gutiérrez *Practicarum Quaestionum Civilium*, III, quaestio 17 [Gutierr. d. lib. 1 qu. 17, n. 160]. This *quaestio* was the one Gutiérrez copied from Poza's tract on this subject.

Bibliography

Main Sources

Crónica de las siete casas de Vizcaya y Castilla. Escrita por Lope García de Salazar, año 1454, introd. by Juan Carlos Guerra (Madrid: Sucesores de Rivadeneyra, 1914).

Fontecha y Salazar, Pedro de (attributed), *Escudo de la más constante fe y lealtad del Muy Noble y Muy Leal Señorío de Vizcaya*, ed. and introduction by Jon Arrieta (Bilbao: Universidad del País Vasco / Euskal Herriko Unibertsitatea, Argitalpen Zerbitzua, Servicio editorial, 2015).

García de Saavedra, Juan, *Tractatus de Hispanorum Nobilitate et Exemptione, sive ad Pragmaticam Cordubensem, quae est l. 8. Tit. 11. Lib. 2 Novae Recopilationis, in ultima editione Madriti edita* (Köln: Sumptibus Societatis, 1737) (first ed., Valladolid, 1588).

Poza, Andrés de, *Fuero de hidalguía: Ad Pragmaticas de Toro et Tordesillas*, ed. Carmen Muñoz de Bustillo, transl. M. Ángeles Durán Ramos (Bilbao: Servicio Editorial de la Universidad del País Vasco, 1997).

Poza, Andrés de, *De la antigua lengua, poblaciones y comarcas de las Españas* (Bilbao: Mathias Mares, 1587).

The Old Law of Bizkaia (1452), ed. Gregorio Monreal Zia, transl. William A. Douglass and Linda White, preface William A. Douglass, Basque Classics Series, n. 1 (Reno: Center for Basque Studies, University of Nevada, 2005).

Main Bibliographical References

Aguinagalde, F. Borja de, ed., *El País Vasco, tierra de hidalgos y nobles: Momentos singulares de su historia* (Madrid: Fundación Banco Santander, 2016).

Arrieta, Jon, "El licenciado Andrés de Poza y su contribución a la ubicación de Vizcaya en la Monarquía hispánica", in Jon Arrieta, Xavier Gil and Jesús Morales, eds., *La diadema del rey: Vizcaya, Navarra, Aragón y Cerdeña en la Monarquía de España (siglos XVI-XVIII)* (Bilbao: Servicio Editorial de la Universidad del País Vasco, 2017).

Caro Baroja, Julio, *Los vascos y la historia a través de Garibay* (San Sebastián: Txertoa, 1973); new edition, with introductory essay by Guadalupe Rubio de Urquía (Madrid: Caro Raggio, 2002).

Mañaricua, Andrés de, *Historiografía de Vizcaya (Desde Lope García de Salazar a Labayru)*, 2nd ed. (Bilbao: Gran Enciclopedia Vasca, 1973).

Prieto Lasa, José Ramón, *Las leyendas de los Señores de Vizcaya y la tradición melusiniana* (Madrid: Universidad Autónoma de Madrid, Universidad del País Vasco, 1995).

CHAPTER 4

The Myth of Sobrarbe between Old Europe and the New World

A Reassessment

Angela De Benedictis

1 Introduction

When thinking of foundation myths related to charters and political systems in the early modern period, one such case comes easily to mind, the so-called myth of Sobrarbe, in Aragon, which was crucial in local politics and enjoyed remarkable diffusion in late sixteenth-century European debates on the limits of kingship and was evoked even in the debates around the English and the American Revolutions. This theme has always been particularly fascinating to me and thus I took it into account in a broader study on early modern politics.[1] The starting point in historiography was of course the monograph by Ralph E. Giesey, *If not, not. The Oath of the Aragonese and the Legendary Laws of Sobrarbe* (1968); then Xavier Gil studied the political context of the myth; and the literature on pactism and on the *Herrschaftsverträge* that has developed should be mentioned as well.[2] In addition, having not had the opportunity to study it thoroughly, I suggested the theme to Clizia Magoni as a research topic for her doctoral thesis, which later became a monograph, *'Fueros' e libertà*.[3] The issue of Sobrarbe has received further attention concerning European republicanism.[4]

---

1 Angela De Benedictis, *Politica governo istituzioni nell'Europa moderna* (Bologna: Il Mulino, 2001), 88, 226–7.

2 Ralph E. Giesey, *If not, not: The Oath of the Aragonese and the Fueros of Sobrarbe* (Princeton: Princeton University Press, 1968); Xavier Gil, "Aragonese Constitutionalism and Habsburg Rule: the Varying Meanings of Liberty", in Richard L. Kagan and Geoffrey Parker, eds., *Spain, Europe and the Atlantic World: Essays in Honour of J.H. Elliott* (Cambridge: Cambridge University Press, 1995), 160–87; De Benedictis, *Politica*, 287–95.

3 Clizia Magoni, *'Fueros' e libertà: Il mito della costituzione aragonese nell'Europa moderna* (Roma: Carocci, 2007); Spanish translation: *Fueros y libertades: El mito de la constitución aragonesa en la Europa moderna*, translation by Antonio Pérez Martin (Zaragoza: El Justicia de Aragón, 2012).

4 Xavier Gil, "Republican Politics in Early Modern Spain. The Castilian and Catalano-Aragonese Traditions", in Martin van Gelderen and Quentin Skinner, eds., *Republicanism: A*

 | DOI:10.1163/9789004549159_006

Why, then, go back to the topic? In other words, from what point of view resume the research on such a wide and complex topic within the little space of a presentation first, and an essay later? What is worth doing is to reconsider an aspect of the myth or, rather, of the founding text of the myth of the *fueros* of Sobrarbe, which certainly has been investigated already, but perhaps not yet in its full potential. I am referring to the problem of the archaic language of the text in its graphic form as well that calls attention to fundamental issues of the political-legal culture of the XVI century (such as the discovery of the *fueros* of Sobrarbe), or at least of the time between the "conquest" of Navarre in 1513 (an event that plays a decisive role in the whole matter) and the monarchomach Huguenot treatises, which make of the *fueros* and the Aragonese liberties a specific object of political-constitutional claim in the France of the time.

If the partial reassessment of this issue is currently possible, it is mainly because recent historiography has thoroughly investigated several issues that are crucial to understand the emblematic value of the Aragonese freedoms and the myth of Sobrarbe. Firstly, the problem of tyranny;[5] then the remedies to tyranny and the supervisory magistrates (Ephorate);[6] the mixed government.[7]

Shared European Heritage, vol. I: *Republicanism and Constitutionalism in Early Modern Europe* (Cambridge: Cambridge University Press, 2002), 263–88. I will be making a few specific references to other studies on the said liberties.

5 For an overview on the problem of tyranny, see an important essay by Diego Quaglioni, presented at the opening conference of the European Society for the History of Political Thought: "Sovereignty versus Tyranny in Medieval and Early Modern Political Thought", in Janet Coleman and Paschalis M. Kitromilides, eds., *In the Footsteps of Herodotus: Towards European Political Thought* (Florence: Olschki, 2012), 65–75.

6 Above all concerning the *Politica methodice digesta* by Johannes Althusius (1614) and its chapter XXXVIII: i.e., Robert von Friedeburg, "Von den Ephoren als Institut ständischer Mitbestimmung zur Fundamentalverfassung des Gemeinwesens: Die Entwicklung von Calvin bis hin zu Althusius, Besold und Boxhorn um die Mitte des 17. Jahrhunderts", in Heinrich de Wall, ed., *Reformierte Staatslehre in der Frühen Neuzeit* (Berlin, 2014), 79–98. For a complete bibliographical overview, see now Lucia Bianchin, *Diritto, teologia e politica nella prima età moderna: Johannes Althusius (1563–1638)* (Foligno: Il Formichiere, 2017).

7 Martin van Gelderen, "Aristotelians, Monarchomachs and Republicans: Sovereignty and *respublica mixta* in Dutch and German Political Thought, 1580–1650"; and Hans Erich Bödeker, "Debating the *respublica mixta*: German and Dutch Political Discourses around 1700", both in van Gelderen and Skinner, eds., *Republicanism*, I, 195–218 and 219–46, respectively; Diego Quaglioni, "La souveraineté partagée au Moyen Âge"; Christian Nadeau, "Les constitutionnalistes français face au problème de la constitution mixte: Claude Seyssel et Jean Bodin"; Isabelle Bouvignies, "Monarchie mixte et souveraineté des États chez le monarchomaques huguenots"; Michael Stolleis, "La *respublica mixta* au XVIIe siècle. Reception de l'idéal de la constitution mixte en Allemagne"; Giuseppe Duso, "La constitution mixte et le principe du gouvernement: le cas Althusius"; and Jean Terrel, "Hobbes: la critique du gouvernement mixte", all six in Marie Gaille-Nikodimov, ed., *Le gouvernement*

Also, it is because of the consolidation of a research method in constitutional as well as legal history that pays specific attention to symbols, ceremonies and rituals.[8] Besides, it is necessary to mention that even the most recent studies on "monarchomach" literature provide fundamental suggestions for the (extremely partial) reassessment which I am proposing in this essay.

I mainly refer to the huge monography of Paul-Alexis Mellet, *Les Traités monarcomaques*, who dedicates a great part of his thoughts to the function of history in the monarchomach treatises, and therefore also in Hotman's *Francogallia*.

It is from these thoughts that I would like to start, before going to the text of the *fueros* reproduced in the *Francogallia* and in other writings that might help to understand his (Hotman's) concern. Before moving, in other words, to sources that are coeval to the 'conquest' of Navarre above mentioned.

Mellet of course is conscious of the role played by the Aragonese oath in the *Francogallia*, since the obligations resulting from the oath constitute a central aspect of the ideal political regime for all the Monarchomachs. For them, it was a kind of oath that "deserved to be introduced in France because it allowed the nature of the obligations of the king to be fixed, enhancing the States". The study of the past and the use of history were intended to "search for remedies to the present situation", meaning that history represented "a set of examples to follow, that is a set of norms".[9]

Such normative value is inherent to the second of the three functions that are attributed to history in monarchomach treatises, the institutional one (together with the moral and the predictive ones). The aim, in other words, is to "show the nature of the institutions of the past, and to suggest, implicitly or explicitly, that those ancient models constitute a remedy to the problems of the XVI century France. This is the case – frequently mentioned – of the Ephors of Sparta". In a table comparing monarchomach treatises and pamphlets, Mellet shows how the example of the Ephors is necessary to discourses on conditional obedience, on the deposition of the king in case of abuse, on the opposition to the king, in case he violates the law. The Ephors are the "brakes" on kings,

---

mixte: De l'idéal politique au monstre constitutionnel en Europe (*XIIIe-XVIIe siècle*) (Saint-Étienne: Université de Saint Etienne, 2005), 15–24, 95–115, 117–38, 153–73, 139–51, 175–89 respectively.

8 For some references, see below, footnotes 66–67.

9 Paul-Alexis Mellet, *Les traités monarcomaques: Confusion des temps, résistance armée et monarchie parfaite* (*1560–1600*) (Geneva: Droz, 2007), 410, 457. Here, as in the following lines, the quotations are drawn from the translated original French version.

to prevent the risk of tyranny; they are the essential condition to preserve the kingdom, against the flatteurs.[10]

Therefore, the use of history "not only enables an institutional form modelled after the past, but it also makes it real showing that it has already existed. In order to do this though, it is necessary that ancient examples can serve as valid laws for the present or for the future, that is to say they produce universal obligations". On the other hand, the "study of the institutional function of history leads to confirming the idea that the study of the past … represents a set of norms aimed at the future".[11]

Speaking about historical law (valid for the past, the present and the future), Mellet conveniently mentions the definition of historical myth given by Donald R. Kelley, one of the most expert scholars in the analysis of Renaissance political thought, French political thought and of the relationship between history and law: "not a nonevent, but a kind of Hyper-event".[12]

What is being investigated, then, is the relationship between the past and the present just like it was conceived and analysed in a political thought that reflected on the nature and functions of monarchy. Historical research on European institutions helped to show what France lacked: "the (limited) right of election, the role of Parliament, the obligations connected to the oath".[13] The ideal framework of a temperate monarchy led the Monarchomachs to endorse "ancient (biblical and historical) and contemporary (European) regimes in order to compare them to the French situation of the XV and XVI centuries". Their political project led them to "create historical and original myths".

With respect to this, Mellet significantly recalls the not-so recent – but nonetheless extremely valid – thoughts expressed by Pocock in *The Ancient Constitution and the Feudal Law*. It is worth reading them again directly, also because this allows me to go immediately after to the heart of the matter. Pocock poses the problem of what is and up until what point the contemporary concept of "constitutionalism" can coincide with the peculiar problems of European political thought between the XVI and XVII centuries:

---

10 Mellet, *ibidem*, 454–5.

11 Mellet, *ibidem*, 457, 460.

12 Mellet, *ibidem*, 457; as regards Donald R. Kelley, "Martyr, Myths and the Massacre: The Background of St Bartholomew", in his volume *The Writing of History and the Study of Law* (Aldershot: Routledge, 1997), V, 1334.

13 Mellet, *Les traités*, 485.

> There existed, therefore, in a number of European nations a kind of political thought which cannot satisfactory be termed 'constitutionalism', since it involved a more intensive use of historical and antiquarian thinking than the use of that term normally implies. It may be provisionally defined as the attempt to settle fundamental political questions, notably that involving law, right and sovereignty, by appeal not directly to abstract political concepts, but to the existing 'municipal' laws of the country concerned and to the concept of custom, prescription and authority that underly them, as well as to the reverence which they enjoyed by reason of their antiquity – an attempt which necessarily involved the study, critical or otherwise, of their origins and history. One may reasonably claim that the history of European political thinking, at any rate in the sixteenth to eighteenth centuries will be incomplete until we know more about this branch of thought than we now do. To call it 'constitutional antiquarianism' would perhaps do less justice to the quality of the historical thought which its practitioners sometimes displayed; and the South Italian scholars, who appear to be the only historians who have studied its evolution as naturally forming part of the history of their states, use such term as 'cultura storico-giuridica' and 'tradizione giuridica', which do not go well into English.[14]

Provided that now instead "cultura storico-giuridica" e "tradizione giuridica" "go well into English",[15] it is Pocock's comment on the characteristic approach of that political thought "notably that involving law, right and sovereignty, by appeal not directly to abstract political concepts, but to the existing 'municipal' laws of the country concerned and to the concept of custom, prescription and authority"[16] that brings us straight to the heart of the problem.

---

14 J.G.A. Pocock, *The Ancient Constitution and the Feudal Law: A Study of English Historical Thought in the Seventeenth Century. A Reissue with a Retrospect* (Cambridge: Cambridge University Press, 1987), 17–18.

15 As shown in the extensive essay written by Diego Quaglioni, "Italy, 1. From Medieval Jurists to Machiavelli", in Howell Lloyd, Glenn Burgess and Simon Hodson, eds., *European Political Thought, 1450–1700: Religion, Law and Philosophy* (New Haven and London: Yale University Press, 2008), 55–74.

16 Pocock, *The Ancient Constitution*, 17.

2 "Ad perpetuam rei memoriam"

NOS QVI VALEMOS TANTO COME VOS, Y PODEMOS MAS QVE VOS, VOS ELEGIMOS REY: CON ESTAS Y ESTAS CONDITIONES: INTRA VOS Y NOS, UN QVE MANDA MAS QVE VOS.[17]

> We, who are of as great Value as you, and can do more than you, do elect you to be our King, upon such and such Conditions: Between you and us there is *one* of *greater Authority* than you.[18]

The words reported by the great French Huguenot jurist François Hotman, already in the first edition of his *Francogallia* (1573), meant to underline the "extraordinary and most singular fortitude" of the Spanish "in disciplining the king", that is the king of Aragon, have been widely known to constitutional historiography for a long time. It refers to the role in a "kind of play" that the Spanish "enact ... when they appoint a king of Aragon in their general council ... to keep the issue constantly in mind". The Nos is "a man whom they name 'the Law of Aragon'", which "by a decree of the people" is declared "to be greater and more powerful than the king". The "words" are used to "harangue the king, who is appointed with fixed laws and conditions". Amongst all the "laws of nearly all nations" that subordinate laws and decrees enacted by kings to the agreement and consent of the kingdom expressed in Parliament, the Spanish law is, in Hotman's view, the most "remarkable",[19] even when compared to that of the English, of which he has previously spoken.

---

17 François Hotman, *Francogallia* ([Geneva]: Ex officina Iacobi Stoerij, 1573), ch. X, *"Qualis Regni Francogallici constituendi forma fuerit"*, 85.

18 Here, I am quoting from the first English translation of 1711, Francis Hotoman, *Franco-Gallia, or Or, An Account of the Ancient Free State of France, and Most Other Parts of Europe, Before the Loss of Their Liberties* (London: printed for Timothy Goodwin, 1711), ch. X, "The Form and Constitution of the Francogallican Government", 71. The modern translation by J.H.M. Salmon in the edition by Ralph E. Giesey is of course, different: *Francogallia*, Latin text by Ralph E. Giesey, translated by J.H.M. Salmon (Cambridge: Cambridge University Press, 1972), 307–9: "We, who are worth as much as you and can do more than you as king upon such and such conditions, between you and us there is one whose authority is greater than you".

19 In this case, the quotations are drawn from the translation by Salmon: Hotman, *ibidem*, 307. Despite being the translation of a great expert, it is nevertheless worth reporting the original Latin version, at least to show that "instituta" in Hotman 1573 becomes "laws" in Hotman 1972, and that "insigne memoratur" referred to "instituta" becomes "remarkable". It is worth noting that the English translation of 1711 interpreted "instituta" as "Law and Customs": Hotman, *Franco-Gallia* (1711), 71.

Among all the Aragonese political writings which, after Hotman, make use of the essential sources to prove the validity of the Aragonese liberties while they are heavily threatened by Philip II's policy, there is the *Discurso y alegaciones de derecho* of the jurist Pedro Luis Martínez (1591).[20] It is a long and well-supported defence of the role of the Justicia de Aragon, in the context of the Aragonese "rebellion" of 1591 and the sequence of events linked to the former secretary of the king Antonio Pérez.[21]

The comment to the text of the Fueros de Sobrarbe, as it has been reconstructed by Jerónimo Zurita and Jerónimo Blancas,[22] constitutes a fundamental element of Martínez' *Discurso*, on which the jurist insists several times. With respect to the pacts, conditions and laws under which kings were elected, Martínez writes that all historians support it. To reinforce this claim thoroughly, Martínez mentions a series of jurists: Bartolus of Saxoferrato (ca. 131–1357), Nicolò de' Tudeschi known as Panormitanus (1386–1445), Felino Maria Sandeo (1444–1503), Guillaume Benoît (1455–1516), Filippo Decio (1454–1535 ca.), Pietro Paolo Parisio (1473–1545), Giovanni Francesco Porporati (1485–1544), Giuseppe Mascardi (1540/1545–1587/1588).[23] The quoted passages of these jurists, or in some cases the very titles of their works recall the question of the validity of chronicles and histories as proof in the decision of legal cases. That is, if and to what extent it is possible to use chronicles and histories as proof in the decision of legal cases.

The problem was certainly – and had always been – controversial. A number of jurists still maintained that chronicles and histories were trustworthy. It was

---

20 Pedro Luis Martínez, *Discurso y alegaciones de derecho … en que trata y declara el origen, y principio del reyno de Aragon, y la excelencia de su govierno y leyes, y justicia que tiene, en el pleyto en que defiende en el consistorio del Justicia de Aragon, que la magestad del rey no puede nombrar Virrey estrangero para su govierno, ni conviene a su real servicio* (Zaragoza: Lorenzo Robles, 1591). The significance of the *Discurso* is shortly underlined by Eliseo Serrano Martín, "*No demandamos sino el modo.* Los juramentos reales en Aragón en la Edad Moderna", *Pedralbes*, 28 (2008), 446, 448; and by Jon Arrieta Alberdi, "Las formas de vinculación a la Monarquía y de relación entre sus reinos y coronas en la España de los Austrias. Perspectivas de análisis", in Antonio Álvarez-Ossorio Alvariño and Bernardo J. García García, eds., *La Monarquía de las naciones: Patria, nación y naturaleza en la Monarquía de España* (Madrid: Fundación Carlos de Amberes, 2004), 317.

21 There is an enormous bibliography on this subject. See above all Jesús Gascón Pérez, *Alzar banderas contra su rey: La rebelión aragonesa de 1591 contra Felipe II* (Zaragoza: Prensas Universidad de Zaragoza, 2010). He mentions the role played by the jurist Pedro Luis Martínez: 166, 176, 339, 341, 531.

22 See at least Giesey, *If not not*, 57–60; 131–7.

23 Martínez, *Discurso y alegaciones de derecho*, 21–2.

the case, for example,[24] of Giovanni Francesco Porporati, whom I recall here because in his *Lectura* of 1526 used by Martinez, the jurist from Pinerolo maintained that among public writings, the ones that could be considered trustworthy were those carved in marble gravestones.[25] In turn, Porporati based himself on the authority of Ippolito Marsili's (1450–1529) *De probationibus*,[26] according to whom letters that were written, carved into gravestones or marble could constitute proof only when proving something ancient.[27] Marsili's authorities were, in turn, other previous jurists, among whom Bartolus of Saxoferrato and Baldus de Ubaldis (1327–1400).

In the *Francogallia* Hotman has the sentence "Nos qui valemos tanto como vos" spoken by the Justicia de Aragon. These words are written in the archaic Latin of the Law of the Twelve Tables, the founding text of Roman law, and they possess the characteristic features of marble inscriptions. This is well-known and repeatedly underlined by historiography, as much as the fact that Blancas's reconstruction (who was familiar with the *Francogallia*) of the text of the fueros presents the same features.[28] Furthermore, it is also known that Hotman stepped into a well-established research path[29] by devoting an entire work to the issue of the Twelve Tables's text reconstruction.[30] As far as I know though, no historiography related to the Aragonese freedoms and the *fueros* of Sobrarbe has paid any attention yet to what Martinez' *Discurso,* that clearly includes Blancas among his sources, emphasizes in the extract mentioned above,[31] even though he does it indirectly by means of the work of other jurists. Probably, Hotman – who had investigated the tradition of the Twelve Tables – was familiar with the legal literature that Martínez used to support the validity of chronicles and histories as proof. It would be sufficient to read the other works of Hotman as a civil lawyer[32] to prove it.

---

24 It is impossible, of course, to report here all the passages quoted in Martínez' *Discurso*.

25 See, for instance, the commented edition by Giason del Maino, *In primam-secundam Digesti veteris partem commentarii* (Lugduni: Apud Hugonem a Porta, 1569).

26 Ippolito Marsili, *Aurea repetitio iuris … rubrice Codice de probationibus* (Bononiae: Impressa per Benedictum Hectoris bibliopolam Bononiensem, 1508).

27 Marsili, *Aurea repetitio,* col. 40: "probatio enim fit per litteras scriptas seu sculptas in lapidibus seu in marmore & tales littere probant & hoc quando tractatur de re antiqua probanda".

28 Giesey, *If not not*, 61–2.

29 Kelley, *François Hotman.*

30 François Hotman, *De Legibus Duodecim Tabularum tripartita … commentatio* (Lugduni: Tornaesius, 1564).

31 Martínez, *Discurso y alegaciones de derecho*, 21–2.

32 Perhaps legal historians have already confirmed this. However, exploring this aspect further would go beyond the nature and purposes of this essay.

The carving of words into marble and gravestones proved their validity and authenticity, according to a *communis opinion doctorum*. This was well-known to those jurists who discussed "fundamental political questions, notably that involving law, right and sovereignty" – to quote Pocock again[33] – in that very year when the problem arose – dramatically – for the Kingdom of Navarre, and therefore for the *fueros* of Navarre as well.[34] In 1513, when Niccolò Machiavelli posed an ancient problem in an undoubtedly new way – that of the power of the *princeps* – driven by his experience of the "horrible" wars of Italy, the jurist Mario Salamonio degli Alberteschi wrote a treatise in six books, in the form of a dialogue, *De Principatu*,[35] that was published and spread later in France, which was devastated by religious wars.[36]

The underlying problem in the *De Principatu* by Salamonio is the distinction between the prince and the tyrant, that is problem of the *potestas* and the *ius* of the prince, which is dealt with through the *quaestio* of the *solutio a legibus* of the prince. It is discussed by a jurist, a theologian, a philosopher and

33 Pocock, *The Ancient Constitution*, 17.

34 See the most recent studies on the subject in Alfredo Floristán Imízcoz, ed., *1512. Conquista e incorporación de Navarra: Historiografía, derecho y otros procesos de integración en la Europa renacentista*, (Barcelona: Ariel, 2012); and in his "Conquista e incorporación de Navarra a la Monaquía de España", in Jon Arrieta, Xavier Gil, Jesús Morales, eds., *La diadema del rey: Vizcaya, Navarra, Aragón y Cerdeña en la Monarquía de España (siglos XVI-XVIII)* (Bilbao: Publicaciones Universidad del País Vasco, 2017), 307–45.

35 The most complete study on Salamonio is still the one by Mario D'Addio, *L'idea del contratto sociale dai sofisti alla riforma e il "De Principatu" di Mario Salamonio* (Milan: Giuffrè, 1954), who also published the modern edition of the Mario Salamonio degli Alberteschi, *De Principatu libros septem; nec non Orationes ad priores florentinos*, recognovit Marius D'Addio (Milan: Giuffrè, 1955), from which the quotations will be drawn, from now on. Salamonio is also one of the protagonists of the work by Quentin Skinner, *The Foundations of Modern political Thought*, I. *The Renaissance*, 148–52; II. *The Age of Reformation*, 131–4. The recent studies that have been published on the occasion of the 500th anniversary of Machiavelli's *Prince* have produced a new-found attention for Salamonio: Paolo Carta, "Salamone degli Alberteschi Mario", in Italo Birocchi, Ennio Cortese, Antonello Mattone and Marco Nicola Miletti, eds., *Dizionario biografico dei giuristi italiani (XII-XX secolo)* (Bologna: Il Mulino, 2013), 1766–7; Lucio Biasiori, "Salomonio degli Alberteschi, Mario", in *Machiavelli: Enciclopedia machiavelliana*, II (Roma: Istituto della Enciclopedia Italiana, 2014), 473–4; Angela De Benedictis, "Principato civile e tirannide: il capitolo IX del *Principe* e il *De Principatu* di Mario Salamonio degli Alberteschi", in Gian Mario Anselmi, Riccardo Caporali and Carlo Galli, eds., *Machiavelli Cinquecento: Mezzo millennio del* Principe (Milano: Mimesis, 2015), 57–72; David Jiménez Castaño, "*Princeps non est legibus solutus*. La negación contractualista de Mario Salomonio a la sentencia de Ulpiano", in Alberto Maffi, ed., *Princeps legibus solutus* (Torino: Giappichelli, 2016), 63–76.

36 Mario Salamonio degli Alberteschi, *De principatu libri sex. Ad Pomponium Beleurium, regis in Sacro Consistorio consiliarium* (Parisiis: excudebat Dionysius du Val, 1578).

a historian. The historian explicitly has the function of going through actions, new and old facts that can explain the problem.

The debate between the philosopher, the jurist, the theologian and the historian examines everything that legal-theological-philosophical doctrine had developed until then with regard to principality and tyranny, ever since Aristotle and Thomas Aquinas, on specific issues such as the power of the *populus romanus* transferred to the prince temporarily or permanently. The discussion then focuses on the *Lex Regia de imperio*, and consequently on the nature and validity of the agreements between the prince and the *populus*. And it is the historian who reminds the other speakers what no one seemed to know. That is to say that the *lex* had to be confirmed and renewed every time there was a new prince, as it was clearly stated in the bronze table into which the text was carved and that still lied in the Lateran Basilica. Otherwise, that *lex* would be useless.[37] And after the historian has read and repeated the whole text of the *lex de imperio Vespasiani* as it is in the bronze table, the jurist – who had been sceptical at first – recognises that the prince cannot be unbound by that law: the power of the people is greater than that of the prince.[38]

What the historian from Salamonio proved, also on the basis of the materiality of the document/monument onto which the *lex regia* was carved, had already occurred a few years before. It had happened in Bologna, where the jurist Ippolito Marsili, already above mentioned with regard to the validity as proof of marble inscriptions, served as law professor at the *Studium*.[39] "Reconquered" by Pope Julius II in 1506, the city government had negotiated the conditions of its renewed loyalty to the Pope, trough agreements.

The first time, in 1507, the agreements were supervised by a Senate of aristocratic nature. The second time in 1510, because of a shift in alliances of the "warrior" Pope in the context of the ever-changing relationship with the France of Louis XII. In this case, the agreements had been supervised by the tribunes of the plebs, the people's magistrates (even polemical of/in opposition to the Senate). As usual, the recognition of the agreements was officialised by a papal bull. In the bull, the contractual validity of the agreements was explicitly recognised (*per vim contractus*). The tribunes of the plebs immediately decided

37 Salamonio, *De Principatu* (1955), 64.

38 "Ex ultimo capite in perspicuo ponitur illa populi potestas ac maior ipso Principatu de qua me disserentem irridere videbamini": Salamonio, *De Principatu* (1955), 65.

39 Marsili, *Aurea repetitio*, col. 40: "probatio etiam fit per litteras scriptas seu sculptas in lapidibus seu in marmore & tales littere probant & hoc quando tractatur de re antiqua probanda".

to fixate the content of the papal bull in an indelible way. They had the text summarised in the language and style of the law of the Twelve Tables and they had it engraved in a marble board that was placed between two chapels in the Basilica of San Petronio, the patron saint of the city. Some decades later, when in some cases the pontiffs' who succeeded Julius II had already shown uncertainty and hostility in reaffirming that kind of agreements, the Senate charged a jurist of the *Studium*, Annibale Monterenzi, with printing a commented edition of the city statutes (municipal laws), both civil and criminal (the last edition dated back to 1454, with some later addictions). The text of Julius II's bull was contained in the third volume, published in 1574,[40] with glosses by Monterenzi. At the end of the glossed text, the jurist copied the complete text of the existing inscription in San Petronio, both in content and form, *ad perpetuam rei memoriam,* so that the memory of it would be undying.[41] The meaning is that the city's freedoms cannot expire. The marble engraving is still in the Basilica of San Petronio.[42] In European – and non-European – libraries, there are as many copies of Monterenzi's commentary to the bull of 1510 and of the reproduction of San Petronio's board, as there are of the edition of the statutes of 1574.

3 Lex Regia *and Mixed Government*

The digression on a case study that certainly cannot aspire to the exemplarity of the *fueros* de Sobrarbe presents, however, common elements with a European political-legal culture which developed through that *civilis sapientia*[43] that is the interpretation of roman-canon law.

---

40 Annibale Monterenzi, *Statutorum inclitae civitatis studiorumque matris Bononiae … Tomus tertius* (Bononiae: apud Ioannem Rossium, 1574).

41 Monterenzi, *Statutorum inclitae civitatis*, 17: "Haec ad perpetuam rei Memoriam summatim / aureis literis in quodam Divi Petronii / peristillo pone sacellum S^{mi}. Cor / poris Christi insculpta / visuntur".

42 Angela De Benedictis, *Repubblica per contratto: Una città europea nello Stato della Chiesa* (Bologna: Il Mulino, 1995), 190–3; *Eadem*, "Identità politica di un governo popolare. La memoria (culturale) dei Tribuni della Plebe", in her edited volume *Diritti in memoria, carità di patria: Tribuni della plebe e governo popolare a Bologna* (XIV-XVIII *secolo*) (Bologna: CLUEB, 1999), 40–8; and "Popular Government, Government of the *Ottimati* and the Language of Politics. Concord and Discord, 1377–1559", in Sarah Rubin Blanshei, ed., *A Companion to Medieval and Renaissance Bologna* (Leiden-Boston: Brill, 2018), 302.

43 Quaglioni, *"Italy, 1. From Medieval Jurists to Machiavelli"*.

The idea that negotiated laws were considered as inviolable contracts was inherent to that culture. Furthermore, in case they were sworn laws, they obtained a greater strength: originating from the consent of the subjects (legally subordinate to the prince), they were founded on that consent.[44] The appeal to those laws which in different parts of early modern Europe were called *privilegia, libertates, usus et consuetudines,* and of course, *foros,* was founded on this principle. I am referring to a well-known issue in historiography: that is, the appeal to privileges, freedoms, customs, rights and their safeguard was a common feature, and therefore a fundamental feature, of political action all over Europe between the XV and the XVIII centuries.[45] And it did not make any difference if those liberties were claimed in Aragon, or in a city pertaining to the Church like Bologna, or in Rome itself (as we are going to see shortly), or elsewhere.

Claiming the validity of liberties, privileges, etc, in the relationship between the prince and his subjects involved consequences on the conception of the monarchy, whose superiority, however, was not questioned. Monarchy was thought to be an essential component of the government of a kingdom, though just like aristocracy and democracy. The most suitable form of government to supervise the consensual relationship between the prince/king and his subjects was the mixed-government. Furthermore, the mixed-government was what Hotman in the Francogallia believed as the most suitable for France, right in the chapter where he glorified the exemplar value of the institution of the Aragonese Justicia.[46]

The *maiestas* and the power of the king were not diminished at all if the king respected the agreed and "sworn" laws. The jurist Pedro Callixtus Ramirez claimed this too, in relation to the *Justicia,* in his *Analyticus Tractatus de Lege*

---

44 See Heinz Mohnhaupt, "Erteilung und Widerruf von Privilegien nach der gemeinrechtlichen Lehre vom 16. bis 19. Jahrhundert", in Barbara Dölemeyer, Heinz Mohnhaupt, eds., *Das Privileg im europäischen Vergleich,* 1 (Frankfurt am Main: Klostermann, 1997), 93–121; *Idem,* "Confirmatio privilegiorum", in Barbara Dölemeyer and Heinz Mohnhaupt, eds., *Das Privileg im europäischen Vergleich,* 2 (Frankfurt am Main: Klostermann, 1999), 45–63; and "Vertragskonstruktion und fingierte Vetrag zur Sicherung von Normativität: Gesetz, Privileg, Verfassung", in Jean-François Kervégan and Heinz Mohnhaupt, eds., *Gesellschaftliche Freiheit und vertragliche Bindung in Rechtsgeschichte und Philosophie / Liberté sociale et lien contractuel dans l'histoire du droit et la philosophie* (Frankfurt am Main: Klostermann, 1999), 1–33. For Navarra, see Rafael García Pérez, *Antes leyes que reyes: Cultura jurídica y constitución política en la Edad Moderna* (*Navarra 1512–1808*) (Milan: Giuffrè, 2008).

45 I have discussed this in De Benedictis, *Politica,* 279–85.

46 Hotman, *Francogallia* (1573), 78–80.

Regia, qua in Principes suprema & absoluta potestas translata fuit: cum quadam corporis politici ad instar phisici, capitis & membrorum connexione (1616),[47] dedicated to Philip III of Spain (but II of Aragon) who had visited Zaragoza in 1599, after that in 1592 Philip II had confirmed – despite the repression of the "rebellion" of 1591 – that the *fueros* could not be altered unless all Aragonese laws were taken into consideration.

In the chapter dedicated to the origins of monarchy in Aragon, and to the way in which the *lex regia* had been transferred into it,[48] the jurist claimed that, even though the monarchic principality was the best, the mixed government was the most useful, because of the imperfection of men, who wished to participate in the exercise of power. In fact, in the mixed government, when the prince wanted to enact laws or deliberate on important issues of the *Res Publica,* he asked for the opinion of the most powerful citizens, consulting with them and deciding with them on public issues. Aristotle and others had taught that aristocracy, if well-instituted, excelled over royal power and over a monarchy that was mere and absolute, since there was nothing better than a principality bound by laws and, on the contrary, there was no plague worse than a principality unbound by laws. Therefore, the ancestors – in order to build a monarchy that lasted long and forever, and in order to make it holier and blessed – made sure (imitating Romulus) to protect the kingdom that they had decided to build with laws, rather than walls. And they had established that it would not be lawful for the kings alone to change those laws, or to make new ones if the passing of time required it, but instead that they must consult the people, who was represented in the four estates of the realm (commonly called "brazos"): the senatorial estate, of the nobles; the militar, of the *milites*; the popular or plebeian one, of the cities; eventually, the ecclesiastical one.

---

47 Petrus Callixtus Ramirez, *Analyticus Tractatus de Lege Regia, qua in Principes suprema & absoluta potestas translata fuit: cum quadam corporis politici ad instar phisici, capitis & membrorum connexione* (Caesaraugustae: Lanaja Quartanet, 1616). On this treatise see Pablo Fernández Albaladejo, "*Lex Regia Aragonensium.* Monarquía compuesta e identidad de reinos en el reinado de Felipe III", in his *Materia de España: Cultura política e identidad en la España moderna* (Madrid: Marcial Pons, 2007), ch. 3; Jon Arrieta Alberti, "Ubicación de los ordinamientos de los reinos de la Corona de Aragón en la Monarquía hispánica: concepciones y supuestos varios (siglos XVI-XVIII)", in Italo Birocchi and Antonello Mattone, eds., *Il diritto patrio tra diritto comune e codificazione, secoli XVI-XIX* (Roma: Viella, 2006), 143–5; and now Xavier Gil, "De diademas y circumferencias, de provincias y periferias", in Arrieta, Gil and Morales, eds., *Diadema del rey*, 34–5. Some shorts comments, in De Benedictis, *Politica*, 227–8.

48 Ramirez, *Analyticus Tractatus*, § 4: "Monarchicus Principatus unde fluxerit, & in Aragonia quomodo, & qualis in suos Reges lege regia translates", 49–56.

It is worth underlying that in the previous paragraph of the *Analyticus tractatus,* dedicated to the origin and nature of the *Lex Regia* among the Romans,[49] Ramírez made explicit reference to the bronze table located in St. Peter's Basilica in which the *lex* was described as proof – according to some – that the *potestas* granted to the emperor by the people was not supreme and absolute. He based himself also on the authority of Mario Salamonio degli Alberteschi: not so much on the *De Principatu,* but on his comment to the passage by Ulpian *Quod principi placuit, legis habet vigorem,* included in the commentary to the Pandects printed in 1530.[50]

At this stage, it is worth giving a context to the writing of the *De Principatu* by Salamonio, especially since the historian taking part in the conversation had rapidly mentioned it, taking it for granted.[51] In the summer of 1511 Salamonio had played an important role in the solution of a conflict that, especially after Pope Julius II's illness and rumours about his death, had united – even though with different positions – the great roman nobility represented by the Orsini and the Savelli, both to the members of the city government and to the people. A conflict that had resulted into a riot against Pope Della Rovere's policy. The reasons behind it were precise requests made by the College of Cardinals to restore the honour of the main families in Rome and to bestow the cardinalate on some of those families. In fact, Julius II had eliminated the prerogative that was so dear to the romans, unlike the policy carried out in this respect by his predecessors Pope Sixtus IV, Innocent VIII, Alexander VI. On the other hand, also the citizens involved in the government of the city were particularly affected by the limitation of their authority on the part of the Governor of Rome, the delegate of the Pope in the city government. Under those circumstances, there occurred an agreement between the barons and the citizens involved in government, also thanks to the efforts of some of the leading citizens, among whom the noble Mario Salamonio degli Alberteschi. This resulted later in the agreement called *Pax Romana,* signed in the Palazzo dei

49 Ramirez, *ibidem*, § 3. "In suprema saeculari potestate, quot sunt species regendi; quae excellentior; & quae fierit apud Romanos lex Regia; & de aliquis urbis Romanae laudibus", 36–48: 42.

50 Mario Salamonio degli Alberteschi, *In librum Pandectarum iuris civilis commentarioli* (Basileae: Andreas Cratander, 1530), "De constitutione principum", cc. 40v-41v. Salamonio is one of the many sources of Ramírez, also in other passages of the *Analyticus Tractatus:* § 23 "Potestatis plenitudo in Principe, quae absoluta appellantur, quid sit, & singulae diffinitionis partes explicantur; & an, & quando eam exercere Principem oporteat, & quae urbes regiae appellentur", 184–206: 189.

51 Salamonio, *De principatu* (1955), 46–7.

Conservatori and sealed with an oath on the 28th of August, through which the subscribers swore to "defendere, augmentare l'onore e la reputatione di tutti i gentiluomini, cittadini e abitanti della città", as well as the rights, jurisdiction, privileges, immunities and statutes granted and confirmed more than once by Julius II and his predecessors in the Roman Republic.

With the agreement they committed to defending every citizen, belonging to any class, from violence, injustice, oppression, tyranny and persecution. The agreement between the barons e the citizens involved in government was strengthened by a wide popular participation: the *Pax Romana* then, was a city peace, signed even by representatives of all the districts. Afterwards, when Julius II had suddenly recovered, in August 1511, the pontiff had ordered the barons to leave the city. Pompeo Colonna had been the last. Many nobles reacted to the pontiff's policy by choosing exile from Rome by themselves. Those who had believed the *Pax* completely continued to believe that it should become effective, in the fight against the papacy of all the forces that were interested in limiting the power of the Pope. The mediation role of the Commune, and especially of Conservators, had been essential in this respect. Given the difficulties that Julius II was facing (from the Council of Pisa and the preparation of the future Lateran Council), he had eventually accepted the requests that had been submitted to him. Between March and April 1512, he had issued *motu proprio* on justice administration, reinstatement of roman officials in the exercise of some jurisdiction rights, on the destination of a tax increase to the restoration of the city walls and of the Trevi Fountain. All this had meant, then, that Rome had reacquired its liberties. After the death of Julius II, newly elected Leo X had confirmed them by means of a bull of 19 March 1513. To Leo X, Salamonio had dedicated, soon afterwards, his treatise written in the form of dialogue.

Reminding Leo X the *lex regia* through the *De Principatu* did not have a substantially different aim than reminding, a century later, to Philip III of Spain the same *lex* through the *Analyticus Tractatus.* Neither did the treatise by Andrés de Poza *Escudo de la mas costante fe y lealdad* when presenting the constitutional role of Vizcaya in the monarchy of the Habsburg of Spain, in the context of the "Flemish tragedy" as it has been recently analysed by Jon Arrieta.[52]

52 Jon Arrieta, "El licenciado Andrés de Poza y su contribución a la ubicación de Vizcaya en la Monarquía hispánica", in Arrieta, Gil and Morales, eds., *Diadema del rey*, 207–8. See also Arrieta's chapter in this volume.

4 Sobrarbe, Navarre and Aragon in the New World

As it has been shown by Clizia Magoni the Aragonese liberties and the Aragonese constitution formed part of the intense constitutional debate of the English Revolutions of the XVII century[53] as well as of the newly founded United States of America. This is apparent in the work published in London between 1786 and 1787 by the future president John Adams: the three volumes of the *Defence of the Constitution of Government of the United States of America*.[54] Nevertheless, this is not the *New World* I am referring to in the title of the essay, but rather Mexico, where the bishop Juan de Palafox, originally from Navarre, bishop of Puebla and general visitor of New Spain in 1648–1649, tries – without success – to enact a reform that would give new strength to the Habsburg of Spain monarchy, particularly strained by the Thirty Years' War and by the Catalan crisis. It is a complex jurisdictional conflict that is attested by an especially evocative historical-legal memoir.

Here are the facts, briefly and rapidly.[55] After the patent failure of his protector the Count-Duke de Olivares' attempt to unify the composite Spanish monarchy, as bishop of Puebla and visitor, Juan de Palafox (former Council of War attorney and counsellor in the Council of the Indies) develops a reform programme that involves devolving powers to municipal governments controlled by Creoles. The program was considered a serious threat to the viceregal government system. Also because of the Jesuits' opposition, somehow involved in the reform project, Palafox' policy wasneutralised. In 1649, the consecration by Palafox of the La Puebla cathedral in Los Angeles is the meaningful and conclusive moment of the complex sequence of events. The bishop has insignia hung in the royal chapel, among which is the coat of arms of the Kingdom of Sobrarbe, the red cross picture on a green tree, settled in a golden field. This presence is considered harmful to the majesty of the Spanish Crown by the Crown attorney, who orders to remove the insignia at the end of the year.

Memoirs came in succession from the two sides (the attorney and the bishop, as well as the city council) in favour and against this decision. In 1651 the *Memorial y discurso Històrico, Polìtico, de la S. Iglesia Catedral de la Puebla*

53 Magoni, *'Fueros' e libertà*, 108–34 (Magoni, *Fueros y libertades*, 141–72).

54 Magoni, *'Fueros' e libertà*, 152–6 (Magoni, *Fueros y libertades*, 193–8).

55 See the detailed reconstruction by Cayetana Álvarez de Toledo, *Juan de Palafox obispo y virrey*, prologue by Sir John Elliott (Madrid: Marcial Pons, 2011) (original English edition: *Politics and Reform in Spain and Viceregal Mexico: The Life and Thought of Juan de Palafox, 1600–1659*, Oxford: Oxford University Press, 2004).

de los Angeles, en la Nueva España is published under the name of the jurist Juan Alonso Calderón,[56] in fact written by Palafox[57] himself to explain to the king the rightfulness of his conduct.

Since the arguments of the memoir[58] make use of the previous literature on Sobrarbe and are part of the debate concerning the origin of the kingdom, it is not possible to unfold all of them in this essay. Instead, it is important to call attention to the motivations that the memoir puts forward to prove the correct employment order for the collocation of the mentioned coat of arms of Sobrarbe.[59] The followed orders were those of heraldry and of law. According to the law, the crown of Castile and Leon comes before the crown of Aragon and Navarre. As regards heraldry, the author says that the doctrine of Bartolus de Saxoferrato in the *de insignis et armis* and that of Barthélémy de Chasseneuz in the *Cathalogus gloriae mundi* have been followed.[60] He also provides – as usual in this kind of literature – the specific excerpts.[61]

---

56 Juan Alonso Calderón, *Memorial y discurso Histórico, Jurídico, Político, de la S. Iglesia Catedral de la Puebla de los Angeles, en la Nueva España. Sobre restituirla las armas reales de Castilla, León, Aragón, y Navarra, que puso en la capilla mayor de su Iglesia, de que ha sido despoiada iniustamente, al Rey* N.S (*s.l:* 1651).

57 Eva Botella-Ordinas, "Fruto, cruz y árbol. Diseño castellano de un reino de Sobrarbe", *Espacio, Tiempo y Forma. Serie IV, Historia Moderna*, 11 (1998), 203. http://revistas.uned.es/index.php/ETFIV/article/view/3365.

58 Extsensively examined by Botella-Ordinas, "Fruto, cruz y árbol", 204–13.

59 Calderón, *Memorial y* discurso, cc. 2v.-3r: "si se pusiessen por menor todos los de las Coronas que componen la Monarquia de V.M. parecia formar estos dos escudos, eligiendo papa ellos las principales Coronas de España respeto de la America, que son Castilla, y Leon, Aragon, y Navarra, y que toto lo ciñesse la Corona Imperial de la Casa de Austria, orlando el Escudo la Cadena de eslabones del Tuson de oro de V.M. por las Casas de Borgoña, y Flandes, en la forma que se acostumbra. ... por los Serenissimos Reyes de Navarra la Crux roxa sobre el Arbol verde en campo de oro, como mas *Antiguas, Milagrosas, y Misteriosas* de aquella Corona, y la de Aragon. *Antiguas*, porque començaron el ano de 724, en los primeros passos de la restauracion de España. *Milagrosas*, como embiadas del Cielo al Señor Rey Don Garci Ximenez, Glorioso, y primero Fundaddor destas Coronas. *Misteriosas*, porque le ofrecio Dios en ellas la Cruz, señal de nuestra Redempcion, Y tan propia para colocarla en los Escudos Reales de aquel santo Templo".

60 Calderón, *ibidem*, 3r: "En la preferencia de los Escudos, y quarteles Reales, se guardò la orden de *Armeria*, y *Derecho*. La del *Derecho*, entre estas Coronas prefiriendo Castilla, y Leon, à Aragon, y Navarra. La de *Armeria*, porque conforme à la doctrina de Bartulo, Y Casaneo".

61 Calderón, *ibidem*, 3r: "Bart. de Insig. & Arm. num. 23. Cas. Catal. Glor. mûd. concl. 96. fol. 31".

Both works are fundamental legal texts, one dating back to the half of the XIV century,[62] the other printed for the first time in 1529,[63] which had a wide circulation and great influence also on the political literature on the early Modern Age.

According to the memoir, it is possible to justify the choice made, because in legal issues, it necessary to trust the words of historians and heraldry experts.[64] When quoting the *De iure insignorum* by Hopking, it maintains that the effect of the union of several arms in the same coat of arms would mean offering the symbol of an agreement.[65]

The interesting elements, on which it would be worth dwelling, offered by the arguments of the memoir and by the employed sources would be many. However, for the purposes of this exposition of some ideas to resume the study of the theme of the "myth of Sobrarbe", it is enough to underline that this sort of "anatomy of Spain"[66] leads to attributing constitutional relevance to acts of symbolic communication like coats of arms.

This is an issue that has been recently examined, also in methodological terms, by several studies, among which are the ones by Barbara Stollberg-Rilinger on the feudal investiture rituals and on crowning oaths in the Holy Roman Empire of the German Nation.[67]

---

62 See the recent edition, with an English translation, published by Osvaldo Cavallar, Susanne Degenring and Julius Kirshner, eds., *A Grammar of Signs: Bartolo da Sassoferrato's Tract on Insignia and Coats of Arms* (Berkeley: University of California Press, 1994).

63 Barthélémy de Chasseneuz, *Cathalogus gloriae mundi* (Lugduni: impressum per Dionysium de Harsy, 1529). It is well known among legal historians that Bartolus de Saxoferrato's *de insignis et armis* had been both a source and an *auctoritas* for Chasseneuz's *Cathalogus*: Giovanni Rossi, "Il mondo in un libro: cultura giuridica e sapere enciclopedico nel *Catalogus gloriae mundi* di Barthélemy Chasseneux", in Giovanni Rossi, ed., *Il Rinascimento giuridico in Francia: Diritto, politica e storia* (Roma: Viella, 2008), 238.

64 Calderón, *Memorial y discurso*, c. 31v: "siendo tan constante en derecho la fee que se deve dar a los Historiadores y Coronistas".

65 Calderón, *ibidem*, c. 70v.: "uno de los utiles, y honestos efectos de la mezcla, de unas Armas con otras en un mismo Escudo, la significacion, y simbolo de la conformidad, y dizelo con estas palabras: *Quartus effectus huius coniunctionis est, foederis quandoque praebere symbolum*".

66 See the fundamental essay by Bartolomé Clavero, "Anatomía de España.Derecho hispano y derecho español entre fueros y codigos", in Bartolomé Clavero, Paolo Grossi and Francisco Tomás y Valiente, eds., *Hispania: Entre derechos proprios y derechos nacionales* (Milano: Giuffrè, 1991), 47–86.

67 Barbara Stollberg-Rilinger and André Krischer, eds., *Herstellung und Darstellung von Entscheidungen: Verfahren, Verwalten und Verhandeln in der Vormoderne* (Berlin: Dunker & Humblot, 2010); *Barbara Stollberg-Rilinger*, "On the Function of Rituals in the Holy

It seems appropriate to finish with a quotation drawn from an essay by Stolberg-Rilinger, since they are thoughts that – in my opinion – can apply also the case of the "myth of Sobrarbe" as a problem of the history of political thought and of constitutional history. First, "rituals do not merely *say* something; they *do* something".[68] And this is because "Premodern European history is filled with rituals of rulership; in monarchies as well as in republics, there were royal coronations or changes of republican councils, investitures and homages, court days and assemblies of the estates of the realm. The swearing of oaths was almost always at the center of these acts and took place on all levels of the hierarchical order, holding the entire society together by justifying and limiting rule. The royal coronation oath at the head of the hierarchy formed only 'the heart of an interwoven system of rulership contracts'".[69]

Bibliography

Main Sources

Calderón, Juan Alonso, *Memorial y discurso Histórico, Jurídico, Político, de la S. Iglesia Catedral de la Puebla de los Angeles, en la Nueva España. Sobre restituirla las armas reales de Castilla, León, Aragón, y Navarra, que puso en la capilla mayor de su Iglesia, de que ha sido despoiada iniustamente, al Rey* N.S. (*s.l.*: 1651).

Hotman, François, *Francogallia*, Ex officina Iacobi Stoerij, 1573.

Luis Martínez, Pedro, *Discurso y alegaciones de derecho … en que trata y declara el origen, y principio del reyno de Aragon, y la excelencia de su govierno y leyes, y justicia que tiene, en el pleyto en que defiende en el consistorio del Justicia de Aragon, que la magestad del rey no puede nombrar Virrey estrangero para su govierno, ni conviene a su real servicio* (Zaragoza: Lorenzo Robles, 1591).

Ramirez, Petrus Calixtus, *Analyticus Tractatus de Lege Regia, qua in Principes suprema & absoluta potestas translata fuit: cum quadam corporis politici ad instar phisici, capitis & membrorum connexione* (Caesaraugustae: Lanaja Quartanet, 1616).

Roman Empire", in R.J.W. Evans, Michael Schaich and Peter Wilson, eds., *The Holy Roman Empire, 1495–1806* (Oxford: Oxford University Press, 2011), 359–73; and *Rituale* (Frankfurt am Main: Campus, 2013).

68 Barbara Stollberg-Rilinger, "Much Ado About Nothing? Rituals of Politics in Early Modern Europe and Today", *Annual Bulletin of the German Historical Institute*, 33 (2011), 8.

69 Stollberg-Rilinger, *ibidem*, 14. The last quotation in Stollberg-Rilinger's book alludes to the fundamental work by Paolo Prodi, *Il sacramento del potere: Il giuramento politico nella storia costituzionale dell'Occidente* (Bologna: Il Mulino, 1992).

Salamonio degli Alberteschi, Mario, *De Principatu libros septem* [1513]; *nec non Orationes ad priores florentinos,* recognovit Marius D'Addio (Milan: Giuffrè, 1955).

Main Bibliographical References

Arrieta, Jon; Xavier Gil; Jesús Morales, eds., *La diadema del rey: Vizcaya, Navarra, Aragón y Cerdeña en la Monarquía de España (siglos XVI-XVIII)* (Bilbao: Publicaciones Universidad del País Vasco, 2017).

Giesey, Ralph E, *If not, not: The Oath of the Aragonese and the Fueros of Sobrarbe* (Princeton: Princeton University Press, 1968).

Mellet, Paul-Alexis, *Les Traités monarcomaques: Confusion des temps, résistance armée et monarchie parfaite (1560–1600)* (Geneva: Droz, 2007).

Quaglioni, Diego, "Sovereignty versus Tyranny in Medieval and Early Modern Political Thought", in Janet Coleman and Paschalis M. Kitromilides, eds., *In the Footsteps of Herodotus: Towards European Political Thought* (Florence: Olschki, 2012), 65–75.

Stollberg-Rilinger, Barbara, "Much Ado About Nothing? Rituals of Politics in Early Modern Europe and Today", *Annual Bulletin of the German Historical Institute,* 33 (2011).

CHAPTER 5

Law, Wisdom, and Politics in Making Süleyman "The Lawgiver"

Fatma Sinem Eryılmaz

1 Introduction*

The long reign of Sultan Süleyman (r. 1520–1566) offered ample material to fashion a legendary image. In Western Europe, his vast domains and the material and human resources to which he had access gave him a reputation for magnificence. Though this was also repeated in contemporaneous Ottoman documents, it was not the principal aspect of his rule that was emphasized. In its stead, it was justice, the *sine quo non* virtue of an ideal ruler, that was cultivated for his contemporaneous and posterior reputation as "the Lawgiver" ("Kanuni").[1] His justice was orchestrated through the regulations, which, under his leadership and supervision, organized the state, determined the status of its subjects, and regulated the relationships between them. At the same time, the largely successful efforts to create a 'perfectly' ordered realm reinforced the spirit of the times that saw the epoch as extraordinary and Süleyman as a major contender for being its ruler.

As the sultan and a close group of high state officials established standards and regulated paths, especially but not exclusively, in Ottoman administration and installed legal codes and practices, in the larger Mediterranean and its Euroasian hinterland apocalyptic expectations trespassed religious denominations and linguistic barriers.[2] These expectations incubated an amalgam of

---

* Only quoted texts from primary sources are fully transcribed.

1 For his reputation for justice, see Halil İnalcık, "Süleyman the Lawgiver and Ottoman Law", *Archivum Ottomanicum*, 1 (1969), 15–106. Poems protesting his decision to have his popular firstborn, Mustafa, killed (1553) fiercely question his reputed justice. See Mustafa İsen, *Acıyı Bal Eylemek: Türk Edebiyatında Mersiye*, (Ankara, 1994), 283–323; especially those by Sami and Nisayi (305–7 and 308–11 respectively).

2 Cornell H. Fleischer. "The Lawgiver as Messiah: the Making of the Imperial Image in the Reign of Süleyman", in Gilles Veinstein, ed., *Soliman le Magnifique et sons temps* (Paris: Documentation Française, 1992), 159–77; "Shadow of Shadows: Prophecy in Politics in 1530s İstanbul", *International Journal of Turkish Studies*, 13.1–2 (2007), 51–62; and "Ancient Wisdom and New Sciences: Prophecy at the Ottoman Court in the Fifteenth and Early Sixteenth Centuries", in Farhad Massumeh and Serpil Bağcı, eds., *Falnama: the Book of Omens* (London: Thames

 | DOI:10.1163/9789004549159_007

sentiments ranging from the fear of total chaos to the longing for universal order and peace; from a heightened historical consciousness accompanied by a hyperawareness of extraordinary natural incidents to the need for protection.[3] In this psychological environment, Süleyman's image as the establisher and protector of order and justice, as well as the ruler of an extensive and multi-religious empire, promoted him as an ideal candidate for universal leadership. His main rivals were Charles V (r. 1519–1556) of Habsburg Spain and Shah Tahmasb (r. 1524–1576) of Safavid Iran, both of whom cultivated similar ideological discourses of divinely bestowed political and spiritual authority over the known world.

Concurrently, an empire spread over several continents presented major problems in administration and maintenance. In the territories conquered in the first decades of the sixteenth century Ottoman authority was yet to be consolidated.

The former Mamluk territories of Syria and Egypt, conquered in 1516 and 1517 respectively, were such areas. Sources of great financial revenues, especially in the case of Egypt, and equally great prestige, these lands had also been the foremost centres of learning. Consolidating the relatively new authority of the Ottoman state over lands with rich administrative and cultural traditions required more than brute force. Indeed, under Süleyman a series of measures were taken in order to organize the social, economic, and cultural life of the empire, giving priority to these recently conquered lands. The most significant of them were legislative in nature.[4]

The leading administrators of the time, like Celalzade Mustafa Çelebi, prepared legal and administrative codes, put the already existing laws into a coherent order, and added new ones. The preambles especially to the codes composed in the first decades of Süleyman's reign also provided the textual space to describe the nature of the new sultan's rule. They promoted his authority among the state officials, who were to read and use them for their

---

and Hudson, 2009), 232–43; Kathryn Babayan, *Mystics, Monarchs, and Messiahs: Cultural Landscapes of Early Modern Iran* (Cambridge, MA: Harvard University Press, 2002); Sanjay Subrahmanyam, "Turning the Stones over: Sixteen-century Millenarianism from the Tagus to the Ganges", *Indian Economic Social History Review*, 40.2 (2003), 129–61.

3 The sack of Rome in 1527 and the repeated occurrence of the plague sharpened these sensitivities.

4 See for example, James E. Baldwin, *Islamic Law and Empire in Ottoman Cairo* (Edinburgh: Edinburg University Press, 2018), where the author discusses the plurality of law practices and institutions in Cairo addressing issues such as centre-periphery relations, Ottoman perception of royal justice, and the great tradition of Islamic scholarship in the Egyptian capital.

daily tasks. In fact, some of these texts went beyond their formal function and were copied and read separately among the bureaucratic and scholarly elite as fundamental texts of Ottoman state culture.[5]

Here, I will discuss two of these preambles. The one of Egypt was composed in 1525 after the suppression of the rebellion of a former vizier. The preamble of Bosnia was written in 1530 as the region was losing its frontier status. Before proceeding any further, however, it would be worthwhile to revise the mechanism and terminology of law in Islamicate societies, focusing on the Ottoman case.

2 Problems of Terminology: fiqh and Shari'ah

Law in early modern Islamicate societies involved a synthesis of sorts.[6] Rather than a synthesis that became fixed in time, this was one that was essentially interpretive and dynamic. In the Ottoman case the various practices constituting it differed in their origins but did not necessarily contradict in their purpose or practice. Most importantly, each claimed jurisdiction over a vast variety of areas, occasionally overlapping with one another.

The main judiciary frame was the practice of Shari'ah based interpretations of jurisprudence (*fiqh*). Among the four major schools (*madhab*) of Sunni Islamic jurisprudence, namely the Shafi'i, Hanafi, Maliki, and Hanbali, it was the Hanafi *madhab* that the Ottoman state favoured. Hanafi courts were disseminated throughout the empire. In regions like Syria and Egypt, where legal life was traditionally dominated by other *madhabs*, alongside Hanafi courts, the authority of the relevant *madhab* was generally respected, though not without tensions.[7]

5 Snjezana Buzov, "The Lawgiver and his Lawmakers: The Role of Legal Discourse in the Change of Ottoman Imperial Culture", unpublished Ph.D. dissertation (Chicago, 2005), 30. Ahmet Akgündüz lists five copies for the preamble to the Egyptian *qanunname* separate from the law code it introduces, four in Istanbul (Süleymaniye (1) and Topkapı (3) libraries) and another copy in Paris (Bibliothèque Nationale). Ahmet Akgündüz. *Osmanlı Kanunnâmeleri ve Hukukî Tahlilleri. Kanunî Sultan Süleyman Devri Kanunnâmeleri*, volume 6 (Istanbul: OSAV, 1993), 82.

6 I owe much of my understanding of Ottoman law to Snjezena Buzov, who generously shared with me the unpublished manuscript of her brilliant book, "State Law and Divine Law under the Ottomans: Encounters between Shari'a and the Sultan's Law".

7 Reem Mashal challenges the idea of Ottoman preservation of local legal customs and culture in conquered lands and argues that in Süleyman's reign, Ottomans manipulated both *qanun* and *fiqh* to homogenize law, hence trespassing the plurality inherent in the system and constructing a legal culture that was "at once more individualistic and more

Here, it is important to clarify some issues concerning terminology. Firstly, as Snjezana Buzov has rightly noted, the distinction between Shari'ah and *fiqh* has often been ignored in Ottoman legal studies.[8] While Shari'ah is Divine law revealed in the Quran and Hadith literature, where the practices and teachings of Muhammad (*Sunnah*) are narrated, *fiqh* is its human interpretation expanded by Islamic jurists. Due to its divine nature, Shari'ah can never be completely or perfectly known, let alone be realized in action. In order to attain practical significance for the Muslim community, Shari'ah needs human understanding and interpretation; in other words, it needs *fiqh*. *Fiqh*, on the other hand, always remains open ended and plural, for it is the output of human experts, who are conditioned by the perspectives and limitations imposed on them by social and political circumstances and by nature. Hence, *fiqh* cannot constitute a uniform system of legal thinking, but involves a variety of, often inconsistent, interpretive positions on specific issues.

The plurality in the nature of *fiqh* does not signify a total and uncontrolled freedom, either. When there are no direct passages in the Qur'an or the Hadith referring to the case at hand, the judicial decisions are made using the other two 'roots' of Islamic jurisprudence (*usul al-fiqh*): consensus (*ijma*) and analogy (*qiyas*).[9] While analogy makes the fundamental religious texts relevant once again, consensus of the community of legal experts brings legitimacy to the final decision(s).

Related to the confusion in terminology, is the common error in scholarship to see Ottoman law as a dual system of sacred and secular law. According to this view, *fiqh*, often inaccurately named Shari'ah, constituted the sacred law, and *qanun* represented the sultan's secular political authority. While religious law was timeless and static, the secular one evolved with respect to the needs of the situation, determined by social, economic, and political circumstances.[10]

---

conformist": "Antagonistic Sharīʿas and the Construction of Orthodoxy in Sixteenth-Century Ottoman Cairo", *Journal of Islamic Studies*, 21.2 (2010), 4 and elsewhere.

8 Buzov, "The Lawgiver and his Lawmakers", 13.

9 There are other supplementary principles for the four legal *madhabs* in Sunni Islam, such as preferability, which the Hanafis use arguably more extensively than other *madhabs* to expand on personal judgment (*ra'y*). Marshall G.S. Hodgson. *The Venture of Islam: Conscience and History in a World Civilization*, vol. 1 (Chicago: University of Chicago Press, 1974), 326–36.

10 The conception of Islam as static reinforced Orientalist and Weberian portrayals of its law. Among Turkish historians there have been two interrelated factors nurturing the dual system argument. One is the republican and nationalist impulse of blaming Islam for the eventual failure of the Ottoman Empire in achieving modernity. The other is the search for sources of secular progress in the overemphasized connections to a Central Asian past in all aspects of life, including legislative practices. See for example, Ömer Lütfi Barkan, *XV ve XVıncı Asırlarda Osmanlı İmparatorluğunda Ziraî Ekonominin Hukukî ve Malî Esasları*

As opposed to this view still dominant in scholarship, historians such as Haim Gerber, Dror Ze'evi, and Snjezana Buzov, have offered more nuanced explanations recognizing the contextual character of any legislative action including *fiqh*-based jurisprudence.[11] As Ze'evi notes, the perceived differences between *qanun* and *fiqh*-based legal interpretation should not be interpreted "as two conceptions of law, but rather as evolution within the same legal and cultural sphere".[12]

Just as any other interpretation, *fiqh* also evolved. Not only the corpus of interpretative jurisprudence included new additions, but the traditional decisions and formulations also gained or lost popularity with changing times and circumstances. Effectively the sixteenth century intellectual and bureaucrat Mustafa 'Ali (d. 1600) refers to jurists who did not contextualize law but only repeated the oldest traditions as the lowest group among the learned: "*fundamentalists who hold so firmly to the words of the oldest authorities that they refuse to consider that new insights or new works are possible. They sin in the direction of fanaticism and blindness, like the Jews and Christians who refused to acknowledge the authority of the Prophet*".[13]

As in cases involving regulations established during pre-Ottoman (often Byzantine) periods, *fiqh* even came to accommodate some non-Islamic practices and traditions while rejecting others for not necessarily legal reasons. The great Ottoman Chief *Mufti* (*Shayk al-Islam*) Ebu's-suud's legal

---

(Istanbul: Bürhaneddin matbaası, 1943); Halil İnalcık, "State, Sovereignty and Law during the Reign of Süleyman", in Halil İnalcık and Cemal Kafadar, eds., *Süleyman the Second* (sic.) *and His Time* (Istanbul: İsis, 1993), 59–93; Uriel Heyd, *Studies in Old Ottoman Criminal Law*, ed. V.L. Ménage (Oxford: Clarendon, 1973) and "Kanun and Sharia in Old Ottoman Criminal Justice", *Israel Academy of Sciences and Humanities. Proceedings* (Jerusalem, 1967); Colin Imber, *Ebu's-suud: The Islamic Legal Tradition* (Edinburgh: Edinburg University Press,1997); Richard Repp, "Kanun and Shari'a in Ottoman Context", in Aziz al-Azmeh, ed., *Islamic Law: Social and Historical Contexts* (London: Routledge, 1988), 124–45.

11 Boğaç A. Ergene, "Qanun and Sharia", in Rudolph Peters and Peri Bearmen, eds., *The Ashgate Research Companion to Islamic Law* (Burlington: Ashgate, 2014), 109–22; Buzov, "The Lawgiver and his Lawmakers". Ergene offers a more comprehensive analysis of the debate on Ottoman law summarized here.

12 Dror Ze'evi, *Producing Desire: Changing Sexual Discourse in the Ottoman Middle East, 1500–1900* (Berkeley: University of Los Angeles Press, 2006), 69.

13 Paraphrased in Cornell H. Fleischer, *Bureaucrat and Intellectual in the Ottoman Empir: The Historian Mustafa Ali, 1541–1600* (Princeton: Princeton University Press, 1986), 259–60, from Mustafa 'Ali, *Künh ül-Ahbar*, vol. 1, (Istanbul: 1861/1277), 34–9. See also 109–110 in http://ekitap.yek.gov.tr/urun/kunhu'l-ahbar--1-2-ciltler-_733.aspx Last accessed: 17 October 2022.

recommendations (*Ma'ruzat*) presented to Sultan Süleyman fall into this latter category.[14] These were a collection of legal decisions on a variety of topics preferred over other legitimate alternatives, mainly for practical reasons. In sum, the part denominated as "sacred" in the dual system concept was neither exclusively sacred nor static.

Furthermore, the dual system idea misled to an inherent tension formed by the unchangeable and timeless tenets of Islam and the dynamic secular laws represented by *qanun*. In fact, the *fiqh*-based tradition already recognized the right of political authorities to legislate, especially when dealing with administrative, financial, and military issues. Ahmed Akgündüz lists the three areas where Islamic law permits a political authority to exercise its right to legislate. The first is when a ruler decides to integrate decisions included in books of *fiqh* into *qanun*. The second is when a legal practice for a social issue is preferred over other choices and is incorporated into the corpus of *qanun*.

The final category is independent from previous decisions. It includes cases where the political authority takes legislative and judiciary decisions in order to establish and maintain social order (*niẓām-ı 'ālem*), punish crimes against the state, enforce legal, administrative, financial, and military regulations, and implement regulations for the administration of non-royal lands.[15] This last category, also known as *siyasat*, signifies the potentially most ample use of political authority in matters of justice. With the legislative reforms of Süleyman's reign and exercising the legitimate right of *siyasat*, the state introduced economic punishments, such as forced labour and progressive fines, and social castigation, none of which were included among *fiqh*-based castigation.

3 Other Participants: Fermans, Fetwas, and Pre-ottoman Legislation

The royal edicts (*fermans*) were essential participants in Ottoman legislation. They were issued by each sultan as an extension of his suzerainty and a reaffirmation of his relationship with his subjects. Through them, the sultan authorized, confirmed, and protected his subjects' rights and duties with respect to the state, the land, and to one another. In this way, they served two essential functions of Ottoman law: to maintain an orderly society and to underline the sultan's role as the implementer and protector of order.

14 Ebu's-suud served the state as Chief Military Judge of Rumelia (*Kadıasker*) from 1537 until his appointment as *shayk al-islam* in 1545.

15 Akgündüz, *Osmanlı Kanunnâmeleri ve Hukukî Tahlilleri*, volume 4, 31.

The religious opinions (*fetwas*) that the jurist scholars (*muftis*) issued within the framework of the *Shari'ah* were also taken into account. Even though the authority that issued them was different, like many *fermans*, they treated specific concerns. The weight of the *fetwa* depended largely on the personal authority of the religious scholar issuing it. In trials their usage was not obligatory for decision-making, and even infrequent.

Occasionally, the *shayk al-islam* issued a *fetwa* in response to a legal/ethical question of the sultan. In such cases, these legal opinions were often utilized politically as permissions, reasons, or pretexts for important state decisions and to avoid popular protests.[16]

Though seldom, a *shayk al-islam*'s *fetwas* entered the main body of Ottoman law (*qanun*). In judicial cases where there was an urgent need for reform requiring the sultan's approval, *muftis* and *qadis* prepared written petitions, named *Ma'ruzat* (pl. for *ma'ruz*) and presented them to the Grand Vizier or the sultan. This practice pertains to Akgündüz' second category of cases mentioned above, where *fiqh* allows political authority to legislate. Then jurisprudents advised the sultan on frequently encountered cases needing a standardization of legal practices to attain efficiency and maintain order. Their recommendation indicating a single interpretative decision over other legitimate alternatives followed administrative protocol, and the exercising of their legal advice depended solely on the will and authority of the sultan. In other words, such cases exemplified a collaboration of the religious and political authorities where the initiative arrived from the former while the final legislative authority, from the latter.

The most famous Ottoman case of this practice is the above-mentioned collection of *fetwa*s Ebu's-suud prepared for Süleyman's approval on a variety of social and economic issues. Ebu's-suud composed his *Ma'ruzat* with the most appropriate legal opinions he selected and compiled for "the order of the religion and state and the correct organization of the matters of the realm".[17] These responded to cases ranging from religious practices to divorce, from runaway slaves to court testimonial. The compilation is also significant in revealing the

16 For the transcribed text of Ebu's-suud's *fetwas* for the accusation of Prince Bayezıd, see appendix x in *Şerafettin* Turan, *Kanuni Süleyman Dönemi Taht Kavgaları* (Ankara, 1997), 180. Ebu's-suud and, before him, Hamza Saru Görez and Kemalpaşazade had issued *fetwas* legitimizing war against the Safavids, designating them as infidels. For the latter, see nos. 6401 and 12077, Topkapı Palace Archives in Şehabettin Tekindağ, "*Yeni Kaynak* ve Vesîkaların Işığı Altında Yavuz Sultan Selim'in İran Seferi", *Tarih Dergisi / Turkish Journal of History*, 17.22 (Istanbul, 1967), 55.

17 "Niẓām-ı dīn ü devlet ve intiẓām-ı aḥvāl-i memleket", in Akgündüz, *Osmanlı Kanunnâmeleri ve Hukukî Tahlilleri*, v. 4, 35.

effective communication between him and the sultan on legal issues, making the latter's participation in legislature extraordinarily extensive for a principally political authority.

The remarkably high number of extant manuscripts of this document suggests a readership with a more general profile than merely experts in law.[18] According to Akgündüz, all were copied from an original most probably prepared by Ebu's-suud's successor Hamid Efendi (tenure 1574–1577),[19] who seems to have needed the new sultan's confirmation to continue the practice. This need for confirmation after the death of both Ebu's-suud (d. 1574) and Süleyman (d. 1566) suggests that the *Ma'ruzat,* was first and for most seen as a contract between them. After the compilation was approved, it became a classical reference for Ottoman law.

The local practices of recently conquered lands were other important participants in the Ottoman legislative system. In some cases, even in not-so-recently-conquered lands, rules and regulations dating from pre-Ottoman periods were maintained. They were approved and incorporated into the corpus of laws (*qanun*) and protected by the authority of the sultan as the highest legislator. As long as they did not contradict *fiqh*, their possible non-Islamic origin was not considered relevant. They served the interests of the subjects and the state and regulated their activities.[20]

In short, the Ottoman synthesis was not a composite system formed as a mosaic of different and individually more limited parts. Rather, it was the outcome of a dynamic negotiation and harmonization of various judiciary traditions.[21] Judiciary interpretations of the Qur'an and the Hadith literature, Islamic legal opinions concerning determined issues, as well as already existing legislations inherited from past Muslim or non-Muslim states were all integrated into a corpus of laws and regulations that aimed at establishing and

18 Akgündüz gives a partial list of thirteen manuscript copies: *ibidem*, v. 4, 34.

19 Akgündüz, *ibidem*, v. 4, 33. Here, there is a slight problem with the name of the sultan to whom the compilation was presented. By the time Hamid Efendi assumed his post, Selim II had already been ruling for eight years; so I find it doubtful that the new sultan was Süleyman's son Selim II (r. 1566–1574) as Akgündüz states.

20 For arguments against the view of a pacific and smooth incorporation of local laws and customs in conquered lands, see Mashal, "Antagonistic Sharīʿas".

21 Buzov, "State Law and Divine Law under the Ottomans". Similarly, Kristin Stilt and Yossef Rapoport argue for a synthetic judicial system integrating *fiqh* and legislative authority of the ruler (*siyasa*) in the Mamluk context: Kristin Stilt, *Islamic Law in Action: Authority, Discretion, and Everyday Experiences in Mamluk Egypt.* (New York: Oxford University Press, 2011); Yossef Rapoport, "Royal Justice and Religious Law: Siyāsah and Sharīʿah under the Mamluks", *Mamluk Studies Review*, 16 (2012) 71–102.

maintaining an ideal order. Changing times and specific political, social, or economic necessities and gender relations led to the natural evolution of this corpus and its interpretive execution.[22]

Compilations of preferred legal opinions presented by the *shayk al-islam* and legislated by the sultan, such as Ebu's-suud's *Ma'ruzat*, exemplified how the system enabled the cooperation of religious and political authorities when practicality and efficiency were at stake. These types of initiatives answered the need for a more modern and standardized practice of justice. They were facilitated by the agility within the system allowing for synthesis and harmonization of a variety of practices from different origins. Ironically, they also worked against this flexibility by turning theoretically open-ended decisions into solidified laws leaving less room for interpretation.

The sultan's role of protecting this legally governed perfect order formulated and regulated by *qanun*s added a new dimension to the natural tension between absolute and legal governance. The ideal sultan's role as the refuge of the weak and the protector of justice, paradoxically, glorified his royal persona and confirmed his authority. Sultan Süleyman's reign was often projected as one such period both during and after his life. The fervent legal and administrative activity led by the *Shayk al-islam* Ebu's-suud Efendi and the secretary-Chief Secretary-and-then-Chancellor Celalzade Mustafa Çelebi with the sultan's approval and participation resulted in the formation of a characteristic Ottoman legal manner distinct from those of other Islamic states preceding it.

4 "Süleymanic" Law and Order

Ebu's-suud Efendi's work is largely responsible for Süleyman's reputation as a legislator. He applied concepts, principles, and terminology from the *Hanafi* law to the areas of landholding, taxation, criminal punishment, and charitable endowments.[23] We have seen an example of this cooperation in his *Ma'ruzat* when he standardized *fiqh*-based decisions on various frequently encountered issues into the Ottoman Book of Laws and Regulations (*qanunname*). Simultaneously, Ebu's-suud was also doing the inverse by recasting "practices that were part of the Ottoman legal and administrative repertoire in the language of Islamic jurisprudence", that is *fiqh*.[24] This should not simply be considered an effort to translate the sultan's will into religious idiom. The efforts to

22 Ze'evi, *Producing Desire*, 48–76.
23 Ergene, "Qanun and Sharia", 112.
24 Ergene, *ibidem*.

create a legislative system with up to date *qanun* books and issuing new edicts that synthesized the existing practices and *fiqh* with the current needs of the Empire were jurisprudential in nature.

The oft-studied Ottoman practice of cash endowments is a telling example for the relationship between *fiqh* and *qanun*.[25] These were simple interest-bearing loans guaranteed by pawns of real estate. Even though interest was forbidden in Islam, cash endowments were an accepted part of Ottoman economic life as early as the second half of the fifteenth century. They had an important function of capital distribution and helped finance social projects in health, education, and general welfare. Three years before his appointment as the *shayk al-islam* in 1548, Ebu's-suud wrote a twenty-eight-page treatise justifying the practice. The document proved both his professional rigour and acumen in integrating his expertise in fiqh with the social and economic interests of the realm.

Another interesting area is criminal punishment. In Ottoman courts, some lighter crimes were dealt with fines instead of the physical punishment typically assigned by many classical jurists. Most non-violent sexual transgressions, such as adultery, received progressively designed fines, forced labour, and banishment; and rarely heavy physical chastisement.[26] When a criminal act was seen as a serious threat to public order or abhorrent, however, the courts generally opted to mete out harsher punishments rather than lesser ones. In violent cases involving pederasty, for example, the verdict was often execution rather than blood money that *fiqh* allowed the perpetrator to pay to the victim's family.[27]

Whether the Ottoman courts inclined towards more religious sources or more pragmatic ones, and whether they became more lenient or stricter as a result, an ideal of perfect order remained arguably the principle aim of the legal

25 See Murat Çizakça, "Cash waqfs of Bursa, 1555–1823", *Journal of the Economic and Social History of the Orient*, 38.3 (1995), 313–54; Jon E. Mandaville. "Usurious Piety: The cash Awqaf Controversy in the Ottoman Empire", *International Journal of Middle Eastern Studies*, 10.3 (1979), 289–308; Haim Gerber, *Economy and Society in an Ottoman City: Bursa, 1600–1700* (Jerusalem: The Hebrew University, 1988), 128–9. For the social reception of cash *awqaf* and the influence of public opinion, see Haim Gerber, "Public sphere and civil society in the Ottoman Empire", *The Public Sphere in Muslim Societies* (Albany: SUNY Press, 2002), 72–4.

26 Ze'evi. *Producing Desire*, 64–5.

27 The principal reference on Ottoman criminal law is still Uriel Heyd's posthumous book *Studies in Old Ottoman Criminal Law*, ed. V.L. Ménage (Oxford: Clarendon, 1973). For a summary on the execution of law and the system of checks and balances, see also Rudolph Peters, *Crime and Punishment in Islamic Law: Theory and Practice from the Sixteenth to the Twenty-first Century* (Cambridge: Cambridge University Press, 2005), especially 69–102.

system. The cases of sexual transgression reveal the priority of maintaining social order over moral chastisement *per se*. They also underline the social and economic role of law and legislation. The Ottoman *qanun*, especially after the reformulation and standardization activities in Süleyman's reign, designated the household, extended family, the village and town quarters as legal bodies responsible for controlling its members, cooperating in rendering culprits, and contributing to the financial punishment its members received.[28] Social exclusion was used in the form of banishment from community. Finally, the fines and forced labour benefitted the state and, in the long run, were supposed to benefit its subjects, for whom the state offered protection and infrastructure.

With its servants trained in the military, administration, and/or the religious/scholarly establishment, the state was to provide safety for all its subjects, Muslim and non-Muslim, and to ensure the efficient functioning of their religious and economic activities, travelling, and communication. Despite the checks and balances of the system corruption existed, and neither safety in the extensive realm nor the idealized system of meritocracy was perfect. The institutions and career paths established during Süleyman's reign were to become overcrowded already in the last quarter of the sixteenth century posing serious problems of maintenance. Nevertheless, Süleyman's reign was marked by an expansive program of reforms, institutional development, and standardization. In this environment, it is no coincidence that the legacy of the civilizing prophet-king Solomon, after whom the sultan was named, became a major reference for comparison and source of inspiration in making the persona of the sultan.

5 Solomon in Islamic Tradition

The image of the prophet-king Solomon in the Islamic and the Judeo-Christian traditions have many similarities. He is the archetype of the powerful and just ruler, who was divinely endowed with insightful knowledge. He ruled a prosperous kingdom and was famous for his architectural patronage. While in both traditions Solomon's wisdom and justice are intertwined, the exemplary story given differs.

In the Judeo-Christian tradition, Solomon has to decide between two women's claims of motherhood and choose the authentic one. The Qur'an refers to the dispute of two men. The plaintiff is a farmer, and the defendant, a shepherd.

28 Ze'evi. *Producing Desire*, 60.

In the story, the farmer appears before King David, Solomon's father, complaining that the shepherd's sheep entered his field, trampled over his crops and grazed, causing him financial damage. He demands compensation from the animals' owner. The shepherd is poor and the damage he caused exceeds his sheep's value.

Hearing the case, David promptly decides that the shepherd should hand over his flock to the farmer. David's teenager son, Solomon, also present at the tribunal, offers an alternative solution. With prudency and respectful words, he suggests that only the right to use the milk and wool of the shepherd's sheep be given to the farmer. The shepherd should work in the farmer's damaged fields to restore them to their previous condition. Afterwards, the farmer should return the sheep to the shepherd.

David finds his son's solution more suitable than his own and orders its implementation. The Qur'anic passage ends, "And We made Süleyman understand (the case); and unto each of them We gave judgement and knowledge".[29]

How the story of Solomon's judgment in the Judeo-Christian tradition ends is well-known. Solomon orders the child be cut in half so that he could be shared between the two women. This order then reveals the identity of the authentic mother, who prefers to lose her rights on her child instead of seeing him perish. Solomon's indirect way of determining the truth reveals his shrewd intelligence and capacity for solving problems using his understanding of human psychology.

Solomon in the Islamic tradition also solves the problem with finesse. To be exact, David's monolithic decision was just, however, it lacked Solomon's insight to the human condition and his resulting compassion. Were all his flock taken from the shepherd, he would have been left destitute. Neither was David's alternative economically effective: the value of the shepherd's flock could not sufficiently cover the farmer's damage. Solomon's more complex solution benefited both parties. Aside from safeguarding the shepherd's ownership of the animals, it also promised fuller economic compensation to the farmer by providing him free milk and wool to use and sell, as well as free service for his fields.

Solomon's justice also preserved the peace and *status quo* the incident temporarily disturbed and avoided a possible future confrontation between the two sides. In a desperate effort of self-preservation, the shepherd might have disobeyed David's law and even shown physical resistance creating both legal and social disharmony.

---

29 The Qur'an 21:79.

Solomon's wise judgement has more implications when the two sides are seen as representative members of larger socio-economic groups: the farmer of settled communities and the shepherd of nomadic or semi-nomadic ones. From this perspective Solomon's judgement brings and secures harmony to the potentially volatile relationship between the nomadic and settled populations. He displays a governing wisdom that will guarantee harmony in his future realm.

The narrative structure of the story includes yet another important element for the description of an ideal king: the capability of recognizing sound counsel even when it comes from someone inferior. If Solomon shows God-given judgment and knowledge with his counsel, David exhibits the same qualities with his ability to take his son's counsel. The story's pre-modern audience, for whom differences of age and social standing mattered significantly, would have noticed the mismatch between the social positions of the giver and the receiver of advice. Their awareness would have underlined such messages as the possibility of good advice arriving from an inferior source or the importance of the good ruler to recognize sound counsel.

6 The Legacy of Solomon during the Reign of Sultan Süleyman

Albeit being widely known, the story of the litigation never became a popular topic for illustrations. In its stead, Solomon was often represented with his impressive court composed of ministers, jinns, and a motley of animals, highlighting his universal authority. On the other hand, the concept of the wise vizier as the indispensable companion of a discerning king became a *topos* in text and image throughout Islamicate civilization. However, it was Solomon, and not his father who became the model ruler heeding good counsel, and his vizier, Asaf, the humbler source of sound advice.

References to Solomon and Asaf were particularly rampant during the reign of Sultan Süleyman.[30] Lutfi Pasha (grand vizier between 1539–1541) composed a book of advice for ministers after his dismissal and titled it "The Book of Asaf" (*Asafname*), thereby comparing himself to the reputed vizier, and the sultan to Solomon. Occasionally, these flattering comparisons arrived from

30 Paul Losensky examines a parallel manipulation of the legacy of the prophet-king for the Safavid Shah Solayman (1647–1694): "Coordinates in space and time: architectural chronograms", in Colin Paul Mitchell, ed., *New Perspectives on Safavid Iran: Empire and Society* (Abingdon: Routledge, 2011), 203–7. See also Colin P. Mitchell. *The Practice of Politics in Safavid Iran* (London, New York, 2009), 120–137.

foreign sources. Such was the case with the letter Shah Tahmasb's delegate Kemaleddin Ferruhzade presented to the sultan on the 21st of May 1555 on occasion of a peace treaty. After referring to Süleyman as "*Süleymān-ı Zamān*" (the Solomon of the Age) twice in verse, the Safavid scribe had written on behalf of the shah, that an earlier "venerable letter has been delivered" to him "from [Prophet] Solomon", i.e., his Ottoman namesake.[31]

It was in the literary circles where comparisons between the two Süleymans/ Solomons were the most common. Contemporaneous poets, such as Yahya Beg, Baki, and 'Arif, drew parallels between the two in terms of justice, authority, wealth, and generosity.[32] We know that the sultan was well aware of these flattering comparisons and approved them. In fact, he made similar references in his own poems.[33]

In the fields of art and architecture, the situation was no different. Gülru Necipoğlu provides a detailed report of the associations drawn by the contemporaneous Ottoman and foreign visitors between the artistic programme of the Süleymaniye mosque complex on the one hand and paradise, Haghia Sophia, and the Dome of the Rock (Jerusalem), on the other. After highlighting the similarities between the decorative and architectural programs of the mausoleums of the sultan and his wife in the Süleymaniye mosque complex to those of the Dome of the Rock, Necipoğlu notes the possibility "that the similarities are meant to be a reference to the legendary Temple of Solomon".[34] After all, "it is known that the sultan intended to renovate the Dome of the Rock, that he frequently made allusions to passages in the Koran where Solomon is

31 Feridun Ahmed Bey. *Münşe'ât üs-Selâtin*, I., 508–9. https://babel.hathitrust.org/cgi/pt?id=uc1.c070909290&view=1up&seq=546&size=125 Last accessed: 17 of October 2022; also quoted in Colin Paul Mitchell, "The Sword and the Pen. Diplomacy in Early Safavid Iran", unpublished Ph.D. dissertation (University of Toronto, 2002), 356–7.

32 See, for example, the poems of Fuzuli (on justice, wealth, and power), Lami'i (on power), Hayali (on power, wealth, and generosity), Yahya Bey (on power) in Ali Yıldız, *Kanuni Sultan Süleyman'a Yazılan Kasideler* (Ankara: Kültür Bakanlığı, 1996), 178, 70, 188, 208, 216, 272, 340 respectively. See also Hüseyin Akkaya, *The Prophet Solomon in Ottoman Turkish Literature and the Süleymâniyye of Şemseddin Sivâsî*, ed. Şinasi Tekin and Gönül Alpay Tekin (Cambridge, MA: Harvard University Press, 1997); Şükri-i Bitlisi, *Selim-name*, ed. Mustafa Argunşah (Kayseri: Erciyes Ü.Y., 1997), 52–3.

33 See Sultan Süleyman, *Dîvân-ı Muhibbî* (*Kanunî Sultan Süleyman'ın Şiirleri*), ed. Vahit Çabuk, 3 volumes (Istanbul: Tercüman, 1980), numbers 550 (vol. 2), 727, and 953 (both in vol. 3).

34 A similar case is made for Philip II and his architectural program for the Escorial. René Taylor, "Architecture and Magic: consideration on the *Idea* of the Escorial", in D. Fraser, H. Hibbard and M. Lewine, eds., *Essays in the History of Architecture Presented to Rudolf Wittkower*, eds. (London: Phaidon, 1967), 81–109.

mentioned, and that he was referred to as "*Süleymān-ı Zamān*" (the Solomon of the Age) in his endowment deed (*waqfiyya*) and in inscriptions on public fountains".[35]

The small fountain behind the Reception Hall (*Arz Odası*) of the Topkapı Palace is one example to these fountains. Here, the inscription reads: "Sultan of the worlds, Solomon of his time, who gives the water of life to the members of his court". A similar reference is inscribed in a water fountain built during the sultan's restoration project in Jerusalem's Temple Mount (*Haram al-Sharif*).[36] The six-pointed star known in Islamicate civilization as the Seal of Solomon was inserted in the Jerusalem city walls rebuilt by Sultan Süleyman.

In an enigmatic single page representation currently preserved in the Los Angeles County Museum of Art [Figure 5.1], we see the same inscription, "*Süleymān-ı Zamān*" as part of the distich: "He is Solomon of his time / he has the kingdom of Solomon in his days". Using the inscription, the hoopoe bird perched at the top of a tower,[37] the physiognomy of the figure and his personalized turban, Rachel Milstein identified the painting's principal figure as Süleyman presented as the haloed prophet-king Solomon.[38]

In the image, we see three older men crowned with lesser haloes sitting before Süleyman in a setting resembling his chambers in the Topkapı Palace. They look like religious scholars. Six others are conversing, perhaps debating among themselves, in two groups of three. We can discern a book and an astrolabe in their hands. The style of the painting invites close association with the images of a particular corpus of dynastic literature (*shehnames*) prepared by the Sufi poet and historian 'Arif for Süleyman in the late 1550s.

We still do not know much more about this unattached page; yet it stands as proof to a particularly direct association made between the sultan and the prophet-king Solomon: a wise and just civilizing governor, who keeps company with scholars and discerns sound counsel; the head of a prosperous empire on earth, protected and revered by the angels above.

---

35 Gülru Necipoğlu-Kafadar, "The Süleymaniye Complex in Istanbul: An Interpretation", *Muqarnas*, 3 (1985), 100–1.

36 For the inscriptions on these fountains see Rachel Milstein, "King Solomon's Temple and Throne as Models in Islamic Visual Culture", in Bianca Kühnel, Galit Noga-Banai and Hanna Vorholt, eds., *Visual Constructs of Jerusalem* (Turnhout: Brepols, 2014), 192; and "King Solomon or Sultan Süleyman?" in Eyal Ginio and Elie Podeh, eds., *The Ottoman Middle East. Studies in Honor of Amnon Cohen* (Leiden: Brill, 2013), 21.

37 The hoopoe is associated with Solomon in Islamic lore.

38 Milstein, "King Solomon or Sultan Süleyman?", 15–24.

FIGURE 5.1 Sultan Süleyman as prophet-king Solomon, LACMA, M. 73.5.446

7 Süleyman as a Prophet-Like Sultan in Legal Texts

Solomon was not the only prophet to whom the sultan was compared. Ottoman bureaucrats, historians, and poets made analogies between Süleyman and other prophets and saints and employed astral and mystical imagery in their texts to describe his nature and historical mission. In 1530, in the previously mentioned preamble to the *Qanunname* of Bosnia, Celalzade described the sultan as the

> King of all nations, Caliph of God in the domain of knowledge, protector of the lands of the People of the Faith, eraser of the traces of infidelity and tyranny, distributor of justice and beneficence and equity, destroyer of the bases of tyranny and oppression and injustice, patron of God's followers, vanquisher of God's enemies, possessor of all worldly dominions, announcer of God's exalted word, Shadow of God in East and West, Sultan of the Sultans in East and West, lion of East and West in combat and war, one who is *Sahib Qiran* (i.e. Lord of the Auspicious Conjunction of Saturn and Jupiter), the son of *Sahib Qiran*, pride of the Ottoman dynasty, who was given the name of the prophet Süleyman (Solomon)—peace be upon him—Sultan Süleyman, … may the most exalted God spread the carpets of his caliphate over the earth forever, and establish his foundation above Ursa Minor until the Day of Resurrection.

With these words, Celalzade combined universal political and religious authority in his persona. He based the sultan's authority on his administration of justice and divine knowledge. His military prowess and auspicious birth, coinciding with the major astrological conjunction, confirmed his divinely given mission as the Caliph of the Islamic community—both as the Successor of Muhammad, and the Representative of God. The text continued, "in the time of the vizierate of the minister of celestial revolution, Asaf of the time, named after Khalilu'r-Rahman (i.e., Abraham)", referring to his wise grand vizier Ibrahim.[39]

Five years prior to the law code of Bosnia, in his preamble to the *Qanunname* of Egypt, Celalzade had composed an analogous formulation of the sultan's authority and aura using expansive metaphors for the sultan. From mystical and celestial allusions ("the sovereign destined for paradise", "the felicitous sultan of the celestial throne that is the threshold of the universe and the abode of the

39 Buzov, "The Lawgiver and his Lawmakers", appendix B, 234–5.

lotus tree of the seventh heaven"), his metaphors first descended to the astrological sphere as he compared Süleyman to "the Sun in opposition to the Sun in Pisces, the Moon of youthfulness and possessor of the victorious signs, Jupiter the vizier, Mercury of the right course, Saturn the guardian of the Universe, Mars in fatality", and then continued with a list of pre-Islamic prophets starting with Adam. The sultan was hence "Adam the Pure in sincerity, Noah the Saved of noble deeds, Enoch in learning", as well as "Ishmael in submission to God, Moses in eloquence, Jacob in pleasing God, Joseph in Preciousness, David in caliphate". The comparison to Solomon was with respect to his authority.

In the Egyptian preamble, Celalzade also likened him to Muhammad and the four Rightly Guided Caliphs: he was "Ahmad (Muhammad) in honour, Sıddık (Abu Bakr) in devotion, Faruq (Omar) in justice, Uthman in forbearance, Ali in knowledge". According to Celalzade,

> While he is not a prophet, to that distinguished creature
> The Creator gave all moral qualities of the prophets
> All saints recognized his saintly power
> If the shah (i.e., the sultan) is called "holy", that suits the notion of holiness.[40]

The Egyptian law code and its preamble were written at a crucial time for Süleyman, who was yet to consolidate his authority. His appointment of his favourite, Ibrahim, to the grand vizierate in 1523 had antagonized the Second Vizier Ahmed Pasha, who had been waiting for his promotion after Piri Mehmed Pasha's (grand vizier between 1518–23) dismissal. Now, as the Governor of Egypt, Ahmed Pasha, thereafter known as the Treacherous (*Hain*), organized a rebellion against the young sultan and declared his independence. After the rebellion of Janbardi al-Ghazali in Syria immediately after Süleyman's ascension (1520), this was the second rebellion in the former Mamluk territories.

The sultan sent his new Grand Vizier with forces from Istanbul and the rebellion was routed in 1524. Nevertheless, it was not sufficient to quench the uprising; Egypt had to be integrated to the rest of the empire economically and legally. That is why a group of administrators accompanied the military forces sent from the capital. Their principal aim was to confirm Ottoman authority over this recently acquired territory of formidable state and cultural tradition. The administrative team included the treasurer İskender Çelebi and the secretary Celalzade.

40 Buzov, *ibidem*, appendix A, 210. Buzov translated and examined the full text.

In this context, the preamble's ambitious presentation of the sultan was not merely common eulogy taken a pitch or two higher, but part and parcel of Celalzade's response to the need of establishing the sultan's authority. Celalzade's success in Egypt made him the Chief Secretary (*Re'is ül-Küttab*) in 1525, very soon after his return to the capital.[41]

The Egyptian Preamble launched Süleyman's historical mission as a divinely chosen universal ruler of the age. Sometime after its composition, it acquired a 'textual life' of its own and was copied many times separate from the law code it formally introduced. The mission Celalzade described for the sultan also had a long life.

More than fifty years after the preamble's composition, the dynastic writer 'Arif used the same ploy of the order of Creation and prophetic comparisons that Celalzade utilized to project Süleyman's mission as the spiritual and political leader of the epoch.[42] In his first *shehname* project of universal history in five volumes circa 1558, his description was longer, more subtle and elaborated in a theo-philosophical discourse. In the first volume, he began human history with the first Caliph of God, Adam; in the fifth, he concluded with the reign of the last Caliph of God, Süleyman.

About five years later, in the Imperial Scroll (*Tomar-ı Hümayun*), the same idea was represented in a different format, making visual references to the mythic celestial scroll where humanity's destiny was allegedly written [Figure 5.2].[43] Once again the sultan's significance for humanity was conceived within a universal history starting with Creation. Here too, astral imagery was employed. The Scroll projected an ecumenical vision of Islam by its inclusion of the twelve imams revered by the Twelver Shi'a. Furthermore, Süleyman was connected to Muhammad, and the early prophets in the central branch of the

41 For the life and career of Celalzade Mustafa and an evaluation of Süleyman's reign, see Kaya Şahin, *Empire and Power in the Reign of Süleyman: Narrating the Sixteenth-Century Ottoman World* (Cambridge: Cambridge University Press, 2013).

42 Fatma Sinem Eryılmaz, "From Adam to Süleyman: Visual Representations of Authority and Leadership in 'Ārif's *Şāhnāme-yi Āl-i 'Os̱mān*", in H. Erdem Çıpa and Emine Fetvacı, eds., *Writing history at the Ottoman Court. Editing the Past, Fashioning the Future* (Bloomington: Indiana University Press, 2013), 100–28.

43 For 'Arif and Eflatun's careers and more on the Scroll, see Fatma Sinem Eryılmaz, "The *Shehnamecis* of Sultan Süleyman: 'Arif and Eflatun and Their Dynastic Project", unpublished Ph.D. dissertation (University of Chicago, 2010); "The Manipulation of Ancient and Medieval Knowledge in the Ottoman Court", in Godefroid de Callataÿ, Mattia Cavagna and Baudouin Van den Abeele, eds., *Intersective Perspective on Mediaeval Encyclopaedism / Regards Croisés sur l'encyclopédisme médiéval* (Turnhout: Brepols, 2021).

FIGURE 5.2 The beginning of the genealogical section of the Ottoman Imperial Scroll, *Tomar-ı Hümayun*, Topkapı Palace library, A. 3599

Scroll's genealogical scheme vis-à-vis his inheritance of Divine knowledge, transmitted to the Ottoman dynasty by Ibn Sina (Avicenna, 980–1037).

Between 1563–1565, as the Imperial Scroll was being prepared, Kınalızade Ali Çelebi, then Chief Military Judge in Damascus, was writing his book on the ethics of family and state, *Ahlaq-i 'Ala'i,* which became a reference in the field shortly after its conclusion. Kınalızade's main references were the classical works of Nasir al-din al-Tusi (1201–1274), Jalal al-din al-Davvani (1426–1502), and Abu Nasr al-Farabi (c. 870-c. 950) on ethics, as well as those attributed to Aristotle, Plato, Socrates, and Ibn Sina (Avicenna). In the section on the exceptional king, whom he described as the Ruler of Hidden Meanings (*ḥākim-i mānī'*), Kınalızade expounded on the nature of kingship: "he is the one who is distinguished by Divine support and upon whom is bestowed unending Divine accord (*tevfīq*) such that he is able to order the welfare (*ṣalāḥ*) of the domain and also to perfect the souls of the people".[44] This is the same ruler that the "moderns" called "Caliph" and the Shi'i called "Imam",

44 Here, I am principally using Shahab Ahmed's translation: *What is Islam? The Importance of Being Islamic* (Princeton: Princeton University Press, 2016), 473–5. For the text of the 1832 Cairo edition of Kınalızade's work see https://ia800203.us.archive.org/3/items/ahlakialaiooali/ahlakialaiooali_bw.pdf.

and Plato, "the prudent Manager of the World" (*müdebbir-i ʿālem*). He added that this ruler, who spread justice and was free from any form of tyranny or injustice, was "perfect (*kāmil*) among his kind" and "fit to be called Shadow of God on Earth, and merits possession of and distinction by the quality of the Caliphate of Real-Truth", i.e., God. Kınalızade did not articulate the name of the exceptional ruler of his time. Yet his frequent intersections of the narrative with examples from Sultan Süleyman's actions and words as ethical models of perfection strongly hint at the identity of the Ruler of Hidden Meanings of the age.

8 Conclusion

In the Ottoman world of letters of the sixteenth century, it was common to find many of the same writers composing universal histories, law codes, poems, and ethical treatises. These intellectuals shared similar visions of the world and history and envisioned their contemporaneous ruler's special role in the unfolding of God's plan for humanity. References to one another in their writings as well as in other sources, such as the biographical dictionaries, highlight the similar professional and intellectual backgrounds they shared and the social and intellectual networks they constituted. It is hence not so surprising to find the formulations of Süleyman's special historical role in the preamble of an important law code or the description of his spiritual and political leadership in an ethical treatise from the pen of the Chief Judge of Damascus, one of the most important provinces of the Empire. In order to understand the minds that set the remarkable Ottoman state apparatus, it is imperative to understand the intellectual parameters of these writers who also ideated divinely approved universal leaders acting as God's viceroys in delivering humanity through the threshold of an exceptional epoch.

Indeed, those who codified the imperial administrative and legal institutions also formulated the nature of the sultan's authority and significantly contributed to his legacy. Ebu's-suud brought order and harmony to different judicial traditions already present in Ottoman legal practice. With his jurisprudential work, he defined a strong and agile legal system capable of answering the empire's needs. With his *fetwas* on critical issues, such as war against the Safavids or capital punishment for Prince Bayezıd, he provided the sultan legitimate freedom to exercise his political will. With his extensive *Ma'ruzat*, he involved Süleyman in law-making thereby activating his legislative authority as caliph allowed by the Shari'ah. He cultivated Süleyman's authority both as the successor or Caliph of Muhammad and as the Caliph of God.[45]

Celalzade Mustafa Çelebi, on the other hand, composed Ottoman laws in the official language that he himself helped create. At the same time, like Ebu's-suud, he gave shape to the young sultan's image and legacy. Especially after becoming the Chancellor in 1534, he worked in tandem with the *shayk al-islam* in preparing a harmonious legal tradition. Both worked for the order of the realm, which they called 'the order of the world' (*niẓām-ı 'ālem*), and the success of its protector, the sultan. Both developed a relationship of trust and interdependence with Süleyman.

While not the creator or the sole innovator of the Ottoman state or the legal system, Sultan Süleyman was personally involved in the construction and implementation of the institutionalization program during his reign. He was the legislative head of the state and protector of the institutions. The Ottoman state and legal system continued evolving after him. Yet his reign and reforms remained as foundational references.

Bibliography

Main Sources

Akgündüz, Ahmet, *Osmanlı Kanunnâmeleri ve Hukukî Tahlilleri. Kanunî Sultan Süleyman Devri Kanunnâmeleri*, vols. 4 and 6 (Istanbul: 1992, 1993).

Ahmed Bey, Feridun, *Münşe'ât üs-Selâtin*, 1. https://babel.hathitrust.org/cgi/pt?id=uc1.c070909290&view=1up&seq=546&size=125.

'Ali, Mustafa, *Künh ül-Ahbar*, vol. 1. http://ekitap.yek.gov.tr/urun/kunhu'l-ahbar--1-2-ciltler-_733.aspx.

Sultan Süleyman, *Dîvân-ı Muhibbî* (*Kanunî Sultan Süleyman'ın Şiirleri*), ed. Vahit Çabuk, 3 volumes (Istanbul: Tercüman, 1980).

The Qur'an.

Main Bibliographical References

Buzov, Snjezana, "The Lawgiver and his Lawmakers: The Role of Legal Discourse in the Change of Ottoman Imperial Culture", unpublished Ph.D. dissertation, University of Chicago, 2005.

45 Imber, *Ebu's-su'ud,* ch. 4, 105. Imber mentions the role of the law books of Buda (1541), Skopje, and Thessalonika (1568) in defining the sultan's caliphate vis-à-vis Muhammad; and the preamble to his treatise on ablution and the Süleymaniye mosque's inscriptions, vis-à-vis God.

Ergene, Boğaç A. "Qanun and Sharia", in Rudolph Peters and Peri Bearmen, eds., *The Ashgate Research Companion to Islamic Law* (Burlington, 2014), 109–122.

Eryılmaz, Fatma Sinem, "From Adam to Süleyman: Visual Representations of Authority and Leadership in 'Ārif's *Şāhnāme-yi Āl-i 'Os̱mān*", in H. Erdem Çıpa and Emine Fetvacı, eds., *Writing history at the Ottoman Court: Editing the Past, Fashioning the Future* (Bloomington: Indiana University Press, 2013), 100–28.

Fleischer, Cornell H., "The Lawgiver as Messiah: The Making of the Imperial Image in the Reign of Süleyman", in Gilles Veinstein, ed., *Soliman le Magnifique et sons temps* (Paris, 1992), 159–177.

İnalcık, Halil, "Süleyman the Lawgiver and Ottoman Law", *Archivum Ottomanicum*, 1 (1969), 15–106.

SECTION 2

Governance and Change

CHAPTER 6

After Revolts

Moments for Constitutional Refashioning in Early Modern Europe

Xavier Gil

1

At the start of *The Prince*, Machiavelli reflected on how to govern the various sorts of principalities and made a particular remark:

> Of course, it is true that, after a ruler has regained power in rebel territories, he is much more likely to hang on to it. For the rebellion gives him an excuse, and he is able to take firmer measures to secure his position, punishing delinquents, checking up on suspects, and taking precautions where needed.[1]

He was not specifically referring to the introduction of new forms of government, but rather to strengthening rulers' authority. Then, when he wrote about plots in his *Discourses*, he pointed to the psychological aspect of the matter: "Those [rulers] who survive become more unbearable and more bitter". Decades later, in 1561, at the start of the French Wars of Religion, Étienne de la Boétie offered his thoughts on how to put an end to that conflict and recommended exemplary punishments for those responsible for the most brazen disobedience toward the crown, including destruction of their dwellings and dismantling their municipal structures and legality. Though he also suggested other remedies, he had no doubt as to the efficacy of these in persuading people to accept royal law: "It is hard to believe, after this terror, how much more manageable, pliable, and willing to conform the people are".

A generation later, Ottavio Sammarco expressed similar views in a treaty that went through several editions, where he warned about the multiple occasions and ways in which change – always a negative thing – threatened states. One of these occasions was popular revolts; if the prince could smother them,

1 Niccolò Machiavelli, *The Prince*, ed. and translation by David Wootton (Indianapolis and Cambridge: Hackett, 1995), ch. 3, 8.

 | DOI:10.1163/9789004549159_008

he said, "he would become more proud and more cruel, like someone unexpectedly provoked". Finally, according to Thomas Hobbes, in a passage concerning the chain of consequences following all human acts and the natural punishments deriving from them, "negligent government of princes [is naturally punished] with rebellion; and rebellion with slaughter". In a more general vein, he concluded that sooner or later all civil conflicts lead to reinforced power in the hands of the victor.[2]

Machiavelli, La Boétie, Sammarco, and Hobbes represent different political and cultural settings, and each offered distinct perspectives. But they all appear to have shared one assumption: defeating a rebellion or being victorious in a civil war led to a more authoritarian government over a more docile and subdued society. To some extent the historiography has agreed with this, having established a causal relationship, be it explicit or implicit, between revolt, repression, and absolutism in the sense that the aftermath of a crushed revolt generally consisted of two phases: punishment followed by political and governmental changes aimed at shoring up the authority that had been challenged.[3]

Even so, the variety of such episodes throughout the sixteenth and seventeenth centuries prompts us to ask if this general rule did indeed prevail and if it did so both in the realm of government practice and in terms of political-juridical thought. Taking into account the variety of arguments and situations, we can suggest that in fact the general rule was not quite as general as has been thought.

Machiavelli provided thoughts on the issue in two pieces he wrote while working as secretary to the Council of Ten under the orders of the Signoria of Florence. In "On the matters of Pistoia" (1502) he wrote about a conflict two years earlier that had broken out after the local pro-Florentine faction was expelled from the city. Florence reacted with a series of measures: subduing

2 Niccolò Machiavelli, *Discorso sopra la prima deca di Tito Livio*, ed. Francesco Bausi (Rome: Salerno, 2001), book 3, ch. 6, 583; Étienne de la Boétie, *Mémoire sur la pacification des troubles*, ed. Malcolm Smith (Geneva: Droz, 1983), 54, 63; Ottavio Sammarco, *Della mutatione de' regni* (Turin: Gio. Dom. Tarino, 1629), 121 [additionally: Naples 1628, Turin and Venice 1629, Milan 1630]; Thomas Hobbes, *Leviathan*, ed. Richard Tuck (Cambridge: Cambridge University Press, 1991), ch. 31, 253–4; on his conclusion see Salvo Mastellone, *Storia del pensiero politico europeo dal XV al XVIII secolo* (Turin: UTET, 1999), 132.

3 Perez Zagorin, *Rebels and rulers, 1500–1660* (Cambridge: Cambridge University Press, 1982), vol. 1, 110, 274; vol. 2, 85–6, 220; Jack A. Goldstone, *Revolution and rebellion in the early modern world* (Berkeley: University of California Press, 1991), 41, 451. See also Francesco Benigno, *Specchi delle revoluzioni: Conflitto e identità politica nell'Europa moderna* (Rome: Donzelli, 1999), viii-ix for a critical appraisal of this assumption.

Pistoia, punishing those responsible for the expulsion, stripping the city of its artillery, and tearing down its walls. After describing these efforts, and by way of conclusion, Machiavelli expressed his reservations: "It remains to be seen how to move forward, especially concerning reform of the city".[4]

Submission had indeed to be followed by political reform. The following year Machiavelli returned to the topic in another report, "On the Method of Dealing with the Rebellious Peoples of Valdichiana" (1503). The report began by summarizing Livy's commentary on the rebellion of towns in Lazio against Rome and the latter's response, which in some cases involved punitive measures (destruction, exile, repopulation by outsiders) though in other cases Rome offered pardons and compensation. The middle road was rejected as being counterproductive. As was his wont, Machiavelli drew lessons from Roman history, especially being that both Lazio and Valdichiana underwent "uprisings followed by reconquest". As in the past, the Signoria's response was sometimes benign (e.g, Cortona and other towns), which met with Machiavelli's approval ("you were clever to win them over with benefits") while in other cases, such as that of Arezzo, Florence levied partial punishments, which Machiavelli criticized as a halfway approach.[5]

Once Machiavelli had retired from active political life and was writing his major works, he could address the question of which political measures were most advisable in certain situations. Along the quote with which this essay begins, he made other observations, some of them well known, concerning the steps necessary for preserving newly acquired states (but not after a rebellion) that previously had had their own laws. In one passage he pointed to two options: exterminating the former prince's family and leaving laws and taxes intact. Elsewhere he pointed to three more: destroying those states; having the prince move there to live; and, third, preserving the laws, appointing a favorable government, and exacting tribute. In certain cases, he said, the best solution was destruction, given the possibility of future rebellions, while in others one had two options: destruction or living there.[6]

The crisp clarity of Machiavelli's solutions may well have been inspired more by the turbulent times in Italy than by international events, which he was also well informed about, given that then, as well as later, the most common recourse by composite monarchies was the third option he listed, which in the end he rejected. In any case, Machiavelli was equally clear in describing

---

4 Niccolò Machiavelli, *L'arte della guerra. Scritti politici minori*, ed. Jean-Jacques Marchand, Denis Fachard, and Giorgio Masi (Rome: Salerno, 2001), ch. 3, 442.

5 *Ibidem*, ch. 6, 463.

6 Machiavelli, *The Prince*, ch. 3, 8–9; ch. 5, 17–8.

the difficulties involved in introducing new political institutions. His words of warning concerned the case of conquered principalities but also could be applied generally: "One ought to pause and consider the fact that there is nothing harder to undertake, nothing more likely of failure, nothing more risky to pull off, than to set oneself up as a leader who plans to found a new system of government". This difficulty helps us to understand his praise for Cesare Borgia for having forced Romagna into obedience by giving it "a good government", first through a cruel and decisive ruler and then by installing a new court of law. In the *Discourses* he once again warned of the dangers of constitutional and political reorganization, which he illustrated by pointing to the changes undergone in Florence after the events in Arezzo, after which the Republic itself disappeared in 1512 and the Medicis returned.[7]

Well-known as they are, these observations are presented here as a way of introducing the two matters to be addressed in this chapter: first, writers' considerations regarding the proper amount of political-institutional change after political crises, especially failed rebellions; and then, a few practical examples to see how solutions were applied. Such situations constituted a moment of political refashioning, even in those cases in which the status quo remained almost untouched.

2

Revolts were an ever-present topic in political and juridical treatises since the Middle Ages. Commentators of the *Corpus Iuris Civilis* and the *Decretales*, and a long list of authors from Rolando de Lucca in the early thirteenth century to Luca da Penne and Bartolus de Saxoferrato in the mid-fourteenth century wrote about whether or not resistance to authority could be licit and what its modalities and limits were. Some of these reflections originated in arguments defending either the authorities or those who challenged them, and therefore much of this genre had a forensic and jurisprudential nature. The basic issue was the relationship between obedience and disobedience or, put another way, the question of sovereignty. The terminology to describe the various events and acts was deeply nuanced, thanks to which one could distinguish between *iuste resistens*, on the one hand, and, on the other, the gradations of misdeeds

7 *Ibidem*, ch. 6, 19; and ch. 7, 24; Machiavelli, *Discorso*, book 1, ch. 2, 18.

from *inobedientia* to *crimen rebellionis* to *crimen laesae maiestatis*, with various mitigating and aggravating circumstances in both cases.[8]

It should be noted that the term "revolt" did not belong to this juridical tradition, though it would become more frequent in treatises concerning reason of state, which were more political and used the term in a decidedly negative way. The late sixteenth century, with the appearance of new types of disobedience (for example religious dissidence and tax revolts) and the ease with which disobedience could lead to civil war, witnessed a change in the political mood as there was a twofold tendency to reinforce, on the one hand, theories of sovereignty and revive, on the other, theories regarding the right to resist (which found inspiration both in the Neo-scholastics and in Calvinism). Both theories appealed to the common good, but while the former emphasized the obligation to obey the prince, the latter (which never equated resistance and rebellion) was presented as a second-order form of obedience. While reflections on disobedience and legitimate resistance certainly would not disappear, the tendency would be to stress the obligation to obey the prince, who was the incarnation of religious orthodoxy. Obedience was judged to be essential for the social order.[9]

A key objective in the jurisprudential genre was to determine who could perpetrate actions defined as crimes and who could be accused of being a delinquent. In principle, everyone except the emperor and the pope was susceptible to the charge of disobeying a superior. And both Emperor Henry VII and Pope Clement V were quite clear on the matter on the occasion of a conflict between the former and several cities of Lombardy in 1313: the imperial *Edictum de crimine laesae maiestatis* and *Declaratio quis sit ribellis* established the equivalency between disobedience and rebellion, while the papal decree *Pastoralis cura*, which favoured the cities, declared that certain of the emperor's actions were contrary to natural law. Bartolus later used this latter argument to point out differences between *resistere* and *rebellare*.[10]

This debate would continue well into the early modern era. The establishment of new Renaissance states led to more than a few noble uprisings against the crown, events defined as rebellion, and the corresponding capital punishment seemed clear. While these were not exactly individual actions, given

8 Angela de Benedictis, *Tumulti: Moltitudine rebelli in età moderna* (Bologna: Il Mulino, 2013), 11–4, 258. English translation: *Neither Disobedients nor Rebels: Lawful Resistance in Early Modern Italy*, translation by Alexandra Mary Lawrence and Robert Fredona (Rome: Viella, 2018).

9 De Benedictis, *Tumulti*, 9, 11–2, 15–17, 144, 153; Rosario Villari, *Politica barroca: Inquietudine, mutamento e prudenza* (Rome: Laterza, 2010), 15–7.

10 De Benedictis, *Tumulti*, 17, 115.

that the perpetrators were heads of noble houses, the royal judiciary wasted no time in punishing them. Punishment increasingly included the demolition of their houses and dwellings, so that the family suffered also physical losses.[11]

Another sort of action was the rising up of a multitude or a large group. In this case the juridical definition of collective perpetrator was ill defined, and in practice it was difficult, if not impossible, to capture and punish a mob. Thus, it was recognized that the crime (once it had been established that indeed it was a crime) might go unpunished: *ob populum multum crimen pertranseat inultum*, according to one of Gregory IX's decretals invoked on a wide variety of occasions and which generated a long textual tradition. One contributor to this principle was André Tiraqueau, whose 1562 treatise on punishment attempted to define a delinquent multitude and concluded that its members, though not its leaders, had to go unpunished. The principle was to be found also in chronicles on revolts. Writing in 1566 on the uprising of the *agermanats* in Valencia (1519–22) the notary Martín de Viciana stated that the law established that a rebelious multitude had to be pardoned. Similarly, the Augustinian monk Guillermo de Santa María arguing in favor of the Chichimeca people in the northern part of the viceroyalty of New Spain, who tenaciously fought the Spaniards, invoked the papal decrees to deny that a community's or people's sins or crimes could justify the punishment of all its members.[12]

Punishment of ringleaders in the hope that that would teach a lesson, along with broad or restricted general pardons for everyone else, appeared frequently in practice and in treatises. Machiavelli, with his eye on immediate efficacy, suggested that the prince apply exemplary and speedy punishments and not waste his compassion, which, if misapplied, would only bring about circumstances requiring even greater cruelty.[13]

Lastly, a third case was that of a *universitas delinquens*, another concept going back to the Middle Ages frequently commented upon by erudite writers. It refers to cities or corporations: how could a *universitas* or corporation commit a crime, given that it was a *persona ficta*, and in any case, how should

11 Christopher R. Friedrichs, "House-destruction as a ritual of punishment in Early Modern Europe", *European History Quarterly*, 50.4 (2020), 599–624.

12 De Benedictis, *Tumulti*, 139, 144, 147–8; Viciana, quoted by Juan F. Pardo Molero, "La 'justice d'Almudévar': confisquer, punir et pardonner les comuneros et agermanats (Espagne, 1521–1528)", in Yves Junot and Violet Soen, eds., *Confisquer, restituer, redistribuer: Punition et réconciliation matérielles dans les territorires des Habsburg et en France* (XVIe et XVIIe *siècles*) (Valenciennes: Presses Universitaires de Valenciennes, 2020), 49; Guillermo de Santa María, *Guerra de los chichemecas* (*México 1575-Zirosto 1580*), ed. Alberto Carrillo Cázares (Zamora: Colegio de Michoacán, 2003), 229–30.

13 Machiavelli, *The Prince*, ch. 17, 51.

it be punished? Should all members pay for the crimes of a few? One essential factor pointed out by Bartolus was if authorities had formally decided upon criminal conduct after proper deliberation and according to the usual procedures. In such a situation, both the city and its inhabitants were guilty, and punishment consisted in the suppression of the statutes and privileges that gave the *universitas* its identity, towers and walls were demolished and communal goods were confiscated, with which the *persona ficta* disappeared. But if the action had emerged from groups of people gathering informally outside the structures of government, then individual actors could receive capital punishment. Despite the clarity of these two options, the casuistry could go on forever, involving a variety of aggravating and mitigating factors. Among the former was the eventuality that rebel leaders sought protection from another prince or, even worse, from a rival prince; the most usual mitigating factors were self-defense or licit resistance in the face of unjust orders and the accompanying moderate use of force to that end.[14] Later on, Jean Bodin consolidated the doctrine; after affirming that colleges and corporations were one of society's organizational bases, he openly resolved that cities and communities that had rebelled or undertaken seditious actions in a legitimate assembly were "punished in their corporations by the loss of privileges, and the right of community, by fines, burdens, servitude, and other punishments according to the quality of the offense". Equally clearly however, he pointed out that such a punishment would not be appropriate if the conduct were not the result of a formal decision by the community.[15]

The renewed doctrine of the prince's absolute sovereignty in no way undercut erudite affirmations in defense of cities and corporations accused of such offenses. Also, the notion of political change, *conversio rerumpublicarum*, was of keen interest to writers drawing up catalogs of changes of all sorts. Though Christian eschatological ideas regarding the evolution of human affairs were not going to disappear, two other visions acquired new importance: the naturalist, which posited the birth, development, and decline of all human works, including the political; and Polybius's theory of anacyclosis, the cyclical change of political regimes, notably monarchy, aristocracy, and democracy, into, respectively, degenerate forms of tyranny, oligarchy, and demagogy.[16]

---

14 De Benedictis, *Tumulti*, 108–10, 127–9, 138–40, 143ff, 259–60.

15 Jean Bodin, *Les six livres de la république*, ed. Cristiane Frémont, Marie-Dominique Couzinet, and Henri Rochais (Paris: Fayard, 1986) [facs. of the 1576 ed.], book 3, ch. 7, 193.

16 Diego Quaglioni, "Il 'secolo di ferro' e la nuova reflessione política", in Cesare Vasoli, ed., *Le filosofie del Rinascimento* (Milan: Mondadori, 2002), 329, 334.

Machiavelli and Francesco Guicciardini clearly belonged to that world, especially given their interest in the changes undergone in Rome and Florence since the fourteenth century. Guicciardini, in particular, devoted the first book of his *Dialogue on the government of Florence* (1524) to a discussion among four friends regarding the most appropriate form of government for Florence in light of the crises and political changes from the Ciompi revolt of 1378 to the fall of the Medicis in 1494, the year when the conversation is situated. Following an introductory statement of the topic's importance ("How splendid and honourable it is to meditate on government and public administration"), the writer recognized how habitual and sudden these political changes were, "thanks to the unexpected occurrences that happen daily in human affairs".[17]

The dialogue starts off focusing precisely on the proper word with which to describe these changes. The participants distinguished between *alterazioni*, which entailed a redistribution of power within the elites, and *mutazione di stato*, or "the mutation of one species of government into another". Guicciardini mentioned the six conventional types of government according to Polybius, as well as the oligarchy/democracy dyad, which was frequent in Italian debates, but he leaned toward other more appropriate ways of representing his vision of Florentine political life. He distinguished between more open forms of government (*largezza*) and more closed forms (*stretezza*), describing the city's constitutional evolution as a continual fluctuation between one and the other. Generally speaking, this fluctuation reflected both the finite nature of things and the way in which the world was constituted, and these brought about "changes and deteriorations". Speaking more precisely, the fluctuation also responded to leadership acts which, in any case, were influenced by Fortune and by cities' life cycles:

> A new born or a young city … is easy to form and set up, and receives the habits given to it without any difficulty. When cities are old, it is difficult to reform them, and once they have been reformed, they soon lose their good set-up and always remember their original bad habits.[18]

The speaker who offered this opinion, the old and experienced Bernardo del Nero (Guicciardini's alter ego), believed that Florence was an old city undergoing a process of decadence, making him skeptical regarding the right reforms

17 Francesco Guicciardini, *Dialogue on the Government of Florence*, ed. and translation Alison Brown (Cambridge: Cambridge University Press, 1994), 1–2.

18 *Ibidem*, 6–7, 10, 16, 79, 140, 153; regarding his options more suited to local politics, see Brown's introduction to this volume, xxvi.

for setting the city straight. He also observed generally that revolutions tended to end up harming a city's life, and he specifically stated his disagreement with the changes undergone in Florence in 1494. In any case, Del Nero agreed that civil conflicts generally led to stronger government:

> The troubles caused by civil discord give rise either to a new tyranny or to the return of the old tyranny, or they encourage depravity and license among the people and the plebs which tumultuously shake the city.

Similarly, another discussant, Pagolantonio Soderni, despite being in favor of the 1494 events, and therefore disagreeing with Del Nero's distrust of changes, commented that the outcome of *alterazioni* might be that "the authority of the ruler [is] increased by the civil disturbances".[19]

After the *Dialogue* was written, Florence underwent still more political changes, which drew the attention of Bodin as he wrote his long treatises on history, law, and politics, *Method for the Easy Examination of Histories* (in Latin, 1566), and the *Six Books of the Republic* (in French, 1576). Bodin was especially interested in political change as the outcome of the mutable nature of political orders. No country, he saw, had undergone quite so many changes as Italy, and Machiavelli, Guicciardini, and several other Italian historians therefore accounted for much of his reading.[20]

Quoting Herodotus, Bodin referred to the well-known tripartite classification of regimes and their corresponding corrupted forms, the latter phases being more subject to the "winds of civil strife". But all regimes could be affected by instability on account of the passage of time. Their various combinations gave rise to six perfect changes and six imperfect changes. Given that, as theologians and philosophers agreed, nothing in this world happened by chance, Bodin wrote that the causes of "the changes and ruin of the commonwealth" might be divine, human, or natural. Though in the last case, natural causes such as climate or geography were questions of God's will, human will was free, theologians averred, with Bodin arguing cautiously, "at least with regard to the civil realm". Given that human will was mutable and uncertain, it was impossible to base upon it any opinion regarding the changes and ruin that states might undergo in the future. But this stark uncertainty was offset with chronological patterns throughout time, whose recurrences and regularities

19 *Ibidem*, 7, 48, 79, 81.

20 Quaglioni, "Il 'secolo di ferro'", 340–2; Howell A. Lloyd, *Jean Bodin, "This Preeminent Man of France": An Intellectual Biography* (Oxford: Oxford University Press, 2017), 85, 127–8.

Bodin carefully outlined in a demonstration of his well-known passion for numerology.[21]

The origin of such changes might be external, as in the case of foreign invasion, or internal, such as an illness suffered by the body politic. As for their nature, this might consist of a *changement de république* or *état*, on the one hand, or of *lois*, on the other. The latter would amount to only an *alteration*, given that sovereignty would remain intact. Bodin drew up lists of causes for change: in the *Method* he mentioned the abolition of slavery (because emancipation led to great poverty which brought about changes) and religious differences, while in the *Six Books* he offered a longer list including interruptions in royal succession – a circumstance that prompted quarrels among nobles for the control of the state–, grandees' ambitions, too much wealth or poverty, unfair distribution of offices and honours, acts of revenge among factions, foreign interference, and changes in laws or religion. Along with commonplaces, in this second list one can detect the instability of contemporary France. Elsewhere, in a passage on tyranny, Bodin mentioned another sort of change: while categorically denying that subjects had the right to resist or commit tyrannicide, he admitted that a foreign prince might intervene to overthrow a tyrant.[22]

In other words, there was a notable variety of possible constitutions, leading Bodin to admit: "The ancient question of wise politicians is yet not well resolved, namely, whether a new law, even if better than the old one, should be preferred to an old law, because as good as it may be, it is worth nothing if it carries a contempt of itself". New laws, he argued, must be strong enough to be enacted, but continuity in old laws bestowed authority upon them. In short, "there is nothing more difficult to deal with, nor more doubtful to succeed, nor more dangerous to manage, than to introduce new ordinances", an advice in terms very close to that of Machiavelli quoted above. Additionally, "every change of law that touches the state is dangerous" because that would affect the foundations thereof. But the same thing happened when laws were changed, evoking "the ancient maxim of wise politicians" that a stable republic's laws should not be changed even in an effort to improve them. In the case of truly necessary changes, it was best to imitate nature and proceed slowly.[23]

---

21 Bodin, *Les six livres*, book 2, ch. 2, 27; book 4, ch. 1, 12, 52. On the chronological patterns see Lloyd, *Jean Bodin*, 74.

22 Bodin, *Les six livres*, book 4, ch. 1, 1, 8, 16–7, 37; ch. 3, 100; book 2, ch. 5, 80; Lloyd, *Jean Bodin*, 86, 149.

23 Bodin, *ibidem*, book 4, ch. 3, 101. For Machiavelli's quote, see n. 7.

In his chapters devoted to change, Bodin did not mention uprisings by cities or by part of the body politic, concentrating instead on the whole republic. As we have seen, he did mention local revolts when discussing corporations. In another passage on rebellions, he heartily recommended that the prince cut them off at the roots.[24] A rebellion immobilized before it got going, it would seem, would not develop into a situation requiring later legal modifications in the dissident political entity.

England during the Rising of the North of 1569–70 would seem to confirm this assumption. The uprising, inspired by Catholics and put down relatively quickly with hundreds of executions, was followed by an intense campaign of printed and oral homilies preaching political and religious obedience to the crown and discrediting resistance not only because it was illegal but because it was useless. Elizabeth I's position was strengthened with a conformist discourse blending loyalty to kingdom, nation, and the Anglican Church.[25] However the fusion of politics and religion might also inspire opposition, as occurred famously with the Dutch Calvinist resistance to Philip II, summarized neatly in William of Orange's *Apology* of 1581.

In this context, it comes as no surprise that political writers reflecting the dominant currents of neo-Tacitism and reason of state showed growing interest in rebellions, their causes, and their remedies. The old question of conservation, which Machiavelli had understood above all to apply to government rule, was now everywhere a matter of great interest and concerned the body politic as a whole. Giovanni Botero fully embodied this new stage; in the first few pages of *Della ragion di stato* (1589) he outlined the causes of the ruination of states and, like Guicciardini before him and Francis Bacon and Hobbes later on, he distinguished between the intrinsic and the extrinsic. Among the former were "envy, rivalry, discord, ambition among the great, fickleness, inconstancy and passion in the people and the inclination of both to favor a different rule". Revolts against the prince, whether by nobles or commoners, were clearly included in this list. Elsewhere Botero returned to the issue of popular rebellions by discussing how to avoid them: the ruler "must remove whatever may occasion and facilitate rebellion". But he said nothing about how to confront them nor, once they were extinguished, about punishment and the subsequent political situation. Generally speaking, he recommended "the avoidance of novelty" in matters of politics and government, because changes

24 Bodin, *ibidem*, book 4, ch. 4, 112–3.

25 Kevin Sharpe, *Selling the Tudor Monarchy: Authority and Image in Sixteenth-Century England* (New Haven: Yale University Press, 2009), 345–7, 351–2, 402; Glenn Burgess, *British Political Thought, 1500–1660* (Basingstoke: Palgrave, 2009), 96–9.

generally inspired resentment. But if they were necessary, he recommended – as Bodin had – that they be slow and imperceptible.[26]

Justus Lipsius offered more detailed analyses in his *Six Books on Politics*, also from 1589. An eyewitness to relentless religious and political conflicts in the Low Countries and an admirer of Roman civil and military discipline, Lipsius subscribed to the commonplaces of inherent instability in all states and the advisability of punishing a few to quell the many, but he stood out for preaching moderation as the best recipe for stability. He acknowledged that in some cases – for example if powerful individuals committed treason – then punishment must be severe, but he advised the prince not to over-use *crimen laesae maiestatis*. Elsewhere he stated that if vassals enjoyed privileges that undercut princely authority, the prince could violate those privileges, though here he did not mention the aggravating factor of rebellion as a justification. He devoted considerable space to warning that excessive punishment could be counterproductive, as it endangered political stability, and he repeatedly recommended that reprisals be delayed or reined in. For the sake of the *constantia* Lipsius so frequently invoked, he also favored respecting existing laws instead of enacting new ones, even if they might be regarded as an improvement.[27]

The last of Lipsius's six books was devoted to civil war, which he defined as a "war started by [the prince's] subjects against the prince or among each other". The immediate causes were factionalism, rebellion (*seditio* in Latin), and tyranny. He defined rebellion in almost the same way as he did civil war: "A sudden and violent action of the populace against the prince or magistrate". His association of rebellion with civil war might reflect contemporary events in France and the Low Countries, where the former had led to the latter. In any case, he stated that civil strife could end in two ways: "by a pact and by victory" and he argued in favor of the former: "To me, every peace with fellow citizens seems to be more advantageous than civil war, even if [the peace] is temporary and insufficiently strong". Moreover, he warned, "victory produces many evils, as well as most certainly tyranny".[28]

26 Giovanni Botero, *The Reason of State*, translation by P.J. and D. P. Waley (New Haven: Yale University Press, 1956). The quotations are from book 1, part 4, 5; book 4, part 1, 82; and book 2, part 8, 51.

27 Justus Lipsius, *Politica: Six Books of Politics or Political Instruction*, bilingual ed. and translation by Jan Waszink (Assen: Royal Van Gorcum, 2004), 393–5, 411, 427–9, 451, 459, 465–7, 471, 475, 529, 689.

28 *Ibidem*, book 6, chs. 1–7, 667, 679, 705–7. Note that tyranny appears both as a cause and as a probable outcome of civil war.

This opinion can be added to those we saw earlier that linked the defeat of sedition with strengthened royal authority. But Lipsius's principal goal, good Stoic that he was, was to provide political lessons regarding prudence and morality, always with the aim of practical instruction. Attention to these themes was a feature of the first treatises on the jurisprudence of war. Baltasar Ayala, a Catholic, and Alberico Gentili, a Protestant, both of them influenced by Bodin, believed that a rebel was not a *legitimus hostis* and therefore was not protected by the laws of war and deserved harsher punishment. Specifically, Ayala thought the Roman practice of disarming rebels was a measure that could be used to pacify and punish Dutch Calvinists, while Botero wrote that that conflict as well as the French Wars of Religion were encouraging the use of weapons among subjects, which could favor revolts.[29]

Thus, these writers considered – sometimes in a rather undifferentiated way – the causes of revolts, measures to avoid them, how to resolve them once under way, and, with fewer details, the situation that emerged as a result. This was not the case, however, with Francis Bacon, who in his well-known essay, "Of seditions and troubles" (1625), concerned himself only with preventative measures.[30] In contrast, Johannes Althusius produced possibly the most detailed treatment concerning this issue, chapter 31 of his *Politica methodice digesta* (1603 and 1614), called "How to Preserve Peace (*concordia*)". Heavily based on Biblical passages along with quotes from Bodin (especially book 4 of the *Six Books*), the Bodin disciple Pierre Grégoire, Botero, and, to a lesser extent, Lipsius, Althusius outlined a vast range of situations and the appropriate measures for each of them from punishing perpetrators of the *crimen laesae maiestatis*, disarming rebels, and constructing fortresses from which to suppress them, on the one hand, to, on the other, pacifying rebels with gifts, calming rulers down, increasing or diminishing punishments, and other measures designed to calm the waters. "Revenge must be tempered, and above all one must keep security in mind", he declared; it was desirable to seek agreement through pacts and mediation even if the peace were temporary and unstable, a judgement previously put forward by Lipsius. The classical world was always a good guide, from Greek *amnistia* to Roman *decimatio*.

29 On Ayala, Gentili and others, see Xavier Gil, "Guerra justa y derechos de guerra a finales del reinado de Felipe II: la obra de Baltasar de Ayala (1582)", in Alberto Marcos and Carlos Belloso, eds., *Felipe II ante la historia: Estudios de la Cátedra Felipe II en su 50 aniversario* (Valladolid: Universidad de Valladolid, 2020), 262ff; Botero, *The Reason of State*, book 9, part 2, 171.

30 Francis Bacon, "Of seditions and troubles", in *The Essayes or Counsels,Civill and Morall*, ed. Michael Kiernan (Oxford: Clarendon, 2000), ch. 15, 43–50.

Althusius used the concept of *multitudo delinquens* and carefully pointed out the particular gravity of revolts led by dignitaries, provincial governors, and local authorities, but he did not mention the suppression of provincial and municipal privileges. Rather, in a general way, he recommended that no legal innovations be undertaken and that those who were overly enthusiastic about novelties be punished.[31]

Rigor and leniency, as well as (despite Machiavelli) a combination of the two, could be found in the pages of these treatises and, increasingly, in the minds of rulers as the Thirty Years' War caused serious dislocations to the governments of the belligerent nations. Adam Contzen in 1629 and Johann Wilhelm Neumair von Ramsla in 1632 wrote about the unrest, considering it alongside taxation and economic development. A bit later, in 1639, Gabriel Naudé made a singular contribution with his notion of *coups d'état*, which he differentiated from the *maximes* or *raison d'état*. Though the definition was the same ("an excess of common right, for the public good … bold and extraordinary actions that princes are forced to carry out in difficult and desperate cases against the common right without keeping even any order or form of justice"), the difference lay in the fact that coups were planned in secret and their execution preceded their justification.

One reason a *coup d'état* might be legitimate, Naudé wrote, was the following: "When it concerns weakening or breaking certain rights, privileges, franchises, and exemptions which some subjects enjoy to the prejudice and diminishment of the prince's authority". As an example, he offered that of Philip II and the Aragonese constitutional uprising of 1591. In that case, the king, wishing to abolish Aragon's privileges, which cut into his own authority, used Jesuits to stir up a popular uprising in favor of the privileges, during which time the king raised an army. Next, again with the help of the Jesuits, who by then were defending the angry king and pointing to the rebels' weaknesses, the monarch unloaded his full arsenal: executions, banishments, demolition of homes, construction of a fortress, and the general ruin of the province, which as a result "is now the most subjected and most submissive of the king of Spain's provinces".[32]

Neither Naudé's account of the events nor his conclusions concorded with reality. But in any case, a similar machination had been considered a few years

31 Juan Altusio, *Política metódicamente concebida e ilustrada con ejemplos sagrados y profanos*, ed. and translation Primitivo Mariño (Madrid: Centro de Estudios Constitucionales, 1990), ch. 31, 438–54, numbers 69, 71.

32 Gabriel Naudé, *Considérations politiques sur les coups d'état* [Rome, 1639], ed. Frédérique Marin and Marie-Odile Perulli (Paris: Les Éditions de Paris, 1988), 101–118.

earlier, when the Count-Duke of Olivares wrote his "Great Memorial" for the young Philip IV in 1624. His project of strengthening the king's authority both domestically and abroad involved legislative harmonization among the kingdoms of the Spanish monarchy. He proposed three ways of achieving this goal, the third of which ("not as justifiable, but the most efficient") consisted in the king visiting one of his kingdoms duly accompanied by troops, stirring up a popular revolt and then, with the pretext of restoring order, using all his force to impose Castilian law.[33]

Olivares had read his Tacitus and was fond of maxims that encapsulated the rules of government. But he was also well aware that the changing nature of government "makes it necessary to one day have one opinion and the next day have an entirely different one", as he admitted in his memorandum to Philip IV.[34] The art of politics, especially during wartime, required adapting rules to a multitude of circumstances and eventualities. Writers and rulers were immersed in this inevitable ambivalence, and therefore it is no surprise that contemporary political practice provides us with examples, some of them contradictory, of measures taken after revolts.

3

Several cases illustrate the variety of responses by princes and rulers whose authority had been challenged. Beginning with punitive measures, a few cases stand out. Charles V's repression of his birthplace, the city of Ghent, in 1539–40, was especially notable given the city's turbulent history of uprisings. It was now subject to the usual array of punishments: execution of local leaders, the suppression of municipal privileges, and the construction of a fortress. Similar examples can be found with the revolt of Urbino against Duke Guidobaldo della Rovere in 1572–73, which ended with loss of privileges and the establishment of a harsh judicial regime; and the resistance by various French towns – the Huguenot base of La Rochelle (1628), Marseilles (1660), and Rennes, during the *bonnets rouges* rebellion (1675) – against Louis XIII and Louis XIV, which all also lost their privileges. Another clear example of punishment was Messina, declared a *universitas delinquens*, with the additional aggravating factor of having conspired with the French (1674–78). Additionally, Bohemia's "new

33 John H. Elliott, José F. de la Peña, and Fernando Negredo, eds., *Memoriales y cartas del Conde Duque de Olivares*, 2 vols. (Madrid: Centro de Estudios Europa Hispánica and Marcial Pons, 2013) [revised ed.], vol. 1, doc. 4, 121–2.

34 *Ibidem*, 79, 120.

constitution" in 1627 put an end to the religious tolerance extended in 1609 and also established new measures clearly favorable to Habsburg authority: hereditary royal succession, greater abilities for the emperor to appoint officials and enact laws, and the use of German along with Czech. The severe new constitution was imposed after several years of forcible land transfers and emigration, and it was succeeded in 1629 by the Edict of Restitution concerning ecclesiastical properties.

These and similar cases show that successfully putting down municipal or provincial revolts might clear the way for punishments constituting an important step toward the consolidation of the monarchy's authority, with fiscal and religious repercussions as well. The inverse examples make the same point: the duke of Alba's failure to put down the Dutch, leading to his replacement in 1573, was clearly a setback in this regard.

Still other factors came into play in the above-mentioned cases in later years. William of Orange restored Ghent's municipal privileges in 1577, but the city did not return to its former existence; rather the prince established a new, long-lasting order. The new duke in Urbino issued a pardon and undertook to reconcile with the city. In Bohemia, the new constitution benefitted from a wide range of more general factors including the *pietas austriaca*, pro-Catholic campaigns in Central Europe, and changes in local society. In Messina, as well, relationships with authority evolved toward renewed cooperation. In all these cases, after experiencing periods of crime and punishment, both the absolute monarchy and the local ruling groups had to figure out ways of managing the new circumstances.[35]

But there are other cases that show that the defeat of a rebellion and a strengthening of absolutism might not be quite so clearly linked, and in fact might not be linked at all, at least with regard to punitive political reforms. Some rulers opted not to punish rebels to the extent permitted by the laws or counseled by treatise writers, choosing restraint instead, which, as we have seen, was an option favoured by some treatises. One can assume that many varied factors went into these choices: the ruler's character, the degree of victory he enjoyed over the rebels, operative capacity in the current circumstances, the geopolitical situation of the region, other priorities, distance, contingency, etc. In any case, just as the absence of revolt during times of crisis is as eloquent as the revolt itself, cases in which rebellions were not followed by

35 Geoffrey Parker, *The Dutch Revolt* (Harmondsworth: Penguin, 1979), 185–6; De Benedictis, *Tumulti*, 97; R. J. W. Evans, *The Making of the Habsburg Monarchy, 1550–1700: An Interpretation* (Oxford: Clarendon Press, 1979), 70, 198–200; Luis A. Ribot, *La Monarquía de España y la guerra de Messina (1674–1678)* (Madrid: Actas, 2002), 612–5, 622–7.

notable changes in political organization can also be significant. For a proper analysis, one must distinguish between executions and physical repression, as a first step, and constitutional changes, as a possible second step.

Juan II of Aragon was unusually benign with the Generalitat of Catalonia, Barcelona, and other cities and their respective officials when he won the civil war of 1462–72, during which he had been repudiated by Catalan authorities and supplanted by other princes. The Capitulation of Pedralbes, in 1472, omitted any reference to the events, and a generous general pardon ended the conflict.[36] The defeat of the urban uprising of the Comunidades in Castile in 1521 against Charles V was a military one that brought about transformations in Castilian political life, but the institutional system itself did not undergo formal modification. Rather, when Charles returned to Spain after being proclaimed emperor, he adopted the rebels' political program, in large part putting it into effect though, of course, under the crown's firm control. In the medium run, Castilian cities consolidated their role as the principal political protagonists.[37] By the same token, Aragon after the 1591–92 uprising against Philip II did not undergo a constitutional dismantling; rather, the king, with the support of the Cortes, implemented a few critical changes aimed at ensuring social stability under stronger crown rule, measures decisively aided by the new attitude of the Aragonese ruling class, which had been chastened by the grave events.[38] Henry IV of France in 1598 put an end to the Wars of Religion with a combination of measures ranging from the conquest of towns such as Amiens and the elimination of their municipal privileges, to the direct purchase of loyalty and, of course, the promulgation of the Edict of Nantes for the benefit of the Huguenot minority. Occasionaly he restituted urban privileges, a gracious measure with which he exercised not only the virtue of clemency but also, and more precisely, absolute power. The variety of local situations and degrees of loyalty was such that there was no single solution, though one commonality was that the crown backed the rise of oligarchies in municipal government (especially in Limoges after a tax revolt), which aided general pacification.[39]

36 Alan Ryder, *The Wreck of Catalonia: Civil War in the Fifteenth Century* (Oxford: Oxford University Press, 2007), 222–5.

37 Stephen Haliczer, *The Comuneros of Castile: The Forging of a Revolution, 1475–1721*, (Madison: University of Wisconsin Press, 1981), 205–6 and ch. 9; Pablo Sánchez León, *Absolutismo y comunidad: Los orígenes sociales de la guerra de los comuneros de Castilla* (Madrid: Siglo XXI, 1998), 236–8.

38 Xavier Gil, "Crown and Cortes in Early Modern Aragon: Reassessing Revisionisms", *Parliaments, Estates and Representation*, 13 (1993), 109–22.

39 A. Annette Finley-Croswhite, *Henri IV and the Towns: The Pursuit of Legitimacy in French Urban Society, 1589–1610* (Cambridge: Cambridge University Press, 1999); Olivia Carpi,

Well into the seventeenth century, and with increasing wars and domestic political instability, there were more than a few cases in which kings and rulers were forced to or chose to give in to rebels at one point or another and grant their fiscal or political demands, just as there were concessions after religious conflicts, resulting in *de facto*, if not *de iure*, religious tolerance. While the principle of *necessitas* had pushed governments to intensify demands on local and provincial powers, such demands were often met with resistance, but now that same *necessitas* forced them to give in, willingly or otherwise. Dissimulation and the hope that things might be more favorable for them in the future led rulers to concede and appease with short-term measures that sometimes became permanent. This can be seen with the revolts that broke out in the Spanish monarchy during a period when wars were being fought on multiple fronts: Palermo (1647), Naples (1648), and Barcelona (1652). Elsewhere, tax concessions were used to forestall greater uprisings in areas affected by grain riots.[40] This was most evident with two kings, Philip IV of Spain and Charles II of England, who, with the aim of recovering kingdoms they claimed, solemnly declared their willingness to rule them in accordance with their existing laws and customs; the former did this unsuccessfully in 1658 with Portugal, and the latter did so successfully in 1660 with the better known Declaration of Breda.

Such concessions might turn out to be counterproductive in that they might encourage others to rebel: rulers, feared that outcome,[41] and treatise writers were likewise aware of this. Bodin made a comment to that effect in his long list of rebellions, running from the Old Testament to Rome to the recent past, to which kings and princes responded with what he considered to be either excessive cruelty or excessive leniency. He resolved that the best solution was the intermediate one, "which is the means of true justice, as law should be

---

"L'exception comme instrument de pacification: le roi et la privation des privileges urbains au temps de la Ligue (France, 1589–1596)", in Junot and Soen, eds., *Confisquer, restituer, redistribuer*, ch. 2.

40 Geoffrey Parker, *Global Crisis: War, Climate Change and Catastrophe in the Seventeenth Century* (New Haven: Yale University Press, 2013), 286, 398, 439–40, 528–32; Rosario Villari, *Un sogno di libertà: Napoli nel declino di un impero, 1585–1648* (Milan: Mondadori, 2012), 534, 540, 546; Ruth MacKay, "Catalonia, revolt of", in Jonathan Dewald, ed., *Europe, 1450 to 1789: Encyclopaedia of the Early Modern World* (New York: Charles Scribner's Sons, 2002), vol. 1, 209–10. See also Gibran Bautista Lugo, "*Constantia et clementia.* El lenguaje de la gracia real en cuatro ciudades en rebeldía: Quito, México, Nápoles y Barcelona (1592–1652)", *Pedralbes. Revista d'Història Moderna* 40 (2020), 211–56.

41 John H. Elliott, "Rebellion", in Evonne Levy and Kenneth Mills, eds., *Lexicon of the Hispanic Baroque: Transanlantic Exchange and Transformation* (University of Texas Press, Austin, 2013), 275; Parker, *Global Crisis*, 264, 270, 283, 424, 528.

respected when offenses are punished, both if it is a matter of punishing a multitude acting as a political body [*communeauté*] or not".[42]

Though Bodin had witnessed religious civil war in his country, his attitude toward the question was above all scholarly. In contrast, Diego Saavedra Fajardo, a diplomat and writer who played an important role in drawing up the Peace of Westphalia, displayed a more sensitive understanding of the contradictory demands of the real world, which he knew first-hand after living in Central Europe. Like other writers, he paid attention to sedition, for example in his *Idea of a Politico-Christian Prince Represented in One Hundred Emblems* (1640; revised edition, 1642), warning that rioters always asked for more. In a more precise vein, he argued that when the people, "under the pretext of freedom and conservation of privileges", dared to challenge the prince's authority, it was best "not to play down the importance of their contempt" lest they sense encouragement. But he also said the prince must always be inclined toward pardons, especially when "it is the multitude that sins", and he furthermore recognized that deceit might be licit. "In large cases there is rarely any remedy without some injustice, which is offset by the common good", he wrote. Sedition and civil war were such grave events, he concluded, "it is prudent to resolve them at any price".[43]

Such ambivalence was inevitable for a Tacitist writer such as Saavedra Fajardo. Hobbes, on the other hand, was more resolute. Once the Leviathan had been constituted through the exercise of reason, achieving sovereignty through rebellion was contrary to reason. "Rebellion is war renewed", he wrote, the collapse of the community, and the return to original war. For that reason, punishment must be all the more severe. John Locke employed the same image, with a notable difference: rebels act in opposition to the laws of the kingdom and likewise "bring back again the state of war".[44]

Hobbes and Locke believed rebellion was tantamount to warfare, and indeed there was a relationship between the two in practice, though not always in a cause-and-effect manner.[45] Similarly, nor was the connection between rebellion and increased princely authority a mechanical one, through the medium- and long-run tendency went in that direction, with the assistance of other cultural and social factors. As we know, obedience and resistance, whether

42 Bodin, *Les six livres*, book 3, ch. 7, 200.

43 Diego de Saavedra Fajardo, *Idea de un príncipe político-cristiano representada en cien empresas*, ed. F. Javier Díez de Revenga (Barcelona: Planeta, 1988), *empresa* 73, 509–17.

44 Hobbes, *Leviathan*, ch. 28, 219; John Locke, *Two treatises of government*, ed. Peter Laslett (Cambridge: Cambridge University Press, 2003), ch. 19, n. 226, 416.

45 Parker, *Global Crisis*, 53–4.

as arguments or conduct, were not incompatible, a situation encouraged by the coexistence of diverse legal systems. A clear example was military recruitment: invoking the language of obedience, Castilians up to a point managed to evade military duty by using litigation, delays, and outright breaches of duty, always pointing to the contractual nature of political power.[46]

From the ambivalence of principles to the casuistry of their materialization in practice, revolts were a main feature in both reflection and action in the early modern era. Writers and rulers both, faced with the prospect of revolt, had to carefully examine what the constitutive foundations of their polities were and which reformulations might be admissible.[47] A victorious revolt or revolution marked a clear constitutional moment for the newly formed regime. Likewise, a failed revolt created its own constitutional moment, opening up opportunities to tinker with the prevailing order. Writers and political actors faced with this opportunity responded in different ways, and though their words were not as visible as revolutionary upheaval, they were no less eloquent.

Bibliography

Main Sources

Bodin, Jean, *Les six livres de la république*, ed. Cristiane Frémont, Marie-Dominique Couzinet, and Henri Rochais (Paris: Fayard, 1986) [facs. of the 1576 ed.].

Guicciardini, Francesco, *Dialogue on the Government of Florence*, ed. and translation by Alison Brown (Cambridge: Cambridge University Press, 1994).

Lipsius, Justus, *Politica: Six books of politics or political instruction*, bilingual ed. and translation by Jan Waszink (Assen: Royal Van Gorcum, 2004).

Machiavelli, Niccolò, *The Prince*, ed. and translation by David Wootton (Indianapolis and Cambridge: Hackett, 1995).

Saavedra Fajardo, Diego, *Idea de un príncipe político-cristiano representada en cien empresas*, ed. F. Javier Díez de Revenga (Barcelona: Planeta, 1988).

46 Andrew Wood, *Riot, Rebellion and Popular Politics in Early Modern England* (Basingstoke: Palgrave, 2001), 38–48; Ruth MacKay, *The Limits of Royal Authority: Resistance and Obedience in Seventeenth-Century Castile* (Cambridge: Cambridge University Press, 1999), 3–4, 9, 13, 59, 99, 161ff, 174.

47 Laura Manzano Baena, *Conflicting Words: The Peace Treaty of Münster (1648) and the Political Culture of the Dutch Republic and the Spanish Monarchy* (Leuven: Leuven University Press, 2011), 30, 236.

Main Bibliographical References

De Benedictis, Angela, *Tumulti: Moltitudine rebelli in età moderna* (Bologna: Il Mulino, 2013).

Elliott, J.H., "Rebellion", in Evonne Levy and Kenneth Mills, eds., *Lexicon of the Hispanic Baroque: Transanlantic Exchange and Transformation* (Austin: University of Texas Press, 2013).

Junot, Yves; and Violet Soen, eds., *Confisquer, restituer, redistribuer: Punition et réconciliation matérielles dans les territorires des Habsburg et en France* (*XVIe et XVIIe siècles*) (Valenciennes: Presses Universitaires de Valenciennes, 2020).

Parker, Geoffrey, *Global Crisis: War, Climate Change and Catastrophe in the Seventeenth Century* (New Haven: Yale University Press, 2013).

CHAPTER 7

Accommodatio in the Jesuit Constitutions

Jaska Kainulainen

In this chapter, I focus on aspects of Jesuit *Constitutions* that reflect the Jesuit principle of *accommodatio* ('adaptability'). "Constitution" is used here to mean "the basic principles and laws of a nation, state, or social group" that contain "the fundamental rules of a political or social organization".[1] It is a commonly held notion that constitutions embody a set of fixed rules which are difficult to change. In line with these observations, Ignatius Loyola regarded Jesuit constitution as a collection of rules which dealt with issues that were "important, permanent, and applicable at all times and places", and, although General Congregations of the Society of Jesus have made changes to the *Constitutions*, these changes have nevertheless always been formulated as decrees of a given General Congregation and thus separate from the original, sixteenth-century *Constitutions*.[2] It has been pointed out, however, that the Jesuits are free to make changes to their *Constitutions* insofar the changes "do not run counter to any major provisions of the bull" *Exposcit debitum*—published in 1550—which contains the so-called *Formula of the Institute*, "the equivalent of 'the Rule' in other religious orders".[3]

Loyola completed the first version of the *Constitutions* between 1547 and 1551.[4] As soon as the draft was completed, he spent several weeks discussing its content and form with such leading Jesuits as Francis Borgia, Diego Laynez, Nicolas Bobadilla and Alfonso Salmerón. Over the next few years, Loyola would continue revising the *Constitutions*, although, aware of the urgent need for unified rules in the rapidly expanding Society, he sent Jérôme Nadal to Sicily, Spain and Portugal to promulgate and explain the existing version of the

1 *Merriam-Webster's Dictionary of Law*, s.v. "Constitution".

2 George E. Ganss, "Introduction", in *The Constitutions of the Society of Jesus*, translated, with an introduction and a commentary, by George E. Ganss (St. Louis: Institute of Jesuit Sources, 1970), 46. All references to the Constitutions are to this edition, giving the paragraph rather than page number.

3 John O'Malley, "Introduction", in John O'Malley *et al.*, eds., *The Jesuits II: Cultures, Sciences, and the Arts, 1540–1773* (Toronto: University of Toronto Press 2006), xxiii.

4 Ganss, "Introduction", 50–1, 53; Silvia Mostaccio, *Early Modern Jesuits Between Obedience and Conscience During the Generalate of Claudio Acquaviva (1581–1615)* (Ashgate: Routledge, 2014), 63.

 | DOI:10.1163/9789004549159_009

Constitutions.[5] Loyola continued to make corrections to the *Constitutions* until his death in 1556. The Spanish version of the *Constitutions* was then ratified at the first General Congregation of the Jesuit order in 1558, and, according to George E. Ganss, published in Polanco's Latin translation in the same year. Silvia Mostaccio notes, however, that the "official Latin version" was only published in 1581 and approved by Gregory XIII in 1583.[6]

Loyola's final version of the Jesuit *Constitutions* consists of four parts: 1) the General Examen, 2) Declarations on the Examen, 3) the Constitutions of the Society of Jesus, and 4) the Declarations of the Constitutions. By '*Constitutions*', it is thus possible to refer specifically to the third part of Loyola's constitutional writings, but, in this study, I refer to the whole, which consists of all four parts listed above. The different parts of the *Constitutions* complement one another and were understood to have equal juridical value.[7]

In what follows I suggest that the Jesuit Constitutions are a flexible set of rules which comply with the principle of *accommodatio*. Furthermore, I suggest that the adaptable nature of the Constitutions reflects some of the key aspects of the early Society of Jesus. As a recent study puts it, the Jesuit *Constitutions* amounted to a "legal fulfilment" of "the legacy of the *Spiritual Exercises*", emphasizing the "development of missionary and pastoral activities" of the Society "according to the practice of *accommodatio*".[8] Jesuits, in keeping with the practice of *accommodatio*, were expected to adapt their speech and activities to pertinent "times, circumstances, and persons", and the *Constitutions* identified such behaviour as "a hallmark of 'our way of proceeding'".[9]

Some passages in the *Constitutions* nevertheless imply a rigid rather than flexible way of thinking. Statements such as the following are worth considering: "as far as possible, we should all think alike and speak alike"; "even in regard to things which are to be done, diversity ... should be avoided as far

5 Nadal's visits were well received, as we can judge from a letter by Michael de Torres (Lisbon, 1553): "*Mucho nos avemos todos consolado con lo que avemos entendido de las constitutiones, especialmente con la viva voz del P. Nadal*" (*Epistolae P. Hieronumi Nadal*, vol. 1, Madrid 1898, p. 774).

6 Ganss, "Introduction". 53; Mostaccio, *Early Modern Jesuits*, 63.

7 Ganss, "Introduction", 35–6.

8 Mostaccio, *Early Modern Jesuits*, 68.

9 John O'Malley, *The First Jesuits* (Cambridge, Mass.: Harvard University Press 1993), 255. In his *Saints or Devils Incarnate? Studies in Jesuit History* (Leiden: Brill 2013), 179, O'Malley defines "our way of proceeding" as something "geared to 'helping souls' ... as they here and now are". This meant that "the details of 'our way of proceeding' had to yield the ultimate principle of accommodation to the needs of the people in front of them". At the same time, O'Malley notes that, by "our way of proceeding", the early Jesuits referred to such "primary documents of the Society" as the *Constitutions*.

as possible". Both of these passages suggest that the *Constitutions* encouraged uniformity and obedience to an extent that would have precluded any aspiration toward a flexible adherence to the rules.[10] It should be noted, however, that these and other similar passages served the *Constitutions*' aim to ensure and maintain the unity of the Society. While the unity of the Jesuit body was an end and a fixed ideal, the means—the everyday activities of the Jesuits and the rules and regulations which guided such activities—maintained a certain degree of flexibility. Both passages also include the qualification "as far as possible", which immediately softens the otherwise categorical nature of the regulation. Rightly, therefore, John O'Malley remarks about the Jesuit *Constitutions* that "almost every provision in that remarkable document is accompanied by qualifications", making it "a document filled with escape-clauses".[11]

While Jesuit activities such as proselytization or zealous engagement in confessional disputes—both activities remarkably hostile to the idea of *accommodatio*—were guided by fixed ideals, in practice the Jesuit "way of proceeding" was marked by adaptability and a belief in the importance of well-functioning governance and hierarchy, "relations of command and obedience", and not necessarily in "laws as such".[12] While the *Constitutions* represented "the laws" of the Society, the need for unity and a functional governance of what had quickly become a global organization necessitated such legislative formulations which did not demand uniform application, but, instead, allowed for adaptation to the pertinent time, place and audience. We should remember that the Jesuits arrived at Goa already in 1542, only two years after the founding of the Society. This means that, from the beginning and already before starting to write the *Constitutions*, Ignatius Loyola had to adapt his vision of the Society to the reality of its global reach.

In the early modern period, Jesuit adaptability instigated accusations of moral laxness and relativism, and Jesuit obedience to the papacy and to the Society's own Superior General only exacerbated the negative qualities that Protestant observers ascribed to the Society.[13] I argue that the characteristic principle of *accommodatio* in their *Constitutions* reflects the sensitivity of early Jesuits to the reality of the Society's challenging position as an organization

10 *The Constitutions of the Society of Jesus*, 273.

11 O'Malley, *Saints or Devils Incarnate?* 41.

12 Harro Höpfl, *Jesuit Political Thought* (Cambridge: Cambridge University Press, 2004), 5.

13 Peter Burke, "The Black Legend of the Jesuits: An Essay in the History of Social Stereotypes", in Simon Ditchfield, ed., *Christianity and Community in the West: Essays for John Bossy* (Aldershot: Routledge, 2001), 165–82; Sabina Pavone, "Between History and Myth: The *Monita secreta Societatis Jesu*", in *The Jesuits II*, 55–8.

whose activities had spiritual and civic implications in both national and transnational contexts, within and without different jurisdictional, cultural and geographic borders. *Accommodatio* and obedience are central principles in Jesuit *Constitutions* and, although they often seem contradictory and even mutually exclusive (the tension between *accommodatio* and obedience is evident for example in the adaptation of Christian practices to Chinese and Indian customs by Jesuit missionaries such as Matteo Ricci and Roberto de Nobili), it was through the interplay and interdependence of *accommodatio* and obedience that the *Constitutions* fulfilled their aim to provide Jesuit order with such regulations that guaranteed the success of their activities in both the spiritual and the civic sphere. While the council of Trent may have adopted "discipline" as its "operative word", the Jesuit approach to obedience was marked by a constant recourse to *accommodatio*.[14]

The successful coupling of the principles of *accommodatio* and obedience in the *Constitutions* guaranteed the establishment and administration of an organization which operated on a transnational level and in regions as remote and varied as India, China and Paraguay. The aim of the *Constitutions* was to guarantee the unity and obedience within the Society, but it also allowed—at least in theory—for members of the Society of Jesus to maintain a check on the Superior General: after declaring that Jesuit superiors "should have much authority over the subjects" and the General "over the individual superiors", the *Constitutions* asserts that "the Society should have much authority over the general" so that, in case "they perform poorly, they may be kept under complete control".[15] As Harro Höpfl points out, however, the Jesuit Superior General was "virtually irremovable and uncontrollable from within the Society" and, regardless of what the *Constitutions* stated about the "authority" that the Society entertained over the Superior General, in practice, these statements were little more than a "mirror for generals" or a collection of "desiderata".[16] Despite the indisputable authority enjoyed by the Jesuit Superior General, the *Constitutions* often delegated authority to other Jesuit superiors. While it is hardly surprising that a global organization should incorporate such delegations of authority in its internal regulations, the fact nevertheless demonstrates how important it was to the Jesuit *Constitutions*—and, in fact, to the

14 O'Malley, *Saints or Devils Incarnate?* 91.

15 Höpfl, *Jesuit Political Thought*, 34; the translation of the relevant passage of the Constitutions is Höpfl's. See also Silvia Mostaccio, "A Conscious Ambiguity: The Jesuits Viewed in Comparative Perspective in the light of Some Recent Italian Literature", *Journal of Early Modern History*,12 (2008), 413.

16 Höpfl, *Jesuit Political Thought*, 35–6.

Jesuit order—that *accommodatio* and obedience were woven into its stipulations in order to adapt the otherwise strict hierarchy of authority to the reality of particular geographic, temporal and interpersonal contexts.

In what follows, I first discuss the nature of Jesuit *accommodatio* with reference to its spiritual, humanistic and global characteristics, demonstrating that Jesuit spirituality encompassed the nucleus of Jesuit adaptability and that Jesuit spirituality was largely incompatible with the notion of fixed and rigid formulations of constitutional texts. Secondly, I suggest that the early Jesuit reception of Renaissance humanism enabled them to envision *accommodatio* as a rhetorical principle and device. I support my discussion of the adaptable nature of Jesuit *Constitutions* with passages that are particularly demonstrative of the principle of *accommodatio*. These passages are written in a way that allows for the circumvention of the regulation stipulated in the passage. Thirdly, I suggest that Jesuit *Constitutions* were shaped by and accommodated the multicultural composition and global reach of the Society. This means that the spiritual, humanistic and global characteristics of the Society guided Loyola's writing of the *Constitutions* and resulted in a remarkably flexible and, consequently, durable collection of organizational rules. I conclude, however, with few remarks on the fact that the *Constitutions* and especially the additional decrees of the General Congregations of the Society were criticized by a number of individual Jesuits.

1 Spiritual, Humanistic and Global Aspects of Jesuit Adaptability

What does Jesuit *accommodatio* or adaptability mean? In his recent study Jeffrey Muller concludes that "Jesuit accommodation was political, and its method was Machiavellian".[17] Muller makes the conclusion in reference to certain events and personalities in the history of the Jesuits—for example, the Jesuit infiltration into the Swedish court in the 1570s—while the main emphasis of his study is on accommodation in the context of overseas missions. In contrast to the reading of Jesuit adaptability in terms of Machiavellian politics, the current study takes its cue from John O'Malley's observations of certain civic and spiritual aspects of Jesuit accommodation. Emphasizing the impact of rhetoric, "good judgment" and spirituality on the formation of Jesuit accommodation, O'Malley argues that the principle of *accommodatio* informs Jesuit

17 Jeffrey Muller, "The Jesuit strategy of accommodation", in Wietse de Boer, Karl A.E. Enenkel and Walter Melion, eds., *Jesuit Image Theory* (Leiden: Brill, 2016), 479. Muller also acknowledges the connection between rhetoric and Jesuit accommodation.

Spiritual Exercises and their *Constitutions*, the latter defining the ideal Jesuit as "a person of sound judgment", and that early Jesuits adopted humanistic rhetoric, which, in turn, was guided by "its imperative for accommodation".[18] Thus, the principle of accommodation manifests in good judgment, which, in turn, is related to the rhetorical principle of arguing on both sides, *in utramque partem*. While the conscious use of accommodation, good judgment and arguing *in utramque partem* was intended for persuasion, it was generally understood during the Renaissance period that 'even the deepest wisdom' needed to be supplemented by "the force of eloquence".[19] Jesuit accommodation thus reflected the Ciceronian ideal of coupling wisdom with the art of persuasion, an ideal, which at once promoted moral virtue and the skill of arguing on both sides of a case or question. Such an approach—i.e., persuasion through accommodation and rhetorically skilled argumentation—was marked by sensitivity to the particular circumstances which varied from place to place, time to time.

As discussed above, *accommodatio* was "a hallmark" of the Jesuit "way of proceeding". The conscious and constant adaptation to time, place and audience was thus an essential characteristic of the Society of Jesus. This principle guided Jesuit spirituality as much as it marked their *Constitutions*. The most important source for Jesuit spirituality is Loyola's *Spiritual Exercises*, which he composed in the 1520s and which was first published in 1548. Being the first Jesuit publication, the *Spiritual Exercises* preceded the *Constitutions* by eleven years. From the point of view of my argument about the flexibility of the Jesuit *Constitutions*, it is therefore important to note that, already in his *Spiritual Exercises*, Loyola instructs his fellow Jesuits to "adapt" the exercises "to the disposition of the persons who desire to make them—that is, to their age, education and ability".[20]

Furthermore, as observed by John O'Malley, the *Spiritual Exercises* are non-prescriptive. They allow room for flexibility in the actual practice of the exercises. Instead of a fixed set of rules that would apply regardless of the character and specific needs of the person going through the exercises, Loyola emphasized the importance of a direct spiritual connection between God and the

---

18 O'Malley, *The First Jesuits*, 81, 112, 145, 255. For a discussion of 'O'Malley's rhetorical principle of accommodation', see Stephen Schloesser, "Accommodation as a Rhetorical Principle: Twenty Years after John O'Malley's *The First Jesuits* (1993)", *Journal of Jesuit Studies*, 1.3 (2014), 347–72.

19 Quentin Skinner, *Reason and Rhetoric in the Philosophy of Hobbes* (Cambridge: Cambridge University Press, 1996), 98–9.

20 *Monumenta Ignatiana series secunda, exercitia spiritualia*, vol. 1, Rome 1969, 157: "*Secundum dispositionem eorum qui volunt recipere exercitia spiritualia, hoc est, secundum eorum œtatem, literas, ingenium, debent eis aptari exercitia*".

person performing the spiritual exercises. In line with the assumption that the exercises were based on this kind of spiritual connection, Loyola instructed the director of the exercises to allow "the Creator to deal directly with the creature and the creature directly with Him".[21] The director of the exercises was thus someone who facilitated rather than prescribed. It has been suggested that these two aspects of the *Spiritual Exercises*—accommodation to the person doing the exercises and the idea that "the Creator" deals directly with the "creature"—show that the *Spiritual Exercises* are "a quintessentially sixteenth-century document" which expresses a "subjective individualism" similar to that of such "religious reformers and humanist rhetoricians" as Luther, Calvin and Erasmus.[22]

Besides the adaptable characteristics of the *Spiritual Exercises*, Jesuit spirituality embraced *accommodatio* through Loyola's reading of the Apostle Paul. When he sent his confreres Paschase Broët and Alfonso Salmerón to Ireland in 1541, Loyola provided them with instructions on how to converse with different kinds of people, asking the two Jesuits to imitate the manners and style of speaking of the people they would encounter in order to observe Paul's dictum: "I was made to be all things to all men".[23] Loyola reiterated this idea later in his correspondence—for example, in a letter to Diego Miro in 1553: "according to our vocation", he wrote, "we must converse with everyone" and follow St. Paul's principle: "I became all things to all men, that I might save all".[24] Similarly, the Jesuit *Constitutions* instructed new members of the order to "seek god ... in all things".[25] This aspiration to become united with all of mankind, to be all things to all men and to see God in all things led Jérôme Nadal to conclude that "the world is our house".[26]

Secondly, besides the accommodating features of Jesuit spirituality, Jesuit adaptability was influenced by Renaissance humanism. For several decades

21 *Monumenta Ignatiana series secunda*, vol. I, 154: "*Quapropter dictanti exercitia standum est in quodam æquilibrio, sinendumque, ut citra medium Creator ipse cum creatura sua, et hæc vicissim cum illo rem transigat*". For O'Malley's observation, see his *Saints or Devils Incarnate?* 124.

22 Schloesser, "Accommodation as a Rhetorical Principle", 356.

23 *Monumenta Ignatiana series prima, epistolæ et instructiones*, vol. I, Madrid 1903, 179: "*En el negociar con todos ... tomar el modo dellos con ellos, porque aquello es lo que les agrada;* omnia omnibus factus sum".

24 *Monumenta Ignatiana series prima*, vol. IV, 627: "*según nuestra vocación, conversamos con todos; antes, según de sí dezia S. Pablo:* omnia omnibus fieri debemus, ut omnes X. lucri faciamus".

25 *The Constitutions of the Society of Jesus*, 288.

26 O'Malley, *The First Jesuits*, 46.

now, historians have studied different aspects of Jesuit humanism.[27] While these aspects include issues relating to language, rhetoric and history, the Jesuit contribution to humanistic ideals and practices was most evident in their system of education. This was a system organized according to the model of the humanist educators of the fifteenth and sixteenth centuries, one that consisted of the *studia humanitatis*—i.e., grammar, poetry, history, moral philosophy and rhetoric. In the Jesuit curriculum, religious writings (including those of the church fathers) were secondary, while the key readings consisted of the writings of such pagan authors as Cicero, Virgil, Sallust, Quintilian and even the comic playwrights Aristophanes and Terence.[28]

How does Jesuit education relate to the idea of *accommodatio*? In short, Jesuit educators introduced their students to the principle of accommodation through the teaching of classical rhetoric and literature. Classical rhetoric taught students of the humanities to consider problems, as we have seen, *in utramque partem* and also stressed the importance of a well-rounded education, which in turn supported the aim of learning to think from different points of view. Classical rhetoric also echoed the imperative to reflect on the specific characteristics of one's audience: Cicero, Quintilian and other champions of classical rhetoric urged their readers to adapt one's speaking and writing to match the audience, to adapt oneself to the time, place and people. While the chief aim of classical rhetoric was to persuade, this could only be achieved, as ancient and Renaissance theorists of rhetoric argued, by addressing the audience according to the principles of *kairos* and *decorum* (i.e., timeliness and appropriateness of speech).[29]

---

27 For example, Marc Fumaroli, *L'âge de l'éloquence: Rhétorique et 'res literaria' de la Renaissance au seuil de l'époque classique* (Geneva: Droz, 1980); O'Malley 1993; Paul Nelles, "Historia magistra antiquitatis: Cicero and Jesuit history teaching", *Renaissance Studies*, 13.2 (1999), 130–72; Robert A. Maryks, *Saint Cicero and the Jesuits: The influence of the liberal arts on the adoption of moral probabalism* (Ashgate: Routledge, 2008); Stefania Tutino, *Shadows of Doubt* (Oxford: Oxford University Press, 2014); Cinthia Gannett and John C. Brereton, eds., *Traditions of Eloquence: The Jesuits and Modern Rhetorical Studies* (New York: Fordham University Press, 2016).

28 On this, see, Hannibal du Coudret's letter to Juan de Polanco (14 July 1551) in *Monumenta pædagogica*, vol. I, Rome 1965, 93–106, and *Monumenta pædagogica*, vol. V, Rome 1986, which contains the 1586, 1591 and 1599 versions of the Jesuit *Ratio studiorum*. For secondary literature on Jesuit education, see François de Dainville, *L'éducation des jésuites, XVIe-XVIIIe siècles* (Paris: Éditions de Minuit, 1978); Aldo D. Scaglione, *The Liberal Arts and the Jesuit College System* (Amsterdam: John Benjamins, 1986); Vincent J. Duminuco, ed., *The Jesuit Ratio Studiorum: 400th Anniversary Perspectives* (New York: Fordham University Press, 2000).

29 For classical rhetoric, see, for example, Thomas Conley, *Rhetoric in the European Tradition* (Chicago: University of Chicago Press, 1990); G.A. Kennedy, *A New History of Classical*

It is easy to see how well these characteristics of classical rhetoric correspond with the Jesuit aim "to be all things to all men". While the fundamental goal of the Jesuit order was to "help souls"—that is, to help other people towards salvation through such ministries as preaching and teaching—the means to achieve this goal was marked by the skilful use of rhetoric and the readiness to accommodate oneself and one's speech to different times, places, and audiences. The need to accommodate became all the more pressing with the rapid expansion of the Jesuit order to Asia, Africa and the Americas. Not only had the Society of Jesus become a global organization, it also encompassed members of different national backgrounds who spoke different languages. This leads to the third and last aspect of Jesuit *accommodatio*: the transnational and global nature of the Society.

Although most of the original companions of Ignatius Loyola were Spanish—the two exceptions being a Savoyard and a Portuguese—the Jesuits quickly embraced new members from different nationalities and established colleges within and without Europe.[30] Today, Jesuits operate in 112 different countries across six continents.[31] Given the quality of sixteenth-century communications technology, how was it possible for a spiritual brotherhood to turn into a successful global and multinational organization, one that managed not only to survive but to remain as a unified and coherent group which worked together on common goals? How is it possible that the Jesuit organization did not falter before the challenge of having members of different nationalities, customs and languages? And if we also consider the ambulatory lifestyle of the Jesuits, often traveling to geographically remote and culturally alien places, it is no mean feat that the order survived its own expansion.

As suggested in this study, the Society's coping with its own rapid expansion depended on the flexibility of its *Constitutions*. Although often stipulating precise regulations with regard to everyday affairs, the *Constitutions* at the same time allowed for local decision-making. Without questioning the leadership of the Jesuit Superior General, the *Constitutions* acknowledged that a global

Rhetoric (Princeton: Princeton University Press, 1994); Brian Vickers, *In Defense of Rhetoric* (Oxford: Clarendon, 1988). On *kairos* and *decorum*, see Phillip Sipiora and James Baumlin, eds., *Rhetoric and Kairos: Essays in History, Theory, and Praxis* (New York: State University of New York Press, 2002).

30 On the expansion of the network of Jesuit colleges, see Oskar Garstein, *Rome and the Counter-Reformation in Scandinavia: Jesuit Educational Strategy, 1553–1622* (Leiden: Brill, 1992), 63–4.

31 John Bowden, *Christianity: The Complete Guide* (London: Continuum, 2005), 1023.

organization could not be managed without the delegation of authority, nor without sufficient room to adapt its rules to different times, places and peoples.

It is a specific feature of the Jesuit *Constitutions* that they were designed and written with the aim to support and maintain an expanding international organization. For example, part eight of the *Constitutions* provides instructions on how to maintain unity in a situation in which the members of the Society are "scattered among the faithful and among the unbelievers in diverse regions of the world", because "the Society cannot be preserved, or governed" unless the members are "united among themselves and with their head".[32] The preamble to the *Constitutions* also states that "the purpose of the constitutions is to aid the body of the Society as a whole and also its individual members toward their preservation and development for the divine glory". In order to achieve the preservation of the Society, the preamble goes on to assert that the *Constitutions* should have the following three characteristics: "first, they should be complete, to provide for all cases as far as possible"; secondly, "they should be clear, to give less occasion for scruples"; and thirdly, "they should be brief, as far as the completeness and clarity allow".[33] These characteristics—completeness, clarity and brevity—issued from the pragmatic need to provide such regulations as could be understood and observed universally, among the Jesuits based in Poland as well as those in India or Ethiopia.

Since a detailed discussion of specific issues was impossible within the *Constitutions*, "completeness"—i.e., the aspiration to cover all possibilities—was achieved by flexibility and (to a certain degree) the delegation of authority. For example, in reference to the countless details involved in the process of sending missionaries, the *Constitutions* states the following: "in regard to all the details, the superior will consider the greater edification of the neighbour and the service of God our Lord and then decide what should be done".[34] Elsewhere, the *Constitutions* states that "it will always be safer for him (i.e., the individual Jesuit) to confer with his nearest superior about the means to be used".[35] In practice, this meant that a Jesuit based, for example, in Goa was encouraged to discuss his problems with the local Jesuit superior rather than with those residing in Rome. With regard to different ways in which the Jesuit houses and colleges could "help their fellowman", the *Constitutions* explicitly states that, "since it could happen in some places", "these means" might

32 *The Constitutions of the Society of Jesus*, 655.

33 *The Constitutions*, 136.

34 *The Constitutions*, 625.

35 *The Constitutions*, 635.

not seem appropriate, unless the local superior specifically "thinks that such means should be used".[36]

2 Accommodatio *in the Jesuit Constitutions*

The expansion of the Society of Jesus to new regions and the undertaking of new ministries such as education resulted in concerns about how to administer such a heterogeneous and global organization. By the 1550s the need for a written constitutional document had become urgent. However, when Loyola finally produced the *Constitutions*, the reception was not all positive. In 1557, the Jesuit Nicolas de Bobadilla complained in a letter to the pope Paul IV that the Jesuit *Constitutions* were, first of all, written solely by an "absolute father and patron", and, secondly, they were a "confused labyrinth", too difficult for the members of the order to understand, let alone to observe.[37] While Bobadilla has been described as "a somewhat controversial figure" in the Society,[38] the more official view of the *Constitutions*, expressed for example by the fifth Jesuit Superior General Claudio Acquaviva was clearly favourable: according to Acquaviva, the *Constitutions* were based on "spirit and celestial light" and consisted of rules that were "complete, clear and perfect".[39] Bobadilla was known for his readiness to challenge his superiors, but the fact that he and Acquaviva held such opposing views on the *Constitutions* might also reflect the different circumstances of a Jesuit priest working alone in foreign territories and the Superior General working alongside close allies, all of whom, in the words of Bobadilla, sat "comfortably in their garden or kitchen in Rome".[40]

Bobadilla's quarrelsome attitude within the Society was precisely what the *Constitutions* sought to eradicate. Aware of the challenges posed to the Society by its multicultural and global characteristics, Loyola furnished the *Constitutions* with reminders of such challenges and with the general advice to apply the principle of *accommodatio:*

36 *The Constitutions*, 646.

37 *Epistolae P. Hieronumi Nadal*, vol. IV, Madrid 1898, 733: "*Le constitutione … le ha fatte solo M. Ignatio, perchè era Padre et padrone absoluto et faceva quanto voleva … Le constitutione e declaratione fatte sonno un laberinto confusissimo, e sono tante, che non bastano, nè li inferiori, nè superiori, a saperli, non che ad observarli*".

38 O'Malley, *The First Jesuits*, 155.

39 Acquaviva, *Ad provinciales societatis, de quibusdam mediis …* in *Epistolæ præpositorum generalium ad patres et fratres societatis* (Antwerp, 1635), 194: "*Habeamus Constitutiones tanto spiritu, ac cœlesti lumine conditas, regulasque tam plenas, claras, atque perfectas*".

40 Quoted in O'Malley, *The First Jesuits*, 334.

> In general, they (future members of the Society) ought to be instructed in the way of proceeding proper to a member of the Society, who has to associate with so great a diversity of persons throughout such varied regions. Hence, they should foresee the inconveniences that may arise and the opportunities that can be grasped for the greater service of God by using some means at one time and others at another.[41]

The principle of *accommodatio* is present already in the beginning of the *Constitutions*, in a section which focuses on the question of who should be admitted to the Society. In his treatment of this question, Loyola first delineates the desirable qualities of candidates—e.g., good judgement, good memory and sufficient physical health—after which Loyola blurs his point by adding that "the more an applicant is distinguished for those qualifications, the more suitable he will be for this Society" and "the less he is distinguished by them, the less suitable he is".[42] The terms "more" and "less" relativize the passage, suggesting that there is no fixed way to measure or deliberate over a candidate's judgement, memory or physical health. While these were desirable virtues, for example in the case of not having many candidates it might have been acceptable for a Jesuit superior to welcome a candidate of "less" distinguished qualities given the Society's ongoing need for new teachers and missionaries. The passage thus demonstrates how *accommodatio*, as incorporated in the *Constitutions*, catered to the pragmatic needs of the Society. The suitability of the candidates was assessed with the help of "testing experiences". These "experiences" could then be "advanced, postponed, adapted" and "replaced by others, according to the persons, times, places and their contingencies".[43]

Nothing is ever spelled out in black and white in the Jesuit *Constitutions*. In case any of the Jesuit superiors—provincials, rectors, visitors and so on—struggled with the ambiguity of a given rule, the *Constitutions* consoled them with the promise that "the holy unction of divine wisdom will teach the means which should be retained in all this to those in charge of the matter".[44] In other words, the *Constitutions* promised that divine wisdom would help the local Jesuit superiors decide which candidates should be admitted to the novitiate. To make the rules on the suitability of individual candidates even more flexible, Loyola concluded that, "if someone lacks one or another of those qualifications" or "if it is judged in the Lord that this lack is compensated for by his

---

41 *The Constitutions of the Society of Jesus*, 414.

42 *The Constitutions*, 161.

43 *The Constitutions*, 64.

44 *The Constitutions*, 161.

other qualities", then "authority to give him dispensation will be possessed by the Superior General" or "by the other superiors to the extent that he has communicated his authority to them".[45]

While the regulations on admitting candidates to the Society were marked with flexibility, it is worth pointing out that the candidates themselves were expected to be of a flexible nature. The Society only welcomed candidates who already demonstrated some degree of *accommodatio* in their personality and way of thinking and expressing themselves. In his list of sixteen desired qualities for future members of the Society, Juan de Polanco ranks flexibility third after academic abilities ("*letras o habilidad*") and good judgement ("*buon juicio*"): "both in speculative and pragmatic reasoning", the candidate "should be flexible", because "hard heads" are "not suitable for the Society".[46] The budding *accommodatio* discerned in new members of the Society was then continuously supported and amplified by the *Constitutions*, the structure of which assumed—in the words of John O'Malley—"emotional and psychological development of the Jesuit from the time he entered until he reached full maturity".[47]

Addressing the question of who can be dismissed from the Jesuit order and in whom the authority to dismiss members of the Society is invested, the *Constitutions* stipulates that such authority resides, firstly, in a General Congregation, secondly, with equal effect, in the Superior General, and, thirdly, each individual member of the order, to the extent that this authority is communicated to them by the Superior General. In terms of communicating such authority to the provincial and local superiors, the *Constitutions* states that "it is wise that it be communicated amply", because clearly established authority contributes to general obedience within the order. However, the *Constitutions* continues, "even if the Superior General communicates ample authority" to individual superiors, "this authority may nevertheless be restricted and limited by means of private letters according to what seems expedient".[48] Offering guidelines on the hierarchy of authority was a crucial aspect of the *Constitutions*. At the same time, however, the addition that such authority may be limited by private letters demonstrates that questions relating to authority and obedience were also approached with a degree of *accommodatio*.

45 *The Constitutions*, 162.

46 *Polanci complementa*, vol. II, 730: "*3.a* (*Flexibilidad*) – *Tanto en el speculativo quanto en el práctico entendimiento, debe ser flexible; porque los más duros de cabeça … no son para la Compañia*".

47 O'Malley, *Saints or Devils Incarnate?* 112.

48 *The Constitutions of the Society of Jesus*, 206–7.

Prior to the publication of the *Constitutions*, individual Jesuits felt the need for regulations which would unify the varying practices of different Jesuit communities. Jesuits such as Bobadilla no doubt thought that the *Constitutions* solved very little in this respect, and it is easy to see why. For example, Juan de Polanco wrote in 1552/1553 that the lack of specific instructions about which books to use had led to an overwhelming variety in the curricula of Jesuit colleges.[49] How was this problem dealt with in the *Constitutions*? Not surprisingly, the *Constitutions* does not contain any specific lists of books which should be used in classrooms. Instead, the rules merely stipulate that, in each faculty, the students should follow "the doctrine" and "authors" that are "safer and more approved". It is then the responsibility of the rectors of Jesuit schools to ensure that the curricula conform "to what is decided on in the Society as a whole for the greater glory of God". More specifically, in so far as "the books of humane letters by pagan authors" are concerned, "nothing immoral should be lectured on", and "what remains can be used by the Society like the spoils of Egypt".[50]

While the *Constitutions* clearly encourages the use of books which comply with Christian doctrine and values, it avoids naming such books, delegating this task to an unspecified authority and time, merely stating that "it is good to determine in detail the books which should be lectured on and those which should not".[51] Instead of addressing Polanco's concerns about the Society's failure to specify which books to use, the *Constitutions* simply reiterates the concern, concluding that, "in each university, these should be individually designated".[52] True to the principle of *accommodatio*, the *Constitutions* states that, while "the master of sentences" (i.e., Peter Lombard) should be lectured on, if "it seems that the students will draw more help from another author", this can "be permitted" after "much weighing of counsel and examination" by "the persons deemed fit in the whole Society".[53] Similarly, the *Constitutions* asserts that, in the humanities, lecturing on "any book which contains matters harmful to good habits of conduct should be avoided *as far as possible*, unless the books are previously expurgated of objectionable matters and words".[54] While the vagueness that marks the *Constitutions* may have stirred frustration

49 *Polanci complementa*, vol. 1, 84: "*No hay hecha determinatión en los libros que se han de usar en la Compañia, de una facultad y de otra; y asi ay variedad harta*".

50 *The Constitutions of the Society of Jesus*, 358–59.

51 *The Constitutions*, 359.

52 *The Constitutions*, 464.

53 *The Constitutions*, 466.

54 *The Constitutions*, 468 (emphasis mine).

among individual Jesuits, in the long run, such flexibility no doubt contributed to the Society's survival under the divergences that emerged due to its own expansion.

Part five of the *Constitutions* discusses the Jesuit novitiate, the period which precedes full membership and which usually lasted more than two years. The *Constitutions* first asserts that such a period "should always be more than two years" but then continues with escape-clauses which declare that the period "can be prolonged" in case "more complete satisfaction" is needed or, just as well, "may be shortened in some cases".[55] Similarly, the *Constitutions* first states that before anyone can be "admitted to the profession" (i.e., full membership), that person should have "exercised himself in theology" for a "four-year period". This statement is, however, followed by the qualification that "one who has sufficient learning" or "other outstanding qualities" can be "admitted to the profession" without "that proficiency".[56] Not only does the qualification justify the circumvention of the rule according to which full membership would necessitate four years of theological experience, it does so in a way that seems to completely discard the point in question—namely, that theological experience is required—by opening the full membership to anyone of "other outstanding qualities". One wonders if, for example, the possession of "outstanding" connections to powerful and wealthy people could compensate for the lack of theological knowledge or experience.

One should not, however, underestimate the impact of the pragmatic needs of the Society on the flexible characteristics of the *Constitutions*. The Society constantly needed new sources of funding and new members to manage the expanding network of Jesuit houses and colleges. On the one hand, the Jesuits were guided by their vow of poverty and their principle of not taking up prelacy or any "position that entailed benefices",[57] while, on the other, they required the means to meet the increasing costs of their organization. In the *Constitutions*, this tension is reflected in the following passage that discusses the question of whether the Jesuits should accept bishoprics: the Society "does not oblige itself to undertake this helpful activity each time" an individual Jesuit is offered a bishopric, "but it remains free to omit this activity or to take it up" depending on whether "it is judged to be of great importance for divine service".[58]

---

55 *The Constitutions*, 514–15.
56 *The Constitutions*, 518–19.
57 O'Malley, *The First Jesuits*, 286.
58 *The Constitutions*, 818.

It should be noted, however, that, while bishoprics were lucrative and influential positions, Jesuits seldom took up such offices. Peter Canisius, for example, refused the bishopric of Vienna in 1554, while Edmund Tanner accepted that of Cork and Cloyne in 1574 (at which point he left the Society of Jesus). Robert Bellarmine, besides becoming cardinal in 1599, was the archbishop of Capua in 1602–1605.[59] According to O'Malley, it happened only once that Loyola violated the principle of rejecting bishoprics: when João Nunes Barreto, Andrés de Ovieto and Melchor Carneiro were nominated bishops of Ethiopia.[60] It was therefore through skilful networking and diplomacy rather than through the taking up of prelacies that the Jesuits maintained their influence among potential patrons of the Society. The way the *Constitutions* discussed the question of bishoprics, however, leaves the door open for a Jesuit bishop, provided such a nomination benefitted "divine service". Although early Jesuits were, in principle, uncomfortable with the idea of becoming prelates, the *Constitutions* implies that the question of bishoprics should always be deliberated on with regard to particular circumstances. The problem of Jesuit bishops was similar to that of Jesuit rectors. In part six, the *Constitutions* reaffirms the ideal of poverty, stating that "the professed should live on alms in the houses" and refrain from holding "the ordinary office of rectors of the colleges or universities of the Society". The statement is, however, immediately followed by the qualification "unless this is necessary or notably useful for these institutions".[61]

Rather than regarding these and other similar passages in the *Constitutions* as further evidence for the stereotype of the Jesuits as Machiavellian tacticians who were keen on promoting their own financial and political interests, I have here sought to approach Jesuit *accommodatio* as a manifestation of the Jesuit sensitivity to the complexities which issued from their own position as a brotherhood whose activities were guided by both religious and civic objectives. The Jesuit *Constitutions* thus reflect the daily balancing act that individual Jesuits performed between the conflicting demands of religious and civic life.

---

59 Giacomo Fuligatti, *Vita del Patre Pietro Canisio della Compagnia di Giesu* (Rome, 1649), 52–3, depicts the misery of Canisius when Paul IV appointed him to the bishopric. With the help of Loyola, Canisius managed to avoid the office, though he temporarily undertook the position of administrator of the diocese of Vienna (O'Malley, *The First Jesuits*, 275). On Tanner, see Thomas McCoog, *The Society of Jesus in Ireland, Scotland, and England, 1541–1588* (Leiden: Brill, 1996), 67, 118. On Bellarmine, see *Biographical Dictionary of Christian Theologians*, ed. Patrick Carey and Joseph Lienhard (Westport: Greenwood Press, 2000), 65.

60 O'Malley, *The First Jesuits*, p. 327.

61 *The Constitutions of the Society of Jesus*, 557.

3 *Jesuit Critics of the* Constitutions

Notwithstanding the adaptable characteristics of the Jesuit *Constitutions*, many early modern Jesuits felt that the *Constitutions* failed to appreciate the heterogeneous and changing nature of the Society. Their criticism was directed against the fact that, in writing the *Constitutions*, Loyola composed rules and regulations which he considered permanent. In his *Discurso de las enfermedades de la Compañia*—first published in French in 1625—the Spanish Jesuit Juan de Mariana (1536–1624) writes that the laws of the Society were created in similar fashion as if "a father", who immediately "after the birth of his son", would prepare all the future clothes for the child so that they would be "cut for all the ages". It would be "a great mistake", Mariana continues, to expect that the son would use clothes which would not fit him. It would be equally mistaken, Mariana concludes, to expect a "Society" which has become 'different from what its founder imagined' to follow "the same laws which were made at the beginning" and "for a different body".[62]

Mariana complains that the Society of Jesus had too many laws and, because it was impossible to "observe all of them", the laws started to lose their authority.[63] Emphasizing the importance of past experience to the process of making laws Mariana remarks that "our laws" are based on "speculation rather than experience" and this, he concludes, is "a fountain of errors and blindness".[64] Having based their laws on speculation rather than experience, the Jesuits constantly needed to revise their legislation. According to Mariana, such revisions

62 Juan de Mariana, *Discurso de las enfermedades de la Compañia* (Madrid, 1768), 217–18: "*Es como si el padre luego que le nace el hijo, le cortáse vestidos para todas las edades ... y sería mayor yerro porsiar á que usáse de aquellos vestidos porque se los dexó su padre cortados. Que si el cuerpo de la Compañia se diferencia de como su Fundador lo imaginó, y trazó, grande yerro sera porsiar que se vista de las mismas leyes, que al principio se hicieron para cuerpo desemejable*". According to Harald E. Braun, Mariana's *Discurso* was first published in French in 1625 and in Spanish only in 1768: *Juan de Mariana and Early Modern Spanish Political Thought* (Aldeshot: Ashgate, 2007), 43.

63 Mariana, *Discurso de las enfermedades*, 216: "*Las Leyes de la Compañia son muchas en demasía; y como no todas se pueden guardar ... á todas se pierde el respéto*". Braun points out that Mariana complained about the "great multitude of laws" already in his *De rege et regis institutione* (1598): *Juan de Mariana*, 43–4.

64 Mariana, *Discurso de las enfermedades*, 85: "*Nuestras leyes ... mas salieron de la especulacion, que de la practica, fuente caudalosa de yerros, y cegueras*". On page 217 de Mariana specifies that this applies in particular to the *Constitutions* and the *Formula of the Institute*: "*La mayor parte ha salido de la especulacion. Por lo menos las Constituciones, y Reglas que se publicaron en Roma año de 1550*".

damaged the authority of their laws.[65] While Mariana's criticism of the Jesuit legislation suggests that he considered the *Constitutions* too rigid, his solution to the problem implies that the principal target of his attack was not the original *Constitutions*, but the subsequent additions and new regulations made by Jesuit superiors and General Congregations. In order to remedy the legislative chaos of the Society, he suggests that the "orders from Rome" should be in line with the *Constitutions* and the *Formula*. This, Mariana continues, was the practice of the Jesuit General Everard Mercurian (1514–80) who did not make "new commentaries on them, or new orders".[66] Although critical of the idea that the Society could have permanent laws, made "speculatively" at the birth of the Society, Mariana nevertheless preferred the original *Constitutions* to the contemporary practice of making new additions to the existing legislation. He seems to be implying that the solution could be found in a flexible observance of the *Constitutions*. This reading of Mariana's comments on the Jesuit legislation suggests that while he may have deemed the *Constitutions* lacking in adaptability, he nevertheless advised his confreres to be flexible when interpreting and applying them to the Society's daily practices.

As Bobadilla's acerbic description of the *Constitutions* as a "confused labyrinth" suggests, early Jesuits found it difficult to interpret the rules and regulations of their Society. Francis Borgia, the third Superior General of the Jesuits, wrote in 1569 that while "discord" can issue from a number of sources, one of its principal causes was the error of "neglecting the spirit of the *Constitutions*".[67] Borgia's remark suggests that he, like Mariana, advocated a flexible reading of the *Constitutions*, one that emphasized the spirit rather than the letter of the document.

The former Jesuit Giulio Clemente Scotti (with the help of the Hungarian Jesuit Melchior Inchofer) criticized the Society of Jesus in the satire *Monarchia solipsorum*, first published in 1645.[68] In the book Scotti remarks sarcastically

---

65 Mariana, *Discurso de las enfermedades*, 216–17: "*Hanse mutado muchas veces en especial las Reglas, cosa que deshache mucho la autoridad de las leyes*".

66 Mariana, *Discurso*, 221–2: "*Que la visita y las ordenes de Roma se enderezasen solo à que las Constituciones y Reglas se guardasen, que es lo que practicaba nuestro Padre Everardo, sin hacer nuevos comentarios sobre ellas, ni nuevas ordenes*".

67 *Monumenta Borgia*, vol. v (Madrid, 1894), 73: "*Aunque por diversas vias y con diversos ardides puede entrar la zizaña en nuestro campo, como uno de los primeros y no menos principales se deve temer el descuido de no guardar el spiritu de las constitutiones*".

68 Sabina Pavone, "The History of Anti-Jesuitism: National and Global Dimensions", in Thomas Banchoff and José Casanova, eds., *The Jesuits and Globalization: Historical Legacies and Contemporary Challenges* (Washington, DC: Georgetown University Press, 2016), 119.

that in the Monarchy of the "*solipsorum*" there are "no legal studies", because all decisions are based on "the authority of the monarch", instead of "laws and reason".[69] It follows from this, Scotti concludes, that "nobody is versed in the laws" of the monarchy, but, instead, laws are discussed in a "confused" manner.[70] The monarchy—ie., the Society of Jesus—is ruled with a great number of laws and "unless some moderation intervenes", this number continues to increase "infinitely".[71] The laws require "that everyone subjects" their "will and judgement" as well as their "intellect and reason" to the "will and judgement of the monarch", to the extent that they "no longer are human beings, but tamed beasts".[72]

Guillaume Pasquelin, another disappointed member of the Society of Jesus, asked in 1614 "are we true or artificial Jesuits" and "if true, why are we different from" the first generation of Jesuits?[73] Discussing the gradual alienation of the seventeenth-century Jesuits from the virtues of Loyola and Francis Xavier, Pasquelin advocates a return to the original agenda of the Society. In order to promote the "renaissance of the early Society", Pasquelin attached the Jesuit *Formula instituti* to his pamphlet.[74] Although Pasquelin does not specifically refer to the *Constitutions*, his contribution to the self-reflective Jesuit literature further demonstrates that seventeenth-century Jesuits longed for a legislative and institutional reform, one that would have restored the original—and, allegedly, simpler—Society of Jesus. For this purpose, it was necessary to refrain from producing further laws and, instead, to return to the original spirit and legislation of the first generation of Jesuits.

---

69 Giulio Clementi Scotti, *Lucii Cornelii Europaei Monarchia solipsorum* (Venice, 1645), 27: "*Iuris studium apud eos nullum, quando iudicia non legibus, & ratione, sed solius Monarchae auctoritate constant*".

70 Scotti, *Monarchia solipsorum*, 35: "*Neminem prorsus Solipsorum leges Monarchiae universim callere, sed confuse de iis loqui, & sentire*".

71 Scotti, *Monarchia solipsorum*, 53: "*Leges, & statuta Solipsorum … abitura in infinita, nisi moderatio intersit*".

72 Scotti, *Monarchia solipsorum*, 58–5: "*Non solum voluntatem omnem, & iudicium suum subdendum esse voluntati, & iudicio Monarchae, sed etiam intellectum, & rationem … non se hominem, sed cicuratam bestiam esse*".

73 Guillaume Pasquelin, *Protocatastasis seu prima Societatis Iesu Institutio restauranda summo Pontifici* (s.l., 1614), 7: V*eri ne sumus an affícti Iesuite, si veri, cur primis dissimiles sumus?*" .

74 Pasquelin, *Protocatastasis*, 13: "*Quo renascentem primam Societatem intueri licebit?*". The *Formula instituti* is on pages 18–21.

4 Conclusion

Besides addressing the pragmatic needs of a multicultural and global organization, the Jesuit *Constitutions*, I have suggested, owed its flexible characteristics to both the spiritual outlook and the humanistic aspirations of the early Jesuits. Following the principle of the Apostle Paul to be "all things to all men" and embracing the flexibility advocated in classical rhetoric and by Renaissance humanists, Loyola and his closest associates envisaged a Society that was marked by pragmatism and adaptability. The integration of the principle of adaptability (*accommodatio*) in the Jesuit *Constitutions* guaranteed the survival of the Jesuit organization during the order's rapid expansion from a small congregation of a few friends into a multinational, global enterprise, one that could only have been effected with and maintained by regulations that carefully aligned a set of clearly stated unified objectives with the pragmatic need to accommodate to different times, places and peoples. However, from the beginning, the *Constitutions* also faced severe criticism from individual members of the Society. Jesuits such as Bobadilla, Mariana, Scotti and Pasquelin claimed that the Society had too many laws and regulations. Their criticism suggests that—from Bobadilla's early remarks in 1557 to Scotti's satire in 1645—some members of the Society called for a simplification of the existing rules and regulations, a restoration of the original, Ignatian spirit and legislation, and a more flexible approach to the *Constitutions*. It seems that rather than in the *Constitutions* themselves, the problem that these critics were pointing at lay in the constantly increasing number of new decrees stipulated by the General Congregations of the Society.

Bibliography

Main Sources

The Constitutions of the Society of Jesus, translated, with an introduction and a commentary, by George E. Ganss (Saint Louis: Institute of Jesuit Sources, 1970).

Monumenta Ignatiana series secunda, exercitia spiritualia, vol. I (Rome, 1969).

Monumenta Ignatiana series prima, epistolæ et instructiones, vol. I (Madrid, 1903).

Mariana, Juan de, *Discurso de las enfermedades de la Compañia* (Madrid, 1768).

Polanci complementa, Epistolae et commentaria, vol. II (Madrid, 1916).

Main Bibliographical References

Fumaroli, Marc, *L'âge de l'éloquence: Rhétorique et 'res literaria' de la Renaissance au seuil de l'époque classique* (Geneva: Droz, 1980).

Ganss, George E., "Introduction", in *The Constitutions of the Society of Jesus*, translated, with an introduction and a commentary, by George E. Ganss (Saint Louis: Institute of Jesuit Sources, 1970).

Höpfl, Harro, *Jesuit Political Thought* (Cambridge: Cambridge University Press, 2004).

O'Malley, John, *The First Jesuits* (Cambridge MA: Harvard University Press, 1993).

Schloesser, Stephen, "Accommodation as a Rhetorical Principle: Twenty Years after John O'Malley's *The First Jesuits* (1993)", *Journal of Jesuit Studies*, 1.3 (2014), 347–72.

CHAPTER 8

The Monarchical Moment

Constitutionalism, Lutheran Political Thought, and the Rise of Danish Absolutism

Brian Kjær Olesen

1

On the eve of the monarchical revolution of October 1660, a party of burghers and clergymen, who called themselves the Conjugates under the Freedom of Copenhagen, walked in procession through the streets of the Danish capital. The spectacle was led by the bishop of Zealand, Hans Svane, who was accompanied by the burgomaster of Copenhagen, Hans Nansen. Their purpose was political, their demand hereditary monarchy. The immediate context surrounding the procession and the demand for hereditary monarchy was the financial recovery of the realm following the wars against Sweden from which the kingdom had barely survived. Frederik III, who had summoned the Estates to Copenhagen, seized the moment. He ordered the gates of Copenhagen closed and doubled the guards, thus entrapping the nobility within the walls of the Danish capital. The nobility realised their defeat and surrendered to the demands for hereditary monarchy. On 13 October 1660, the Council of State was dissolved, and the coronation charter was annulled and returned to the king. On 18 October 1660, representatives of all the estates swore an oath of allegiance to Frederik III and left it up to the king alone to define a new political regime. In January 1661, each estate in Denmark signed an *Act of Sovereignty* that granted absolute power to the king, and by 1662, what began as a political revolution in Copenhagen had reshaped an entire empire, as the estates in Norway, Iceland and the Faroe Islands signed similar acts consenting to the revolutionary changes in the form of government.[1] Nansen and Svane had so

1 Sebastian Olden-Jørgensen, "Enevældens indførelse 1660 – en københavnsk revolution", *Historiske Medelelser fra København* (2011); Michael Bregnsbo and Kurt Villads Jensen, *Det danske imperium*, 2nd edition (Copenhagen: Aschehoug, 2005), 141–43; Michael Bregnsbo, "Copenhagen – the capital of an empire", in Søren Bitsch Chistensen and Jørgen Mikkelsen, eds., *Danish Towns during Absolutism: Urbanisation and Urban Life, 1660–1848* (Aarhus: Aarhus University Press, 2008), 142–43.

 | DOI:10.1163/9789004549159_010

far achieved what they wanted,[2] but they no longer belonged to the circle of people in whose hands the future of the monarchy rested. On 14 November 1665, the constitutional framework of the absolute and hereditary monarchy was codified in the *Lex Regia*, originally drafted by Peder Schumacher, librarian and secretary to the king. Unique amongst contemporary European monarchies, Danish absolutism rested not on the personal ambitions of the monarch, nor on the ebb and flow of power struggles at the royal court, but was founded on a constitutional document, an absolutist monarchical constitution. Danish monarchs thus possessed absolute sovereignty not only *de facto*, but also *de jure*.

The introduction of absolutism in 1660 is a milestone in the history of Danish political thought. Yet three interconnected misconceptions concerning the justification, sources, and nature of Danish absolutism persistently cloud a deeper historical understanding of the main intellectual currents in which the *Lex Regia* was ingrained. As this article argues, prevailing historical interpretations of Danish absolutism are not only misleading, they also fail to address the central issue, namely in what sense monarchical power was considered absolute. Seeking to gain a deeper historical understanding of the Danish theory of absolutism, the article situates the *Lex Regia* in its constitutional and intellectual contexts and recovers a particular strand of Lutheran political thought which in combination with a Bodinian language of sovereignty sheds light on the meaning and scope of Danish absolutism in the seventeenth century.

2

In the sixteenth and early seventeenth century "the Kingdom of Denmark" was considered "a free Elective Kingdom", governed in concert by king and council according to the rights and privileges stipulated in the coronation charter of each monarch.[3] The protagonists of this constitutional order drew on humanist and Lutheran ideas about political authority.[4] Associating princely office

2 Sebastian Olden-Jørgensen, "Den politiske proces på stændermødet 1660", *Historie* (1993).

3 *Samling af Danske Kongers Haandfæstninger og andre lignende Acter* (Copenhagen: Selskabet for Udgivelse af Kilder til Dansk Historie, 1974), 89; Paul Douglas Lockhart, *Denmark 1513–1660: The Rise and Decline of a Renaissance Monarchy* (Oxford: Oxford University Press, 2007), 6–7.

4 Sebastian Olden-Jørgensen, "Scandinavia", in Howell A. Lloyd, Glenn Burgess and Simon Hodson, eds., *European Political Thought, 1450–1700: Religion, Law and Philosophy* (New Haven and London: Yale University Press, 2007).

with moral philosophy, especially humanist and Philippist writers emphasised the classical and Christian virtues of the monarch. The towering figure within this tradition of thinking was Niels Hemmingsen, a Christian humanist of Philippist leaning. In his *De Lege Naturæ Apodicitica Methodus* (The Law of Nature based on the Apodictic Method), first published in Wittenberg in 1562, Hemmingsen sets out to show "how far reason can go without the prophetic and apostolic word".[5] Moral philosophy, on Hemmingsen's account, is thus not founded on scriptural sources, but on the precepts of natural law, which further informs the Decalogue. Drawing especially on humanist and Ciceronian conventions, he argues that the prince must be in possession of the four cardinal virtues, "prudence, temperance, fortitude, and justice", for it is by these virtues that "human society is preserved, that is, households and polities".[6] Being in possession of the cardinal virtues, the prince is obliged to care for "the common good" as well as the "safety of the Commonwealth".[7] Hence it is the "effects of virtues", as Hemmingsen further asserts, that "preserve the status and dignity of Man" and "strengthen Commonwealths and households".[8]

Hemmingsen, furthermore, advocated the right of resistance. When he first addressed the issue of resistance in the *De Lege Naturæ*, he embraced a doctrine of passive resistance and endurance, arguing that "he who rules is not to command anything against God, and he who obeys is not to obey the Prince in illegal things, that is, things that goes against Natural and Divine Law".[9] Returning to the issue of resistance, however, in his Latin commentary on Psalm 84, which first appeared in 1569, Hemmingsen offered a deeper analysis of the right of resistance, centred on the role of popular magistrates. Popular magistrates are "placed of God" in order to fulfil two central functions, that is, "to be the keepers of the first and second tables", and to "moderate", and, if necessary, "with weapons to defend godlie subiectes, and remoue-awaie idolatrie & restore true Religion".[10] It is thus the duty of "popular magistrates" to take up armed resistance, should moderation, "counsel", "wisedome", and persuasion fail. "[O]utward violence", he writes, "which is offered to religion by tyrants, maie by the magistrate placed betweene the cheefe head, and priuate men,

5 Niels Hemmingsen, *Om naturens lov 1562*, 4 vols., Richard Mott, ed. (Copenhagen: Forlaget Øresund, 1991–1995), §291.

6 Hemmingsen, *Om naturens lov*, §111.

7 Hemmingsen, *Om naturens lov*, §250.

8 Hemmingsen, *Om naturens lov*, §247.

9 Hemmingsen, *Om naturens lov*, §139.

10 Niels Hemmingsen, *The faith of the Church Militant, Moste effectualie described in this exposition of the 84. Psalme*, Thomas Rogers, trans. (London: H. Middleton, 1581), 432.

be repelled by force. Which thing both nature teacheth, and the office of the popular magistrate requireth, and the example of holie men doe confirme". On Hemmingsen's account, active resistance is thus justified against the prince's violation of "the lawes and religion".[11]

The humanist language of virtues and vices was further developed by Arild Huitfeldt, historian and chancellor. Huitfeldt not only contrasted what he called a "legal Regiment", characterised by a contractual relationship between ruler and subjects, to a government founded on "Fear", he further juxtaposed "Hereditary Kingdoms" to "free Elective Kingdoms".[12] Since "no Kingdoms or Principalities were [originally] Hereditary", Huitfeldt asserts, "the People" must elect the "most Virtuous, Wise and best Suited" amongst themselves to be king.[13] The status of the prince is that of a *primus inter pares*, a person who "exceeds others in Virtues and Piety", and, like "the Sun", shins brighter than "other Stars".[14] Yet virtues alone cannot ensure good government, as not even the most virtuous and capable "Captain" can ever hope to navigate a "Ship" on his own.[15] A prince must therefore – and this is the central point he wished to make – gather around him "reasonable, wise and noble People, their advice he must use".[16] Contrasting tyranny and hereditary kingdoms to legal regiments and free elective kingdoms, Huitfeldt not only emphasises the active political role of the councillors in the government of the kingdom, he also underscores the contractual relationship between the two central governing bodies that constituted the post-Reformation constitutional order.

3

The humanist tradition of constitutionalist thought was rivalled by a tradition of thinking about political authority, which rejected the main components of the humanist tradition, that is, the emphasis on princely virtues, the contractual relationship between the ruler and the council of state, and the right of resistance. The overall framework of this rival tradition of thinking about political

11 Hemmingsen, *Church Militant*, 431–2.

12 Arild Huitfeldt, *En kaart Historiske Beskriffuelse/ Paa hues merckeligt/ som sig Aarlige under Kong Christian den Tredie/ Danmarckis/ Norgis/ Vendisoc Gottis Konning/ etc. haffuer tildragit* (Copenhagen: Matz Vingaard, 1595),):ij verso –):iij recto.

13 Huitfeldt, *En kaart Historiske Beskriffuelse*,):ij verso –):iij recto.

14 Huitfeldt, *En kaart Historiske Beskriffuelse*,):iij recto.

15 Huitfeldt, *En kaart Historiske Beskriffuelse*,):iij verso.

16 Huitfeldt, *En kaart Historiske Beskriffuelse*,):iij verso.

authority was the two-kingdom theory, as Martin Luther had outlined it in the 1520s.[17] In 1567, the clergyman and court chaplain Niels Nielsen Colding published a work entitled *De Besynderligste Historier/ Sententzer oc Exempler/ som findis i den Hellige Scrifft/ om Øffrighedz Kald/ Regiment oc Bestilling* (The Most Specific Stories, Sentences, and Examples Contained in the Holy Scriptures about the Calling, Regime, and Work of the Magistrate), in which he drew on scriptural sources in order to emphasise the divine character of monarchical power. Ordained to "such a Regime" by the "LORD and God", Colding writes in the Preface, "all Magistrates" must govern justly.[18] When "Kings and Princes" govern and maintain their "Subjects" by "Just Laws", Colding goes on to argue, they are "like a Housefather to his Children and Flock", to be known as "*Patres patriæ*".[19] The emphasis on justice and divine ordination had two implications for the understanding of political authority. Firstly, "Kings and Princes must not with Violence and force take from their Subjects any Land, Property, or anything else, however little it may seem to the World",[20] and, secondly, in what regards the Christian faith, the principal task of the prince is to preserve and defend "Churches and the Worship of God".[21] Political power is divine in origin, but its arena is strictly limited to earthly or temporal matters. Colding's contentions were shared by a group of writers, who emphasised obedience and interpreted political authority along Lutheran lines. In 1596, at the coronation of Christian IV, bishop Peder Vinstrup interpreted monarchical power as ordained by God and referred to Christian IV as "an Absolute Monarch",[22] and in the early seventeenth century, bishop Hans Poulsen Resen argued that "Christian Kings" embodied "a sacred Office".[23]

---

17 Quentin Skinner, *The Foundations of Modern Political Thought*, 2 vols. (Cambridge: Cambridge University Press, 1978), II, 3–19; W. D. J. Cargill Thompson, *Studies in the Reformation: Luther to Hooker* (London: Athlone, 1980), 42–59.

18 Niels Nielsen Colding, *De Besynderligste Historier/ Sententzer oc Exempler/ som findis i den Hellige Scrifft/ om Øffrighedz Kald/ Regiment oc Bestilling: Vddragne aff Bibelen ordentlig/ fra den Første Mose Bog/ oc indtil enden i det Ny Testament/ met en gantske kort Paamindelse til Øffrighed forklarede* (Copenhagen: Lorentz Benedicht, 1567), Preface.

19 Colding, *De Besynderligste Historier*, 169verso.

20 Colding, *De Besynderligste Historier*, 108verso.

21 Colding, *De Besynderligste Historier*, 144verso.

22 August Erich, *Klarlige oc Visse Beskriffuelse/ Om dend Stormectige/ Høybaarne Førstis oc Herris/ Herr Christians den Fierdis* ..., A.B. Dallin, trans. (Copenhagen: Heinrich Waldkirch, 1598), 56.

23 Hans Poulsen Resen, *Om den Hellige Tro til Den sande Gud, Oc den hand sende, Jusum Christum, Oc at Luthers rette Catechism bør icke at lastis, tillige. Imod nogle Nestorianiske Klafferj* (Copenhagen: Salomone Sartorio, B., 1614), Preface.

Despite their different implications for the interpretation of political authority, the division between the Lutherans and the humanists were often blurred. Hemmingsen, for instance, not only praised Colding's ideas in a preface he wrote to Colding's *De Besynderligste Historier*,[24] he also placed many of his later discussions of political matters within a Lutheran framework. In *Liffsens Vey* (The Way of Life), which first appeared in 1570, Hemmingsen described the "Worldly Authority" as the "*Custos vtriusq*[*ue*] *tabulæ*, the Guardian of the two Tables", and placed religious concerns at the heart of his discussion.[25] Should a person act in violation of God's law, it is the duty of the worldly authority to punish this person, and should the ruler refrain from inflicting such punishment, he shall himself be guilty of the sins committed. "For it is a relentless grace", he argues, "to spare one for the depravity and injury of the multitude".[26]

Moreover, the arguments for resistance advocated by Danish writers from Hemmingsen onwards seem to have emerged not in the context of Calvinist and monarchomach theories of revolt, as scholars mistakenly suggest,[27] but out of later developments in Lutheran political thought. In the 1530s, when the position of the Protestant princes in Germany, and thus the fate of the Reformation was threatened by the turn of political events,[28] Luther and his followers reinterpreted the office of political authority and its place in the earthly kingdom. Without abandoning the theory of obedience to a lawful authority, the Lutheran reformers drew a crucial distinction between the office of the prince and the political order more generally, justifying revolt against a tyrant as a means of preserving the political order, i.e., the ordinance of God. Moreover, the Lutherans revised their interpretation of chapter 13 of St Paul's epistle to the Romans, commonly invoked in favour of non-resistance, to include lesser as well as superior magistrates in the definition of legal and divinely ordained political authority. Should a superior magistrate exceed his

24 Niels Hemmingsen, "Fortalen", in Colding, *De Besynderligste Historier*.

25 Niels Hemmingsen, *Liffsens Vey: Det er, En vis oc Christelig Underuisning om huad det Menniske skal vide, tro oc giøre, som det euige Liff vil indgaa* (Copenhagen: Lorentz Benedicht, 1570), 30verso–31recto.

26 Hemmingsen, *Liffsens Vey*, 32recto.

27 Knud Fabricius, *Kongeloven: Dens tilblivelse og plads i samtidens natur- og arveretlige udvikling* (Copenhagen: H. Hagerups Forlag, 1920), 75; Leon Jespersen, "Knud Fabricius og den monarkiske bølge: nogle kommentarer til de statsretlige brydninger i 15–1600-tallets Danmark", *Historie*,1 (1997), 69; Leon Jespersen, "The Constitutional and Administrative Situation", in Leon Jespersen, ed., *A Revolution from Above? The Power of State of 16th and 17th Century Scandinavia* (Odense: Odense University Press, 2000), 61–4.

28 Robert von Friedeburg and Michael J. Seidler, "The Holy German Empire of the German Nation", in Lloyd, Burgess and Hodson, eds., *European Political Thought, 1450–1700*, 114–20.

office, it is the duty of lesser magistrates to resist his rule.[29] These contentions informed not only the later writings of Hemmingsen, they also underpinned central constitutional developments in the seventeenth century.

On this account, which bridge the contractual interpretation of political authority and the Lutheran or Pauline doctrine that all authority is of God, the Council of State takes centre stage, representing the voice of divine providence. Monarchical authority is sanctioned by God, who acts indirectly through the council. This contention was most clearly expressed by the leading nobleman and councillor Christian Skeel, who in 1658, just two years prior to the monarchical revolution, insisted that the Council of State is part of God's ordained order, "instituted by God in order to govern and rule with His Royal Highness".[30] Sanctioned by God, the Council could legitimately oppose tyrannical rule without thereby opposing the will of God, Skeel argued, seeking to rally a revolt against Frederik III for violating the terms of his coronation charter.

4

Against this background, the monarchical revolution signalled significant intellectual changes as well as continuities. The turbulent days in October 1660 had left the kingdom in a constitutional vacuum, leaving a number of issues unresolved.[31] The *Act of Sovereignty* had granted the king the liberty to design the "Right of Succession, Sovereignty and absolute Government", which was to be stipulated in a political testament or a "last Will".[32] Rather than opting for an arbitrary form of absolutism, leaving the issue of heredity to be decided by the monarch himself in a political testament, Frederik III took the advice of Dietrich Reinkingk and the German Chancellery in Glückstadt. The issue

29 Skinner, *The Foundations of Modern Political Thought*, II, 74, 199–206.

30 Christian Skeel, *Som jeg har ment mit fædreland det vel..: Rigsråd Christian Skeels politiske optegnelser*, Leon Jespersen, ed. (Copenhagen: Selskabet for Udgivelse af Kilder til Dansk Historie, 2004), 191.

31 Sebastian Olden-Jørgensen, "Enevoldsarveregeringsakten og Kongeloven: Forfatningsspørgsmålet i Danmark fra oktober 1660 til november 1665", *Historisk Tidsskrift*, 93.2 (1993); Ditlev Tamm, "De statsretlige aspekter", in Allan Tønnesen, *Magtens besegling: Enevoldsarveregeringsakterne 1661 og 1662 underskrevet og beseglet af stænderne i Danmark, Norge, Island og Færøerne* (Odense: Syddansk Universitetsforlag, 2013), 22.

32 *Kongeloven og dens Forhistorie: Aktstykker*, A. D. Jørgensen, ed. (Copenhagen: C. A. Reitzel, 1886), 2–3.

was to be settled in a constitution.[33] In the aftermath of the monarchical revolution, a number of constitutional projects were launched. In 1663, two civil servants, Søren Kornerup and Rasmus Vinding, drafted a royal constitution entitled *Lex Regia Frederici Tertii*, in which they sought to ground the authority of the king in divine rights theory, thus stressing that the king held absolute power directly from God.[34] The *Lex Regia Frederici Tertii* was rejected and the task of writing the final draft fell to a young and ambitious civil servant, the archivist and librarian Peder Schumacher, who was working as the king's secretary.[35] When the *Lex Regia* was signed in 1665 it contained not only a law of heredity, but also a new constitutional arrangement. Like absolutists elsewhere in Europe,[36] Schumacher was a committed constitutionalist, seeking to redescribe rather than to abolish existing constitutional structures.

Comprised of a preamble and forty paragraphs, the *Lex Regia* outlines the constitutional foundation of the absolute monarchy as well as the law of heredity. The preamble, especially, has received much scholarly attention, as it interprets the introduction of absolutism in 1660 along the lines of what is commonly perceived as two distinct and contradictory models of justification, one secular, the other religious. On the one hand, one group of scholars has argued, the justification of absolute monarchy is provided by reference to a *translatio* or a popular transfer of power in the style of a Roman *lex regia*, that is, the transfer of power from the people to the emperor Augustus.[37] When Schumacher penned his draft of the *Lex Regia*, he may well have been following a tradition of thinking about the origins of absolute power already in place. As early as 18 October 1660 and coinciding with the estates swearing a new oath of allegiance to Frederik III, the pastor to the German congregation at Copenhagen Daniel Pfeiff had interpreted the monarchical revolution as a modern parallel to the Roman *lex regia*. Out of appreciation of the king's

33 Olden-Jørgensen, "Enevoldsarveregeringsakten og Kongeloven", 311–3.

34 The draft is reprinted in *Kongeloven*, 33–7.

35 Sebastian Olden-Jørgensen, *Kun navnet er tilbage – en biografi om Peter Griffenfeld* (Copenhagen: Gads Forlag, 1999).

36 Mark Goldie, "Absolutism", in George Klosko, ed., *The Oxford Handbook of the History of Political Philosophy* (Oxford: Oxford University Press, 2011).

37 Olden-Jørgensen, "Scandinavia", 322–3; Olden-Jørgensen, "Enevoldsarveregeringsakten og Kongeloven", 300; Sebastian Olden-Jørgensen, "Ind i enevælden", in Thomas Lyngby, Søren Mentz and Sebastian Olden-Jørgensen, *Magt og pragt. Enevælde 1660–1848* (Copenhagen: Gads Forlag, 2010), 51–2, 69; Leon Jespersen, "Teokrati og kontraktlære: Et aspect af de statsretlige brydninger ved Frederik 3.s kroning", in Carsten Due-Nielsen *et alii*, eds., *Struktur og funktion. Festskrift til Erling Ladewig Petersen* (Odense: Odense Universitetforlag, 1994); Jespersen, "Knud Fabricius"; Jespersen, "The Constitutional and Administrative Situation", 50.

heroic defence of the realm against the Swedish invasion, Pfeiff observed, the estates wanted not only to imitate the Romans by granting the monarch supreme authority and power, but also to surpass the Romans by granting him the right of heredity.[38]

The idea of the monarchical revolution as a historical parallel to the Roman *lex regia* was further emphasised by the *Act of Sovereignty*, in which the popular transfer of power took pride of place. "[O]f their own free Will" the estates had granted the king supreme authority.[39] In the preamble to the *Lex Regia*, Schumacher rehearses the argument of the *Act of Sovereignty* almost to the point. Acting "of their own free Will", the estates surrendered to the king "the Hereditary Right to these our Kingdoms Denmark and Norway as well as to all Jura Majestatis, absolute Power, sovereignty, and all Royal Privileges and Regalia".[40]

By contrast, a competing tradition of scholarship has interpreted the *Lex Regia* as an expression of the divine justification of absolute power.[41] The appeal to divine providence plays a crucial role in the *Lex Regia*. At length, the central passage reads,

> the great and almighty God rules over all kings and princes as well as their subject kingdoms and lands according to the counsel of his inscrutable wisdom and thereby governs and orders everything; this perceptibly inasmuch as His divine omnipotence has paternally delivered us from the danger of almost apparent and imminent utter ruin and collapse which was hovering over our royal house and these our kingdoms and lands, and has acted to such an end that not only have we been saved and placed in the desired state of peace and tranquillity but also that He has caused our then existing Council of the Realm and all the estates, noble and non-noble, spiritual and secular, to give up their previous prerogatives and rights of election and to consent to render the capitulation previously signed by us, with all of its transcripts, points and clauses, null and void; and to declare us, in all ways and without any exception, rid and

38 Olden-Jørgensen, "Scandinavia", 322–23; Sebastian Olden-Jørgen, *Poesi og politik: Lejlighedsdigtningen ved enevældens indførelse 1660* (Copenhagen: Museum Tusculanum Forlag, 1996), 52.

39 *Kongeloven*, 2.

40 *Kongeloven*, 39.

41 Fabricius, *Kongeloven*; Svend Erik Stybe, *Fra folkevækkelse til enevælde af Guds nåde: Den danske reformations idéhistorie* (Copenhagen: Berlinske, 1975); Carl Henrik Koch, "Enevælde af Guds nåde", in Sven Erik Stybe, ed., *Politiske ideologier: Fra Platon til Mao* (Copenhagen: Politiken, 1974), 105–8.

> free of the oath to which we bound ourselves when we began our reign; and thus, uncompelled and without any instigation, request or command from us, of their own free will and after mature deliberation, most humbly to surrender to us, as the head and first possessor, and to our descending male and female lines born of lawful marriage, as long as any of them are alive, the hereditary right to these our kingdoms Denmark and Norway as well as to all Iura Majestatis, absolute power, sovereignty, and all royal privileges and regalia.[42]

Much historical scholarship has been devoted to the task of deciphering which model represents the real ideological orientation of the monarchy as opposed to mere pompous flattery.[43] Such endeavours are, however, misleading. Both models of justification are clearly present, making it difficult to hinge any real ideological orientation on either one of them. Thus, in so far as we wish to understand the nature of the absolutist thinking in the *Lex Regia*, the questions we ought to consider concerns not the true ideological orientation of the absolute monarchy, but rather the intervention in current political thought resulting from the combination of the two models.

Schumacher drew on a range of commonplaces in contemporary European political thought. The idea that the *lex regia* entailed a popular transfer of power was widespread amongst early modern commentators on Roman law.[44] Moreover, the models of justification to which Schumacher referred in the preamble had wide currency in European political thought – not only in absolutist circles, but also amongst the advocates of elective monarchy.[45] In Denmark, as we have seen, these models featured in different ways in the works of Hemmingsen, Huitfeldt, and Skeel. Especially Skeel, who defended the rights of election and considered the Council of State a part of God's

42 *Kongeloven*, 38–39; Ernst Ekman, "The Danish Royal Law of 1665", *Journal of Modern History*, 29:2 (1957), 105.

43 Compare Knud J. V. Jespersen, "Absolute Monarchy in Denmark: Change and Continuity", *Scandinavian Journal of History*, 12:4 (1987), 313–15, and Olden-Jørgensen, *Kun navnet er tilbage*, 99–100.

44 Julian H. Franklin, *Constitutionalism and Resistance in the Sixteenth Century: Three Treatises by Hotman, Beza, & Mornay* (New York: Pegasus, 1969), 12.

45 J. P. Sommerville, "Absolutism and royalism", in J. H. Burns and Mark Goldie, eds., *The Cambridge History of Political Thought, 1450–1700* (Cambridge: Cambridge University Press, 1991); J. P. Sommerville, *Royalists and Patriots: Politics and Ideology in England 1603–1640*, second edition (London and New York: Routledge, 1999), esp. 9–54; Cesare Cuttica, "Absolutism, History of", in James D. Wright, ed., *International Encyclopedia of the Social and Behavioral Sciences*, 2nd edition (Oxford: Elsevier, 2015), 1, 6–11.

ordained authority, was keen to stress that whilst all authority is divine in origin, the person of the king was designated to his office by the councillors.

The upshot of the preamble to the *Lex Regia* was not an argument about the justification of absolute monarchical power, be it divine or popular, but its intervention in a constitutional controversy. In this context, Schumacher's combination of the divine and popular models of justification was intended to ensure that the act of surrendering the charter and the right of election was definitive. Even if one accepted the fact that the councillors once possessed by divine ordination the rights of election and resistance, they had now surrendered those rights for all posterity. Moved by God, the estates had wilfully surrendered all their powers, liberties, and rights to the monarch, who would be for all posterity the sole possessor of political power.

In so far as the task at hand is to understand the meaning of absolutism, there is a further question to be asked, namely what contemporaries meant by such concepts as "Jura Majestatis, absolute Power, [and] sovereignty".[46] Much scholarship has been concerned with the intellectual sources of Danish absolutism, seeking to decipher the influence on the *Lex Regia* and its author of such political philosophers as Hobbes,[47] Grotius and Bodin.[48] Whilst there is little to be said of a Hobbesian influence, Schumacher knew the works of both Grotius and Bodin, with which he became familiar during his stay in Oxford in the late 1650s.[49] Although the historical works of Bodin were widely known in Denmark,[50] and although Heinrich Ernst, a German professor of Jurisprudence, lectured on Grotian natural law at the Academy of Sorø,[51] where Christian IV had unsuccessfully offered a professorship to Grotius,[52]

---

46 *Kongeloven*, 39.

47 J. A. Fredericia, "Betragtninger over Enevælden i Danmark fra 1660 til 1720", *Tilskueren* (1886), 766; Paul Kléber Monod, *The Power of Kings: Monarchy and Religion in Europe, 1589–1715* (New Haven and London: Yale University Press, 1999), 207; E. Ladewig Petersen, "War, Finance, and the Growth of Absolutism", in Göran Rystad, ed., *Europe and Scandinavia: Aspects of the Process of Integration in the 17th Century* (Lund: Esselte Studium, 1983), 46.

48 Knud Fabricius, *Griffenfeld* (Copenhagen: J. L. Lybecker, 1910), 90–92; Fabricius, *Kongeloven*, 1–20; Thomas Munck, *Seventeenth Century Europe: State, Conflict and the Social Order in Europe 1598–1700* (London: Palgrave, 1990), 341.

49 Fabricius, *Griffenfeld*, 50, 90–91.

50 Karen Skovgaard-Petersen, *Historiography at the Court of Christian IV (1588–1648): Studies in the Latin Histories of Denmark by Johannes Pontanus and Johannes Meursius* (Copenhagen: Museum Tusculanum Press, 2002).

51 Olden-Jørgensen, "Scandinavia", 314.

52 Olaf Carlsen, *Hugo Grotius og Sorø Akademi. En kritisk studie* (Taastrup: Handelstrykkeriet, 1938).

these philosophers had no direct influence on the nature of Danish absolutism. The German political theorist Henning Arnisaeus, who took up a position as the physician to Christian IV in 1619, may however establish a connection between Bodin's ideas and the *Lex Regia*.[53] Before coming to Denmark, Arnisaeus had lectured on politics and jurisprudence at Frankfurt an der Oder and at Helmstedt, and he was heavily engaged in the German discussions of Bodin's political philosophy, from which he sought to distance himself. Two of his main political works, the *Doctrina politica* and the *De Republica*, published in 1606 and 1615 respectively, became foundational works for German political Aristotelianism,[54] but he also authored a work on monarchy. First published in 1610, his *De Jure Majestatis* picks up the semantics of *iura majestatis* from Bodin and puts forth a theory of monarchy in which the king embodies "all the rights of the Majesty", limited only by divine and natural law as well as the pacts or contracts of his predecessors.[55]

Though Arnisaeus may have introduced the political philosophy of Bodin to a Danish readership, the connection remains vague. Moreover, Arnisaeus's engagement with Bodin predates his time in Denmark, and historians have so far not been able to establish any such connections.[56] Even so, the scholarly interest in the philosophical influences on the *Lex Regia* tells us very little about the theory of absolutism that went into in the *Lex Regia*. Thus, in order for us to understand the meaning of Danish absolutism we need to consider not the philosophical influence behind the *Lex Regia*, but languages in which the document is written.

The language of sovereignty in which the *Lex Regia* was engrained carried a range of Bodinian traits. Especially the sections of the *Lex Regia* concerned with the rights of majesty or *iura majestatis* are embedded in the political philosophy of Bodin. In the *Six Books of the Commonwealth*, Bodin put forth a

53 Stybe, *Fra folkevækkelse*; Fabricius, *Kongeloven*, 45–57, 315.

54 Horst Dreitzel, *Protestantischer Aristotelismus und Absoluter Staa:. Die 'Politica' des Henning Arnisaeus (ca. 1575–1636)* (Wiesbaden: Franz Steiner, 1970); Martin van Gelderen, "Aristotelians, Monarchomachs, and Republicans: Sovereignty and *respublica mixta* in Dutch and German Political Thought, 1580–1650", in Martin van Gelderen and Quentin Skinner, eds., *Republicanism: A Shared European Heritage*, 2 vols. (Cambridge: Cambridge University Press, 2002), I, 208–10; Annabel Brett, *Changes of State: Nature and the Limits of the City in Early Modern Natural Law* (Princeton: Princeton University Press, 2011), chs. 6–7; Richard Tuck, *Philosophy and Government,1572–1651* (Cambridge: Cambridge University Press, 1993), 124.

55 Henning Arnisaeus, *De Jura Majestatis*, in *Opera Politica Omnia*, 2 vols. (Strasbourg [Argentorati]: Lazari Zetzneri, 1648), II, 33.

56 Dreitzel, *Protestantischer Aristotelismus*, 408.

novel theory of "Sovereignty", which he understood as "the absolute and perpetual power of a commonwealth".[57] Belonging to a single person or a uniform body or group of persons, the defining feature of Bodin's theory of sovereignty was the notion of indivisibility.[58] As Bodin insists in Book I, chapter 10, "the notion of a sovereign (that is to say, of someone who is above all subjects) cannot apply to someone who has made a subject his companion".[59] Sovereignty cannot be shared by two or more separate political bodies such as a king and a council. "Mixture, then", Bodin further stresses in his discussion in Book II, chapter 1 of the forms of commonwealth, "is not a state, but rather the corruption of a state".[60] In addition to the indivisibility of sovereignty, Bodin offered a list of *iura majestatis* or sovereign rights. These marks of sovereignty comprised (i) "the power of making and repealing law"; (ii) the right of "declaring war or making peace"; (iii) the right of "hearing appeals"; (iv) the right to appoint and remove "the highest officers"; (v) the power to impose "taxes and aids on subjects or exempting them"; (vi) the power to grant "pardons and dispensations against the rigor of the law"; (vii) "determining the name, value, and measure of the coinage"; and finally (viii) the right to demand and receive homage and loyalty from "subjects and liege vassals".[61]

In the *Lex Regia*, the king is described as the possessor of a similar list of *iura majestatis*, though it does not correspond entirely to the one listed by Bodin. The two first paragraphs deal with the king's supremacy and his relation to God. "The best beginning to everything is to begin with God", it reads in the opening line, after which the *Lex Regia* obliges the king to "honor",

> serve, and worship the only just and true God in that manner and fashion which He has revealed in His holy and true word; and make known our Christian faith and creed clearly according to the form and manner in which it was presented, pure and undefiled, in the Augsburg Confession of the year 1530, and hold the inhabitants of the country to the same pure

57 Jean Bodin, *On Sovereignty: Four chapters from The Six Books of the Commonwealth*, Julian H. Franklin, ed. (Cambridge: Cambridge University Press, 1992), 1.

58 Julian H. Franklin, "Sovereignty and the mixed constitution: Bodin and his critics", in J. H. Burns and Mark Goldie, eds., *The Cambridge History of Political Thought, 1450–1700* (Cambridge: Cambridge University Press, 1991), 298; Julian H. Franklin, "Introduction", in Bodin, *On Sovereignty*, Franklin, ed.

59 Bodin, *On Sovereignty*, 50.

60 Bodin, *On Sovereignty*, 105.

61 Bodin, *On Sovereignty*, 58–9.

> and undefiled Christian faith and defend it by force and shield it in these lands and kingdoms against all heretics, fanatics, and mockers of God.[62]

Paragraph II establishes the supremacy of the king, who "shall hereafter be, and by all subjects be held and honored as, the greatest and highest head on earth, above all human laws and knowing no other head or judge above him, either in spiritual or secular matters, except God alone".[63] Acting as supreme judge, the king is "a free and unfettered Absolute King", as it reads in paragraph XVII, who "cannot be bound by his subjects to any Oath or prescribed obligations".[64] The king thus possessed, as it reads paragraph III, the "supreme power and authority to make laws and ordinances according to his own good will and pleasure", a right which also includes the "laws previously made by himself or by his forefathers".[65] Elevated above all human laws, the only exception to the king's power was the *Lex Regia* itself, which had the status of a "fundamental, that is, an unchangeable Constitutional Law".[66] Moreover, whilst paragraph IV grant the king the "supreme power and authority to appoint and dismiss officials, high and low", paragraph V sets out his "right to wage war, to conclude and dissolve alliances", and "to impose duties", "levies", and taxes.[67] Finally, paragraph VI establishes the king's "supreme power over the clergy".[68]

These *iura majestatis*, which collectively constituted the king's indivisible and absolute power, placed the monarch directly under God and everything else directly under him. The king is above the law, unlimited in all his relations. Especially the contention in paragraph II that the monarch is above all human laws has caused historians to misinterpret the nature of Danish absolutism as an essentially unlimited and arbitrary form of power.[69] Yielding unlimited power in theory, historians further assert, monarchical sovereignty was often curbed by administrative practices.[70] Yet, like Bodin's account of absolute sovereignty came with certain restrictions on sovereign power in relation to

---

62 *Kongeloven*, 43; Ekman, "Royal Law", 105–6.
63 *Kongeloven*, 43–44; Ekman, "Royal Law", 106.
64 *Kongeloven*, 51; Ekman, "Royal Law", 106.
65 *Kongeloven*, 44; Ekman, "Royal Law", 106.
66 *Kongeloven*, 40–41.
67 *Kongeloven*, 44–45; Ekman, "Royal Law", 106.
68 *Kongeloven*, 45; Ekman, "Royal Law", 106.
69 Olden-Jørgensen, "Ind i enevælden", 71.
70 Thomas Munck, *The Peasantry and the Early Absolute Monarchy in Denmark, 1660–1708* (Copenhagen: Landbohistorisk Selskab, 1979), 49–53; Olden-Jørgensen, "Ind i enevælden", 64–72.

private property, the laws of the land, and the doctrines of faith,[71] the *Lex Regia* placed a number of restrictions on monarchical power. As was the case anywhere else in Europe, monarchical power was limited in relation to natural and divine law. But the *Lex Regia* places further limitations on absolute power. Just as it is beyond his powers to alter the *Lex Regia*, the king cannot abandon the Augsburg Confession, change the line of succession, divide up the kingdom, or by any other means decrease the king's absolute power.[72] The most crucial limitations concerned the king's relationship with the church and the private property of his subjects. But although Bodin's notion of sovereignty also carried with it certain limitations, the restrictions that the *Lex Regia* placed on monarchical power on these two areas were rooted in the Lutheran tradition of thinking about political authority.

5

In the second half of the seventeenth century, a group of prominent theologians offered discussions of politics that accepted the Bodinian description of the *iura majestatis* as marks of sovereignty into the broader framework of Luther's two-kingdom theory. Between 1663 and 1672, Johann Wandal, bishop of Zealand and professor of theology at Copenhagen, published his magnum opus, the *Juris Regii libri VI* (The Rights of Majesty in Six Books), in which he offered a systematic account of the divine origin and nature of political authority. Corresponding, largely, to a series of lectures which Wandal delivered at Copenhagen on the rights of sovereignty, the *Juris Regii* provides us with an ongoing commentary on a broad range of writers, including Hobbes and Grotius, and on the most pressing political issues of the 1660s and early 1670s.[73] An intervention in the debates in the early 1660s over how to interpret the monarchical revolution, Wandal argued that the power of the king was instituted not by a popular transfer of power, as Daniel Pfeiff's allusions to the Roman *lex regia* suggested, but by the grace of God.[74] This interpretation of the divine character of monarchical power was further emphasised by Wandal

71 Julian H. Franklin, *Jean Bodin and the Rise of Absolutist Theory* (Cambridge: Cambridge University Press, 1973), 70, 84, 86–90; J. H. Burns, "The Idea of Absolutism", in John Miller, ed., *Absolutism in Seventeenth-Century Europe* (London: Macmillan, 1990).

72 Munck, *The Peasantry*, 50.

73 Paolo Borioni, "Suverænitetsbegrebet i Bog IV af H. Wandals *Jus Regium*" (Ph.D. Dissertation, University of Copenhagen, 2003), 67–71.

74 Stybe, *Fra folkevækkelse*, 145.

in his sermon at the coronation of Christian V in 1671. On Wandal's account, monarchical power was instituted by 'the holiest *Anointment*'.[75] In his sermon, Wandal moreover offered a biblical analogy to the transition of power from Frederik III to Christian V:

> What the Spirit of God informs us of the deathly departure of the Lord's most dear Friend and King, David, and his Son's entry after him in the Royal Regiment, to this we could rightly add: *now David rests with his Fathers, and was buried in his City: but our Solomon sits again on his Father's, our David's Throne and his Kingdom is already much Constituted* [...] *Our Solomon, King Christian the Fifth, may he live long and be happy*.[76]

As a modern Solomon, Christian V had inherited the throne of Frederik III, who, like David, had slain the Goliath of his time, i.e., the Council of State. The biblical analogy thus offered a rival interpretation of the monarchical revolution, interpreting key events and actors not in light of Roman history, as had Pfeiff, but the biblical story of David and Solomon, who are offered as models of kingship. Wandal was not the only theologian to offer such comparisons. Amongst seventeenth-century theologians, the Old Testament played a crucial role in the discussion of politics and government. In 1667, the largely unknown writer Hans Jensøn Alan described Frederik III and Solomon as "Twins",[77] and in 1648, in his coronation sermon to Frederik III, Jesper Rasmussen Brochmand invoked the example of the "Judges, who should rule Israel", thus emphasising the divine origin of political authority.[78] Contrasting the "Order of God" to "Human Affectations" and the "Manners of the Heathens", the "Office of Kingship" is meant to eradicate all "severe Sins" and to promote that which is "good, Pious and Just".[79]

---

75 Johann Wandal, *Den Stormægtigste og Høybaarne Arffve-Konnings og Monarchs/ HER CHRISTIAN DEN FEMTES* ... (Copenhagen: Hendrick og Jørgen Gøede, 1671), Aii recto.

76 Wandal, *Den Stormægtigste*, B verso.

77 Hans Jensøn Alan, *Catena methodica Salomonis. Det er: Salomon adspreedt, samblet aff hans Ordsprocker, Prædicker oc Høysang effter Joseph Hals Methodum udi tre gudelige Konster, som ere Ethica ... Politica ... Oeconomica aff Hans Jensøn Alan* (Copenhagen: Daniel Paulli K. M. B., 1667), Dedicatio.

78 Jesper Rasmussen Brochmand, *Den Stormectige Høybaarne Førstis oc Herris/ Her Frederich dend Tredies Danmarckis/ Norgis/ Wendis oc Gottis Konnings/ Hertug udi Sleßvig/ Holstein/ Storman oc Dimersken: Greffue udi Oldenborg oc Delmenhorst: Hans Majestets Kongelige Kroning/...* (Copenhagen: Georg Lamprecht, 1650), Cii recto.

79 Brochmand, *Den Stormectige*, Ciii recto, Civ recto, Kiv recto.

Reaching back to the Pauline contentions central to such sixteenth-century Lutheran political thinkers as Colding, Vinstrup, and Resen, the seventeenth-century representatives of this tradition were concerned as much with the question of the origin of secular power as with its limits and scope. To Wandal and Brochmand not only the distinction between the earthly and the heavenly kingdom, but also the division of the earthly kingdom into three estates was considered essential to the discussion of political power. Based on a functional difference, Luther first explained in his circular disputation on the right of resistance against the Emperor from 1539,[80] God had ordained three regiments or estates that should govern the earthly kingdom: the *ordo economicus* (the household or the *Nehrstand*), the *ordo politicus* (the commonwealth or the *Wehrstand*), and the *ordo ecclesiasticus* (the church or the *Lehrstand*). Whilst political power is divine in origin, its arena is strictly limited not just to the earthly kingdom, but specifically to the *ordo politicus*.

Wandal and Brochmand were amongst the most influential political thinkers in the seventeenth century. Hans Svane, for instance, who played a crucial role in the monarchical revolution was a pupil of Brochmand, and Peder Schumacher, who authored the *Lex Regia* had been part of Brochmand's academic household in his youth. It is thus no coincidence that their way of thinking about political authority informed central aspects of the Danish theory of absolutism. This tradition of thinking had two major implications for the contemporary view of the meaning and scope of absolute power. First, the monarch, whose place in the earthly kingdom is the *ordo politicus*, possesses no dominion over the private property of the subjects, that is, the *ordo economicus*. As it reads in the *Lex Regia*:

> The king alone shall have control over the armed forces and the raising of arms, the right to wage war, to conclude and dissolve alliances with whom and when he sees fit, and to impose duties and all other levies; since everyone well knows that kingdoms and lands cannot securely be held without armed power, and military power cannot be maintained without stipend, and stipend cannot be raised without taxation.[81]

This formulation was in line with the Lutheran tradition of thinking about the household or the *ordo economicus*. As Wandal explained in his sermon, the subjects owed to their king three sets of obligations, "Submission and Obedience",

80 Robert von Friedeburg, "Church and State in Lutheran Lands, 1550–1675", in Robert Kolb, ed., *Lutheran Ecclesiastical Culture, 1550–1675* (Leiden and Boston: Brill, 2008), 369.

81 *Kongeloven*, 44–45; Ekman, "Royal Law", 106.

"Honour and Fear", and finally "Taxes and Customs".[82] Considering taxes and customs amongst the "*Jura Majestatis* and *Regalia*, which belongs solely to the Highest Ruler in the Country", the king's right to levy taxes and customs is far reaching, but never arbitrary.[83] The king's right over "the persons of his subjects" and their "Estates and property", Wandal asserts, is restricted to what is necessary "for his and his Armies' *conservation*, and for the defence of the common Welfare against his own and the Kingdom's Enemies".[84]

Secondly, the king should refrain himself from interfering with the inner affairs of the Church. As it reads in the *Lex Regia*, the domain of the monarch was the external, earthly realm, within which the king alone holds "supreme power over the clergy from the highest to the lowest to order and arrange all ecclesiastical and divine services; to enjoin or forbid, when he considers it advisable, meetings, assemblies, and conventions on religious matters".[85] The *ordo ecclesiasticus*, though, remains free in its domain, which relates to salvation, faith, and the inner intentions of man. Commenting on this distinction in his sermon to Christian v, Wandal reinterprets the role of the clergy within the confessional state, following intellectual trends within the German tradition of *politica Christiana*.[86] The division between the three earthly regiments, Wandal argued, places upon the *ordo ecclesiasticus* a duty to critically assert the moral grounding of the king's actions. The purpose of the *ordo ecclesiasticus* was to be the moral watchdog over the *ordo politicus*. Wandal was, in other words, defending the right of the theologian to perform moral criticism of secular rulers.

> When a Priest and Servant of God by himself must remember, warn and urge a King, on behalf of God and his Office, about those Cases that concerns God's honour and right worship as well as the utility and education of his Christian Congregation: then, when it happens with sufficient reverence and well-intended servility, a Christian King ought to take it into account.[87]

---

82 Wandal, *Den Stormægtigste*, Civ recto.

83 Wandal, *Den Stormægtigste*, Biv verso.

84 Wandal, *Den Stormægtigste*, Ciii recto.

85 *Kongeloven*, 45; Ekman, "Royal Law", 106.

86 Luise Schorn-Schütte, *Evangelische Geistlichkeit in der Frühneuzeit: Daren Anteil an der Entfaltung Frühmoderner Staatlichkeit und Gesellschaft* (Heidelberg: Gütersloher, 1996); Luise Schorn-Schütte, "Obrigkeitskritik und Widerstandsrecht: Die *politicachristiana* als Legitimitätsgrundlage", in Luise Schorn-Schütte, ed., *Aspekte der politischen Kommunikation im Europa des 16. und 17. Jahunderts: Politische Theologie – Res Publica-Verständnis – konsensgestützte Herrschaft* (München: De Gruyter Oldenbourg, 2004).

87 Wandal, *Den Stormægtigste*, Div recto.

Describing the office of the theologian as the only true advisor to the king in matters pertaining to morality and religion, Wandal offers his advice to the new monarch, urging him to banish all false religion. "A Christian King", he argues, "must ward off and avert from his subjects all Heresy, all false, erring and seductive teachings, [and] hinder and ward off those *false Prophets who show up in cheeps clothing, but internally are tearing Wolves*".[88] Referring to "the holy Mosaic Royal Law", Wandal reminds Christian v of his duties to "God", "who alone appoints Kings, and removes them again".[89] The intellectual foundation of the theory of public criticism was the division between the inner and the external government of the church, excluding the secular ruler from interfering in the internal matters of the faith whilst simultaneously subjecting the ruler to moral criticism. The Lutheran political thinkers thus intended to steer the monarchy in the right direction, ensuring the protection of the true doctrines of faith. As the court chaplain Hector Gottfried Masius explained in his *Interesse Principum Circa Religionem Evangelicam* (The Interest of the Prince Concerning the Evangelical Religion), which first appeared in 1687, "AS LONG AS THE LUTHERAN RELIGION REMAINS, THE MAJESTY IN DENMARK WILL BE SUPREME AND ABSOLUTE".[90]

6

This article has been concerned with the rise and meaning of Danish absolutism as it came to be expressed in the *Lex Regia* of 1665. Rejecting three common misinterpretations concerning the justification, the sources, and the nature of Danish absolutism the article has situated the *Lex Regia* in its intellectual as well as its constitutional context. Danish absolutism rested on twin pillars. On the one hand, absolute monarchical power was understood in connection with a Bodinian language of sovereignty, centred on indivisibility and sovereign rights. On the other, absolute monarchical power was strictly limited to the *ordo politicus*, and the limits that were placed on absolute power corresponded to Luther's two-kingdom theory, as it was interpreted by the Lutheran political thinkers in the seventeenth century. To Danish absolutists, the *Lex Regia* never instituted anything like unlimited power. To the extent that the king exceeded his office, he did so only in practice, and always against the constitutional

88 Wandal, *Den Stormægtigste*, E recto.

89 Wandal, *Den Stormægtigste*, Diii recto.

90 Hector Gottfried Masius, *Interesse Principum Circa Religionem Evangelicam Ad Serenissum ac Potentissimum Daniæ Regem* (Copenhagen: Joh. Phil. Bockenhoffer 1687), 168.

foundation upon which Danish absolutism rested. The notion of political authority embodied in the *Lex Regia* does not amount to the all-embracing notion of absolute monarchical sovereignty, entertained by modern scholars. Monarchical power was considered absolute only within the *ordo politicus*, and what makes the office of kingship absolute within this realm is the possession of a range of specific sovereign rights or *iura majestatis*. Unlimited absolute power that encroaches upon all aspects of human life is a historical myth. This does not however entail – as Nicholas Henshall polemically claims in *The Myth of Absolutism* – that absolutism is a myth. Though Henshall rightly shows that the concept of absolutism carries with it a nineteenth-century intellectual baggage, which places the concept in the context of modern totalitarianism,[91] absolutism is still a useful historiographical concept in so far as we use it to historicise the languages employed by early modern absolutists.

Bibliography

Main Sources

Brochmand, Jesper Rasmussen, *Den Stormectige Høybaarne Førstisoc Herris/ Her Frederich dend Tredies Danmarckis/ Norgis/ Wendisoc Gottis Konnings/ Hertug udi Sleßvig/ Holstein/ Storman oc Dimersken: Greffue udi Oldenborg oc Delmenhorst: Hans Majestets Kongelige Kroning/* … (Copenhagen: Georg Lamprecht, 1650).

Hemmingsen, Niels, *Om naturens lov 1562*, 4 vols., Richard Mott, ed. (Copenhagen: Forlaget Øresund, 1991–1995). A Danish/Latin edition of Hemmingsen's *De Lege Naturæ Apodicitica Methodus* (1562).

Huitfeldt, Arild, *En kaart Historiske Beskriffuelse/ Paa hues merckeligt/ som sig Aarlige under Kong Christian den Tredie/ Danmarckis/ Norgis/ Vendisoc Gottis Konning/ etc. haffuertildragit* (Copenhagen: Matz Vingaard, 1595).

Kongeloven og dens Forhistorie: Aktstykker, A. D. Jørgensen, ed. (Copenhagen: C. A. Reitzel, 1886). A collection of sources, including, most importantly, the *Act of Sovereignty* (pp. 1–4) and the *Lex Regia* (pp. 38–67).

Wandal, Johann, *Den Stormægtigste og Høybaarne Arffve-Konnings og Monarchs/ HER CHRISTIAN DEN FEMTES* … (Copenhagen: Hendrick og Jørgen Gøede, 1671).

Main Bibliographical References

Ekman, Ernst, "The Danish Royal Law of 1665", *Journal of Modern History*, 29:2 (1957).

91 Nicholas Henshall, *The Myth of Absolutism. Change and Continuity in Early Modern European Monarchy* (London: Routledge, 1992), 119–212. This case is argued more forcefully in Nicholas Henshall, "The Myth of Absolutism", *History Today*, 42 (1992).

Fabricius, Knud, *Kongeloven: Dens tilblivelse og plads i samtidens natur- og arveretlige udvikling* (Copenhagen: H. Hagerups Forlag, 1920).

Jespersen, Knud J. V., "Absolute Monarchy in Denmark: Change and Continuity", *Scandinavian Journal of History*, 12:4 (1987).

Jespersen, Leon, "The Constitutional and Administrative Situation", in Leon Jespersen, ed., *A Revolution from Above? The Power of State of 16th and 17th Century Scandinavia* (Odense: Odense University Press, 2000).

Olden-Jørgensen, Sebastian, "Scandinavia", in Howell A. Lloyd, Glenn Burgess and Simon Hodson, eds., *European Political Thought, 1450–1700: Religion, Law and Philosophy* (New Haven and London: Yale University Press, 2007).

CHAPTER 9

A Model Republican Constitution? Guicciardini vs. Machiavelli on the Roman Example

Nikola Regent

Exactly two and a half centuries after Machiavelli's death, in the first half of 1777, Domenico Cimarosa's opera *Il fanatico per gli antichi Romani* was first performed in Naples.* Its *librettista*, Giuseppe Palomba, certainly did not have Machiavelli in mind when writing the libretto for the comical opera, though the most praised aria, "Nel vedervi così armati", has some Machiavellian overtones, reminding the listener (or the reader) of *armi proprie*, Machiavelli's "refrain" (as Meinecke aptly called it).[1] While Guicciardini probably would not go that far, to declare Machiavelli a "fanatic for the ancient Romans", it is without doubt that he regarded his older friend and co-citizen as too obsessed with the Roman example, as his remark from the *Ricordi*, on those who *a ogni parola allegano e' romani*, vividly confirms.[2]

This chapter will focus on Guicciardini's criticism of Machiavelli's model state – "the imperial republic", as Pocock called it[3] – based precisely on the Roman example, examining the younger Florentine's objections to Machiavelli's analysis and conclusions. Pocock, who in *Barbarism and Religion* reiterated the importance of "the problem of *imperium et libertas*" in Machiavelli's opus,[4] had offered its more extensive examination already in *The Machiavellian Moment*, particularly emphasising the significance of the republican choice discussed in the *Discorsi*, I.5 and I.6.[5] This crucial choice, the "republican dilemma" between

* My research on Guicciardini's political thought during 2014–17 was funded by the Australian Research Council grant DE140101358.

1 Friedrich Meinecke, *Machiavellism: The Doctrine of Raison d'État and Its Place in Modern History* (New York: Praeger, 1957 [1924]), 37.

2 See *infra*, 198 and n. 63.

3 J.G.A. Pocock, *Barbarism and Religion*, vol. 3: *The First Decline and Fall* (Cambridge: Cambridge University Press, 2003), ch. 10.

4 *Ibidem*, *passim*; quoted expression is at 210.

5 J.G.A. Pocock, *The Machiavellian Moment: Florentine Political Thought and the Atlantic Republican Tradition* (Princeton: Princeton University Press, 1975), ch. 7, esp. 196ff. John P. McCormick, "Machiavelli against Republicanism: On the Cambridge School's 'Guicciardinian Moments'", *Political Theory*, 31.5 (2003), 615–43, does not discuss Guicciardini himself (nor does it quote a single time any of his works), and is irrelevant for our argument.

 | DOI:10.1163/9789004549159_011

following Rome and following Sparta (and Venice) – as well as its origins – has been closely analysed in my previous work.[6] I have examined Machiavelli's choice of the best form of government, establishing (1) why Machiavelli prefers a republic to a principality, and (2) why he prefers the expansionistic model of republic based on Rome over the non-expansionistic model based on Sparta and Venice. I have shown reasoning behind this choice, and the (ancient) origins of Machiavelli's model state based firmly on the example of the Roman Republic.[7]

Machiavelli's framing of the "republican dilemma" in the *Discorsi* is of highest importance for the development of Guicciardini's views on this issue. Guicciardini adopted Machiavelli's framework, when examining the question of the best (or the most applicable) republican constitution – and opposed his conclusions.[8] Based on the previous examination of Machiavelli's ideas (my own in particular), the chapter will explore Guicciardini's criticism of Machiavelli's analysis and conclusions from the *Discorsi*. While the two greatest Florentines of the period were undoubtedly friends,[9] there is a very noticeable difference in their approach and their mode of thinking.[10] "I see Machiavelli, as he saw himself, as one concerned with the statement of 'ancient' values

6 Nikola Regent, "Machiavelli: Empire, *Virtù* and the Final Downfall", *History of Political Thought*, 32.5 (2011), 751–72.

7 These conclusions, consistent with Pocock's argument, indirectly rebut Skinner's claim about the "priority of liberty" in Machiavelli's republican constructions; cf. *ibidem*, n. 45. For my subsequent direct rebuttal of Skinner's interpretation, see Nikola Regent, "Quentin Skinner, Contextual Method and Machiavelli's Understanding of Liberty", *History of the Human Sciences*, 35.5 (2022), 108–34. Against the whitewashed "good republican" interpretations of Machiavelli, cf. also my argument in Nikola Regent, "Sallust, Machiavelli and the Divorce of *virtus* from *res publica*", *English Historical Review*, 135.575 (2020), 775–803.

8 "Guicciardini's anti-Roman antithesis constantly presupposes the Machiavellian thesis" suggested Pedullà; not "in every detail", though – Guicciardini clearly disagreed with some of Machiavelli's analysis of Roman history. Gabriele Pedullà, "Machiavelli and the Critics of Rome: Rereading *Discourses* 1.4", in David Johnston, Nadia Urbinati and Camila Vergara, eds., *Machiavelli on Liberty and Conflict* (Chicago: Chicago University Press, 2017), 87–112, at 108. And, *pace* Pedullà, already in the *Discorso di Logrogno* we can find very specific criticism of Rome and her "disordine" and at least an instance of explicit "opposition between Rome and Venice". See *Discorso di Logrogno* [*Del modo di ordinare il governo popolare*], in *Dialogo e discorsi del reggimento di Firenze*, ed. Roberto Palmarocchi (Bari: Laterza, 1932), 218–59, at 226, 222, cf. also 221.

9 As their correspondence clearly shows. See 27 surviving letters (17 by Machiavelli, 10 by Guicciardini), in Machiavelli, *Tutte le opere*, ed. Mario Martelli (Firenze: Sansoni, 1971), 1202–48. All of Machiavelli's works will be quoted from this edition; all translations, for both Machiavelli and Guicciardini, are my own.

10 For a more general comparison, see Gennaro Sasso, "Guicciardini e Machiavelli", in *Per Francesco Guicciardini* (Roma: Istituto Storico per il Medio Evo, 1984), 47–158.

under 'modern' conditions", wrote Pocock.[11] The very same thing can be said about Guicciardini;[12] the only difference being that Guicciardini was more concerned with 'modern' conditions, while Machiavelli paid more attention to 'ancient' values. And while Guicciardini was often "a greater realist" than the more idealistic Machiavelli, whose powerful imagination sometimes got so carried away that he would just forget about details that did not fit into the grand picture, Guicciardini also offers a different view on the uses and utility of history for modern politics. Unquestionably unique and original in his political thinking, Guicciardini was still closer to the prevailing ideas of the time, and his disagreements with Machiavelli fully show "the radical nature" of the latter's thought.[13] One of the aims of this chapter is to show how extreme was Machiavelli's position on following the Romans even in his own times. Guicciardini's criticism is here most illuminating: for we deal with the most insightful and most thorough contemporary critic of Machiavelli and his ideas on imitating the ancients.

1 Guicciardini and Machiavelli's Choice

The importance of Guicciardini as a major political thinker was fully revealed over three centuries after his death, when, from 1857 to 1867, Giuseppe Canestrini edited and published his surviving manuscripts and correspondence. Up to then, Guicciardini was known as the author of *Storia d'Italia*, a history of the great early sixteenth-century struggle for European supremacy that took place on the Italian soil, and a significant political actor who himself played a role in this struggle.[14] Averse to publication of any of the products of his contemplative hours,[15] Guicciardini postponed public knowledge of his

---

On Guicciardini as Machiavelli's critic, cf. Ugo Spirito, *Machiavelli e Guicciardini* (Firenze: Sansoni, 1968 [1944]), ch. 4.

11 Pocock, "Afterword", *Machiavellian Moment*, 2nd edition (Princeton: Princeton University Press, 2003), 564.

12 Cf. Pocock, "Machiavelli and Guicciardini: Ancients and Moderns", *Canadian Journal of Political and Social Theory*, 2.3 (1978), 93–109, esp. 107.

13 As Meinecke put it, *Raison d'État*, 38.

14 For a more extensive discussion of the fate of Guicciardini's political writings and their reception, and an overview of the secondary literature, see Nikola Regent, "A 'Medical Moment': Guicciardini and Lycurgus' Knife", *History of European Ideas*, 34.1 (2008), 1–13, at 1–2. On Guicciardini's life, see Roberto Ridolfi, *The Life of Francesco Guicciardini* (London: Routledge and Kegan Paul, 1967).

15 Note that even *Storia d'Italia*, an extensive work in 20 books which made Guicciardini's name as a historian, was published only two decades after his death, against Guicciardini's

theoretical brilliance until the second half of the nineteenth century, and as a consequence simultaneously also harmed his own inclusion into the canon of the great political theorists. Yet, it is clear that as a *cinquecento* political thinker, he is second only to his celebrated older co-citizen and friend Machiavelli. Guicciardini's connection with Machiavelli, and his importance for (re)assessing Machiavelli's writings, was also obvious to Canestrini, who in 1857 started the first of the 10 volumes of *Opere inedite* exactly with *Considerazioni intorno ai Discorsi del Machiavelli*: a work which critically analyses, chapter by chapter, the *Discorsi* of the older Florentine.[16] The following year, the second volume started with the *Dialogo del reggimento di Firenze*, Guicciardini's longest political treatise, where the main interlocutor, Bernardo del Nero, discusses at length, and criticises, Machiavelli's precepts on how to organise a republic.[17]

A few introductory observations on Guicciardini and the ancients, and on his general understanding of human nature, should be made to help the reader grasp better the premises of his arguments. As I had shown over a decade ago, Guicciardini in his youth idealised the Spartan example.[18] This point should be strongly underlined, as it established an idealistic streak in Guicciardini's early political thought (even if already there his cynicism is strongly pronounced) – and it sheds a somewhat different light upon his criticism of the ancient examples as a whole. Yet, this feature makes his criticism of Machiavelli's Romans – the focus of this chapter – even stronger, exactly because it comes from the pen of the man who truly *does* respect antiquity.

In the same work I also uncovered Guicciardini's ideas about the legitimacy of the use of force, in order to reform the body politic in the circumstances of extreme necessity. Nonetheless, despite his readiness to use violence – the so-called "knife of Lycurgus" – if necessity asks for it, Guicciardini is never inclined towards extreme measures and solutions. Guicciardini is risk-averse,

apparent wishes, by the decision of his nephew: see Sasso, "Guicciardini e Machiavelli", 47. Besides this work, only a portion of Guicciardini's *Ricordi* was published before the mid-nineteenth century.

16 *Considerazioni intorno ai Discorsi del Machiavelli sopra la prima deca di Tito Livio*, in *Opere inedite*, ed. Giuseppe Canestrini, vol. 1 (Firenze: Barbèra, Bianchi e comp., 1857), 1–79. Not all the chapters are covered: Guicciardini extensively comments the opening chapters of book I, but later skips more and more chapters (e.g. already chapter 13 is not considered). From book II, only 8 chapters are commented; from book III, just 3.

17 *Del Reggimento di Firenze*, in *Opere inedite*, ed. Giuseppe Canestrini, vol. 2 (Firenze: Barbèra, Bianchi e comp., 1858), 1–234. I shall use Palmarocchi's critical edition, published in *Dialogo e discorsi*, 1–172.

18 Regent, "Medical Moment". See also my further treatment, and re-examination of some important points, in Nikola Regent, "Guicciardini and Economic (In)equality", *European Journal of the History of Economic Thought*, 27.1 (2020), 49–65, esp. 51–5.

and his general attitude is defensive – to protect what one has, rather risking it for further gains. The masses, and men in general, Guicciardini points out, are much easier won over "when they are offered the hope of acquiring, than when they are shown the danger of losing", while the contrary should be the case, "because the appetite to conserve is more natural than to gain".[19] Hope is stronger than fear in most men, that is the reason of this "fallacy": thus men "easily do not fear that what they should fear, and hope that what they should not hope".[20] Guicciardini confessed he is influenced more by fear than by hope,[21] and even suggested that men with "more than mediocre" intelligence are more inclined to worry and anxiety than "more positive" simple minds.[22]

It is no wonder that Guicciardini's mouthpiece Bernardo del Nero, confronted in the *Dialogo del reggimento di Firenze* with Machiavelli's choice from the *Discorsi*, I.5 and I.6,[23] would without any hesitation opt for the

19 "E' popoli communemente e tutti gli uomini si lasciano più tirare quando è proposta loro la speranza dello acquistare, che quando si mostra loro el pericolo di perdere; e nondimeno doverrebbe essere el contrario, perché è più naturale lo appetito del conservare che del guadagnare", *Ricordi*, II.62 (in *Scritti politici e Ricordi*, ed. Roberto Palmarocchi (Bari: Laterza, 1933), 239–336).

20 "La ragione di questa fallacia è, che negli uomini può ordinariamente molto più la speranza che el timore; però facilmente non temono di quello che dovrebbero temere, e sperano quello che non doverebbono sperare", *ibidem*.

21 "Sono varie le nature degli uomini: certi sperano tanto, che mettono per certo quello che non hanno; altri temono tanto, che mai sperano se non hanno in mano. Io mi accosto più a questi secondi che a' primi e chi è di questa natura si inganna manco, ma vive con più tormento", *ibidem*, II.61. For his risk-aversion in financial matters see *ibidem*, II.55; for a decidedly un-Napoleonic (or, un-Clausewitzian) approach to offering a battle, see II.183. Generally, "it is such a madness to play a game in which incomparably more may be lost than won" ("quanta pazzia è giucare a uno giuoco che si possa perdere più sanza comparazione che guadagnare"), *ibidem*, II.51; cf. also I.157.

22 "Lo ingegno più che mediocre è dato agli uomini per la loro infelicità e tormento; perché non serve loro a altro che a tenergli con molte più fatiche e ansietà che non hanno quegli che sono più positivi", *ibidem*, II.60.

23 That Guicciardini was acquainted with the *Discorsi* already when composing the *Dialogo del reggimento di Firenze*, will be evident to any careful reader from the text itself; a fact also confirmed by a cross-reference in the *considerazione* on *Discorsi*, I.4 (see *infra*). The *Dialogo* was highly likely completed in 1524 (see editor's note in *Dialogo e discorsi*, 287), and Guicciardini was undoubtedly acquainted with some of the *Discorsi* much before 1529, as Ridolfi suggested (*Considerazioni* were written in 1530). Indeed, as Sasso points out, "it is almost superfluous to note" that that Guicciardini knew both the *Discorsi* and *Il principe*, before their publication: see his "Guicciardini e Machiavelli", 92–5, criticising Ridolfi. Sasso suggests a reference to the *Discorsi* already in 1521 (the letter with Lysander quoted *infra*), and most plausibly argues that already *Del modo di assicurare lo stato alla casa de' Medici* (written in 1516 or shortly after) shows Guicciardini's reading of *Il principe*; references to acquiring *principato nuovo* and *principe nuovo*, exemplified by Valentino

non-expansionistic model of republic: "If you asked me what would be better for a city, to live content with its freedom, when it could have it secure without wanting dominion, as many territories in Germany do today, or turn the spirit to making an empire, I know what my answer would be".[24] However, under the given Florentine circumstances, this option is excluded, "because we are of those who have the dominion, and after obtaining force, we have lived always in this way, from which there is no retreat".[25]

Notice how Bernardo would immediately and without any doubts go for the peaceful option – his answer almost assumes it as a self-evident choice, and it is given in an implicit form. And if here Guicciardini echoes Machiavelli's judgement, from the *Discorsi*, II.19, on small republics *della Magna*, earlier in the dialogue Bernardo puts the matters even more strongly. To Pagolantonio's claim that to live free and well governed in a city has priority over dominating others, Bernardo retorts:

> you want to divide the things that cannot be divided. If a city that was content with its liberty and with its small territory was left alone by others, you would be right; but this is not [the case] in our house and cannot be, because it must be either in a powerful mode to oppress others or be oppressed by others. If you lost your dominion, you would also lose the liberty and the city itself, which would be assaulted, and you would have no forces to defend it; and to make good justice, to distribute well the magistrates, to have good laws and well observed, would not defend you. ... the dominion lost, and the city remains subjugated and usurped, without any hope of ever being able to rise again.[26]

---

and by Francesco Sforza, beyond doubt concern its chapters VI and VII. See this treatise, in *Dialogo e discorsi*, 267–81, at 270–1 [not 170–1, a mistype in Sasso, n. 99].

24 "Se tu mi dimandassi che sarebbe meglio a una città, o vivere contenta della libertà sua quando potessi averla sicura sanza volere dominio, come sono oggi di molte terre nella Magna, o voltare lo animo al fare imperio, io saprei che rispondere", *Dialogo*, 159. (*Dialogue on the Government of Florence*, trans. Alison Brown (Cambridge: Cambridge University Press, 1994), 154).

25 "...perché siamo noi di quegli che abbiamo dominio, e poi che abbiamo avuto forze siamo vivuti sempre in questa via, dalla quelle non ci posendo più ritirare", *ibidem*.

26 "Se una città che si contentassi della libertà sua e del suo piccolo territorio fussi lasciata stare dagli altri, tu diresti bene; ma questo non è a casa nostra e non può essere, perché bisogna o che sia in modo potente che opprima gli altri, o che sia oppressa da altri. Se voi perdessi el dominio vostro, perderesti ancora la libertà e la città propria, la quale sarebbe assaltata, e non aresti forze da difenderla; ed el fare buona giustizia, el distribuirsi bene e' magistrati, l'avere buone leggi e bene osservate, non vi difenderebbe. ... perduto el dominio, e la città ne rimane soggiogata ed usurpata, sanza speranza alcuna di potere mai risurgere", *ibidem*, 73 (*Dialogue*, 70).

We can again notice a striking resemblance to Machiavelli's analysis from the *Discorsi*, II.19. As he stresses there, "it is impossible for a republic to succeed remaining peaceful, and enjoy its liberty and its narrow confines: because, if it does not molest the others, it will be molested itself; and from being molested it will arise in it the will and the necessity for acquisition".[27] Guicciardini obviously fully shares Machiavelli's opinion on Germany's special conditions – if the German republics have lived for quite a while in this peaceful, non-expansionistic manner, it is "from the certain conditions present in that country, that cannot be found elsewhere"; without them they could not survive with such methods.[28] They can live within their small territory, "within their walls", as the Imperial authority protects them; but, if the conditions in Germany were different, they would have to renounce their ways of peace.[29]

To a casual reader it might even seem that Machiavelli here goes against his own principal division, on an expansionistic and a non-expansionistic republic. Yet, such a reader would be wrong, for the very purpose of this chapter is to show how the republics who do not follow "the Roman virtue" when expanding, work on their own ruin.[30] Guicciardini's criticism in his *considerazione* on the chapter is focused on this very point. Machiavelli's *leitmotiv* of the dangers of expansion for a non-expansionistic republic is reiterated in the *discorso* – the unarmed Italian contemporary cases of Florence and Venice being used as examples. And Guicciardini rebuffs his late friend's arguments:

> Who doubts that the city of Florence, that the republic of Venice, would be weaker and less powerful had they enclosed their territory between narrow confines, as they did not? … I confess that a republic which has its own arms is more powerful and makes more capital from acquisitions, but I will never confess that an unarmed republic becomes weaker

27 "…è impossibile che ad una republica riesca lo stare quieta, e godersi la sua libertà e gli pochi confini: perché, se lei non molesterà altrui, sarà molestata ella; e dallo essere molestata le nascerà la voglia e la necessità dello acquistare", *Discorsi*, II.19.

28 "E se le republiche della Magna possono vivere loro in quel modo, ed hanno potuto durare un tempo, nasce da certe condizioni che sono in quel paese, le quali non sono altrove, sanza le quali non potrebbero tenere simile modo di vivere", *ibidem*.

29 "Possono vivere, adunque, quelle comunità contente del piccolo loro dominio, per non avere cagione, rispetto all'autorità imperiale, di disiderarlo maggiore: possono vivere unite dentro alle mura loro … Ché, se quella provincia fusse condizionata altrimenti, converrebbe loro cercare di ampliare e rompere quella loro quiete", *ibidem*.

30 "Che gli acquisti nelle republiche non bene ordinate, e che secondo la romana virtù non procedano, sono a ruina, non ad esaltazione di esse", *ibidem*. The other possibility is the expansion by the way of leagues: see *ibidem*, II.4.

> when it acquires more, nor that Venice, which now fears neither kings nor emperors, if it were without dominion on land and on sea, would be more secure than it presently is.[31]

Thus Bernardo, after concluding there is "no retreat" from playing the game of power, approves some extra acquisition for Florence, if a clear-cut opportunity arises. If Italy was all in Italian hands, "the acquisition of Lucca or Siena would be as laudable now, as acquiring Pisa and Arezzo was in the time of our ancestors".[32] However, in their days, if these ultramontane powers come to dominate Italy,[33] it would be easier to preserve a *grandezza* of current Florentine size, than a bigger one. The ultramontanes will not fear such a Florence and will satisfy themselves with extorting money from it. Being in a far worse position for extending dominion than Venice is, Florence cannot grow big enough to be thus secure; the Florentines should limit themselves to recapturing Pisa, and embark only on the most secure acquisitive ventures.[34] Living in a difficult neighbourhood, "a province which was full of liberty" – i.e. cities used to republican self-government – the Florentines can expand only "with a greatest fatigue": in contrast to the Venetians who were able to subdue with relative ease "lands used to servitude".[35]

---

31 "Chi dubita che la città di Firenze, che la republica di Vinegia sarebbono più deboli e di minore potenzia se avessino rinchiuso el territorio loro tra piccoli confini che non sono? … Confesso che una republica che ha arme proprie è più potente e fa più capitale degli acquisti, ma non confesserò già che una republica disarmata diventi più debole quanto più acquista, né che Vinegia, che ora non teme de' re né degli imperadori, se fussi sanza dominio in terra ed in mare, fussi più sicura che non è di presente", *Considerazioni*, II.19.

32 "…cosi sarebbe da lodare ora lo acquistare Lucca o Siena, come fu a tempo de' passati nostri Pisa ed Arezzo", *Dialogo*, 159 (*Dialogue*, 154–5).

33 As the dialogue is supposed to take place just few weeks ("poche settimane") after the expulsion of Piero de' Medici (9 November 1494), as Guicciardini tells us in the *proemio* (*ibidem*, 4; *Dialogue*, 3), he gives Bernardo far too extensive knowledge of the future events; Charles VIII only invaded Italy that September. But, of course, Guicciardini wants to discuss the key issues of the foreign policy of the time – even if the dialogue is set thirty years earlier. In the same vein, Piero reconstructs Machiavelli's arguments, etc. "Guicciardini is exercising hindsight here", as Pocock (*Machiavellian Moment*, 265) commented on p. 143 of the *Dialogo*; but not only "here", he does it throughout the work.

34 *Ibidem*, 159–61 (*Dialogue*, 154–6).

35 "…ed è verissimo, che più è stato difficile a' fiorentini a fare quello poco dominio che hanno, che a' viniziani el loro grande; perché e' fiorentini sono in una provincia che era piena di libertà, le quali è difficillimo a estinguere; però si vincono con grandissima fática … E' viniziani hanno avuto a pigliare terre use a servire", *Ricordi*, II.29. Guicciardini here offers a similar judgement on relative difficulties of Florentine and Venetian expansion, emphasising also the Florentine disadvantage of having the Papal States nearby.

2 Against Roman Tumults

While Guicciardini, considering the *Discorsi*, II.19, does not comment on the Romans themselves; *Considerazioni intorno ai Discorsi del Machiavelli* as a whole, and especially the *Dialogo*, offer a full-scale critique of Machiavelli's analysis of the Roman example. In the crucial chapters on the choice between the two models of republic, Machiavelli concludes how Rome could not copy Sparta, and institute a *governo stretto*; wishing to make a great empire, she needed the increase of the number of her citizens.[36] Therefore, "those enmities that developed between the populace and the senate, [I think it is necessary] to tolerate, taking them as an inconvenience necessary to arrive at Roman greatness".[37]

Guicciardini finds such a diagnosis completely false. "The disunity of the Roman plebs and the senate made that republic free and powerful", asserted Machiavelli.[38] How can somebody praise disunity? "But to praise disunity is like praising illness in an ill man, for the goodness of the remedy that was applied to him";[39] Guicciardini characteristically uses a medical metaphor in his comment.[40] In the *Dialogo* Guicciardini gives his father Piero the task to closely reconstruct Machiavelli's arguments from these early chapters of the *Discorsi*:

> accepting that premise which nobody denies or can deny, that its [Roman] militia was good, one has to confess that the city had good orders, otherwise it would not be possible that it had good military discipline. This is also shown because not only in the militia but in all other laudable things that city had infinite examples of the greatest virtue, which would not exist if the education had not been good, nor the education can be good where the laws are not good and well observed, and where this is present, it cannot be said that the order of government is bad. Therefore

36 "...ma non poteva, come lei [Sparta], non crescere il numero de' cittadini suoi, volendo fare un grande imperio", *Discorsi*, I.6.

37 "...quelle inimicizie che intra il popolo ed il senato nascessino, [credo ch'e' sia necessario] tollerarle, pigliandole per uno inconveniente necessario a pervenire alla romana grandezza", *ibidem*.

38 "Che la disunione della plebe e del senato romano fece libera e potente quella republica", *ibidem*, I.4. On tumults in Machiavelli, cf. Gabriele Pedullà, *Machiavelli in tumulto* (Roma: Bulzoni, 2011).

39 "...ma laudare le disunione è come laudare in uno infermo la infermit, per la bontà del remedio che gli è stato applicato", *Considerazioni*, I.4.

40 On Guicciardini's use of medical metaphors, see my analysis in 'Medical Moment'.

> it follows that those tumults between the fathers and the plebs, between the consuls and the tribunes, were more frightening in display than in effect, and that display which arose did not disorder significant matters in the republic.[41]

Meticulous reconstruction of Machiavelli's argument from the *Discorsi*, I.4 is here obvious – a fact also confirmed by a cross-reference in the related *considerazione*.[42] "I have heard somebody arguing the opposite"[43] to what is the majority's opinion on Roman internal affairs, Piero mentions before starting to present this contrary position: that "somebody" is, without any doubts, Machiavelli. In the crucial *discorso* I.4 we find Machiavelli asserting that "where there is a good militia, it follows there is a good order",[44] and how a republic cannot be called disordered, where there are many examples of virtue present, "because good examples come from good education, good education from good laws; and good laws, from those very tumults that many inconsiderately condemn".[45]

The most famous illustration of this logic are surely the lines from *Il principe*, "there cannot be good laws where there are no good arms, and where there are good arms it follows there are good laws".[46] Guicciardini strongly disagrees

41 "…ponendo quello fondamento che nessuno nega né può negare, che la milizia sua [de' romani] fossi buona, bisogna confessare che la città avessi buoni ordini, altrimenti non sarebbe stato possible che avessi buona disciplina militare. Dimostrasi ancora perché non solo nella milizia ma in tutte altre cose laudabili ebbe quella città infiniti esempli di grandissima virtù, e' quali non sarebbono stati se la educazione non vi fussi stata buona, né la educazione può essere buona dove le legge non sono buone e bene osservate, e dove sia questo, non si può dire che l' ordine di governo sia cattivo. Dunche ne seguita che queli tumulti tra e' padri e la plebe, tra e' consuli ed e' tribuni, erano più spaventosi in dimostrazione che in effete, e quella dimostrazione che ne nasceva non disordinava la cose sustanziali della republica", *Dialogo*, 148 (*Dialogue*, 143–4).

42 "I have on another occasion written more extensively, and will pass over it briefly" ("Io ho altra volta scritto più largamente, però ora me ne passerò con brevità"), *Considerazioni*, I.4.

43 "…io ho udito disputare qualcuno in contrario", *Dialogo*, 148 (*Dialogue*, 143).

44 "…and rarely does it happen that there is not good fortune also present" ("dove è buona milizia, conviene che sia buono ordine, e rade volte anco occorre che non vi sia buona fortuna"), *Discorsi*, I.4.

45 "Né si può chiamare in alcun modo con ragione una republica inordinata, dove siano tanti esempli di virtù; perché li buoni esempli nascano dalla buona educazione, la buona educazione, dalle buone leggi; e le buone leggi, da quelli tumulti che molti inconsideratamente dannano", *ibidem*.

46 "…non può essere buone legge dove non sono buone arme, e dove sono buone arme conviene sieno buone legge", *Il principe*, XII. Guicciardini was acquainted not just with the *Disorsi*, but also *Il principe*, before composing the *Dialogo*: see n. 23 *supra*.

with such a conclusion: answering to Piero, Bernardo del Nero thrashes the argument he reconstructed. It was said that good military discipline is a sign of good orders, but "where the effects can be touched by hand, one needs not to seek for signs",[47] Bernardo tells his interlocutors. The extensive answer he gives to Piero contains Guicciardini's own interpretation, and understanding, of Roman history.[48]

The domestic aspects of the Roman Republic were so "tumultuous and full of sedition, that was it not that the military virtue was so vigorous, that republic would have collapsed many times".[49] The principal cause of all the divisions in the city was its partition into two classes: the plebeians and the patricians. The patricians never treated the plebs with moderation; however, in the time of the kings, the plebeians formed a sort of natural alliance with the king, who was protecting them from abuse. Servius Tullius particularly played this "populistic" policy, paying the debts of the poor, introducing more "progressive" taxation,[50] etc. At those times the king was *maestro della bottega*,[51] and the plebs, satisfied with not being abused, did not care about the offices, even more so as the king would many times promote a number of plebeians into patricians' ranks. Once the republic was installed, the patricians gained the upper hand, and all changed. The plebs – the core of the army – was very much needed for Rome's expansionistic policy. But, instead of uniting the Roman population, and abolishing the distinctions between the two classes – the right solution to the problems of repeated disorders according to Guicciardini – the patricians wanted to keep all the power for themselves. Even allowing more "social mobility" for the leading plebeians might have been enough. Pressed over and again by repeated tumults, the patricians gave way little by little; however, these

47 "Piero disse che lo esservi la disciplina militare buona è segno che gli ordini vi erano buoni … che dove gli effetti si toccono con mano, non accade cercare e' segni", *Dialogo*, 156 (*Dialogue*, 152).

48 The following resume is based on Bernardo's answer, *ibidem*, 150–8 (*Dialogue*, 145–54), but cf. also 68 (*Dialogue*, 65–6) and relevant *Considerazioni*, I.3–6.

49 "…el governo di drento fu tumultuoso e pieno di sedizione, che non fussi stata sì vigorosa la virtù militare arebbono molte volte precipitate quella republica", *Dialogo*, 150 (*Dialogue*, 145). Cf. n. 53 *infra*.

50 On Guicciardini and progressive taxation, see Nikola Regent, "Guicciardini's *La Decima scalata*: the First Treatise on Progressive Taxation", *History of Political Economy*, 46.2 (2014), 307–31.

51 ["Master of the shop".] In variant B of the manuscript, *Dialogo*, 351, *nota* to p. 152 (*Dialogue*, n. 376 at 147).

disturbances produced also tribunes – who were to become the most harmful office in the later Republic.[52]

Guicciardini clearly disliked such a situation: Bernardo warns the interlocutors more than once about the dangers of the Roman tumults. The only thing which saved the city from seditions, which brought it to the verge of ruin more than once, was the strong military discipline.[53] Yet, even the disciplined army which formed the backbone of the Roman Republic was in fact instituted by the kings, in earlier times. This was fortunate for Rome, as in the tumultuous period which followed after the Republic was established, that would have been impossible.[54]

The circle is made: if Machiavelli's analysis put the traditional understanding upside – down,[55] Guicciardini put it "back" to its place. The Romans acquired their empire not *because* of, but *despite* tumults and disturbances present in their city, thanks to the exceeding excellence of their *armi propie*. "[They] were military men, and did not know how to live without war, which was the trade from which they drew their riches, honours and reputation".[56] Far from arguing against all of the Roman *ordini*, Bernardo points out how praiseworthy were their customs, patriotism, love of glory and other virtues. Guicciardini uses this moment in the dialogue to broaden his account of the early Roman successes, offering a nuanced, almost "sociological" explanation:

> the city [was] poor and surrounded by enemies who did not allow it to run to delights and to pleasures; in a way that I think that not so much the good laws, as the nature of men and severity of those ancient times, especially in that part of Italy that had prerogatives in this over the others,

52 In contrast, cf. *Discorsi*, I.3: the creation of "tribuni della plebe" in Rome "fece la republica più perfetta"!

53 "...che furono di tale peso che ... se la città non avessi avuto la disciplina militare tanto viva, vivendo con quelle sedizione, sanza dubio precipitava", *Dialogo*, 154 (*Dialogue*, 149). Cf. n. 49 *supra*. Guicciardini is unambiguous about the precarious existence of the early Republic: the incidents such as plebs going to the Mons Sacer were "accidenti che non potevano essere più periculosi e più perniziosi" (*ibidem*; *Dialogue*, 150).

54 "...la disciplina militare fu ordinata da' re e si può dire che nascessi con la città, e sanza dubio se si avessi avuta a ordinare in quelli tempi tumultuosi che furono qualche volta per rovinarla, non si ordinava mai", *ibidem*, 156 (*Dialogue*, 152).

55 See the very first sentence of *Discorsi*, I.4.

56 "...erano uomini militari, e che non sapevano vivere sanza guerra, che era la bottega donde cavavano richezze, onori e riputazione", *Dialogo*, 68 (*Dialogue*, 66).

> produced those so notable virtues and customs and conserved it for a long time clear from any corruption by vices.[57]

Indeed, such diagnosis is confirmed by the later times, when there were better laws, and there was concord in the city; yet the Romans got worse [*imbasterendo*] and "those excellent virtues converted themselves into enormous vices".[58] The riches, the greatness of the empire and too much security that follows helped to corrupt and destroy the Romans; and if there is no particular evident cause, it follows from "the natural cycle of things in the world, that cannot last forever".[59]

The reader will not be surprised to find Bernardo telling his interlocutors "do not cite me the example of the Romans".[60] Their circumstances were different, and hence "one cannot model himself after these examples who does not have things with conditions and qualities which they had".[61] We find a far more famous expression of this thought in Guicciardini's *ricordo*, directed undoubtedly against his "Machiavello carissimo":[62]

> How mistaken are those who at every word cite the Romans! One should have a city with the conditions as theirs, and then behave according to that example; which is for one who has disproportionate qualities very disproportionate, as it would be to wish that a donkey runs like a horse.[63]

---

57 "…la città [era] povera e circundata di inimici che non gli lasciava scorrere alle delizie ed a' piaceri; in modo che io credo che non tanto le legge buone, quanto la natura degli uomini e la severità di quegli antichi tempi, massime in quella parte di Italia che ebbe questa prerogative sopra le altre, producessino quelle virtù e quelli costume tanto notabili e la conservassino lungamente sincera da ogni corruzione di vizi", *ibidem*, 157 (*Dialogue*, 152).

58 "…quelle virtù eccellente si convertirono in vizi enormi", *ibidem* (*Dialogue*, 153).

59 "…la conversione naturale delle cose del mondo che non possono durare perpetue", *ibidem*. Unlike Guicciardini, Machiavelli offers a full description of the mechanism of the downfall: see my analysis in Regent, "Machiavelli: Empire, *Virtù* and Downfall", 769–72.

60 "Né mi allegate … lo esemplo de' Romani", *Dialogo*, 68 (*Dialogue*, 65).

61 "Però non si può regolare secondo questi esempli chi non ha le cose con le condizione e qualità che avevano loro", *ibidem* (*Dialogue*, 66).

62 As Guicciardini often calls Machiavelli in their correspondence.

63 "Quanto si ingannono coloro che a ogni parola allegano e' romani! Bisognerebbe avere una città condizionata come era loro, e poi governarsi secondo quello esemplo; el quale a chi ha le qualità disproporzionate è tanto disproporzionato, quanto sarebbe volere che uno asino facessi el corso di uno cavallo", *Ricordi*, II.110.

As with the Lacedaemonian example, we see again the importance of circumstances, which set limits to the applicability of a given example. In another *ricordo* Guicciardini generalises further:

> It is completely fallacious to judge by examples; for if they are not similar in every smallest detail they are useless, since every slightest variation in the case could be the cause of a greatest variation in the effect, and to discern these variations, when they are small, requires a good and perspicacious eye.[64]

3 Use of Historical Examples

Notwithstanding just quoted passages, it would be a mistake to assume that Guicciardini was entirely against the use of historical examples. "He did share the contemporary view that history taught by example", Gilbert rightly observed.[65] Guicciardini just thought that one cannot generalise the conclusions coming from certain historic situations, as Machiavelli did so often with the Roman example, and think they are a paradigm applicable in *any* given state of affairs. But he never doubted that *historia* is indeed *magistra*, nor about its usefulness. In a letter to Machiavelli, Guicciardini – mentioning the example of Lysander, to whom Machiavelli is compared![66] – puts it most explicitly:

> One can see, only the faces of men and the external colours change, the same things all return; we cannot see any incident that has not been seen

64 "È fallacissimo il giudicare per gli esempli; perché se non sono simili in tutto e per tutto non servono, conciosiaché ogni minima varietà nel caso può essere causa di grandissima variazione nello effetto, ed el discernere queste varietà, quando sono piccole, vuole buono e perspicace occhio", *ibidem*, II.117.

65 Felix Gilbert, *Machiavelli and Guicciardini: Politics and History in the Sixteenth-Century Florence* (Princeton: Princeton University Press, 1965), 230.

66 Whom Machiavelli is compared to, for his solace: as Lysander was given duty to distribute meat to the same soldiers he earlier victoriously commanded, so Machiavelli, after negotiating with so many kings, dukes and princes ("con quanti Re, Duchi et Principi voi havete altre volte negociato"), is now given a task to write annals [*Istorie fiorentine*, written at Leo X's commission]. Cf. Plutarch, *Lysander*, XXIII.7–9, and *Agesilaus*, VIII.1–2; these passages from the *Vitae* are consistent and were obviously the source of Guicciardini's comment. And while here the appointment as a distributor (or carver) of meat is regarded as abasement and humiliation for Lysander, in *Moralia* Plutarch retells the story as the position being an honour for the "foremost men", so that even Lysander accepted it. See *Quaestiones convivales*, II.10.2 (*Moralia*, 644B).

> at other times. But the change of names and forms of things makes them recognisable only to the prudent: and therefore history is good and useful, because she puts one ahead and makes him recognise and see that what one has never known nor seen.[67]

The passage brings to mind Machiavelli's *proemio* to book I of the *Discorsi*, where he tells us how "the heaven, the sun, the elements, the men" have not changed from the times of antiquity. Guicciardini is clear about *utilità* of history, not only the ancient one, but also the Florentine (the statement is made in context of both). An intelligent, prudent man will take his lesson, to be sure, from history ancient and modern; nonetheless, Guicciardini was rather sceptical about contemporary examples. A *ricordo* on two military expeditions Guicciardini participated in illustrates well his thoughts:

> if true, as I largely believe them to be, the things that are written on ancient militia, ours is but a shadow in comparison to theirs. Modern captains have no virtue, no industry; it is proceeded without art, without stratagems, as if walking in slow pace on a main road; so that it was not inappropriate what I said to signor Prospero Colonna, captain of the first expedition, who was telling me that I had never been in any war before; that I was sorry that in this one I have not learnt anything either.[68]

For a reader of *Storia d'Italia*, to see Guicciardini displaying such an attitude towards his contemporaries hardly comes as a surprise.[69] However, what is implicitly put here, is that one can, after all, learn from the examples of antiquity – in military matters at least. For Guicciardini shared, with his

---

67 "Vedi che, mutati solum e visi delli huomini et e colori extrinseci, le cose medesime tutte ritornano; né vediamo accidente alcuno che a altri tempi non sia stato veduto. Ma el mutare nomi et figure alle cose fa che soli e prudenti le riconoschono: et però è buona et utile la hystoria, perché ti mecte innanzi et ti fa riconoscere et rivedere quello che mai non havevi conosciuto né veduto". Letter to Machiavelli, Modena, 18 May 1521 (Martelli, 1205). [*Tu* should be here translated as "one", Guicciardini clearly uses it in that sense; in the letter, he otherwise addresses Machiavelli with *voi*, as always.]

68 "...se sono vere, come in gran parte io credo, le cose che si scrivono della milizia antica, questa a comparazione di quella è una ombra. Non hanno e' capitani moderni virtù, non hanno industria; procedesi sanza arte, sanza stratagemmi, come camminare a lento passo per una strada maestra; in modo che non fuora di proposito io dissi al signor Prospero Colonna capitano della prima impresa, che mi diceva che io non ero stato più in guerra alcuna; che mi doleva anche in questa non avere imparato niente", *Ricordi*, II.205.

69 Gilbert, *Machiavelli and Guicciardini*, 282: "The humanists taught history teaches by example. In Guicciardini's *History of Italy* there are hardly any examples to be imitated".

contemporaries and with Machiavelli, the admiration for the ancients, and did regard them superior in many aspects. Yet, for that very reason he thought that imitation of a number of these aspects is impossible or will bring exactly the reversed effects. Thus, as I have shown, Guicciardini in *La Decima scalata* counsels the Florentines not to follow the Spartan ways, though he specially admires this very example, as following it without *armi proprie* they would cause their own ruin.[70]

Nonetheless, the end of *Discorso di Logrogno* shows plainly that Guicciardini, at least in his earlier years, did think that the arming of Florence is possible, and that gradually his city may – if slowly, and perhaps not pushing to the very extreme – adopt the ways of Lacadaemon; this would also open the path to glory.[71] This kind of hopes must have faded away in his later years; the growing pessimism of older age and, particularly, the adverse political circumstances of the time, clearly made their impact. But, while Guicciardini obviously thinks very highly of Lycurgus' constitution, it is certainly not the case with the Roman one. It must be underscored to what extent different reading of Roman history entails different political ideals and priorities for Machiavelli and Guicciardini. Whether Rome achieved a universal empire *despite* or *because* of its internal constitution does make all the difference! And if Machiavelli's backward induction, that from good arms follow good laws and orders, therefore such orders should be copied, may be quite an easy target for Guicciardini; Machiavelli complements it with an ingenious explanation how the energy produced by these turmoils was externalised and used as a source of expansion.

Paradoxically, Guicciardini, disinclined to *governo troppo largo*, notices more the plight of the Roman plebs, than Machiavelli himself ever did.[72] Indeed, "the government of Rome was mixed, not plebeian",[73] Guicciardini duly observes; then again, he is as averse to tumults and seditions as he is to the rule of the multitude. His reluctance is to be traced not only in his (more aristocratic) *ottimati* background, but also in his nature and character – far more risk-averse and prudent than Machiavelli ever was.

Thus, it comes almost naturally, as the arming of the Florentines and introduction of some sort of Lycurgianesque reforms became an increasingly remote possibility with the ever-growing foreign dominance in Italy, that Guicciardini concentrated on a practical and far more pertinent model: Venice. Bernardo

70 Regent, "Medical Moment", 7–8; cf. "Guicciardini's *La Decima scalata*", 325.

71 See my detailed analysis in "Medical Moment".

72 Cf. Ch. Wirszubski's analysis, *Libertas as a Political Idea at Rome during the Late Republic and Early Principate* (Cambridge: Cambridge University Press, 1950).

73 "...el governo di Roma era misto, non plebeo", *Considerazioni*, I.5.

states it plainly in the *Dialogo*: "It seems to me that the Venetian government is for an unarmed city as fine as any free republic has perhaps ever had".[74] Its durability for centuries, flourishing and united, cannot be attributed to mere chance or fortune.[75] The unity of the city, and the absence of seditions and internal problems, is the key to Guicciardini's choice. Venice is "tempered", by successfully combining the elements of all three types of government.[76] The oration of the doge Lionardo Loredano in the Venetian senate in *Storia d'Italia*, and the *laudatio* for the *Serenissima* Guicciardini puts in his mouth, is most illuminating: without any civil strife and discord, and no blood shed between her citizens for centuries, Venetian concord, "unique praise of our republic", excels all the ancient republics – Rome, Carthage, Athens and Sparta.[77]

4 Concluding Remarks

Guicciardini therefore settles for a contemporary republic. That he came to such a conclusion is not particularly surprising; as Gilbert put it, Machiavelli was "the only Florentine political thinker who was not an admirer of Venice".[78] Being more sensitive to current conditions, more conservative and more

74 "A me pare che el governo viniziano per una città disarmata sia cosí bello come forse mai avessi alcuna republica libera", *Dialogo*, 106 (*Dialogue*, 102). On 138–9 (*Dialogue*, 134) it is put even more strongly: "Venetian government … is the finest and best government not only of our times, but also perhaps that ever a city in ancient times had" ("governo viniziano … è il più bello ed migliore governo non solo de' tempi nostri, ma ancora che forse avessi mai a' tempi antichi alcuna città").

75 "…essendo durato già centinaia di anni florido ed unito come ognuno sa, non si può attribuire alla fortuna o al caso", *ibidem* (*Dialogue*, 102–3).

76 "…perché participa di tutte le spezie de' governi, di uno, di pochi e di molti, ed è temperato di tutti in modo che ha raccolta la maggiore parte de' beni che ha in sé qualunche governo e fuggiti la più parte de' mali", *ibidem*, 138–9 (*Dialogue*, 134).

77 "…la forma del governo che, temperato di tutti i modi migliori di qualunque specie di amministrazione publica e composta in modo a guisa di armonia, proporzionato e concordante tutto a se medesimo, è durato già tanti secoli, senza sedizione civile senza armi e senza sangue tra i suoi cittadini, inviolabile e immaculato; laude unica della nostra republica, e della quale non si può gloriare né Roma né Cartagine né Atene né Lacedemone", *Storia d'Italia*, VIII.10.

78 Felix Gilbert, "The Venetian Constitution in Florentine Political Thought", in Nicolai Rubinstein, ed., *Florentine Studies: Politics and Society in Renaissance Florence* (London: Faber and Faber, 1968), 463–500, at 488. Cf. also Roberto Palmarocchi, "Stato e governo nel pensiero di Francesco Guicciardini", in his *Studi guicciardiniani* (Firenze: Macrì, 1947), 6–30, at 17. Pocock, *Machiavellian Moment*, ch. 8, concentrates in particular on Guicciardini's treatment of Venice.

pessimistic, Guicciardini opts for Venice. He makes such a choice, though, despite being undoubtedly keen on ancient history, and interested in extracting valid political lessons from the Roman example.[79] Indeed, he is – unlike Machiavelli – full of respect for the austere version of classical republican virtue demonstrated by the last great Roman republicans, Cato Minor and Brutus.[80] The analysis of Guicciardini's criticism of Machiavelli's Roman model offered in this chapter reveals more than just a set of astute insights of the other great Florentine political thinker, and his own views: it also vividly shows how extreme was Machiavelli's position on emulating the Romans even in his own time.

Guicciardini's criticism of Machiavelli rejects the discord present in constitutional model based on the Roman Republic: here he certainly had "the weight of tradition on his side", as a commentator put it.[81] Simultaneously, sharp analysis offered by the younger Florentine clearly points to various weaknesses in Machiavelli's theoretical constructions. Perhaps the strongest rhetorical power of Guicciardini's critique is in his repeated emphasis on inapplicability of the ancient examples in changed political circumstances – all in spite of his pronounced respect for the ancients – a more down-to-earth approach which might be ascribed both to his more "limited" vision and a more "realist" grasp of prevailing political reality. However, it is important to stress that Guicciardini criticises not only the expansionistic, Roman model, but also the non-expansionistic republican constitution, suggested as the other alternative by Machiavelli. Following Polybius' comparison of the Roman vs. the Laconian constitution, Machiavelli in the *Discorsi*, I.6 improves the latter type by adding explicit prohibition of expansion, and, moreover, puts Venice in the same class as Sparta.[82] While raising the issue only when commenting the connected chapter of the *Discorsi*, II.19, it is clear that Guicciardini disapproves a

79 This is nicely shown in *Nota di cose da considerarsi* (in Guicciardini's *Opere inedite*, ed. Giuseppe Canestrini, vol. 10 (Firenze: M. Cellini e comp., 1867), 404–6), a list of (mainly political) problems Guicciardini was planning to write about: numerous entries are based on the Roman examples, especially from Livy.

80 See Guicciardini's little-known treatise *Del suicidio per ragione di libertà o di servitù* (in *Opere inedite*, vol. 10, 382–8). Machiavelli was unimpressed by Cato: see my comments in "Sallust, Machiavelli", 793–4 and n. 110.

81 John M. Najemy, "Society, Class, and State in Machiavelli's *Discourses on Livy*", in John M. Najemy, ed., *Cambridge Companion to Machiavelli* (Cambridge: Cambridge University Press, 2010), 96–111, at 103. Cf. here my conclusion in "Guicciardini's *La Decima scalata*", 329, how Guicciardini, with a prominent debate on justice and equality in the examined treatise, is far more representative of the typical concerns of the time, in the Italian republics, than is Machiavelli.

82 Cf. here my analysis in "Machiavelli: Empire, *Virtù* and Downfall", esp. 761–2.

general non-expansion rule no less than the plans for copying Roman modes and orders. Guicciardini is disinclined to both one-sided, extreme solutions: in contrast, Machiavelli unequivocally and repeatedly rejects the middle way [*via del mezzo*].[83] As Guicciardini himself once observed, his older co-citizen was a writer who was always particularly keen on "extraordinary" measures and remedies.[84]

Bibliography

Main Sources

Machiavelli, *Discorsi*.
Guicciardini, *Considerazioni intorno ai Discorsi del Machiavelli*.
Guicciardini, *Dialogo del reggimento di Firenze*.
Guicciardini, *Ricordi*.

Main Bibliographical References

Pocock, J.G.A, *The Machiavellian Moment: Florentine Political Thought and the Atlantic Republican Tradition* (Princeton: Princeton University Press, 1975).
Regent, Nikola, "A 'Medical Moment': Guicciardini and Lycurgus' Knife", *History of European Ideas*, 34.1 (2008), 1–13.
Regent, Nikola, "Machiavelli: Empire, *Virtù* and the Final Downfall", *History of Political Thought* 32.5 (2011), 751–72.

---

83 See e.g. *Discorsi*, I.6, I.26, II.23, III.3, III.40; *Del modo di trattare i popoli dalla Valdichiana ribellati*, 14.

84 "…lo scrittore, al quale sempre piacquono sopra modo e' remedi estraordinari e violenti", *Considerazioni*, I.26.

CHAPTER 10

The Union of Utrecht

An Unfinished Constitutional Definition between Federalism and Particularism in the Low Countries (1579–1621)

Alberto Mariano Rodríguez Martínez

1 In Search of a Constitution for the Republic*

On the morning of 29 January 1779, an audience consisting of judges, professors and students listened to a speech in Latin by Pieter Bondam, Professor of Law at the University of Utrecht, commemorating the 200th anniversary of the signing of the Union of Utrecht. Bondam's words recalled how its authors' determination, political affinity and love for their fatherland had led, two hundred years earlier, to "an eternal consensus being reached among different peoples".[1] This consensus crystallised with the signing, in 1579, of a union or collaboration treaty by the representatives of various cities and territories in the Low Countries.[2] As part of the celebration, students commissioned the artist P. J. Muller to design an arch featuring the *Unio Trajectina*, who was represented as a traditional Dutch Maiden, raising her eyes to the heavens, under the coats of arms of the seven United Provinces, and carrying the liberty bonnet on the tip of a lance. The arch was also to represent an altar, which alluded to the defence of religion, and a bust of William of Orange above the motto *His salvis, salva Republica.* Although it seems that this project never came to fruition, the involvement of the academic community in the bicentenary of the Union of

* This study was carried out within the framework of the research project "Res Publica monárquica. La Monarquía Hispánica, una estructura imperial policéntrica de repúblicas urbanas" (PGC2018–095224-B-I00) based on Universidad Pablo de Olavide (Seville), led by Manuel Herrero Sánchez and funded by the Spanish Ministerio de Ciencia, Innovación y Universidades.

1 Pieter Bondam, *Redevoering over de Unie van Utrecht, ter gelegenheid van derzelver twede eeuwfeest* (Utrecht: 1779), 137.

2 For a detailed reconstruction of the events, Geoffrey Parker, *The Dutch Revolt* (Harmondsworth: Pelican, 1979, 2nd ed.), 194–5; J. C. Boogman, "The Union of Utrecht: its Genesis and Consequences", *BMGN–Low Countries Historical Review*, 94.3 (1979), 377–407; Jonathan I. Israel, *The Dutch Republic: Its Rise, Greatness, and Fall, 1477–1806* (Oxford: Oxford University Press, 1995), 196–205.

DOI:10.1163/9789004549159_012

Utrecht was amply demonstrated by the sermons, firework displays and other festivities that marked the anniversary.[3] These celebrations also reached other cities and provinces: speeches took place and publications exalting the spirit of union and fraternity were published.[4]

A commemoration often involves reflecting on one's own past, and much can be gained from studying how different societies reflect. Centenaries are never an innocent exercise of memory: as pointed out by some scholars, these celebrations invariably serve contemporary needs and purposes.[5] It should not come as a surprise, therefore, that throughout the 18th century the Union of Utrecht was linked closely to the basic principle of the state and the constitution of the Republic. Towards the end of the century, especially with the crystallisation of natural law and contemporary constitutionalist concerns, it became necessary to find a legal and political monument, a compilation of laws and fundamental rights, that historically defined the state's basic premises. At this juncture, the treaty was reinterpreted and realigned to fit the liberal political theory that would triumph within a few decades; the Union was presented as:

> the only foundations on which the famous 'building of the State' stood, the buttress that held its walls, the documents with which its greatness had been achieved, and the pillars that kept it safe before the eyes of the world.[6]

As well as the "Grond-Constitutie van deze Republicq" on which to base the Dutch political structure, the 1579 treaty was also considered a reflection of the prudence and political wisdom of its creators.[7]

During the 20th century, the Union of Utrecht, its constitutional nature and the political genius of its promoters have been viewed in a rather different

3 *Brief aan een vriend, te Rotterdam bij gelegenheid, dat men het tweede eeuwgetijde der Utrechtsche Unie, vierde* (Utrecht: 1779), Knuttel 19330, 12.

4 J. W. te Water, *Redenvoering over de Unie van Utrecht* (Vlissingen, 1779). For the case of Leiden, see the pamphlet *Lierzang op het tweede eeuwgetijde van de Utrechtsche Unie* (Leiden, 1779), Knuttel 19329.

5 L. Dorsman, E. Jonker, K. Ribbens, *Het zoet en het zuur. Geschiedenis in Nederland* (Amsterdam: Wereldbibliotheek, 2000), 9–29. For the use of the past in the formation of identities, see Judith Pollmann, *Memory in Early Modern Europe, 1500–1800* (Oxford: Oxford University Press, 2017), ch. 4. The case of the Low Countries in J. van der Steen, *Memory Wars in the Low Countries, 1566–1700* (Leiden: Brill, 2015).

6 J. W. te Water, *Redenvoering*, 4.

7 Bondam, *Redevoering*, 138; P. Paulus, *Verklaring der Unie van Utrecht*, vol. 1, (Utrecht: 1775), Preface, 4v.

light.[8] The idealised vision, which saw the Union of Utrecht as the foundational document of the Dutch Republic, as well as a key reference for American constitutionalism, was replaced by a more pessimistic perspective, which doubted the document's value as a tool for political innovation. In the 20th century, emphasis was placed on the limitations of a document that could only be interpreted as an *ad hoc* military alliance against a common enemy.[9] If in the 18th century the promoters of the Union had been praised for their political savvy and their almost visionary powers, in the 19th and 20th centuries they were criticised for their inability – or unwillingness – to replace feudal mechanisms with a new order, modernising the Republic on the basis of political centralisation and legal homogenisation. The error of characterising the Union of Utrecht in constitutional terms was stressed: the union was an instrument that looked backwards, rather than forwards. It had been concocted as a practical expedient to face a conflict, and never had any pretensions in terms of political modernisation. According to some, the conservative and highly competitive Dutch elites had eschewed the possibility of creating a strong central authority, preferring instead to preserve their traditional spaces of power in the cities and the provinces.[10]

In the following pages, I shall analyse the role played by the Union's alleged errors and contradictions in the Dutch political model. Historiographical works often represent the Union of Utrecht in relation to its failure to give rise to a modern nation-state. However, rather than examining the text of the Union in search of inconsistencies, I shall begin by exploring the context within which the treaty was written in order to reassess its constitutional nature. As we shall see, the Union was not born with the purpose of becoming the legal foundation of the laws enacted in the Republic within the next two hundred years: it

8 The 400th anniversary of the Union brought the issue to the fore again. The most interesting contributions to the debate were P. Jongeling, *Een vast verbond: de Unie van Utrecht in haar historische context* (Groningen: De Vuurbaak, 1979); J. Baalbergen, *Van opstand tot onafhankelijkheid: de Unie van Utrecht en het ontstaan van een zelfstandige staat (1559–1609)* (The Hague: Staatsuitgeverij, 1979); S. Groenveld and H. L. Ph. Leeuwenberg, eds., *De Unie van Utrecht: Wording en werking van een verbond en een verbondsacte* (The Hague: Martinus Nijhoff, 1979).

9 S. J. Fockema Andreae, *De Nederlandse staat onder de Republiek* (Amsterdam: Noord-Hollandsche Uitgevers Maatschappij, 1973), 3; Boogman, "The Union of Utrecht", 386, 390.

10 For the characterisation of the city as an obstacle for the formation of the modern state, see W. P. Blockmans, "Voracious States and Obstructing Cities: An Aspect of State Formation in Preindustrial Europe", in C. Tilly and W. P. Blockmans, eds., *Cities and the Rise of States in Europe, A. D. 1000 to 1800* (Boulder: Westview Press, 1994), 218–250. A new perspective on the role of Dutch cities in the state-building process in W. Brake and W. Klooster, eds., *Power and the City in the Netherlandic World* (Leiden: Brill, 2006).

was more of a statement of intent, marked from the beginning by the reality of war, the autonomous tradition of cities and provinces, and the pre-eminence of customary law. Under these circumstances, there was little room for the implementation of those articles that aimed to regulate the collective action of the Union's members; for the period 1579–1588, these articles are said to have been "dead letters".[11] In the following years, however, federal action became increasingly important, as the threats to the survival of the Union progressively subsided. This is clearly related to Holland's hegemony within the Republic, a phenomenon halfway between federalism and particularism. The second part of the paper will examine how Holland used the terms of the Union of Utrecht for two, apparently contradictory, purposes: to justify the States General interfering with the internal politics of some provinces whilst also consolidating the primacy of Holland and its privileges in the Union. As such, I shall analyse how, during the period 1588–1616, Holland was able to make compatible the strengthening of the union with the promotion of provincial autonomy. Traditional historiography emphasises the contradictions in the foundational text of the Union. In contrast, I shall highlight how the ambiguous character of the Union of Utrecht facilitated the coexistence between different conceptions of power.

2 The Union of Utrecht: between Myth and Historical Reality

It is not difficult to find examples of the past being idealized by public opinion, and this applies also to the traditional foundational milestones of the Dutch Republic.[12] However, the historical reality of these events is generally much more prosaic. On the one hand, the reservations about the "miraculous" Dutch model as a precedent for democratic governments are, it seems, justified, based on the strong barriers to popular participation in politics that remained. While craftsmen and the popular sectors could sometimes tilt the political balance

---

11 R. Fruin and H. T. Colebrander, *Geschiedenis der Staatsinstellingen in Nederland tot den val der Republiek* (The Hague: Nijhoff, 1980), 179.

12 The Pacification of Ghent (1576), the Union of Utrecht (1579), the Twelve Years' Truce (1609) and the Peace of Münster (1648) were regarded as the constitutional bases of the Republic in C. H. Trotz, *Verklaaring van de Grondwetten der Vereenigde Nederlanden* (Harlingen, 1778). For later compilations of these fundamental laws, S. Groenveld, *Unie-Bestand-Vrede. Drie fundamentele wetten van de Republiek der Verenigde Nederlanden* (Hilversum: Verloren, 2009); Coos Huijsen and Geerten Waling, eds., *De geboortepapieren van Nederland: de Unie van Utrecht, de Apologie van Willem van Oranje en het Plakkaat van Verlating in hedendaags Nederlands* (Amsterdam: Elsevier, 2014).

against the wishes of magistrates, this happened only rarely, and the elites never lost their monopoly over political power. As such, Robert Johnson's comment in his English translation of Botero's *Relationi Universali*, which defined the Republic's political model as one in which "the people and citizens have so much voice and authority", can be countered with less favourable comments.[13] An in-depth analysis of the traditional milestones of Dutch constitutionalism reveals that their real ability to radically undermine the basis of traditional political models was beset with great limitations, and as a result, these models continued largely after the Dutch revolt. It is possible to question the value of the Union of Utrecht and the Act of Abjuration as the trigger of revolutionary changes capable of establishing the unique Dutch Republic. If we do this, it seems that the model embodied by the Dutch Republic was not deliberately or consciously put in writing in a series of texts which aimed to become the constitutional foundation and legal basis of the new regime. All the evidence suggests that implementing political innovations and transformations was never on the agenda of the States, which preferred to keep the traditional model and recognised Philip II as their natural lord until 1581. If the treaty of Union in January 1579 cannot be considered the birth of the Republic of the United Provinces, then the Act of Abjuration did little more than confirm the need for a ruling head and validate a political tradition that exalted the monarchy as the best form of government.[14] In conclusion, the constitution of a republican government in 1588 was related more to the lack of available alternatives than to the existence of real political convictions. The Dutch model, therefore, rather than being shaped by a series of foundational documents, crystallised

---

13 G. Botero and R. Johnson, *Relations of the most famous kingdomes and common-wealths* (London, 1630), 206. For his part, William Temple considered that the United Provinces, "though they retained the name of a free people, yet they soon lost the ease of the liberties they contended for, by the absoluteness of their magistrates in the several cities and provinces and by the extreme pressure of their taxes", in *Observations upon the United Provinces of the Netherlands* (London, 1673), 55. He assured that both aspects were in the Republic "greater than in many of those governments which are esteemed most arbitrary among their neighbours", 108–9.

14 As early as August 1579, William of Orange expressed that "the Netherlands need a prince to take the duties of government upon himself". Soon afterwards, the idea of appointing the Duke of Anjou as "protector of the Low Countries, with full authority in matters of justice, government and war", was circulating. In J. Wagenaar, *Vaderlandsche historie*, vol. 7 (Amsterdam, 1752), 302. For arguments in favour of princely power during the first half of the 17th century, as a constitutive and necessary element of the new regime, see E.H. Kossmann, *Political thought in the Dutch Republic: three studies* (Amsterdam: Koninklijke Nederlandse Akademie van Wettenschappen, 2000), 27–51.

progressively and adapted to the circumstances. In Bentivoglio's words, this Republic seemed to "have grown up before it was born".[15]

With these origins, it was impossible to foresee that the Dutch Republic was destined to become, a century later, a global power capable of expanding its geographical horizons and playing a central role in international relations. However, during the decades that followed the beginning of the revolt, the Low Countries became the only stage in a war in which the survival of the provinces' liberties was at stake. This war could not be won by provinces fighting independently, making union an urgent necessity. The prevailing particularism, however, hampered the provinces effective cooperation in defending their privileges. Traditional inter-provincial conflicts were clearly present in the attitudes of the provinces, which had traditionally opposed to some centralising tendencies represented by their former Burgundian and Habsburg sovereigns.[16] During the late 1570s, under the aegis of the free States General, presided over by Archduke Matthias as governor-general and controlled by William of Orange, the situation remained largely the same. The States' delegates voiced constant, and reciprocal, suspicions of treachery. A pamphlet claimed that some of these delegates appeared to have been chosen "not because they were experienced in state affairs, but because they were enormously stubborn and particularly good at fighting for the rights, exemptions and advantages of their towns and provinces".[17] This was also William of Orange's opinion. In 1579, William regretted that the delegates had completely forgotten the common good. According to the stadtholder, they wanted nothing but to elevate their cities and provinces above the rest, and to look after their own interest, even if this meant the ruin of the others.[18]

As a result, it is hardly surprising that arguments for a Closer Union (*Nadere Unie*) were received with little enthusiasm, if not open hostility, by some

---

15 "Anzi con istupore, [è la Republica] cresciuta quasi prima, che nata", in G. Bentivoglio, *Relatione delle Provincie Unite*, ed. Salvo Mastellone and E. O. G. Haitsma Mulier (Firenze: Centro Editoriale Toscano, 1983), 4r.

16 For a study on the interactions among different ideas of fatherland and the emergence of multi-layered identities, see Robert Stein and Judith Pollmann, eds., *Networks, Regions and Nations: Shaping Identities in the Low Countries (1300–1650)* (Leiden: Brill, 2010); Alastair Duke, "The Elusive Netherlands: The Question of National Identity in the Early Modern Low Countries on the eve of the Revolt", *BMGN-Low Countries Historical Review*, 119.1 (2004), 10–38.

17 *Emanuel-Erneste, dialogue de deux personnages sur l'estat du Païs Bas* (Antwerp, 1580), Knuttel 545, 24.

18 R. Fruin and H. T. Colebrander, *Geschiedenis der Staatsinstellingen*, 183. Regarding provincial particularism during these years, see G. Malengreau, *L' esprit particulariste et la révolution des Pays-Bas au XVIe siècle, 1578–1584* (Louvain: Bibliothèque de l'Université, 1936).

provinces. The cities in Gelderland, for instance, were wary of the Calvinism underlying the proposal. The fact that negotiations concerning the terms of the new union, which took place in September 1578 in Arnhem, were accompanied by a series of iconoclastic practices did nothing but confirm Gelderland's reservations, and this led to a body of troops, commanded by Jan van Nassau as stadtholder of the province, to enter the city in order to force a favourable resolution.[19] Aside from the religious issues, other new tensions did not take long to emerge, when the representatives of Holland conditioned their joining the union to Gelderland and the remaining Catholic provinces' actively contributions both militarily and financially to the common effort. Everyone was aware that, until then, the burden of the war had been chiefly borne by the provinces of Holland and Zeeland,[20] which now sought to collaborate with the northern and eastern provinces to contain the enemy and push the war – which hampered the circulation of goods and persons – outside their own territory. This proposal was not well received by the representatives of Gelderland, who were accused by their counterparts from Holland of lacking solidarity. Despite the endeavours of their stadtholder, who tried to force the union upon the provinces, the States of Gelderland consistently opposed what they deemed to be a sterile, unnecessary and risky *Hollantsche Union*, which put their privileges under threat in the face of the increasing domination of Calvinist Holland.[21]

For their part, the States in the province of Overijssel were too busy with the siege of Deventer to attend those meetings in which the Union of Utrecht was being discussed, first in Arnhem and later in Utrecht, in September and October 1578 respectively: they sent two representatives, but merely as observers. In 1581, during the meeting of the States General in which the acceptance of the Duke of Anjou as sovereign was discussed, the delegate Johan Dorre advised the representatives of Deventer to watch and act prudently, as they had previously done on the occasion of the Union of Utrecht.[22] Meanwhile,

19 For a detailed analysis of the preliminary negotiations in Arnhem and elsewhere, see P. J. van Winter, "De ontwerpen van de Unie van Utrecht", *Bijdragen en Mededelingen van het Historisch Genootschap*, 64 (1943), 108–179; A. van Hulzen, "Achtergronden van de Unie van Utrecht", *Jaarboek Oud-Utrecht 1978*, 24–55.

20 Holland and Zeeland were at least praised for their efforts: "Olandesi e Zelandesi ad ogni prencipe havevano insegnato, che se con lungo tempo manegiar le armi agguerrivano i popoli che difendevano la libertà loro, si facevano divenir insuperabili", in Traiano Boccalini, *De Ragguagli di Parnaso. Centuria seconda* (Venice, 1613), 25.

21 A.E.M. Janssen, "Het verdeelde Huis: Prins Willem van Onranje en graaf Jan van Nassau bij de totstandkoming van de Unie van Utrecht", in Groenveld and Leeuwenberg, eds., *De Unie van Utrecht*, 128–9.

22 In this sense, he said "I think that we are best off in this matter [with respect to Anjou] if we maintain the same posture as we took with respect to the Closer Union. We should

in Friesland cities were completely divided about the possibility of joining the union, which was, at any rate, then rejected outright by the provincial clergy. Finally, the enthusiasm for the union exhibited by the Ommelanden must be related to the possibilities that the new framework might provide to its cities in their competition with Groningen.[23]

The Union of Utrecht was signed on 23 January 1579. It had severe limitations, and it had little chance of garnering the support of provinces, which were not willing to sacrifice their own interests for the common good. The agreement was born into a context where few had high expectations, and it only had the full support of Holland, Zeeland, Utrecht, the Ommelanden, a few nobles from Gelderland and the stadtholder Jan van Nassau. On the other hand, certain Frisian rural authorities (*grietmannen*) and some cities in Flanders and Brabant, which were still fighting the enemy, joined the Union individually in the following months. The fact that some of these cities – for example, Brugge – were isolated or too far away to influence the military operations, and the presence in others of strong social-reformist guild-Calvinist elements – for instance, in Ghent – made their incorporation into the Union appear more as a problem than an advantage to the moderate group of regents who ruled the States of Holland. For his part, Count Rennenberg, stadtholder of Groningen, Friesland, Drenthe and Overijssel, only agreed to sign the Union under strict conditions, after rejecting it for five months, ostensibly because the union had been consummated behind the back of Archduke Matthias and the States General of Brussels.[24] William of Orange expressed similar doubts; he suspected that the signatory provinces would continue to follow their policies and disregard both the general union with the southern Low Countries (*Generale Unie*) and his own policy of religious tolerance. For this reason, he did not join the Union until May 1579.[25] From the military point of view, the Union of Utrecht proved

not make speedy decisions, but rather await the time that the issue is less hot. If, by that time, others are benefiting from it, then we can still join them". In Richard Reitsma, *Centrifugal and centripetal forces in the Early Dutch Republic: The States of Overyssel, 1566–1600* (Amsterdam: Rodopi, 1982), 172.

23 The Ommelanden were all those territories in the province of Groningen that were outside the city of Groningen's direct control. For an analysis of the relationships between Ommelanden and the city of Groningen, and of how they marked the trajectory of a province which was known as *Stad en Lande* because of its twofold nature, see H. Feenstra, *Spinnen in het web: Groningse regenten in relatie tot het omringende platteland tijdens de Republiek* (Assen: Van Gorcum, 2007).

24 P. C. Bor, *Oorsprongk, begin en vervolgh der Nederlandsche oorlogen*, vol. 2 (Amsterdam, 1680), 33.

25 Israel, *The Dutch Republic*, 202.

incapable of stopping Farnesio from advancing and taking Maastricht, at a time when the use of force also became necessary against some cities which refused to join the Union and were in a state of open rebellion. The example posed by the city of Amersfoort (Utrecht), which rejected the province's decision to join the Union, illustrates the internal tensions and the differences of opinion from local contexts that beset the alliance and gravely undermined its efficacy.[26] In this situation, it is little wonder that the first coinage to be issued after the signing of the Union featured, in William Temple's words, a ship "labouring among the Waves without Sails or Oars; and these words: *Incertum quo fata ferant*".[27] It is hard to imagine a better illustration of the difficulties and uncertainty of those times.

3 Contradiction as a Foundation of the Model? Provinces, Generality and the Problem of Sovereignty

When it comes to analysing the failure of this (and future) projects, which might have become precursors to centralisation and political modernisation, the focus is often placed on the traditional particularism of cities and provinces. Indeed, this particularism was the main reason why the articles that emphasised collective military and financial efforts (articles VIII and V, respectively) fell by the wayside. Yet, the inability of the Union to undermine the prevailing particularism may lie in article I. This article made it clear that the fact that the provinces were forming "an alliance, confederation, and union among themselves (…) as if they constituted only a single province" could not undermine their traditional freedoms. The article elaborates further: "each province and the individual cities, members and inhabitants thereof shall retain undiminished its special and particular privileges, franchises, exemptions, rights, statutes, laudable and long practiced costumes, usages and all its rights".[28] As some authors have pointed out, the Union was born to both facilitate cooperation between provinces and protect their integrity, but the former objective was subordinated to and limited by the latter. Put differently: the Union was the means, and the preservation of privileges the end.[29]

26 Wagenaar, *Vaderlandsche historie*, vol. 7, 286.
27 Temple, *Observations*, 54.
28 Bor, *Oorsprongk*, vol. 2, 26–9; Groenveld, *Unie-Bestand-Vrede*, 61.
29 A. Th. Van Deursen, "Tussen eenheid en zelfstandigheid: De toepassing van de Unie als fundamentele wet", in Groenveld and Leeuwenberg, eds., *De Unie van Utrecht*, 138–9.

The opening article of the Union seems to stress the autonomy and sovereignty of the provinces and cities, but we should not forget that other articles were to have a long-term effect on the Dutch model, which may effectively be linked to the eventual development of a federal policy. The text did not expressly indicate the creation of a federal authority, let alone outline its powers. However, the articles that defined the role of the stadtholders and the Generality as arbiters of potential inter-provincial disputes (articles IX and XVI) put the two institutions that (at least in terms of appearance) better represented the Union's policy in a position to exercise enormous authority. Although the stadtholder was still, theoretically, a provincial position, his role as captain general of the Union effectively endorsed it with federal powers. Concerning the States General, certain authors have stressed that their role was merely to serve as an arena for the interaction of seven sovereign and independent entities.[30] In theory, this institution had no authority to interfere with the government of provinces and cities, as it was forced to respect their freedoms and privileges (in keeping with article I of the Union). However, we must not underestimate the practical effects that the need to keep unity at all costs would have had for provincial autonomy in the long term. Although the text entrusted, somewhat imprecisely, the Generality with the role of mediator between the provinces, its role as arbiter gave the institution enormous power, especially from 1588 onwards. The political crises of 1618, 1650 and 1672 are evidence of the ability of the States General to impose a given line of action and challenge the sacrosanct principle of provincial autonomy and its theoretical foundations. The fact that, under those conditions, the States General and the stadtholder invariably referred to the text of the Union reveals that this question was at the heart of the political struggle between provinces and the Generality. The analysis of the practical development of the Dutch model reveals that appeal to the Union of Utrecht and interpretation of its terms were useful resources to claim authority in the context of the coexistence and complementarity of different political stances.[31]

In this regard, sovereignty in the Dutch Republic should not be understood as a closed concept which is linked to the exercise of power by an absolute and

30 Fruin and Colebrander, *Geschiedenis der Staatsinstellingen*, 183.

31 G. de Bruin, "De soeverainiteit in de republiek: een machtsprobleem", *BMGN–Low Countries Historical Review*, 94.1 (1994), 27–40. It seems necessary to stress the importance of those studies which, beyond a formal analysis of authority and the institutional structure of the Republic, emphasise the practical functioning of Dutch political machinery. See also G. de Bruin, *Geheimhouding en verraad: De geheimhouding van staatszaken ten tijde van de Republiek (1600–1750)* (The Hague: SDU, 1991), 133.

well-defined authority, but rather as an argument for a debate in which legal and political ideas used by different forces converged.[32] Often, the relationship between different notions of sovereignty and power was marked by contradiction or rivalries, but it was not always the case. In 1611, Guido Bentivoglio's *Relatione delle Provincie Unite* described the government of the Republic in what many would today define as openly contradictory terms. First, he argued that, after the revolt, "the States of each province became the supreme authority, which theretofore resided with the prince", whilst simultaneously claiming that these States sent "their sovereign decrees" to a council (*Gecomiteerde Raden*), which executed them. However, concerning the States General, he stated that "this great assembly represents the sovereignty of the Union, and is above all other institutions, like the Prince was in the past".[33] William Temple's account of the States General may seem equally confusing: "This counsel is not sovereign, but only represents the sovereignty".[34] It is clear that both authors were aware of the multi-layered nature of the system, and that they tried to describe it without entering into a discussion of matters of internal hierarchy.

The problem is revealed in all its complexity with the questions that came later: Where does sovereignty lie in the Republic? Was the Republic a federation or a confederation? No definitive answers might be forthcoming if we conceive sovereignty in the Republic, as well as in many other early modern political entities, from a modern perspective involving a *summa potestas* emerged from a "restatement of the permanent problem of deciding the basis of government and obligation within a political community".[35] Although this Bodinian notion is still shared today by Daniel Philpott, who considers sovereignty as supremacy within an ordered political constellation, it is difficult to fit in a territory where neither power nor prerogatives were clearly distributed.[36] Therefore, these questions may concern the demands of some scholars aiming to identify the true holder of sovereignty, rather than the practical needs and changing

---

32 Martin van Gelderen, "The Low Countries", in Howell A. Lloyd, Glenn Burgess and Simon Hodson, eds., *European Political Thought, 1450–1700. Religion, Law and Philosophy* (New Haven-London: Yale University Press, 2007), 389. See also Hent Kalmo and Quentin Skinner, eds., *Sovereignty in Fragments: The Past, Present and Future of a Contested Concept* (Cambridge: Cambridge University Press, 2010), 7.

33 Bentivoglio, *Relatione*, 9, 15, 18.

34 Temple, *Observations*, 98–9.

35 F. H. Hinsley, *Sovereignty* (Cambridge: Cambridge University Press, 1986, second edition), 26.

36 Daniel Philpott, 'Sovereignty', *The Stanford Encyclopedia of Philosophy* (Fall 2020 edition), Edward N. Zalta, ed., https://plato.stanford.edu/archives/fall2020/entries/sovereignty/ (last visited on 26/02/2021).

circumstances of a Dutch model for which the meaning of this term was not a precise one.[37] We can thus understand the doubts of the Dutch delegates at the conference held in Plessis-lès-Tours in September 1580, when the appointment of the Duke of Anjou as "lord" (*heer*) of the Low Countries was being discussed, and the French delegation asked to include the term *souverain* in his title. In the event, the Dutch delegation rejected this condition, arguing that the term was quite ambiguous.[38]

As we have already seen, there was also ambiguity in the clauses of the Union of Utrecht, which were open to interpretation by centrifugal and centripetal forces that competed in the Republic. From one perspective, their conflict could be related to the shortcomings of the Union of Utrecht and the eccentric nature of the model which it represented. Despite all of this, this does not mean that the Union automatically triggered a confrontation between two different doctrines on sovereignty, as the Union also emerged as a middle ground and, in a way, made dialogue possible. In this regard, the deficiencies, vagueness, and imprecision of the text become something almost positive, insofar as the Union allowed for the interaction of different approaches to authority and sovereignty, in much less conflictive terms. Except during crises, at all other times all the evidence suggests that dialogue reigned supreme and contributed to the long-term survival of a Republic in which persuasion, not coercion, was the predominant political tool. In a way, those articles of the Union of Utrecht that could be interpreted in multiple ways, which many have used to explain the failure of the Dutch state, may have also contributed to the political stability of the system, although it was riven with paradoxes and anomalies.[39] Although the absence of a clearly defined authority and principle of sovereignty may sound odd from the perspective of 20th century political theory, an analysis of the relationship of powers reveals that this situation could, under some circumstances, be beneficial. As we shall see in the following section, Holland benefited from the Union of Utrecht more than anyone else. The value

37 On the impact that the course of events made on the development of the concept of sovereignty in the Low Countries, which we should study not only from a theoretical but also historical approach, see Erik de Bom, Randall Lesaffer and Werner Thomas, eds., *Early Modern Sovereignties: Theory and Practice of a Burgeoning Concept in the Netherlands* (Leiden: Brill, 2021).

38 Wagenaar, *Vaderlandsche historie*, vol. 7, 399.

39 Something hinted at by Huizinga, despite his criticism of a political system described as faulty (*gebrekkig*) and a Union which considered full of imperfections (*onvolkomenheden*). However, at the same time, he suggested that this lack of definition may have been a benefit rather than a problem in politics. In Johan Huizinga, *Nederland's beschaving in de zeventiende eeuw: een schets* (Haarlem: Tjeenk Willink, 1941), 46.

of the Union did not lie in its theoretical content, but rather in the practical opportunities that it offered.

4 From Theory to Practice: the Union of Utrecht and Holland's Hegemony (1588–1616)

In April 1588, the Earl of Leicester renounced the position of protector of the Netherlands, conferred by the States General years earlier, leaving the Union bereft of a visible head once again. This was not a new situation for the Union, which this time decided to adopt a republican model, marked by the uncontested hegemony of the province of Holland.[40] The leadership of this province had consolidated throughout the 1580s, and was to fully crystallise in the following decades. During this period, the provincial States of Holland not only defended their particular interests with energy, but managed to effectively justify their ascendancy over the remaining provinces: for instance, when they tried to preserve the authority and leadership of William of Orange in the province, against hypothetical encroachments of the Duke of Anjou.[41] In 1587, in the context of the political confrontation between Leicester and the States of Holland, the latter mounted a two-pronged strategy. One the one hand, they vindicated traditional particularism against the possibility of centralising power and authority in the Council of State (*Raad van State*), dominated by Leicester, who had taken up residence in Utrecht.[42] This was supported by the appointment by Holland and Zeeland of the young Maurits van Nassau as provincial stadtholder before Leicester could even think of assuming that role. The intention was to use the new stadtholder as a counterweight to Leicester and thus help preserve the autonomy of the province. Meanwhile, the pensionary of Gouda, François Vrancken, presented strong arguments for the

40 Israel, *The Dutch Republic*, 277. For the weight of the province, traditionally considered *pars pro toto* of the Republic, see H. Wansink, "Holland and Six Allies: The Republic of the Seven United Provinces", in J. S. Bromley and E. H. Kossmann, eds., *Britain and the Netherlands,* vol. IV: *Metropolis, Dominion and Province* (The Hague: Springer, 1971), 133–55.

41 See the letter sent in 1583 by the States of Holland to their counterparts in Utrecht, which aimed to dismiss the risks that this measure could, allegedly, have for the Union, and the idea that Holland and Zeeland were too autonomous. In P. C. Bor, *Oorsprongk*, vol. 2, 187–90.

42 For Leicester's rule of the Netherlands, see F. G. Oosterhoff, *Leicester and the Netherlands, 1586–1587* (Utrecht: HES Publishers, 1988); Simon Adams, *Leicester and the Court: Essays on Elizabethan Politics* (New York: Manchester University Press, 2002), 176–95.

political pre-eminence of the States, laying down theoretical foundations and putting forward a line of argument which was later to be followed by Grotius and Busius. This argument emphasised the role of provincial States as the main repositories of authority and sovereignty in an eminently aristocratic system, based on a mixed republic.[43] Vrancken stressed the role of the States, their sovereignty and authority, in secularly defending and representing the common good against the prince; pitched against him were the arguments of Thomas Wilkes, an English member of the *Raad van State*, and Gerard Prouninck, burgomaster of Utrecht, both loyal followers of Leicester, who defended the need for a "sovereign head" and thought that the prince could not be deprived of his authority by the representatives of the *commonalty*, but only by the *commonalty* itself.[44] However, despite presenting legal arguments for the sovereignty and exclusive authority of the provinces, the States of Holland did not hesitate to promote political union and federation in so far as this benefited their interests. In practice, this strategy involved the utilisation of the Generality's institutional framework, especially the States General, in order to promote Holland's policies and strengthen its hand in its conflict with Leicester. There is little doubt that the move of the States General to The Hague in 1585, to a building but a few metres away to the place where the States of Holland met, offered the delegates of Holland the chance to influence the representatives of the other provinces and effectively steer the policy of the States General. The appointments of Maurits as admiral-general of the Union in 1588, as well as that of Johan van Oldenbarnevelt as *landsadvocaat* of the province in February 1586, aimed not only to put obstacles in the path of Leicester's government but also to consolidate Holland's hegemony.[45] This policy benefited greatly from Oldenbarnevelt's cunning in coordinating the defence of the interests of the province and the promotion of a federal policy under the banner of the Union. The result was the consolidation of Holland's hegemony, incarnated in a figure who theoretically presented himself as a representative of the

43 Hugo Grotius, *Antiquity of the Batavian Republic*, ed. J. Waszink (Assen: Van Gorcum, 2000), 49. For Paulus Busius, see M. E. H. N. Mout, "Ideales Muster oder erfundene Eigenart: Republikanische Theorien während des niederländischen Aufstands", in H. G. Koenigsberger, ed., *Republiken und Republikanismus im Europa der Frühen Neuzeit* (Munich: R. Oldenbourg Verlag, 1988), 186–7; Kossmann, *Political Thought*, 33–6.

44 For a fragment of Vrancken's *Corte Vertoninge*, and other speeches related to this debate on the nature of sovereignty, see E. H. Kossmann and A. F. Mellink, *Texts concerning the Revolt of the Netherlands* (Cambridge: Cambridge University Press, 1974), 269–81.

45 Commision for Maurits as admiral-general, 31/08/1588: Koninklijke Huisarchief, Archief Prins Maurits, VI, 7; H. H. Rowen, *The Princes of Orange: The Stadholders in the Dutch Republic* (Cambridge: Cambridge University Press, 1988), 35.

provincial States, but who in fact exercised considerable power at the federal level. Whoever could manoeuvre within this field of coexistence, playing with the different concepts of power and sovereignty, would have the upper hand.

The following decades were characterised by the combination of both approaches and the close correspondence between the policies advocated by the States of Holland and the Generality. Often, the States General implemented policies which, while theoretically respecting the traditional privileges of provinces and cities, allowed in practice the intervention of the States General when it suited the interests of Holland. Holland's manipulation of the States General and the arguments for unity ran parallel to the strengthening of the doctrine of autonomous provincial sovereignty.[46] The scales tilted one way or the other depending on the circumstances, as Holland's interpretation of the Union of Utrecht changed according to the political situation. Between 1588 and 1616, Holland took advantage of the ambiguous relationship between particularism and federal government. For this reason, it is not strange that those who presented themselves as the strongest advocates of the autonomy of Holland in the context of the political crisis of the period 1616–1618 had previously featured as foremost promoters of the Union and the authority of the States General, understood merely as an instrument of Holland's hegemony.[47] When a delegation from Overijssel went to The Hague in 1592 to complain about a private treaty between the Frisian States and the city of Hasselt, which agreed to reject being garrisoned by troops from other provinces, the States General quickly pointed out that this undermined the privileges of the province of Overijssel and, therefore, the principle of provincial sovereignty as formulated in the Union of Utrecht.[48] It is likely that The Hague's swift reaction was prompted by Holland's wish to curb the increasing influence of Friesland, whose opposition had been instrumental in the rejection of the appointment of Maurits, stadtholder of Holland and future Prince of Orange, to the position of captain general of the Union, in 1589.[49] In 1607, Oldenbarnevelt

46 It is an idea Bentivoglio emphasised: "si vede particolarmente, c'hà proportione e corrispondenza grandissima il governo unito insieme di tutte [the provinces], co'l governo separato di ciascuna di loro", in G. Bentivoglio, *Relatione*, 25.

47 Concerning Grotius, his argument in defence of the sovereignty of the States of Holland appears not to be incompatible with a positive view of the notion of unity and community between the seven provinces. See H. Grotius, *Antiquity*, 123, 139, 144; E. Alexander-Davey, "Nationhood and Constitutionalism in the Dutch Republic: An Examination of Grotius' *Antiquity of the Batavian Republic*", *History of Political Thought*, 38.1 (2017), 64–91.

48 Van Deursen, "Tussen eenheid en zelfstandigheid", 141–2; Israel, *The Dutch Republic*, 245–6.

49 R. Fruin and H. T. Colebrander, *Geschiedenis der Staatsinstellingen*, 211. The States of Holland repeated the same suggestion in 1609, but failed once more with the opposition of Friesland, Groningen and Overijssel.

advocated the strengthening of the authority of the States General over provinces and cities as the only way to force them to keep their commitments with the Union and thus guarantee the survival of the state, because "no Republic may exist, without good order in the general Government".[50] In March 1619, after the provinces had reacted against Holland's supremacy and established control over the States General, Oldenbarnevelt did not hesitate to change the strategy and describe this body as a mere meeting of subordinated delegates, like the Imperial Circles or the parliaments of the Swiss cantons: "[they may] decide only in those affairs which are entrusted to their league (…) while supremacy and sovereignty lie only in awarding authorities".[51] At this juncture, Oldenbarnevelt's interpretation of the Union of Utrecht advocated that provincial autonomy and respect for Holland's privileges and liberties should take precedence over the authority of the Generality. After decades during which Holland's supremacy had rested on the coexistence of different interpretations of power, the years 1616–1618 brought changes to the political scenario. The ambiguous nature of the Union of Utrecht facilitated then partisan uses of its clauses, increasing inter-provincial rivalries as well as inter-urban tensions in Holland. The effects of the Twelve Years' Truce varied from city to city, and this tainted the cities' opinion about religious policy and negotiation with the Spanish monarchy, splitting political positions in the province of Holland and incapacitating the province's influence in the Union; the stadtholder, for his part, used his role as arbiter to strengthen his own position.[52] However, after the 1616–1618 interval, the Union was to resume its role as the central foundation of the relationship between cities, provinces and the Generality – a complex relationship generally based on interdependence, rather than opposition.[53]

---

50 Quoted in M. L. van Deventer, *Gedenkstukken van Johan van Oldenbarnevelt en zijn tijd*, vol. 3 (The Hague: Martinus Nijhoff, 1865), 143. In fact, it is stressed that it was Oldenbarnevelt who strengthened the unity of the state and acted as a unifying factor until the crisis of 1618. See also Fruin and Colebrander, *Geschiedenis der Staatsinstellingen*, 212.

51 In M. Siegenbeek, ed., *Verhooren van Johan van Oldenbarnevelt* (Utrecht: Kemink en Zoon, 1850), 191.

52 For the tensions that sowed seeds of dissent among the cities of the province of Holland, see M. 't Hart, "Intercity Rivalries and the Making of the Dutch State", in Tilly and Blockmans, eds., *Cities and the Rise of States*, 196–217; Jonathan I. Israel, 'The Holland Towns and the Dutch-Spanish Conflict, 1621–1648', *BMGN–Low Countries Historical Review*, 94.1 (1994), 41–69.

53 This relationship between different levels of power revolved around such issues as taxes, defence and political action: James D. Tracy, *The Founding of the Dutch Republic: War, Finance and Politics in Holland, 1572–1588* (Oxford: Oxford University Press, 2008); Griet Vermeesch, *Oorlog, steden en staatsvorming: de grenssteden Gorinchem en Doesburg tijdens de geboorte-eeuw van de Republiek (1570–1680)*, (Amsterdam: Amsterdam University Press, 2006).

5 Conclusion

As previously noted, the Union of Utrecht did not precisely determine a political system that was to oscillate between the integrity of each province and the need to make these provinces work for the common good. Both, seemingly contradictory, principles were included in the original text of the Union, supposedly triggering oppositional approaches to power and sovereignty. However, the analysis of this concept should not be divorced from the practicalities of politics and their development over time; the document of the Union of Utrecht must be viewed in the light of "the experience and practices followed, which must be considered as the best interpreters of the said Union".[54] Contextualization, rather than focusing on its theoretical and constitutional formulation, can be more revealing of the actual impact of the Union on an ever-evolving model; we need to recognise that its improvised institutional apparatus was never immune to changing power relationships.

Based on this premise, if we consider that the "fails" of the Union of Utrecht facilitated the coexistence of different approaches to sovereignty and political power, we shall obtain a different picture of the United Provinces. The political model of the Dutch Republic has been repeatedly described as the result of neverending tensions between the dominant Holland and the lesser provinces, between *prinsgezinden* and *staatsgezinden*, between the sovereignty of the Union and that of the provincial States.[55] Its evolution highlights the various uses made of the Union of Utrecht as a political weapon to be invoke during episodes of institutional conflict in the Republic. However, the example posed by Holland in the period 1588–1616 demonstrates that the system had multiple layers of authority and political action that, most of the time, were able to coexist. Despite these internal contradictions, or probably thanks to them, this flexible system was able to cope with challenges and demonstrated unparalleled resilience for the next two hundred years.

54 As pointed out by the *Raad van State* in 1659. See Van Deursen, "Tussen eenheid en zelfstandigheid", 152.

55 Israel, *The Dutch Republic*, Preface, VI; David Onnekink and Gijs Rommelse, *The Dutch in the Early Modern World: A History of a Global Power* (Cambridge: Cambridge University Press, 2019), 51.

Bibliography

Main Sources

Bentivoglio, Guido, *Relatione delle Provincie Unite*, ed. S. Mastellone and E. O. G. Haitsma Mulier (Florence: Centro Editoriale Toscano, 1983).

Bondam, Pieter, *Redevoering over de Unie van Utrecht, ter gelegenheid van derzelver twede eeuwfeest* (Utrecht, 1779).

Bor, Pieter Christiaenszoon, *Oorsprongk, begin, en vervolgh der Nederlandsche oorlogen, beroerten, en borgerlyke oneenigheden, beginnende met de koomste van Alexander Farnese, Prince van Parma, en eyndigende omtrent het laetste van Junius des Jaers 1587* (Amsterdam, 1679–84), 4 vols.

Temple, William, *Observations upon the United Provinces of the Netherlands* (London, 1673).

Wagenaar, Jan, *Vaderlandsche Historie, vervattende de Geschiedenissen der nu Vereenigde Nederlanden, inzonderheid die van Holland, van de vroegste tyden af* (Amsterdam, 1749–59), 21 vols.

Main Bibliographical References

Boogman, J. C., "The Union of Utrecht: its Genesis and Consequences", *BMGN–Low Countries Historical Review*, 94.3 (1979), 377–407.

De Bom, E.; R. Lesaffer; and W. Thomas, eds., *Early Modern Sovereignties: Theory and Practice of a Burgeoning Concept in the Netherlands* (Leiden and Boston: Brill, 2020).

Fruin, R.; and H.T. Colebrander, *Geschiedenis der Staatsinstellingen in Nederland tot den val der Republiek* (The Hague: Nijhoff, 1980).

Groenveld, S., *Unie, Bestand, Vrede: Drie fundamentele wetten van de Republiek der Verenigde Nederlanden* (Hilversum: Verloren, 2009).

Israel, Jonathan I., *The Dutch Republic: Its Rise, Greatness, and Fall, 1477–1806* (Oxford: Oxford University Press, 1995).

PART 3

The Enlightenment

CHAPTER 11

Ancient Constitutionalism in the Age of Enlightenment

The Case of Denmark-Norway

Håkon Evju

In the preface of his *Introduction à l'histoire du Danemarch* (1755), the young Genevan historian Paul Henri Mallet (1730–1807) sought to enhance the importance of the subject matter of his book. He appealed to what at the time was a historical convention, the notion of the ancient North as the home of the barbarian tribes that had wandered south and eventually overrun the Roman Empire, and to the latest twist given to this migration myth by an established literary authority.[1] Mallet had noticed how Montesquieu (1689–1755), in his *De l'esprit des lois* (1748), a few years earlier heaped praise on Scandinavia as the ancestral home of European liberty.

> The great prerogative of Scandinavia (says the admirable author of the Spirit of Laws) and what ought to recommend its inhabitants beyond every people upon earth, is, that they afforded the great resource to the liberty of Europe, that is, to almost all the liberty there is among men. The Goth Jornandes (adds he) calls the North of Europe the Forge of Mankind. I should rather call it the forge of those instruments that broke the fetters manufactured in the south. It was there those valiant nations were bred, who left their native climes to destroy tyrants and slaves, and to teach men that nature having made them equal, no reason could be assigned for their becoming dependent, but their mutual happiness.[2]

---

1 Colin Kidd, "Northern Antiquity: The Ethnology of Liberty in Eighteenth-Century Europe", in Knud Haakonsen and Henrik Horstbøll, eds., *Northern Antiquities and National Identities* (Copenhagen: Det Kongelige Danske Videnskabernes Selskab, 2008), 19–40; Thor J. Beck, *Northern Antiquities in French Learning and Literature (1755–1855): A Study in Preromantic Ideas*, vol. 1 (New York: Columbia University, 1934). On the very beginnings of this story, see A. S. Christensen, *Cassiodorus, Jordanes and the History of the Goths: Studies in a Migration Myth* (Copenhagen: Museum Tusculanum Press, 2002).

2 Paul Henri Mallet, *Northern Antiquities: Or, A Description of the Manners, Customs, Religion and Laws of the Ancient Danes, and Other Northern Nations; Including Those of Our Own Saxon Ancestors: With a Translation of the Edda, or System of Runic Mythology, and Other Pieces, from*

 | DOI:10.1163/9789004549159_013

In the hands of Mallet, these comments by Montesquieu went beyond mere promotional significance and were to take on special meaning in Denmark-Norway. They became part of a new interpretation of the historical and constitutional basis of the Dano-Norwegian monarchy. Since the introduction of absolutism in 1660, the kings of the House of Oldenborg had been fiercely insistent on heredity and sovereign power, as ancient and constitutive features of the monarchy. With Mallet, this insistence gave way to a different ancient constitution that cast Dano-Norwegian absolutism as heir to a republican political tradition, in which the king had governed together with a free and virtuous citizenry before the latter voluntarily chose to endow the king with sovereignty. As the century progressed, this view of Dano-Norwegian constitutional history became firmly entrenched and was applied also to debates about reform of the Danish manorial economy, on how to improve the condition of the Danish peasantry. Ancient constitutionalism went to the heart of what was among the most heated discussions in the Dano-Norwegian public sphere in the eighteenth century and was central to the Enlightenment drive towards reform and human betterment in Denmark-Norway.[3]

This chapter traces the varieties of ancient constitutionalist arguments in the dual-monarchy of Denmark-Norway in the eighteenth century along the lines sketched above. It focuses on the way such a language was used to discuss state and society in Denmark-Norway, the legitimacy of absolutism and reforms of the Danish manorial economy. My work on this topic builds on that of Henrik Horstbøll, who in recent years has emphasized the role of history in monarchical thought in mid-eighteenth century Denmark-Norway.[4]

---

the Ancient Icelandic Tongue, vol. 1, ed. Thomas Percy (London, 1770), 1: LVI. I refer to the English translation of Mallet's work in the following. For the relation between the original in French and the English translation by Thomas Percy, see Margaret Clunies Ross, *The Norse Muse in Britain, 1750–1820* (Trieste: Parnaso, 1998). Compare Mallet's introductory remark to Montesquieu, *The Spirit of the Laws*, ed. Anne M. Cohler, Basia C. Miller, and Harold S. Stone (Cambridge: Cambridge University Press, 1989), book 17, ch. 5, 283.

3 On the importance of reform and human betterment to the Enlightenment, see most recently John Robertson, *The Case for the Enlightenment. Scotland and Naples, 1680–1760* (Cambridge: Cambridge University Press, 2005). See also Franco Venturi, *Utopia and Reform in the Enlightenment* (Cambridge: Cambridge University Press, 1971).

4 Henrik Horstbøll, "Defending Monarchy in 18th Century Denmark-Norway", in Hans Blom, John Christian Laursen and Luisa Simonutti, eds., *Monarchisms in the Age of Enlightenment: Liberty, Patriotism and the Common Good* (Toronto: University of Toronto Press, 2007), 175–93; Henrik Horstbøll, "Northern Identities and National History – Paul Henri Mallet, Peter Frederik Suhm and Tyge Rothe", in Haakonsen and Horstbøll, eds., *Northern Antiquities and National Identities*. See also Håkon Evju, *Ancient Constitutions and Modern Monarchy: Historical Writing and Enlightened Reform in Denmark-Norway, 1730–1814* (Leiden: Brill, 2019).

Conditions for historical writing were favourable compared to other forms of political theorizing in an intellectual environment otherwise strictly monitored by a highly centralized absolutist state. Historians such as Mallet, Peter Frederik Suhm (1728–1798), Gerhard Schøning (1722–1780) and Tyge Rothe (1731–1795) took advantage of this and gained a prominent position in the emerging public sphere. In the following I will explore these developments from the perspective of ancient constitutionalism and extend the analysis to include reform politics.

The concept employed in the analysis of this chapter, that of ancient constitutionalism, first gained currency in the historiography following the publication of J. G. A. Pocock's *The Ancient Constitution and the Feudal Law* in 1957. Pocock's book was about the way in which the constitutional struggles between king and parliament in seventeenth century England tended to be argued in historical terms, but he presented this proclivity as part of a broader European development, also highlighting the role of ancient constitutionalism in sixteenth century France. As he presented it, such a language of politics was a product of religious conflict and the process of centralization of power it promoted, i. e. a linguistic weapon in the hands of opponents of the *Machtstaat* in the guise of absolute monarchy encroaching on inherited rights and privileges of estatist institutions.[5] Although well established by now, especially in the English context, ancient constitutionalism has not generated a broad research tradition to the same degree as other strands of Pocock's work.[6] As Pocock himself remarked in one of his recent books, he has had "fewer companions" along the road exploring the relationship between historiography and political thought, compared to his writings on methods in intellectual history and on republicanism.[7]

By applying the concept of ancient constitutionalism to Dano-Norwegian historical and political thought in the eighteenth century, this chapter moves beyond the periodical boundaries first suggested by Pocock's study. In his book, Pocock focused on ancient constitutionalism as a phenomenon of the sixteenth and seventeenth centuries, and this has remained the historical period within which this language of politics has been most thoroughly researched. It is tempting to relate this to the way the textbook understanding of the

5 J.G.A. Pocock, *The Ancient Constitution and the Feudal Law* (Cambridge: Cambridge University Press, 1957), 16.

6 This is also pointed out in Mark Goldie, "The Ancient Constitution and the Languages of Political Thought", *Historical Journal*, 62.1 (2018), 3–34.

7 J.G.A. Pocock, *Political Thought and History: Essays on Theory and Method* (Cambridge: Cambridge University Press, 2009), IX.

Enlightenment as an age marked by criticism of age-old inherited institutions, practices, and beliefs, seems to assign to ancient constitutionalism automatically a somewhat marginal role. In such light, attempts to articulate and appeal to tradition, to argue from history in politics, are prone to appear defensive, if not even reactionary. This might in some cases be correct. Indeed, ancient constitutionalism often get associated with renewed attempts to defend or bring back the institutions and privileges of the nobility. Eighteenth century critics of appeals to the ancient constitution in England and Scotland, such as David Hume (1711–1776) and William Robertson (1721–1793), seems to have regarded them from such a perspective, as attempts to resurrect the liberties of warring feudal barons.[8] Also, the way in which eighteenth-century ancient constitutionalism in France has been tied to the aristocratic reaction to the absolutism of King Louis XIV, especially in the works of Count Henri de Boulainvilliers (1658–1722), might have reinforced this stereotype.[9] Pointing to the customs of the Franks and the constitutional arrangements following their conquest of Gaul, Boulainvilliers asserted famously the right of the old French nobility to political participation and unrestricted ownership of their land, extending even to private jurisdiction over their serfs.

The form of ancient constitutionalism considered here, however, was different from that of Boulainvilliers. It was not aristocratic, but monarchical and developed as part of an attempt to rethink the foundations of Dano-Norwegian absolutism. Indeed, when it was brought to bear on questions of monarchical reform politics, to the possible break-up of the Danish manorial economy, it took on an explicit anti-aristocratic hue. By way of Dano-Norwegian ancient constitutionalism in the Enlightenment, this chapter aims to contribute to our understanding of the different uses to which such a language of politics could be put in the eighteenth century.

8 Duncan Forbes, *Hume's Philosophical Politics* (Cambridge: Cambridge University Press, 1975), 233–307; Colin Kidd, *Subverting Scotland's Past: Scottish Whig Historians and the Creation of an Anglo-British Identity, 1689–c. 1830* (Cambridge: Cambridge University Press, 1993).

9 Robin Briggs, "From the German Forests to Civil Society: The Frankish Myth and the Ancient Constitution in France", in Peter Burke, Brian Harrison and Paul Slack, eds., *Civil Histories: Essays Presented to Sir Keith Thomas* (Oxford: Oxford University Press, 2000), 231–49.

1 Absolutism and Ancient Constitutionalism in Denmark-Norway

The unavoidable reference point for appeals to a prescriptive political past in Denmark-Norway in the Age of Enlightenment was the absolutist form of government, which had been introduced in 1660–1661 following a series of disastrous wars with Sweden. At the meeting of estates in Copenhagen in October 1660, the nobility in the council of the realm had been pressured to give up their right to elect kings and issue coronation charters. The last charter, signed by Frederick III in 1648, was ceremoniously returned to the king by the estates and the king was asked to work out the constitutional arrangements of a monarchy that was now hereditary. This was done by the king and his advisors with the so-called Act of Sovereignty of January 1661, which abolished the council of the realm and lodged sovereignty firmly with the king. Being presented as a fait accompli, the act was approved by representatives of the estates and absolutism was thus established as the form of government in Denmark-Norway. Somewhat later, in the Lex Regia of 1665, it was given a constitutional basis and the line of succession was fixed.[10] Both of these founding documents pointed to various modes of legitimation, stressing how God had intervened to help the King save the realm from extinction in the late wars, how God worked through the king, but also how the estates freely, without the use of force, had agreed to make the crown hereditary and endow the king with absolute sovereignty.[11] As is often repeated in the historiography,[12] these theocratic and contractual elements were to be crucial components for much Dano-Norwegian political theorizing of the late seventeenth and early eighteenth century, sometimes combined as in the Act of Sovereignty, but at times also in conflict.[13]

10 On the constitutional developments in Denmark-Norway in these years, see Sebastian Olden-Jørgensen, "Enevoldsarveregjeringsakten og kongeloven. Forfatningsspørgsmålet i Danmark fra oktober 1660 til november 1665", (*Dansk*) *Historisk Tidsskrift*, 16.2 (1993), 295–321.

11 See Brian Kjær Olesen's contribution to this volume.

12 Edvard Holm, *Om det Syn paa Kongemagt, Folk og borgerlig Frihed der udviklede sig i den dansk-norske Stat i Midten af 18de Aarhundrede* (*1746–1770*) (Copenhagen: Schultz, 1883); Jens Arup Seip, *Teorien om det opinionstyrte enevelde* (Oslo: Universitetsforlaget, 1958); Sebastian Olden-Jørgensen, "Scandinavia", in Howell Lloyd, Glenn Burgess and Simon Hodson, eds., *European Political Thought, 1450–1700: Religion, Law and Philosophy* (New Haven: Yale University Press, 2007), ch. 9.

13 For the most obvious example of a conflict between theocratic and natural law based arguments, see Frank Grunert, "Zur aufgeklärten Kritik am theokratischen Absolutismus: Der Streit zwischen Hector Gottfried Masius und Christian Thomasius über Ursprung und Begründung der summa potestas", in *Christian Thomasius: Neue Forschungen Im Kontext der Frühaufklärung*, ed. Friedrich Vollhardt (Berlin: De Gruyter, 1997), 51–78.

Although it has received less attention from specialists working in Danish and Norwegian intellectual history, advocates of the Dano-Norwegian absolute monarchy were eager also to legitimate the form of government in historical terms. They sought to deny that what happened in 1660–1661 had been a constitutional innovation and to present the former *monarchia mixta*, in which the aristocratic council of the realm had shared sovereignty with the monarch, as a deviation from tradition and a usurpation of power. Such a historical theory developed gradually. The notion of heredity, rather than election, as an ancient and constitutive feature of the Dano-Norwegian monarchy came to the fore in the historical writing of the two royal historiographers Tormod Torfæus (1636–1719) and Vitus Bering (1617–1675) towards the end of the 17th century.[14] As late as in the 1730s it was taken up and defended in the works on Danish and Norwegian history by the foremost man of Enlightenment in Denmark-Norway, Ludvig Holberg (1684–1754).[15] At that point, however, it was not only focused on heredity, but also sovereign power as defining characteristics of the Dano-Norwegian ancient constitution. Holberg had won royal patronage early on as a writer of textbooks in natural law and history and established his literary credentials among a wider audience in the 1720s as a playwright and steady provider of plays for the Danish stage. In 1730, he had become professor of history at the University of Copenhagen, and the year before he had released his historical-statistical *Danmark og Norges Beskrivelse* (An Account of Denmark and Norway). In it, Holberg treated the introduction of absolutism and took care to present the events of 1660–1661 as a restoration. "Everyone therefore realized how highly necessary it was to restore to his Majesty the sovereign power, which his ancestors in antiquity had possessed, and under which government Denmark had flourished and been the terror of all its neighbours".[16] The introduction of absolutism was in accordance with Dano-Norwegian constitutional tradition.

A few years later, Holberg reiterated this claim in more detail in his three volume *Danmarks Riges Historie* (History of the Realm of Denmark, 1732–1735). He referred the different arguments over whether the Danish monarchy had

14 On Bering, see Karen Skovgaard-Petersen, "Klassikerimitation og danmarshistorie i den tidlige enevælde. Om Vitus Berings Florus Danicus", *Danske Studier*, 1990, 72–7, see esp. 76; On Torfæus, see Ellen Jørgensen, *Historieforskning og historieskrivning i Danmark indtil aar 1800*, 2nd ed. (Copenhagen: Gyldendal, 1960), 144.

15 For a recent, broad treatment of Holberg, see Knud Haakonsen and Sebastian Olden-Jørgensen, eds., *Ludvig Holberg (1684–1754): Learning and Literature in the Nordic Enlightenment* (London: Routledge, 2017).

16 Ludvig Holberg, *Dannemarks og Norges Beskrivelse* (Copenhagen, 1729), 61.

been hereditary or elective systematically in his introduction to his third volume, supposedly in a neutral way, but at that point his own views had already been made evident as part of his narrative. He had for instance stressed how the practice of issuing coronation charters was a late development, belonging to the era of the Kalmar Union.[17] Holberg, however, went beyond the issue of heredity also in his narrative and argued that the first kings of Denmark had possessed absolute authority. Summing up his thoughts on the form of government in Denmark in the period up until King Sweyn Forkbeard (d. 1014), he claimed that the different kings had been unusually civil and cultivated the company of commoners. He admitted that there were many episodes of men of humble origins who behaved impolitely before the king. That, however, was a result of "the impoliteness of the Age, more than the limited character of government". According to the university professor, other instances told of "royal authority being much more unlimited than it would later become".[18]

2 Molesworth, Montesquieu, and Mallet

When Holberg wrote his history of Denmark, the ancient constitutionalist argument was no longer primarily directed towards the old Danish nobility and their wish for a restoration of the *monarchia mixta*. The absolute monarchy had become more entrenched and the threat from its former enemies had receded. A new more purely ideological challenge to Danish absolutism had arisen in 1694 however, with the publication of *An Account of Denmark as It was in the Year 1692*, by the former English ambassador to the court of Christian V, Viscount Robert Molesworth (1656–1725).[19] Although directed mainly towards English political debate,[20] Molesworth's account was highly unfavourable to Denmark and focused on the events of 1660–1661 and the absolutist form of government, which the former ambassador considered an instance of

17 Ludvig Holberg, *Dannemarks Riges Historie* (Copenhagen, 1732–35), 1:184–85, 215.

18 Holberg, 1:113, see also 196.

19 Sebastian Olden-Jørgensen, "Robert Molesworth's 'An Account of Denmark as It Was in 1692': A Political Scandal and Its Literary Aftermath", in Haakonsen and Horstbøll, eds., *Northern Antiquities and National Identities*, 68–87.

20 D. W. Hayton, "The Personal and Political Contexts of Robert Molesworth's *Account of Denmark*", in Haakonsen and Horstbøll, eds., *Northern Antiquities and National Identities*, 41–67.

a French malaise threatening ever more European realms,[21] England included. According to Molesworth absolutism constituted a deviation from the ancient Gothic constitution that had been established in England and elsewhere in Europe, by the peoples that had emerged from the north, wandered south and eventually overwhelmed the Roman Empire, most often simply called Goths.[22] In line with this narrative the fact that Denmark had succumbed to absolutism was in a sense especially tragic, as the Goths were perceived to have hailed from the North, from Denmark, as well as from Norway and Sweden.

Molesworth had mixed his Gothic ancient constitutionalism with a republican critique of the effects of being subject to absolute or arbitrary power, emphasizing how the Danes gradually had become accustomed to slavery and lost their former virtue.[23] Notably, this critique was reiterated by Montesquieu in his *Considérations sur les causes de la grandeur des Romains et de leur decadence* (1734). In it he declared that "the Kings of Denmark are the most despotic Sovereigns in Europe", and attributed the Danish losses in the wars with Sweden to the slavish despondency that was a consequence of being subjected to arbitrary power.[24] Denmark-Norway thus gradually gained a reputation for despotism, which was acerbated by Montesquieu's novel tripartite classification of forms of government in *De l'esprit des lois*. The French nobleman distinguished between republics, monarchies, and despotic governments, emphasizing how monarchies were defined by the presence of "intermediate, subordinate and dependent powers"[25] that could check the sovereign and moderate his rule. The lack of such powers in Denmark led many to conclude that Dano-Norwegian absolutism would fall into the category of despotism, against which several intellectuals in Denmark-Norway protested.[26]

As we have seen in the introduction, this perceived, implicit charge of despotism occurred against the backdrop of what seemed like praise for the ancient North. Like Molesworth, Montesquieu was fascinated by Gothicism and involved himself in French ancient constitutionalist controversy, most notably between l'Abbé Du Bos (1760–1742) and Count Boulainvilliers, over

21 Robert Molesworth, *An Account of Denmark as It Was in the Year 1692* (London, 1694), 223–225.

22 Molesworth, 42.

23 Molesworth, 75.

24 Montesquieu, *Reflections on the Causes of the Grandeur and Declension of the Romans* (London, 1734), 154, 194.

25 Montesquieu, *The Spirit of the Laws*, book 1, ch. 1, 10; book 2, ch. 4, 17.

26 See in this regard Ditlev Tamm, "The Danish Debate about Montesquieu: Holberg, Kofod Ancher, Sneedorff, Schytte and Stampe", in Haakonsen and Horstbøll, eds., *Northern Antiquities and National Identities*, 163–80.

the origins of the French monarchy, leaning towards the side of the latter.[27] His high praise of Scandinavia as the ancestral home of European liberty was related to this, as the Frankish founders of monarchy in France ultimately were descended from the ancient Northerners. As mentioned, Montesquieu's comments on the very distant Northern past proved an important clue for the further development of Dano-Norwegian ancient constitutionalism and for what constituted one of the most sophisticated answers to Molesworth and Montesquieu's criticism of absolutism in Denmark-Norway.

The key figure in this regard was the aforementioned Paul Henri Mallet, who was called to Denmark in 1752 by the leading ministers of the incapable King Frederik V, Adam Gottlob Moltke (1710–1792) and Johann Hartwig Ernst Bernstorff (1712–1772). Mallet was to lecture at court on *belles letre* and instruct Dano-Norwegian nobles and intellectuals in Francophone culture.[28] He published his own journal, *Mercure Danois*, and he was asked to write a history of Denmark in French. Mallet's Danish history eventually comprised multiple volumes, but it is best known for its two first instalments, for his *Introduction à l'histoire du Danemarch* (1755) and the companion volume, *Monuments de la mythologie et de la poesie des Celtes* (1756) consisting of a collection of excerpts from the Poetic Edda and the Prose Edda, as well as from Old Norse poetry more broadly, giving readers a glimpse of Old Norse religion and mythology. In his introductory volume, Mallet drew a picture of the politics of the ancient Northerners not far removed from that of Molesworth and Montesquieu. He emphasized the centrality of public assemblies and popular royal election for what was in fact not only an ancient Danish, but an ancient Nordic constitution.[29] Like Montesquieu, Mallet was indebted to Tacitus and described the men taking part in politics as independent and freedom-loving, defiant of authority and restraint.[30] Crucially, however, he was also influenced by the republicanism of his native Geneva and went further than Montesquieu in

27 Annelien de Dijn, *French Political Thought from Montesquieu to Tocqueville: Liberty in a Levelled Society?* (Cambridge: Cambridge University Press, 2008), 20–32; Michael Sonenscher, *Before the Deluge: Public Debt, Inequality, and the Intellectual Origins of the French Revolution* (Princeton, N.J.: Princeton University Press, 2007), ch. 2.

28 Mallet was not the only Genevan intellectual to settle in Copenhagen in the middle of the eighteenth century, see Henrik Horstbøll, "Mellem despoti og demokrati. Den schweiziske forbindelse: Roger, Mallet og Reverdil om den danske enevælde", *Fund og forskning* (2005), 153–176; Julius Clausen, "Franske literater i København på Frederik den femtes tid", *Historisk Tidsskrift*, 7 (1897), 1–81.

29 Mallet, *Northern Antiquities*, 1:160–161.

30 See the author's preface to Mallet, *Northern Antiquities*.

classicizing the ancient Nordic political past. The free men of the North came close to being citizens, as Mallet described them.

The basis for such claims, the Genevan historian found above all in the Old Norse-Icelandic saga tradition and the scholarship on Northern history that had accumulated over the years. It was in his depiction of Iceland, drawn from this literature, that his republicanism came through most vividly. A key event in this regard, based on the thirteenth century skald and historian Snorri Sturluson (1179–1241), was the supposed unification of the Norwegian realm under King Harald Fairhair in the late ninth century, and the consequent expulsion of his enemies to Iceland, where they settled and founded what Mallet described as an Icelandic republic. Mallet presented Harald as a classic conqueror, with all the allusions to feudalism that this implied. He described him flat out as a tyrant and his reign as a form of tyranny that many freedom-loving Northerners would not endure.[31] The Genevan historian was full of praise for the orderly, republican government they established in Iceland, centred as it was on the assembly of free men.

> The whole settled into form as it were of itself, and fell into order without any effort. In like manner as bees form their hives, the new Icelanders, guided by a happy instinct, immediately on their landing in a desert island, established that fine constitution wherein liberty is fixed on its proper basis, viz. a wise distribution of the powers of government. An admirable discovery, which at first sight, one would think must have been the masterpiece of some consummate politician; and which nevertheless, according to a remark by a great genius of this age, was compleated here, as in other countries, by savages in the midst of forests.[32]

In fact, he argued that the decision by the Icelanders to organize their society in such a way mirrored how a constitution would have been formed if left to the calm deliberations of civilized and wise politicians. It was so well-ordered that it was hard to believe that it had been put in place by what "a great genius" had called savages in the midst of forests, Mallet wrote with a veiled allusion to Montesquieu's choice of words about the English constitution.

In spite of this praise of ancient Nordic politics, the Genevan historian was not blind to its broader societal context. When Mallet ventured outside the field of politics, his depiction of Northern antiquity became more ambivalent.

31 Mallet, 1:172.
32 Mallet, 1:173.

He stressed how the freedom-loving and martial spirit of the Northerners also made it hard for them to truly settle down and devote themselves to agriculture. Accustomed to resolving conflicts with violence, they lacked a proper understanding of law and an appreciation of the fruits of peace and order. They were barbarians, cultivating a life of war and plunder.[33] In Mallet's eyes, an important reason for this was Old Norse religion, and the belief that you needed to die a violent death in battle in order to reach the halls of Valhalla. Honour was tied to the display of heroic virtue on the battlefield.[34] Consequently, it was only with the coming of Christianity that the Northerners settled and started to enjoy the fruits of peace and civilization.

Mallet never reconciled this bleak and historicised picture of the life of the ancient Northerners with the praise he reserved for their politics. In fact, his narrative thrived on such paradoxes, on stressing the barbarism evident in their love of war and their lack of concern for agriculture, while at the same time praising their skills in navigation and maritime expeditions. He had, however, made the contemporary political implications of his work rather clear in his preface. Like Molesworth and Montesquieu, he used the migration myth to picture a contrast been the slavish and despondent South and the freedom-loving and vigorous North. Unlike them, though, this martial and libertarian spirit had never left Europe and the North, according to Mallet.

> Is not this, in fact, the principal source of that courage, of that aversion to slavery, of that empire of honour which characterise in general the European nations; and of that moderation, of that easiness of access, and peculiar attention to the rights of humanity, which so happily distinguish our sovereigns from the inaccessible and superb tyrants of Asia?[35]

Absolutism and despotism were not the same thing. Contrary to what Molesworth had feared, in Europe and the North, there was a peculiar republican inheritance that served to moderate monarchy. Even the Danes after the introduction of absolutism still in a sense watched over their liberty. They had not, as Montesquieu had suggested, succumbed to arbitrary power. The kings of the Oldenborg line merely held their subjects' liberties in custody, and like other absolute sovereigns had to behave differently from oriental despots, staying attuned to the wishes of their subjects. Mallet then, drew on critics of

---

33 Mallet, 1:252.

34 Mallet, 1:119, 122.

35 Mallet, 1: LIII.

Dano-Norwegian absolutism to reconstruct a form of ancient constitutionalism better suited to meet the charge of despotism.

3 European Feudalism and Northern Allodial Liberty: Tyge Rothe

The men in power in Denmark-Norway were pleased with Mallet's work,[36] which also received favourable reviews in the main review journals.[37] In Dano-Norwegian intellectual circles, however, the interest in the Genevan historian's Danish history seems to have been more limited, especially as the historical culture at the time was more erudite than philosophical, focused on questions of origins and descent, on attempts to reconcile Biblical, Classical and Old-Norse Icelandic sources on the most distant and dark Northern past.[38] At the same time, it seems clear that the Genevan historian opened up for a different interpretation of the ancient Nordic political past than that propagated by Holberg. He demonstrated that it was possible to not only mention in passing popular assemblies, royal elections or depositions of kings, but that Dano-Norwegian absolutism actually allowed for a systematic description of ancient Nordic politics as republican. The absolutist ancient constitution of Holberg had been superseded. This was picked up by the two foremost Dano-Norwegian historians of the second half of the eighteenth century, Gerhard Schøning and Peter Frederik Suhm, who further entrenched the new interpretation in Dano-Norwegian historiography in their regnal histories of Norway and Denmark.[39] Schøning and Suhm, however, did not treat the constitutional question in a systematic manner and the intellectual who developed the ancient constitutionalist argument one step further, was the aforementioned Tyge Rothe.

36 Horstbøll, *Northern Identities and National History*, 214.

37 Anonymous, "Introduction à l'histoire de Dannemarc", *Kiøbenhavnske Nye Tidender om lærde og curieuse Sager no. XLVII* (1758): 369–74; Anonymous, "Monumens de la Mythologie", *Efterretninger om Nye Bøger og Lærde Sager i Danmark og Norge* (1756): 309–36; Anonymous, "Indledning udi Danmarks Riges Historie", *Efterretninger om Nye Bøger og Lærde Sager i Danmark og Norge* (1756): 643–5.

38 Evju, *Ancient Constitutions and Modern Monarchy*, 91–7.

39 Gerhard Schøning, *Norges Riiges Historie*, 3 vols (Sorø and Copenhagen, 1771–1781); Peter Frederik Suhm, *Historien af Danmark, Norge og Holsten udi tvende Udtog til den studerende Ungdoms bedste* (Copenhagen, 1776). Especially the latter work by Suhm, which became part of the curriculum for future civil servants in grammar schools, helped popularize the new ancient constitutionalism introduced by Mallet.

Although, the landowner and historian's main contribution to Dano-Norwegian ancient constitutionalist discourse was his *Nordens Statsforfatning* (The Nordic Constitution, 1781–1782), the publication of this treatise was part of a larger project. He had in the early 1770s started to publish a multivolume philosophical history on the effects of Christianity on the peoples of Europe,[40] and it was following his fourth volume, when he considered the meeting of barbarism and religion after the fall of Rome, that he found special reason to linger on the North. According to Rothe, Northern barbarism had taken on a special character and was in a sense less barbarous than what was the case elsewhere in Europe at the same time. He followed what by then had become conventional wisdom about Northern antiquity. The form of government had been what he called "a monarchy tempered by a democracy".[41] Popular assemblies had been central and the people had taken part in legislation, elected kings and held them accountable if they overstepped. Compared to Mallet, however, Rothe went even further in classicising his image of the ancient North, stressing how the role of the free man had been reserved for property-holders. His own independent contribution to exploration of the distant Nordic political past had to do with his insistence on the prevalence of individual property rights to land early on in the North.

Tyge Rothe had come to the realization about the legal basis of popular liberty in the ancient North partly by studying Tacitus and the Old-Norse saga tradition. The landowner and historian was however also influenced by Montesquieu's historical approach to law and paid close attention the medieval Nordic law codes and their later interpreters, most notably the professor of law at the University of Copenhagen, Peder Kofoed Ancher (1710–1788).[42] In his studies into Danish and Nordic legal history Ancher had noticed the Old Norse concept of *óðal*, which he equated with allodium, as described in feudal

40 Tyge Rothe, *Christendommens Virkning paa Folkenes Tilstand i Europa*, 5 vols (Copenhagen, 1774–1783).

41 Tyge Rothe, *Nordens Staetsforfatning før Lehnstiden, og da Odelskab med Folkefriehed – I Lehnstiden og da Birkerettighed, Hoverie, Livegenskab med Aristokratie*, vol. 1 (Copenhagen: Gyldendal, 1781), 47.

42 See in this regard Ancher's *History of Danish Law* and his *Danish Feudal Law* in Peder Kofoed Ancher, *Samlede juridiske skrifter*, ed. Johan Friedrich Wilhelm Schlegel and Rasmus Nyerup, 3 vols (Copenhagen, 1807–1811); Ancher planed a separate treatise on the relation of odel and allodium, see Peder Kofoed Ancher, "Beviis paa Sprog-Konstens virkelige Nytte, Som en Fortale til den Afhandling der er destinered til følgende Tome om Oprindelsen til det Ord: Adel, Forklared af vores gamle Nordiske Allodial-Ret", *Skrifter, som udi Det Kiøbenhavnske Selskab af Lærdoms og Videnskaberns Elskere ere fremlagte og oplæste i Aarene 1751, 1752, 1753 og 1754* 6 (1754): 57–78.

law, more precisely in the Lombard *Libri Feudorum* (Book of Fiefs). Rothe took this observation made by Ancher and elevated it into a central and defining feature of the ancient North. Together with the fact that there was no written code of feudal law in the North, this was proof for him that feudalism had developed late and through a protracted autochthonous process in the Nordic countries. There had been no foreign conquest in the North, similar to what had happened in England, in France or in Lombardy. In a more direct sense than for Mallet, King Harald Fairhair's unification of Norway was a key event in this regard. Rothe stressed that what Harald had done, was merely to establish his suzerainty, and demand that his subjects paid taxes.[43] He had not, like William the Conqueror in England, claimed dominion over the land, and distributed it to his vassals as fiefs. Divisions of property rights into ownership and use-rights were alien to the North. Consequently, Rothe also claimed that the ancient North was thoroughly egalitarian, in the sense that there had been no hereditary nobility with political privileges and private jurisdiction over other men. In his eyes, the development of such distinctions and such classes of men were the result of a conquest, of a fundamental division between conquerors and conquered.[44] Given that Rothe could identify no such single event in the history of the North, he could assign the feudal baron a more limited and alien role in Nordic history than what he found elsewhere.

Rothe was obviously proud of his "discoveries" and situated them in a broader European and global context, referring to the expanding genre of philosophical history. As Henrik Horstbøll has pointed out,[45] Rothe sought to argue that the society he had unearthed in the distant Nordic past, was proof that the North had experienced an era of liberty and allodial landholding in between that of Tacitus wandering barbarians who had practiced communal ownership of land and the feudal barons of the *Libri Feudorum*.[46] As for the political implications of Rothe's work, he did not call for a return to Northern antiquity. He never fully explained his theses of the autonomous development of feudalism in the North, but he made it clear that the existence of slavery and the legal distinction between free men and slaves had prepared the way in this regard.[47] Through slavery the spirit of feudalism had crept in early, during Northern antiquity, only later to flourish when models of feudal relations were imported from abroad through the foreign conquests of King Sweyn Forkbeard

43 Rothe, *Nordens Staetsforfatning*, 40.
44 Rothe, 69–70.
45 Horstbøll, *Defending Monarchy*, 184–6.
46 Rothe, *Christendommens Virkning paa Folkenes Tilstand i Europa*, 5:56–57.
47 Rothe, *Nordens Staetsforfatning*, 1:22–23, 29.

and King Cnut the Great and when civil wars later made free men give up their land in exchange for protection. Rothe insisted however that the freeholders had never formally surrendered their right to legislate and take part in assemblies and royal elections. As landholding became more centralized, their political role had merely been taken over by the nobility in the council of the realm, without a formal legal sanction. In 1660, at the meeting of the estates, "the middle estates", the burghers and the clergy, had therefore been able to take on the role of the ancient freeholders, and exercise their ancient rights, when they brought about the change of government.[48] Absolutism in Denmark-Norway then not only rested on a contractual and consensual basis. It had also been introduced in a way that was in accordance with tradition. Although others would later interpret Rothe's work in a way that might seem critical of absolutism and favourable to the French revolutionaries,[49] the landowner and historian had on the surface reconciled his ancient constitutionalism with the current form of government.

4 Ancient Constitutionalism and Reforms of the Danish Manorial Economy

Rothe himself seems in fact to have been more eager to engage with the debate on economic improvements in Denmark-Norway, that to argue for or against absolutism. Such improvements came on the agenda across Europe during the eighteenth century, partly driven by the need to develop the economy in order to muster more human and financial resources and survive in an increasingly competitive state system.[50] They received an important impetus from the rise of patriotic societies and from different governmental initiatives.[51] In Denmark-Norway public discussions about economic reforms came to the fore after 1755, when the government of King Frederik v issued an invitation for all "patriots" to come forward with proposals for reform and thereby signalled

48 Rothe, 1:134–135.

49 On this particular use of Rothe, see Evju, *Ancient Constitutions and Modern Monarchy*, 163–164.

50 See in this regard Istvan Hont, *Jealousy of Trade: International Competition and the Nation-State in Historical Perspective* (Cambridge, Mass.: Belknap Press, 2005); Sonenscher, *Before the Deluge*.

51 Koen Stapelbroek and Jani Marjanen, eds., *The Rise of Economic Societies in the Eighteenth Century* (Basingstoke: Palgrave Macmillan, 2012).

that the censorship regulations would be practiced more leniently.[52] Debates about improvements in the Danish manorial economy soon dominated the emerging public sphere in the second half of the eighteenth century, and while the topics aired for many years mostly were about technical improvements, the issues gradually turned towards the more fundamental organization of rural life in the 1770s and 80s.[53] Increasingly, more controversial issues were discussed, issues such as adscription, the ban on peasantry leaving their manors before the age of 40, forced labour service on the demesne and the different rights of the landlords that gave the peasantry an extremely precarious hold of the land they were farming.[54]

This was the context in which the ancient constitutionalism that had become entrenched in Dano-Norwegian historical writing acquired its most immediate relevance. Such a mode of argument can be found already in the early 1770s, during the Struensee interregnum, but it rose especially to prominence after several initiatives by *Det Kongelige Danske Landhusholdningsselskab*, the royal Danish society for agriculture, late in the decade and in the early 1780s.[55] A string of critical and conservative landowners sought at that point to question the need for reform or to argue for reforms initiated locally by the seigneurial landlords themselves. Some claimed that Danish agriculture already was improving and that a liberation of the peasantry would lead to a mass exodus and breakdown in agricultural production. Others were less gloomy but argued that an abolition of adscription and forced labour service should be followed by giving landlords free reins to dispose of their property as they saw fit. Almost everyone despised the idea of government intervention in their affairs and had little sympathy for the endeavours of the reformers in the

52 This development is discussed in depth in Jakob Maliks, "Vilkår for offentlighet. Sensur, økonomi og transformasjonen av det offentlige rom i Danmark-Norge 1730–1770" (Norges teknisk-naturvitenskapelige universitet, 2011).

53 On the debate over agricultural reforms, see Edvard Holm, *Kampen om Landboreformerne i Danmark i Slutningen af 18. Aarhundrede* (Copenhagen: Gad, 1888); Hans Jensen, *Dansk jordpolitik 1757–1919*, vol. 1 (Copenhagen: Gyldendal, 1936); and for the last phase of the debate, see most recently Eva Krause Jørgensen, "Breaking the Chains: An Intellectual History of the Discursive Struggles over the Danish Agrarian Reforms, 1784–1797" (Aarhus University, 2015).

54 The literature on the great agrarian reforms in Denmark from the perspective of political, social and economic history, is voluminous and will not be dealt with here. For an introduction to the literature, see Claus Bjørn, ed., *Landboreformerne – forskning og forløb* (Landbohistorisk selskab, 1988). See also the recent treatment of the agrarian reforms by Birgit Løgstrup, *Bondens frisættelse: De danske landboreformer 1750–1810* (Copenhagen: Gads forlag, 2015).

55 On these initiatives, see Holm, *Kampen om Landboreformerne*, 47–48.

Copenhagen-intelligentsia, especially as one of them put it, for their wish to return to "the era of Odin".[56] The supporters of reform themselves had for long used arguments from political economy, stressing the dismal conditions in which the peasantry laboured and the beneficial effects of giving them greater incentives to improve their condition by developing their own farms. Giving them more personal freedom and a more secure hold of their land, would benefit the peasantry, landlords and state alike. Increasingly, however, such language was combined with ancient constitutionalist arguments that not only underlined the benefits of reforms, but also their legality.

One of the central contributors in this regard was Tyge Rothe, who already had given significant clues in his *Nordens Statsforfatning* to his position in these debates, a position he developed further in a series of pamphlets.[57] The sharp contrast drawn by Rothe and other historians between Northern antiquity and the present in terms not only of politics, but also of more general social and economic conditions, served to denaturalize the present state of affairs and lower the bar for reform. Rothe had indeed suggested that adscription, forced labour service as well as the private jurisdiction enjoyed by some landlords over their peasants, were late developments in Denmark, and not part of the ancient constitution.[58] They lacked proper legal foundations in his eyes. Rothe however, had been careful not to dispute the legality of the centralization of landholding. He did not question the present distribution of property. He was in favour of giving the peasantry greater personal freedom, but he did not want to grant them freehold or hereditary tenancy. His ideal was English style commercial agriculture based on existing manors, but with an emancipated class of leasehold farmers. He was after all not that far removed from some of the conservative landlords that voiced their opposition to the reform

---

56 Friderich Wilhelm Wedel-Jarlsberg, *Veiledning til rigtige Begreb om de Danske Jorde-Godsers Indretning i Hoved-Gaarde og underliggende Hovnings-Bønder, med Tvende Breve i samme Materie.* (Copenhagen, 1782), 36; Evju, *Ancient Constitutions and Modern Monarchy*, 244–9.

57 Tyge Rothe, *Dansk Agerdyrkeres – især den til Hovedgaard hæftede Festbondes Kaar og borgerlige Rettigheder, for saavidt samme ere bestemte ved Lovene; eller vort Landvæsens System, som det var 1783, politisk betragtet* (Copenhagen, 1784); Tyge Rothe, *Tanker om den danske Bondes Pligt at pleye Fødestavn, fremsatte med Hensyn paa den Meening, at Pligten har Grund i Jorddrottens lovlige Rettighed* (Copenhagen, 1784); Tyge Rothe, *Vort Landvæsens System, som det var 1783, politisk betragtet: Anden Deel* (Copenhagen, 1785); Tyge Rothe, *Er Staeten best tient med Stoere, eller med smaa Bøndergaarde? Og var det en rimelig Bøn til Regieringen, at smaa Jordlodder – enhver Festers Ret uforkrænket – maatte legges sammen, for at udgiøre stoere?* (Copenhagen, 1785); Tyge Rothe, *Hvorfor skulle vi ønske Landvæsens Systemets Forandring?* (Copenhagen, 1786).

58 Rothe, *Nordens Staetsforfatning*, 2:265, 320, 343–6, 386, 399, 403.

movement. Indeed, he emphasized how giving the peasantry a more secure hold of their land, turning them into freeholders, would amount to a conquest. It would amount to the conquest Denmark and the North had been spared in the past.[59]

Unfortunately for Rothe, there were others that did not see things his way. He was criticised by the civil servant Christian Albrecht Fabricius (1734–1815), another friend of reform who did not think Rothe went far enough. Fabricius radicalized Rothe's ancient constitutionalism by suggesting that the landlords' hold of the land farmed by the peasantry was a result of usurpation, lacking a proper legal basis. Strengthening the position of peasants vis-à-vis their landlords and making their tenancy hereditary was not an infringement of anyone's legitimate privileges, but a restoration of ancient rights. "Our ancient constitution has remained and to a large extent is still in existence",[60] as the civil servant explained. It was merely necessary to revive it. As the debate progressed, it was Fabricius' point of view which was victorious. Following a coup d'etat in 1784, new, more reform minded men had come to power in Denmark, and a commission to propose reforms of the manorial economy was appointed shortly afterwards, in 1786. Both within the commission and in the public debate that ensued after its appointment, ancient constitutionalist arguments along the line of Fabricius were prominent.[61] This is not surprising as the issue no longer was whether or not Danish agriculture ought to be reformed, but how far the government could go in their intervention into the affairs of landlords and peasants. The debate was now about the limits of Dano-Norwegian absolutism itself, and in this regard the historical and legal basis of the current organization of Danish agriculture was crucial.

The utility of ancient constitutionalist arguments in the final phase of the debates over reforms of the Danish manorial economy, came through most forcefully in the opening statement made by the secretary, and for all practical purposes, the leader of the reform commission, the jurist and civil servant Christian Colbjørnsen (1749–1814). He took time to give his fellow members a lecture in history, telling them that:

> In antiquity, the peasantry of Denmark was a free people. The country's fields were divided into equal lots among its inhabitants; these had a perfect right of property, were free citizens and were not subject to anyone

59 Tyge Rothe, *Dansk Agerdyrkeres*, 49.

60 Christian Albrecht Fabricius, *Noget til Oplysning at vore Fæstebønder ei er Trællenes Afkom. En Fortsættelse af Tankerne om de nye Indretninger i Landvæsenet* (Copenhagen, 1785), 57.

61 Evju, *Ancient Constitutions and Modern Monarchy*, 282–94.

> but the laws and highest power of the state [...] But towards the end of the 15th century, when the power of kings was limited as a result of the predominance of the nobility, adscription and serfdom were introduced, however not by any law, neither over the entire country, but alone by abuse in Zealand, Møen, Falser and Lolland.[62]

As Colbjørnsen portrayed it, adscription and what he called serfdom, was a novel and alien element in Danish history, something that was evident in the patchy nature in which it had been implemented. It lacked a proper legal foundation and they now had the chance to restate the peasantry into their rightful position, into the small-scale self-sufficiency agricultural arrangements that had prevailed in the distant Danish past. Although controversial, Colbjørnsen's views proved influential in a commission composed in a way that favoured reform and in which members from among the sceptical landlords gradually stopped attending meetings. It was reforms along the lines of Colbjørnsen that in the end was proposed and enacted in 1787–88, abolishing adscription, giving the peasantry a more secure hold of their land and a stronger position vis-à-vis their landlords. Even though the reforms were not without compromises, especially when it came to the issue of forced labour service, they were seen as a victory for the writers and civil servants of the Copenhagen intelligentsia, who for long had advocated improvements. As we have seen, it was a victory in which the form of ancient constitutionalism developed by Paul Henri Mallet and Tyge Rothe proved increasingly important as the struggle intensified. On the one hand, the appeals to a prescriptive Nordic political past served the cause of the established form of government, paving the way for the monarch to use his absolute power to intervene in the relationship between landlords and their peasants. On the other hand, it undermined traditional, inherited institutions and practices of the manorial economy. In order to attack central elements of *l'ancien régime* in Denmark, many reformists appealed to a past even more ancient.

5 Concluding Remarks

In the prominent form discussed in this chapter then, eighteenth century Dano-Norwegian ancient constitutionalism, differed from the European pattern

62 *Den for Landboevæsenet nedsatte Commissions Forhandlinger*, vol. 1 (Copenhagen, 1788), 32–3.

often associated with such a mode of argument. It was not a defence of aristocratic privileges or institutions, nor an attempt to bring them back. Rather, ancient constitutionalism was monarchist and anti-aristocratic geared towards a restitution of what Tyge Rothe called "popular liberty". This serves to underline a central point in this chapter, how ancient constitutionalism could mutate, take different forms and be used for a variety of purposes. We have seen how an insistence on heredity and absolute sovereignty as ancient and constitutive features of the Dano-Norwegian monarchy gave way around the middle of the eighteenth century for a different articulation of tradition. Following the work of Mallet, the kings of the House of Oldenborg were cast as heirs to a political legacy in which a people of freedom-loving, virtuous, and patriotic citizens had an important role. In this way ancient constitutionalist arguments contributed to renew monarchist ideology and answer the charge of despotism, levelled at the Dano-Norwegian absolute monarchs by the likes of Molesworth and Montesquieu.

On a surface level, Tyge Rothe's exploration of the distant Nordic political past, served much of the same purpose as that of Mallet, reconciling the ancient Nordic constitution with absolutism by portraying the events of 1660–1661 as a matter of the people exercising their ancient rights. At the same time, Rothe's stress on an egalitarian distribution of landed property and what he called allodial liberty as a defining feature of the political arrangements of the ancient North, reveals his intention of intervening also in the ever more intense debates over agricultural improvements in Denmark. In what was one of the most contested issues in the Dano-Norwegian public sphere in the Age of Enlightenment, arguments from history, appeals to tradition, had an important role alongside arguments from political economy about the benefits of improving the situation of the peasantry, giving them greater autonomy and more of a chance to work for their own benefit. Radicalized by Fabricius and Colbjørnsen, Rothe's ancient constitutionalism became not just an attack on adscription and the different legal restraints on the liberty of the peasantry, but an attack on the existing distribution of property as well. They envisioned a more thorough break with the manorial economy, a transition to small-scale family based agriculture of independent freeholders sitting on equal size lots. Although there were marked differences over the exact lessons to be drawn from the past, it was certainly seen as useful for making the case for reform. The enlightened push for improvement and human betterment in this world, was not only based on an abstract science of man and society, but also on a historical understanding of the predicament that marked rural Denmark, how it had come about and the degree to which it was legitimate.

Bibliography

Main Sources

Den for Landboevæsenet nedsatte Commissions Forhandlinger, 2 vols. (Copenhagen: Johan Fredrik Schultz, 1788–1789).

Fabricius, Christian Albrecht, *Noget til Oplysning at vore Fæstebønder ei er Trællenes Afkom* (Copenhagen: J. F. Schultz, 1785).

Mallet, Paul Henri, *Introduction à l'histoire du Dannemarch* (Copenhagen: Philibert, 1755).

Rothe, Tyge, *Nordens Staetsforfatning før Lehnstiden*, 2 vols. (Copenhagen: Gyldendal, 1781–1782).

Rothe, Tyge, *Vort Landvæsens System, som det var 1783, politisk betragtet* (Copenhagen: Gyldendal, 1784).

Main Bibliographical References

Evju, Håkon, *Ancient Constitutions and Modern Monarchy: Historical Writing and Enlightened Reform in Denmark-Norway, 1730–1814* (Leiden: Brill, 2019).

Goldie, Mark, "The Ancient Constitution and the Languages of Political Thought", *Historical Journal*, 62.1 (2018), 3–34.

Haakonsen, Knud; and Henrik Horstbøll, eds., *Northern Antiquities and National Identities* (Copenhagen: Det Kongelige Danske Videnskabernes Selskab, 2008).

Horstbøll, Henrik, "Defending Monarchy in 18th Century Denmark-Norway", in Hans Blom, John Christian Laursen, and Luisa Simonutti, eds., *Monarchisms in the Age of Enlightenment: Liberty, Patriotism and the Common Good* (Toronto: University of Toronto Press, 2007), 175–93.

Pocock, J.G.A., *The Ancient Constitution and the Feudal Law* (Cambridge: Cambridge University Press, 1957).

CHAPTER 12

Rousseau and Poland

Pragmatic Rebirth Rather than Idealistic Reforms?

Mark J. Hill

Poland in the eighteenth century faced two problems that made a constitutional project akin to that found in the *Social Contract* impossible: First, it was under threat from its neighbours, aided by internal political instability. Second, the country was, ironically, too well established. With a constitution which had been maintained (and thus, maintained itself) for centuries, the character, moeurs, manners, traditions, and beliefs of the Polish people were too well established. Jean-Jacques Rousseau, therefore, had to develop proposals that satisfied both of these issues: a solution, which took into account Poland's history and existing institutions, that aimed to unify Poland in the face of encroaching enemies, and ultimately reinforced the Polish character so that it could continue to exist – even without Poland, if necessary.

In this way, Rousseau's writings for Poland are radically different from his political proposals found elsewhere. In the *Social Contract* and his writings for Corsica, Rousseau provides his reader with reflections on the founding of a new polity with ideal constitutions. In fact, Rousseau explicitly states that Corsica is the only country in Europe capable of receiving the laws laid out in the *Social Contract*.[1] In response to this apparent incongruity, many commentators have claimed that, in writing his *Considerations on the Government of Poland*, Rousseau revised or abandoned his previous theories.[2] This position

1 Jean-Jacques Rousseau, *Du contrat social, Œuvres complètes*, vol. 3, Bibliothèque de La Pléiade (Paris: Gallimard, 1964), 391. Page references to Rousseau's works are to the Pléiade editions. Most quotes use translations taken from *The Plan for Perpetual Peace, On the Government of Poland, and Other Writings on History and Politics* (Hanover: Dartmouth College Press, 2005) and *The Social Contract and Other Later Political Writings*, ed. Victor Gourevitch (Cambridge: Cambridge University Press, 1997).

2 Jerzy Michalski and Richard Butterwick-Pawlikowski, *Rousseau and Polish Republicanism* (Warsaw: Tadeusz Manteuffel Institute of History, Polish Academy of Sciences, 2015), 45–9; Gordon McNeil, "The Anti-Revolutionary Rousseau", *The American Historical Review*, 58. 4 (1953), 808; W. Kendall, "Introduction: How to Read Rousseau's 'Government of Poland'", in *The Government of Poland*, by Jean-Jacques Rousseau, ix–xxxix (Indianapolis: Hackett Publishing, 1985), xiv, xvi; Jeffrey A. Smith, "Nationalism, Virtue, and the Spirit of Liberty in

 | DOI:10.1163/9789004549159_014

ignores the extent to which Rousseau engages with Poland's pre-existing historical condition, however. In fact, when his concerns for Poland's existing political norms are taken into consideration, the text instead reiterates many of Rousseau's earlier claims.

This argument is divided into three parts. First, Poland's political and constitutional history is examined. Second, the Polish intellectual context is examined, asking what Rousseau's actual task and goals may have been. Finally, comparisons between the proposals for Poland and those in Rousseau's other works are offered, highlighting exactly why the Polish were an inappropriate people to be given new laws. In doing this it is shown how the project must be understood as particular to Poland and its own historic constitutional moment.

1 History of Poland

There are two moments in the history of Poland that are worth highlighting in the context of this paper: the establishment of its political relationship with Lithuania, and the extraction of rights from Polish kings by nobles, culminating in the *pacta conventa*. With regard to the former: In 1385 Poland entered a union of crowns between the Grand Duke of Lithuania, Władysław II Jagiełło and Queen Jadwiga of Poland, initiating the Jagełłonian dynasty. The union allowed both nations to maintain political independence while expanding their collective territories and defeat the Teutonic Knights. By 1490 they had managed to extract allegiances from most of Central and Eastern Europe. External successes resulted in internal strife, however, and the Polish nobility grew concerned that their privileged position would be weakened as the king's successes were cemented.

While the king exercised power over one sixth of Polish land, had greater military and economic resources than the Sejm (Poland's bicameral parliament), gave royal favours and tenancies to royal land, and chose officers of the state (amongst other official temporal and spiritual powers), his powers began to be limited by the gentry who, witnessing the emergence of absolute monarchs in neighbouring countries, began to offer their own military support only in exchange for expanded privileges and rights. Amongst these rights were: the creation of provincial dietines; legal immunity; freedom of faith; a monopoly over land-ownership; the 1505 *Nihil Novi* ('nothing new') statute,

Rousseau's 'Government of Poland'", *The Review of Politics*, 65.3 (2003), 420; Franco Venturi, *Utopia and Reform in the Enlightenment* (Cambridge: Cambridge University Press, 1970), 129.

which forbade any new laws or taxes from being introduced without the consent of both chambers of the Sejm; the 1569 Union of Lublin, which ended the political independence of Poland and Lithuania; and in 1573, when the last of the Jagełłonian dynasty died, the right to elect monarchs. This right was formalized in the *pacta conventa*, a signed agreement between newly elected kings and "society" (in reality the gentry) that, in addition to forbidding the establishment of a hereditary monarchy, enumerated specific rights and duties a particular king would enjoy and be expected to fulfil.[3] The political history of Poland, therefore, is a series of protracted discussions and arrangements that came to form the basis of the Polish constitution and was instituted by a sort of social contract (the *pacta conventa*).

While the emerging political system is often referred to as the "noble democracy" or "golden liberty", it has also been identified as a cause of instability in Poland.[4] As the gentry made up a large portion of the population (roughly ten percent), this unusual political body gave Poland a reputation for chaos – one that is captured in a popular Polish phrase from the time: "it is by unrule that Poland stands".[5]

After a century consolidating internal power, external problems re-emerged. While the end of the sixteenth century saw successful wars with Russia and Sweden, and the putting down of sporadic uprisings by Cossack peasants in modern Ukraine, the seventeenth century began with conflicts with the Ottoman Empire and Baltic losses to Sweden. This set a pattern for an era that has become known as the Deluge. Starting roughly with the Khmelnytsky Uprising in modern Ukraine (1648–1657), the era included wars with, and territorial losses to, Russia (1654–1667), Sweden (1655–1661; 1700–1721), and the Ottoman Empire (1672–76). Ironically, in the face of these existential threats, rather than unite, the most powerful families moved to buttress their own positions turning to foreign powers.[6] This was made possible with two established constitutional arrangements: the *liberum veto* and confederacies – two things Mably and Rousseau would come to argue were the cause of Poland's "most perfect state of anarchy".[7]

3 P. Skwarczyński, "The Constitution of Poland before the Partition", in William Fiddian Reddaway, ed., *The Cambridge History of Poland* (Cambridge: Cambridge University Press, 1950), 49–55.

4 Norman Davies, *God's Playground: A History of Poland*, volume 1: *The Origins to 1795* (Oxford: Oxford University Press, 2005), 256–7.

5 Davies, 246.

6 Neal Ascherson, *The Struggles for Poland* (New York: Random House, 1991), 20–2.

7 Gabriel Bonnot de Mably, *Du gouvernement et des loix de la Pologne* (Paris: Volland, 1781), 51.

2 Liberum Veto

An important institutional rule attached the Sejm, the *liberum veto* demanded consensual agreement from all members to pass a session's slate of legislative work. As a rule, it quickly became problematic: those elected to take part in legislation were sent to discuss – and agree on – only the topics that they had been authorized. Thus, as it could be claimed by any particular deputy that they had no right to negotiate on an issue, every member had a veto on proceedings.

Unsurprisingly this was a disruptive power: from 1697–1733 eleven out of twenty sessions were ended by veto; from 1733–1763, only one session was successfully concluded. The threat posed by the *liberum veto* was compounded by Poland's enemies' use of it. It is claimed that every European power had at least one deputy in their pay and these corrupt nobles were encouraged by foreign powers to use the *liberum veto* when particular sessions threatened their relative position.[8] As Walicki notes, this ultimately resulted in the state becoming "a passive object and not subject in European politics".[9] In the end, a right designed to protect Poland from an absolutist leader became a tool of foreign absolutists.

Despite the clear threat posed by the *liberum veto* nobles remained supportive of it. When king Stanisław August Poniatowski (1732–1798), a would-be enlightened despot himself, manoeuvred to modernize the Polish political system by increasing crown power and limiting the veto's use, "confederations" emerged – the other constitutional practice noted as a cause of instability.

3 Confederations

Confederations were *ad hoc* quasi-military organizations which emerged to fulfil a legitimate constitutional need: the enforcement of the terms of a *pacta conventa* between the gentry and king. They were made up of nobles who shared political aims and agreed to work together to achieve their limited goals, or act in their collective self-defence. Their legitimacy was tied to the idea of the "omnipotence of the gentry" – the theory that the gentry as a whole stood above the king, and thus had the right and duty to enforce the king's

8 Davies, *God's Playground*, 265–6.

9 Andrzej Walicki, *The Enlightenment and the Birth of Modern Nationhood: Polish Political Thought from Noble Republicanism to Tadeusz Kościuszko* (Notre Dame: University of Notre Dame Press, 1989), 7.

obligations to society.[10] Their necessity was further compounded by the need for some other method of maintaining order due to the inability to institutionally legislate during moments of crisis caused by the *liberum veto*. The result was, for all intents and purposes, "a legalized form of civil war".[11]

During Stanisław's rule a number of confederations emerged. In March 1767 the protestant Confederation of Toruń and the Orthodox Confederation of Słuck were founded with the aim of re-establishing political rights that had been attacked during the Counter-Reformation and lost when Catholicism was declared the confession of Poland (in 1766, and again in 1768). In June of the same year, the Catholic Confederation of Radom emerged. All three were sponsored by Russia. In response, the Catholic Confederation of Bar was formed in 1768, and opposed Russian interference, political reforms that would strengthen the king's power, and the extension of political rights to non-Catholics.[12]

While the causes of confederations were multi-faceted, involving both internal and external actors, and both temporal and spiritual conflict, the outcome was a state in the grip of a constitutionally legitimate anarchy, and the once powerful Poland was economically, administratively, and socially hindered by the nobility's opposition to reforms. It was during this time that count Michal Wielhorski (1730–1794), a member of the Confederation of Bar, made contact with Rousseau.

We do not have the original correspondence between Rousseau and Wielhorski, although one is able to piece together the essential problem and proposal: as Wielhorski saw it, the long-standing Polish fear of their monarchy was legitimate, and the very reforms being proposed by Stanisław were evidence of this.[13] Wielhorski, therefore, recruited Rousseau with the goal of protecting Poland from both its neighbours and itself. To further grasp what this task was, however, it is necessary to reconstruct the intellectual culture of, and around, Poland that Rousseau would have been engaging with.

10 Skwarczyński, "The Constitution of Poland before the Partition".

11 Davies, *God's Playground*, 260.

12 Daniel Z. Stone, *The Polish-Lithuanian State, 1386–1795* (Seattle: University of Washington Press, 2014), 271–2.

13 Jerzy Lukowski, "Recasting Utopia: Montesquieu, Rousseau and the Polish Constitution of 3 May 1791", *The Historical Journal*, 37.1 (1994), 70.

4 Intellectual Culture, Rousseau, and Poland

The "Polish Enlightenment" – which roughly coincided with the reign of Stanisław, but more broadly ran from the 1720s, continued through the partitions, and concluded with the November Uprising in 1830 – was made up of somewhere between 700–800 direct participants publishing "in the spirit of belonging to the Enlightenment" and upwards of 2000 people if one incudes "those individuals who played a role as a lively literary audience, and thus participated in the intellectual ferment, even if only passively".[14] This is a miniscule number in relation to the population, and the influence of this group is questionable. Even amongst Poles there was a conception of the nation being comparatively backwards. In 1790 Stanisław Staszic exclaimed: "How far behind Poland is! What efforts have been made by other countries … Poland has just entered the fifteenth century while the rest of Europe is almost finished with the eighteenth".[15] Reflections on the cause of this, and how it could be overcome, were not uncommon – and unsurprisingly, at least one source noted was the "noble democracy".

As early as the sixteenth-century Poland's unique political organization was linked to its perceived backwardness. Conservative critics, such as Piotr Skarga (1536–1612), argued for the absolute divine right of kings and embraced the Counter-Reformation, while more progressive critics, such as Andrzej Frycz Modrzewski (1503–1572), "fearlessly condemned the oppression of the peasants, the exclusion of the bourgeoisie, the ignorance of the clergy, the luxury of the nobility". One can find similar criticism from Mikołaj Rey (1505–1569), Grzegorz Paweł z Brzezin (1525–1591), Stefan Garczyński (1690–1756), Stanisław Staszic (1755–1826), and Hugo Kołłątaj (1750–1812).[16] Thus, by the eighteenth century there was a strong sense that what was wrong with Poland was tied to its political norms. Others, however, looked further inwards for solutions to political problems, and particularly pervasive amongst nobles was the counter-Enlightenment Sarmatian ideology.

---

14 Barbara Grochulska, "The Place of the Enlightenment in Polish Social History", in J.K. Fedorowicz, *A Republic of Nobles: Studies in Polish History to 1864* (Cambridge: Cambridge University Press, 1982), 245, 249.

15 Quoted in Grochulska, 250.

16 Davies, *God's Playground*, 272–73; Grochulska, "The Place of the Enlightenment in Polish Social History", 250–1; Adam Ulam, "Andreas Fricius Modrevius--A Polish Political Theorist of the Sixteenth Century", *The American Political Science Review*, 40.3 (1946), 485. https://doi.org/10.2307/1949322.

Sarmatianism was a mythical history that claimed that the Polish nobility were descendants of a Persian people who came to the Black Sea steppe during the first centuries of the common era, before expanding into regions between the Dnieper and Vistula rivers where they enserfed the local population. A hybrid ideology, stories of "heroic deeds of old [...] and vivid only in the ethnically Polish environment" were mixed with "tales of conquest by the Sarmatian sword in times prior to the reign of the first Piasts", the ideas functioned as both myth of unification amongst the nobles and as ideological support for their political rights.[17] It was an ideology that saw the Polish form of politics as "exceptional, specific, and superior to all foreign forms of political life".[18] From their perspective, the inconveniences caused by their political system paled in comparison to the tyrannies they witnessed amongst their neighbours, and despite recognizing that some of Poland's problems may be institutional, they felt that specific noble solutions were necessary, rather than borrowing practices from other states.

This perspective meant that the Polish people were also distinct to foreigners – its history, political institutions, and ideologies, made it "an object of bewilderment, if not contempt, to outside observers".[19] Pufendorf noted that they were "inclined to an uncontroled liberty, or rather licentiousness and petulancy".[20] Voltaire described the country as not being "our part of Europe" in the *Essai sur les mœurs et l'esprit des nations* (1756), and elsewhere he links this to the nobles having maintained the manners of "*l'ancienne Sarmatie*"– being "fierce and idle [*oisive*]" – and that this had allowed them to maintain a system of government that had been "corrected" everywhere else. The noble democracy to him was nothing more than an oligarchy, the confederations rebellions, the country suffering from religious fanaticism, and the peasantry enslaved.[21]

---

17 Janus Tazbir, "Polish National Consciousness in the Sixteenth to the Eighteenth Century", *Harvard Ukrainian Studies*, 10.3/4 (1986), 318, 321.

18 Henryk Hinz, "The Philosophy of the Polish Enlightenment and Its Opponents: The Origins of the Modern Polish Mind", *Slavic Review*, 30.2 (1971), 345. https://doi.org/10.2307/2494244.

19 Jerzy Lukowski, "Political Ideas among the Polish Nobility in the Eighteenth Century (To 1788)", *The Slavonic and East European Review*, 82.1 (2004), 2.

20 Samuel von Pufendorf, *An Introduction to the History of the Principal Kingdoms and States of Europe*, edited by Michael J. Seidler, translated by Jodocus Crull (Indianapolis: Liberty Fund, 2013), 397.

21 Voltaire, *Histoire de Charles XII, roi de Suède, divisée en huit livres, avec l'Histoire de l'empire de Russie sous Pierre-le-Grand, en deux parties divisées par chapitres* (Geneva: Cramer, 1768), 92–3. http://gallica.bnf.fr/ark:/12148/bpt6k65533779. The section in which he describes their Sarmatian heritage was not included in the first edition (1731). Earlier criticisms which we know Rousseau was familiar with include: Bodin's *Six livres de la*

Not everyone saw Poland negatively, however. Calvin's successor, Theodore Beza, wrote positively of the *pacta conventa*, and Huguenot philosopher Stephen Junius Brutus praised the nation in the *Vindiciae contra tyrannos* (1579).[22] Gabriel-François Coyer, in his *Histoire de Jean Sobieski, Roi de Pologne* (1761), noted that: "The Romans who conquered all, never bested the Sarmatians".[23] As Wolf notes, Eastern Europe as a whole was an "intellectual object under construction", but in the case of Poland, a "perfect innocence and ignorance of the nation" meant one could "theorize imaginatively".[24] This theorizing meant that interest had grown enough by 1770 to allow Baudeau to write that Poland had "*enfin*" become a "*nation célèbre*" as the whole of Europe pitied its fate.[25] However, the unifying theme amongst commentators was Poland's need to reform. As Davies wrote, "[i]n such an atmosphere, it was a bold spirit indeed who dared to say anything favourable of the Polish constitution. Even apologists [...] and the proponents of Reform, from Baudeau to Mably, were given to blackwashing Poland in the hope of provoking change".[26]

In the case of Mably, who was also invited by Wielhorski to write for Poland, proposed reforms included: the establishment of a hereditary monarch (although one that did not have the right to distribute royal privileges, and whose funds were to be limited); freeing the peasants; reforming the *liberum veto* so as to require the unanimous dissent of all envoys, and restricting its use to bills rather than sessions; ending the legitimately of confederations; and economic reforms to encourage commerce.[27] These radical suggestions – perhaps seen

République (1566); Pufendorf's *Introduction à l'histoire* (1695); and Montesquieu's *Lettres persanes* (1721) and *De l'esprit des loix* (1748).

22 Hinz, "The Philosophy of the Polish Enlightenment and Its Opponents"; Larry Wolff, *Inventing Eastern Europe* (Toronto: University of Toronto Press, 2006); Edward Andrew, *Patrons of Enlightenment* (Toronto: University of Toronto Press, 2006).

23 Gabriel François Coyer, *Histoire de Jean Sobieski, roi de Pologne* (Chez Duchesne, libraire, 1761), 2.

24 Wolff, *Inventing Eastern Europe*, 236, 360. For example, Defoe's satirical poem *The Dyet of Poland* (1705) turned the state into an allegory for England's own dysfunctional politics. Poland's literary potential for early eighteenth-century readers, the extensive details Defoe felt were necessary to provide for them, and the mistakes that he himself made in doing so, all say something about Poland's place in eighteenth century popular culture.

25 *Éphémérides du citoyen, ou Chronique de l'esprit national*, vol. 2 (Paris: N. A. Delalain, 1770), 16. http://gallica.bnf.fr/ark:/12148/bpt6k1044676q. Baudeau's works in the *Éphémérides* included the *Avis économiques aux citoyens éclairés de la République de Pologne, sur la manière de percevoir le revenu public* (t. XI [1770]; t. I [1771]) and the *Lettres historiques sur l'état actuel de la Pologne, et sur l'origine de ses malheurs* (t. II, III, IV [1770]; t. III, IV, V [1771]).

26 Davies, *God's Playground*, 281.

27 Mably, *Du gouvernement et des loix de la Pologne*.

as attacks on Poland's noble democracy – were unsatisfactory to Wielhorski; although Mably's *Observations* was completed on 31 August, 1770, Rousseau was contacted soon after and began his work in October 1770.[28]

Rousseau – like most – had a minimal knowledge of Poland. He notes that the majority of what he knew came from a six-month study made possible by resources provided by Wielhorski. The exact contents of these resources are not known, but a "copy-book" that contains "a dossier of [Wielhorski and Mably's] cooperation on the projected reform of the Polish system of government" exists.[29] While Michalski argues that it is difficult to know if Rousseau had access to these specific works, it is clear that Rousseau was engaging directly with many of the ideas and propositions put forward by both Wielhorski and Mably in them (as one would expect if they shared the same historical source material). Fabre has also noted that Rousseau made use of "abundant physiocrat productions", including the previously mentioned Baudeau works from *Ephemerides*, and notes on Poland by "Mirabeau, Dupont de Nemours, Maurice de Saint-Leu, Quesnay de Saint-Germain and many others".[30] Christian Pfeffel's *État de la Pologne* appears to have been seen in some form, and, although the *Histoire de l'anarchie de Pologne* was not published until after Rousseau's own work was completed, Rousseau was in contact with Claude-Carloman de Rulhiere.[31]

This is all to say that, while Rousseau was not an expert on Polish politics, he was also not in a state of "perfect innocence and ignorance". This is important as a recurring theme in Rousseau's political writings is the necessity of thoroughly knowing the people one is legislating for – "even more so when it is a question of a nation already completely instituted, whose tastes, morals, prejudices and vices have taken root too much to be easily stifled by new seeds".[32] The Polish people were "completely instituted". Even if the details of this community were not thoroughly, or even correctly, known to Rousseau, his proposals had to take his understanding of their history into consideration. Therefore, if one wants to understand his proposals fully, they must measure them against

28 Michalski and Butterwick-Pawlikowski, *Rousseau and Polish Republicanism*, 14–5.

29 Michalski and Butterwick-Pawlikowski, 22.

30 Rousseau, *Œuvres Complètes*,3: *Du contrat social; Écrits politiques*, 1736, 1740, 1783.

31 On Pfeffel's influence see: *Œuvres Complètes*, 3: *Du Contrat social; Écrits politiques*, 1735–42; Michalski and Butterwick-Pawlikowski, *Rousseau and Polish Republicanism*, 21–3. For more on Rulhiere see: Michalski and Butterwick-Pawlikowski, 44; Tomasz Szkudlarek, "On Nations And Children: Rousseau, Poland And European Identity", *Studies in Philosophy and Education*, 24.1 (2005), 21–2. https://doi.org/10.1007/s11217-004-6528-3; Wolff, *Inventing Eastern Europe*, 272.

32 Rousseau, *Œuvres complètes*, vol. 3: *Considerations on the Government of Poland*, 953.

the history of the Polish people as he could have known it. Rousseau's proposals took all of Poland's mystery, absurdity, and instability – that which made everyone else see Poland as awkward, dangerous, and politically problematic – as his starting point.[33] Thus, while the conclusions he draws may be markedly different from those found in his other works, this should not be a surprise; the work is a specific response to a specific set of conditions (imagined or not). In this way, the work can also inform our understanding of Rousseau's system as a whole – it is a case study in the application of his thought to a particular scenario. To move forward, then, we must look at what those particular conditions were, and how they fit into Rousseau's political system as a whole.

5 An Inappropriate People

Let us begin with Rousseau's description of a people who are ready to be legislated for:

> What people, then, is fit for legislation? One which, while finding itself already bound together by some union of origin, interest, or convention, has not yet borne the true yoke of laws; one with neither deep-rooted customs nor deep-rooted superstitions; one which is not in fear of being overrun by a sudden invasion; which without taking part in its neighbors' quarrels can resist each one of them by itself, or enlist the help of one to repulse the other; one whose every member can be known to all, and where one is not forced to charge a man with a greater burden than a man can bear; one which can do without all other peoples and without which every other people can do; one which is neither rich nor poor, and can be self-sufficient; finally, one which combines the stability of an ancient people with the docility of a new people.[34]

Poland did not fit this pattern. While Poland had been in a long-standing union, this was a political and legal union. The Polish people had diverse and deep-rooted customs and superstitions in terms religious beliefs (Catholic, Judaic, Calvinist, Lutheran, Islamic, Eastern Orthodox, and Uniate), ethnic backgrounds (being made up of Poles, Lithuanians, Jews, Germans, Ukrainians, Belarusians, Ruthenians, Tartars, and even a substantial Scottish population),

33 Rousseau, *ibidem*, 953–4.
34 Rousseau, *Social Contract*, 390–1.

and Sarmatianism.[35] There was almost no sense of "being" Polish – from the sixteenth century "inhabitants of the Commonwealth shared neither a single language nor the same religious convictions or customs. The term 'Poland' was used interchangeably with 'Commonwealth'".[36] When one includes the burghers and peasants, there was even less which united the people. Additionally, Poland had long felt the "yoke of laws"; it had a remarkably well-established and stable constitution, and the Sejm had been meeting for nearly three hundred years.

Size was also an issue. By the seventeenth century Poland covered almost a million square kilometres and contained around six million people – this was much too large by standards set in the *Social Contract*.[37] Additionally, the country was "a natural invasion route for those entering Europe from the East and those attacking Russia from the West", having no natural borders across this axis.[38] This problem was compounded by a lack of strict self-sufficiency. While Poland had fertile land and had become an important regional exporter, it was also prone to droughts, floods, and crop-killing frosts. Thus, in good times, Poland's neighbours relied on it for exports, and in bad times, Poland relied on others.[39]

Finally, there was an emerging affinity amongst the Poles and the French that Rousseau was unsupportive of. Their royal and aristocratic families intermarried, the polite language was French, and the Enlightenment itself was a source of inspiration to those (few) who were aware of it. This led Rousseau to warn the Polish to refrain from embracing French (or other foreign) customs less they become just another corrupted European people.[40]

For these many reasons Poland, from the outset, could not be given the Rousseauvian constitution contained in the *Social Contract* and Rousseau was explicit about this. In section five of *Poland*, he warns his readers that they

35 Skwarczyński, "The Constitution of Poland before the Partition", 68; Ascherson, *The Struggles for Poland*, 5, 18; Grochulska, "The Place of the Enlightenment in Polish Social History", 248; William Lithgow, *The Totall Discourse, of the Rare Aduentures, and Painefull Peregrinations of Long Nineteene Yeares Trauayles from Scotland, to the Most Famous Kingdomes in Europe, Asia, and Affrica* (London: Nicholas Okes, 1632), 422.

36 Tazbir, "Polish National Consciousness in the Sixteenth to the Eighteenth Century", 317.

37 Skwarczyński, "The Constitution of Poland before the Partition", 51; Rousseau, *Œuvres Complètes. 3, Du Contrat Social ; Écrits Politiques*, 386.

38 Ascherson, *The Struggles for Poland*, 3–4, 17.

39 Rousseau offers further reflections on these specific deficiencies in both the *Social Contract* (390) and *Considerations on the Government of Poland* (959).

40 Rousseau, *Considerations on the Government of Poland*, 962; Ascherson, *The Struggles for Poland*, 8.

must avoid "rushing from the very outset into chimerical projects" – specifically, the "enterprise" of "giving to the constitution of a large kingdom the solidity and vigor of that of a small Republic". Instead, Rousseau notes, there are two options: devolve or retrench; become smaller or abandon the "chimerical" project of modifying Poland's constitution. With regard to the former option, Rousseau writes: "The first reform you need is that of your extent … Begin by compressing your boundaries if you want to reform your government. Perhaps your neighbors are considering doing this service for you".[41] However, it was the latter option that Rousseau seriously suggested:

> [I]t is amazing that the vast extent of Poland has not already a hundred times over brought about the conversion of the government into despotism, debased the souls of the Poles, and corrupted the mass of the nation. It is an example unique in history that after centuries such a State is still only in anarchy. The slowness of this progression is due to advantages inseparable from the inconveniences from which you want to free yourselves. Ah, I cannot say it too many times; think well before touching your laws, and above all the ones that made you what you are.[42]

Plans for maintaining Poland as it already existed were Rousseau's focus in the text. The remainder of this paper will explore the ways in which Rousseau thought this could be done.

6 A Polish People

6.1 *The Problem*

The prime task of the historical and mythical lawgiver was to recognize what was unique about a people and establish legal institutions that use these qualities to form a lasting, and unique, national character.[43] Rousseau was explicit in the *Social Contract* that once a national character had been set it could not

41 Rousseau, *Considerations on the Government of Poland*, 971. If his advice was too unpalatable, Rousseau offered the half-way solution of a federal system, although the details of how this would work were left to the Poles – this was not Rousseau's task, nor did he suspect it had much chance of success.

42 Rousseau, *ibidem*, 971.

43 Bonnie Honig, *Democracy and the Foreigner* (Princeton: Princeton University Press, 2001), 21–2.

be transformed – and warned that anyone who attempted such a task be prepared to fail.[44]

In the case of Poland, then, neither the founding of a national character, nor the establishment of legal institutions, were possible. Instead, the existing qualities and constitution needed to be worked with. With regard to the former, the existing national character (at least amongst the nobles) was communicated explicitly to Rousseau in Wielhorski's *Essai sur les mœurs et le caractère des Polonais*, and this is what he worked with.[45] With regard to the latter issue, Rousseau noted two constitutional aspects of Poland's institutions which were causes of anarchy: the *liberum veto* and confederations.[46] However, while these parts of Poland's long standing constitutional order were identified as causes of its turmoil, they could not easily be abandoned. This is in spite of having written in the *Social Contract* that a sovereign who was limited was not sovereign, and that by allowing particular wills to dominate the general one risked exactly the type of conflict Poland faced. That is, despite pragmatic and theoretical concerns, Rousseau did not argue for the abolishment of these causes of anarchy. Instead, he wrote that the *liberum veto* "is not in itself a vicious right, but as soon as it exceeds its bounds it becomes the most dangerous of abuses: now it is nothing but the instrument of oppression". The veto was a part of the Polish constitutional system and therefore Rousseau called for it to be maintained – although every use of it to be scrutinized, and abuses be punished by death. Confederations, similarly, were to be seen as shields, refuges, and sanctuaries for the constitution; "instead of abolishing the confederations, determine the cases in which they can legitimately take place, and then regulate their form and effect".[47]

What we are presented with in *Poland*, then, conforms neither to the *Social Contract*, nor the genre of law-giving more generally.[48] The foundational laws

---

44 Rousseau, *Social Contract*, 385. Book II, chapters VII-XII overview the task and problem. There is an exception to this rule (for which Lycurgus was an example), but it required the destruction of a people.

45 Michalski and Butterwick-Pawlikowski, *Rousseau and Polish Republicanism*, 82.

46 Rousseau, *Considerations on the Government of Poland*, 994. Rousseau also noted the threat posed by private armies. Being a distinctly private – rather than legal – matter, however, Rousseau argues that they must be eliminated.

47 Rousseau, *Considerations on the Government of Poland*, 995–8.

48 Kendall has pointed to a number of specific arguments from the *Social Contract* which have been either dropped, or flipped around, in *Poland*. These include: the general will and popular sovereignty; civil religion; the role of a civic education; the importance of natural law; and the problem of a peoples' given political history. See Kendall, "Introduction: How to Read Rousseau's 'Government of Poland'", xiv–xv.

for Poland existed, and therefore proposals were limited. Rousseau was explicit on this point, noting that his topic was "the administrative regime", and that he would be "leaving the foundation of your laws virtually untouched".[49] This distinction is clear even in the language Rousseau deploys; while he elsewhere described the founding of a nation in terms of a birth, and its collapse as its death, for Poland he speaks of reinvigorating the national character through a "second birth".[50]

6.2 *National Character*

Since Rousseau could not change the constitution, nor form the people, he turned to buttressing both. However, he warned: "No constitution will ever be good and solid unless that law rules the citizens' hearts. So long as the legislative force does not reach that deep, the laws will invariably be evaded".[51] Thus, the greatest threat facing Poland came not from its existing laws, but from a lack of patriotic unity that encouraged the Poles to obey them. Therefore, Rousseau wanted to encourage patriotic love amongst the people, and for their political institutions. This was not a political project as one would imagine it, but instead, a programme of social engineering – education rather than legislation; re-founding rather than founding.

This led to his peculiar proposals: "How, then, can one move hearts, and get the fatherland and its laws loved? Dare I say it? With children's games; with institutions which appear trivial in the eyes of superficial men, but which form cherished habits and invincible attachments".[52] He did not claim to have invented these methods, however: "The same spirit guided all ancient Lawgivers and their institutions. All of them sought bonds that might attach the Citizens to the fatherland and to one another, and they found them in distinctive practices".[53] These were not only theoretical or historical reflections – the description echoes Rousseau's writings on his own childhood in Geneva, and the celebrations of Le Régiment de St. Gervais in particular.[54] However, the goal was not to recreate public celebrations as they existed elsewhere, but instead establish and re-establish those specific to Poland – ancient and new

49 Rousseau, *Considerations on the Government of Poland*, 961.

50 Rousseau, *Social Contract*: 424; Rousseau, *Considerations on the Government of Poland*, 969.

51 Rousseau, *Considerations on the Government of Poland*, 955.

52 Rousseau, *ibidem*, 955.

53 Rousseau, *ibidem*, 958.

54 Jean-Jacques Rousseau and Jean Le Rond d'Alembert, *Letter to D'Alembert and Writings for the Theater*, edited by Allan David Bloom, Charles E. Butterworth, and Christopher Kelly (Lebanon, NH: UPNE, 2004), 123–4.

practices that "have the advantage of making the Poles fond of their country and give them natural revulsion to mingling with foreigners".[55]

He offered the example of bullfighting in Spain as a suitable event, but called for one that would be more Polish – possibly involving a more nationally suitable activity such as horsemanship. The exact details of these practices, however, were not an essential topic from Rousseau's perspective (he was not an expert on Polish history). What was essential was that "games must be devised, festivals, solemn occasions so distinctive of this particular Court that they are found at none other".[56] Differentiating Poland was seen as so key that even national dress was discussed.

Nobles sympathetic to Sarmatianism would likely have been receptive to this advice – there was an already existing tendency to see themselves as distinct from other Europeans which verged on an "intense xenophobia ... They came to believe that everything foreign was a potential threat to their language, traditions, and, what was most important, their class liberties".[57] And they would have also appreciated his position on public displays and the authority they endow.[58] He noted that these ceremonies should not be "exclusively for the Great and the rich" and instead, they should hold "spectacles in the open, where ranks are carefully distinguished but the entire people participates equally, as among the ancients".[59] However, in this vein Rousseau continued further than Sarmatian tastes would have appreciated: he argued for the possibility for all to become nobility via a graduated class system attached to patriotic duty – although, importantly, the peasants were not initially to be included.[60] There would be two upshots to this: first, it meant that inequalities were not ossified and thus result in resentment, and second, since distinctions were rewards for patriotism, externalities from inequalities would be positive.[61]

55 Rousseau, *Considerations on the Government of Poland*, 962.
56 Rousseau, *ibidem*, 962.
57 Tazbir, "Polish National Consciousness in the Sixteenth to the Eighteenth Century", 330–1.
58 Rousseau, *Considerations on the Government of Poland*, 964.
59 Rousseau, *ibidem*, 963.
60 Wielhorski's description of the Polish peasantry was that of 'drunks, idlers and layabouts, but also insolent'. It was said that they were '[b]lindly attached to relations that had existed for centuries and suspicious of all novelties, they were incapable of "se former une juste idée des douceurs de la liberté", preferred serfdom and the *corvée* to the "freedom" under which they would have to fend for themselves.' While this position is obviously problematic, Wielhorski's use of custom may have had rhetorical sway over Rousseau. See: Michalski and Butterwick-Pawlikowski, *Rousseau and Polish Republicanism*, 36; Rousseau, *Considerations on the Government of Poland*, 974.
61 The aims of these proposals are similar to those found in Rousseau's other works (in particular for Corsica). See Rousseau, *Œuvres Complètes*, vol. 3: *Constitutional Project for*

Again, the end of Rousseau's proposals in *Poland* was to create a feeling of membership amongst the Polish people – but this membership was not to be born from a new constitution but in the rediscovering of an original Polish character. Poland was "already a fully instituted nation, whose tastes, morals, prejudices and vice are too deeply rooted to be easily stifled by new seeds".[62] Therefore, Rousseau told them: "Correct the abuses of your constitution, if it is possible to do so; but do not despise the constitution that made you what you are".[63]

6.3 *Public Education*

To be secured, the Polish people needed to embrace their historical founding and constitution (albeit, as described by Wielhorski). For Rousseau, the method of doing this, and which made up 'l'article important' in his text, was a national education.[64]

Education was not a topic ignored by Rousseau, nor his contemporaries. As Gill has shown, the Enlightenment project was itself, to some extent, a belief in that transformative power of education.[65] However, one of the key tensions within this genre was the contradiction between an individualistic education respecting a child's dignity and potential enlightenment, and the creation of a systematic mass education system that produced social virtues. Rousseau's, perhaps sophistic, response to this problem was to build upon the longstanding body-politic metaphor and treat the nation as the individual. If one were to recognize each *nation* as a unique body that required its own particular system of education, that acknowledged the dignity and potentiality of that particular people, one could also develop a system aimed at social unity: "It is education that must give the national form to souls, and direct their opinions and their tastes so that they will be patriots by inclination, by passion, by necessity".[66] In this way, Rousseau took a tenet of the Enlightenment – the belief that men are universally malleable – and argued for it to be used to reinforce, in the Polish people, their own non-universal qualities.

Corsica, 918–20. For more on Rousseau's proposals for Corsica see Mark J. Hill, "Enlightened 'Savages': Rousseau's Social Contract and the 'brave People' of Corsica", *History of Political Thought*, 38.3 (2017), 462–93.

62 Rousseau, *Considerations on the Government of Poland*, 953.

63 Rousseau, *ibidem*, 954.

64 Rousseau, *ibidem*, 966.

65 Natasha Gill, *Educational Philosophy in the French Enlightenment: From Nature to Second Nature* (Farnham: Ashgate Gower, 2010), 4–5.

66 Rousseau, *Considerations on the Government of Poland*, 966.

The importance of such a system for Poland was also made explicit in Wielhorski's *Essai sur les mœurs*. There we read that, due to a taste for foreign education "one can see Poland as divided into two nations of which principles and *mœurs* differ essentially".[67] In *Poland*, Rousseau aims to correct this:

> National education belongs only to free men; they are the only ones who have a common existence and are truly tied together by Law. A Frenchman, an Englishman, a Spaniard, an Italian, a Russian are all just about the same man: he leaves school already completely formed for license, that is to say, for servitude. At twenty years of age a Pole ought not to be a different sort of man; he ought to be a Pole.[68]

Education, as proposed by Rousseau, was a political good that, in the face of foreign enemies, encouraged the formation of a patriotic citizenry that would make an 'indigestible' people. To achieve these ends Poland needed to abandon the systems of education practised elsewhere – including foreign tutors and religious teachers. The only person truly qualified to educate the Pole would be the Pole. Teaching would not become a profession, however. Poland should instead make use of citizens who had demonstrated exemplary Polish qualities and turn teaching into one step of his proposed graduated class system – a civic process that every worthy citizen would take part in as they progressed through the varying levels of society and government. The teacher was someone and something that all children would, and should, become.

Rousseau also turns to the educational theories developed in *Émile*, arguing that in Poland education should be "negative". By this he meant that education should not be a form of social training in which children are provided with rules and maxims used to overcome bad or evil inclinations – this was to make being good the outcome of mental calculations rather than innate qualities. Such an education at best frustrated children, and at worse taught them about vices they may not have otherwise come to know. Instead, and born out of his belief that humans are naturally good but corruptible, good actions should be natural inclinations, and thus Rousseau advised Poland that to "[p]revent vices from arising, you will have done enough for virtue".

Just as celebrations were to be public, education and play was also to be visible to all (as, from Rousseau's perspective, the two were the same thing) so

67 Quoted in Michalski and Butterwick-Pawlikowski, *Rousseau and Polish Republicanism*, 34–35. Michalski identifies the division between the richer magnates and the nobility more generally.

68 Rousseau, *Considerations on the Government of Poland*, 966.

as to "accustom them from early on to rule, to equality, to fraternity, to competitions, to living under the eyes of their fellow-citizens and to seeking public approbation".[69] As with classes, playful competition amongst children was designed to encourage positive social ends.

Rousseau concludes his discussion on education by noting that if he were ignored here, all other reforms would be superfluous: "However wise, however farsighted they might be, they will be evaded and vain, and you will have corrected some abuses that wound you, only in order to introduce others that you will not have foreseen. These are the preliminaries that I consider indispensable".[70]

6.4 *Polish Freedom*

Perhaps the clearest distinction between Rousseau's proposals for Poland and those found in his other texts can be identified in his definition of a free Poland. He does not attempt to create the conditions allowing for civic or republican freedom developed in the *Social Contract* – the freedom to be part of, and obey, self-imposed laws. Nor does he propose conditions to create moral freedom – the freedom to obey one's own self-imposed moral imperatives.[71] He also denied Poland the spiritual freedom he identified as key for Geneva – a "saintly, sublime, genuine religion, [in which] men, *as children of the same God*, all recognize one another as brothers, and the society that unites them does not dissolve even at death".[72] And, in Rousseau's most clear break with the Polish nobility, Rousseau also dismissed Sarmatian freedom. While, for Wielhorski, the way in which the efficacy of the state was measured was tied to how particular institutions "guaranteed the inviolability of rights and freedom" of the nobles, for Rousseau, the view that noble liberty was "the highest good and the principal criterion for evaluating governmental institutions" stood in the way of Polish stability.[73] Instead, Rousseau called for reforming

69 Rousseau, *ibidem*, 968. Here too proposals emulate those found in *Émile*; in one case the tutee was under the everpresent eye of Rousseau-the-tutor, in the other case, children are to be under the watchful eye of the public.

70 Rousseau, *ibidem*, 969.

71 Rousseau, *Œuvres complètes*, vol. 3: *Second Discourse*, 156–7; Rousseau, *Social Contract*, 328–9.

72 Rousseau, *Social Contract*, 464–5; Richard Whatmore, "Rousseau and the Representants: The Politics of the Lettres écrites de la montagne", *Modern Intellectual History*, 3.3 (2006), 406. Interestingly, the topic of religion is essentially ignored in the text. There are only two mentions of it, and both are found during the discussion on Numa.

73 Michalski and Butterwick-Pawlikowski, *Rousseau and Polish Republicanism*, 30.

some of the gentry's most valued institutions by increasing the power of the monarch while limiting the power of the *liberum veto* and confederations.[74]

Thus, civic, moral, spiritual, nor Sarmatian freedom, are taken up by Rousseau as his ends. Instead, he proposed a new type of freedom – a freedom akin to that which Moses gave the Jews – the freedom to *continue to be* Polish in spite of the threats facing Poland:

> In the present state of things, I see only a single means of giving [Poland] the stability it lacks: that is to infuse, so to speak, the soul the confederates into the whole nation: that is to establish the Republic so much in the hearts of the Poles that it continues to exist there in spite of all its oppressors' efforts. That, it seems to me, is the only refuge where force can neither reach nor destroy it … You might not be able to keep them from swallowing you; at least make it so they cannot digest you … Its citizens' virtue, their patriotic zeal, the distinctive form which national institutions can give their souls, that is the only rampart always ready to defend it, and which no army could force.[75]

Unsurprisingly, this proposal has raised questions. Platter argues that Rousseau appears to abandon his previous position on "the almost insuperable barriers to making freedom and virtue reign in large states". Smith has called the idea – that Poland could become more free as it became closer to disappearing as a state – a paradox of liberty; he asks: "If the Poles' extensive liberty were less threatened (or completely secure), would Rousseau hold them to be less 'truly' free (or not free at all)?" These questions miss the point, however. Freedom, as Smith is trying to construct it – and not surprisingly, as this is how Rousseau had elsewhere described it – is civic or republican freedom, and this was not a possibility for Poland.[76] As a people, the Polish were on the brink of entering the wilderness. While it would be ideal to prevent this from happening, Rousseau's work for Poland was not idealistic in this sense. Again, the ideal scenario would be a reinvigorated Polish state with institutions built upon, and supported by, Polish patriotism. However, as Polish republican freedom could

74 See sections eight and nine of *Poland*.

75 Rousseau, *Considerations on the Government of Poland*, 959–60.

76 Marc F. Platter, "Rousseau and the Origins of Nationalism", in Clifford Orwin and Nathan Tarcov, eds., *The Legacy of Rousseau* (Chicago: University of Chicago Press, 1996), 194; Smith, "Nationalism, Virtue, and the Spirit of Liberty", 10. See also Pierre Hassner, "Rousseau and the Theory and Practice of International Relations", in *The Legacy of Rousseau*, 209.

not exist without a Polish republic, Rousseau's proposals were independent from the republic. He developed a set of proposals that would, ultimately, provide Poland with the ability to exist without a government – a freedom that allowed for a people without political leaders, rulers, or even borders – an anarchic freedom.

7 Conclusion: Constitutions and Founding Myths

The importance of the historical founding of a political regime is perhaps one of the few aspects of Rousseau's work that is not disputed. Hendel wrote: "The great law-givers, Lycurgus and Numa, told in the Lives of Plutarch, were among the boyhood admirations of Rousseau; and Moses of the Old Testament could scarcely have been absent from the fancies of the youth of Geneva".[77] The link between this admiration and his political theory is well documented; many have noted that Rousseau's legislator in the *Social Contract* shared much with these historical figures.[78] As Shklar wrote: "The Great Legislator must not only invent [laws], but create the moral climate that is needed for their acceptance … That was the way of those ancient political paragons, Moses, Lycurgus, Numa, and Solon".[79] The link between constitutions, legislators, and foundational moments is made explicit by Rousseau in the *Social Contract*. Establishing a constitution is, by definition, something that happens during extra-constitutional moments; established during a time of loose association between a people. It becomes, however, defining – both legally and as a foundational part of a people's morals, customs, and opinions. It is the immovable keystone that holds society together.[80] All of this led David Wisner to conclude that Rousseau was the "writer who best explored the logical potential" of the legislator, having made it central to his own political system.[81]

---

77 Charles Williams Hendel, *Jean-Jacques Rousseau: Moralist* (Indianapolis: Bobbs-Merrill, 1962), 320.

78 Byron Wells, "Rousseau's Legislators and the Exemplar of Sparta", in Ruth Grant and Philip Stewart, eds., *Rousseau and the Ancients / Rousseau et les anciens*, Pensée Libre, 8 (Montreal: North American Association for the Study of Jean-Jacques Rousseau, 2001); Keller, "Plutarch and Rousseau's First Discours", *PMLA*, 54.1 (1939), 212–22. https://doi.org/10.2307/458634; Peter D. Jimack, *La genèse et la rédaction de l'Emile de J.-J. Rousseau*, vol. 13 (Geneva: SVEC, 1960).

79 Judith N. Shklar, *Men and Citizens: A Study of Rousseau's Social Theory*, 2nd ed. (Cambridge: Cambridge University Press, 1985), 155–6.

80 Rousseau, *Social Contract*, 394.

81 David A. Wisner, *The Cult of the Legislator in France, 1750–1830: A Study in the Political Theology of the French Enlightenment* (Oxford: Voltaire Foundation, 1997), 4.

Despite this, Rousseau did not attempt to put any of these ideas into practice in *Poland*. In fact, an early draft of *Poland* was prefixed with "*Constitution et République*", but he later crossed these three words out and replaced them with *gouvernement*.[82] The importance of this is made clear in his text:

> One should not lose sight of what I said in the *Social Contract* about the state of weakness and anarchy in which a nation finds itself while it establishes or reforms its constitution. In that moment of disorder and excitement it is in no state to offer any resistance and the least shock can topple everything. It is therefore important at all costs to secure for oneself an interval of tranquility during which to work on oneself without risk and *rejuvenate one's constitution*.[83]

The task for Poland, then, was not the same as that found in the *Social Contract* – it was not the establishment of a polity that fulfilled the "*principes du droit politique*". Instead, it aimed to secure Poland's existing political norms.

In this context it may be surprising that Rousseau began *Poland* with a short chapter on ideal lawgivers (in the examples of Moses, Lycurgus, and Numa). While one may initially suspect Rousseau is turning to this topic to prepare his readers for his own foundational proposals – to set the scene for his own entrance – this was not the case. Instead, he was drawing his Polish reader's attention to the historical moments that every established people had *already* experienced – including Poland. These ancient examples highlight what was so difficult about the situation Poland faced, and why it was necessary to look to history for future solutions. Again, in the *Social Contract* Rousseau warned: "What makes the work of legislation difficult is not so much what has to be established as what has to be destroyed".[84] It was this threat of destruction when presented with an established people that necessitated Rousseau's conservative proposals (and perhaps led to him making any proposals at all). Although radical in thought, Rousseau was not a revolutionary. To understand how these proposals fit into Rousseau's system as whole, one must return to the first task facing the would-be legislator outlined in the *Social Contract*: "Just like an architect, before putting up a large building, observes and tests the ground to see whether it can support the weight, so the wise institutor does not begin by drawing up laws good in themselves, but first examines whether

82 Rousseau, *Considerations on the Government of Poland*, 1733.
83 Rousseau, *ibidem*, 1036–37. Italics added.
84 Rousseau, *Social Contract*, 391.

the people for whom he intends them is fit to bear them".[85] The architectural foundations of Poland – awkward as they were – had already been set, and although the structure upon them was in a wretched state, facing both collapse from the inside and incursion from out, the foundations remained.

Bibliography

Main Sources

Bonnot de Mably, Gabriel, *Du gouvernement et des loix de la Pologne* (Paris: Volland, 1781).

Pufendorf, Samuel von, *An Introduction to the History of the Principal Kingdoms and States of Europe,* edited by Michael J. Seidler, translated by Jodocus Crull (Indianapolis: Liberty Fund, 2013).

Rousseau, Jean-Jacques, *Oeuvres complètes*, Bibliothèque de La Pléiade (Paris: Gallimard, 1964), vol. 3: *Considérations sur le governement de Pologne*; *Project de constitution pour la Corse.*

Main Bibliographical References

Davies, Norman, *God's Playground: A History of Poland* (Oxford: Oxford University Press, 2005; first ed., 1981).

Fedorowicz, J.K., *A Republic of Nobles: Studies in Polish History to 1864* (Cambridge: Cambridge University Press, 1982).

Michalski, Jerzy; Richard Butterwick-Pawlikowski, *Rousseau and Polish Republicanism* (Warsaw: Tadeusz Manteuffel Institute of History, Polish Academy of Sciences, 2015).

Shklar, Judith N., *Men and Citizens: A Study of Rousseau's Social Theory,* 2nd ed. (Cambridge: Cambridge University Press, 1985).

Walicki, Andrzej, *The Enlightenment and the Birth of Modern Nationhood: Polish Political Thought from Noble Republicanism to Tadeusz Kościuszko* (Notre Dame: University of Notre Dame Press, 1989).

Wisner, David A., *The Cult of the Legislator in France, 1750–1830: A Study in the Political Theology of the French Enlightenment* (Oxford: Voltaire Foundation, 1997).

85 Rousseau, *ibidem*, 384–5.

CHAPTER 13

The Lawgiver in Eighteenth-Century Neapolitan Political Thought

Charting Mediterranean Liberalism

Adriana Luna-Fabritius

Since the end of the Neapolitan Republic of Masaniello (1647–1648) late seventeenth-century political thinkers had sought to develop an idea of a monarch capable of procuring happiness for his people; but by the eighteenth century they had extended this to the figure of a strong and prudent legislator. These parameters created a framework for analysing, limiting, and sustaining the authority of the monarch. It was in this context that the ideal represented by Lycurgus of Sparta was revived: proposed in Naples by Paolo Mattia Doria's *La Vita Civile* (1709),[1] passing on to Antonio Genovesi's *Delle lezioni di commercio o sia d'economia civile* (1765)[2] and then to his most prominent disciple Gaetano Filangieri, who consolidated this ideal in his *Scienza della legislazione* (1780).[3] They shaped a line of thought around core ideas. Historical commentary has seen the eighteenth century as a century of great political transformations. These Neapolitan political philosophers presumed that only strong monarchs such as Lycurgus, who guided his people towards happiness, could realise any ambitious programme. Yet they insisted that transformations have to follow a specific arc within a given framework: one provided by a small number of unambiguous laws regarding the happiness of the people.

Although recent research has stressed the relevance of Gaetano Filangieri during the initial constitutional moments in Spain and its former Atlantic dominions after 1812,[4] arguments over the limits of a monarch's action as a

1 Paolo M. Doria, *La Vita Civile … aggiuntovi un trattato della Educazione del principe* (Agusta: Daniello Hopper, 1710) (henforth, *Vita Civile*).

2 Antonio Genovesi, *Delle lezioni di Commercio o sia D'Economia Civile da leggersi nella Catedra Interiana* (Naples: Fratelli Simone, 1765–1767), 2 vols. (henceforth *Lezioni*).

3 Gaetano Filangieri, *La scienza della Legislazione* (Naples: Stamperia di Amato Cons, 1780–1785), 5 vols. (henceforth *Scienza della legislazione*); and *La scienza della legislazione*, ed. Vincenzo Ferrone (Venice: Centro di Studi sull'Illuminismo Europeo G. Stiffoni, 2003), 7 vols.

4 Juan Carlos Chiaramonte, "Gli illuministi napoletani nel Rio de la Plata", *Rivista Storica Italiana*, 86.1 (1964), 114–32; Adriana Luna González, "La recepción de ideas de Gaetano Filangieri en José María Luis Mora: un primer acercamiento al contexto constitucional

 | DOI:10.1163/9789004549159_015

lawgiver as conceived in this period have yet to be explored. The primary objective of this chapter is to chart these boundaries. This study argues that scientific debates on human fallibility informed the core of Neapolitan thought,[5] and will then consider its impact within the Hispanic space as a Mediterranean-Atlantic form of liberalism.[6]

This study reconstructs the way in which Lycurgus came to be the ideal lawgiver for an important branch of political thought initiated in late-seventeenth century Naples in the *Accademia degli Investiganti* (1650–1683), subsequently consolidated in the eighteenth century, especially in the texts of Doria, Genovesi and Filangieri. It assesses the preference for this model of lawgiver as against others available at that time, for example influential models derived from Grotius and John Locke, amongst others.[7] I show the forms in which this model was appropriated by deputies – members of the Tribunal who met in Cadiz and promulgated the 1812 Constitution – via the translations of Neapolitan political economy texts that became available in Spain. It then concludes by suggesting that the constitutional moment in Cadiz was the highest point in this line of thought regarding Lycurgus as a model. Hence, I argue that Neapolitan political thought and the Lycurgus model had a crucial place in the shaping of Spanish liberalism. Finally, given the configuration of the Cadiz deputations and the presence of their representatives in the Courts, this study argues that this constitutional moment was one of the channels through which this line of thinking was disseminated through the Hispanic-Atlantic space.

---

mexicano", *Istor. Revista de Historia Internacional*, 29 (2007), 120–49; *Eadem*, "El modelo constitucional Napolitano en Hispanoamérica", in Adriana Luna-Fabritius, Pablo Mijangos and Rafael Rojas, eds., *De Cádiz al siglo XXI. Doscientos años de tradición constitucional en Hispanoamérica* (Mexico: Taurus, 2012) pp. 123–149; Jesús Astigarraga, "The great success of Filangieri's *Scienza della legislazione* in Spain (1780–1839)", *Nuevo Mundo, Mundos Nuevos*, 6 (2006); *Idem.*, "La ilustración napolitana imputada: críticas y censuras a la *Scienza della legislazione* de Gaetano Filangieri en la España de finales del siglo XVIII", *Nuevo Mundo, Mundos Nuevos*, 7 (2007).

5 Corrado Ocone and Nadia Urbinati, "Introduzione", in their edited volume *La libertà e i suoi limiti. Antologia del pensiero liberale da Filangieri a Bobbio* (Rome: Laterza, 2006); Adriana Luna-Fabritius, "Limits of Power: Gaetano Filangieri's Liberal Legacy", *Pléyade*, 20 (2017) 61–83.

6 Luna-Fabritius, "Limits of Power".

7 Patrick Riley, "Consent and Natural Law in Locke's Philosophy", in Enrico Pattaro, Damiano Canale, Paolo Grossi, *et al.*, eds., *A Treatise of Legal Philosophy and General Jurisprudence: A History of the Philosophy of Law in the Civil Law World, 1600–1900* (Heidelberg: Springer, 2009), vol. 9, 49–50.

I argue here that the power of the executive was reinforced by the Constitution of Cadiz not unintentionally but was the consequence of an understanding of human fallibility. This study provides an account of Filangieri's conception of the limits of monarchical power which can be traced back via Naples to Doria's *Vita civile*, together with some other members of his generation. Additionally, it reconsiders Filangieri's contribution to Spanish constitutional thought during the early nineteenth century.

1 Doria (1167–1746), Lycurgus and the Revision of Republican Tradition

Doria made a significant contribution to early modern Italian constitutional tradition. His political thought has been associated with that of Gian Vicenzo Gravina, and distinguished from that of Vico and Giannone, supporters of an administrative monarchy.[8] Recent scholarship has confirmed that Doria's constitutional contribution rests on his critique of absolutism, of power politics and on his analysis of the British system.[9] Building on this work, I argue that Doria developed his former ideas on the limits of authority and happiness into a constitutional framework, and likewise elaborated Lycurgus as a model legislator in his *Vita civile* (1709),[10] his *Ragionamenti* (1716),[11] and his *Filosofia* (1728).[12] Doria's thinking continued to be developed throughout the eighteenth century in Naples by Antonio Genovesi and Gaetano Filangieri.

In *Vita Civile* Doria argued that to create a virtuous civil life human beings not only had to participate in civil society, but also needed the assistance of virtuous laws provided by a wise legislator, and the division of society into orders.[13] For him the prince epitomises authority, insofar as his action is

8 Marcello Capurso, *Accentramento e costituzionalismo. Il pensiero italiano del primo Settecento di fronte al problema dell'organizzazione dello stato* (Naples: Pironti, 1959).

9 V. Ivo Comparato, "Platonismo e antidispotismo in P. M. Doria", in Lea Campos Boralevi, ed., *Challenging Centralism* (Florence: Firenze University Press, 2011), 99.

10 Doria, *Vita Civile.*

11 Paolo M. Doria, *Ragionamenti indirizzati alla Signora D. Aurelia D'Este Duchessa di Limatola ne' quali si dimostra la donna, in quasi che tutte le virtù più grandi, non essere all'uomo inferiore* (Frankfurt [but Naples], 1716), henceforth *Ragionamenti.*

12 Paolo M. Doria, *Filosofia* (Amsterdam [but Geneva]: Tournes, 1728), 2 vols.

13 On the different types of binding reasons of state, commerce, religion, and the contradictions between them prior the formation of modern states, see Paolo Sarpi, *Opere* (Milan-Naples: R. Ricciardi, 1969), 107; Maurizio Viroli, *From Politics to Reason of State: The Acquisition and Transformation of the Language of Politics, 1250–1600* (Cambridge: Cambridge University Press, 1992).

directed by the principles of honesty. This contrasted with the authority of the tyrant, unconstrained by reason of state, honour, or commerce.[14] For Doria, as in classic political writing, a virtuous prince was the opposite of a tyrant, and Lycurgus – whose actions could guide contemporary rulers – served to emphasise this.

In Doria's analysis, although Lycurgus's passion made him the most excellent defender of his Patria, his acts may be considered heroic only because he led the Spartans to follow and love their laws. Lycurgus's desires were passions that became virtuous acts in their context, for the benefits they brought to the Patria. Doria's conclusion echoes Machiavelli's lessons; however, it could also be read alongside the proto-utilitarian principles that began to circulate in Europe during the closing decades of the seventeenth century, continuing with Bernard Mandeville's works and much later, in 1789, with Jeremy Bentham's *Principles of Morals and Legislation*.[15] Lycurgus's acts became virtuous when he left his Patria to consult the oracle of Delphi, making Spartans loved swear to obey the law during his absence. Lycurgus did not return from Delphi, but the Spartans retained their adherence to his laws following their pledge. For Doria, Lycurgus espoused a love of glory; he did however emphasise that without love of virtue, love of glory leads to weak and vile actions that, instead of being virtuous, are only acts of arrogance, envy, and vainglory. He considered that the passions – far from shaping a virtuous government – lead to the highest forms of malice. He warned his readers that his approach to human passions in politics was not appropriate for weak and vile men, for weak rulers could be seized by their passions, leading the republic towards its most illicit forms.[16]

Doria continued his analysis of Lycurgus in his *Ragionamenti to Aurelia D'Este* (1716), where Lycurgus's performance as lawgiver and his laws were central. He maintained a love of the laws and the equal capacity of men and women. Here Doria argued that women were equal to men in all the highest republican virtues, as founders of empires and fierce warriors, and defenders of their Patria.[17]

---

14 Doria, *Vita Civile*, 93. For a contemporary construction of tyranny, see Gian Vincenzo Gravina, *Opera seu Originum iuris civilis libri tres, De Romano Imperio liber singularis, eiusque Orationes et Opuscula Latin, reecensuit et adnotationibus auxit Tottfridus Mascovius* (Lipsiae: Joh. Frid. Gleditschii B filium, 1737; Venice: Franciscum Pitteri,1739; Venice: Franciscum Pitteri, 1750; Naples: Josephus Raimundus, 1756), Fabrizio Lomonaco, ed. (Naples: Liguri, 2004).

15 On Doria's conception of utility and the possibility of it being a proto-utilitarian theory see Adriana Luna González, "From Self-preservation to Self-liking in Paolo Mattia Doria: Civil Philosophy and Natural Jurisprudence in Early Italian Enlightenment", (Florence: European University Institute), 2009.

16 Doria, *Vita civile*, 80–81.

17 Doria, *Ragionamenti*, 75.

Using historical examples Doria claimed that women had defended a true idea of liberty and given virtuous laws to those building civilised nations. Women were just as capable as were Perseus, Theseus, Lycurgus, Cyrus and Romulus of founding empires that could compete with, and acquire the same glory, as those founded by men.[18] In the *Ragionamenti* Doria revealed his awareness of the implications of Lycurgus's model of lawmaker and criticised the immoderate love of his contemporaries for mysterious or divine arguments, ignoring the potential of classic historical examples. He condemned lawmakers' use of divine arguments to create reverence for the laws in the people's hearts.[19]

Doria's choice of the Lycurgus model seems to be twofold: it allowed him to distance himself from current theological debates on legislators, and to conceive a higher and more abstract conception of freedom and gender equality. Numa Pompilius, Solon, and Lycurgus represented the classic models of a legislator that returned in seventeenth- and eighteenth-century Europe, specifically associated with the revival of Machiavelli's *Discourse*. In circles associated with atheistic discussion on the role of the legislator Machiavelli's approach was an alternative to the influential Grotian and Lockean models that had been associated with theological disputes.[20] In Naples Doria was one of the leading promoters of a new reading of the lessons of Machiavelli. In his argument concerning higher forms of liberty and women's equality Doria also proposed the *Republic* of Plato. His rationale was that Plato had gone even further than Lycurgus, making women free and attributing to them the capacity to be rulers. Like Machiavelli, Doria defined liberty as the absence of any form of domination over a person.[21] However, discussion of the lawgiver along these lines was not unproblematic.[22]

In his *Filosofia* (1728) Doria argued that creating a sacred image of the legislator was a constant in Western history. For instance, Moses always appears as a legislator inspired by God. Alternatively, Grotius presented Moses as lacking direct communication with God, and Doria offered the example of Strabo the

18 *Ibidem*, 75–6.

19 *Ibidem*, 75–80.

20 Justin A. I. Champion, "Legislators, Impostors, and Political Origins: English theories of 'imposture' from Stubbe to Toland", in Silvia Berti, Françoise Charles-Dauber and Richard H. Popkin, eds., *Heterodoxy, Spinozism, and Free Thought in Early Eighteenth-Century Europe. Studies on the Traitè des Trois Imposteurs* (Heidelberg: Springer, 1996), 338.

21 Doria, *Vita Civile*, 81; Doria, *Ragionamenti*, 347; and Luna González, *From Self-preservation to Self-liking.*

22 Adriana Luna-Fabritius, "Per una definizione del potere legislativo: sulla possibilità di un linguaggio liberale condiviso tra Napoli ed Spagna nella età moderna", *Diciottesimo Secolo. Rivista Italiana della Società Italiana di Studio sul Secolo XVIII*, 5, (2020) pp. 69–80.

Greek geographer, philosopher and historian, a simple man following the principles of philosophy and religion of his Patria.[23] Instead of engaging theological discussion, Doria commented on Moses's virtues as a human being, concluding that Pagans have exceeded Christians in the civil and human virtues.[24]

Doria's discussion of the virtues of the Pagans allowed him to develop his analysis of human passions and his proposal for civil life. He revisited the virtues and errors of the republics through historical examples: the moment when Athenians became soft and effeminate from the excessive luxury in which they lost themselves; the moment when Spartans became servants to the love of gold promoted by Lysander; or when Rome became subordinated to the ambition of the heroes that had formerly expanded the empire. Likewise, Doria examined the Assyrian, Persian and other great empires that had been extinguished for lack of virtue, and he noted that Pagans, Lycurgus being the first, knew that Sparta was a republic sustained by the virtues of fortitude and temperance, and so he introduced severe laws to preserve them.[25] Moreover, Lycurgus also allowed women freedom to have civil conversations with men.[26] According to Doria, the valuable lesson from Pagan societies was their use of the laws. Hence the constitutions of nations should address human fallibility. He noted the case of the Romans who reunited around Romulus, a group of fugitives and debtors in need of strict edicts. It was important to make the Romans obey laws embodying virtuous maxims that were especially designed to oppose their vices. For Doria, the use of punishment was the last resort.

In his *Filosofia* Doria insisted on the importance of the secular foundations of the legislator's authority being peacefully transferred from the people to the legislator. The legislator should possess the authority to use force when needed. The legislator should be strong and brave, the wisest and strongest man. Along the lines of Plutarch, Doria argued that, despite legislators knowing the maxims of justice, passions rendered them unable to adhere to them and deliver justice to the people. Given the suspicion of corruption the laws should remain suspended, but the persistent suspension of their execution of law and justice, Doria warned, rendered laws impotent, putting the republic at risk.[27] The efforts of legislators were never sufficient to secure a perfect republic, and so the people must be virtuous, educated in the virtues and principles of justice, temperance, and fortitude. Here, in contrast with his earlier writings, Doria

23 Doria, *Filosofia*, 296.
24 Doria, *Filosofia*, 124.
25 *Ibidem*, 575.
26 *Ibidem*, 228–9, 552.
27 Doria, *Filosofia*, 31–4.

argued that people should be educated in the love of God, otherwise the efforts of the legislator would be in vain. There is a shift in Doria's attitude towards the love of God; in 1728 he considered it more useful for maintaining the virtue of the republic. In Doria's *Filosofia* the legislator could also be the prince. The lawmaker should know how to defend his people and acknowledge his duty to employ force to defend the republic's happiness. The legislator may be able to unite all the virtues necessary for the formation and preservation of the perfect republic.[28]

Doria's complex approach to passions, based on his geopolitical typology[29] and his idea of the love of country, allowed him to relocate the analysis of political acts from a former framework, fashioned by the languages of republicanism and natural law, to a new one more suited to passionate beings. In his search for a solution to the problem of human sociability in his time, that undermined human moral psychology – the capacity of being free, and to establish and maintain political communities by binding them to the laws – Doria proposed a new principle of sociability, based on honour. In 1709 he introduced honour in his *Vita civile,* where he detached the foundations of politics from their religious underpinning and replaced them with maxims for a new science of man and woman (1716). For him, duties of honour generate stronger bonds among human beings in civil society than those of religion. The principles that derived from laws founded upon honour are the duty to defend the Patria, the defence of the prince and of the weak, the fulfilment of promises, constancy in upholding the truth, and verbal commitments. In so doing *Vita civile* created a comprehensive political philosophy which in 1716 Jean Le Clerc reviewed at length in his *Bibliothèque universelle*.[30]

---

28 *Ibidem*, 33.

29 Bodin started this line of political writing upon a comparative and empirical approach to history, jurisprudence and the climatic conditions, braking with medieval tradition. It reached its maximum expression in Montesquieu's *De l'Esprit des Loix* (1748): V. Ivo Comparato, "El pensamiento político de la Contrarreforma y la razón de estado", in Adriana Luna-Fabritius, ed., "Los conceptos y proyectos de Reforma y Contrarreforma en el pensamiento político católico de los siglos XVI y XIX", *Hispania Sacra*, 68 (2016), 13–30; *Idem*, "Readers of Bodin in Italy: From Albergati to Filangieri", in Howell A. Lloyd, ed., *The Reception of Bodin*, (Leiden: Brill, 2013); Johann P. Sommerville, "Absolutism and Royalism", in J. H. Burns, ed., *The Cambridge History of Political Thought,1450–1700* (Cambridge: Cambridge University Press, 1991), 347–73. On Montesquieu's interest on Doria's human characters theory, Robert Shackleton, "Montesquieu et Doria", *Revue de Literature Comparée*, 29 (1955), 173–83.

30 Jean Le Clerc, *Bibliothèque ancienne et moderne … Bibliothèques universelles et choisie* (Amsterdam : Chez David Mortier, 1716), v.

In 1728 Doria took up the analysis of Moses's and Lycurgus's passionate actions, showing the possibility of attributing to them different moral values. He softened the image of Lycurgus, giving a different reading to the well-known severity of his laws, the factions, his political changes, and the vigilant government of the Ephorate that had been considered to be destructive of the development of commerce and arts.[31] Lycurgus gave Doria the key example to demonstrate the possibilities of his approach and political philosophy, most significantly the creation of a framework for evaluating the performance of rulers/lawmakers, and the design of new laws aimed at seeking people's happiness and freedom.

2 Antonio Genovesi (1713–1769): the Foundations of Neapolitan Political Economy

During the 1750s Antonio Genovesi – who held one the first chairs of political economy in Europe (1754)– wrote one of the most influential texts in the Hispanic-Atlantic space, the *Lezioni di economia civile* (1769), which dealt with the characteristics of the legislator and his understanding of human nature. His concern with human fallibility continued a branch of Neapolitan political thought reaching back to the late-seventeenth century in the *Accademia degli Investiganti* (1650–1668).

Like Doria, the approach to human nature taken in *Lezioni* took in differing climatic, cultural, but also physiological contexts. Genovesi's account included the newest discoveries about the human nervous system and its response to basic *stimuli* such the avoidance of pain, annoyance, and irritation. Genovesi argued that it was crucial for the legislator ruling a nation to know what motivates his people during each moment of the civilising process. For instance, barbarian peoples were stimulated by crude energy and sensations, rather than by reason, reflection, and refined passions. Genovesi's political economy drew also on Vico's account of the historical process. His anthropological and historical account included the most recent studies by the Swiss writer Paul Henri Mallet (1730–1807) in his *Introduction à l'Histoire de Dannemarc* (1755–1756).[32] Such studies allowed Genovesi to compare Orpheus, Muhammad, and

31 Romano Molesti, *Economisti e accademici nel Settecento veneto: una visione organica dell'economia* (Milano: Franco Angeli, 2006), 141.

32 Paul Henri Mallet, *Introduction à l'histoire de Dannemarc, où l'on traite de la religion, des loix, des moeurs & des usages des anciens Danois* (Copenhague: De l'imprimerie des Héritiers de Berling, 1755).

Northern civilisations that he considered to be primitive in comparison with Mediterranean cultures.[33]

Along the lines of Doria, Genovesi argued that wise and enlightened nations move by finer springs – the conferral of titles to nobility, distinctions, and honours – because they exist in a different moment of the civilising process. For instance, the French nation was more responsive to honour and military glory, and therefore it supported Louis XIV's undertakings. Similarly, Genovesi gave examples from the Spanish, British, and German nations, demonstrating that human beings are motivated by personal interests, reasoning, and physical energy.[34] According to Genovesi, pain included energetic enthusiasm, sympathy, and antipathy; there were different ways of relieving this kind of pain, and although they run counter to human happiness, those should address the principles of justice and honesty. By taming energetic enthusiasm people increase their virtuous actions, improving arts and commodities and rendering nations peaceful and prosperous. Genovesi stated that the legislator should also know how to coerce by using punishments to create dishonour and infamy, or any other forms of irrational and tiresome sensations.

The legislator should be aware of the roots of all the forms of vices caused by human unsociability,[35] since they depopulate, disunite, and render unhappy the political body. Unsociability could lead people to decide not to join a political community. In these passages Genovesi's account of sociability acquired a new dimension, including the geo-climatic and economic conditions needed for a social group to survive in a particular time and place.

As with Doria and Vico, Genovesi's legislator was to provide the conditions necessary to improve the human spirit and increase the opulence of the nation. There are three arts that legislators should promote: i) the primitive and necessary arts that produce human subsistence (hunting, fishing, metalworking, pasture and agriculture); ii) the arts that improve the materials originating in the soil, in the seas, plus the arts to improve wool and textiles; and iii) the arts of voluptuousness and luxury intended to promote a pleasant life (sculpture, painting).[36] For Genovesi the study of abstract and unusual ideas was not frivolous, but a way of improving people's lives.[37] As for which art should be the priority of legislators, Genovesi argued that the individual should have liberty to choose. Hence there were no arts contrary to the interest of the state or to

33 Genovesi, *Lezioni*, 50–52.
34 *Ibidem*, 51.
35 *Ibidem*, 56, 70.
36 *Ibidem*, 77–78.
37 *Ibidem*, 105.

custom. However, some made a greater contribution to the livelihood of the republic since they produced immediate benefits. A more pressing matter for the legislator was to understand which science could bring more utility to the Patria, the political body and the public happiness.[38]

For Genovesi the first law of politics was to address the problems of human sociability, maintaining the unity of the political body and improving public welfare. Laws with these foundations could gather peoples under the rule of law. Laws founded by the principles of civil economy might not be 'moral', but they were aimed at procuring wellbeing and the reduction of harm to the public.[39]

The critical matter for Genovesi was to master nature, including in this human fallibility. Legislators should favour and trust physical rather than metaphysical methods, understanding that human beings are born and grow in the physical world, leading their education towards a knowledge of nature.[40] The prime objective of legislators and magistrates should be the encouragement of industry, and secondly adoption of the two means for perfecting the arts and the sciences: honour and rewards.

As Doria, Genovesi argued that passions are the principal engine of the soul in improving the happiness of the people and insisted there would be no progress in the arts and sciences without promise of future reward. Here Genovesi recalled Cicero's statement that *honos alit artes*, a maxim valid for the entirety of human history;[41] that the history of humankind had shown that nations could not develop without the impulse of creativity and the human spirit.[42] Those who make the lives of others easier should be rewarded for promoting public utility and happiness, especially those that invent new manufactures, new instruments, machines, perfect the old ones, travel to cultured nations to learn of the perfection of their arts so as to introduce them in their own Patria. The new honours and prizes should be distinguished from the existing ones to arouse the spirit and creativity of the nation. Human beings only became aware of their creative power when they find themselves in situations where they can test their 'resourcefulness'.

For Genovesi civil liberty was not enough for the development of civil life. Honour and prizes would contribute to preserving the virtue of citizens, which

38 *Ibidem*, 172–3.

39 *Ibidem*, 130.

40 *Ibidem*, 206.

41 Marcus Tullius Cicero, *Tusculan Disputations*, John Edward King, transl., (London: William Heinemann, 1927), 1, 2, 4.

42 Genovesi, *Lezioni*, 209–10.

was the purpose of civil empires.[43] The promotion of the principles of honour and the conferral of prizes should not be exclusive to the republics, but expand to all kinds of governments, especially monarchies. Reward may be the incentive to virtue, knowledge, and industry in all kinds of states.[44]

In his *Lezioni* Genovesi explained that the evolution of commerce made civil life more complex, rendering sociability of peoples even more difficult. Complex situations had to be regulated. He developed a more detailed discussion of the particular laws that legislators should enact to encourage the development of industry. Economic laws should be the most important of all, for they supported all the others.[45] Commerce, agriculture and industry and their development were crucial for the nation. Genovesi concluded that the wise legislator should not govern the state with reference to the poorly educated, but by considering the general wellbeing of the nation.[46]

Lycurgus was an outstanding model lawmaker for Genovesi; his laws were supported by physical and moral education, with physical education making up two-thirds. This emphasis on physicality was perhaps the reason why the Spartans were the best regulated amongst all the Ancients. Genovesi also cited the example of Mosaic law, centred upon wise and gentile education. This had led in many European countries to the foundation of colleges of arts, children being given a mechanical training and with that, the possibility of training their spirit and manners.[47] This is what Vico had defined as *civiltà*. Genovesi ended his commentary by stressing that despite the laws of the nations being formed by two principal parts, economics and dicastics, very few had been devoted to the first. There might be many learned specialists in our constitutions and pragmatics, but only very few on the economy of the state: study of the propagation of the human species, education, industry, commerce, and the administration of the land.[48]

3 *Gaetano Filangieri (1753–1788) and the* Scienza Della Legislazione

In Gaetano Filangieri's *Scienza della legislazione* the diverse character of nations informs the diversity of political and moral bodies. Along Doria and

43 *Ibidem*, 210.
44 *Ibidem*.
45 *Ibidem*, 207ff.
46 *Ibidem*, 268–70.
47 *Ibidem*, 347–8.
48 *Ibidem*.

Genovesi, he argued that each form of government had its own motivating factor, yet as with Vico, some functioned at one time but not at others. The customs of one century were not those of another before or after. The interests of nations quickly shift for each generation, the elements useful in one period soon ceasing to be so. Filangieri reflected on whether the laws should follow the resulting inconsistency and concluded that legislators should consider the best way to remedy such inconsistencies. Holistic understanding of the system was, indeed, the ultimate justification for legislation, since a republic dedicated to lasting happiness and strength was an object of universal admiration.[49] Legislators had to adapt to different times, changing their opinions according to the period. One legislator might protect commerce, others promote arts, agriculture, or industry. Genovesi argued that legislators should ensure that every citizen had an occupation and seek to preserve their means of subsistence, citizens being free to choose their occupation. Idleness should be punished as a crime, women could be economically active, and the legislator should try to correct the corruption of customs in relation to wealth and luxury. Then the republic should be rich, happy and powerful, and even if it did not preserve its laws for all time, it would have won glory in surviving in freedom.

In *Scienza della legislazione* Filangieri compared Lycurgus's Sparta with Solon's Athens. He emphasised that the outcomes of legislation in each case were similar, despite their differences and the diversity of their causes. Both were opportune in that their republics maintained the relationship between laws and the character of each nation, Filangieri conceptualising this as *bontà relative* (relative goodness).[50]

Likewise Doria, Filangieri noted that the wisest legislator had always resorted to the use of reflective and mysterious elements to achieve adherence to the laws. Filangieri noted the example of Homer's story of Minos, who every eighth year visited Jupiter so that Cretans could believe his laws had divine inspiration. Homer referred to Jupiter as the *Novennalis* Legislator *Supremi Numinis*. Filangieri also took account of the Greek lawgivers Zamolxis from Thrace[51] and Zaleucus from Locri,[52] who looked for support for their laws in the heavens. Filangieri suggested that Lycurgus likewise understood the need

49 Filangieri, *Scienza della legislazione*, 89. On Benjamin Franklin's interest in Filangieri's *Scienza della legislazione*, see Luna-Fabritius, "Limits of Power", 67.

50 Filangieri, *Scienza della Legislazione*, 90.

51 Filangieri is referring to Herodotus's account of Zalmoxis (in his *Histories*, 2, 13, ch. 24) in *Scienza della legislazione*, 101.

52 Claudio Eliano, *Varia Historia*, 2, 37 and book 13, 24.

to make use of the ignorance and superstition of the plebs to gain their favour, attributing his laws to Apollo.[53] He finally noted the Roman cases of the nymph Egeria, and the deities who taught Romulus and Numa Pompilius to be wise legislators.[54]

Filangieri distinguished between young and mature nations and suggested that while Romulus and Numa knew how to gain favour in a young nation, their successors manipulated a mature nation. As with Gravina, Filangieri argued that in time Romans had established the rule that consuls, tribunes of the people and superior magistrates did not propose a new law without the advice of the wisest jurisconsult of their time.[55]

Filangieri thought that to win the favour of his people a legislator had to encourage his people to demonstrate their virtue through useful actions to the benefit of the Patria. Those capable of enhancing the virtue of the people were heroes. If William Penn, for instance, had lived in the days of Solon and Lycurgus he could have outshone their glory. Penn had transformed Pennsylvania into a Patria of heroes, an asylum of freedom and admired throughout the universe. He understood that the primary object of legislation was the union of private and public interests, and that the only means to achieve this in free governments was through popular election and the distribution of public employments, of magistrates and ministers. For Filangieri these were the best means of transforming a love of power into an endless source of merit and virtue; more so than through a Senate, for while an entire nation is rarely wrong or corrupted, a Senate is normally exposed to both dangers. Filangieri thought that Penn understood how to solve the problems of human fallibility. The solution was to be found in the laws prescribed in a democracy.[56]

Filangieri argued that in antiquity legislators such as Lycurgus prevented wealth and luxury in Sparta since they saw in opulence the source of vice, the instrument of corruption and slavery. Hence, they promoted frugality through poverty, courage, strength, patience, and severity of manners. However, his era was in the past, and today's politicians were engaged in the pursuit of wealth, promoting agriculture and the progress of arts and commerce. Wealth was the new happiness. Consequently, rulers should know that to maintain peace in

53 Plutarch, "The Life of Lycurgus", in *Plutarch's Lives*; and Livy, *The History of Rome by T. Livius*, G. Baker transl. and ed. [1823], Liberty Fund, 2018, 6 vols.

54 Numa was considered to be the author of several 'sacred books' of divine teaching, mostly from Egeria and the Muses: Plutarch, "The Life of Numa" in *Plutarch's Lives*.

55 Gian Vincenzo Gravina, *De Origene Juris Civilis*, lib, 1, XXIX, in Filangieri, *Scienza della Legislazione*, 102.

56 Filangieri, *Scienza della legislazione*, 167ff.

their dominions they had to avoid indigence since it would undermine their rule, exposing their territories to the disparagement and pillage of neighbouring powers. Opulence was the element that would make their government feared and respected, and their alliance courted.

The fact that for Filangieri the spirit of wealth had prevailed implied that love of opulence and the superiority of the nation no longer rested on physical strength, courage or military heroism, but on the wealth of its people. The richest are the happiest, so the legislator should give his whole attention to increasing it, employing agriculture, arts, commerce, and the acquisition and preservation of wealth. Legislators should derive the principles of legislation from this idea of the dominium of the spirit of wealth and the character of their nations.

To the belief of Doria and Genovesi that the geopolitical character of nations renders them naturally diverse in their genius and disposition Filangieri added the common features of European nations – the feudal system, the early romantic system of chivalry and gallantry, the code of honour, and the harmony of a moral system derived from a common religion. Considering the utility of maintaining this religion he argued that despite the revisions that it had suffered in some nations, certain moral precepts had been a constant. The legislator should therefore take all these elements into account, given their influence on the spirit of laws.

4 Cadiz's Constitution: the Elements of a New Narrative

Although the constitutional moment in Cadiz began with the proclamation of God as the supreme legislator of society, deputies had discussed the role of the legislator using Lycurgus as their model. Their proceedings were conducted according to the influential line of Neapolitan political philosophy initiated by the *Investiganti* and which had reached its highest point with Filangieri's *Scienza della legislazione*. The Cadiz constitutional moment had wider repercussions: as consequence of the crisis of the Spanish monarchy caused by Napoleon's invasion of the Iberian Peninsula in 1808, this line of thought quickly spread throughout the Hispanic space.[57] The deputies drafting the constitution for the Spanish monarchy represented all the Atlantic kingdoms of the monarchy, albeit disproportionally.[58] There were of course

57 Bartolomé Clavero, *Evolución histórica del constitucionalismo en España* (Madrid: Tecnos, 1984); José María Portillo, *Crisis atlántica* (Madrid: Marcial Pons, 2006).

58 Pilar Chavarri Sidera, *Las elecciones de diputados a las Cortes Generales y Extraordinarias (1810–1813)* (Madrid: Centro de Estudios Constitucionales, 1988); J.M. García León, *Los*

differences among the deputies, but some common ground emerged from their discussions.[59] Here I emphasise they were aware they were introducing new elements to the Spanish constitutional tradition, principally new forms of representation, and a new science of legislation based on Neapolitan ideas of human fallibility.

Despite the cultural and geographical differences among the Cadiz deputies, textual analysis of the debates reveals the existence of a shared normative language within the Spanish monarchy. Most evident is the case of the Neapolitans examined above, the detachment from the Aristotelian *zoon politikon* leading to a new conception of human sociability that informed two leading questions of human fallibility.[60] First, the need to create limits of action for the ruler that was discussed along the lines of happiness and tyranny; and second, the need to counterbalance the power of the ruler. Cadiz's deputies agreed on the need for a new science of legislation rather than a codification of old laws; and that this should be developed in a language understandable to everyone and dealing with the public happiness of the nation. Although these discussions coincided with the emergent language of political oeconomy in Europe, the privileged circulation of Neapolitan texts in original and in several translations suggests that we should pay especial attention to Neapolitan political thought in this constitutional moment. Neapolitan texts were available in the Iberian Peninsula before similar texts from elsewhere.[61]

While the kingdom of Naples had officially been separated from the Spanish monarchy since 1714, it had retained a privileged channel of communication with the Iberian Peninsula since 1734, when it had been declared an independent kingdom by Charles of Bourbon. After he was crowned Charles III of Spain

---

diputados doceañistas … Cortes Generales y Extraordinarias (1810–1813), (Cádiz: Quorum, 2006); Joaquín Varela Suanzes, "Nación, representación y articulación territorial del Estado en las Cortes de Cádiz", *Criterio Jurídico*, 11.1 (2011), 11–49; Marie Laure Rieu-Millán, *Los diputados americanos en las Cortes de Cádiz* (Madrid: CSIC, 1990), 31–57.

59 José Antonio Maravall, "Las tendencias de reforma política en el siglo XVIII español", *Revista de Occidente*, 52 (1967), 70–1; Antonio Elorza, "Estudio preliminar", in *Cartas político-económicas al Conde Lerena* (Madrid: Ciencia Nueva, 1968), 72–3; Joaquín Varela Suanzes, "El debate sobre el sistema británico de gobierno en España durante el primer tercio del Siglo XIX" (Alicante: Biblioteca Virtual Miguel de Cervantes, 2005); Marta Lorente and Carlos Garriga, *Cádiz, 1812. La Constitución jurisdiccional* (Madrid: CEPC, 2007); Luna-Fabritius, *et al.*, *De Cádiz al siglo XXI*.

60 Adriana Luna González, "Naturaleza humana y 'amor propio'. Descifrando el lenguaje de la jurisprudencia natural en Cádiz", *Revista Internacional de Filosofía Política*, 32 (2008), 24–36.

61 Jesús Astigarraga and Javier Usoz, "The Enlightenment in Translation: Antonio Genovesi's Political Economy in Spain, 1778–1800", *Mediterranean Historical Review*, 28.1 (2013) 24–45.

in 1759 this connection was reinforced. The new monarch travelled from Naples to Madrid accompanied by some of his former ministers with the intention to introduce improvements to the Spanish monarchy. At the same time new libraries were established, chairs were founded in Spanish Academies and universities canvassed new political and economic plans for the improvement of the monarchy. Here the ideas of Neapolitan political economists like Antonio Genovesi and Gaetano Filangieri had a leading role.[62]

Naples and Cadiz shared an understanding that the passions and interests of human beings should be the starting point of all legislative enterprise. Legislators presumed that, due to natural fallibility, men and women lacked *philia* towards their fellows, compromising the binding nature of the laws. This is what in the language of natural law was known as the problem of human sociability; Neapolitans discussed this extensively during the eighteenth century, and in the emergent liberal tradition this would become known as human fallibility.[63]

Following the example of Lycurgus some Cadiz deputies turned to this solution. Like Neapolitans, they maintained that to ensure obedience to the laws Lycurgus had resorted to the drastic solution of leaving his country and renouncing a Patria to which he never returned, so that he might guarantee the continuity of his institutions. For those in Cadiz this solution was considered radical; one deputy did cite Lycurgus, Romulus and even Muhammad as persons claiming contact with spiritual deities who prescribed laws securing obedience.[64] But there was otherwise in Cadiz consensus that the emerging science of legislation could supplant the practices suggested by these classic examples.[65]

Like the Neapolitans, some deputies knew that for the lawmaker to determine the laws most suited to the people they needed the empathy to analyse

62 Richard Herr, *The Eighteenth-Century Revolution in Spain* (Princeton: Princeton University Press, 2015 [1958]); José Luis Peset and Mariano Peset, *Carlos IV y la Universidad de Salamanca* (Madrid: CSIC, 1983) and Adriana Luna-Fabritius, "Cameralism in Spain *Polizeywissenschaft* and the Bourbon Reforms", in Ere Nokkala and Nicholas B. Miller, eds., *Cameralism and the Enlightenment: Happiness, Governance and Reform in Transnational Perspective* (New York-London: Routledge, 2020).

63 Adriana Luna-Fabritius, "Visions of Sociability in Early-Modern Neapolitan Political Thought", in Jonas Gerlings, Ere Nokkala and Martin van Gelderen, eds., *Processes of Enlightenment. Essays in Honour of H.E. Bödeker* (Liverpool: Oxford Studies in the Enlightenment, forthcoming).

64 José Miguel Guridi y Alcocer, *Diario de las discusiones y actas de las Cortes* (Cádiz: Imprenta Real, 1812), 11: 330–1 (henceforth, *Diario*).

65 Conde de Toreno, *Diario,* 11: 309.

and discover the springs motivating human actions. Laws should be capable of taming human desires by identifying the *stimuli* moving action. Some deputies defended the idea that men sought society to protect their lives, liberty, and property. Human beings knowing themselves needed the free exercise of their faculties and the freedom to dispose over their property.[66]

Hence the study of human nature should be the starting point and the criterion for laws and legislation. Their considerations of human passions and interests made them aware that laws, rulers, and legislators were fallible. Consequently, laws once appropriate in the past had to be revised for the present. Additionally, some of the deputies believed that the language of ancient laws was outdated and incomprehensible to most Spaniards. They urged the creation of new laws, especially criminal laws.[67]

It was the duty of legislators clarify and explain the laws.[68] But given the fallibility of lawmakers, when a law was issued, they should not pretend that it was perfect. Legislators should consult and consider as many cases and circumstances as possible. Likely, they should remember that a law can only be perfect at the moment of its promulgation, as it is the expression of the cases and circumstances consulted by its authors.[69] Given the emphasis on rulers' and legislators' fallibility, laws should be subject to constant correction and adjustment,[70] taking account of prevailing circumstances. Their validity and legitimacy depended on the fact that they were intended to protect people's lives, honour and property.[71] Some deputies believed that the task of lawmakers did not end with the elaboration of the laws, but that they should also secure their observance, authority and binding force,[72] all of which could be ensured if they address people's happiness.[73]

To promote public happiness legislators should achieve a positive balance,[74] ensuring the prosperity of all nations of the Hispanic monarchy, based on an understanding of the spirit, character and geopolitical conditions of all provinces.[75] This concern was shared by others who believed that lawmakers

66 Oliveros, *Diario,* 1811, 5: 205.

67 Oliveros, *Diario,* 1811: 5: 205; Alejandro Agüero and Marta Lorente, "Penal Enlightenment in Spain: from Beccaria's reception to the first Criminal Code", in Jesús Astigarraga, ed., *The Spanish Enlightenment revisited* (Oxford: Voltaire Foundation, 2015), 235–64.

68 Anér, *Diario,* 1811: 7, 55; and Villagómez, *ibidem*, 7: 62.

69 Anér, *Diario,* 1811: 7, 55.

70 Oliveros, *Diario,* 1811, 7: 205.

71 Bárcena, *Diario,* 1811, 5: 261, and Gordillo, *ibidem*, 5: 455–7.

72 Bárcena, *Diario,* 1811, 5: 261.

73 *Ibidem*, and García Herreros, *Diario,* 1811, 6: 553ff.

74 Larrazábal, from Guatemala, *Diario*, 1812, 11: 465.

75 Conde de Toreno, *Diario,* 1812, 11: 309.

should have expert knowledge of all the lands of the monarchy, their climate, extent, fertility, characteristics and conditions of their populations, their mental disposition, habits, traditions and customs. Cadiz deputies did not however recognise, as did Genovesi or Filangieri, that the pursuit of wealth was central. They defined public happiness as the need to avoid pauperism and promote the industry and agriculture of the provinces.[76]

It was the duty of lawmakers to oversee every link in the chain, ensuring the laws served people's circumstances, and if they did not, then correct them. Some deputies even maintained that the legislator could consult his people to make sure the laws did further the general wellbeing of the people, for if not the legislator could be replaced.[77]

This all led to the creation of a system of legislative check and balances; and if the expected results were not achieved, the people could treat the pact with the ruler and the lawmaker as broken.[78] This idea of a guarantee, of a social pact between the monarch and the people, was supported by reference to natural law but it was founded indeed on happiness. Although imprecise, here Grotius was cited to reinforce the social pact argument.[79] Some of the deputies radicalised the argument, arguing that if the monarch did not properly consider public happiness his power would be considered contrary to the fundamental laws of the kingdom and, consequently, his right to rule nullified.[80]

As with Doria and Filangieri, the legitimacy and authority of the laws is endorsed when the people can elect their magistrates. Regular elections would correct and prevent possible cases of corruption caused by the appointment of friends and relations. This was intended to protect the life, honour, and property of the people[81] and correct excessive privilege which was a relic of the arbitrary despotism of the past. Some deputies went so far as to argue that a monopoly of privileges should be treated as yet one more element breaching the pact between monarch and people.[82]

This prompted extensive discussion of the absolutist power of the Spanish monarchy. One deputy argued that the kings of Spain had never possessed such absolute dominium, for they had always been subject to the framework provided by law. He argued that they had always been bound, like any other

76 García Herreros, 1811, 6: 553ff.
77 Oliveros, *Diario*, 1811, 5: 265; and Gutiérrez Huerta, *ibidem*, 5: 408.
78 Llanera, *Diario*, 1811, 5: 359.
79 Gordillo, *Diario*, 1811, 5: 455–457.
80 García Herreros, *Diario*, 1811, 6: 553ff.
81 Gordillo, *Diario*, 1811, 5: 455–457.
82 Gordillo, *ibidem*.

individual in society, by the laws. Evidence of this was that they could not alter the laws relating the common good without usurping a right they did not possess. Spanish monarchs had never possessed more authority than that prescribed in law, the administration of justice and the meticulous observance of good order. The power of Spanish monarchs had been limited in this way to avoid any degeneration into despotism, and with the intention of preserving the civil liberty of the people. This line of argument cited the jurisprudence of the Visigoth laws, the *Fuero Juzgo,*[83] and the Fourth Council of Toledo,[84] which had prescribed the duties and the limits of princes.[85]

However, despite all of this, the public happiness of the people became the standard prescribing and delimiting the duties of monarchs, the parameters of their practices and the rights of individuals. These rights included the prosperity of the nation and emphasised the intimate union between people and government. As in seventeenth-century Naples, the laws became the site for the resolution of conflict.

5 Conclusion

That the classical example of Lycurgus was so prominent in the Cadiz constitutional moment is significant. It is no small thing that after expressly declaring the constitution to be subject to the Catholic confession, the Cadiz deputies in fact followed a secular path in their discussions that was shielded by their former open declaration of a bond to Catholicism.

More importantly, the example of Lycurgus, in conformity with Neapolitan ideas, made it possible for the Cadiz deputies to discuss the problem of human sociability together with the fallibility of monarchs, lawmakers, magistrates, and the binding force of the laws. Instead of appealing to God's grace the deputies assembled in Cadiz adopted the arguments of Neapolitan political philosophers, opting for the creation of a new science of legislation shaped by human fallibility.

The form taken by constitutional discussion at Cadiz confirms the powerful part of Neapolitan political thought there. This can be seen in the above reconstruction of Lycurgus as a lawmaker, developed out of the emergent science of legislation as conceptualised by the generation of Doria, Vico, and Gravina,

83 The Spanish codex enacted in Castile in 1241 by Fernando III has been considered as a translation of the *Liber ludiciorum* formulated by the Visigoths in 654.

84 García Herreros, *Diario*, 1811, 6: 553ff.

85 García Herreros,1811, 6: 557–559.

continued by Genovesi and then culminating in Filangieri. Here the limits of power were discussed in the context of conceptions of public happiness and tyranny, exactly as had been done in Naples since the late seventeenth century. Insistence on the obsolescence of the laws and the need to design new guidelines for the work of legislation pervaded the Cadiz constitutional moment: the study of geopolitical conditions, the character of the people in guaranteeing sociability and public happiness. These principles set the limits of action by monarchs and lawmakers, but they also underwrote the legitimacy of the laws and their binding force, in addition to guaranteeing the social pact between monarch and people. This was the solution minted in Naples, and which shaped discussion in Cadiz.

Bibliography

Main Sources

Diario de las discusiones y actas de las Cortes (Cadiz: Imprenta Real, 1811–1812) 21 vols.

Doria, Paolo M., *La Vita civile … aggiuntovi un trattato della Educazione del principe* (Agusta: Daniello Hopper, 1710).

Filangieri, Gaetano, *La scienza della legislazione* (Naples: Stamperia di Amato Cons, 1780–1785), 5 vols.; *La scienza della legislazione*, ed. Vincenzo Ferrone (Venice, 2003), 7 vols.

Gravina, Vincenzo, *Opera seu Originum iuris civilis libri tres, De Romano Imperio liber singularis, eiusque Orationes et Opuscula Latin, reecensuit et adnotationibus auxit Tottfridus Mascovius* (Lipsiae: Joh. Frid. Gleditschii B filium, 1737; Venice: Franciscum Pitteri,1739; Venice: Franciscum Pitteri, 1750; Naples: Josephus Raimundus, 1756), Fabrizio Lomonaco, ed. (Naples: Liguri, 2004).

Genovesi, Antonio, *Delle lezioni di Commercio o sia D'Economia Civile da leggersi nella Catedra Interiana* (Naples: Fratelli Simone,1765–1767), 2 vols.

Main Bibliographical References

Comparato, V. Ivo, "Platonismo e antidispotismo in P. M. Doria", in Lea Campos Boralevi, ed., *Challenging Centralism* (Florence: Firenze University Press, 2011), 99.

Comparato, V. Ivo, "El pensamiento político de la Contrarreforma y la razón de estado", in Adriana Luna-Fabritius, ed., "Los conceptos y proyectos de Reforma y Contrarreforma en el pensamiento político católico de los siglos XVI y XIX", *Hispania Sacra*, 68 (2016): 13–30.

Comparato, V. Ivo, "Readers of Bodin in Italy: From Albergati to Filangieri", in Howell A. Lloyd, ed., *The Reception of Bodin*, (Leiden: Brill, 2013).

Luna-Fabritius, Adriana, Pablo Mijangos and Rafael Rojas, eds., *De Cádiz al siglo XXI. Doscientos años de tradición constitucional en Hispanoamérica* (Mexico: Taurus, 2012).

Ocone, Corrado; and Nadia Urbinati, "Introduzione", in their edited volume *La libertà e i suoi limiti. Antologia del pensiero liberale da Filangieri a Bobbio* (Rome: Laterza, 2006).

CHAPTER 14

From Masterpiece of Modern Legislation to an Aristocratic Oligarchy

Contemporary European Appraisals of the Swedish Constitution of the Age of Liberty (1719–1772)

Ere Nokkala

1 Introduction*

It is often pointed out in the scholarly literature that the Swedish Constitution of 1719/1720 was praised by several influential contemporary thinkers such as Gabriel Bonnot de Mably (1709–1785), Rousseau (1712–1778), and Voltaire (1684–1778).[1] However, their accounts of Sweden have never been systematically analysed. Furthermore, it has gone practically unnoticed that the Swedish Constitution received broad contemporary criticism from significant thinkers like Johann Heinrich Gottlob von Justi (1717–1771) and Jean-Louis De Lolme (1741–1806). The aim of my chapter is to provide a balanced analysis of contemporary European appraisals of the Swedish Constitution. I argue that, depending on the context in which the Swedish Constitution was commented on, it was either criticized as a constitution that supported aristocratic oligarchy or praised as a response to the crisis of the republics. Special attention will be paid to Mably and De Lolme, who both enjoyed considerable influence in the eighteenth century. Unlike many of the other commentators on the Swedish Constitution, Mably and Delolme were quite systematic in their admiration and critique of Sweden. In other words, commenting on the Swedish Constitution of the Age of Liberty was not merely tendentious in their literary production. Both Delolme and Mably have been rediscovered as

---

* I want to thank Jonas Nordin and Mark J. Hill for their comments and suggestions to improve this chapter.

1 For two influential examples see Michael Roberts, *The Age of Liberty: Sweden 1719–1772* (Cambridge: Cambridge University Press, 1986), 59; Franco Venturi, *The End of the Old Regime in Europe, 1768–1776: The First Crisis* (Princeton: Princeton University Press, 1989), 279–339. See also Eric Cyril Bellquist, "Foreign Governments and Politics: The Five Hundredth Anniversary of the Swedish Riksdag", *American Political Science Review*, 29 (1935), 857–65.

 | DOI:10.1163/9789004549159_016

political thinkers and philosophers since the 1990s.[2] However, very little has been written about their commentaries on the Swedish Constitution, which, although not a dominant theme in their work, certainly had a central place in the conceptual underpinnings of their thought.

"Age of Liberty" (1719–1772) may sound like a later historical label for a period in history. The very phrase Age of Liberty (*frihetstiden*) appears to have been used for the first time in the 1750s, but the concept was much older and had already been invoked by the 1720s in such forms as "this time of freedom" (*denna tid av frihet*) or our "recovered liberty" (*vår återvunna frihet*). The same designation was used by both parties: the Hats and the Caps. Hats in particular used it to praise their own rule.[3]

The Hats' interpretation of the Constitution and of their own rule emphasized that the Swedish Constitution prevented the misuse of royal power. The Constitution of 1719/1720 had been legislated to put an end to royal absolutism, as practised by the late Charles XII. During the Age of Liberty, power in the Diet was held by four Estates: the nobility, clergy, burghers and peasants. The Diet was, in practical terms, independent of the king. The 16-strong Council of the Realm acted as the government of the country. The king chaired the Council but he was not, strictly speaking, a member. The composition was 16 members from the Estate of nobility plus the king with two votes, which gave a total of 18 votes.[4]

The Age of Liberty has been subject to numerous historical interpretations.[5] In Sweden, most recent interpretations dealing with the Age of Liberty tend to emphasize how progressive the political culture of the Age of Liberty was. The role of the Estates has been seen as a forerunner to "popular sovereignty" and "representative democracy".[6] Anglophone scholars such as Michael Roberts

---

2 On Mably, see Peter Friedemann, *Die politische Philosophie des Gabriel Bonnot de Mably (1709–1785): Eine Studie zur Geschichte des republikanischen und des sozialen Freiheitsbegriffs* (Münster: LIT Verlag, 2014). On Delolme, see Iain McDaniel, "Jean Louis Delolme and the Political Science of the English Empire", *Historical Journal*, 55 (2012), 21–44, 23.

3 On the concept of liberty in Swedish political culture, see Jonas Nordin, "Von 'fremder Unterdrückung' zur 'Freiheitszeit'. Die Vorstellung von Freiheit im frühneuzeitlichen Schweden", in Georg Schmidt, Martin van Gelderen and Christopher Snigula, eds., *Kollektive Freiheitsvorstellungen im frühneuzeitlichen Europa (1400–1850)* (Frankfurt am Main: Peter Lang, 2006).

4 Roberts, *The Age of Liberty*; Michael F. Metcalf, ed., *The Riksdag: A History of the Swedish Parliament* (Stockholm: Sveriges Riksdag & Riksbankens Jubileumsfond, 1987).

5 Pasi Ihalainen, Michael Bregnsbo, Karin Sennefelt and Patrik Winton, eds., *Scandinavia in the Age of Revolution: Nordic Political Cultures, 1740–1820* (Farnham: Ashgate, 2009).

6 For examples of these assessments, see Pasi Ihalainen, "The 18th-Century Traditions of Representation in a New Age of Revolution", *Scandinavian Journal of History*, 40 (2015), 70–96, at 71.

and Michael Metcalf have echoed these positive interpretations.[7] In Sweden, a broader segment of the population than in Britain were able to participate in political decision-making. One of the high points of the Age of Liberty was the legislation of the Freedom of Press Act of 1766, which was the first of its kind in the world.[8] This Act made access to public documents a constitutional right. There is a long tradition of these positive interpretations of the Age of Liberty in Swedish historical writing. The most prolific historian in this sense was Fredrik Lagerroth, whose weighty and influential book *Frihetstidens författning* (The Constitution of the Age of Liberty, 1915) depicted the Age of Liberty as a forerunner – defined by parliamentary democracy – to the reform of the Swedish Constitution in the 1910s.[9] Because Lagerroth's thesis was written in the pre-parliamentarian age, the Age of Liberty was still a relevant point of comparison. To Lagerroth, it was one empirically tested way of arranging popular politics.[10] In Finland, interpretations of the Age of Liberty have been quite different. First, there has been reluctance among Finnish historians to use the term "Age of Liberty" because it connotes an inherently positive evaluation of the period. Rather, Petri Karonen, for example, has suggested that "The Age of the Estates" or the "Autocracy of the Estates" would be a more apt title for the rule of the Estates during the years 1719 to 1772.[11] The Finnish tradition of negatively evaluating the period must be seen in historical context as well. When Sweden lost Finland to Russia, the law of 1772 with its 1789 amendments – the very same constitution that ended the Age of Liberty in Sweden – came to play an important role in the Grand Duchy of Finland (1809–1917). It was the "constitution" that "guaranteed" the autonomy of Finland and the continuation of the administration of the country according to the Swedish tradition. As a corollary, instead of defending the Constitution of 1719/1720, Finnish historians

7 Roberts, *The Age of Liberty*; Ihalainen, "The 18th-Century Traditions", 88.

8 Kristina Örtenhed and Bertil Wennberg, eds., *Press Freedom 250 Years: Freedom of the Press and Public Access to Official Documents in Sweden and Finland – a Living Heritage from 1766*. See in particular the chapter by Marie-Christine Skuncke called "Press Freedom in the Riksdag 1760–62 and 1765–1766", 109–44. See also *Eadem*, "Freedom of the Press and Social Equality in Sweden, 1766–72", in Ihalainen, Bregnsbo, Sennefelt and Winton, eds., *Scandinavia in the Age of Revolution*, 133–44.

9 Fredrik Lagerroth, *Frihetstidens författning: En studie i den svenska konstitutionalismens historia* (Stockholm: Bonnier, 1915), 733–35; Fredrik Lagerroth, "En frihetstida lärobok i gällande svensk statsrätt", *Statsvetenskaplig Tidskrift*, 40 (1937), 185–211; Ihalainen, "The 18th-century traditions", 86.

10 Jonas Nordin, *Frihetstidens monarki: Konungamakt och offentlighet i 1700-talets Sverige* (Stockholm: Atlantis, 2009), 17.

11 Petri Karonen, *Pohjoinen suurvalta: Ruotsi ja Suomi 1521–1809*, 3rd ed. (Helsinki: WSOY, 2008), 405–8.

and politicians from the nineteenth century onwards were more inclined to defend the Constitution of 1772 and to depict the preceding era as a period of corruption characterized by oligarchic and arbitrary rule by the nobility. The Constitution of 1772 later came to serve as an intellectual resource for the strong presidential executive that was realized in independent Finland (1917–). Well into the 1980s, the necessity of having a strong executive was emphasized at the expense of the parliament.

In this chapter, I show that the arguments about the character of the Age of Liberty used in later "constitutional moments" in Finland (especially during the constitutional reform 1917–1919) and in Sweden (1809, 1917) were in many ways similar to those used by contemporaries. Depending on their own political conviction, they decided either that the benefits outweighed the drawbacks, or alternatively, that the deficiencies were of such a serious nature that a *coup d'état* was necessary, or at least unavoidable.

2 Masterpiece of Modern Legislation: between Limited Monarchy and Aristocratic Republic

Naturally, the new Constitution of 1719/1720 had to be justified by the Estates. There were several strategies for accomplishing this. One was to highlight that the 1680–1718 period of autocratic rule by the monarch were totally exceptional in Swedish history. In this line of legitimisation of the new rule of the Estates, the emphasis was on pointing out that a strong tradition of *monarchia mixta* had existed for a long time in Sweden.[12] Another way to justify the new Constitution was to build on natural law contract theories: the people had justly taken power back from the arbitrary unlimited ruler and legislated a new order. In this spirit, the state ordered an official translation of John Locke's *Second Treatise*.[13] The third way to legitimize the new order was to refer to the classical republican tradition.[14]

---

12 See Nils Runeby, *Monarchia mixta: maktfördelningsdebatt i Sverige under den tidigare stormaktstiden* (Stockholm: Svenska bokförlaget, 1962).

13 Sami-Juhani Savonius, "The Swedish Translation of John Locke's *Second Treatise*, 1726", *Locke Studies*, 1 (2001), 191–220.

14 Charlotta Wolff, *Noble Conceptions of Politics in Eighteenth-Century Sweden* (Helsinki: Finnish Literature Society, 2008); *Eadem*, "Aristocratic Republicanism and the Hate of Sovereignty in Eighteenth-Century Sweden", *Scandinavian Journal of History*, 32 (2007): 358–75; Ere Nokkala, "Debatten mellan J.H.G von Justi och Heinrich Ludwig von Hess om frihetstidens författning", *Historisk Tidskrift för Finland*, 94 (2009), 20–55.

The Age of Liberty endured for a relatively long period of time, and how the country was ruled changed significantly during these more than fifty years. It can be argued that the rhetorical strategies in defence of the "parliamentary regime" of Sweden shifted from limited monarchy via *monarchia mixta* to arguments in favour of a *de facto* aristocratic republic.[15] Once the aristocratic Hat party had established its rule, the interpretation of Sweden as an aristocratic republic became the dominant narrative among the Hats.[16] The aristocratic republicanism of the Age of Liberty aimed at making the executive power independent of the person of the monarch. Abolishing the monarchy as an institution was out of the question due to its strong standing among the broader population.[17] The goal was a republic with a king. A free state could have a king as long as the power of the king was limited.[18] This rhetoric of limiting the power of the monarch can be read in its clearest form in the Hat Party's mouthpiece, *En ärlig Swensk* (An Honest Swede), which was the first political periodical in Sweden, published between 1755 and 1756.[19] *An Honest Swede* defined the "freedom" of the Age of Liberty (*frihetstiden*) as freedom from sovereignty. Freedom from sovereignty was equated with freedom from the autocracy of a single ruler. *An Honest Swede* went so far as to state that the Swedish Constitution worked like the Bible. The Bible liberated mankind from the dominance of Satan, while the Constitution of Sweden liberated the Swedes from the whim of an autocratic tyrant. The Constitution became regarded as Holy scripture that would be challenged only by infidels.[20]

An Honest Swede presented the Swedish Constitution as an ideal that surpassed foreign theories of government, and therefore should be emulated elsewhere. "Foreign theories" referred, in the first place, to Montesquieu's concepts of the separation and balance of power. The German translation of *An Honest*

15 Jonas Nordin, "The Monarchy in the Swedish Age of Liberty (1719–1772)", in Ihalainen, Bregnsbo, Sennefelt and Winton, eds., *Scandinavia in the Age of Revolution,* 29–40.

16 Wolff, *Noble Conceptions,* 35. See also Pasi Ihalainen, *Agents of the People: Democracy and Popular Sovereignty in British and Swedish Parliamentary and Public Debates, 1734–1800* (Leiden: Brill, 2010), 170.

17 Nordin, *Frihetstidens monarki,* 45, 47, 273.

18 Bo Lindberg, *Den antika skevheten: Politiska ord och begrepp i det tidig-moderna Sverige* (Stockholm: Kungl. Vitterhets Historie och Antikvitets Akademien, 2006), 61–2.

19 [anon.] *En ärlig Swensk* (Stockholm, 1755). The last censor and a supporter of the Hat party, Niclas von Oelreich (1699–1770) is most commonly regarded as the editor of *The Honest Swede*. According to Josef Edström, the periodical was an initiative of the leading Hat politician Carl Fredrik Scheffer. See Josef Edström, "En ärlig Svensk som politisk tidskrift", in Ulf Jonsson and Johan Söderberg, eds., *Från vida fält* (Stockholm: University of Stockholm, 1987), 34.

20 [anon.] *En ärlig Swensk* (Stockholm, 1755), 100–1.

Swede, titled *Eigentliche Staatsverfassung des Reichs Schweden unter seiner gesetzmäßigen Freyheit beschrieben und wider Uebelgesinnte gerettet von dem ehrlichen Schweden* (1758), was addressed primarily to the German-speaking subjects of Sweden in Pomerania in order to educate them to become free, virtuous and honest Swedes.[21] Still, the book was widely distributed in the German-speaking region, as is clear from the list of subscriptions printed in the book. The title of the translation indicated that the aim of the book was to save the Swedish Constitution from evil-minded critics and demonstrate how the Constitution was able to produce freedom in accordance with law. The main message was republican in the sense that giving the king stronger executive power would lead to the enslavement of his subjects, who would become dependent on his arbitrary will.

The author who took the mission of defending the Swedish Constitution furthest – making it a universal ideal – was Heinrich Ludwig von Hess (1719–1784).[22] Von Hess was considered a foreigner by the Swedes, but he considered himself a free Swede. He was born in Gothenburg, but was of Pomeranian origin, and German was his mother tongue (although he did speak Swedish, most of his publications were in German). Von Hess is most explicit in his use of republican terminology. One of his pamphlets, which addressed the power struggle between the Council of the Realm and King Adolf Fredrick of Sweden, bears the title *Der Republickaner* (1754).[23] In this pamphlet, Hess defended the Hat Party's conception of liberty as liberty from autocracy. The pamphlet is a dialogue between a monarchist and a republican. Without hesitation, Hess favours the republican path. Granting the king wider executive rights, Hess

21 [Niklas Oelreich], *Eigentliche Staatsverfassung des Reichs Schweden unter seiner gesetzmäßigen Freyheit beschrieben und wider Uebelgesinnte gerettet von dem ehrlichen Schweden* (Stralsund and Greifswald, 1758). On the German translation of *Ärlig Swensk* and on its reception in Germany, see Per Nilsén, *Att "Stoppa munnen till på bespottare": Den akademiska undervisningen i svensk statsrätt under frihetstiden* (Lund: Institutet för rättshistorisk forskning, 2001).

22 On Hess, see Ere Nokkala, "Rewriting Eighteenth-Century Swedish Political Thought: Heinrich Ludwig von Hess's *Der Republickaner*", *History of European Ideas*, 42 (2016), 502–15.

23 *Der Republickaner* was first circulated as a handwritten manuscript in Sweden in 1754. It was first printed in Hamburg in 1754 and translated into French the same year and into Swedish in 1756. None of these first printed editions seem to have been preserved. The first printed edition of which I have managed to find a copy is the second edition of 1762 printed in Hamburg. *Der Republickaner* is further printed in Hess, *Satyrische Schriften* (Hamburg, 1767); Hess, *Vermischte Schriften* (Hamburg, 1770), 295–330; Hess *Staatsschriften* (Hamburg, 1772), 93–124. In addition, there also exists a modern edition in Gunter Grimm, ed., *Satiren der Aufklärung* (Stuttgart, 1975), 67–88.

argues, would lead to slavery. Thus, Hess presented the contemporary Swedish regime in a most favourable light.

Hess elaborated on his republican conception of freedom in another publication, deeply embedded in the context of the Seven Years War, called *Betrachtungen über das elfte Stück von des Herrn von Justi sogenannten neuen Wahrheiten zum Vortheile der Naturkunde und des gesellschaftlichen Lebens des Menschen, durch welche die Freyheit der schwedischen Reichsraths wider Uebelgesinnte vertheidiget werden* (1760/61). This publication attacked Johann Heinrich Gottlob von Justi's critique of the Swedish Constitution, to which we will return later. In his *Betrachtungen,* Hess applied Montesquieu's ideas of the balance of power in favour of the Swedish government. Hess stated that a perfect balance prevailed in Sweden thanks to its formidable Constitution: the Senate (Council of the Realm), which kept the king in control, was itself controlled by the Estates summoned to the Diet. The Estates were bound by the Constitution and by subsequent generations of the Estates.[24] This was, without doubt, a republican trope of the wisdom of the ages, in contrast to the immediacy and thus, the unreliability – of the individual decision-maker. Equally decisively, Hess set himself against the royal veto, arguing that it erased the independence of the parliament and the courts. Its very existence was enough to endanger the existence of the republic. Hess asked how freedom could prevail if the king were able to stop the legislature – or even the judiciary – from making decisions. Thus, the power of law and justice would depend solely on the king's whim. If the king used his veto wisely, it would not reflect the merit of the form of government, but the person of the sovereign. Again, Hess reiterated that the virtue or personal conscience of the monarch was not a sufficient guarantee of freedom. Hess referred to the events of the early 1750s, when King Adolf Fredrick argued that he could not ratify the decisions he disapproved of because he had to follow his conscience.[25] That is what Hess commented on when he pointed out that the conscience or any personal virtue of the leader was an unreliable criterion,[26] for the conscience of even the best princes may be mistaken. If the prince were free to follow his conscience, it would replace the law. In other words, the ruler would be above the law, and a people at the

24 Heinrich Ludwig von Hess, *Betrachtungen über das elfte Stück von des Herrn von Justi sogenannten neuen Wahrheiten zum Vortheile der Naturkunde und des gesellschaftlichen Lebens des Menschen, durch welche die Freyheit der schwedischen Reichsraths wider Uebelgesinnte vertheidiget werden* (1760/61). Printed in Hess's *Satyrische Schriften* (Hamburg, 1767), 331–462, 387.

25 Wolff, *Noble Conceptions,* 60.

26 Hess, *Betrachtungen,* 449–52.

mercy of a king would have lost their freedom. Hess raised the question of whether it would be more likely that one person would be more easily misled than the plurality of the Estates and the Senate. Hess emphasized that if the members of the Council of the Realm did not act reasonably, they could be dismissed by the next regime. He further pointed out that a councillor who had lost the trust of the Diet could be dismissed (*Licentierung*).[27] According to Hess, the Councillors of the Realm only advised; they did not rule. This is a massive understatement against the backdrop of the political reality of the 1750s.

Hess's republican writings can be considered a variant of the same project as *An Honest Swede*. Hess defended the concept of freedom of the Hat Party in German as freedom from the sovereignty of a single ruler and as freedom to do what the law did not forbid. He also placed the Senate (i.e., the Council of the Realm, consisting only of members of the Hat Party) in a most favourable light. What has remained understudied, even in the latest studies on Swedish aristocratic republicanism, is the role of the "third concept of liberty", wherein freedom is conceptualized as non-dependence on the arbitrary will of others. Hess and *An Honest Swede* define freedom as non-dependence on the arbitrary will of a ruler. In the neo-Roman civic humanist tradition, liberty and slavery were generally opposed to one another. This was also the case with the Swedish aristocratic republicans.[28]

The aim of presenting the Swedish Constitution as being ideal had some success beyond the German-speaking region. Jonathan Israel has argued that the Swedish political system of the Age of Liberty was greeted with nearly universal enthusiasm by the French *philosophes*.[29] Thus, the French appraisals of the Swedish Constitution deserve closer scrutiny. The case for Rousseau as an admirer of the Swedish Constitution is the weakest. Fahlbeck and Lagerroth, both in the 1910s, referred to the anonymous author of *Wåra grundlagars förswar, uti et bref til Rousseau* (Our Constitution's Defence, from a Letter to Rousseau, 1771) as the source of Rousseau's admiration. According to the author of the pamphlet, Rousseau had refused to send him the plan for the Constitution of Corsica, because the Swedes already had such a great example

27 Hess, *Betrachtungen*, 342.

28 On opposing freedom with slavery, see Hess, *Republickaner*, 99, 107–9. On the neo-Roman "third concept of liberty", see Quentin Skinner, *Liberty Before Liberalism* (Cambridge: Cambridge University Press, 1998).

29 Jonathan Israel, "Northern Varieties: Contrasting the Dano-Norwegian and the Swedish-Finnish Enlightenments", in Ellen Krefting, Aina Nøding and Mona Ringvej, eds., *Eighteenth-Century Periodicals as Agents of Change* (Leiden: Brill, 2015), 17–45, at 26. Lagerroth already highlighted how the Constitution of the Age of Liberty was admired by foreign, and especially French, writers: *Frihetstidens författning*, 734.

of perfection in their fatherland's constitution that nothing new would be found in Rousseau's plan, which was based on the same principle insofar as different natures and circumstances allowed.[30] This statement, from a pamphlet written in the turbulent year of 1771, does not truly suffice to prove that Rousseau would have been a great admirer of the Swedish Constitution. Above all, it is insufficient because it is a second-hand source of low value, but there is yet another reason why it is insufficient: even if the quote were authentic – and nothing about it stands out as being obviously false – Rousseau was a strong believer in constitutions being tied to their people. In this way, the best constitution for Sweden could only be a Swedish constitution, and not Corsican ideas.[31]

Voltaire's massive *oeuvre* contains several references to the Swedish Constitution. However, to conclude from these that he would have been a committed admirer of the Swedish Constitution overstretches the argument. It is true that Voltaire praised Sweden as the freest kingdom on earth in his essay *Sur les moeurs* (1756).[32] What Voltaire found admirable at this point was the freedom that the Diet enjoyed. At the same time, he was an admirer of the previous autocratic king, Charles XII, who to him was kind of an enlightened despot. Above all, Voltaire was an admirer of Charles XII's personal qualities. After the coup d'état of Gustav III, Voltaire praised the new king in a poem. It is important to notice that even in his praise of the "freedom" of the Age of Liberty, Voltaire praised Sweden as a monarchy and not as a republic. There is no contradiction here, since a limited monarchy could also be considered a free state: a republic with a king. The crucial point was the presence of some sort of representative assembly that counterbalanced the executive. Voltaire was not an isolated case. In the French *Éncyclopédie* Louis de Jaucourt (1704–1779) writes under "*monarchie limitée*":

> Limited monarchy (Government). A sort of monarchy in which the three powers are so melded together that they use one another to balance and counterbalance. Hereditary limited monarchy appears to be the best

---

30 [anon.], *Wåra grundlagars förswar, uti et bref til Rousseau* (Stockholm, 1771). Loaned after Erik Fahlbeck, "Studier öfver frihetstidens politiska idéer", *Statsvetenskaplig Tidskrift*,19 (1916), 125. Fahlbeck's article was published in three parts in a folllowing manner: *Statsvetenskaplig Tidskrift* 18 (1915): 325–44; *Statsvetenskaplig Tidskrift* 19 (1916): 31–54 and 104–26.

31 I am grateful to Mark J. Hill for pointing this out to me. See his contribution to this volume.

32 Voltaire, *Essai sur les moeurs et l'esprit des Nations* (1756), ch. 165: *Cette Suède, despotiquement gouvernée, est devenue de nos jours le royaume de la terre le plus libre, et celu ioù les roissont le plus dependants.*

> form of monarchy [...] It seems that in Sweden we enjoy this precious advantage, as far as we are far from Denmark; but the monarchy of Russia is pure despotism.[33]

Voltaire would have agreed with de Jaucourt's assessment. Monarchy *per se* was not considered a bad form of government.

The republican authors who used the Swedish Constitution most actively as an argument in their debates were the Italians. In Naples, one of the leading republicans, Paolo Mattia Doria (1662–1746), was concerned about the freedom of peoples. In his manuscripts *Il politico alla moda* (1739) and *Il commercio mercantile* (1742), Doria argued that only the Swedes had managed to recover their ancient liberty. It is noteworthy that Doria's conception of the Swedish Constitution links it with ancient, rather than modern, liberty. In general, Italian writers regarded the Swedish political system as "a monarchy with a mixed government according to the Venetian Republic's model".[34] The interest that the eighteenth-century Italian writers showed in Sweden during the Age of Liberty is elaborated on by Franco Venturi, who devotes a whole chapter of his book to Sweden. The chapter is titled "Between Republican Monarchies and Monarchical Republics: Sweden".[35] Sweden appears as an exceptionally interesting case in that it illustrates how the monarchical and republican elements were intertwined in the eighteenth century. Sweden resembled England in applying republican values to a monarchical state – although, of course, much less attention has been paid to Sweden.

The republican political thinker who engaged himself most systematically with the Swedish Constitution was Mably. Mably is a central figure in

---

33 Louis de Jaucourt, "Monarchie limitée", in *Encyclopédie, ou dictionnaire raisonné des sciences, des arts et des métiers, etc.*, ed. Denis Diderot and Jean le Rond d'Alembert, University of Chicago: ARTFL Encyclopédie Project (Autumn 2017 Edition), Robert Morrissey and Glenn Roe, eds., http://encyclopedie.uchicago.edu/. [accessed 1 April 2018], X: 637: "Monarchie limitée (*Gouvernement*), sorte de monarchie où les trois pouvoirs sont tellement fondus ensemble, qu'ils se servent l'un à l'autre de balance & de contrepoids. La *monarchie limitée* héreditaire, paroît être la meilleure forme de monarchie [...] Il paroît qu'on jouit en Suede de ce précieux avantage, autant qu'on en est éloigné en Danemark; mais la *monarchie* de Russie est un pur despotisme".

34 For the quotations and a short overview, see Salvo Mastellone, "Italian Enlightenment and the Swedish Constitution during the Age of Liberty (1719–1772)", in Nils Stjernquist, ed., *The Swedish Riksdag in an International Perspective* (Stockholm: Bank of Sweden Tercentenary Foundation, 1989), 112–7. On Doria, see Adriana Luna González's Ph.D. thesis "From Self-preservation to Self-liking in Paolo Mattia Doria: Civil Philosophy and Natural Jurisprudence in the Early Italian Enlightenment", EUI, Florence, 2009.

35 Venturi, *The End of the Old Regime*, 279–339.

the history of eighteenth-century French political thought and an author of the most comprehensive and influential treatises on republicanism to be produced in eighteenth-century France. His significance as an intellectual source for the key intellectual figures of the French revolution has been established. Indeed, in his lifetime, he competed in fame with Voltaire and Rousseau. Measured against his collected writings, Sweden was not a dominant theme. However, Sweden played a crucial role in his argument in favour of turning the French monarchy towards a more equalitarian state. Hence, the primary context in which Mably engaged himself with Sweden was France of the 1760s and 1770s. Mably dealt at length with Sweden in two of his publications, which took him many years to complete. In his "postulate of equality", *De l'étude de l'histoire* (1775), which he had already started to write in the 1760s, he called the Swedish Constitution "a masterpiece of modern legislation" (*chef-d'œuvre de la législation moderne*) and stated that the people of Sweden were the freest in all of Europe (*le plus libre de l'Europa*).[36] Mably's "plea for equality and social justice as a foundation of a constitution", titled *De La Législation ou Principes des lois* (1776), was a dialogue among a Swedish philosopher, an Englishman, and the author. This work, which Mably described as his most considered political statement, was written in the late 1760s, but published only in 1776.[37] Mably left no doubt that, in his view, the Swedish republican form of government advocated by the fictitious Swedish philosopher in his book, was superior to the British monarchy in every respect. To quote George Armstrong Kelly in 1986, "Sweden was somewhat the same kind of beacon for him as for certain Western socialists today".[38] Mably's interest in the Swedish Constitution coincides with the period, from 1750s onwards, when he became a committed republican.[39] Sweden was an example of establishing a republican system of government suitable for a large territorial state.

36 Gabriel Bonnot Mably, *De l'étude de l'histoire*, texte revu par Barbara Negroni (Paris: Fayard, 1988), 188. "*C'est le chef-d'œuvre de la législation moderne, et les législateurs les plus célèbres de l'antiquité ne désavoueroient pas cette constitution où les droits de l'humanité et de l'égalité sont beaucoup plus respectés qu'on auroit dû l'espérer dans les temps malheureux où nous vivons*". See Johnson Kent Wright, *A Classical Republican in Eighteenth-Century France: The Political Thought of Mably* (Stanford, CA: Standford University Press, 1997), 162–3.

37 Gabriel Bonnot Mably, *De la législation, ou principes des lois* (Amsterdam, 1776); Friedemann, *Die politische Philosophie*, 108; Michael Sonenscher, *Before the Deluge: Public Debt, Inequality, and the Intellectual Origins of the French Revolution* (Princeton: Princeton University Press, 2007), 241.

38 George Armstrong Kelly, "Mortal Man, Immortal Society? Political Metaphors in Eighteenth-Century France", *Political Theory*, 14 (1986): 5–29, at 24.

39 Wright, *A Classical Republican, passim.*

What, then, did Mably find so admirable in the Swedish form of government? First, Mably was a realist: he preferred the Swedish Constitution over the English Constitution because he regarded improvement of the French monarchy according to the model of Sweden as a more realistic scenario than the English variation.[40] Turning France into a country ruled by the Estates seemed plausible to Mably. Second, according to Mably, the Swedish Constitution of 1719/1720 had the most important preconditions for a rightful constitution: the separation of powers and control of the executive power by the Diet (parliament), which held all the legislative power.[41] Mably saw the Swedish Constitution in the same republican light as Hess had done before him. He highlighted that in Sweden the executive power was exercised by the Council of the Realm, which was dependent on the Diet. The king only presided over the Council of the Realm. Hence, the relationship between the hereditary monarchy and the Diet was perfect. As an anti-monarchist, Mably was very pleased by this fact. It is worth emphasizing that Mably defined freedom in terms of equality. To him, equality was the only possible foundation of a just constitution and society in general. Mably's conviction was that Sweden was the freest state because it was the most equal. This was evidenced by the fact that the Swedish peasants had a vote among the other Estates at the *Riksdagar*. Equality in Sweden was much more widely distributed than in other European forms of government. Mably also favoured the strict commercial regulation that the Hat regime exercised in Sweden until the second half of the 1760s. The strict sumptuary laws legislated in Sweden had their place as a tool to prevent the excessive proliferation of wealth – which, again, would be bad for equality. Like the character of the Swedish philosopher in *De la législation ou principes des lois,* Mably was not totally against trade, but he was highly critical of commercial society, and especially of the modern commercial and colonial monarchy of England, which was a beacon for many of his contemporaries. Mably argued for a society founded on helpfulness, solidarity and respect for the third party.[42] The English model of expanding beyond Europe, growing rich, and engaging in commerce was based on greed, which was to be avoided.[43] In sum,

40 Wright, *A Classical Republican*, 162–3.

41 This was not exactly right. According to the Constitution of 1720, the king was the sole legislator. The right to stipulate laws was *de facto* transported to the Diet in the course of the age, but it was a slow process. For the discussion of the formal side of this process, see Nordin, *Frihetstidens monarki*, 39–41.

42 Friedemann, *Die politische Philosophie*, 109.

43 Venturi, *The End of the Old Regime*, 328.

according to Mably, the path to be chosen was the egalitarian way of Sweden, without which there would be no real liberty in France.

3 Aristocratic Yoke

In the history writing that has celebrated the Constitution of the Age of Liberty as an important milestone in the history of Swedish and Western parliamentarianism, it has gone almost unnoticed that Mably was far from being a mere naive admirer of the Swedish Constitution. Because Mably's treatises dealing with Sweden were published only after the royal coup d'état of Gustav III (1772) it was natural that Mably tried to explain why the coup had taken place. Still, it is quite striking that Mably stayed loyal to the main principles of the Constitution of the Age of Liberty and continued to admire it even after 1772. Whereas Voltaire, the physiocrats and several French philosophers greeted the coup with enthusiasm, Mably planned to publish a treatise in which he would denounce the revolution. Mably stated self-consciously that the king of Sweden had changed the Constitution of Sweden; however, the king could not change the content of Mably's book.[44] The virtues of the Constitution of 1719/1720 remained valid to Mably.

Although Mably's books present a defence of the Constitution of the Age of Liberty after its abolition, he does suggest how the Constitution could have been altered in order to prevent the royal coup. Mably agreed with the royalist critics that the main problem with the Constitution had been that power was concentrated in the hands of the aristocrats. However, the solutions that he suggested were far from monarchical. Mably suggested countermeasures to balance the power of the aristocrats. First, he proposed that the Councillors of the Realm coming from the Noble Estate should have been appointed for a limited period of time only, and not for life. This would have prevented the concentration of power in their hands. Second, Mably advocated the abolition of the exclusive privileges of the nobility, and finally, he suggested that the Diet should have concentrated in its legislation on *lois generales* and left the particulars to the executive.[45] Mably was of the opinion that republics were always in danger of transforming into aristocracies. In his analysis of the royal coup, he argued that it was the privileges of the nobles that had led to the loss of freedom and concentration of power into the hands of an absolute monarch

44 Wright, *A Classical Republican*, 163.

45 This is interestingly well in line with the political changes that were being discussed and tried in Sweden in the 1760s and early 1770s.

in 1680 and that the same had happened in 1772. Establishing a strong monarchical rule appeared to be the only solution to avoid unjust aristocratic rule.[46] For a committed anti-monarchist such as Mably, this was out of the question, and it is noteworthy that none of his suggestions for the improvement of the Constitution of 1719/1720 proposed that a stronger royal executive power could have prevented the rise of oligarchs. According to Mably, one should not build a state that relies on the arbitrary will of a single ruler. The balance of power could be achieved with other means introduced to curb the power of the Noble Estate.

Mably's reassessment of the Swedish rule of the Age of Liberty was foreshadowed by Peter Forsskål (1732–1763). Forsskål was a Swedish thinker educated in Uppsala and Göttingen who recognized the threat of Sweden developing into an aristocracy as early as 1759. By then, he had written and anonymously published a pamphlet called *Thoughts on Civil Liberty* (*Tankar om borgerliga friheten*).[47] Although he does not mention anywhere that he had written the pamphlet as a protest against the ruling aristocratic Hat Party, this was the contemporary interpretation.[48] In a speech in his own defence, Forsskål referred to the peril of degenerating into an aristocracy:

> Our freedom has not yet reached so far that it could not degenerate into a noxious aristocracy [*degenerera til en skadelig aristocratie*]. But, however, it seems to me that in the future, self-interest among the most powerful will find room enough to hurl our country into it, when all the business of those who rule can be defended with their own highest power.[49]

In 1759, Forsskål was still optimistic that the fall into an aristocracy was not inevitable. As a countermeasure, he suggested freedom of the press and limited government. Limitation of the government in this sense did not mean limiting only the power of the king, but that of the aristocracy as well.

A foreign author who was most convinced about the aristocratic and tyrannical nature of the Swedish Constitution was the German cameralist

46 Mably, *De la législation*, 237–49. See also Venturi, *The End of the Old Regime*, 328–9.

47 Peter Forsskål, *Tankar om borgerliga friheten* (Stockholm: Lars Salvius, 1759).

48 Ere Nokkala, "Peter Forsskål: Freedom to Write and the Principle of Public Access to Official Documents", in *Press Freedom 250 Years*, ed. Örtenhed and Wennberg, 61–76.

49 P. Forsskål to Chancellery Councilor M. V. Hermansson with a defence of his pamphlet Borgerliga friheten, Uppsala, 29 June 1759. Printed in Claes Annerstedt, *Upsala universitets historia, Appendix 4: Handlingar, 1749–1776* (Uppsala: Uppsala University, 1912), 123.

and political writer Johann Heinrich Gottlob von Justi (1717–1771).[50] Justi was familiar with the German translation of *An Honest Swede*. In addition, he and Forsskål lived at the same time in Göttingen and knew each other. Therefore, it is likely that Justi's appraisal of the Swedish Constitution was informed by Forsskål's views. Justi's and Forsskål's writings were later discussed in the same meetings of the Chancery Board, the highest organ responsible for censorship. Both Justi's and Forsskål's writings were banned in Sweden in 1760. No official defence was required, and it was mentioned that a foreign writer had already defended the Swedish Constitution. The foreign writer that the Chancery Board referred to was Heinrich Ludwig von Hess.

The main context of Justi's writings on the Swedish Constitution was the Seven Years War, in which Sweden was fighting against Prussia. Justi was hired by the Prussians to write in favour of the Prussian–English coalition. Justi's first critique of Sweden was published in his periodical *New Truths*[51] (Neue Wahrheiten, 1758). However, Justi's critique of the Swedish form of government is not of a tendentious nature and it is found not only in his war pamphlets, but also in his political writings such as *Natur und Wesen der Staaten*[52] (Nature and Essence of the States, 1760) and *Grundriß einer guten Regierung*[53] (Groundwork of a Good Government, 1759). In these books, Justi emphasized that the main rule in establishing a mixed government was to restrain the power of the aristocracy. Were power to be concentrated in the hands of the aristocrats, there would be nothing left of the freedom and welfare of the state. Justi asked his readers simply to compare the constitutions of Sweden and England. Both were mixed forms of government (*Regierungsformen*), composed of democratic, monarchical and aristocratic parts. According to Justi, the English form of government was the most perfect under the sun, whereas the Swedish was perhaps the worst of all possible forms of government. In Sweden, the hereditary nobility was in a position to tyrannize the entire nation.[54] He noted that, in Sweden, every faction that had a majority in the Diet – he clearly had the Hats in mind – could tyrannize people and corrupt the real

50 On Justi, see Ere Nokkala, *From Natural Law to Political Economy: J.H.G. von Justi on State, Commerce and International Order* (Münster: LIT Verlag, 2019).

51 Johann Heinrich Gottlob von Justi, *Neue Wahrheiten zum Vortheil der Naturkunde und des gesellschaftlichen Lebens der Menschen* (Leipzig, 1754–1758), 503–553.

52 Johann Heinrich Gottlob von Justi, *Natur und Wesen der Staaten als die Quelle aller Regierungswissenschaften und Gesetze.* Mit Anmerkungen herausgegeben von D. Heinrich Godfried Scheidemantel (Mittau, 1771 [1760]).

53 Johann Heinrich Gottlob von Justi, *Der Grundriß einer guten Regierung in fünf Buechern verfasset* (Frankfurt und Leipzig, 1759).

54 Justi, *Grundriß*, 151–152.

interest and welfare of the nation in favour of foreign powers. Because of this, Sweden had unwisely joined the war against Prussia. In sum, in Sweden the nobility ruined all the good that the combination of democracy and monarchy brought: the king of Sweden was powerless to act effectively, and the freedom of the citizens was tyrannized by the factions of the *Riksdag*. Furthermore, the Swedish Constitution had nothing left of balance. Therefore, Justi foresaw as early as 1759 that a happy revolution (*glückliche Revolution*) would take place in Sweden because the nobility, which was overrepresented in the *Riksdag* and was in position to change the Constitution, refused to do so.[55] Justi's interpretation of the English Constitution was inspired by Montesquieu, but their conceptions of the role of the aristocracy differed significantly. According to Justi, the strong royal executive was the real balancer in a properly functional government. To him, the aristocracy represented the main threat. The main context of Justi's critique of the Swedish Constitution was the Seven Years War, and his account can be regarded as a defence of a strong authority according to the model of the Prussian monarchy, although he was not unequivocal in his admiration of Frederick II. Justi wrote at a time when Frederick II was planning to turn Prussia into a trading nation, a modern commercial monarchy inspired by the success of England.[56]

Justi's line of interpretation of the Swedish and English constitutions was taken further by Jean-Louis De Lolme, who is well known as an analyst of the English Constitution. He elaborated on it in his *The Constitution of England* (1775), originally published in French in 1771. De Lolme was born in Geneva, and the origins of his critical views on aristocrats were based on his experiences in his native town. He moved to England in 1768. In the scholarly literature, De Lolme has often been portrayed as a conservative royalist.[57] In recent years, however, more attention has been paid to the contextual underpinnings of his thought. In this respect, one of the main sources is a work published in the immediate aftermath of Gustav III's coup called *Parallel between the English Constitution and the former government of Sweden: containing some observations on the late revolution in that kingdom; and an examination of the causes that secure us against both aristocracy, and absolute monarchy* (1772). Whereas

55 Justi, *Grundriß*, 395–399; Justi, *Natur und Wesen*, 197, 219.

56 Marco Cavarzere, "The Rise of a Trading Nation: Prussia and the *Convention préliminaire de commerce* with France (1753)", in Antonella Alimento and Koen Stapelbroek, eds., *The Politics of Commercial Treaties in the Eighteenth-Century* (London: Palgrave, 2017), 295–320. Florian Schui, "Prussia's 'Trans-Oceanic Moment': The Creation of the Prussian Asiatic Trade Company in 1750", *Historical Journal*, 49 (2006), 143–60.

57 McDaniel, "Jean Louis Delolme", 23.

Mably wanted to show how the royal coup could have been avoided in Sweden by republican constitutional improvements, De Lolme's intention with this book was to show that the English Constitution did not possess the same deficits that the former Swedish Constitution had. Therefore, a revolution like the one that had just taken place in Sweden would not occur in England. According to De Lolme, the great advantage of the English Constitution was the broad executive power of the king.

On the one hand, De Lolme's *Parallel* was written in the larger framework of his critique of republican political thought; on the other hand, it was also a denunciation of Montesquieu's conception of the separation of powers. Contrary to common assumptions, De Lolme was a clear critic of Montesquieu, in particular regarding the role of aristocracy in a properly functional society. Like Montesquieu, he combined the separation of powers with a balance between king, nobility and people. However, according to De Lolme, the nobility were the true threat and source of disorder in all republics, whereas the king and the people were on the same side. What was required was a strong royal executive who would function as a counterpoise to aristocratic tyranny. In this sense, a king was the protector of the people.[58] De Lolme's position was very close to that of Justi. According to De Lolme, in Sweden, the king could not fill his counter aristocratic function as the balancer. In fact, Sweden did not even deserve to be called a kingdom:

> The Government of Sweden, therefore, because it had what they called a King, may have been mistaken for a monarchical one, by those who judge of things, from their outward appearance, or for being popular, because even peasants had a seeming share in it. But the executive and military powers centring in the Nobles, with the reality of the legislative authority, it was merely aristocratical, consequently subject to all the evils that necessarily attend that sort of Government.[59]

De Lolme was clearly very familiar with Swedish rule during the Age Liberty. Namely, *de jure* on paper, the king still held the executive power in Sweden during the Age of Liberty. However, *de facto* the power lay in the hands of the councillors and the Diet. According to De Lolme, this was the state of affairs against which the liberty produced by the Constitution was to be evaluated:

58 Luke Mayville, *John Adams and the Fear of American Oligarchy* (Princeton: Princeton University Press, 2016), 37–8.

59 Jean Louis De Lolme, *A Parallel between the English Constitution and the Former Government of Sweden* (London, 1772), 19.

> In our disquisition on the liberty of a Nation, we must indeed pay a great attention to the description of the outward form of its Government; but it is at the distribution of real power that has been introduced, we must chiefly look. Governments are the work of force: like the treaties between Princes, they only subsist by the continued effect and weight of force; and it may be laid down as maxim, that, in any shape of Government, whatever may be got on the side of form, never can compensate what is lost in point of real strength.[60]

De Lolme noted that "All places of trust and profit are, at last, openly and expressly reserved to the Nobles".[61] Several times, Delolme used the expression "aristocratic yoke" in relation to Sweden's former government.[62]

In De Lolme's view, a revolution like the one that had taken place less than a year ago in Sweden would not take place in England, because in England the active executive power was concentrated in the hands of the king, which enabled him to annul the power of the British aristocracy, and this was a source of constitutional stability:

> But the English Constitution is founded upon entirely different principles. It has not made the King the servant and ostensible tool of aristocratical Assembly: it has vested him with prerogatives that make him truly and really King.[63]
>
> It is to the Crown, to its weight and invisible authority, we owe the keeping down the hundred-headed Power that has laid Poland in ashes and reduced the Swedes to desperation.[64]

De Lolme's preference for monarchy over republic becomes visible in his opposition to the idea that a republican government would lead to the liberty of all, and that monarchy would inevitably be a government of slavery:

> Branding Royalty with being, necessarily and on itself, the Government of slavery, and crying up the Power of a few, as being, necessarily and of itself likewise, the liberty of all.[65]

60 De Lolme, *A Parallel,* 13.
61 De Lolme, *A Parallel,* 20.
62 De Lolme, *A Parallel,* 28, 46.
63 De Lolme, *A Parallel,* 23.
64 De Lolme, *A Parallel,* 54.
65 De Lolme, *A Parallel,* 22.

De Lolme's original application of the balance of power was hailed by John Adams as the best defence of the concept,[66] and De Lolme left a legacy for the defenders of the presidential executive in the United States. What has remained so far almost unnoticed is that the conceptual underpinnings of this conception were partly developed in relation to the Swedish Constitution of 1719/1720.

4 Conclusion

The Constitution of the Age of Liberty – and the Age of Liberty in general – has been interpreted in Swedish history predominantly in a positive light. Historians' references to foreign authors have so far remained largely linked with the somewhat teleological conceptions of the Age of Liberty as a period of parliamentary democracy and of parliamentary sovereignty. The negative evaluations of contemporaries have fallen into oblivion. However, as this article has shown, the negative characteristics of the rule of the Estates were well known to contemporary foreign commentators. The critiques of the Swedish Constitution are comparable in number to those that praise it. Taking both the critical and positive interventions into account helps us form a more balanced interpretation of the Age of Liberty. The Age of Liberty can be easily regarded either as a progressive period or as a period of oligarchic rule, depending on what one emphasizes. If one is seeking to find a basis for a negative interpretation of the Age of Liberty, one will find a lot of support for this interpretation in the aristocratic rule of the Estates during the Hat regime. Power was concentrated in the hands of the aristocrats, who enjoyed privileges that were not part of the Constitution, *stricto sensu*, but they could be altered only with the consent of the affected party (i.e., the nobility). In effect, this made it possible to change them only with full consensus between the Estates – just like the Constitution. This made upward social mobility practically impossible for non-nobles. Corruption was common in the Diet and many injustices were perpetrated in the courts. However, if one wanted to emphasize the positive features of the Age of Liberty, one would do well to highlight a certain level of equality in Swedish society. For instance, the Freedom of Press Act (1766) would not have been possible had the three non-noble Estates not been able to overrule the Nobles in legislation. The Diet as an institution made the legislation of the Freedom of Press Act possible. In sum, whether one wants to

66 Mayville, *John Adams*, 37.

present the Age of Liberty as a success story or as a failure is, to a great extent, a narrative choice. The political reality of the period provides sufficient support for both narratives.

My aim in this chapter has been to show that, even in the eighteenth century, foreign republican and monarchist thinkers were aware that the Swedish example could serve as a tool in their debates, either in favour of or against the republican constitution. The main debate concerned whether granting the king wider executive power leads to slavery or whether it in fact creates the required constitutional balance of power that protects the people from the yoke of the aristocrats, and thus is the true saviour of liberty. As the case of De Lolme demonstrates, the foreign commentators were also aware that the Swedish Constitution *de facto* should not be equated with the original Constitution of 1719/1720 *de jure*. Although Sweden was a monarchy on paper, it had developed into a *de facto* aristocratic republic. Moreover, the Swedish Constitution was to be evaluated based on the real power relations, of which De Lolme was no admirer. To conclude, Swedish freedom and equality was admired by foreign intellectuals, such as Jaucaurt and Mably, but the admiration was not unequivocal. According to Justi and De Lolme, Sweden did not show Europe the way to freedom; on the contrary, choosing the Constitution of the Age of Liberty as the model to be followed would lead only to aristocratic oligarchy.

Bibliography

Main Sources

[anon.] *En ärlig Swensk* (Stockholm, 1755).

Delolme, Jean-Louis, *Parallel between the English Constitution and the former government of Sweden: containing some observations on the late revolution in that kingdom; and an examination of the causes that secure us against both aristocracy, and absolute monarchy* (London, 1772).

Hess, Heinrich Ludwig von, *Der Republickaner* (1754), printed in Gunter Grimm, ed., *Satiren der Aufklärung* (Stuttgart, 1975), 67–88.

Justi, Johann Heinrich Gottlob von, *Natur und Wesen der Staaten als die Quelle aller Regierungswissenschaften und Gesetze*. Mit Anmerkungen herausgegeben von D. Heinrich Godfried Scheidemantel (Mittau, 1771 [1760]).

Mably, Gabriel Bonnot de, *De la législation, ou principes des lois* (Amsterdam, 1776).

Main Bibliographical References

Ihalainen, Pasi, *Agents of the People: Democracy and Popular Sovereignty in British and Swedish Parliamentary and Public Debates, 1734–1800* (Leiden: Brill, 2010).

McDaniel, Iain, "Jean Louis Delolme and the Political Science of the English Empire", *Historical Journal*, 55 (2012), 21–44.

Nordin, Jonas, "The Monarchy in the Swedish Age of Liberty (1719–1772)", in Pasi Ihalainen, Michael Bregnsbo, Karin Sennefelt and Patrik Winton, eds., *Scandinavia in the Age of Revolution: Nordic Political Cultures, 1740–1820* (Farnham: Ashgate, 2009), 29–40.

Wolff, Charlotta, "Aristocratic Republicanism and the Hate of Sovereignty in Eighteenth-century Sweden", *Scandinavian Journal of History*, 32 (2007), 358–75.

Wright, Johnson Kent, *A Classical Republican in Eighteenth-Century France: The Political Thought of Mably* (Stanford, CA: Standford University Press, 1997).

PART 4

The Nineteenth Century

CHAPTER 15

"Dark Spots of Our History"

Martínez Marina and Foundational Myths in Eighteenth-Century Spain

Pablo Fernández Albaladejo

Francisco Martínez Marina (1754–1833) was a cleric and a foundational figure in Spanish constitutional historiography, of which he was a firm defender.* His career during a time of constitutional crisis exemplified an effort to establish a political practice and culture befitting that moment. His early denunciations of the excesses of Bourbon absolutism, his active and committed participation in political debates during the Cortes of Cadiz and, last but not least, the reprisals to which he was subject after the restoration of Ferdinand VII represent an unanimously accepted anti-absolutist stance. Nevertheless, his ideological positions suffered from the transitional nature of his time as he wavered, subject to a constitutive ambiguity, between tradition and revolution, and between scholasticism and liberalism.[1]

Grounding himself in assumptions of civic Christianity and adopting a tone we are calling *nacionista*, Martínez Marina's rereading of the past joined liberal assumptions with a careful consideration of the role of tradition.[2] Through that filter, institutions such as the Cortes of Cadiz or, indeed, Castilian law, exemplified a historical tradition marked by its capacity of resistance against the maneuverings of despotic power.[3] Analyses of his work display gaps, however, and some of his writings remain essentially unknown. In what follows

* This project was conducted under the MINECO research project "La nación traducida: Ecologías de la traducción, 1668–1730" [PGC 2018-095007-B-100]. Translated from the Spanish by Ruth MacKay.

1 Marina represents a strain of liberalism combining individual liberty and strong community ties: Brendon Westler, "Between Tradition and Revolution: The Curious Case of Francisco Martínez Marina, the Cadiz Constitution, and Spanish Liberalism", *Journal of the History of Ideas*, 76 (2015), 394–416, and the bibliography cited therein.

2 *Nacionista* in this context refers to the understanding of "nation" in Old Regime political language. It is based on medieval Christianity and quite different from the vision of nation as a constituent political subject that would triumph with the liberal-bourgeois revolution.

3 Pablo Fernández Albaladejo, "El cristianismo cívico de Martínez Marina", in his *Materia de España. Cultura política e identidad en la España Moderna* (Madrid: Marcial Pons, 2007), 323–50; Francisco Tomás y Valiente, *Martínez Marina, historiador del Derecho* (Madrid: Real Academia de la Historia, 1991).

 | DOI:10.1163/9789004549159_017

I shall address two of these neglected works: *Antigüedades hispano-hebreas convencidas de supuestas y fabulosas. Discurso histórico-crítico sobre la primera venida de los judíos a España* (1799), and *Ensayo histórico-crítico sobre el origen y progreso de las lenguas, señaladamente del romance castellano* (1805).[4]

These two essays are different from each other and would appear to have been unrelated to the constitutional climate of the times, but appearances can be deceiving. There were connections. From the perspective of the waning moments of the Spanish Enlightenment, Marina presented a few of the concepts of the new discourse of Spanish identity that he would later formalize in *Teoría de las Cortes* in 1813. But before sketching this constitutional country, he carefully delineated a series of points that were essential for correctly understanding his proposal. These points suggested a revision of some of the foundational myths of Spanish history itself. Showing no hesitation, Marina proposed a new reading of the obscure beginnings of the nation and its "antiquities", and in his second essay he turned to the status of language, or *romance*. In both cases, his contribution was one of deconstruction and clarification, and it was crucial for understanding some of the principal arguments underlying the political scene that emerged after the Cadiz revolution.

•••

The first of the two essays, *Antigüedades hispano-hebreas*, reflected new approaches to long-ago times, or *tiempos remotos*. It explored generic antiquities subject to intense debates emanating from a crisis in European consciousness in which the Bible came to assume a central role.[5] Biblical criticism gave way to what F. Laplanche has called the "rewriting of the Christian myth", a task that for a long time kept leading members of the Republic of Letters very busy and which inevitably pointed to basic contradictions between Biblical knowledge and the new science (contradictions concerning the first language,

4 The *Discurso crítico* was published in *Memorias de la Real Academia de la Historia*, vol. 3 (Madrid: Imprenta de Sancha, 1799), 317–468; the *Ensayo* was published in vol. 4 of the *Memorias* in 1805, 1–63. On the latter, see Emilio Ridruejo, "Los tratados de historia del español bajo el reinado de Carlos IV: las obras de Vargas Ponce y Martínez Marina", in José Bustos and José Luis Girón, eds., *Actas del VI Congreso Internacional de la Lengua Española* (Madrid: Arco, 2006), vol. 2, 825–37.

5 François Laplanche, *La Bible en France entre mythe et critique, XVIe-XIXe siècle* (Paris: Albin Michel, 1994), 33–48; Daniel Droixhe, "La crise de l'hebreu langue-mère au XVII siècle", in Chantal Grell and François Laplanche, eds., *La République des Lettres et l'histoire du judaisme antique, XVI-XVII siècles* (Paris: Sorbonne, 1992), 65–99; Paolo Rossi, *I segni del tempo* (Milan: Feltrinelli, 1979), ch. 2.

the origin of nations, sacred chronology, and geography). Marina was situated in the wake of that debate, only logical in accordance with the tradition of the Royal Academy of History, of which he was a member and director since 1796. The way in which he saw matters was in accordance with his *nacionista* perspective: antiquities should not be seen as merely Hispano-Hebrew but rather as "ours", as purely Hispanic. In fact, the presence of Jews in the far-distant Spanish past was just a "fairy tale" (*fábula pueril*) and therefore Jews could not be admitted as historical fellow travelers since the origin of time. Certainly, they could be "celebrated for their religion", but they were "contemptible for their backwardness and ignorance in commerce, arts and sciences". It was that polarity with modernity, and not their religion, that made them an insufferable "dark spot" (*lunar*) in "national history".[6]

Inspired by the same vivid "national love" that had moved leading scholars before him (for example Nicolás Antonio and the marquis of Mondéjar), Marina specified that the history of "our antiquities" was in need of considerable repair. Given that he was acting in the name of the "integrity" that must underlie "our national history", Marina suggested exposing the "tales" that Spaniards and foreigners had spread regarding antiquities which – aside from those of the Phoenecians, Trojans, Greeks, Assyrians, Chaldeans, Persians, Carthaginians, and Romans – now also included those of the Jews. Much of the responsibility for having made "darkness" so dense "in these times of intense enlightenment" lay with such "modern" writers as the Rodríguez Mohedano brothers and Francisco Masdeu.[7] Marina criticized them for having lent credibility to a history and texts such as the Spanish *Tarsis* that could only be regarded as "alleged and imaginary", especially considering that since the seventeenth century writers including the marquis of Mondéjar (*Cádiz Phenicia*, 1805) had expressed serious doubts in that regard.[8] He therefore rejected the

6 *Antigüedades*, 318–19. On the birth of that tradition, see F. Javier Perea Siller, "Esteban de Garibay y la hipótesis hebraico-nabucodonosoriana", *Estudios de Lingüística del Español*, 36 (2015), 178–95.

7 Rafael and Pedro Rodríguez Mohedano, *Historia literaria de España desde su primera población hasta nuestros días* (Madrid: Imp. Francisco Xavier García, 1766–91), 11 vols.; Francisco Masdeu, *Historia crítica de España y de la cultura española* (Madrid: Imp. Antonio Sancha, 1783–1805), 20 vols.

8 Gaspar Ibáñez de Segovia, marquis of Mondéjar, *Cádiz Phenicia, con el examen de varias noticias antiguas de España, que conservan los escritores Hebreos, Phenicos, Griegos, Romanos y Árabes* (Cadiz: Imp. Don José del Collado, 1805), 3 vols., with a complete list of the authors who had written earlier on the subject, probably drawn up at the end of the seventeenth century. On the author and the broader context see Pablo Fernández Albaladejo, "'Spanish Atlanteans': Crisis of Empire and Reconstruction of the Spanish Monarchy (1672–1740)", *Culture and History Digital Journal*, 4 (December 2015).

existence of "journeys and commerce with Spain" that Jews supposedly had been conducting "since the time of Solomon". In particular, by arguing that Tarsus and Ophir had been in Spain, where Solomon's fleets were bound, the Rodríguez Mohedano brothers in fact were misinterpreting the Holy Book itself.[9] One hundred years after experts such as Samuel Brochart and Pierre Daniel Huet had raised similar questions, Marina felt obliged to attack the surprising continuity of a state of affairs which, in the Spanish cultural realm, should long since have expired.[10]

It is quite true that there also were more traditional interpretations. Among them were *España en la Santa Biblia: Exposición historial de los textos tocantes a Españoles*, by Fray Pablo Yáñez de Avilés, a Cistercian who, when the book was published in 1733, held the post of royal chronicler. In his book, with its expressive title, Yáñez gave credence to the "names of Spain" in the Bible. According to him, there was no reason to deny the Jews' presence in Spain "before the spreading of the Gospel", and even less to think that their arrival had been "dishonorable for Spain".[11] Without referring specifically to the Cistercian's work and confining himself to the "healthiest of criticism", Marina pointed clearly to the Holy Book's silence regarding the "geographic location" of the places in question. The placement of Tarsis in Spain should rightly be considered a clear case of fantasy (*en el orden y catálogo de las fábulas.*) He had a similar view of the presence of patriotic artifacts such as the Hebrew inscriptions discovered in Murviedro (Sagunto), presented as unmistakable proof of "the truth of Solomon's empire in Spain". Simply by applying the "rules of criticism and good judgment" it was clear these inscriptions were "apocryphal" and the logical outcome of times in which "good philosophy and the rules of criticism"

9 On this tradition see M. Rosa Lida de Malkiel, "Túbal, primer poblador de España", *Ábaco: Estudios sobre Literatura Española*, 3 (1970), 11–37. The discovery of America made this geographic identification even more complicated, particularly in the case of Ophir: Juan Gil, *Mitos y utopías del descubrimiento* (Madrid: Alianza, 1980), 226–50; Giuliano Gliozzi, *Adamo e il Nuovo Mondo* (Florence: La Nuova Italia, 1977), 177–247. For a general view, Claudine Pouloin, *Le temps des origines* (Paris: Champion, 1998), 234–65.

10 Samuel Brochart, *Geographia Sacra* (1646), within the logic of "total geography" which attempted to "inscribe in the 'material reality' the 'reality' emanating from the Bible". Continuing in this line of thinking, Pierre Daniel Huet in 1698 wrote his *Commentarius de navigationibus Salomonis*, which in 1701 was followed by *Traité sur la situation du Paradis Terrestre*, and, in 1716, *Histoire du commerce et de la navigation des Anciens*. For more on the author and his works, see Pouloin, *Le temps*, 253–67, 314; and Laplanche, *La Bible en France*, 39.

11 Pablo Yáñez de Avilés, *España en la Santa Biblia: Exposición histórica de los textos tocantes a España* (Madrid: Imprenta de Juan Muñoz, 1733), part 1, ch. 9–10, for references to Tarsis and Ofir; see also 105, 180, and 185.

were ignored. According to Marina, it was precisely the reestablishment of "good taste and literature in Spain" that had allowed the marquis of Mondéjar to reject the fraudulent "ancient arrival of the Jews in Spain". This approach was where he wished to situate himself, convinced as he was that he was on a mission against "schemers" who undermined the "integrity and purity of our national history".[12]

Aside from clearing up the matter of the Jews' presence in Spain's past, Marina also turned to questions of historical methodology. He attacked close colleagues who, ignoring "rules of criticism", lent the tale continuity and credibility as a key element in the story of Spain's antiquities. It is likely that the fact that the Royal Academy in 1796 had republished *Disertación sobre si la Mitología es parte de la Historia y cómo deba entrar en ella* was not unrelated to his uneasiness.[13] The author of that work, Francisco Manuel de la Huerta (1697–1752), was a member of the Royal Academies of both Language and History, and from 1738 to 1740 had published *España Primitiva. Historia de sus reyes y monarcas desde su población hasta Christo*, which at the time drew devastating criticism from such outstanding figures as Gregorio Mayans and Martín de Sarmiento. Huerta's *Disertación* was hardly an audacious exploration of unknown territory. In fact it dealt with one of the key issues in the debate between the "moderns and the ancients" since 1680 regarding the possibility that myths and characters of fantasy might be used as testimony with which to build a narrative in accordance with the new historiographic epistemology's requirement of certainty.[14] Somewhat tracking the steps of the French Académie des Inscriptions et Belles-Lettres, the Spanish academy, by

12 Marina, *Antigüedades*, 320, 395, 405–18, with a detailed analysis of stylistic and linguistic contradictions. See also Gloria Mora, "Los estudios hebraicos en la España ilustrada: Francisco Pérez Bayer y el origen de las lenguas y escrituras en España", in *Estudios en Homenaje a L. García Iglesias* (Madrid: UAM, 2010), 425–54, esp. 446–7. Marina referred specifically to authors such as Benito Arias Montano and Esteban de Garibay, though he reserved most of his attention for Juan Román de la Higuera. See Mercedes García-Arenal and Francisco Rodríguez Mediano, *Un Oriente español. Los moriscos y el Sacromonte en tiempos de la Contrarreforma* (Madrid: Marcial Pons, 2010), 222–28; and Katrina B. Olds, *Forging the Past: Invented Histories in Counter-Reformation Spain* (New Haven: Yale University Press, 2015), ch. 4.

13 Francisco Manuel de la Huerta, *Disertación sobre si la Mitología es parte de la Historia, y como deba entrar en ella* (Madrid: Real Academia de la Historia, 1796), 1–42, a re-issue of the version published in *Fastos de la Real Academia Española de Historia* (Madrid, 1740), 63–195.

14 Carlo Borghero, *La certezza e la storia. Cartesianismo, pirronismo e conoscenza storica* (Milan: Franco Angeli, 1983), ch. 1–3.

publishing the *Disertación*, gave signs it wished to enter the debate and used Huerta as its introducer.

Huerta's *España primitiva* could be called, as Mayans did, *España imaginaria*, but Huerta's reputation as a fraud owing to his historiographic machinations should not blind us to other facets of his work, particularly the new possibilities in the history of origins. Displaying a militant strain of Euhemerism, his history of the Spanish "Atlántidos" who lived in "primitive Spain" uncovered an incomparable national family tree whose heroic deeds confirmed them as founders. Huerta thus was part of what Pierre Vidal-Nacquet has called "Atlantic nationalism", a strain of thought epitomized by Olaus Rudbeck's four-volume treatise, *Atlantica sive Manheim* (1679), which resolutely argued for European roots apart from the Greek inheritance.[15] Rudbeck's case in favor of Northeners coincided with the growing role of Eastern peoples, as described by Bochart in his *Geographia*, a strain of Orientalism that gave European culture Egyptian roots and attracted such erudite Spaniards as Tomás de León and Mondéjar himself, whose *Cádiz Phenicia* was a solid early example. Phoenicians were usually included in historiographic narratives, but their presence and role in the Iberian Peninsula was increasingly visible during the first half of the eighteenth century.[16]

Ancient history thus occupied a strategic place in the construction of a new narrative of identity. Huerta's *España*, as we said, was situated right at the crux, as was a work published in 1759 by Luis José Velázquez, marquis of Valdeflores, the *Anales de la nación española desde el tiempo más remoto hasta la entrada de los romanos*. Valdeflores was connected to the orbit around the marquis of Ensenada, who had risen to power in 1747. He himself was a member since 1752 of the Royal Academy of History, and he played an important role in Ensenada's and the Academy's project of cultural reconstruction. As a member of the academic commission overseeing recovery of the nation's historical

15 H. Laurena, "Orient et Origine", in *Primitivism et mythes des origines dans la France des Lumières, 1680–1720* (Paris: Sorbonne, 1989), 205–18; this book's introduction by Chantal Grell should also be consulted. On Atlántida, see Pierre Vidal-Nacquet, "L'Atlantide et les nations", *Représentations de l'origine, Cahiers CRLH-CIRAOI*, 4 (1987), 9–28; *Idem, L'Atlantide: Petite histoire d'un mythe platonicien* (Paris: Les Belles-Lettres, 2005); Gunnar Eriksson, *The Atlantic Vision: Olaus Rudbeck and Baroque Science* (Canton MA: Science History Publications, 1994).

16 Gonzalo Cruz Andreotti and Fernando Wulff Alonso, "Tartessos en la historiografía del XVIII al XIX: creación, muerte y resurrección de un pasado utópico", in José Beltrán and Fernando Gascó, eds., *La historiografía como argumento* (Seville: Scriptorium, 1993), 171–89. By the same authors, "Ancient History and Enlightenment: Two Spanish Histories of the Eighteenth Century", *Storia della Storiografia*, 23 (1993), 75–94.

legacy, Valdeflores was assigned the part concerning civil history, and he spent the next eighteen years working tiressly on it, finally producing *Noticia del viage a España* in 1765. In that work he outlined a plan for "a new general history of Spain" that would include "not just History itself but also proof", that is, "ancient foundational documents". As he wrote, this was "the first time that the History of Spain has been subject to analytical method and the philosophical spirit present in all sorts of writings". Here we can detect the tension present throughout the European Enlightenment between erudition and philosophy, and it is important to take account of these different premises.[17]

In accordance with the above, Valdeflores proposed a methodology that would systematize "all the smallest articles of the Nation's ancient History" according to branches (diplomacy, inscriptions, medals, painting, sculpture, architecture, furniture, civilian utensils, etc.). Each of these sections included the word "science", that is, "news and theory concerning the knowledge and use of [these documents]". Rather than base his reading of the remote past on literary evidence, Valdeflores proposed what we might call an archaeological perspective. His proposal was coherent with a European trend starting in the mid-seventeenth century, brilliantly explained by Arnaldo Momigliano, whose objective was to construct historical narratives with evidence "based on coins, inscriptions, and archaeological artifacts".[18] The use of non-literary proof became widely accepted as being among historians' tasks, to the point that documents, inscriptions, and coins were considered just as reliable, if not more so, than traditional literary evidence.[19]

Works such as *Ensayo sobre los alfabetos de las letras desconocidas que se encuentran en las más antiguas medallas y monumentos de España* (1752) and *Conjeturas sobre las medallas de los Reyes Suevos y Godos de España* (1759) illustrate the changes in how ancient history was now analyzed. Valdeflores showed

17 On Valdeflores, see Manuel Álvarez Martí-Aguilar, *La Antigüedad en la historiografía española del siglo XVIII: El Marqués de Valdeflores* (Málaga: Universidad de Málaga, 1996). The citations come from *Noticia del viage de España hecho de orden del Rey de una nueva historia general de la nación desde el tiempo más remoto hasta el año de 1516* (Madrid: Imp. Gabriel Ramírez, 1765), 29–30.

18 Arnaldo Momigliano, "Ancient History and the Antiquarian", *Journal of the Warburg and Courtland Institute*, 13 (1950), 293, 298, 304.

19 Within certain limits, of course. As Alain Schnapp has noted, the objective was to "reach history by a more direct path" and a more true path than that of texts, but always subject to philological rather than purely archeological interpretation: "Modèle naturaliste et modèle philologique dans l'archéologie européenne du XVI au XIX siècles", in Javier Arce and Ricardo Olmos, eds., *Historiografía de la arqueología y de la historia antigua en España* (Madrid: CSIC, 1991), 19–23.

the possibilities of the new methodology being used in certain French circles, and he himself was a correspondent of the Académie Royale des Inscriptions et Belles-Lettres. His *Anales de la Nación Española*, which aimed to reach the most remote times, clearly is distinct from *España*, by Huerta. Valdeflores was not hesitant to embrace mythology as a necessary formal framing device, nor did he reject Varron's chronology. But in establishing a timeline, Valdeflores looked to Newton's controversial proposal in *The Chronology of Ancient Kingdoms Amended* (1729), whose system he attempted to apply to ancient Spanish history.[20]

Starting in unknown times, ancient history was written in terms of the "Nation's origins". It was true that the Spanish nation suffered the same "vain efforts" of other nations to locate their "earliest origins in a far-off time", which to Valdeflores confirmed "human weakness" when people "abandon reason and philosophy".[21] Given that those times were "beyond memory, and there is no monument left of its things", the highly doubtful sources one might consult made it impossible to do the numbers. In any case, bowing to the need to establish a beginning, it was possible that Spaniards were descended from Tarshish, Noah's great-grandson, an option that challenged the long tradition of assigning Noah's grandson Tubal with this foundational role but, more important, gave a name to Spain's first inhabitants and established Tartessos as a "country" located on the "coast of Baetica". Tartessos was the key reference point at this civilizing moment. Not only did it incarnate the origin of the monarchy itself, it pointed to independence from the less ancient Greek culture. Following Newton's orientalism and chronology, Valdeflores proceeded to outline Spaniards' cultural genealogy separate from the Jews' influence, establishing its roots with the arrival of the prestigious civilization of the Phoenicians. As he himself said, the role of the Phoenician *curetes* was similar to that played by druids and bards in Celtic cultures, or the descendants of Salius in Italy. Thus, the peninsula gained a reference point for the Spanish nation on this new map of origins, just as Father Pezron was proposing for the Celts.[22]

20 Álvarez Marti-Aguilar, *La antigüedad*, 104; on the broader context see Chantal Grell, *Le Dix-huitième siècle et l'antiquité en France, 1680–1789* (Oxford: Voltaire Foundation, 1995), 809ff.

21 Rossi, *Segni del tempo*, 199–210, for a general view.

22 On Tartessos and Valdeflores see *ibid*; references from Valdeflores come from *Noticia*, 113, 119–20; on the Celts and Paul Pezron, see Grell, *Le Dix-huitième siècle*, 1119–23.

The Phoenician connection, which diminished interest in primary genealogy and the Bible, was the object of a series of works.[23] Inevitably, construction of the Phoenician narrative opened the doors to a reflection about the Carthaginian presence, also now seen with new assumptions. Carthage's protagonism was European and it formed part of the struggle for continental hegemony between French absolutism and British constitutionalism, the latter of which presented Carthage as an early republican and commercial model along the lines of the British Isles.[24] Allowing for differences, the 1756 edition of *Antigüedad marítima de la República de Cartago con el periplo de su General Hannon* by Campomanes tried to show the excellence of this model. This work, often referred to as the *memorias*, contained "many antiquities" linked to "Commerce and Navigation by primitive Spaniards", and these antiquities could be "the basis for the Maritime Empire fitting for Your Majesty's Crown". These were primitive peoples worthy of interest, for they lay at the origin of the subsequent "memorable undertakings and faraway discoveries" by the "Spanish Nation".[25]

Aside from this *nacionista* premise, publication of the book about Hanno's journey confirmed the consolidation of Orientalism in Spain in the second half of the eighteenth century, fomented by the Academies of both History and Language. One of the most outstanding members of the Academia de la Lengua, Francisco Pérez Bayer, undertook a study of Hebrew, convinced that the language contained the key to deciphering the writing on so-called "unknown" Spanish coins, "in other words, Iberian and Celtiberian".[26] Shortly beforehand, in a similar vein, Cándido María Trigueros wrote in his *Discurso persuadiendo el estudio de la lengua hebrea* (1773) that "those dark times in which our writers sold us fantasies about Tubal and Tarshish" had come to an end, and now, on the contrary, "our Spain" knew that its "earliest inhabitants

23 Alfredo Mederos Martín, "Los estudios fenicios en la España ilustrada", in Martín Almagro-Gorbea and Jorge Maier Allenda, eds., *De Pompeya al Nuevo Mundo. La Corona española y la arqueología en el siglo XVIII* (Madrid: Real Academia Española, 2012), 15–33.

24 Edmond Dziembowsky, *Un nouveau patriotism français, 1750–1770: La France face à la puissance anglaise à l'époque de la Guerre des Sept Ans* (Oxford: Voltaire Foundation, 1998), 182–91, 238–47.

25 Pedro Rodríguez de Campomanes, *Antigüedad marítima de la República de Cartago, con el periplo de su General Hannon, traducido del griego e ilustrado* (Madrid: Imp. Antonio Pérez de Soto, 1756), especially prologue and introduction; also Martín Almagro Gorbea, "Pedro Rodríguez Campomanes y las 'antigüedades'", in *Campomanes en su segundo centenario* (Madrid: Real Academia de la Historia, 2003), 117–59.

26 Mora, *Estudios hebraicos*, 440–7; Jorge Eiroa Rodríguez, "Las antigüedades hebreas en el siglo XVIII", in *De Pompeya al Nuevo Mundo*, 245–53.

were either the Celts by land or the Phoenicians or Carthaginians by sea". Furthermore, "our primitive memories" could be reduced to the languages of the latter two peoples, knowledge of which could be attained only through Hebrew.[27] There was an even more radical proposal, formulated most strongly by the Jesuit Esteban Terreros in the prologue to his *Diccionario* of 1786, where he argued that regardless of what Spain's primitive language was, and whether it came with Tubal or with Tarshish, the passage of foreign nations through the peninsula had ended up creating a 'lingua franca', a "jumbled language" with many roots, so that the resulting "mixture of words" gave way to a rich language that contained the words "of sciences and the liberal mechanical arts".[28]

•••

Pérez Bayer himself did not conceal his optimism regarding the new directions opened up by the discussion on origins, particularly with regard to matters that could be researched immediately. As he himself said in 1781, his interest in monetary affairs was simply a way of better understanding "our primitive literature and population". He participated in Enlightenment debates regarding the origins of language, and finally ended up endorsing Martínez Marina's *Ensayo* on the Castillian *romance* mentioned at the start of this essay. In 1710, Leibniz, in his *Brevis designatio meditationum de originibus gentium ductis potissimum ex indicio linguarum*, pointed to languages as true documents of antiquity that allowed for investigations of peoples' remote origins.[29] However Nicolas Fréret must get credit for having seen that the history of languages was an essential tool for rewriting the universal history of origins. In the 1740s, his *Vues générales sur l'origine & mélange des anciennes nations* summed up his research on the peoples of India and Italy, on the Cimmerians, Greeks, and ancient Gauls. His principal contribution concerned the heuristic status of language in establishing the origins of a nation: "la connaissance du langage que parloit une nation nous conduit à celle de son origine & du pays où elle a dû

---

27 See Francisco Aguilar Piñal, *El académico Cándido María Trigueros (1736–1798)* (Madrid: Real Academia de la Historia, 2001), 85.

28 E. Herreros y Pando, *Diccionario castellano con las voces de Ciencias y Artes y sus correspondientes en las tres lenguas, Francesa, Latina e Italiana* (Madrid: Viuda de Ibarra, 1786–93), 4 vols. The citations are from the prologue, i-v.

29 Daniel Droixhe, *La linguistique et l'appel de l'histoire (1600–1800): Rationalisme et révolutions positivistes* (Geneva: Droz, 1978), 126–42; Raffaele Simone, "Seicento e Settecento", in Giulio Lepschy, ed., *Storia della linguistica* (Bologna: Il Mulino, 1990), vol. 2, 350–55.

sortir d'abord".[30] Fréret's notion of interaction between language and nation was a precursor of a debate centered on the origins of language that, as is well known, would attract some of the best minds of the second half of the eighteenth century, including Condillac, Momboddo, Turgot, Rousseau, and even Lorenzo Hervás y Panduro. Thus, to quote Mercier-Faivre, there was a break with the past, which had "mixed languages and nations in one sole origination myth bound to Biblical tradition". The definition of nation "was no longer tied to divine right or mythical genealogies but rather was based on observable facts and history". In this way, a synchronic and comparative approach won out, strengthening the concept of nation and, in the end, defining language, which, in turn, would acquire a higher role.[31]

The debate around "primitive language" had been developing in Spain at least since the early seventeenth century, as evidenced by the exchanges between Gregorio López Madera and Bernardo de Aldrete.[32] The decline of the monarchy throughout the seventeenth century brought about reflections that included language as an example of the corruption supposedly brought about by Baroque excess. The new dynasty, with its own narrative to distinguish itself from the Habsburgs, embraced the notion of regenerating language. Indeed, this was the context in which the Real Academia Española was established in 1713 in order to combat "the errors that have sullied the Spanish language with the introduction of many unsuitable and barbaric words", "novelties" that had gravely damaged the "Nation's reputation and glory". The Bourbons thus acquired a certain cultural legitimacy that allowed them to present themselves as effective restorers of the nation through language, following guidelines

---

30 On Fréret, who died in 1749, see Chantal Grell and Catherine Volpilhac-Auger, eds., *Nicolas Fréret, légende et verité. Colloque 1991* (Oxford: Voltaire Foundation, 1994), esp. the article by Grell, "Nicolas Fréret, la critique et l'histoire ancienne", 51–73. The citation is from p. 70. See also, by the same author, *L'Histoire entre érudition et philosophie* (Paris: PUF, 1993), 84–92.

31 Anne-Marie Mercier-Faive, "La nation par la langue: philologie, nationalisme et nation dans l'Europe du dix-huitième siècle", in Michael O'Dea and Kevin Whelan, eds., *Nations and Nationalisms: France, Britain, Ireland and the Eighteenth-Century Context* (Oxford: Voltaire Foundation, 1995), 164, 169–70.

32 This debate was based on assumptions that had nothing to do with Fréret's. On the two positions see Kathrin Woolard, "Is the Past a Foreign Country? Time, Language Origins, and the Nation in Early Modern Spain", *Journal of Linguistic Anthropology* 14 (2004), 57–80; Vicente Lledó-Guillem, "¿Compañera o rebelde? La lengua y el imperio según Bernardo de Aldrete", *Bulletin of Hispanic Studies*, 87 (2010), 1–16; Lucia Binotti, "Historicizing Language, Imagining People: Aldrete and Linguistic Politics", in *Cultural Capital, Language and National Identity in Imperial Spain* (Woodbridge: Tamesis, 2012), 149–72.

from the king's home country. But that was a far cry from announcing linguistic sovereignty in order to establish complete control over a well-established language that was allegedly unique.[33] In part, as Lázaro Carreter pointed out, this was because the Academy itself "did not have a correct opinion on the origins of language".[34] The way in which "Spanish" and "Castilian" were used interchangeably in the dictionary was evidence of this indeterminacy and worked to contradict the alleged exclusivity of the former term. The preliminaries of the *Diccionario* stated that, given how the Castilian language was formed, it was but an "aggregate or accumulation of words" that had grown out of the peninsula's medieval linguistic intermarriages (*mestizaje*), a way of saying that Castilian did not exclude the presence of words from other provincial dialects.[35] In any case, and speaking generally, *castellano* meant "Spanish from Spain". Rising above provincial diversity, a memory of nation enabled the construction of language.[36]

Gregorio Mayans's crucial work, *Orígenes de la lengua española* (1737), part of a larger plan to reform "Spanish letters", was an early response to these issues. He accepted Aldrete's proposal, and the erudite Valencian critic also rejected the possibility of just one primitive language in Spain, considering that *castellano* was the result of the *dominaciones* that had affected the peninsula. His belief that "there are as many languages as there are *dominaciones*" required him to adopt the historian's presentist stance; in studying a living language, he said, "we must understand the people as they are today, not how they were".[37] Such a dangerous proposal was quickly attacked by the *Diario de los Literatos de España*, which countered that "seeking the origins of a language in a nation's civil body is the most sensible anatomy … that can be performed

33 On these connections see Pablo Fernández Albaladejo, "*Fénix de España*. Decadencia e identidad en la transición al siglo XVIII", in his *Materia de España*, 125–47. See also Mª José García-Folgado, "Motivaciones para el estudio de la gramática española en el siglo XVIII", *Analecta Malacitana*, 1 (2004), 91–116. For a point of view contrary to the general tendency, see Hélène Merlin on the French case: "Langue et souveraineté en France au XVII siècle: La production autonome d'un corps de language", *Annales, ESC* (1994), 369–94.

34 Fernando Lázaro Carreter, *Crónica del Diccionario de Autoridades (1713–1740)* (Madrid: Real Academia Española, 1972), 25; my thoughts on the matter are drawn from this work.

35 This echoed Aldrete's proposals and later on would inspire Terreros's introduction to the *Diccionario*.

36 The *Diccionario* (1734) defined *lengua* as "a collection of sounds and terms, voluntarily chosen, with which each Nation explains its concepts".

37 Gregorio Mayans y Siscar, "Orígenes de la lengua española", in his *Obras completas*, ed. Antonio Mestre (Oliva: Ayuntamiento de Oliva, 1984), vol. 2, 313–419; see also in that volume the prologue by J. Siles.

in the theater of history".[38] This reply was written by Martínez Salafranca, a member of the Academy, showing that regardless of personal opinions, there was a growing tension between the Academy and Mayans, who had made clear his considerable doubts about the *Diccionario*. The conflict spilled over into other arenas as well.[39]

The conflict indicated how important grammar had become.[40] The situation was similar in Portugal. Luis Antonio Verney around this time overcame a series of problems to publish *Verdadeiro método de estudar para ser útil à República e à Igreja*, a denunciation of traditional Jesuit teaching methods, saying "any Grammar of a language that is not national" should be "explained in the language that one knows".[41] The Spanish edition of Verney's book, published in 1760, attempted to consolidate that viewpoint. One supporter was Fray Benito de San Pedro, whose *Arte del romance castellano* (1769) stated that "the basis for the revival of all arts, letters and sciences is the cultivation of one's own language". With the assumption that contemporary grammar manuals were "defective in their rules and observations and especially in their general principles", San Pedro aimed at "tying [language] to rules".[42] While not ignoring his debt to Mayans, the author clearly embraced the assumptions of rationalist grammarians, making clear, as M. Lliteras has said, the proper correspondence "between logical categories and grammatical categories" such that "all good

38 Mayans, "Conversación sobre el *Diario de los Literatos de España*", *ibidem*, 421–83, esp. 427; Jesús Miguel Ruiz Veintemilla, "La polémica entre Don Gregorio Mayans y el *Diario de los Literatos de España*", *Revista de Literatura*, 1 (1979), 69–130.

39 Summarized in José Luis Valls Toimil, "Una polémica gramatical del siglo XVIII", in Jesús Antonio Bartol, Juan Felipe García Santos and Javier De Santiago Cuervós, eds., *Estudios filológicos en homenaje a Eugenio Bustos Tovar* (Salamanca: Universidad de Salamanca, 1992), vol. 2, 925–40; Fernando Lázaro Carreter, *Las ideologías lingüísticas en España durante el siglo XVIII* (Barcelona: Crítica, 1983), 191–2; Mª José Martínez Alcalde, "Mayans y la gramática española del siglo XVIII", in Antonio Mestre, ed., *Actas del Congreso Internacional sobre Gregorio Mayans* (Oliva: Ayuntamiento de Oliva, 1999), 329–45.

40 Mª José Martínez Alcalde, "El retorno de la gramática: Los textos de 1743 (Benito Martínez Gómez Gayoso) y 1769 (Benito de San Pedro)", in José Jesús Gómez Asencio, ed., *El castellano y su codificación gramatical* (Burgos: Instituto Castellano y Leonés de la Lengua, 2011), vol. 3, 159–93; Mª José García Folgado, "La gramática a finales del siglo XVIII (1769–1800). Objetivos y fuentes", in *Nuevas aportaciones a la historiografía lingüística. Actas del IV Congreso Internacional de la SEHL* (Madrid: Arco Libros, 2004), vol. 1, 561–72.

41 The Verney quote in García Folgado, *Motivaciones*, 106–7; Elena Gallego Moya, "La enseñanza del latín en el *Verdadero método de estudiar* de Verney", in Esteban Calderón, Alicia Morales and Mariano Valverde, eds., *Koinòs Lógos. Homenaje al profesor José García López* (Murcia: Universidad de Murcia, 2006), 237–46.

42 Prologue, *Arte del romance castellano dispuesta según sus principios generales i el uso de los mejores autores* (Valencia: Imprenta Benito Monfort, 1769), vol. 1.

Spaniards know their language by principle and by reason".[43] Essential as this was, knowledge of language "with reason and science" had to coexist with language according to "speech and use", a balance that constituted a sort of "symmetry of reasoning". It was therefore necessary to diligently read the "works of good Authors". In fact, the ability to become "a good *Romancista*" depended on a tacit circularity between the two approaches: "No reading [*lección*] of good Spanish books without Art, nor Art without the reading of Spanish books". The books in question involved *lección* but also *elección*, the choosing of a space of time that was deliberately set apart and stable. There was no doubt that the sixteenth century had marked the time of "greatness and perfection of our language", the period when there was a cast of writers worthy of constituting the nation's canon, the canon for a nation defined by its language. Recognizing the essential influence that the "extension of empire" had had in this regard, Fray Benito emphasized that his grammatical "method" was of strict "utility to the Nation". In the last analysis, languages had always followed the "condition of peoples", and the splendor of language reflected "the nation's original genius". Patriotic projection of this assumption fed political interests themselves: everyone knew "how important it was to the State to develop patriotism in its citizens", with the culture of language being "one of the most powerful means" to that end.

The Piarist's linguistic-national emphasis coincided to a large degree with the monarchy's efforts since the 1760s, though the latter were more coercive. They included primary literacy, Latin, and rhetoric in Castilian, along with requirements that instructors be "carefully observant and diligent in extending the Nation's general language".[44] One needs to see the priority given to the Castilian language in its proper terms. One after another, laws and orders made clear the effort to broaden Castilian's place in the curriculum, even within a cultural system that was predicated on Latin and Jesuit education up to the time of the order's expulsion. Mayans's university reform plan of 1767 combined support for the vernacular with a defense of classic Latin.[45] Twenty years later, grammarian Juan Pablo Ballot said that "knowledge of a nation's own language beyond speaking it purely and correctly" was merely the first step toward learning Latin, which at that time was still the international language

43 Margarita Lliteras, "Benito de San Pedro frente a la tradición nebrisense", *Bulletin Hispanique* 94 (1992), 506–27.

44 Real Cédula, 23 June 1768 (from García Folgado, *Motivaciones*, 97).

45 Martínez Alcalde, *Mayans y la gramática*, 343–45.

in arts and sciences.[46] Official introduction of Castilian in schools would not take place until 1813, and even then there were a few regressions.[47]

The 1771 publication of the *Gramática de la lengua castellana compuesta por la Real Academia Española* made the new orientations official.[48] Shifting the focus away from the *Diccionario*, thirty years after *Orthographia Española*, the *Gramática* inaugurated the codification of Castilian and would go through four editions by 1796. It proposed an "art of speaking well" whose rules were acquired through "observation of speech" that deemed itself self-referential and canonical. The assumption was of permanent interaction between language and the current use of language. Linguists of the Enlightenment debated the roles of linguistic theory and the practice of language, a conflict that was finally settled through negotiation. Enlightenment thinkers drawing up rationalist grammar books were less interested in establishing a "grammatical code" than in "defining language use" in line with the practices of the best writers.[49] Therefore usage as "owner and arbitrator" was the underlying assumption of the Academia, which stated that it was allying itself with the criteria of "celebrated modern grammarians".[50]

As can be seen in the works of Mayans and Valdeflores, it was increasingly believed necessary to establish a canon of authors. The Academy had been conducting lexical cleansing as a reaction to Baroque excess, but contrary to what was happening in France, it was difficult to revive authority figures about whom little was remembered.[51] Neoclassicism in part filled the gap, though at the price of *casticismo*, or exaggerated authenticity. The search for and use of archaicisms by practicioners of *casticismo* became the central point of the debate during the last third of the eighteenth century and the first half of the nineteenth century, as a result of which *purismo* was seen as a "negative facet".[52]

---

46 García Folgado, *Motivaciones*, 108–109.

47 On the regressions, see J. Gutiérrez Cuadrado, "La sustitución del latín por el romance en la universidad española del siglo XIX", *Universidades españolas y americanas: Época colonial* (Valencia: CSIC, 1987), 237–52; García Folgado, *Motivaciones*, 103–14.

48 See Ramón Sarmiento's introduction to the facsimile edition of the *Gramática* (Madrid: Editorial Nacional, 1984), 19–23; Félix San Vicente Santiago, "Filología", in Francisco Aguilar Piñal, ed., *Historia literaria de España en el siglo XVIII* (Madrid: Trotta, 1996), 593–669, esp. 606–11.

49 Georges Gusdorf, *Les sciences humaines au siècle des Lumières* (Paris: Payot, 1973), 319–28.

50 Sarmiento, introduction to *Gramática*, 39–45.

51 Gusdorf, *Les science humaines*, 318–28.

52 Lázaro Carreter, *Ideologías lingüísticas*, 255–90, esp. 234–37. For an analysis of the phenomenon in the nineteenth century, see Fernando Durán López, who distinguishes between *arcaísmo neologista*, as innovative, and *arcaísmo casticista*, which was purist and

The tendency was noticeable within the Academy, which Martínez Marina's *Ensayo Histórico-Crítico* made clear. Many of its arguments were aimed at rebutting José de Vargas Ponce's *Declamación contra los abusos introducidos en el castellano*, a report presented to the Academia de la Lengua in 1790 and published anonymously in 1793; the book's cover indicated it had been "presented but not given a prize". Marina referred to him as the "anonymous author" of the *Declamación*, but it is difficult to imagine that the Academy's director did not recognize the writer who, the same year the competition was announced (1791), himself had been appointed as a new member of the Academy. Vargas Ponce's *Declamación*, a manifesto of *casticista* archaicism, received a sharp review by Juan Pablo Forner, who in a 1795 pamphlet accused Vargas of plagiarism and also criticized his use of antiquated style and language.[53]

Marina's *Ensayo* did not get overly involved in the battles between neoclassicists and purists. His objections were more methodological and historiographic than literary. He was concerned that the rise of *casticismo* might send us back to Babel, an option he made very clear he was not considering. It is significant that his work regarded "the noble and excellent faculty of speech" to be "a prerogative and gift of men", showing that the Creator (*Criador*) had placed men above animals. This was a "machine … as simple in its principles [as it was] complex in its effects". It raised a host of questions: What does it mean that men speak? How were languages formed? How have they changed and divided, and why do they become more perfect or more corrupt? It was essential to find answers to these questions in order to opine about "the formation, alteration, and perfection" of our language, that is, of Castilian. Condillac and Rousseau were Marina's principal reference points, and he recognized his differences with Condillac's "system" which, though it had been "accepted by the most celebrated psychologists" (*psicologistas*), seemed to him to be "completely incomprehensible".

Marina made no secret of his preference for Rousseau, favoring "consent in common" over "the mechanical formation of languages". The faculty of speech, far from being a "gift of nature", was "a talent or art acquired just like all the rest". The key to the process was education. It was impossible to imagine "a more excellent theory of language", in Marina's view. It was a theory that made

---

nacionalist: "Arcaísmo, casticismo y lengua literaria: alrededores de algunas cuitas de José de Vargas Ponce y sus contemporáneos", in Victoriano Gaviño and Fernando Durán, eds., *Gramática, canon e historia literaria (1750 y 1850)* (Madrid: Visor, 2010), 117–80, esp. 118.

53 Besides the work by Durán López already cited, see his introduction to the *Obras escogidas* of José de Vargas Ponce (Seville: Fundación Manuel Lara, 2012), lx-lxxxi, esp. lxx, for the points referenced here.

nonsense of those who rejected this conclusion and instead investigated this "rare phenomenon of the origin of languages". Given that it was impossible to recognize the "nature and circumstances" of that primitive language, it was necessary to look at things from another angle, and it helped to keep in mind that humans, "by nature of their constitution, liberty, organization, and perfectibility" were able to receive, rectify, or forget "different ideas".[54] This was the beginning of the transformation of primitive language and the later formation of dialects. Similarly to Valdeflores, Marina's "more philosophical spirit" won out over those who continued down paths of "forced and capricious erudition".[55]

Beyond the private sphere, human beings' indivisible social condition and their capacity to create relationships had necessarily shaped the dynamic of changes in languages. Progress in the arts and sciences, political revolutions, and their growing interrelationships with industry and commerce made it clear that "languages cannot be enriched except through the intelligible exchange of ideas and thoughts". The richest languages of the universe were but "traces and relics of others that were older, unknown and forgotten … rivers that have swelled with brooks and streams". That was why the "Roman language" had grown, and the same was true of "our Castillian". Those were the points one must keep in mind when asking which language might have been spoken by "ancient Spaniards in the fabulous times of our history". "Research" by "our men of letters" about the period before the arrival of the Carthaginians and Romans added up to nothing but a "*fábula*". Simply by applying "the principles of good philosophy" one could assume at most that this was a "poor, miserable, and very limited" language. Thus, those who lived in a state similar "to that of the Antilles and other newly discovered countries" eagerly accepted the sciences, arts, customs, and ideas of "virtue, law, and sociability" of the "Roman conquerors", to the point that "the language of Latium became universal, unique, and invariable in the peninsula" and Spaniards "became Romans".[56]

Marina thus was openly opposed to the "anonymous author" of the *Declamación* and the latter's defense of an ancient "national language" prior to the Roman era whose traces could be found in "the use of certain words native to the country". Such a possibility was in no instance backed up by a single monument or inscription. On the contrary, everything pointed to the fact that "the common language of the nation, of both the wise and the commoners, was the Latin language". The academician, along the lines of Nebrija,

54 *Ensayo*, 10.

55 On this critical debate between philosophy and erudition, see Grell, *L'histoire*, 19–52.

56 *Ibidem*, 11–3.

argued that the fate of languages was linked to that of the arts and sciences, which were, in turn, linked to the fate of empires. Therefore "the arrival of barbarians from the north" put an end to Latin's purity and beauty, though this had to be finessed somewhat with regard to the peninsula. In contrast to Aldrete's notion of a general corruption of Latin, Marina posited its continuity on the peninsula as a result of the invaders having earlier been contaminated by the Romans, a solution corroborated by an endless number of "monuments" and the language of the Visigothic "legislative corpus". "Barbarisms" and "alterations" that might have appeared thus were unable to corrupt "our ancient language". That was not the case with the Arab invasion, "the most extraordinary, rapid and violent revolution that had ever been seen". The Latin language quickly collapsed, to the point that in the mid-ninth century it was considered gone.[57]

Obviously, the complete version of these events involved not losing sight of the "small numbers of independent Spaniards" who opted to defend themselves "in the harsh Asturian mountains". One could credit them with having slowly altered their "ancient language" as they laid the foundations of "a new monarchy". *Roman*, or castellano, was gestated in this context, in which "ignorance, negligence, and carelessness" in the cultivation of Latin was accompanied by political developments that undermined recognition of "just one legislative code and just one scepter". Such particularism led to an endless series of "domestic and civil wars" that in the early thirteenth century made the language of Latium entirely unrecognizable. Along the way language had been solidified "without artifice and entirely independent of the rules of grammar", with a "simple order" akin to the "naturalness" of Oriental languages and increasingly distant from the mother tongue. The reign of Alfonso VI in the mid-eleventh century and the conquest of Toledo, the "center of Spain", allowed for "one sole dominion" and promoted "the common happiness of the nation".

Echoes of "such a serious and sacred undertaking" reached foreign lands and inspired the arrival of Gascons, Franks, and Germans drawn by welcoming conditions.[58] But the visible tracks of that influence were far fainter than those left by the Arabic language of the Muslims, "the most erudite and cultured [nation] in the world in the twelfth and thirteenth centuries", and their linkages "both moral and political" with Spaniards were evidence of their greater reach and penetration. Though to differing degrees, Latin and Arabic formed the foundation of its splendor. For Marina, the Castilian romance as it

57 *Ibidem*, 5–18.
58 *Ibidem*, 22, 34.

appeared in the early thirteenth century had risen "upon the ruins of the Latin language", though "enriched with loans and numerous gifts from the abundant Arabic". The "wealth" of the Spanish language, Marina insisted, its "genius, constitution, grammar, syntax, elements, and words" were owed proportionately to these two languages: three-quarters Latin and the rest Arabic. There were no other debts.

Arguments by José de Vargas Ponce and other *casticistas* in favor of Punic, Celtic, and Gothic words made no sense. With a few exceptions, most of those words came from Latin or Arabic. Throughout the thirteenth century, Ferdinand III and Alfonso X continued and completed the process. Alfonso "made his name and the Castilian language eternal with the code of law" (the *Partidas*).[59] Extending his argument in his favored direction, Marina went on to magnify the importance of "political revolutions at the end of the fifteenth century that continued no less successfully in the sixteenth". These political changes were accompanied by equally important transformations in technology, commerce, and geography, as a result of which "the majesty of the Spanish nation reached the apex of its prosperity". This was also when both the name of Castile and its language "occupied the entire globe".[60]

Though it had been enriched "with words and signs of ideas heretofore unknown", efforts by "learned Spaniards" to make the language reach "the peak of perfection" were still required. His fascination with Greece and Rome led him to regard *romancistas*, men such as Ambrosio de Morales and Fray Luis de León, who had never regarded the Spanish language as inferior to *ático* or *romano*, "with a certain disdain". It was the efforts of such distinguished writers that finally pushed him to "perfection", a key term for him.[61]

Martínez Marina thus formalized a point of inflexion whose importance we must take note of. His deep cultural roots in the Enlightenment metalanguage of nature excluded any option of Babelic dreams concerning a language of their own. And that language had demonstrated its ability to play a straightforward, self-referential role in any regenerative process; in other words, to become its own phoenix. Moving forward with this approach did not depend solely on the internal force of language. Nebrija's words once again were invoked: given the "essential and unbreakable [union] … between the prosperity of states and that of arts, sciences, and languages", success necessarily involved many parts arranged into a precise hierarchy. Languages indeed had been companions of

---

59 *Ibidem*, 37–40, 44–52.

60 *Ibidem*, 54–5.

61 *Ibidem*, 57–8.

empire, and that was the role corresponding to the "national language" as the monarchy attempted to rebuild the foundations of its traditional power. In the linguistic sphere, the operation was finished. A century after the arrival of the "august Philip of Bourbon", the Real Academia Española, that "body of select wise men", had fulfilled the task assigned to it: "Its grammar and spelling established forever [the rules of] writing, pronunciation, order, and syntax"; and "its great dictionary raised an eternal monument to the Spanish language". Inspired by national "genius", the codification of the language, which was tantamount to a kind of *constitution*, had happily been put in place. Martínez Marina's usual designation as a political mythmaker of nation should not blind us to the importance of this earlier undertaking; with *Ensayo sobre el romance*, he made it possible for the subject *nación* not only to constitute a language but also to constitute its own political order.

Bibliography

Primary Sources

Huerta, Francisco Manuel de la, *Disertación sobre si la Mitología es parte de la Historia, y como deba entrar en ella* (Madrid: Real Academia de la Historia, 1796), 1–42.

Martínez Marina, Francisco, "Antigüedades hispano-hebreas convencidas de supuestas y fabulosas: Discurso histórico-crítico sobre la primera venida de los judíos a España", *Memorias de la Real Academia de la Historia*, 3 (1799), 317–468.

Martínez Marina, Francisco, "Ensayo histórico-crítico sobre el origen y progreso de las lenguas, señaladamente del romance castellano", *Memorias de la Real Academia de la Historia*, 4 (1805), 1–63.

Mayans y Siscar, Gregorio, "Orígenes de la lengua española", *Obras completas*, ed. Antonio Mestre (Oliva: Ayuntamiento de Oliva, 1984), vol. 2, 313–419.

Rodríguez de Campomanes, Pedro, *Antigüedad marítima de la República de Cartago, con el periplo de su General Hannon, traducido del griego e ilustrado* (Madrid: Imp. Antonio Pérez de Soto, 1756).

Main Bibliographical References

Fernández Albaladejo, Pablo, *Materia de España: Cultura política e identidad en la España Moderna* (Madrid: Marcial Pons, 2007).

Laurena, H., "Orient et Origine", in *Primitivism et mythes des origines dans la France des Lumières, 1680–1720* (Paris: Sorbonne, 1989).

Lázaro Carreter, Fernando, *Las ideologías lingüísticas en España durante el siglo XVIII* (Barcelona: Crítica, 1983).

Tomás y Valiente, Francisco, *Martínez Marina, historiador del Derecho* (Madrid: Real Academia de la Historia, 1991).

Westler, Brendon, "Between Tradition and Revolution: The Curious Case of Francisco Martínez Marina, the Cadiz Constitution, and Spanish Liberalism", *Journal of the History of Ideas*, 76 (2015), 394–416.

CHAPTER 16

The Metamorphoses of a Historical Constitution

Longue durée *Developments in Nineteenth-Century Hungarian Constitutional and Political Thought*

Ferenc Hörcher and Thomas Lorman

1 Overview of the "Long Nineteenth Century" in Hungary

The long-standing claim that Hungary possesses a historical constitution (*ősi/történeti alkotmány*) is an ill-defined and contested assertion but, at its core, reveals that the concept of the historical constitution was also remarkably adaptable and influential. This article will concentrate on the politically and theoretically most important period in the development of this concept, the "long nineteenth century" from 1790–1918.[1] This was the period when pressure groups, both political and intellectual and mobilized by the key movements of the age, revolutionary, liberal and/or national, sought to radically transform, or even completely discard, Hungary's legal framework. In contrast, many leading statesmen, and the majority of the legal profession were confident that Hungary possessed a long-established constitution which preserved the distinctiveness of their kingdom and could easily be made to conform with the need for reform without abandoning its character and its essence. This clash between those who sought to preserve the historic constitution, if necessary, by means of reform, and those who sought to overthrow the constitution, if necessary, by means of revolution, shaped not only Hungary's constitutional debates but also her wider political debates throughout the period.

The first half of the story – from 1790 to 1848– took place within the "ancien regime" and was determined by the exchange between the Habsburg court (the crown) and the representatives of the country (the *ország*) in the chambers of the ancient Diet in Pozsony (Bratislava). Reformist challenges first emerged after the death of Joseph II in 1790, when – on the basis of their reading of

1 For the use of the term, see György Bebesi, ed., *A hosszú 19. század rövid története* (Pécs, 2013) and Miklós Lojkó, ed., *Hungary's Long Nineteenth Century: Constitutional and Democratic Traditions in a European Perspective. Collected Studies by László Péter* (Lieden and Boston: Brill, 2012) (hereafter, Lojkó, ed., *Hungary's Long Nineteenth Century: Collected Studies by László Péter*).

 | DOI:10.1163/9789004549159_018

Montesquieu – Hungarians suddenly realised that they also possessed a constitution, comprised of laws and customs which had developed over almost a millennium.[2] In the shadow of the French Revolution they tried to rebuild this ancient edifice, inspired by the new ideas flowing out from Paris (and to a lesser extent by the American and Polish constitutions). This reform movement of the 1790s was, however, brutally crushed by the crown, which, fearful of revolution, opposed all constitutional efforts that threatened its grip on power. Nevertheless, a second wave of Hungarian reformers had greater success. Between 1825 and 1848, they included among their demands the restoration of constitutional governance and the fulfilment of nationalist aspirations, such as the establishment of a genuinely autonomous Hungarian government and a European model of parliamentary representation. They also called for the wider reorganisation of society, including the abolishment of serfdom, the end of tax privileges for the nobility and the relaxation of censorship.

These measures were finally enacted with the April Laws of 1848, which were pushed through the constitutional machinery by the charismatic leader of the opposition, Lajos Kossuth, and were made possible by the backdrop of revolutionary outbreaks and constitution-making across Europe. Remarkably, the Hungarian lawmakers in 1848 did not intend to destroy the historical constitution, or to introduce a charter constitution according to the fashionable bourgeois-liberal and nationalist thinking of the time. Instead, they carried out these reforms in strict accordance with their understanding of the constitution by, for example, insisting that both houses of the Hungarian Diet and the Habsburg emperor had to endorse what István Deák has called a "lawful revolution".[3] Some reformers, however, wanted to go even further. Provoked by the revolt of Count Josip Jelačić von Bužim, who challenged the Hungarian government's authority with the support of the imperial court, Kossuth proclaimed Hungary's independence in Debrecen in April 1849. As a reaction to this transgression of the legal framework the new emperor, Francis Joseph, in accordance with the earlier agreement of the Holy Alliance, invited the Russian tsar to help him restore Habsburg rule by force, and the Hungarian army surrendered in August 1849.

Although many of the reforms enacted in 1848 remained in force, from 1849 there followed a decade of direct and initially brutal rule by Vienna. Much of Hungary's elite was, however, unwilling to accept this suspension of their

2 László Péter, "Montesquieu's Paradox on Freedom and Hungary's Constitution, 1790–1990", in Lojkó, ed., *Hungary's Long Nineteenth Century: Collected Studies by László Péter*, 153–82.

3 István Deák, *The Lawful Revolution: Louis Kossuth and the Hungarians, 1848–1849* (New York and London: Columbia University Press, 1979).

historical constitution and refused to cooperate with the crown. Their demand for another restoration of constitutional governance was bolstered by the changes of fortune in international affairs following the defeat of the Habsburg armies in 1859 by Sardinia and France and in 1866 by Prussia. The early eighteen-sixties witnessed, therefore, first unofficial, then official talks between the two partners, which led to what is best described as the Settlement ("kiegyezés" and German "Ausgleich"), of 1867, and the transformation of the centralized Habsburg empire into the decentralized Austro-Hungarian Dual Monarchy.

Heated debates over the legitimacy of this reformed constitutional framework, and its scope for further modification, continued throughout the second half of the nineteenth century both between the political parties in Hungary, and between Vienna and the Hungarian Parliament. Nevertheless, although plans for a radical break with the historical constitution were drawn up – including the exiled Kossuth's utopian vision of a Danube Confederation – the period between 1867 and 1918 was characterised by both rapid societal changes and constitutional stability. Catastrophic defeat in the First World War, as well as surging nationalist agitation, and political incompetence, led directly to the dissolution of the Dual Monarchy and the dismemberment of Hungary in 1918–1919, which was then endorsed by the victorious Great Powers with the Treaty of Trianon in 1920. Notably, however, while both the country's territory and the population were severely reduced in size, the constitutional arrangements which had been established by 1867 survived in certain respects the dissolution of the Habsburg empire and remained in force until 1944.[4]

This summary of the main outlines of constitutional developments in Hungary allows this paper to address the following issue: which were the most important constitutional moments of this period in Hungarian history, and how did the country's ancient constitution manage to endure these moments of radical transformation? We shall concentrate on three such moments: the early 1790s, 1848–49 and 1865–1867. As we shall demonstrate, none of these moments could produce a complete break with the historical constitution, or a total transformation of its contents, and none could initiate the creation of a new constitutional framework. This was because the bulk of the Hungarian political elite, particularly the lower and middle nobility and the politically

4 See Oszkár Jászi, *The Dissolution of the Habsburg Monarchy* (Chicago: University of Chicago Press, 1929). For the constitutional debate over the survival of the monarchy even without a legitimate king, see István Szabó, "Law I of 1920 and the Historical Constitution", in Ferenc Hörcher and Thomas Lorman, eds., *The History of the Hungarian Constitution: Law, Government and Political Culture in Central Europe* (London, New York: IB Tauris, 2019), 160–83.

engaged aristocracy (for different reasons), never sought the historical constitution's destruction. Instead, they strove successfully to preserve legal continuity and the essence of the historical constitution which they regarded as one of their country's distinguishing hallmarks. In what follows we shall look for the reasons behind this phenomenon, drawing especially on László Péter's insight that what actually took place in this period was the "conversion" of the constitution that underscored both its adaptability and its continuing importance.[5] We shall, thus, explain how the actual contents of the constitution could dramatically change while its essential features remained intact, and its "aura" (essence) endured until the middle of the twentieth century.

2 The Historical Constitution of the Hungarian Kingdom

To identify what exactly was referred to in Hungarian politics, jurisprudence, constitutional law literature and historical writing by the term "historical constitution" of the Kingdom of Hungary is no easy task. While the term constitution in the Hungarian context was loosely defined as "the fundamental rules of the social and political order",[6] the precise catalogue of these rules and customs was always difficult to discern, especially as the general term "constitution" was not used in the modern sense before 1780. Moreover, the constitution was embedded in the customary law context of the kingdom.[7] Constitutional lawyers and politicians in Hungary generally referred to sundry rights and privileges that they traced all the way back to at least the establishment of their kingdom in 1000 AD.

The difficulties of grasping the content of the constitution can be illustrated by reference to the work of one of the doyens of the study of Hungary's historical constitution, László Péter. He made three cautionary points in this connection. First he noted that there was not only no single constitutional charter among the laws of historical Hungary, but that even the authority of the entire corpus of statuary law should not be over-estimated because "well

5 See, for example, Péter, "Montesquieu's Paradox on Freedom and Hungary's Constitution 1790–1990".

6 Lojkó, ed., *Hungary's Long Nineteenth Century: Collected Studies by László Péter*, 193. For a longer and more refined definition, adapted to the particular case, see C. A. Macartney who describes it as "an agglutination of laws, privileges and concessions, and unilateral acts on the part of the monarch or the nation", C.A. Macartney, *Hungary* (London, 1934), 126.

7 See Martyn Rady, *Customary Law in Hungary: Courts, Texts and the Tripartitum* (Oxford: Oxford University Press, 2015).

into the nineteenth century the foundation of the social order was not based on statute law but on customary rules".[8] Even a royal decree (*decretum regni*) or a decision of the *Diet* could not be taken as actual law unless it was incorporated into the *consuetudo*. Customary law was, therefore, stronger than the laws of the Diet and *consuetudo* could not be overridden by statutory law.

Péter's second cautionary point refers to the binary structure of constitutional power in historical Hungary, which he termed "the dualism of political authority", in which a very clear division of labour prevailed from very early on between the Diet, as the representative body of the country, and the crown which prescribed the domain of both these institutions' prerogatives.[9] This bipolar structure of the law-making process created conflict: the two sides had to bargain and find common ground. and this was made more difficult by the fact that the Diet and the crown had very different interpretations of what the constitutional arrangement actually was. As Peter puts it:

> Before 1848 the Court, the aristocracy of the Upper House, the Church hierarchy and the university jurists understood the political system as a *monarchia pura* in which authority was solely in the hands of the monarch who was constrained only by his duty to govern in accordance with the laws and customs of his kingdom. (...) The gentry of the Lower House and their jurists held, however, that authority was divided between the monarch and the nation, in fact, the constitution was *monarchia mixta*.[10]

This sharp difference in the understanding of the constitutional standing of the country led to the absurd situation that there was no "official" jurisprudential doctrine (such as a handbook of constitutional principles) which would have been accepted by both sides as the basis for a consensus and facilitated agreement between crown and Diet.

The difference between the two interpretations of Hungary's historic constitution was again bridged by custom as Habsburg emperors at least nominally deferred to Hungary's distinct customs and laws. For example, at their separate coronation as king of Hungary, each emperor was required to swear to uphold the privileges of the various strata of the nobility, and to accept the customs of the country, as collected in Stephen Werbőczy's *Tripartitum* and

8 Lojkó, ed., *Hungary's Long Nineteenth Century: Collected Studies by László Péter*, 4.
9 *ibidem*.
10 *ibidem*, 5.

other legal collections.[11] Only Joseph II refused, pushing Hungary to the brink of revolution. All subsequent Habsburg rulers sensibly recognized that in the long-term Hungary could only be effectively governed by acknowledging the kingdom's distinct constitutional traditions.

Finally, Péter emphasizes that the historical constitution did not provide much constitutional protection for the inhabitants of Hungary particularly as regards abuses by the state. Although the privileges of the nobility provided a check on absolutist rule, nineteenth century liberals, across Europe, demanded explicit curbs on the growing powers of the state. In Hungary, however, such safeguards were not provided by the historical constitution with one significant exception. The Golden Bull of 1222, one of the first Hungarian legal sources to become widely known and accessible, had been enacted as a result of the nobility's demands that the king should publicly oblige himself and his successors to safeguard their privileges, and was thus with good reason celebrated by nineteenth century legal scholarship as an important early check on absolutist rule. In particular, the "right of resistance" (*ius resistendi*) in the Golden Bull, which permitted the nobility to resist the king if he disregarded their liberties, was reiterated in the *Tripartitum* in the early 16th century, was formally abolished in 1687 but continued to be invoked as a customary right into the twentieth century.[12]

In spite of these problems with the constitutional arrangement, both parties generally handled the internal tensions smoothly. The eighteenth century, in particular, appeared to be a period of constitutional peace and collaboration.[13] This is especially noteworthy because the century started with a failed rebellion against Habsburg rule led by count (later prince) Francis II Rákóczi, followed by the peace treaty of Szatmár which created a framework that satisfied both parties. It was only as a result of the radical reforms of Joseph II

11 See, for example, János M. Bak, Péter Banyó and Martyn Rady, eds., *The Customary Law of the Renowned Kingdom of Hungary: A work in three parts rendered by Stephen Werbőczy (The "Tripartitum")* (Idyllwild and Budapest; Central European University, 2005).

12 Martyn Rady, "Law and the Ancient Constitution in Medieval and Early Modern Hungary", in Hörcher and Lorman, eds., *The History of the Hungarian Constitution*, 40–1.

13 See István M. Szijártó, "The Integration of Hungary into the Habsburg Monarchy at the Beginning of the 18th century", in Robert Bartczak, Adam Perlakowski and Anton Schindling, eds., *Die Reiche Mittel und Osteuropas: Integration und Herrschaft: Liber Memorialis Jan Pirozynski* (Kraków, 2009), 225–9; and "The Birth of the Constitution in Eighteenth-Century Hungarian Political Thought", in Hörcher and Lorman, eds., *The History of the Hungarian Constitution*. For a classic account of eighteenth-century Hungary, see Henrik Marczali, *Hungary in the Eighteenth Century; with an Introductory Essay on the Earlier History of Hungary, by Harold W. V. Temperley* (Cambridge: Cambridge University Press, 1910).

(whose refusal to have a separate coronation as king of Hungary, because he did not want to take the coronation oath, meant he was not accepted by most Hungarians as a legitimate ruler) that after his death the representatives of the Hungarian nobility were understandably keen to reaffirm their longstanding rights and privileges, and to regain their political powers via the Diet and the local county assemblies. Their chief tactic, which encouraged lively discussions both inside and outside the Diet, was to draw on enlightenment thinking to challenge Habsburg absolutism.

As Péter observes, Article X of 1790, "was the first statutory reference to the constitution". According to this law "the kingdom had to be 'ruled and governed according to its own laws and customs' because it had 'its own character and constitution' (*propriam habens consistenciam et constitutionem*)".[14] The aim of this law was obvious: the constitution's function was to preserve the autonomy of the country.

The Hungarian term for a constitution, *alkotmány*, was used in a different sense earlier, but by the 1780s it had been refined as a translation of the Latin *constitutio*.[15] This does not mean, however, that an interest in the constitution only emerged in this period, merely that a new term was now employed to describe a practice that dated back centuries, but which became much more self-reflective as a result of the increasingly vigorous debates about Hungary's position within the wider Habsburg Empire.

3 Reasons behind the Constitutional Reform Efforts (1790–1848)

Although the elaborate mechanisms, controlled by custom, which determined the process of law-making in the kingdom were not new, and only the description of this mechanism as a constitution was innovative (and as noted above, borrowed primarily from Montesquieu's classic work), there were, nevertheless, new motivations evident in the constitutional reform efforts of the early 1790s. This became evident during the two short Diets held during Leopold II's reign (1790–1792).[16] Notably, there was widespread repugnance against the

14 Lojkó, ed., *Hungary's Long Nineteenth Century: Collected Studies by László Péter*, 193.

15 On the popularization of the concept of the constitution in late eighteenth century Hungary, see Philip Barker, "Resurrecting the Past, Reshaping the Future: The Rise of the 'Ancient Constitution' at the Diet of 1790/1", in Hörcher and Lorman, eds., *The History of the Hungarian Constitution*, 63–91.

16 For a classic summary of the reform movement of the 1790s, see Győző Concha, *A kilencz-venes évek reformeszméi és előzményeik* (Budapest, 1885; republished 2005).

centralising and "Germanising" tendencies of Joseph II's absolutist reforms enacted in the previous decade. For example, Károly Koppi, József Hajnóczy and Gergely Berzeviczy, were all strongly influenced by the French Revolution, their own enlightened convictions and even, paradoxically, Joseph II's own botched attempt at reform, which inspired them to draw up their own radical reform proposals. Yet this reform movement was not successful – initially because of opposition from their fellow nobles and later because the violent revolutionary conspiracy by Ignác Martinovics and his companions, who were executed by the authorities in 1795, led to a period of absolutist oppression. Even though the Hungarian nobility loyally supported the crown's efforts to defeat Napoleon, the Diet was not re-convened until 1825.

Nevertheless, the work of the nine committees (*regnicolaris deputatio*) which had produced in 1793 written reports (*operatum*), underscoring the need for significant reform, could not be permanently ignored. These reports were finally published during the Diet of 1825–27, and their updated versions inspired widespread debate at the general assemblies of the counties in the early 1830s. The lengthy and vigorous debates about these reports underscored the resolve of the country's political elite to fundamentally reform the entire legislation and government of the kingdom, as well as changing the legal status of both serfs and nobles, and facilitating the creation of a market economy.

According to a simplistic narrative, the two slogans which summed up the wishes of the political and intellectual elite were "haza" (fatherland, patria) or more precisely that Hungary should not be directly governed from Vienna and "haladás" (progress), meaning reform of the social structure and economic institutions of the country which still possessed feudal characteristics, including the maintenance of serfdom. Both terms were famously popularized in a farewell speech given in 1835 by the poet, politician, and orator Ferenc Kölcsey, author of the Hungarian national anthem (*Himnusz*) in which he claimed that the slogan of his generation was "fatherland and progress".[17] Usually, Hungarian historiography regards these two concepts as contradictory. In fact, for Kölcsey the two terms were logically connected, and he managed to synthesize in this speech the political aspirations of both liberals and conservatives by arguing that at certain times preservation required reform, while a failure to reform would only lead to depression and stagnation (*senyvedés*) for the fatherland.

17 Lajos Kossuth, *Országgyűlési tudósítások*, 5 vols, (Budapest, 1948–1961), vol. IV, 1835. február 9. Kerületi ülés. Tárgy: A végleg hazatérő Kölcsey és Eötvös Mihály búcsúja a rendektől.

Unfortunately, many of Kölcsey's contemporaries failed to understand this interconnectedness. Fatherland remained a slogan of nationalist critics of Habsburg rule, for whom independence and self-government was the first priority, while progress remained the slogan used by proponents of a new civil society with its own self-governing bodies and distinct customs and rights. Holding these two aspirations together was immensely challenging, and in fact the next generation (after Kölcsey) was ultimately unable to prevent the proponents of these two ideas separating into two separate and opposing camps.

4 The Long Road to the Austro-Hungarian Settlement (1790–1867)

Plausibly, the reason behind the delay in modernizing nineteenth century Hungary was the entrée of a new ideology, nationalism. Hitherto, existing constitutional arrangements had been predicated on (smooth) relations between the crown and the Diet. For example, in 1687 and 1723, Hungary's political elite reaffirmed its endorsement of rule by the Habsburg dynasty even though they were still regarded as a foreign royal family. This state of affairs raised serious political issues. The Diet, representing the *natio Hungarica*, had a different political culture from the ruling family and its entourage, the elite of the court. Vienna became the centre of Continental politics after the fall of the Napoleonic empire, and Metternich, a guiding figure of the Holly Alliance, enjoyed a European-wide reputation for his self-styled defence of autocracy, opposed, for example, to any concessions to the Hungarian Diet.[18]

In contrast, Hungary's politically active elite struggled to prevent their kingdom becoming increasingly integrated into the wider Habsburg empire. As the Diet was only convened sporadically, they were dispersed among the county assemblies which were the self-governing bodies that helped oversee each of the counties of the kingdom in conjunction with a *főispán* (sheriff) appointed by the crown. While some Hungarian noblemen, especially those who were knowledgeable about wider European political culture, recognized that institutional reorganisation was required to remain competitive in an age of technological development embodied by the industrial revolution, social and demographic changes and urbanisation, the bulk of the nobility simply wanted to enjoy the benefits of their centuries-old feudal privileges.

18 For a recent overview, see Alan Sked, *Metternich and Austria: an Evaluation* (New York: Palgrave Macmillan, 2008).

They had trouble recognizing that the potential short-term loss of their privileges (such as their tax exemptions and the benefits they derived from the wider feudal system) would be in their own common and even individual self-interest, because they could then benefit from a flourishing market economy that would transform Hungary into a prosperous, modern European country.

Likewise, the Habsburg dynasty did not recognise that the modernization of Hungary, socially, economically, and indeed politically, could serve the interests of the court and the wider empire. Vienna was consumed by a constant suspicion that the Hungarian nobility was instinctively rebellious and could not imagine how the crown could retain its authority if Hungary was allowed genuine autonomy. Metternich was particularly distrustful of the Hungarian nobility, whose language he did not speak, and whose political culture appeared to him incomprehensible.[19]

The crown, therefore, obstructed the Hungarian reformers and distrusted the Hungarian Diet. The anti-Josephinist sentiments of Hungarians cast a long shadow in Vienna as did the revolutionary turmoil of 1848/49. Kossuth seemed to be even more dangerous than Ignác Martinovics as he found large crowds of sympathizers not only in Hungary but also in Vienna, London, and America, both in the revolutionary days of 1848 and later in exile following the failure of the War of Independence. In North America, for example, the Hungarian 'freedom fighter' was even received by the United States Congress as a global public celebrity.[20]

In reality, the transformation of Hungary in 1848–1849 was the result of the combined efforts of two generations of enlightened aristocrats, politically-engaged noblemen, and well-educated, self-sacrificing intellectuals (*honoratiors*) who, as János Mazsu notes, were "growing professional groups, of varying social and ethnic origin but chiefly nonprivileged, themselves constituted a sort of feudal corporation or estate. … Their social status gradually improved until it approached that of the lesser nobility. For instance, at the beginning of the 1840s the honoratiors gained the right to vote. Until then this had been the privilege of the nobility which it jealously guarded".[21] These reformers were all

19 On the lack of trust between the Hungarian nobility and Vienna, see Ferenc Hörcher, "Trust, Credit and Commerce: Count Széchenyi's Vision of How to Build Social Cohesion in 19th Century Hungary", in Sándor Laczkó, ed., *A bizalom* (Szeged, 2015), 102–18.

20 John H. Komlós, *Kossuth in America 1851–1852* (Buffalo: East European Institute, 1973).

21 Janos Mazsu, "The Intelligentsia in Hungary prior to World War I", *Hungarian Studies Review*, 24.1–2 (1997), 87; See also Károly Vörös, "A modern értelmiség kezdetei Magyarországon", *Valóság*, 10 (1975).

aware that the country's future was grim unless its institutional infrastructure was reformed and radical amendments to its constitutional-legal framework were enacted. This continuity required, in particular, the overlapping efforts of Count István Széchenyi in the 1830s and Lajos Kossuth in the 1840s who were both able to mobilize distinct but overlapping groups of their contemporaries with their vision of social, economic, and later political reforms.

Széchenyi's innovative ideas of private financing for culture, leisure, and entertainment (including the establishment of the Hungarian Academy of Sciences, as well as a Casino which served as a new meeting place and debating forum for the nobility, and a racecourse), and his path-breaking book on the theory of social trust, "Credit" (Hitel, 1830), fostered discussion, new thinking, capitalist entrepreneurship, and legal reforms. His venture to build the first bridge across the Danube in Hungary to connect the two cities of Pest and Buda (the *Lánchíd*, opened in 1849) opened up new vistas for trade within the country and abroad, and facilitated the later unification of Buda and Pest into a major European capital city. Most importantly, Széchenyi's example gave tremendous spiritual energy to the political and intellectual elite, boosted their self-confidence, and encouraged them to also participate in the effort to modernize the country.[22] Kossuth, on the other hand, developed the politically more confrontational language of the 1840s, took a leading role in drafting the April Laws, became a major figure in the Diet in 1848–1849, took part (with Széchenyi) as a minister in the first autonomous Hungarian government, and later served as Governor of the country in 1849 when he enforced the Declaration of Independence.

If Széchenyi was successful in providing ideas about how to strengthen and revitalise civil society, Kossuth was a more robustly political creature. Széchenyi, a member of a leading aristocratic family, was not particularly interested in the daily workings of the political machinery, and pictured himself as a benevolent modern Maecenas standing aloof from the political struggles of the country.[23] In contrast, Kossuth came from the lower rank of the nobility, the gentry, and earned his reputation as a brilliant lawyer, journalist and orator determined

22 For an overview of how two generations of Széchenyis inspired their countrymen by sponsoring national cultural institutions and establishing spaces for social gatherings, see Ferenc Hörcher, "Enlightened Reform or National Reform? The Continuity Debate about the Hungarian Reform Era and the Example of the Two Széchenyis (1790–1848)", *Hungarian Historical Review*, 5.1 (2016), 22–45.

23 For the changing concepts of sponsorship in the activity of the Széchenyis, see Ferenc Hörcher, "Intézményalapítás és polgári kultúra: A Széchenyiek útja a főúri mecenatúrától a Bildungsbürger eszményéig", in Ferenc Hörcher, Mátyás Lajtai and Béla Mester, eds., *Nemzet, faj, kultúra: A hosszú 19. században Magyarországon és Európában* (Budapest: MTA Bölcsészettudomány Kutatóközpont, Történettudományi Intézet, 2016), 147–77.

to transform the feudal Diet into a modern representative institution and to transform Hungary into a modern European state.[24] His published reports on the sessions of the Diet, inspired the wider population to take a new interest in politics, and used politics to transform the wider population through the new ideology of nationalism and an agonistic view of modern party politics inspired by a compelling vision of mass democracy and popular sovereignty.

Kossuth, therefore, distanced himself from the dualism of the ancient constitution, to which Széchenyi and much of his generation remained wedded. Kossuth's vision of a largely homogeneous and self-governing nation-state clashed with Hungary's reality as a multi-ethnic kingdom embedded within the larger Habsburg empire. Nevertheless, he was willing to compromise when drafting the April Laws of 1848 in order to obtain the widest possible support in the Diet and obtain the approval of the King. He too proved himself a constitutional architect who discovered the common fields of interest between the various parties involved, and thereby proposed innovative constitutional solutions to achieve a constitutional balance between the two poles of the legislative machinery, the crown, and the Diet.[25]

The constitutional achievements of 1848 were then demolished in 1849 after Kossuth pushed the National Assembly to proclaim Hungary independent. The success of the April Laws could only be saved by Ferenc Deák, the ingenious and charismatic architect of the 1867 settlement, known as "the wise man of the nation". Already before 1848 he had defended Miklós Wesselényi, another leading proponent of reform when he was put on trial for sedition, and Deák had also endeavoured to reconcile the competing aspirations of Széchenyi and Kossuth.[26] He was Minister of Justice in the first government of Hungary appointed after the April Laws, although he subsequently resigned from the government due to its growing radicalisation. While a member of the government, he was already seeking to sustain the spirit of the April Laws and foster cooperation between Vienna and his radical cabinet colleagues.

Deák's withdrawal from politics after 1849 symbolized the "passive resistance" of the 1850s against the crown's neo-absolutism. When he returned to public life after the Austrian army's defeat in Italy in 1859, Deák sought to find

24 For an overview of Kossuth's activity, see László Péter, Martyn Rady and Peter Sherwood, eds., *Lajos Kossuth sent word ... Papers delivered on the occasion of the bicentenary of Kossuth's birth* (London: University College London, 2003).

25 Ferenc Hörcher, "Reforming or Replacing the Historical Constitution? Lajos Kossuth and the April Laws of 1848", in Hörcher and Lorman, eds., *The History of the Hungarian Constitution*, 92–121.

26 Bela K. Kiraly, *Ferenc Deák* (Boston: Twayne, 1975).

an alternative to both the understandable but impractical anti-Habsburg sentiment and the willingness of some Hungarians to collaborate with the crown, in spite of all the authoritarian tendencies of Viennese rule in the past decade. In particular, he recognized the areas of common interest for both Hungary and Vienna, staked out both the constitutional terms of the settlement, and lead the Hungarian delegation through the negotiations that, in 1867 created the Austro- Hungarian Dual Monarchy.

In connection with this political process two questions need to be asked: what exactly was the practical knowledge that helped Deák to negotiate between these opposing interests, and how did his activity advance the movement for constitutional reform which was already evident in the early 1790s?

His tactics were akin to those that pragmatic Hungarians had pioneered – notably in Transylvania – in response to earlier foreign invasions: to find the right moment and the right arguments and offer a deal which looked like a win-win situation. Revealingly, a Transylvanian baron, Zsigmond Kemény, who was an experienced journalist as well as a "conservative, pessimistic, far-seeing Hungarian writer",[27] was Deák's direct help. It is also important that Deák was a conservative-minded noble, with a traditional upbringing in the law, conditioned to rely on the laws and customs of the kingdom in order to advance his political objectives. His practical knowledge of Hungarian legal customs came from his experience as one of the opposition's leaders in the national Diet in the pre-1848 reform era and from his long participation in the local assembly of Zala county.

The county assemblies were an ancient institution of the Hungarian state, where members of the nobility learnt in practice the traditional language and manners of politics. Deák, who took over the role of county representative from his brother, used his legal expertise to organize the proponents of reform on the national level and consolidate their political programme. Due to his impressive knowledge of Hungarian customary law (which had first been compiled by Stephen Werbőczy in the beginning of the sixteenth century, and developed by subsequent generations of jurists),[28] he supported attempts at legal reform before 1848 and helped draft both the 'Opposition Manifesto (*Ellenzéki Nyilatkozat*) of 1847 (that summarized the demands of the reformers), and the April Laws in 1848. This gave him an unparalleled practical experience in public law. During the drafting of the laws which made up the 1867 settlement he was able to slowly allay the suspicions which had burdened

27 The assessemnt is provided in John Lukacs, *Budapest 1900: A Historical Portrait of a City and Its Culture* (New York: Grove Press, 1988), 116.

28 Rady, *Customary Law in Hungary.*

earlier attempts to reconcile the crown and Hungary's political elite, and thus grew to be trusted by both sides.

Although Hungarian historiography has usually celebrated its revolutionary heroes, such as Rákóczi and Kossuth, and underestimated the value of humble but solid compromise, a recent trend – following in the footsteps of Gyula Szekfű, who introduced a new tone in historical narratives after the catastrophe of the First World War – has endeavoured to show the other side of the coin.[29] László Péter has, for example, persuasively argued that the long series of nuanced transactions between the crown and the Hungarian Diet, were the result of an institutional mechanism which encouraged both sides to strive for partnership up until the unparalleled historical shocks of the twentieth century.[30] R.J.W. Evans, another leading historian of the Habsburg empire, has also highlighted how recurring periods of cooperation and compromise were evident in both the Austrian and Hungarian halves of the Habsburg empire.[31]

It is in the context of these revisionist historiographical efforts that the congenial efforts of Deák to find a modus vivendi between the opposing camps, in order to dislodge the frozen political field, and to mobilize the administration, public opinion and the entrepreneurial civil capacities of both the wider empire and the Kingdom of Hungary deserve celebration. The political and constitutional arrangement he orchestrated with the emperor, Francis Joseph was not only an impressive, albeit controversial, achievement,[32] but should also be recognized as both a rational and traditionally legitimised solution to a historical deadlock, which had become a burden for both parties involved.

5 The 1867 Settlement

The 1867 settlement, placed on the Hungarian statute books as Law XII of that year, in essence granted Hungary autonomy within the Habsburg empire. The guiding principle was that in domestic affairs she would henceforth govern

29 See, in particular, István Szijártó, *A 18. századi Magyarország rendi országgyűlése* (Budapest: Országgyűlés Hivatala, 2016); and Géza Pálffy, *The Kingdom of Hungary and the Habsburg Monarchy in the Sixteenth Century* (New York: Columbia University Press, 2009).

30 Lojkó, ed., *Hungary's Long Nineteenth Century. Collected Studies by László Péter*, 1–14.

31 R.J.W. Evans, *Austria, Hungary and the Habsburgs. Essays on Central Europe, c.1683–1867* (Oxford: Oxford University Press, 2006).

32 Although it was harshly criticised by 20th century progressive thinkers like István Bibó. See also Alan Sked, "Historians, The Nationality Question, and the Downfall of the Habsburg Empire", *Transactions of the Royal Historical Society*, 31 (1981), 178–181.

herself, whereas in those matters that clearly affected both the Hungarian and Austrian halves of the empire, such as the state debt, tariffs and taxations to fund the imperial government and the army, there would be negotiations between delegations from the Hungarian parliament and the Austrian *Reichsrat* in Vienna. The crown did, however, maintain its exclusive prerogative in certain areas (namely military and foreign policy).[33]

Historians have repeatedly attacked this settlement. It has been described as a self-interested deal by the Austrian and Hungarian elites that blocked radical reform for the next fifty years and alienated much of the population who remained excluded from political influence.[34] Alternatively, the settlement has been denounced as a betrayal of the Hungarian desire for independence (Kossuth called it "the death of the nation"), which bound Hungary to the wider empire and ensured that she too would be implicated in the disastrous foreign policy that led to military defeat and territorial dismemberment in 1918.[35]

In fact, the settlement marked not the end but the continuation of a process of dramatic reform that was constrained only by the ingrained caution of Hungary's ossified political elite rather than the normative limitations imposed by the 1867 settlement. The settlement, in fact, permitted Hungarian governments considerable freedom of action by restoring the traditional "bipolar" arrangement that had existed up until 1848, embodied by the *dietalis tractatus,* the negotiations that had traditionally shaped the legislative process between the crown and the Diet. As László Péter has noted, those who drafted the settlement, particularly on the Hungarian side, derived the new dualist system "from the mutual rights and obligations that had bound the Habsburg crown and the *ország* [nation] together".[36]

Immediate evidence of this restored duality came with the emperor Francis Joseph's consent to finally agree to undergo a separate coronation as king of Hungary, nineteen years after he had been crowned Habsburg emperor. In return, the crown continued to exert its influence on Hungary's domestic affairs. The secret Punctation of 17 March, 1867 provided the emperor with what Steven Beller has called a "prophylactic veto" on all legislation and

33 The clearest account of the contents of the settlement is again given in Lojkó, ed., *Hungary's Long Nineteenth Century: Collected Studies by László Péter*, 251–58.

34 See, for example, Sked, "Historians, The Nationality Question, and the Downfall of the Habsburg Empire". For a Marxist critique of the Ausgleich, see Endre Kovács and László Katus, *Magyarország története, 1848–1890*, 6/2 (Budapest: Akademiai Kiadó, 1979), 777–8.

35 Quoted in László Péter, "Introduction. Lajos Kossuth sent word", in *Lajos Kossuth sent word*, 8.

36 Lojkó, ed., *Hungary's Long Nineteenth Century. Collected Studies by László Péter*, 215.

allowed him to appoint all ministers in the Hungarian government and all of the top officials in the bureaucracy whose responsibility therefore was theoretically to him rather than to parliament.[37] Nevertheless, the crown tended to appoint as prime minister the leader of the most popular party who was tasked with forming the government. It was a rare occasion when a prime minister was appointed who lacked obvious support in parliament (such as the professional soldier Géza Fejérváry in 1905 and the ever-loyal Sándor Wekerle in 1906). Equally, the crown had the formal right to veto legislation, such as the first attempt, in 1894, to introduce compulsory civil marriages alongside an optional religious ceremony. When, however, fresh elections endorsed the government's proposed reform, the crown provided its royal assent.[38]

On occasion, the relationship between crown and nation came close to breaking down, particularly over proposed increases in taxation, for Hungarian public opinion was generally opposed to handing over additional sums to fund the imperial government in (Austrian) Vienna. Troops even had to be sent into the Hungarian parliament in 1912 to force the tax increase through. The question of whether Hungary should have its own army was also a source of contention. Alongside the imperial army, Hungary was permitted to set up a "home guard", but its size, role, uniforms, and even the army's language of command continued to be the subject of bitter debates for the duration of the 1867 settlement.[39] Generally, however, the settlement worked as its architects had envisioned. Relations between the Hungarian political elite and the crown were business-like and even, most of the time, mutually loyal. There was genuine (later cultish) affection for the Emperor's wife, Elizabeth, and a renewed awareness that Hungary's security was dependent on the survival of the empire.[40]

---

37 Steven Beller, *The Habsburg Monarchy, 1815–1918* (Cambridge: Cambridge University Press, 2018), 129.

38 Katalin Ibolya Koncz, "A polgári házasságról szóló törvényjavaslat vitája a képviselőház előtt", *Publicationes Universitatis Miskolcinensis. Sectio Juridica et Politica*, 31 (2013), 55–65; see also Christopher Clark and Wolfram Kaiser, eds., *Culture Wars. Secular-Catholic Conflict in Nineteenth-Century Europe* (Cambridge: Cambridge University Press, 2004), 313–35.

39 Gunther Rothenburg, *The Army of Francis Joseph* (West Lafayette: Purdue University Press, 1976), pp.74–85.

40 Judith Szapor, "From 'Guardian Angel of Hungary' to the 'Sissi look-alike contest': The Making and Remaking of the Cult of Elizabeth, Queen of Hungary", in Agatha Schwartz, ed., *Gender and Modernity in Central Europe* (Ottawa: University of Ottawa Press, 2010), 235–47.

Moreover, successive Hungarian governments were well aware that the settlement had not only re-established an autonomous Hungarian government but also empowered it to modernize the country. From 1867 onwards a wave of legislation transformed Hungary, instilling a new confidence in the political elite, and creating what László Kontler has called "a mirage of greatness" but which, as John Lukacs observed, still resulted in "the great, liberal, capitalist, material flourishing of Hungary, and especially of Budapest".[41] Parliament churned out legislation and though it was often vague and/or poorly drafted it could be supplemented by explanatory decrees that had previously been used by the crown in Vienna to the chagrin of generations of Hungarian politicians, and now became the purview of the government in Budapest. The various ministries proceeded to ruthlessly exploit the custom that where the legislation was silent the authorities were free to act as they wished.[42] Substantial areas of the law were also reformed, with the government making full use of its freedom to draw on best practices elsewhere in Europe as well as existing Austrian legislation.[43] The reincorporation of Transylvania into Hungary in 1867 and the granting of limited home rule to Croatia in 1868 were merely two of the starkest examples of the Hungarian government's new freedom of action after 1867, which permitted it to both grant and revoke autonomy.

The chauvinism of the post-1867 Hungarian political elite also cannot be blamed on the constraints of the settlement. Rather than inspiring the agressive attempt to assimilate Hungary's "nationalities" (*nemzetiségek*), the official term for the non-Magyar peoples of Hungary, the settlement actually resulted in a genuine but flawed attempt to forge a rapprochement with them. As C.A Macartney persuasively argued, the Hungarian politicians who negotiated the settlement were "genuinely anxious ... to reach an acceptable settlement with the nationalities" and the 1868 nationalities law formally granted the non-Magyars in Hungary cultural autonomy.[44] The law was, however, ambiguously worded and largely disregarded by the increasingly nationalist bureaucracy. It was instead replaced by a policy of "Magyarization" that was inspired by the idea, already evident at the beginning of the nineteenth century, that the entire population of the country should be transformed into patriotic Hungarian citizens through a process of assimilation. It was this ambition, which manifested

41 Lászlo Kontler, *A History of Hungary* (Basingstoke: Bloomsbury, 2002), 279; Lukacs: *Budapest 1900*, 117.

42 Martyn Rady, "Nonnisi in sensu legume? Decree and Rendelet in Hungary (1790–1914)", *Hungarian Historical Review*, 5.1 (2016), 5–21.

43 Rady, *Customary Law in Hungary*, 230–40.

44 C.A. Macartney, *The Habsburg Empire* (London: Weidenfeld and Nicholson, 1968), 559–60.

itself most obviously in chauvinistic rhetoric, attempts to magyarize the education system and the occasionally brutal but also haphazard repression of the cultural associations of the "nationalities", which provoked considerable resentment and fuelled the dismemberment of Hungary after 1918.

Likewise, the failure to modernize the electoral system, which was marred by a narrow franchise, unequal constituencies, rampant electoral corruption, and a bureaucracy that was generally committed to ensuring the government's re-election, can only partially be linked to the 1867 settlement. A fear that electoral reform would empower populist advocates of complete independence who would then tear-up the settlement and plunge the country into a new crisis or even civil war, was certainly evident among some of Hungary's more astute politicians.[45] Revealingly, however, even opponents of the settlement were reluctant to enact a major electoral reform because they feared that the Social Democratic Party and the representatives of Hungary's various "nationalities" would be the greatest beneficiaries of universal suffrage.[46]

6 1918/1919 and the Constitution

For Hungarian constitutional lawyers the fact that Hungary had secured a uniquely privileged position within the empire was testament to the virtues of the Hungarian constitution which had secured autonomy for Hungary in 1867.[47] Support for the settlement was boosted by the subsequent decades of rapid economic growth driven both by rising agricultural exports, the beginnings of industrialization, and massive investments in infrastructure.[48] Comprehensive reform of Hungary's legal framework was, therefore, dismissed as unnecessary while the problems that the country faced were usually blamed on either historical legacies, scurrilous propaganda, or the machinations of Vienna.

In contrast, radical critics of the government tended to idealize Kossuth's revolutionary anti-Habsburg actions in 1848–49 and were contemptuous of

45 This point is concisely made in András Gerő, *Imagined History: Chapters from Nineteenth and Twentieth Century Hungarian Symbolics Politics* (New York: CHSP, 2006), 48–51.

46 See, for example, Jenő Gergely, ed., *Magyarországi pártprogramok, 1867–1998* (Budapest, ELTE Eötvös Kiadó, 2003–2005).

47 See the discussion of this triumphalism in Paul Lendvai, *The Hungarians: A Thousand Years of Victory in Defeat* (Princeton: Princeton University Press, 2003), 306–7.

48 A thoughtful summary of Hungary's economic growth in this period can be found in Robin Okey, *The Habsburg Monarchy, c.1765–1918: From Enlightenment to Eclipse* (Basingstoke: Macmillan, 2001), 233–47.

the 1867 settlement. They demanded both Hungary's independence and the dismantling of what they called "feudal Hungary".[49] Their chance came with the military defeat of the Dual Monarchy in the First World War, which led to both its dissolution and the dismemberment of Hungary, the majority of which was annexed by neighbouring states. In the revolutionary turmoil radical reformers, socialists and eventually militant Bolsheviks briefly seized power between October 1918 and August 1919. The Left was, however, unable to handle this catastrophe, which was compounded by further military defeats, attendant economic collapse and the "red terror" of Bolshevik rule. As a result, its attempt to modernize Hungary's legal framework, including the enactment of a new constitution in June 1919, was easily presented by the traditional political and academic elite as illegitimate and was immediately annulled.[50] In response, post-Trianon Hungary was dominated by a Christian conservative political discourse that was determined to preserve the historical constitution albeit with some modifications. The traumatised nation's and its elite's historical delusion that the clock could eventually be turned back resulted in what one of its sharpest observers, the historian and ideologue Gyula Szekfű called a frozen "neo-baroque society".[51] Thus, unlike all of the other successor states to the Habsburg empire, interwar Hungary refused to enact a new, chartered constitution and, its historical constitution remained in force. For example, although the House of Habsburg was formally dethroned in 1921, the new regent, Miklós Horthy, was granted the powers formally exercised by earlier emperors as kings of Hungary. Likewise, the electoral system was expanded but still excluded around seventy per cent of the population, while the upper house of parliament, largely composed of representatives of Hungary's traditional aristocratic elite, was re-established to provide a further check on the elected lower house. At the same time, all interwar Hungarian governments, even though they were appointed by the regent, were expected to have a majority in the lower house of parliament, and to submit all legislation to parliament for scrutiny, open debate and possible modification. The dualist system that existed until 1918, exemplified by the relationship between

49 See, for example, György Litván, *Twentieth Century Prophet: Oszkár Jászi, 1875–1957* (Budapest: Central European University, 2006), 150.

50 For a recent and insightful discussion of this turn to the Right after 1918, see Paul Hanebrink, "Christianity, Nation, State: The Case of Christian Hungary", in Bruce Berglund and Brian Porter-Szűcs, eds., *Christianity and Modernity in Eastern Europe* (Budapest: Central European University, 2010), 66–72.

51 Gyula Szekfű, *Három nemzedék és ami utána következik*, harmadik kiadás, Királyi Magyar Egyetemi Nyomda, Budapest, é.n. (1934). See, in particular, the section entitled "Trianon óta" ("Since Trianon").

the Habsburg monarch and the Hungarian parliament, was, therefore, echoed by the relationship between regent and parliament in interwar Hungary. It was only after the German invasion of Hungary in March 1944 that the new puppet government was able to close parliament, ban rival parties, eviscerate the rule of law, and render the historical constitution defunct.[52] It was during this time that the Holocaust in Hungary took the lives of more than half a million Jews, who were Hungarian citizens as well.

The radical Left represented by Communists and Social Democrats throughout the interwar period continuously dismissed Hungary's constitutional framework as anachronistic, illegitimate, and then seized power with the support of the invading Soviet Union. They regarded the historical constitution as responsible for the catastrophe that befell Hungary during the Second World War. Helped by the presence of the Red Army in the country, they blackmailed the democratically elected post-war government and imposed a new constitutional framework on the country. During direct communist rule, until the settlement of the National Round Table in 1989, the historical constitution was dismissed, in the words of one of Hungary's leading Marxist historians, Győző Ember, as a "bastion" that merely protected "the rights and advantages of the feudal ruling class".[53] The chartered constitution that was enacted in 1949 was inspired instead by the constitution of the Soviet, totalitarian state. This constitution was then substantially modified in 1989, but in accordance with the constitutional standards of contemporary Western parliamentary democracies rather than revitalising the historical constitution. Remarkably, however, the Basic Law (*Alaptörvény*), which was enacted by the second Orbán government in 2012, formally restored the constitutional framework that emerged in the "long nineteenth century" with its explicit declaration that "we honour the achievements of our historic constitution … [and] we do not recognize the suspension of our historic constitution due to foreign occupations".[54] It also

52 For a counter-argument that the historical constitution did exert a brief but significant influence on legal developments in Hungary in the immediate aftermath of the Second World War, see Balázs Fekete, "Law I of 1946 and Law XX of 1949: Continuity or Discontinuity in Traditional Hungarian Constuitutionalism", in Hörcher and Lorman, eds., *The History of the Hungarian Constitution*, 185–210.

53 Győző Ember, "A Magyar történelmi társulat száz éve", *Századok*, 1967, 1146.

54 For the official translation of the preamble to the Basic Law, see Hörcher and Lorman, eds., *The History of the Hungarian Constitution*, 341–3. For a nuanced interpretation, see Ferenc Hörcher, "'The National Avowal': An Interpretation of the Preamble, from the Perspective of the History of Political Thought", in András Zs. Varga, András Patyi and Balázs Schand, eds., *The Basic (Fundamental) Law of Hungary: A Commentary of the New Hungarian Constitution* (Dublin: Clarus Press, 2015), 35–56. See also the relevant analyses by Kálmán Pócza and Ferenc Hörcher in Hörcher and Lorman, eds., *The History of the*

required that the historical constitution should provide the starting point for the interpretation of the Basic Law: "The provisions of the Fundamental Law shall be interpreted in accordance with their purposes, the National Avowal contained therein and the achievements of our historic constitution".[55]

7 Conclusion

This article has argued that the legal framework that was reformed in 1848, 1867 and survived even the turmoil of 1918–1919, and remained generally referred to as the historical constitution of Hungary until the end of WW2, had a remarkable flexibility and adaptability. For a surprisingly long time it had proved to be an able instrument to legally support, control and legitimate the economic, social and political transformation of the kingdom. The relationship between crown and Diet, elected and hereditary institutions, was traditionally shaped by both a respect for the customs that had informed Hungary's legal development for centuries, and by the accommodation of certain demands for modernization from below. In particular, a group of remarkable politicians, notably Széchenyi, Kossuth and Deák, were able to provide (through their combined and often competing efforts) a compelling example of how the desire for modernization could coexist with the preservation of constitutional continuity.

The history of the Hungarian constitution, in the period examined in this article (1790–1918) can, therefore, be described not as a development, or simply progress, but rather a kind of Hegelian dialectical *Aufhebung*; it was both preserved and changed at the same time, evolving and advancing while retaining the essence of its earlier character, its basic identity. As this article has demonstrated, the declaration of the Basic Law recognizes and endeavours to build upon the constitutional traditions of Hungary's "long nineteenth century". In this sense the constitutional heritage of the age of Kölcsey, Széchenyi, Kossuth, Deák and Eötvös, the Golden Age of Hungarian political thought, which we tried to summarize here still represents the common treasury of this political

Hungarian Constitution, 211–36, 237–46. For references to the historical constitution in the new Basic Law, see the rather critical account of Zoltán Szente, "A 2011. évi Alaptörvény és a történeti alkotmány összekapcsolásának mítosza", *Közjogi Szemle*, 1 (2019), 1–8, as well as the more balanced assessment provided in Gábor Attila Tóth, ed., *Constitution for a Disunited Nation: On Hungary's 2011 Fundamental Law* (Budapest: Central European University, 2012).

55 For references to the Basic Law, we used the following online resource: The Fundamental Law of Hungary. English translation of the consolidated version of the Fundamental Law of Hungary, https://www.parlament.hu/documents/125505/138409/Fundamental+law/73811993-c377-428d-9808-ee03d6fb8178.

community, which serves even today as the foundation of Hungary's constitutional architecture.

Bibliography

Main Sources

Bak, Janos B.; Banyó, Péter; and Rady, Martyn, eds., *The Customary Law of the Renowned Kingdom of Hungary: A work in three parts rendered by Stephen Werbőczy* (*The "Tripartitum"*) (Idyllwild and Budapest, 2005).

Concha, Győző, *A kilenczvenes évek reformeszméi és előzményeik* (Budapest, 1885; republished 2005).

Hörcher, Ferenc; and Lorman, Thomas, eds., *The History of the Hungarian Constitution. Law, Government and Political Culture in Central Europe* (London, New York: IB Tauris, 2019).

Kossuth, Lajos, *Országgyűlési tudósítások*, 5 vols. (Budapest, 1948–1961).

Szekfű, Gyula, *Három nemzedék és ami utána következik*, harmadik kiadás, Királyi Magyar Egyetemi Nyomda, Budapest, é.n. (1934).

Main Bibliographical References

Deák, István, *The Lawful Revolution: Louis Kossuth and the Hungarians, 1848–1849* (New York and London: Columbia University Press, 1979).

Evans, R.J.W., *Austria, Hungary and the Habsburgs: Essays on Central Europe, c.1683–1867* (Oxford: Oxford University Press, 2006).

Kiraly, Bela K., *Ferenc Deák* (Boston: Twayne, 1975).

Lojkó, Miklós, ed., *Hungary's Long Nineteenth Century: Constitutional and Democratic Traditions in a European Perspective. Collected Studies by László Péter* (Lieden and Boston: Brill, 2012).

Macartney, C.A., *The Habsburg Empire* (London: Weidenfeld and Nicholson, 1968).

CHAPTER 17

Constitutional Imagination and "Catholic" Political Anthropology

The Grammar of the Mixed Constitution in the Mid-19th Century Crisis of Spanish Liberalism

Pablo Sánchez León

1 Introduction*

In his inaugural lecture as Doctor in Philosophy at the Universidad Central in Madrid in March 1856, Ramón Anglasell discussed the relationships between law, philosophy and history. According to his view, the "science of legislation" had not yet "descended from the philosophical sphere", but instead remained dominated by a "cosmopolitan" school reluctant to take into consideration "the special conditions of each nation".[1] In practice, the academician was targeting especially those from the ranks of so-called *moderados*—conservatives—who regarded the British system of government as "a beautiful ideal for political organizations (…) transplantable to all states".[2] In dismissing such claims, he praised the political system of Britain, though from a historical perspective. According to Anglasell, from the 13th century onwards the Magna Carta had "solidly established the basis of the English government on that mysterious trinity that for so many years binds fraternally together monarchy, aristocracy and democracy".[3]

Anglasell's discourse is of relevance to this volume because he shows the extent to which later 19th century political discourse still referred to the

* This text is a partial result of my participation in two research projects: "Aproximación interdisciplinar a los lenguajes jurídico-políticos de la modernidad euroamericana. Dimensiones espacio-temporales" (HAR2017–84032-P) and "Tradición y constitución: problemas constituyentes de la España moderna y contemporánea" (DER2014-56291-C3-2-P), both financed by the Spanish Ministry of Economy and Competitiveness (Mineco).

1 Ramón Anglasell, *Discurso leído en la Universidad Central en el acto de recibir la investidura de Doctor en la Facultad de Filosofía, Sección de Administración* (Madrid: Salustiano Ríos y Cía., 1856), 6.

2 *Ibidem*, 10.

3 Thanks to which they have since been "free at once of monarchic despotism, aristocratic tyranny and popular anarchy and misgovernment", 11.

 | DOI:10.1163/9789004549159_019

language of the mixed constitution or government. Classically formulated by Polybius in book VI of his *Historiae*, the mixed constitution had been originally forged in Antiquity as a desirable—albeit hazardous—political ideal to be achieved through the balanced combination of three basic elements—monarchy, aristocracy and democracy—that respectively represented unity and coordination, sage and excellence, quantity and force.[4] Reappraised and renovated by Humanists during the Renaissance, in the 18th century the concept was usually deployed as a yardstick for measuring the standards of actual political systems and social orders, mostly thanks to the fame and influence of Montesquieu, who employed the concept in charting historical, existing and foreseeable polities.[5]

Notwithstanding the growing acknowledgement of its "recurrent presence" in Early Modern philosophical debates, historians have, however, tended to disregard the relevance of this trope for the understanding of the Western political tradition.[6] Certainly, political philosophers have recently started to fix their eye on the mixed constitution, but generally for the sake of unearthing alternative approaches to current democracy.[7] Legal historians have also begun to examine its relevance in the formation of modern political culture; yet many scholars—including intellectual historians—regard it as a heritage from Antiquity that was superseded by written constitutions and the rise of political and social sciences between the 18th and 19th centuries.[8]

In line with recent developments in conceptual history, the speech by Ramón Anglasell reveals that a discussion of mixed constitution was far from

4 Chiara Carsana, *La teoria della "Costituzione mista" nell'età imperiale romana*, (Como: New Press, 1990); see also the works gathered in Domenico Felice, *Governo misto: Ricostruzione di un'idea* (Naples: Liguore, 2007).

5 J. S. McClelland, *A History of Western Political Thought* (London and New York: Routledge, 1996), 315–38.

6 Maries Gaille-Nikodimov, "Introduction", in M. Gaille-Nikodimov, ed., *Le gouvernement mixte, de l'ideal politique au monstre constitutionnel, siècle XIII-XVIII* (Saint-Etienne : Publications de l'Université, 2005), 7–14; quote, 7, my translation.

7 One topic of interest has been distinguishing the mixed constitution from the modern notion of separation of powers. See Morgens Hansen, "The Mixed Constitution versus the Separation of Powers: Monarchical and Aristocratic Aspects of Modern Democracy", *History of Political Thought*, 31.3 (2010), 509–31; and Ivan Matiç, "The Concept of Mixed Government in Classical and Early Modern Republicanism", *Belgrade Philosophical Annual*, 29 (2016), 179–97.

8 Of relevance has been its reappraisal by legal historian Maurizio Fioravanti, *Costituzione* (Rome: Il Mulino, 1999). Among Spanish historians, see Antonio Rivera García, "La constitución mixta, un concepto político premoderno", *Historia y Política*, 26 (2011), 171–97.

an obsolete discursive practice well into the period of classical Liberalism.[9] And his was certainly not a marginal approach in its context: on the contrary, as shown in the coming pages, it was to preside over the debates following a major political crisis erupting in Spain in July 1854 that swept away the last of a ten-year series of *moderado* cabinets.[10] In the wake of the so-called 1854 Revolution, a constituent parliament was summoned, the elected members of which for nearly two years tried to reshape the institutional edifice of Spanish representative government. In a context witnessing the rise of new political forces, the language of the mixed government was recurrently deployed by both traditional and emerging participants, especially when dealing with major constitutional issues.

The aim of this chapter is to underline the liveliness of the mixed constitution *after* the promulgation of modern constitutions as a means of both enriching the understanding of Liberalism in general—and particularly the Spanish—and enhancing its status in modern political-philosophical language. My overall contention is that, irrespective of ideological alignments, the mixed constitution remained the main repository of tropes for reflecting on political-constitutional issues during the 19th century: it helped to shape the "constitutional imagination" and provided a framework to regulate "the relations between thought, text and action" both at the symbolic and normative level in modern constitutions.[11] In this view, rather than just a concept, the mixed government appears to function as a form of grammar that allowed for the conjugation of a set of fundamental categories—namely, monarchy,

9 Henk te Velde, "Democracy and the Strange Death of Mixed Government in the Nineteenth Century: Great Britain, France and the Netherlands", in Jussi Kurnmäki, Jeppe Nevers and Henk te Velde, eds., *Democracy in Modern Europe: A Conceptual History* (London, Berghahn, 2018), 42–64.

10 A general overview in the classic by Victor Kiernan, *The Revolution of 1854 in Spanish History* (Oxford: Clarendon, 1966). On the popular dimension of the mobilization, see María Zozaya, "'Moral Revenge of the Crowd' in the 1854 Revolution in Madrid", *Bulletin for Spanish and Portuguese Historical Studies*, 37.1 (2012), 18–46.

11 Reaching beyond the actual legal texts and activating "the power of narrative, symbol, ritual and myth", constitutional imagination regulates the supply of basic interpretive resources that allow citizens to appropriate the language of politics. In the period establishing representative government and modern citizenship, the semantic tropes of the mixed constitution seem to have played the role of projecting "an account of political existence in ways that shape—and re-shape—political reality": Martin Loughlin, "The Constitutional Imagination", *Modern Law Review*, 78.1 (2015), 1–25; quotes from 3. An account of the emergence of constitutional imagination, in James A. Epstein, "The Constitutional Idiom: Reasoning, Rhetoric and Action in Early Nineteenth-Century England", *Journal of Social History*, 23.3 (1990): 553–74.

aristocracy and democracy and their corresponding counter-concepts, despotism, oligarchy and demagogy or anarchy—to be declined according to national traditions of discourse, ideological standpoints and political sensibilities. Considered in their interrelations and as a whole, those concepts appear to conform a meta-conceptual device deserving exploration.

In the case of 19th-century Spain, historical contextualization implies inserting the mixed constitution in the enduring Catholic tradition of organic imagery on the Body Politic and a holistic understanding of the social and institutional relations, that was transferred to modernity through the first Liberal Constitution of 1812.[12] Such tradition of political anthropology did not merely derive from the status the Church in Spain, but also resulted from a series of features embedded in the cultural and legal framework of the Hispanic Monarchy which ultimately referred to a fundamentalist approach to Catholic morals and theology: mainly, a transcendentalist conception of unity—and of its antinomy, division, anticipating anarchy—which was applied to both all communities, from the nation to the family; a meta-political rationality operating behind ideological disputes, which affected the relations among political elites and between these and citizens at large; and a heteronomous understanding of individual consciousness, which touched upon limitations to freedom of thought and the definition of civil rights.[13]

---

12 See on this the seminal studies by José María Portillo, *Revolución de nación: Orígenes de la cultura constitucional en España, 1780–1812* (Madrid: CEPC, 2000); and Marta Lorente and Carlos Garriga, *Cádiz, 1812: La Constitución jurisdiccional* (Madrid: CEPC, 2007). A wider historical approach in António M. Hespanha, "O direito e a imaginaçao antropológica da cultura europeia do início da Era Moderna", in Julio A. Pardos *et alii*, eds., *Historia en fragmentos: Estudios en homenaje a Pablo Fernández Albaladejo* (Madrid: Universidad Autónoma, 2017), 275–92. On its sequels in 19th-century Spanish political culture, see Gregorio Alonso, "Corporations, Subjets, and Citizens: The Peculiar Modernity of Early Hispanic Liberalism", *Journal of Iberian and Latin American Studies*, 22 (2016), 7–22.

13 The 1812 Constitution defined the Spanish as the "Catholic Nation". On the dynamics of the Enlightenment in this milieu, see Ulrich L. Lehner, *The Catholic Enlightenment: The Forgotten History of a Global Movement* (New York: Oxford University Press, 2016). On unity as a core identity referent for Spanish Liberals, see Mari Cruz Romeo, "De patricios y nación: Los valores de la política liberal en España a mediados del siglo XIX", *Mélanges de la Casa de Velázquez*, 35.1 (2005), 119–42; on the problems of political exchange among Liberal elites, expressed in a distrust of political parties, see Ignacio Fernández Sarasola, *Los partidos políticos en el pensamiento español: De la Ilustración a nuestros días* (Madrid: Marcial Pons, 2009), 11–67; on the limits to autonomous conscience in the passage to Liberalism in Spain, see Pablo Sánchez León, "Science, Customs, and the Modern Subject: From Emulation to Education in the Semantics of Spanish Enlightenment", *Contributions to the History of Concepts*, 12.1 (2017), 98–120.

In dealing with mid 19th-century Spanish Liberalism, the mixed constitution approach offers a vantage point for assessing the differences between monarchy and its alternative form of government—republic. Moreover, it also provides for a more rigorous understanding of the semantic field of democracy in a context in which Spanish *demócratas* [democrats], having just been formed as a political faction in 1849 out of the *progresista*—or Liberal—party, acquired for the first time an independent political status in parliament.[14] Beyond that, it also offers insights on the semantic evolution of the notion of aristocracy, which influenced constitutional issues such as the design of the Senate. In all, an approach to the grammar of the mixed constitution offers an alternative understanding of the logic of checks and balances that relates to its hybridization with the inherited "Catholic" political anthropology, accounting for both juridical innovation and continuities.

2 The Struggle between Constituent Powers and the Role of Monarchy

The 1856 Constitution eventually failed to be promulgated and thus it came to be known as *non nata,* "unborn". Law historians have tended to interpret the 1854–56 constitutional settlement as a combination of features from the 1837 Constitution and the 1812 Constitution of Cadiz.[15] Certainly the memory of past legal texts was explicit in some of its proposals, starting with the recovery of "national sovereignty" as a foundation of legitimacy, first coined in 1812 though abandoned later in the 1837 and 1845 constitutions; yet often

14 Florencia Peyrou, "1848 et le Parti démocratique espagnol", *Mouvement Social*, 234 (2011), 17–32. On the interplay between *progresistas* and *moderados* that hegemonized Spanish politics up to the 1854 crisis, see Mari Cruz Romeo, "Lenguaje y política del nuevo liberalismo: moderados y progresistas, 1834–1845", *Ayer*, 29 (1998), 37–62.

15 Isabel Casanova Aguilar, *Aproximación a la Constitución nonnata de 1856: Presentación general y primera publicación del texto* (Murcia, Publicaciones de la Universidad, 1985); *Eadem*, *Las constituciones no promulgadas de 1856 y 1873* (Madrid: Iustel, 2008), 43–5, 58–60. The constitutional text can be found in http://www.cervantesvirtual.com/obra-visor/constitucion-no-promulgada-de-1856/html/1fc321e3-664c-4fdf-87ca-56c806904fd8_2.html. See an approach to the difficulties of the 1854–56 representatives to refound Spanish Liberalism in Bartomé Clavero, *Manual de historia constitucional de España* (Madrid: Alianza, 1989). An account of the achievements of the parliamentary debates, in José Fernando Merino Merchán and Oscar I. Mateos y de Cabo, "La 'Vicalvarada' 140 años después: aproximación al significado jurídico-constitucional del Bienio Progresista (1854–1856)", *Revista de la Cortes Generales*, 32 (1994), 121–76.

debates did not end in choosing from either one or another juridical tradition but favored innovation.

Partially due to the onset of new ideological stances struggling for recognition, the language of the 1854 constitutional debates revolved around the semantics of "principles".[16] Democrats, in particular, presented themselves in parliamentary discussions as a party to be judged "by its integrity, rectitude, doctrines and principles".[17] On the other hand, compared to their forerunners from the 1830s, Spanish Liberals from the 1850s were more aware of the threats of disunity for the stabilization of order as much as the prospect of progress, a sensibility that crystallized in the emergence of a new party—the Unión Liberal [Liberal Unitarians]— founded on the ideal of bridging over the differences between moderates and progressives that had marred their relations since the late 1830s.[18] Certainly, their continental counterparts had also been recently shaken by revolution in 1848, yet the Catholic overtones of Spanish culture exposed Liberals to a particularly crude perception of struggles as a clash between opposing principles or forces that ultimately risked escalating into a fight to the death. Accordingly, all thinkers and orators urged cooperation among the diverse ideological and political groupings in response to a vision of powers as ceaselessly striving for the encroachment of the others.[19]

It was in trying to cope with both the urgency for unity and the acknowledgement of unlimited competition that the mixed government offered a persuasive set of interpretive resources. Its presence stemmed from the depiction of eclecticism itself, now regarded as a problem rather than a solution

16 This reaffirmation of principles was injected into the parliamentary debates about whether organic laws previously excluded from constitutions —such as the electoral legislation, municipal law, and freedom of speech, among others—, should be considered as fundamental and incorporated into the constitutional text. As one newspaper proclaimed, "organic laws are to the Constitution of a State what impeller force is to a steam engine", to the extent that their elaboration "determines their possible undermining, twisting or even subversion of the principles" of a constitution. See *El Clamor Público*, 3344 (June 17th 1855), 1, quoted from Casanova, *Aproximación*, 29. The journal was one of the main organs of the *progresista* party.

17 *Diario de las Sesiones de las Cortes Constituyente: Legislatura de 1854, 1855 y 1856* (Madrid, Imprenta Nacional, 1856), December 19th, 1854, 810, Miguel Ferrer y Garcés.

18 See on this party Francesc Martínez Gallego, *Conservar progresando: la Unión Liberal (1856–1868)* (Valencia: UNED, 2001). On the wider issue of unity among Liberals in this context, Pablo Sánchez León, *Popular Political Participation and the Democratic Imagination in Spain: From Crowd to People, 1766–1868* (London and New York: Palgrave, 2020), ch. 5.

19 In the words of young radical *progresista* deputy José Moreno Nieto, "God placed in all powers the desire for expansion, not only for conservation": *Diario*, January 10th, 1855, 1258.

for political-philosophical coherence: in effect, the 1837 and 1845 Constitutions appeared as flawed due to their taking of "a bit of the monarchy, another bit of aristocracy and of the people" and, "once this confusion was achieved" declaring that "here is unity and the best from each".[20] The challenge of the new political elite elected to the Cortes in the fall of 1854 was how to compromise with competitors and adversaries without feeling they were relinquishing their principles.

From the perspective of 1854, previous Liberal settlements appeared as having been pushed too much by an urgency for combining the elements of the triad monarchy-aristocracy-democracy without first acknowledging their respective autonomy. Integrity was now understood as a perquisite for establishing a relationship between powers that prevented them from degenerating into their negative counter-images that would endanger representative government. Elaborating on these insights, the 1854–56 "constitutional moment" can be regarded as an attempt to reinforcing each of the elements of the mixed constitution while at the same time seeking an equilibrium between them in order to guarantee the overall stability of the system. This was in line with a mantra that many Spanish Liberals espoused then: namely, that no authority could be assumed prior to the proclamation of a new constitution, a standpoint that allowed for a pioneering parliamentarian debate on the Monarchy as a form of government suitable for Spain.[21]

Through their conjugation of the mixed government tropes, democrats distanced themselves from declared *republicanos* [republicans]—also obtaining for the first time seats in the Cortes—and accepted the maintenance of a constitutional monarchy, which in turn encouraged accommodation with

20 Critical distancing from eclectic approaches to constitutional issues was probably the main consensus among the 1854–56 political elites, in reaction against the dominant "doctrinaire" orthodoxy of the previous decades. *Progresista* deputy Higinio Arriaga defined eclecticism as a philosophical "absurdity", which implied "choosing in everything the best" but "lacking any true principle", in practice it involved "confusing everything" and "making from the good and the bad a unity difficult to realize": *Diario*, January 23rd, 1855, 1576.

21 The debate was forced at the opening of the parliamentary sessions by several *demócratas*, who questioned the traditional prerogative of the monarchy to sign legislation with the argument that the institution itself had not been constitutionally defined yet. It included rhetorical phrases such as: "Must the monarchy continue existing? (…) Or can its sentence to death be pronounced in an Assembly, in the calmness of a discussion, as a verdict of justice or a solemn decree of the national will?": *Diario*, January 10th, 1855: 1255, José Moreno Nieto.

progresistas.[22] Resorting to the concepts of the mixed constitution allowed democrats place democracy above the republican form of government. As a *demócrata* deputy declared: "I am more than a republican: I am a democrat", and went on to stress that the "great difference" between one and the other was that "in the democratic form there is no space for tyrannies as happens with republics".[23] Accordingly, in the democratic agenda a republican form of government should not be taken as "inevitable", "systematic" or "an essential condition of the system". Consequently, "as much as despotism may be found in a Republic, democracy can be found in monarchy".[24] *Progresistas* also elaborated on this perspective.[25] In general, however, for many of these, as well as the *unionistas* and average *moderados*, the Monarchy possessed "special conditions" and "attributes", even "eternal principles".[26] Still, in trying to define the Monarchy they resorted to the repertoire of the mixed government: as opposed to the "aristocratic and democratic powers", which may "sometimes rule as sovereign and others obey as subjects", the Monarchy "must always rule".[27]

Through a comparison with the other powers, the grammar of the mixed constitution thus offered decisive interpretive resources for defining Monarchy. The effectiveness of the mixed government stemmed, however, from its framing of the constitutive elements in a relation of mutual recognition and harmony securing order and unity. This entailed applying Montesquieu´s formula of "checks and balances" to issues different from the separation of powers. Certainly, there were important issues in the 1856 Constitution openly referring to the division of powers, such as the limitations to the royal prerogative, the reenactment of the Diputación General—providing for autonomy of the legislative *vis-à-vis* the executive—, the establishment of a calendar for the debates on the annual budget—providing with autonomy of the executive against the legislative—or the different measures instituted to guarantee the

---

22 On the relations between *demócratas* and *republicanos* in the period, and between them and other forces, see Florencia Peyrou, *Tribunos del pueblo: Demócratas y republicanos durante el reinado de Isabel II* (Madrid: CEPC, 2007), 267–349.

23 *Diario*, May 15 1855: 4784, Eduardo Ruiz Pons.

24 This allowed for a relevant distinction between principles and forms: "What we systematically proclaim is the principle of democracy, what we do not systematically proclaim is the form of the Republic": *Diario*, December 16th, 1854, 616, José Ordax Avecilla.

25 Deputy Fernando Corradi from the progressivist bench, for instance, declared: "I believe that true democracy is in the institutions, not in the form of government": *Diario*, November 30th, 1854, 275.

26 *Diario*, December 20th 1854, 854, Patricio de la Escosura. The argument for "eternal principles" was by Antonio Ros de Olano: *Diario*, February 6th, 1855, 1919. They both were *moderados* veering towards the Unión Liberal.

27 *Diario,* January 10th, 1855: 1258, Moreno Nieto, *progresista*.

protection of the rights of citizens, and the autonomy of the judiciary from the executive and the legislative.[28] Yet some of the most heated debates of the 1854 constituent Cortes dealt with issues with little relation to the division of powers—such as the *Milicia Nacional* [the voluntary civic army for policing order and liberties] or the election of municipal authorities—or that reached beyond arguments for institutional checks.

Initially, in the debates there were numerous speeches in favor of a rather proactive exchange between the triad of monarchy-aristocracy-democracy; in particular radical *progresistas* and *demócratas* argued for extending the influence of democracy over the other powers, starting with the Monarchy. As expressed by a democrat deputy: considering that Queen Isabella II "owes its Throne to popular sovereignty",[29] the goal was to strengthen the "bond" and "consistency" between the "Throne and freedom". This implied combining and tainting the former with the latter, as posed by another representative: "We want a Monarchy that is true, plain, popular and democratic".[30] *Demócratas* founded this bid on principle, but also profited from equating the democratic element with progress.[31] *Progresistas* largely agreed with this view, but emphasized the need to balance progress with conservation, identifying the latter with the monarchic element.[32] Despite these differences, both were acknowledging that the balanced combination of the different elements provided the whole social and institutional order with overarching unity, cohesiveness and stability—or, to put it in the negative fashion favored in the context, it was the only means for overcoming "the rival spirits of the Throne, the aristocracy and the people in their ceaseless struggle" that "brings chaos to political and social order".[33]

This approach was underpinned by the widespread belief that the nation was the ultimate source of legitimacy, an issue in which the rationale of the mixed constitution showed its capacity to adapt to the vernacular. The establishment

---

28 Casanova Aguilar, *Las constituciones no promulgadas*, 45–6.

29 *Diario*, December 19th 1854, 852, Martín de los Heros.

30 *Diario*, January 10th, 1855, 1252, Ordax Avecilla.

31 "Democracy is the principle of these times" which could be found "in the atmosphere we live, in the air we breathe, and against which it is futile to fight against", so that "today any barrier placed to oppose it will finally disappear and the current will follow its path": *Diario*, December 16th, 1854: 616, Ordax Avecilla.

32 As proposed by a *progresista* deputy: Monarchy "long time ago ceased to represent progress and only stands for stability and order": *Diario*, January 10th, 1855, 1258, deputy Moreno Nieto.

33 *Diario*, March 17th 1855: 3034, intervention by *progresista* deputy Antonio de los Ríos Rosas.

of the "national spirit" as the basis of sovereignty expressed on the one hand the inability of democrats to propose a more radical alternative—popular sovereignty—; on the other hand, it was inspired by their relying on an organic conception of the Body Politic. From this shared assumption, differences in stress followed ideological lines: whereas conservatives and unionists gave priority to unity for the system and to maximizing the orderly coordination between its parts, democrats and progressives fostered the popular element in different institutions as a means for safeguarding the harmonic internal functioning of the whole. Even radicals upheld this holistic epistemology: when *demócrata* party ideologue José Ordax Avecilla declared he wanted the democratic principle applied "to all relations of social and political life", he justified it as "the sole one that can guarantee the effects of national sovereignty".[34]

3 The Meaning of Democracy in the 1854–56 Parliamentary Debates

Inspired by the tradition of the mixed constitution, for its proponents, democracy was in the first place a bulwark against the efforts of the other powers—monarchy and aristocracy—to encroach on the popular dimension in a constitution: in the words of one of the original founders and forerunners of the Partido Demócrata—José María de Orense—the goal of democracy, aside from "sustaining freedom", had always been "to warn those in government, when they take the wrong trail, that they are following the road to ruin".[35] Behind this was an identification of the people with public opinion on one side, and on the other with the force and quantity required to obstruct extra-limitations by the other powers.

This dialectics of checks and balances can be gauged by considering the discourse from *demócratas*, as expressed in the claim "our principle is popular government".[36] Even when they claimed that "the Spanish nation wants to maintain its throne", they added that their aim was "to surround" the monarchy "with popular institutions".[37] As expressed by Nicolás Rivero, a *demócrata* deputy and one of the leaders of the 1854 Revolution:

34 *Diario*, December 16th, 1854, 616.
35 *Diario*, January 26th, 1855, 1638.
36 *Diario*, December 16th, 1854, 616, Ordax Avecilla.
37 *Diario*, November 30th, 1854, 275, Fernando Corradi.

> Do we want to make disappear such form of antagonism between the Throne and the people that we have been witnessing for many years now? It is as easy as to surround the Throne of democratic institutions.[38]

"Popular" or "democratic", the relevance is not so much in the adjective as in the plural of "institutions". What these expressions meant was to allow commoners to partake in all the different constitutive elements of the Body Politic, either through full membership—in the case of corporations—or by autonomous representation—in the institutions—, a logic that was also applied to the Militia and the Courts through the establishment of the jury.

Further inspiration for this reasoning was not primarily in the English political system; the model was rather the United States. Foreign examples were, however, less influential than a vernacular vein of political culture inherited from early Liberalism and which denounced the maintenance of privileges incorporations or institutions. Nurtured by the memory of the 1812 Constitution—labeled as "democratic" by both its defenders and opponents—, this ideal of 'democracy-within-corporation' is thoroughly distinctive from 20th-century definitions of democracy; its proper understanding requires combining in one single scheme the national tradition of '*doceañismo*' [from the year 12 or *doce* of the early Liberal constitution] with the transnational standards of the mixed constitution, on the premise that in both of them democracy was primarily considered not as a form of government or a type of power singular in its nature, but rather as an element or dimension to be preserved and fostered in any constitution.[39]

The mid-19th century crisis of Liberalism allowed these two visions to hybridize, favoring a discourse on how to partake and be represented inside corporations and institutions. From this vantage point, early Spanish republicans and democrats can be seen as not just striving to empower the people in order to check the excesses from the other powers—which they sought to achieve by limiting the royal prerogative and promoting decentralization—but also trying to stabilize the system through balancing each of the institutions and corporations of the Body Politic, which they pursued by fostering their respective democratic dimension *vis-à-vis* the monarchical and aristocratic ones.

Behind this peculiar 'democratization' was a perception of the social order as a complex set of corporations rather than a civil society. This explains why

---

38 And to make the throne "understand that it is the legitimate representative of Spanish Society", see *Diario*, November 14th, 1855, 8217, Nicolás Rivero.

39 See on this Sánchez León, *Popular Political Participation*, ch. 2.

demócratas tended to disorderly mix into their agenda the promotion of the individual rights of citizens and of the collective power of the people.[40] Notably, universal suffrage was not at the core of their ambitions throughout 1854–56. In effect, *demócratas* and *republicanos* did not focus on generalizing the ballot, but instead sought a wider agenda of measures for assuring a stable, progressive and virtuous constitutional monarchy. Given that their common goal was empowering the democratic element in each institution, universal suffrage was seen as just one among a variety of possible checks and balances rather than the distinctive and exclusive mark of democracy.[41] In general, their discourse on the issue tended to be rather defensive, reminding their opponents that worse than extending the right to voting was "the abuse of the Governments that perpetuate themselves".[42] At best, they regarded universal suffrage as a shield against excesses from the legislative and executive (and judicial alike)—a functional device for representing the many in institutions and corporations in order to prevent the few from forming an exclusive oligarchy that would justify popular revolutions.

"We do not want demagogy, we want democracy".[43] This statement summarizes the extent to which in the wake of the 1854 Revolution the struggle for recognition by radical Liberals referred to both the concepts and counter-concepts supplied by the mixed constitution grammar. Accusations of behaving like demagogues, which democrats utterly rejected, went beyond stereotypes of manipulation of the uncultivated masses, touching upon the role of leadership and authority.[44] They also signal that the usage of democracy

40 As shown in their program for the 1854 election, some of their proposals underlined the autonomy of individuals *vis-à-vis* the State while others favored the empowerment of the people as the backbone of representative government, but without a clear hierarchy and justified order. See the program in Peyrou, *Tribunos del pueblo*, 314–15.

41 This did not contradict that universal suffrage could be seen as a "principle that adapts itself [*se arregla*] to all systems, to all institutions", the superiority of the democratic party being on its part in that universal suffrage matched better with the spirit of democracy: *Diario*, January 24th, 1856, 10174, García López.

42 *Diario*, June 21st, 1855, 5862, Orense, who also argued that in its essence universal suffrage conspired against those "great risk of societies" that were revolutions.

43 *Diario*, January 24th,1856, 10171, García López, who underlined that "there is an immense distance" between them and defined democracy as "the proposal of all the rights, of all those collective rights that constitute the political right".

44 See on this Pablo Sánchez León, "'People', 'Plebs' and the Changing Boundaries of the Political: Assymmetrical Conceptualizations in Spanish Liberalism from a Comparative European Perspective", in Kirill Postoutenko, ed., *Beyond 'Hellenes' and 'Barbarians': Assymmetrical Concepts in European Discourse* (London: Berghahn, 2022), 205–224.

had less to do with ideology than with mastering the available grammar.[45] For, interestingly enough, it was *progresistas* and not *demócratas* who championed the discourse on democracy from within the framework of the mixed constitution. Their spokesmen were a series of intellectuals, one of which was Ramón Anglasell, mentioned above in the opening of this chapter. More respected, however, was Manuel Colmeiro, an expert in political economy, legal science and history. In 1855, Colmeiro published an essay on the history of institutions in Spain in which he established the orthodox position for *progresistas*: they distanced themselves from "pure" democracy, defined as one not properly checked and balanced by the other powers.[46] Anglasell and Colmeiro were thus renewing the mixed constitution as the proper framework for defining the meaning and scope of democracy in a representative government—blaming exclusionary conceptions of popular sovereignty for producing imbalanced polities and institutionally uncontrolled representative systems.

Rival parties as they were, *progresistas* and *demócratas* also found common ground in their interpretation of Spanish history. For decades Spanish Liberals had been collectively building a narrative of the imperial past which underlined the capacity by the monarchy to enroll commoners in the ranks of administration, thus fostering social mobility and diluting the power of the privileged: in spite of differences in stress, the usual account was that the country inherited from its past a "democratic monarchy".[47] Accordingly, by the 1850s it was not necessarily democrats who took as common sense the wisdom that Spain was a democratic society and culture. *Progresista* deputy Servando Ruiz Gómez also claimed that:

> The Spanish society is an essentially democratic society; it is eminently democratic, and there is not another as democratic in the world: it is the democratic society par excellence.[48]

45 Failure to grasp this circumstance risks misleading historians, who usually focus on parties and their ideologies. An example in Peyrou, *Tribunos del pueblo*.

46 He did so through a historical interpretation: "In the first age of the people there appear the simplest governments, such as democracy or monarchy, and only with time there show up the middle terms and the mixed forms, as a remedy to greater needs, or as a fruit of a long experience in the business of States": Manuel Colmeiro, *De la constitución y del gobierno de los reinos de León y Castilla* (Madrid: Librería de Calleja, 1855), I, 43.

47 Pablo Sánchez León, "Aristocracia fantástica: Los moderados y la poética del gobierno representativo", *Ayer* 61 (2006), 77–103; and *Popular Political Participation*, ch. 3.

48 *Diario*, March 7th, 1855: 2725.

Similar statements can also be easily found among *unionistas* and *moderados*.[49] They reveal a common concept of democracy as the possibility for commoners to access all the honors of society and the state, either through membership or representation.[50]

A focus on the grammar of the mixed constitution not only helps to trace semantic analogies between ideological stances, but also reveals the differences that separated them on the issue. For conservatives, democratic mores had been generalized by the kings through the infusing of office-holding with the equalizing ideas of Christianity, the ultimate source of democracy in Spain. Therefore, given that Spain was already a democratic nation, there was no need to further expand the "democratic ideas" in the form "of systems, of codes, of constitutions".[51] In contrast, Patricio de la Escosura, originally a conservative but who had joined moderate *progresistas* (and eventually would *unionistas*), contemptuously affirmed that in constitutional monarchies "governed by the *moderado* party, what rules, what commands society is an oligarchy".[52] To understand this quote, we must now discuss the third element of the mixed constitution triad: aristocracy.

4 The Changing Perception of Aristocracy

In general, in the 1854–56 parliamentary sessions the term aristocracy was used with blatantly negative connotations whenever political actors wanted to denounce what appeared to them as privileges deriving from government policies or institutional dynamics. Yet there were other, more conceptual usages, especially when dealing with the issue of a Senate for the future Constitution.

---

49 "In the light of history, democracy is old in our country": *Diario*, February 6th, 1855, 1919, Antonio Ros de Olano from Unión Liberal.

50 Deputy Manuel Alonso Martínez, then minister of *Fomento* [Improvement] in a *progresista* cabinet (to join the Unión Liberal in 1857), considered that Spain was "essentially democratic" because "always the first offices of the State (…) have been open to all sorts of people, to all classes of citizens": *Diario*, March 15th, 1855, 2896.

51 Democracy had expanded "under the intangible form of the sentiment, of the inspiration, of the spirit": *Diario*, February 9th, 1855, 1854, Gabriel García Tassara. Accordingly, trying to push a political agenda for democracy risked imposing a "rampant" tyranny that would "outstrip all tyrannies": *Diario*, December 18th, 1854, 702, deputy José Joaquín Mariátegui, then minister of Hacienda [Budgeting].

52 *Diario*, January 22nd, 1856, 10060. The debate on the electoral system made him define *moderados* as "oligarchic" and his *progresista* followers as "moderate" for being located "between democratic and oligarchic theory", and thus as "the true middle party": *Diario*, January 31st, 1856, 10439.

When the post-1854 political elites discussed whether one or two cameras suited the principles of representative government and the peculiarities of Spanish society and culture, they openly referred to the mixed government rhetoric—such as when all of the parties spoke of the Senate as "the aristocratic camera".

Positions in favor or against a Senate were not so much marked by ideology as by the transversal influence of *doceañista* sensibility. For Evaristo San Miguel, an older *progresista* deputy and figure of consensus in the 1854 Revolution, the 1837 settlement had opted for a dual camera system by assuming—erroneously from his view—that the "disorders", "agitations" and "collisions" in the wake of the 1812 Constitution had their origins in its "democratic character" which, "doctrinaire" Liberals insisted, required "as principle" a single legislative camera.[53] Such speeches profited from a wide consensus on the historical decline of aristocracy: according to a *demócrata* representative, in Spain aristocracy "does not exist anymore or it´s already confused with the class of the people".[54] The implication of such claims was straightforward: "Where there is not really an aristocracy, there is no reason to give a distinct and special representation to a class which does not exist".[55] Even *moderados* had to acknowledge that Spain lacked "enough aristocratic elements for constituting a Camera like the English".[56] And yet, just like many *unionistas* and moderate *progresistas*, even if there was no traditional aristocracy to stuff it, *moderados* were in favor of an upper house. Their position was not, however, mainly founded on an argument on the division of powers. True enough, some deputies spoke of the "moderating or compensating" attributes of the Senate, which was described "as a force mediating between the power that sanctions and the one that legislates".[57] Yet the core of these debates was a different understanding of the notion of checks and balances: the issue at stake was how to combine the aristocratic and democratic elements *within* the legislative. Here, consensus was neither

53 His counterargument was that the 1812 Constitution "did nor perish" due to its democratic character, neither for designing a one single-camera system; and he went on to stress that by 1812 a second camera "was not popular": *Diario*, March 6th, 1855, 2705.

54 He clarified that the "popular element" was "predominant" in Spanish society: *Diario*, January 25th, 1855, 1615, Carlos Godínez de Paz.

55 *Diario*, March 6th, 1855: 2742, Feijóo Sotomayor.

56 With this diagnose, he did not mean, however, that there could not be a Senate "with a different organization": *Diario*, March 6th, 1855: 2702, Ignacio Yáñez Rivadeneira.

57 *Diario*, March 7th 1855, 2726, Juan Antonio de Padua Florán, Marquis of Tabuérniga. On his part, in his speech against a dual system, San Miguel challenged his opponents to offer "one example in which the camera they call aristocratic" had "ever detained the excesses of Power": *Diario*, March 6th, 1855, 2701.

guaranteed nor even easy to find: as shown by claims that the Senate should be even "more democratic than the Cortes", it was not taken for granted that an "aristocratic camera" meant an institution exclusively shaped by the aristocratic principle or element.[58]

As it can be seen, holistic conceptions of the Body Politic were also predicated on particular organs. Key to the 1854–56 constitutional imagination was that the contents of this inherited political anthropology adapted fairly well to the mixed government tradition. In effect, since the 1830s, even progressive Liberals had concluded that a 'democratic monarchy' was an unbalanced heritage from 1812 which risked veering towards either anarchy or despotism. As they argued, in order to secure freedom and citizenship rights, Spanish Liberalism needed to balance its monarchy and democracy by fostering the aristocratic principle.[59] By the 1850s this view remained influential, reinforced by inspiration from history. Colmeiro described the ancient constitution of Castile as an example of mixed government. According to his account, the Visigoth kings summoned lay and clerical magnates in order to address "challenging business with their counsel", while the "most serious ones" were decided "in the summons of the people as a whole".[60] Eventually, however, the magnates had failed to keep their autonomy *vis-à-vis* the kings, unbalancing the whole constitutional edifice towards autocracy.[61] According to this historical interpretation, long-term subordination to the throne had eviscerated the Spanish aristocracy: even if it still existed as a social reality, "politically speaking" it was "completely void from over three centuries now".[62]

This constituted a major challenge for the stability of a modern social and institutional order, for an autonomous and stable aristocracy adapted to a modern society could not be "improvised" and thus had to be created anew from scratch. By 1854, the way *progresistas* imagined this colossal social engineering

58 See *Diario*, March 7th, 1855: 2726, Marquis of Tabuérniga.

59 Which was behind their acceptance of the rationale underlying the 1837 Constitutional settlement: Sánchez León, "Aristocracia fantástica".

60 Colmeiro, *De la constitución*, 28.

61 In his account, the decisive crossroads of Spanish aristocracy had occurred during the urban revolt against young Charles I in 1520, when "the grandees and lesser nobles" decided not to make "common cause with the towns" against the imperial appetites of the future emperor. Colmeiro concluded that, had the nobles allied instead with commoners "[w]e would then have had a historical constitution without leaning much towards democracy, aristocracy or monarchy, but mixed and in just proportion and suitable for those times", 388.

62 "Aristocracies and woods need the action of centuries to form themselves": *Diario*, March 10th, 1855, 2818, De la Escosura, who added that they required "a series of ancestors", "prestige" and to have a "history" and "breed", attributes that "cannot be bought" with money.

was generating it through the political-institutional machinery. They were persuaded that binding the aristocracy to the procedures of representative government would have the virtuous effect of breeding in it the values of freedom; yet they were also aware that this involved undertaking a whole layer of policies, which explains the hectic activity of the Parliament—in parallel to the constitutional debates—for legislating on issues such as railway expansion, banking, societies of credit and the public sale of common lands. The rationale behind these measures was to increase the sources for business and market relations, so that in the long run ordinary citizens would be admitted to a brand-new aristocracy embodying both private wealth and public virtue—a vision that also appealed to *demócratas*—. The establishment of a Senate was a pressing issue in the short run, however, which required of *progresistas, moderados* and *unionistas* to overcome criticism by *demócratas* against privileging any existing social group, particularly the traditional titled nobility.[63]

They ultimately succeeded in the debate for the Senate by innovating discourse in three ways. First, they expanded on the distinction between the "interests of the moment", as embodied by the lower chamber, and the "constant" interests of the nation—not of any particular group—, which would be represented in the higher camera.[64] Secondly, they argued that permanent interests could be defended by an elective camera that, being subject to "renovation", would represent the people through changes in "opinion".[65] This latter argument was acknowledged by more radical Liberals as both a sign of democratization of the Senate and a means for preventing the transformation of the aristocracy into an oligarchy. Finally, the third and path-breaking argument was to draw a distinction between the individual and the collective. The majority of deputies assumed that, even if there were families owning privileged titles from the past, *as a class* the aristocracy could not be relied on for constituting the Senate; on the other hand, it was also commonly recognized that there existed an "individual aristocracy" that could not be easily discredited

63 A "monarchy democratic by excellence" should be one "in which there are no class privileges": *Diario*, March 24th, 1856, 10174, García López.

64 Another deputy defined "the nature of the popular body" as representing "more cardinally the movable interests", while the Senate stood for "the permanent" ones: *Diario*, March 21st, 1855, 4972, Arriaga. According to Ríos Rosas the function of a Senate was to "moderate" the legislative but also to represent "the moral and general permanent interests" and provide a "constant direction to national politics": *Diario*, March 17th, 1855, 3033.

65 Deputy de la Escosura expressively identified the "interests of the moment" with "public opinion", which he equated with "the expression and the formula of the interests of the people, of its interests in each moment": *Diario*, March 19th,1855, 2818.

as a "privileged class" because it did not found its status on privilege.[66] This combined reasoning allowed progressives and conservatives to argue in favor of stuffing the upper house on such conditions as "merit (...) services (...) science (...) social status (...) capital", that is "the condition of all that gives true influence in every well-ordered society".[67]

In all, the concept of the aristocracy was subject to semantic transformation, being deprived of its class connotations. The resulting discourse secured a middle ground between radicals and conservatives, ultimately remaining within the shared repertoire of the mixed government. The resilience of the mixed constitution grammar can also be seen in that this partial redefinition of aristocracy by moderate *progresistas* was on its part counterbalanced by a redefinition of democracy by *demócratas*, from "a party in opposition to aristocracy" to "a government in which all classes of society are represented, from the higher to the most unhappy".[68] Together, these changes help explain the apparent contradiction of the 1856 constitutional text: compared to previous constitutions it extended the franchise by reducing the minimum income required for political rights as an elector, but on the other it raised the income conditions for candidates to representatives.[69] In effect, the commission designated in the fall of 1855 to draw up the electoral reform assumed the need to "provide an adequate extension to the franchise";[70] on the issue of electors,

66 Moderate *Progresistas* were keen on describing the most popular leader of the 1854 Revolution—Baldomero Espartero, duque of Victory, a hero from the Carlist War and chosen for the Regency in the early 1840s—"not as an example of class aristocracy but of individual aristocracy, for it originates in his merit and in his virtue": *Diario*, March 13th, 1855, 2914, De la Escosura. On Espartero's earlier career, see Adrian Schubert, *Espartero, el pacificador* (Barcelona: Galaxia Gutenberg, 2018); on his popularity, Alberto Cañas de Pablos, "Personificando la revolución. Espartero: Carisma en la Revolución de 1840 y su llegada a la Regencia", *Vínculos de Historia*, 5 (2016), 270–89.

67 *Diario*, March 13th, 1855, 2907, intervention by deputy Modesto Lafuente. Another *progresista* representative spoke of a "legitimate aristocracy" of "feelings" and "aspirations", though he found no contradiction in qualifying the resulting system as a "democracy" of virtuous political emotions: *Diario*, November 8th, 1855, 8021, Ríos Rosas.

68 *Diario*, June 9th, 1855, 5514, Ruiz Pons.

69 María Sierra, María Antonia Peña and and Rafael Zurita, *Electores y elegibles: La representación parlamentaria en la cultura del liberalismo* (Madrid: Marcial Pons, 2010), esp. 189–226.

70 According to one of the members of the commission, if the degree of wealth required for the exercise of voting was "exaggerated", denying the right of "the middle classes, to the class of producers, to the working class, to all those delivering a medium-size contribution" and restricting it "to very few, only the wealthy", then the system as a whole would be "heading towards aristocracy": *Diario*, January 31st, 1856, 10441, Rafael Monares.

however, the members of the commission proceeded in an elitist manner.[71] A similar discourse was deployed when dealing with other institutions like the municipalities—where a further widening of the electoral base was counteracted by limiting candidates to local larger tax contributors—or corporations such as the Militia. These reforms reflected the commitment by the 1854–56 representatives, irrespective of their ideological principles, to strike a balance between the aristocratic and the democratic dimension in each of the organs of the Body Politic, a logic understood on its part as the precondition for their stability, unity, and coordination—the attributes of Monarchy in the language of the mixed government—with the other members of the constitutional setting.

5 Conclusion

The 1856 Constitution would never be promulgated, as it has been said: when the *patres conscripti* were about to finish the debates on the electoral law, the newly designated prime minister General Leopoldo O'Donnell dissolved the Cortes and forced new elections in the fall of 1856; meanwhile, *unionistas* formally organized as a political party and became the crucial force for reproducing a new *moderado* majority that quickly disposed of the works of the constituent Cortes. *Demócratas* on their part felt betrayed by *progresistas*, and started to radicalize their stances: recovering a discourse elaborated in the heat of the 1854 Revolution, they went beyond the traditional identification of monarchy with tyranny and for the first time presented it as a prime cause of disunity and a rival to true democracy.[72] By so doing, they were still arguing within the conceptual repertoire and the meta-conceptual background of the mixed constitution and within the mould of organic and holistic definitions of the Body Politic. In 1868 *demócratas* and *progresistas* would have a new chance

71 The commission accepted the *progresista* dictum that "in purely representative governments the electoral right is not one of the rights of man" but rather "a political function that society entrusts to a certain class of people that will exercise it with prudence, with acumen, with independence and with sage": *Diario*, January 31st, 1856, 10441, Monares.

72 If on one side "Monarchy and national sovereignty reject each other like force and right, like violence and reason", on the other "the dogma of democracy" allowed for "the fusion of all the peoples and races in one sigle family": Fernando Garrido, *El pueblo y el trono* (Madrid: Imprenta de Tomás Núñez Amor, 1854), 9. On the period after 1856 and the political and ideological dynamics of pro-democratic identities, see Guy Thompson, *The Birth of Modern Politics in Spain: Democracy, Association and Revolution, 1854–75* (London: Palgrave/Macmillan, 2009); and Peyrou, *Tribunos del pueblo*, 351–410.

for political influence over the constitutional design when Queen Isabella II was overthrown; this time they openly demanded universal suffrage as their banner.

Traditionally, modern constitutions have been regarded as a combination of checks and balances that assured the mutual independence of the executive, legislative and judiciary. Yet the very notion of check and balances had a different origin and was shaped by a longer tradition of political philosophy. Throughout the 19th century, Liberals made use of it to tackle the relations between the three components or dimensions to mitigate the risk of tyranny, oligarchy or anarchy as referring to the grammar of mixed constitution. This genealogy has been overlooked by both historians of law and political thought although it constitutes a crucial repertoire for modern constitutional and ideological imagination. As this article shows, the vitality of the grammar of the mixed constitution infused new lifeblood to the "Catholic" political anthropology that shaped the political and legal culture of Spanish Liberals. Recovering its heuristic and hermeneutical value offers a vantage point that helps explain how tradition and innovation can coexist in modern cultural and institutional processes.

Bibliography

Main Sources

Anglasell, Ramón, *Discurso leído en la Universidad Central en el acto de recibir la investidura de Doctor en la Facultad de Filosofía, Sección de Administración* (Madrid: Salustiano Ríos y Cía., 1856).

Colmeiro, Manuel, *De la constitución y del gobierno de los reinos de León y Castilla* (Madrid: Librería de Calleja, 1855).

Constitución no promulgada de 1856, http://www.cervantesvirtual.com/obra-visor/constitucion-no-promulgada-de-1856/html/1fc321e3-664c-4fdf-87ca-56c806904fd8_2.html.

Diario de las Sesiones de las Cortes Constituyentes: Legislatura de 1854, 1855 y 1856 (Madrid: Imprenta Nacional, 1856).

Main Bibliographical References

Hansen, Morgen, "The Mixed Constitution versus the Separation of Powers: Monarchical and Aristocratic Aspects of Modern Democracy", *History of Political Thought*, 31.3 (2010), 509–31.

Loughlin, Martin, "The Constitutional Imagination", *Modern Law Review*, 78.1 (2015), 1–25.

Peyrou, Florencia, *Tribunos del pueblo: Demócratas y republicanos durante el reinado de Isabel II* (Madrid: CEPC, 2007).

Portillo, José María, *Revolución de nación: Orígenes de la cultura constitucional en España, 1780–1812* (Madrid: CEPC, 2000).

Sánchez León, Pablo, *Popular Political Participation and the Democratic Imagination in Spain: From Crowd to People, 1766–1868* (London and New York: Palgrave, 2020).

PART 5

The Twentieth and Twenty-First Centuries

CHAPTER 18

The Weimar Constitutional Moment

Constitutionalism, Theoretical Debate and Political Conflict

Ersin Yildiz

> All political concepts arise from a concrete foreign or domestic conflict and are, without this conflict, merely ambiguous, senseless abstractions.
>
> CARL SCHMITT, "Hugo Preuss, His Concept of the State and his Position in German State Theory" (1930).

1 Introduction: Weimar as a Model of Political-Constitutional Conflict

The debate on the political period of Weimar Germany is not limited to specific countries but is widespread in international discourse across a variety of disciplines and an endless number of topics.[1] Even today, theories of Weimar constitutionalism continue to influence legal studies and political theory. That Carl Schmitt in particular has gained significance in today's political thinking cannot be disregarded. Schmitt's Weimar-era work has been influential across a range of scientific fields because both the Schmittian topics and the Weimar constitutional period as a historical-political and specific theoretical discursive context are analytically useful. The reception of his work, which developed rapidly, thus goes beyond merely intellectual history, having become influential in political theory as well.[2] However, there is also a certain obliqueness to the reception which neglects the context of the constitutional discourse

1 For a general historical overview of the Weimar Republic with a special focus on the structure of the political crisis, see also Hans Mommsen, *The Rise and Fall of Weimar Democracy* (Chapel Hill: University of North Carolina Press, 1996).

2 For the enduring importance of Schmitt's political philosophy, cf. Jean-Francois Kervégan, *Que faire de Carl Schmitt?* (Paris: Gallimard, 2011).

 | DOI:10.1163/9789004549159_020

peculiar to the Weimar period. Therefore, in today's discourse, the characteristics of the constitutional-political discourse are thrown out of focus, and in numerous approaches its relevance is not sufficiently considered. This has serious theoretical-analytical implications, obscuring the political context of the theories and posing a challenge for anyone seeking to understand the arguments and opinions of each Weimar theorist.

The historical-political structure and the genesis of concepts and categories must instead be viewed together. What makes this period historically significant is that it led to the rejuvenation and reassertion of categories that had already gained structural stability in a modern constitutional state. Defining the structure of the political discourse of the Weimar constitutional moment, in this respect, is thus beneficial not only in historical terms but also because of its conceptual relevance.

At the core of this analysis will be the discursive structure of the debate on the political foundations of the constitution that was decisive for the Weimar constitutional crisis. Thus, the core social-political problem behind the Weimar constitutional moment will be clarified by considering the theories of Carl Schmitt and Franz Neumann. These two theoreticians are of key importance in comprehending the political polarization in constitutional political discourse. Their constitutional-political positions represented the two main camps dominating Weimar's constitutional discourse. The bourgeois-conservative and socialist positions represented the two main groups in the constitutional-political conflict aiming to determine and define the principles regarding the social order. Disagreement on the historical-political characteristics of the constitution stemmed from the existence of opposed norms based on either socialist or liberal principles. This situation of "open constitutionalism" was the central characteristic of the Weimar constitutional moment. Thus, this chapter will focus on this political antagonism, which has been neglected in recent studies on the Weimar period, providing insight into the structural characteristics of the conflict constellation that provoked the intense political polarization around interpreting the constitution. This constitutional-political context marked the formation of crucial categories and concepts.

However, the dispute went beyond a merely abstract clash between the broad positions of democratic republicans vs. anti-democratic anti-republicans, and instead developed around the social-political order as laid out within the constitution. In interpreting the constitution, the concept of democracy was used in a socialist sense by social democratic theoreticians and jurists, triggering strong reactions on the bourgeois side (represented by bourgeois-conservative theories).[3] This polarization intensified the constitutional crisis. While the social-democratic program – which was basically a socialist one – was reflected most precisely in Neumann's work, the counter-reaction found its specific expression in Schmitt's constitutional writings. Considering his socialist opponents, Schmitt focused on the fundamental concept of the constitution and the question of the basis of legitimation for the constitutional state. This is Schmitt's contribution to the discourse today. His importance and permanent influence are based on his ability to shed light on the central role of constitutionalism as a mechanism of legitimation for the political order.

2 The Main Problems of Contemporary Weimar Reception

Intense reception has yet to lead to an appropriate understanding of the antagonistic structure of the Weimar constitutional moment. The length of time of the reception makes the situation more challenging. This is because the history of the reception is in itself part of intellectual history and therefore cannot be dealt with in detail here. For the question at the heart of this chapter there are two points worthy of note. First, that theorists in the constitutional debate are often styled and understood on the basis of today's conventional political identities. Second, that theories and approaches are often handled on an abstract level, suppressing the historical context.

The most significant element in the various frameworks of reception has been the focus on differences. However, in this respect, a schematic point of view became increasingly dominant in discussions of the Weimar context, in which it is assumed that it suffices to classify theoreticians as conservative authoritarian (Carl Schmitt), liberal positivist (Hans Kelsen) and social-democrat (Hermann Heller) in the present sense of the terms. Yet this categorization is insufficient and also inadequate if we wish to fully grasp the complex structure of the Weimar constitutional-political period and its conceptual and theoretical terms. If dialogue and connections between the theories and the dynamics of such mutual influences are drowned out, there is a risk of

3 However, it should be noted at the outset that the conservative attribution is quite fragmentary in this context. In most cases, the bourgeois theorists were not conservative constitutional theorists according to their self-image. What distinguished them was that they distanced themselves insistently from the positivist tradition and, in contrast to it, decisively rejected the principle of political neutrality. It would thus also be appropriate to call them establishment. For a general overview, see Michael Stolleis, *A History of Public Law in Germany, 1914–1945* (Oxford: Oxford University Press, 2004).

drawing wide-reaching and inaccurate conclusions on Weimar's theories of constitutionalism.

It is not therefore surprising that the most recent contemporary adaptations view the Weimar constitutional moment and especially its crises on a merely conceptual basis. What is positive here is the assumption that the interaction amongst Weimar theoreticians can illuminate today's political and constitutional thought. However, these approaches can be criticized for their inadequate theoretical distinction between the discourse of that period and today's theoretical discourse. In such analyses, the Weimar problem is isolated from its historical-political context and is introduced merely as a conceptual problem. The normative perspective of our day and subjects related to Weimar are intermingled. The constitutional crisis, consequently, is regarded as a result of the insufficiency of theories and concepts. In other words, it is claimed that conceptual problems dragged the constitutional order into a crisis of legitimation.[4] Yet in the Weimar constitutional crisis, the decisive element was not conceptual inadequacy, rather, it was socio-political and ideological political antagonism that intensified political polarization on a theoretical level. When this is ignored and when only the conceptual level is focused on, such an analytically deficient idealist approach arises.

This vagueness concerning the constitutional-political context is a serious problem for intellectual history. This is because the theoreticians are discussed in a contradictory manner within this framework. For instance, Carl Schmitt and Hermann Heller, who is also interpreted as a liberal, are presented as antagonists. In the deliberations on Weimar constitutional theory, Schmitt and Heller are introduced as the representatives of two main opposing theoretical movements: the strongest counter-project to oppose Schmitt's authoritarian project is said to be republicanism, represented by Heller. Here, Kelsen is said to have been weak in his defense of democracy as he was a narrow-minded positivist and a supporter of ethical relativism. An opposing argument could be mentioned, especially by representatives of political philosophy of legal positivism. According to this perspective, Kelsen should be considered as the keenest defender to oppose liberalism and democracy against the authoritarianism of Schmitt's approach. Yet, political philosophies committed to the theoretical perspective of legal positivism are no less ambiguous regarding Kelsen's theory. It is noteworthy that these approaches avoid involving Kelsenian arguments in

4 Such a "pure" theoretical approach is preferred by David Dyzenhaus, *Legality and Legitimacy: Carl Schmitt, Hans Kelsen and Hermann Heller in Weimar* (Oxford: Clarendon, 1997). A similar problematic approach is shown in Peter Caldwell, *Popular Sovereignty and the Crisis of German Constitutional Law* (Durham: Duke University Press, 1997).

their assessment of the Weimar constitutional debate. It is thus unsurprising that there are many contrasting and opposing assessments of Weimar legal and constitutional theories. Sometimes thinkers are adopted by contemporary political thought in a very innovative way whereas sometimes they are rejected entirely.[5] Moreover, the socialist *Rechtsstaat* theoreticians represented by Franz Neumann, Otto Kirchheimer and Ernst Fraenkel and their analysis and criticism of the constitutional and political process are neglected. Again, if one merely breaks down Weimar theoreticians into democrats and anti-democrats and equates the democrats with legal positivists, one cannot grasp the complex constitutional-political constellation of Weimar.[6] In light of this situation, which is created by rather varying interpretations, it is obvious that sufficient clarification regarding the structure of the Weimar constitutional-political moment has not yet been achieved.

The history of the reception points to a need for a new perspective combining the development of the political-historical context and theoretical concepts in the Weimar period. The fact that in this historical-political period, political and social polarization was influential, and that this situation was essential to the constitutional discourse, made this constitutional moment (which developed within a very short period of time) quite productive in theoretical-political terms. At this point, Ellen Kennedy's intervention is very helpful. She justifiably underlines the Schmittian emphasis of John Rawls' late period.[7] The mention of Schmitt and the Weimar period by Rawls is a clear expression of how Rawls concludes that pluralism, which exists in liberal-democratic constitutional states and which is a kind of social foundation of those states, may well turn into a destructive dynamic. Rawls perceives the Weimar experience as a model. However, what should be emphasized here is that the importance of the Weimar context is not limited to merely being a

---

5 See, for an example, David Dyzenhaus' Kelsen interpretation. Dyzenhaus interprets Kelsen's theory as counterproductive for democratic thought: *Legality and Legitimacy*. In a further interpretation, Schmitt has been seen as the most totalitarian thinker of the 20th century. Cf. William Scheuerman, "The Rule of Law Under Siege: Carl Schmitt and the Death of the Weimar Republic", *History of Political Thought*, 14.2 (1993), 265–80.

6 See Duncan Kelly, *The State of the Political. Conceptions of Politics and the State in the Thought of Max Weber, Carl Schmitt and Franz Neumann* (Oxford: Oxford University Press, 2003); and also Gopal Balakrishnan's intellectual biography, *The Enemy: An Intellectual Portrait of Carl Schmitt* (London: Verso, 2000). But still, even these historically-oriented and fruitful studies remain on a general level with regard to the sociopolitical context of the Weimar Republic; Kelly focuses on the general idea of the state concept and Balakrishnan hints at the social conflicts of that time.

7 Kennedy, *Constitutional Failure*.

demonstration of the existence of a political conflict problem in a very general sense. In various other social-historical relations, political conflicts and crises may be observed. Kennedy shows that the main political problems of the time are embedded in the development of constitutional theories, rightly emphasizing that lessons for constitutional practice and political theory should be drawn from the Weimar experience, and pointing out the main problems that stand in the way of this goal in the crisis of the constitutional order. In this regard, her claim that social conflicts have led to deep crises in the political order is correct. But this finding is not precise enough, since the socio-political background remains unclear; what made the Weimar constitutional context and its historical character special was the ideological conflict on the definition of the "societal" nature of a constitution and a political order.

3 The Discursive Structure

The discourse of theory gained extreme importance in establishing the new order, becoming the engine behind the process. Since the constitutional substantializing – that is the method of attributing a sociopolitical program to the constitution – was dominant, the theoretical discourse on constitutional interpretation became the central political issue.[8] Thus, the theoretical debate concerning key legal categories was highly critical. This was the case in the *Kaiserreich*; however, the factor that differentiated the new political era was that it transpired under the conditions of the republican order. In the political culture of the Weimar period, the theory of legal discourse developed under the umbrella of *Staatsrechtslehre,* the discipline of constitutional law, was of great importance.[9] In Weimar, theories of law played a pioneering role in the determination of the new order and therefore the structure of the state. Above all, theoretical discourse influenced the judiciary. The higher judiciary bodies interacted with theories, thus creating a conceptual framework that formed the constitutional and legal order.

8 The emphasis of Jacobsen and Schlink in this respect is very accurate: Arthur J. Jacobson and Bernhard Schlink, eds., *Weimar: A Jurisprudence of Crisis* (Berkeley: University of California Press, 2000). Jacobson and Schlink emphasize that for the Weimar constitution's status, an intensive interpretation conflict process was decisive; however, they do so without offering any explanation of the content of the dispute, which was, as mentioned above, the structure of the societal order and more specifically, whether German society should be transformed in a socialist sense or should continue to exist as a bourgeois-capitalist society.

9 The strong relevance of this political-legal thinking was emphasized by Heinrich Triepel, *Staatsrecht und Politik* (Berlin: de Gruyter, 1927).

Within this discursive framework, constitutional discourse developed along two different fault lines. The socio-political dynamics that emerged during the industrial capitalist stage of bourgeois society and the factors peculiar to the political history of Germany were both influential. The preservation of the unity of Germany as a nation-state was regarded as the most critical political matter by the establishment elites, in addition to the problems of the social order in the face of the socialist challenge.[10] But the class antagonism that had developed in the meantime in a democratic mass society became the most significant dynamic defining the country's reality. The problems that developed in the context of these two subjects were influential. To understand the determining approaches in theories, these two dimensions should not be neglected.

The leading theorists of the bourgeois-conservative course (Heinrich Triepel, Erich Kaufmann, Carl Schmitt) and the high judiciary body made intensive efforts to obtain a monopoly to preserve the political and social order. The activities of the bourgeois theoreticians were directed towards framing the political order within basic principles. However, interpreting the constitution regarding the societal content (substantializing) was not just limited to the establishment. Both the establishment legal theorists (including the judiciary) and the socialist camp aimed at determining the historical-political character of the constitution and its key norms. Although they were not as experienced as the bourgeois-conservative constitutional theorists, socialist theorists also implemented substantializing in their interpretation. The reflection of dominant political polarization in political culture in constitutional discourse could be seen in the mobilization of the substantializing method.

Defining the historical-political character of the Weimar constitution meant defining the entire political order and social order of the republic. The relevance and significance of theories depend on the positions of their authors on this matter. Thus, the development of theories can be explained within the framework of this constitutional-political conflict logic, whereas the larger historical-social background should not remain unconsidered. In the industrial capitalist society of the 20th century, political democracy produced a paradox: the democratic system created opportunities for structural change in the social order. This situation caused anxiety among the bourgeois and state administrative elites in the Weimar Republic. This does not mean

10 The problem of nation-state and national unity was the most disputed issue in discussions among legal scholars concerning the constitution-making process in 1918–19. See Gerhard Anschütz, *Drei Leitgedanken der Weimarer Reichsverfassung* [1922] (Tübingen: J.C.B. Mohr, 1923); Hugo Preuß, *Der Deutsche Nationalstaat* (Frankfurt/M.: Frankfurter Societäts-Druckerei, 1924).

that the elites categorically intended to topple the democratic structure. Rather, the establishment was active for a long time in seeking to paralyze the democratic-socialist demands. The *Sozialstaat* policy of the social democrats was construed as the first phase of the implementation of the Marxist societal-political program, which had been endorsed by the entire left spectrum. Leftist politics were thus regarded as a threat to the societal system. Finally, the political restoration started by dragging the social democratic party outside the political system. This policy was at the core of the emergency government's approach during the last years of the Weimar Republic. Following the end of coalition governments, the period of minority governments began (presidential cabinets). The bourgeois parties terminated the coalition they conducted with social democracy.[11]

Fundamentally, it can be said that the constitutional debate must not be viewed as a direct reflection of the general political situation. Instead, it must be seen as a debate in which issues concerning political order were addressed at the highest intellectual level. The Weimar constitutional discourse was, as mentioned above, primarily polarized in two significant political camps. The two political camps, which opposed one another in their interpretation of the constitution, consisted of the conservative-bourgeois *Staatsrechtslehre* theorists and their antagonists, the socialist legal theorists, who represented the trade unions and the social-democratic movement. In order to understand this constellation, the discourse strategies of the opponents on either side of the debate have to be taken into consideration. First and foremost, the interaction between the two camps must be taken seriously. The socialists, who were the counterparty, focused on how to make use of the institutional legal facilities offered by the Weimar Republic to achieve social justice. The ideas of the socialist legal theorists were based on how the legal framework could benefit policies for social equality. This concept was centered on the idea of improving the constitution with the aim of achieving democratic socialism. Thus, it would be appropriate to define the political program of the Marxist and socialist legal theory as radical reformism (a sort of so-called parliamentary socialism). In setting historical-social goals, the Weimar Left endorsed and positioned the understanding of the concept of "real democracy" against the formal democracy of bourgeois-capitalist order.[12] What is thus intended

11 For the coalition politics and its reflection by Schmitt, see again Kennedy, *Constitutional Failure*, 154.

12 The use of the idea of "real" or "true" democracy in contrast to the concept of bourgeois, formal democracy in the political culture of the Weimar Republic was very common. For the Marxist social philosophy, see Max Horkheimer, *Dawn and Decline: Notes 1926–1931 and 1950–1969* (New York: The Seabury Press, 1978). Horkheimer's position can be understood

is democratic socialism, and the constitutional order had to be interpreted in this direction. Although various statements came from leftist movements, the common goal was the construction of the socialist *Rechtsstaat*. Even though Communist Party circles did not clearly participate in this, it regarded this as a significant step on the road to socialist transformation of the societal order. The purpose of establishing the socialist constitutional state entailed a comprehensive political program.

On the establishment side, the situation was much more complicated. It must be noted however that the foremost motivation of conservative law thinkers should not be regarded merely as defending the order of capitalism, although this was important to them. The conservative-bourgeois camp thought that the unity of Germany as a nation-state was under threat within the Weimar context. Not only did they see it as their duty to protect the capitalist order, but also, more importantly, they believed that the most critical issue was to preserve the political unity of the nation. That the conservatives led by Carl Schmitt identified the concept of constitution as a *politische Existenz* is associated with this situation. Indeed, the most original conception was developed by Schmitt.

Schmitt, who included the term 'political unity' as a basic concept in his constitutional and political theory, elaborated a different concept of interpretation from the mainstream of *Staatsrechtslehre*, basing his discussion of constitutional legitimacy on the tradition of modern constitutionalism. That is, it stresses dynamism immanent within the constitution: according to Schmitt, the constitutional process had created its own basis of legitimacy. As is known, Schmitt's attempt to formulate solutions in view of the constitutional crisis has often been criticized, and beyond that, his Weimar engagement has been often dismissed as anti-modernism.[13] Such an assumption is untenable because it simply does not do justice to the complicated and serious situation of the

as supportive of socialist constitutional politics. Horkheimer's remarks are semantically significant because he used the term "real democracy", which stood for socialism.

13 For an overrated accusation of nihilism, which forms the starting point for the accusation of political and legal nihilism, see John McCormick, *Carl Schmitt's Critique of Liberalism: Against Politics as Technology* (Cambridge: Cambridge University Press, 1997). Critical for this is Andreas Kalyvas, "Review essay: Who's afraid of Carl Schmitt?", *Philosophy and Social Criticism*, 25 (1999), 87–125, 98. From the German discussion, see for this Klaus Roth, "Carl Schmitt – ein Verfassungsfreund? Seine Stellung zur Weimarer Republik in der Phase der relativen Stabilisierung (1924–29)", *Zeitschrift für Politik*, 52.2 (June 2005), 141–56. It should also be pointed out that the theoreticians mentioned in this chapter show in their engagement with Schmitt's Weimar work that the various arguments and ideas Schmitt developed cannot be limited to nihilism.

Weimar context on the one hand and the theoretical content of Schmitt's work on the other. Schmitt's Weimar work is a subject that has many comprehensive connotations. Above all, he develops a concept of legitimacy that is generally valid for the modern constitutional state.

At this point it is possible to mention two points which justify this appraisal. The first is his radical criticism of parliamentarianism, which is accorded too much importance in Schmitt's constitutional theory. The importance of writings on parliamentarianism, which mainly contain exaggerated arguments regarding the conceptual and genealogical relationship between liberalism and democracy, is, however, much lesser for Schmitt's constitutional theoretical and political ideas, for which a general evaluation of parliamentarianism does not play a decisive role. A second point should also be mentioned, which has led to exaggerations in interpretation. It is how Schmitt speaks of "homogeneity", which has led to misinterpretations. But it would be short-sighted to reduce such a complex situation as the Weimar constitutional-political context to the special problem of ethnicity. For Schmitt, in the discourse of the Weimar period as a whole, homogeneity does not mean ethnicism but is supposed to be a positive paraphrase for the idea of subordinating social differences to state authority, according to the state ethics of etatism which he endorses in the Weimar period.[14] As for Schmitt's Weimar constitutional thinking – which is a political constitutional thinking focused on the facets of political modernity – one cannot speak of anti-modernism. It must be emphasized that Schmitt's major work in the Weimar period, his *Constitutional Theory* of 1928, analyzed the Weimar constitutional state within the framework of the Western constitutional tradition.[15] The other important constitutional political writings (*Legality and Legitimacy* and *The Guardian of the Constitution*) dealing with the presidential government system which became the normality in the crisis after 1930, also remain within this framework. What is decisive is that Schmitt acted as a bourgeois antagonist in the constitutional discourse (and also as a public

---

14 See Carl Schmitt, "State Ethics and the Pluralist State" [1930], in Jacobson and Schlink, eds., *Weimar: A Jurisprudence of Crisis*, 300–312. In more conservative rhetoric, other leading jurists formulated their critique of the political situation as decay of the state order and the emergence of the party-state (*Parteienstaat*). However one should consider that this is not really an expression of *Weltanschauung*. Instead, criticism arose from the assumption that the socialist-oriented parties and political forces were a danger to the existing bourgeois order of the nation state and the political unity of Germany.

15 For this point, see Ellen Kennedy, "Forward", in Carl Schmitt, *Constitutional Theory* [1928], ed. Jeffrey Seitzer (Durham: Duke University Press, 2008). Cf. also Jeffrey Seitzer, *Comparative History and Legal Theory: Carl Schmitt in the First German Democracy* (Westport, Conn.: Greenwood Press, 2001).

political intellectual generally). His main argument is historical, placing the bourgeois constitutional state as a historically predetermined political form and principle of social organization at the center of his argument.

Moreover, it should not be overlooked that the assumption that the unity of the German nation-state, which had not yet been consolidated, was endangered was also a leitmotif for him, since he saw socialist universalism as a threat to this laboriously achieved 'political unity' of Germany. This is certainly not intended to play down his advocacy of a fascist-authoritarian transformation of the political order after 1933. Certainly, his entire creative period in Weimar must not be evaluated from the standpoint of his later views. However, with his engagement in the Nazi Movement, Schmitt himself contributed to this perspective when he propagated his hostility to the Weimar Republic in retrospect.[16]

We should also emphasize a matter of decisive importance in the constitutional-political discourse of Weimar. Legal positivism, which opted to remain neutral in disputes over social models, was gradually being excluded. The basic approach adopted by legal positivists was merely the assumption that the political order was a neutral democracy. However, neither the conservatives who represented the bourgeois establishment nor the socialist legal theorists considered this principle of neutrality an approach worth focusing on. This viewpoint was understandable during the Weimar period because the principle of neutrality was based on the claim that the political order was socially neutral. But in the real given situation in which intense polarization was already dominant, this approach meant avoiding a political position. In fact, it would not be inappropriate to consider this as consciously choosing to take an apolitical attitude within the discourse constellation. This is because the concept of a political order free of social content would obviously be ineffective in negotiations on social content. In their basic commentaries on the Weimar constitution, the leading representatives of historical statute positivism Gerhard Anschütz and Richard Thoma were holding back with primary political interpretation of the constitution. As a representative of the new and intensified legal positivism, Kelsen especially preferred to stay in a pure formalistic frame, pedantically avoiding the political discussion on the constitution. This kind of political philosophy of 'unpolitical' legal theory was rejected by the overwhelming majority of Weimar constitutional theorists. An intense debate within the *Staatsrechtslehre* was unavoidable.

16 For an example for this, the title of the volume *Positionen und Begriffe: Im Kampf mit Weimar-Genf-Versailles* [1940] (Berlin: Duncker und Humblot, 1994) should be mentioned.

The constitutional-political discussion clarifies the specific characteristics of the Weimar period as an era of transition, namely establishing a new state order. Nevertheless, transformation of the political landscape led to an exceptional situation. The fact that the final form of the constitutional order was open meant that the social order in particular was up for discussion. This situation resulted mainly from the fact that the founding of the state took place in the epoch of industrial-capitalist class society. Accordingly, open constitutionalism was itself the consequence of a long-lasting 'open statehood'.

4 Argumentation Strategies

The debate that started around the concept of democracy was not limited merely to the concept of constituent power but acquired a deeper and more comprehensive argumentative structure. During the Weimar constitutional moment, the stormy debate on the political character of the constitution led to an intense controversy about the foundations of the political and societal order's legitimacy. The debate on this subject developed in two directions and the two opposing camps preferred diverse ways of determining the constitution's socio-political content. Bourgeois-conservative constitutional and legal theorists emphasized their commitment to the principles of bourgeois society, which was then the historical status quo of the Weimar state. Accordingly, the constitution, and therefore its key norms, did not contain a program of change.

As mentioned above, Carl Schmitt opposed socialist interpreters and described the concept of constitution as the utmost symbolic expression of the existence of a nation. Schmitt emphasizes that bourgeois society should be considered as a historical period and that therefore the bourgeois constitutional state (*bürgerlicher Rechtsstaat*) should be regarded as a form of national existence appropriate for a modern, bourgeois society. The Weimar constitution was decided in favor of a bourgeois national constitutional state and contained a supreme resolution against the socialist and Bolshevik political and societal order. This argument was expressed most frequently in his *Verfassungslehre*. Its conclusion in the last instance expressed the entire conservative-bourgeois position.

Nevertheless, Schmitt could not defend this decisionist argument during his debate with socialist theorists. This is because, in addition to classical liberal-bourgeois principles, the Weimar constitution included numerous norms of socialist politics. The labor movement as a "constituent power" could not accept a decision purely in favor of the bourgeois position. Thus, the socialist theorists were able to assert that according to its original intent, the constitution contained social equality and socialist programs. Franz Neumann led those who favored this argument. Neumann reversed Schmitt's argument, stressing that the Weimar constitution contained a set of ideas that legitimized the socialist process. He based this argument (which he defended vociferously) on historical assumption and on the concept of constituent power which had previously been elaborated by Schmitt. Accordingly, as a result of the reconciliation between the bourgeois and the working classes, socialist norms and content were included in the constitution. Neumann succeeded in developing his argument on this basis and in challenging the bourgeois side, for which Schmitt had become a spokesperson.[17]

According to Neumann, the constitution was aimed at improving democracy. The point, however, was that this interpretation of democracy lay in the socialist sense of democracy as social equality. Historical progress – that is, social evolution – included the abolition of social inequalities. And this process could best be described using the concept of democracy. Neumann's offensive strategy, which could be described as a kind of left-wing political decisionalism, put him in an advantageous position in many respects. His concept diverged in significant respects from other social-democratic legal theorists, such as Hermann Heller or Gustav Radbruch, who were close to the party establishment. In contrast to other theorists of social democracy, Neumann was able to formulate a more appropriate constitutional-political theory because he had developed a consistent approach. Heller often underlined that the constitution is a neutral formal structure (thus taking the same position as the positivists whom he criticized strongly), but at the same time, he argued that the construction of socialism was a social and ethical necessity. Neumann, on the other hand, remains concrete, emphasizing the Weimar constitution contained principles that stem from the socialist tradition. In this perspective, social rights were constructed as the most concrete declaration of this tradition, which meant consciously turning away from the model of liberal society.[18] Consequently, according to this interpretation, Germany's path was intentionally paved for innovations in the direction of socialist democracy.

An important point of reference for the socialist program was the establishment of a national economic council that was anchored in the constitution. Facing the manifold problems of industrial capitalism, the architects of the

17 For the significance of the Weimar constitutional debate for Neumann's socialist legal theory, see the volume Otto Kirchheimer and Franz L. Neumann, *Social Democracy and the Rule of Law* (London and New York: Routledge, 2020).

18 Franz L. Neumann, "The Social Significance of the Basic Laws in the Constitution [1930]", in Kirchheimer and Neumann, *Social Democracy and the Rule of Law*, 27–43.

constitution drafted the formation of the Reich Economy Council in Article 165. This was intended to secure the state control over the capitalist economy (mainly large corporations). Reflecting the view of socialist politics, Neumann emphatically endorsed the concept of "economic constitution". He saw the article's proposed program of cooperation between labor and business in the fundamental shaping of the economy as an exemplary model of postliberal economy.[19]

In this situation, the debate on the problem of *Sozialstaat* was decisive. But the term welfare state must not obscure the fact that what was being debated was not the post-war welfare state. The dispute over the welfare state in the Weimar Republic was primarily ignited because of the program of the socialist transformation of society.[20] The debate that takes place over the content of the social state policies can only be perceived within the framework of the constitutional-political conflict constellation unique to the Weimar context. In this historical constellation, although the construction of social state policies prevailed in daily politics, the disputes in the background centered mainly on transforming the existing social order towards democratic socialism or stabilizing it as bourgeois society.

At this point, one should keep in mind that the concept of the social state in that period had an essentially different meaning than its use in the post-war era. A characteristic of post-war society was its comprehensive social compromise. Therefore, the basic structure not only of the political order, but also of the social order had been established. The Weimar Republic, on the other hand, set no fundamental limits to social change, leaving the political and social order open. From the vantage of constitutional policy, it was possible to perceive of the new order of post-war society as "depoliticized" when compared with the Weimar period.[21]

---

19 Franz L. Neumann, "On the Preconditions and the Legal Concept of an Economic Constitution [1931]", in Kirchheimer and Neumann, *Social Democracy and the Rule of Law*, 44–65.

20 These historical-political specifics are often ignored in the literature and the Weimar welfare state debate is treated as it was in the post-war period. For example: John McCormick, "Legal Theory and the Weimar Crisis of Law and Social Change", in John McCormick and Peter E. Gordon, eds., *Weimar Thought* (Princeton: Princeton University Press, 2013), 55–72; and Peter C. Caldwell, "Is a "Social Rechtsstaat" Possible? The Weimar Roots of a Bonn Controversy", in Peter C. Caldwell and William F. Scheuerman, *From Liberal Democracy to Fascism* (Boston: Humanities Press, 2000), 136–55.

21 Such was the brilliant evaluation of the Federal Republic by Ernst Forsthoff, which can also be extended more generally to the political structures of Western countries: *Der Staat der Industriegesellschaft* (München: C. H. Beck, 1971). In political sociology, the new historical

What is important here is that social democracy aimed at the structural change of the capitalist order, going beyond the intentions of the welfare state. Although this program was not fully implemented in practice, it remained the ultimate goal of socialist politics. Emphasis on this is of great importance for understanding the Weimar constitutional constitutional debate. A consideration of the argumentative maneuvers on this subject will help us to understand both the dynamics of the socialist paradigm and the assertions of the opposing bourgeois-conservative theorists.

The approach by socialist legal theorists cannot be considered without also examining the movement of social democracy. The Social Democratic Party, following a realistic policy, struggled in practice to multiply and protect social state gains. But, besides that, according to the Marxist theoretical-political program that it essentially adopted, historical progress towards a socialist society model was regarded as the goal. According to the concept of social democracy, historical progress would be achieved within the framework of formal democracy. In other words, historical-political progress was to be achieved through reform, and the Weimar constitutional order was of key significance on this path. To summarize, social democracy adopted the concept of radical reformism as a theoretical program. We can attribute the indecisiveness and contradictions amongst theorists affiliated to the movement of social democracy to this fact. Franz Neumann at times stresses that legality is indispensable for radical reformism; nevertheless, he also underlines that the constitutional order is vulnerable. The same is true for Otto Kirchheimer, who even emphasized that the constitution had a transitory value. Particularly striking is Neumann's assumption that progress in society towards social equality was necessary for the perpetuation of the constitutional order, otherwise, the risk of authoritarian restoration would become even more serious.

In this respect, there were two sides to the socialist constitutional theory position on the constitutional order: The socialist democratic position was determined on the one hand by defending formal social democracy and on the other by also acknowledging that formal democracy had a transitory value. Despite the different nuances, the various socialist theorists took the assumption of historical progress as their starting point in this matter. When the development of the dispute between the bourgeois elites and the democratic-socialist camp regarding the constitutional interpretation is examined, the position of the two camps against the constitutional order is revealed. The

situation has been described as the postwar social compromise, which included a class compromise in advanced industrial societies based on a new institutional arrangement.

nature of this constitutional discourse dynamic merely consisted of the interpretation of the constitutional order in line with specific goals. One was progress in the democratic-socialist direction while the other was a restoration to be achieved by the bourgeois elites and state bureaucracy. These aims constituted the two dynamics that would determine the fate of the German constitutional order in the Weimar Republic.

It is not surprising that the bourgeois elites were skeptical about a constitutional order that allowed for the discussion and questioning of the social (capitalist) structure. With the escalation of the crisis, the established authorities preferred to restructure the constitutional order in an authoritarian direction and put that into practice. However, as is known, the emergency government regime they formed was subsequently a fiasco.[22] Eventually, the entire order was seized by the Nazi totalitarian movement. The emergency government and the dynamics of the collapse that it led to are certainly critical dimensions that characterize the Weimar constitutional period. However, there is another dimension that needs to be taken into consideration as well.

The issue that was visible in the constitutional discourse and that was most important for the constitutionalist history of the twentieth century is the concept of legitimacy as developed by bourgeois-conservative legal theorists against the socialist opposition's approach. As pointed out above, openness towards the social order provided opportunities for the socialist and social democratic movement to alter the existing social order within the framework of legality. To eliminate this assumption in particular, the *Staatsrechtslehre* theorists developed a legal concept that protected bourgeois gains – which included national unity within the framework of a centralized nation-state. Accordingly, the political order would not be understood merely in a formal way. Despite this prevailing understanding, political powers would not be able to make changes to the social order, that is, seizing power within the legal framework would not be sufficient for this. In this respect, perceiving the legal order as a neutral factor constituted a threat to the order. Perceiving the current situation in this way, the constitutional theorists shared the same opinion as the bourgeois and state bureaucratic elites who had formed the establishment. The unwillingness to limit the legitimacy of political and social order to legality coincided, therefore, with the political culture. And finally, Carl

22 For a discussion of emergency government process, see Kennedy, *Constitutional Failure*. Statements and discussions from the Carl Schmitt School should also be mentioned here: Ernst Rudolf Huber, "Carl Schmitt in der Reichskrise der Weimarer Endzeit", in Helmuth Quaritsch, ed., *Complexio Oppositorum: Über Carl Schmitt* (Berlin: Duncker und Humblot, 1988), 33–70.

Schmitt prepared the most appropriate concept for re-designing the basis of legitimacy.

The use of the concept of constituent power in favour of an egalitarian and socialist interpretation of the key constitutional norms by the socialist camp was a challenge to the bourgeois-conservative cause. Thus, after observing that this would not be an effective method, Schmitt attempted to position the bourgeois character of the constitutional order on other ground. Schmitt's response was to associate the value system that constituted the basis of legitimacy with the concept of individual rights.[23] This twist was convenient for the leadership of *Staatsrechtslehre*. It was not yet appropriate for the conservative statist theorists to base the constitution and thus the state order only on the principle of popular sovereignty by the constituent power paradigm method. Given that this paradigm had radical democratic aspects, relying solely on that (as Schmitt had initially done) was quite a risky strategy. A concept of justice that transcended the concrete system of law that conservatives like Erich Kaufmann had adopted in the "classical" sense was also proving to be inadequate.

It may come as a surprise to see that Schmitt was looking for political concepts during the Weimar era. Schmitt's preference for a style of philosophical *Zeitdiagnose* and his foregrounding of provocative theses somewhat obscured this fact. His considerations towards the problems and definition of democracy were sobering during the Weimar period. When dealing with democracy, the expansion of democratic procedures, or the act of processing it in an effective manner, was not his focus. Schmitt instead concentrated on a more fundamental problem; his main topic was the fate of the political order in the era of democracy. Accordingly, the mission of the political thought was to develop concepts in the construction and preservation of political order. For him, this had become the most important issue within the Weimar context. To sum up Schmitt's position: there are bourgeois principles that must be kept alive at the time when fragile social relations such as mass democracy and industrial capitalism dominate, and these principles form the intellectual basis of the constitution. Without such principles, the political order would collapse.

The important point here is that Schmitt maneuvered his argument to prove the bourgeois character of the Weimar Constitution. He suggests that the political form (or state structure) of bourgeois modernity in its early period

---

23 Carl Schmitt, *Legality and Legitimacy* [1932], ed. Jeffrey Seitzer (Durham: Duke University Press, 2004). See also Carl Schmitt, "Freiheitsrechte und institutionelle Garantien der Reichsverfassung" [1932], in *idem, Verfassungsrechtliche Aufsätze aus den Jahren 1924–1954: Materialien zu einer Verfassungslehre* [1954], third edition (Berlin: Duncker und Humblot, 1985), 140–73.

contained sufficient legitimacy, but the idea of popular sovereignty could not find success in this form after the radical changes that had occurred since the nineteenth century. Schmitt used a historical argument to come to this conclusion. In the late Weimar period, he asserted the claim that classic fundamental rights (such as individual rights of freedom or property) constituted such a basis of legitimacy. In his thesis, which overlaps with the approaches of the state bureaucratic and industrial elites,[24] Schmitt states that state order can only be sustained through an authoritarian regime of emergency politics during times of crisis. Yet this new situation, a political situation of temporary constitutional dictatorship, had to be a constitutional order in itself, which lead to paradoxical consequences. The intended restoration was thus based on legitimacy. In an authoritarian transformation, the reference to legitimacy is the self-value of bourgeois society, which is symbolized by individual rights.

According to Schmitt, individual rights were central to the development of the modern constitution, since the function of individual rights in the constitutional state was to form the relationship between the state and society. This is not a normative claim. Rather, it is the result of an historical-political (and intellectual-historical) observation. Individual rights "protect" societal space in general. In other words, the function of individual rights as a catalogue categorically separates the domains of society and the state. Concretely, if individual rights protect the individual's private space against the state, exactly the same is true for property rights. The existence of rights precedes the state, and the social space they create as a whole also comes before the state. Schmitt sees this as a structural feature of the constitutional state. What is important here is the nature of the argument: Eventually, liberal norms were referred to as the central character of the constitution. The distinction between state and society and between the spheres of the political and the social was at stake. But describing the social order as a separate category from the political order has far reaching consequences. The social is then driven out of the sphere of influence of political power. Thus, Schmitt developed a concept that negated

---

24 This corresponded first and foremost with the judicial praxis of the higher courts in advocating the societal order. The central medium for this was judicial review. Above all, the higher judiciary played a pivotal legitimating role regarding the ideological basis of the constitutional order. In many court decisions, the judges claimed to interpret legal norms in the sense of the existing status and ownership relationships. This point remains underexamined in recent international studies, while the bourgeois political strategy of the judicial practice of the Weimar courts was emphasized in the neo-Marxist reception of the 1960s and 70s. For example: Helmut D. Fangmann, *Justiz gegen Demokratie. Entstehungs- und Funktionsbedingungen der Verfassungsjustiz in Deutschland* (Frankfurt/M.: Campus, 1979).

the socialist-democratic demands. According to this concept, which had been effective in constitutional development, the idea of democracy could no longer be a legitimate source for the "radical" structural transformation of the societal order. This conceptual construction thus led to serious political consequences. It ensured that society, at least essentially, was kept out of the domain of political normativity.

5 Conclusion

Schmitt's approach to resolving the constitutional crisis indicates the theoretical viewpoints from which one can look back on the Weimar constitutional moment today. Its main characteristic was that it marked a transition from the concept of state to the concept of constitution. The Weimar period must be regarded as an important historical-political moment in the development process of modern constitutionalism, which Martin Loughlin rightly defines as the "age of constitutionalism".[25] With the foundation of the republic, the socialists abandoned their claim of a "state-free" society, which had hitherto been the Marxist paradigm. Meanwhile, the representatives of the *Staatsrechtslehre* also inevitably joined the process of renewing the metaphysical understanding of the state, rejuvenating their own tradition. The two opposed traditions did not limit their debate to the "metaphysics" of the state. In this pursuit, the constitution became the focal point of the discussion.

It is not unreasonable to maintain that the Weimar discourse is a model of the constitutional era that began earlier in the 19th century in the context of the US constitution but took concrete shape in the 20th century. The key categories and concepts of political order in the era of constitutionalism were formed and came to function around the concept of constitutional interpretation. The question of the legacy of Weimar discourse today must be answered on these terms. Certainly, the answer depends both on the analytical perspective and on the political issue, which is regarded as urgent and important, but it is still possible to make (even if only briefly) a concrete statement from a theoretical and conceptual point of view.

First of all, it is necessary to emphasize the centrality of Carl Schmitt's constitutional-political theory for Weimar discourse. Schmitt's importance and his enduring relevance for constitutional and political theory are based mostly on the concept of the constitutional legitimacy of political order. Arguing that

25 Martin Loughlin, "The Constitutional Imagination", *Modern Law Review*, 78 (2015), 1–25.

the social and political values of the bourgeois epoch (political modernity) were the basic principles of the Weimar constitution in the dispute between the socialists and the bourgeois-conservative constitutional and legal theory, Schmitt developed an original method for the social-historical substantialization of the bourgeois-modern society (the social condition of modern civilization) as an intellectual basis for the legitimacy of the Weimar Constitution. This approach left its mark on the Weimar constitutional moment. It follows that it would be incorrect to limit Schmitt's significance for today's political thought to the problem of *Ausnahmezustand* (the state of emergency) and its implications, especially the general problem of sovereignty. On the contrary, in terms of the development of constitutionalism, Schmitt's arguments are based on the "normal" situation. Therefore, it concerns the normality of the constitutional order as well as the emergency government order, which is of primary importance in terms of constitutionalism.

In the debate about defining the historical-political character of the constitution, Schmitt found that the constitutional state could generate its own legitimate basis in a self-reflective manner. This actually imposes restrictions upon political power, as the political domain is limited by the dynamics of judiciary legitimacy. Within this conceptual framework, individual rights are thus conceptualized as a system of values guaranteeing the stability of political order and constituting the basis of legitimacy. What is interesting here is that the concept of a value system constructed from individual rights conforms to the reality of constitutional development in political modernity, which started with the liberal revolutions of the eighteenth century. But while Schmitt develops the argument of individual rights as a concept, he does not directly associate it with the general historical development of the constitutional state because, as seen above, within the dispute he is involved in, he aims to break the arguments of the opposing party and create a concept which is higher than theirs. Nevertheless, it should be emphasized that the idea of individual rights, by representing the basis of legitimacy of the constitution, gradually came to be the cardinal issue of constitutionalism throughout the course of the development of modern society. It is not surprising that these are the factors that constituted the basis of legitimacy in post-war constitutionalism after the middle of the twentieth century. And the conceptualization of individual rights as a legitimizing factor for the constitutional order means that it not only secured the social status quo but also shaped the political structure. As the key element in modern constitutionalism, the idea of individual rights in its manifold diversities of interpretation, has become the most important ideological component of political order.[26]

Bibliography

Main Sources

Anschütz, Gerhard, *Drei Leitgedanken der Weimarer Reichsverfassung* [1922] (Tübingen: J.C.B. Mohr, 1923).

Kirchheimer, Otto; and Franz L. Neumann, *Social Democracy and the Rule of Law* (London and New York: Routledge, 2020).

Schmitt, Carl, *Constitutional Theory* [1928], ed. Jeffrey Seitzer (Durham: Duke University Press, 2008).

Schmitt, Carl, *Legality and Legitimacy* [1932], ed. Jeffrey Seitzer (Durham: Duke University Press, 2004).

Triepel, Heinrich, *Staatsrecht und Politik* (Berlin: de Gruyter, 1927).

Main Bibliographical References

Jacobson, Arthur J.; and Bernhard Schlink, eds., *Weimar: A Jurisprudence of Crisis* (Berkeley: University of California Press, 2000).

Kennedy, Ellen, *Constitutional Failure: Carl Schmitt in Weimar* (Durham: Duke University Press, 2004).

Stolleis, Michael, *A History of Public Law in Germany, 1914–1945* (Oxford: Oxford University Press, 2004).

---

26 This concept became fully developed in the constitutional order in the post-war period. As a valuable study on this subject, see Carl Schmitt, "Die legale Weltrevolution: Politischer Mehrwert als Prämie auf juristische Legalität und Superlegalität", *Der Staat*, 17.3 (1978), 321–39. See also Ernst Forsthoff, "Der introvertierte Rechtsstaat und seine Verortung", *Der Staat*, 2.4 (1963), 385–98.

CHAPTER 19

The Portuguese *Estado Novo* Constitutional Process as a Model for Transitioning to Authoritarianism in the Europe of the New Order

José Reis Santos

In the early 1930's most European nations displayed an evident institutional inability to tackle the economic and social consequences that followed the 1929 New York Stock Exchange crises. Consequently, an intense debate arose around the theory of the State, the role of parliaments and (liberal) institutions and the range of governmental intervention, especially in the sphere of economic planning and social meddling. Portugal, due to the pre-emptive austerity intervention of António Oliveira Salazar as Finances minister (since 1928), was as one of the few countries where the crisis was hardly felt, emerging in the interwar cultural bouillon as the palatine of the Portuguese conservative revolution – a "Revolution of Love", as branded by Mircea Eliade.[1] He symbolized what Manoilescu and others saw as the nations' ability to understand the need to lodge the initiative of social transformation into the hands of selected individuals.[2] By early 1930's Salazar was perceived as a figure that could steer Portugal away from the anarchy instability of the country's First Republic (1910–1926) and through a national revolution and radical constitutional reform promote a new and orderly organised state of public affairs under a corporative *Estado Novo*. By the late 1930's, Salazar' governmental praxis, self-promoted public (and personal) features and political doctrine, frequently referenced in the international press and strongly disseminated in right-wing intellectual circles, earned him a reputation as one of authoritarian corporatism main interpreters and a place in the trans-European conservative constitutional revolution context as an important contributor for the consolidation of interwar political authoritarianism, especially after his nomination

1 Mircea Eliade, *Salazar, a Revolução em Portugal* [1942] (Lisboa: Esfera do Caos, 2011).

2 Mihael Manoilescu, *Le Siècle du Corporatisme. Doctrine du Corporatisme Intégral et Pur* (Paris: Librairie Félix Alcan, 1934); José Reis Santos, "Self-fashioning of a conservative revolutionary: Salazar's integral corporatism and the international networks of the 1930s", in António Costa Pinto and Federico Finchelstein, eds., *Authoritarianism and Corporatism in Europe and Latin America: Crossing Borders* (Routledge: Abingdon-New York, 2018), ch. 4.

 | DOI:10.1163/9789004549159_021

as Portugal's President of the Council (i.e. prime-minister) in 1932 and the advent of the 1933 corporativist Constitution.

In a time when most political regimes re-examined their constitutional parameters, the Portuguese Military Dictatorship transitioned from a self-proclaimed constitutional interregnum (1926–1933) towards a *Estado Novo / New State*, promising in the process to enshrine an ideological corporative-vaticanist and authoritarian model able to simultaneously overcome the dilemmas of excessive (economic) liberalism and the lack of governmental strength, and to socially pacify an overtly divided society and to develop the country under an economic autarchy policy plan.[3] Quickly after its institutional formalization, the Portuguese Propaganda Secretariat (SPN) developed a strategy to export this model as an alternative not only to communism and demo-liberalism but also to Fascism and Nazism, and as a ready-to-use blueprint to countries aiming to overcome the weaknesses of liberalism, sustain and mature their national sovereignty and control the abuses of authoritarian rule as defined by the totalitarian leaders of the New Order. This paper will analyse the Portuguese constitutional process, follow its pre-constitutional debate, appreciate the hybrid liberal-corporative layout and ideological contradictions of the Constitution of 1933 and insert it comparatively in the political and constitutional chronology of the interwar period.

1 A Short Political-Constitutional Radiography of Interwar Europe

In another piece of work, we dealt with the constitutional dynamics of the interwar period.[4] In it we identified the political, social and cultural complexities associated to the double transitions experienced in a significant part of the Old Continent, as most newly born countries embarked in a double journey towards independence and a multi-party liberal democratic systems with no previous experience. This meant a set of intense cultural and social transformations in the years after the Great War, strong migratory movements and population displacement (as by-product of dismantling three multinational European Empires), by the end of the liberal, Eurocentric and imperial *Belle*

3 Of direct inspiration in the *Rerum Novarum* (1891) and *Quadragesimo Anno* (1931) Papal Encyclicals, right-wing intellectuals often categorized the Portuguese *Estado Novo* as corporative-vaticanist regime, cf. José Reis Santos, "Retóricas do Fascismo. Processos de difusão e recepção do Estado Novo no contexto dos processos de transição institucional da Europa da Nova Ordem", Ph. D. thesis, New University of Lisboa, 2018.

4 Reis Santos, "Retóricas do Fascismo".

Époque and by the overture of an era of governmental possibilities, administrative experiences and identitarian explorations.

From the idea of the decline of the West and the collapse of the European Spirit, immediately reflected by intellectuals as Oswald Spengler or Paul Valéry, a new field of political alternatives to classic liberalism and communism would erupt; a frame where dictatorships and authoritarian regimes would be seen as morally acceptable and institutional operative. As such, after a first phase of political vacuum and consequent institutional anarchy, the expected pains of a sturdy reconfiguration of a European map sprinkled with revolutions and counter revolutions (1919–1921), the beginning of the 1920's witnessed the institutional stability derived from the formal legitimation imposed by the peace treaties of Versailles, Sevres, Trianon and Saint Germain. From the point of view of the political alternatives, the cases of Germany (Weimar Republic in 1919), Russia (the Soviet Union after 1922) and Italy (ruled by Mussolini after 1922) will provide the main political models in theoretical appreciation in the interwar period: demo-parliamentarian, communism and authoritarian-fascism.

This period thus witnessed a passionate theoretical debate around the role of the State. Firstly, during the introduction and imposition of liberal multiparty systems during the independence years of 1919–1922. And after, by the impetus of revisionist conservative counter-revolutionary authoritarian right-wing politicians (in their reaction against the established liberal democratic parliamentary procedures), that will gradually take the reins of power in most of new European countries, from Central and Eastern Europe to the Baltic and the Balkans, a tendency where Portugal (and Spain) must be inserted.

From a political constitutional point of view, the interwar period should be divided several phases. The first is distinct by the necessity to dismantle three multi-national Empires in the European space (Austro-Hungary, Russia and Germany), and legitimate new national entities and their respective political models. As a consequence of Wilson's demo-liberal idealism, this will impose constituent transitions and models of parliamentary nature, with multi-party proportional representation electoral systems.[5] These models quickly proved to

5 Due to Russia's early withdrawal from the war, and the Brest-Litovsk treaty, the Baltic countries were the first gaining their independence: Finland in December 1917, then Lithuania, Estonia and Latvia (1918). Finland approved its new Constitution in 1919 without electing a constituent assembly, but Lithuania (Constituent in April 1919, new constitution in August 1922), Estonia (Constituent in April 1919, new constitution in April 1920) and Latvia (Constituent in April 1920, new constitution in February 1922) elected a constituent assembly to draft their primordial texts. Central Europe will follow this scenario: Germany elected a Constituent Assembly in January 1919 (new Constitution in August 1919), Romania also in 1919 (new Constitution in 1923), the Kingdom of the Serbs, Croats and Slovenians in 1920

be unadoptable to the political and social realities of most Post War countries, a situation that led some local right-wing elites, even after some leading the independence processes, to instigate and conspire against what they claimed to be evident institutional deficiencies in the Wilsonian dream, namely the lack of real power of executive branches, the excessive parliamentary control over governmental issues and the inability to produce legislation and policy in excessive fragmented parliaments. To this critique, most right-wing politicians also wished to control the social revolution that erupted during the *biennio rosso* (1919–1921) and introduce authoritarian political models of identitarian-nationalist nature, desires quickly turned reality in Hungary (1920), Italy (1922), Spain (1923–1930, then interrupted by the Second Republic), Portugal, Poland and Lithuania (1926). With the exception of Italy, in all other cases military coups installed military dictatorships that ruled in constitutional interregnums. Then, already in the context of the 1929 crisis, Europe will witness a slow process of authoritarian constitutional settlement (Yugoslavia 1931, Portugal 1933, Austria 1934, Bulgaria 1934, Poland 1935, Estonia 1936, Lithuania 1938, Romania 1938).

The proliferation of such examples will reignite the critic revaluation of the role of the state and its institutions and revamp the theoretical debate around theory of the state, especially after the 1929 crisis led to the evident collapse of *laissez-faire* liberalism. In a brief summary, the main debates revolved around the functions and general organisation of the state and the role it should have in the public and private economic sphere; the role of citizens and institutions in modern societies; and the organisation and articulation between the executive, legislative and judicial bodies.

In this sense, the interwar period, notwithstanding the original domination of parliamentary models of plural representation, quickly became a fertile field for political experimentations, a quasi-permanent laboratory apt to

---

(new Constitution in 1921). Poland and Czechoslovakia will follow a slightly different process, approving first a small Constitution (to frame the newly obtained independence), later evolved to a larger constitutional text (the Polish small constitution is from February 1919 and its larger version of March 1921, the Czechoslovak small text from November 1918, and the new Constitution from February 1920). After the Great War Greece will dive into a turbulent period, oscillating between monarchy and republic. In 1927 the Monarchy was abolished and a short-lived republican Constitution approved in 1927. In 1935 a referendum re-established the monarchy, and in 1938 Metaxas promoted an authoritarian coup d'état. Bulgaria kept its 1878 Constitution until the authoritarian Coup d'état of 1934 brought a new text. Hungary was the only European country deprived of new constitutional procedures, governing Horthy through constitutional decrees and the legal heritage of the statutes of 1848, 1867 and 1869. On the Hungarian case, see Ferenc Hörcher and Thomas Lorman's chapter in this volume.

explore and apply new sets of policy and political solutions that could provide the necessary answers for the main concerns of the ruling elite. And if in a first moment these elites were intent on building a working institutional model that could enable their permanence as transitional gatekeepers (partly to control and restrain any left-wing upraising) later they would venture into manufacturing an idealised version of a monistic society that, under authoritarian rule, could provide national unity, social pacification, economic autarchic development and a ethno-cultural national regeneration, ideologically influenced by the main revisionist political actors of the time, namely Fascism.[6]

In this aspect, there are substantial differences between the early 1920's, moment of intense political and institutional (re)definition in Europe, and the mid 1930's, a time when the dominant political oligarchies, after verifying the incapacity of liberal systems to efficiently generate public policies capable to control post-War social unrest and pacifically frame and discipline the working class, adventured in exploring different forms of authoritarianism, varying from ultra-presidential Caesarism to monarchic dictatorships, fascism or corporative vaticanist models. Most of these new authoritarian models will see themselves as a new type of (contra)revolutionary regimes, taking their legitimacy from a military coup d'état and promoting slow transitional processes. Some, as Portugal, will promote hybrid constitutional texts, as they will not provoke a total rupture with liberal concepts, as were parliamentary structures or formal electoral procedures.

In 1922 the March on Rome and the beginning of the fascist revolution will provide a new centrality and focus of diffusion of an authoritarian model will provide the necessary plaster to unify a formerly disconnected right-wing transnational movement. This moment becomes pivotal, as Rome would define the central elements and theoretical sustenance to be followed by most right-wing authoritarian elites, movements and regimes in the interwar period. Rome will diffuse a new revisionist, post-liberal and anti-Bolshevik paradigm that, with its revolutionary features, will provide an updated and modern version to those searching for alternatives to the traditional formulas of dictatorships and authoritarian regimes, i.e., models essentially concerned on keeping a stratified status quo and social unrest under control with few ambitions to recompose society or create a *New Man*. In this sense, if during the first wave of authoritarianism, time was lacking for a proper appreciation

6 Roger Griffin, "Foreward: Il ventennio parafascista? The Past and Future of a Neologism"; and Aristotle Kallis, "The 'Fascist Effect': on the Dynamics of Political Hybridization in Inter-War Europe", both in António Costa Pinto and Aristotle Kallis, eds., *Rethinking the Nature of Fascism* (London: Palgrave Macmillan, 2014).

of fascist efficiency and proposals, later, fascism would become the blueprint for those searching connections to the new post-liberal, ultra-nationalist, anti-parliamentary, anti-democratic and anti-communist wave.

The first surge of authoritarianism started in Italy (1922), spreading to Spain (1923), Greece (1925), Portugal, Poland and Lithuania (1926), Albania (1928) and Yugoslavia (1929), a chronology that should include the Portuguese experience of Sidónio Pais (1917–1918) as well as Horthy's Hungary (1920). The new political outline provided by Italy was important for the constitutionalising features associated with the second wave of authoritarianism (1933–1934). This period saw democratic systems dismantled in Austria, Germany (1933), Estonia, Latvia and Bulgaria (1934), heated constitutional debates in France and Czechoslovakia (1934), and the impact of Hitler' nomination as German chancellor in January 1933, that quickly shifted from Rome to Berlin the centrality of this movement. Unlike the first wave of authoritarianism, transitions from democracy in the mid 1930's were quickly followed by constitutional and institutional transition processes (as Austria, Bulgaria or Estonia). Before the Second World War, Europe will still witness a third wave of authoritarian transitions (Greece, 1938; Spain, 1939; Romania, 1938 and 1940).

The consolidation of an extended grid of authoritarian regimes in the late 1930's, dully articulated by intricate networks of intellectuals, provided an intense space of emission, diffusion and reception of ideas, political solutions and rhetoric, stimulating a dynamic relation between the main centres (Rome and Berlin) and different peripheries. These peripheries were also defining, experimenting and diffusing new ideals and models of authoritarian nature.[7] An example of this diffusion from the periphery will be Salazar's corporate vaticanist New State.

Within this frame, right-wing politicians, intellectuals and *hommes de lettres* will see Fascism abandon the idea to systematize the complexities in society enshrined in proportional representation electoral systems and take instead the binomial Nation/State as the cornerstone of its systemic building, dropping any legitimation requirements from the liberal citizen-elector contract, and aspire to solve the complex relation between capital, labour and government through the implementation of an authoritarian corporative system of governmental tutelage. Behind such decisions were the consequences that the legal determination to provide wide sectors of society with legitimate capacity to intervene in the political sphere and public affairs brought to political

7 Roger Griffin, *A Fascist Century* (New York: Palgrave MacMillan, 2008); Kallis, "The 'Fascist effect'".

and parliamentary life, i.e., excessive fragmentation and practical ineffectiveness; to which we should add the distrust that right-wing elites and certain economic oligarchies saw in the representation the left, perceived as internationalists and anti-Nation.

Fascism on the other hand claimed to represent the true nature of the Nation, understood as an organic entity. As such, the concept of Head of Family, as the integrated basic-cell of the Nation, replaced the citizen-elector as the central piece of its political system. With this configuration, the system no longer needed a plural party system that elected representatives in a competitive manner and elections became symbolic plebiscites. Instead, all political participation was framed through the hegemony of the Single Party, serving as an aggregating element for all *living forces* of the Nation, those who – in the fascist rhetoric – truthfully deserved the right of representation and participation, relegating the opposition to the outer limits of society or straightforward illegality. Representation would be provided via the corporative system, namely labour, capital and administration. Complementarily, the fascists will also revise the relations between the parliament and the Executive, withdrawing power of interference and governmental control from the Parliament, and reversely empowering the executive.

To this new framework, we should also insert the impact of the intellectual reflections on the decadence of the European moral and philosophical spirit disseminated after the War through the cultural and intellectual imaginary of the right, as well as the advent of new national political entities that in their quest for an identity of their own, after centuries of foreign domination, will venture in developing native projects of ethno-cultural regeneration in this fertile ground to plant the seeds of national authoritarianism.

2 *The* New State *Constitutional Process (1931–1933)*

Portugal' political life in the half of the 20th century will follow the tempo of European events, although the country placed itself at the vanguard of republicanism as it transitioned from monarchic rule to a pluri-party parliamentary model as a result of a revolutionary movement in October 1910. This institutional transition was produced via a Constituent Assembly (1911), that established, as in most new demo-liberal regimes after the Great War, a multi-party semi-presidential system of parliamentary predominance, with non-universal male suffrage, where the executive body depended on the legislative, and a weak Head of State was indirectly elected by the Parliament and the Senate. Following the times, so the Portuguese Republic lived with a highly polarised society, constant social and political (intra and extra-parliamentary) unrest, a fragmented parliament, and a permanent governmental instability with the consequential inability to conclude or instal any relevant set of public policies. A Portuguese peculiarity lies in the fact that most republican elite politicians were staunch anti-Catholic freemasons, in a mostly Catholic country, with loose roots in rural society, with stronger presence in the certain academic and professional circles, and especially in the Lisbon and Oporto areas. As a result, most of their early policies aimed at secularizing the State and on politically isolating the working class (via a restrictive electoral law), both consequences of the distrust that the leaders of the hegemonic Democratic Party had of the right and left wing sectors of society, as well as of their need to overtake the state apparatus and use it to build the new set of citizens through a republican demopedic project.[8]

Consequently, the 1st Republic was a period of high volatility in a constant revolutionary atmosphere. During its existence, no government fulfilled its term; there were two successful right-wing dictatorships (Pimenta de Castro in 1915 and the influential Sidónio Pais between 1917 and 1918), endless rebellions, skirmishes, and putsches.[9] The political reputation of Portugal has reached such a status that the term *Portugaliser* became popular in Paris at the time. It meant a general state of political mess and the inability to manage public affairs.[10] Amongst the different attempts to overthrow the republic, one finally succeeded: on 28th May 1926, in Braga a coup d'état proclaimed the end of the republic and slowly advanced towards Lisbon. A week later the (counter) revolutionary leaders formally took the power from the hands of the President.

Without a pre-revolutionary plan, the leaders of the military coup, after a brief and intense deliberation that saw General Oscar Carmona arise triumphantly, decided to rule under an administrative dictatorship. Due to a lack

8 Among other measures, we highlight the separation of State and Church, the Divorce law, the introduction of the Civil Registration, the end of the Church hegemony in education and the advent of a public education system and policies. The republican demopedic project had the intention of creating the New Republican Men through a civic education model via the public education system and the ideological tutelage of the Education Ministry.

9 As an example of the constant instability, in 1920 Portugal had seven Prime-ministers, six in 1921, two in 1922 and 1923, four in 1924 and five in 1925. There were seven elected parliaments, eight Presidents (only one concluded his mandate) and 45 governments. Two failed attempts to re-install the monarchy (1911 and 1919), failed left wing coups (1913, 1916, 1921, 1926) and the failed right-wing coup of 1925, considered as the pre-emptive attempt of the May 1926 Revolution.

10 At the same time there was also a very popular cabaret song entitled *Encore un'autre révolution au Portugal* ("Yet another revolution in Portugal") (Eliade, *ob. cit.*).

of both a clearly defined leadership and an outlined plan, in a highly unstable political ground branded with constant infighting within their ranks and the need to tame the republican reaction, or the *Reviralho*,[11] this constitutional interregnum lasted until the time of the fourth anniversary of coup, when a new government was sworn in. Headed by General Domingues de Oliveira, amongst its main responsibilities was initiating the constitutional transition process, on hold since 1926. This pivotal task was led by Oliveira Salazar, the (civilian) finance minister, a choice that signalled the failure of the liberal solutions presented by Vicente de Freitas and Sinel Cordes, both former Presidents of the Council and high rank military officials, while it also underlined the impossibility of a transitional process lead by military forces autonomously, without civilian support.

It is not entirely clear when the constitutional works formally started, but sources point out that in by mid 1930, around the time of the presentation of the National Union, the Portuguese Single Party, Salazar took interest in the subject.[12] This version is supported by the speeches of Domingues Oliveira and Salazar during the May 28th celebrations, in which they announced the government's intentions to conclude the constitutional interregnum and take the necessary changes to institutionalize the military dictatorship.[13] As such, during the summer of 1930, Salazar will intensely meet with his select group of confidants and advisers, collecting political and legal advice of some plurality. Within this informal group, most of them colleagues of Coimbra University, the influences of Quirino de Jesus and Fezas Vital were evident, the former as legal and constitutional adviser, the latter playing an eminently political role. In any case, although there were several contributions, the constitution submitted to referendum in March 1933 will bear Salazar's full signature.

Despite this announcement, between mid 1930 and late 1931 the constitutional works made little or no progress, as at the time the main focus of the government was in fighting the recent wave of the *Reviralho*. Only late in 1931 Oscar Carmona, now President of the Republic, decided to jump-start the constitutional matter, taking the issue into his hands by establishing a National

11 The *Reviralho* was the term coined to brand the insurrections that occurred between 1926 and 1934, year of the last violent wave of protests and unrest. During this period, the most significant occurred in 1927, 1928, 1931, 1932 and 1934; cf. Luis Farinha, *O Reviralho: Revoltas republicanas contra a ditadura e o Estado novo (1926–1940)* (Lisbon: Estampa, 1998).

12 António Araújo, *A Lei de Salazar: Estudos sobre a Constituição política de 1933* (Coimbra: Enacitas, 2007).

13 António Oliveira Salazar, "Ditadura Administrativa e Revolução Política" (28 May 1930), in *Discursos, 1928–1934* (Coimbra: Coimbra Editora, 1935), 43–66.

Political Council, a formal political and constitutional body of direct support to the Presidency. In its formative legal document, it was stipulated that:

> the National Political Council will be heard in all political and administrative affairs that are of public interest in the reorganization plan of the State in harmony with the purpose of the 28 of May 1926 movement, especially on the following: 1. Drafting the Constitution and the Administrative and Electoral Codes; 2. Organizing the corporate state system.
>
> Decree-Law 20,643, dated December 22nd, 1931

Further it clarified that «without the prior consultation of the National Political Council the governmental projects referred to in paragraph 1 of this Article cannot proceed» (Decree Law 20.643). The creation of this structure, considered by the British Foreign Ministry as similar to the *Grande Consiglio Fascista*, was an obvious 'move' by President Carmona to take the lead of the transitional process, promoting a sort of constituent board whose purpose was to build the institutional foundations of an authoritarian corporative regime of strong presidential ascendancy, with himself with a central role.[14]

It must be noted that by 1931 it was Carmona, and not yet Salazar, who symbolised the May Revolution, being recently its electoral legitimized Chief.[15] But Salazar, who after balancing the 1929–1930 budget became worldly known as financial wizard, was steadily seen as an indispensable figure in any future of the dictatorship, and showed little willingness to step aside as the pundits hovering the *Belém Palace* attempted to *fascizise* the transitional process. His immediate reaction was to resume the constitutional work and politically boycott the presidential intentions with a visible contemptuous attitude.[16] As such, Salazar, acting upon Carmona's request, will rewrite the President' original proposal and substantially reduce the (political) scope of the Council. He then carefully overlooked the names indicated for the Political Council in order for his faction to have control over any formal voting. In addition, Salazar immediately resumed his own constitutional work, outside the Council's frame, and decided to announce a first Constitutional draft in February 1932, two months after the Council was announced, making clear his intention to marginalize

14 Araújo, *ob. cit.*

15 Searching for popular legitimation, Carmona replicated the plebiscitarian presidential election of Sidonio Pais of 1918 and was elected President without opposition in March 1928.

16 Araújo, *ob. cit.*

the Presidential proposal. Underlying this manoeuvre was not only a struggle for the effective leadership of the transitional process but a political and generational dispute: Carmona represented the old liberal-conservative military republicans and their masonic tradition, while Salazar presented himself as a new type of politician, civil, Catholic-conservative vaticanist, qualified not by force of arms but rather by the value of his intellect and political-ideological stands. Their confrontation was therefore not merely between the military and civilians, or liberals and corporatist, but also a clash between the *old* and the *new* vague.[17]

3 Salazar's Constitutional Notes

Our grasp of the chronology of the Portuguese constitutional process is facilitated by the access to Salazar's constitutional notes deposited in the Torre do Tombo National Archives (IANTT). This set of organized handwritten minutes allow us to closely follow Salazar's working methodology and cross-readings, intellectual and academic reflections, state of mind, key political and ideological concerns, and also to detect the main constitutional influences of the future legal framework of the New State.[18]

The first reference dates back to December 29th, 1931, one week after the presentation of the National Political Council, which confirms Salazar's urgency to react to Carmona's plan. In these early notes, Salazar examined at length, and comparatively, the history of Portuguese constitutionalism, basis from where he waved the first legal considerations to be taken into account in the new text. Complementary, he would also produce a detailed analysis of the principles of the Portuguese 1911 Constitution, as well as a comparative overview of the main European fundamental texts, especially those that were the product of post-World War institutional changes. In his critique of the 1911 Constitution Salazar noted its *old character*, calling it "a text from the nineteenth and not the twentieth century".[19] At the same time, he acknowledged an obvious disproportion between individual rights and duties, and an intolerable legal disregard for the Family, Corporations, Public Opinion and Education.[20] Moreover, in his opinion, the 1911 Constitution established an

17 Araújo, *ibidem*; Reis Santos, *ob. cit.*

18 Out of which we highlight the work of Boris Mirkine-Guetzevitch (*Les Constituitions de l'Europe Nouvele*, 1928), where the Russian exiled in Paris present a consistent summary of most post-war European constitutional texts, cf. Araújo, *ob. cit.*

19 IANTT/AOS/CO/PC – 1.

20 IANTT/AOS/CO/PC – 1.

excessively parliamentary system that skewed the hierarchical relationship between the executive and the legislative, where Parliament could inclusive dismiss Ministers individually. In his mind, the first Republic, with its parliamentary dominance inevitably weakened and conditioned the executive activity of the Government. In short, in Salazar' opinion, the 1911 Constitution was too liberal, extensively coated with an aggressive rationalist positivism that sought to enshrine an individualist, excessively parliamentary democratic regime at the expense of a weak and inconsequential executive branch.

In the comparative analysis of contemporary constitutional processes Salazar, apart from recognizing the predominance of republican forms of government and the constitutional hallowing of advanced social and political arrangements (taken as result of socialist influence and a reaction against Bolshevism), emphasized the practice of a close methodological collaboration between politicians, jurists and legal experts, which, as in the cases of Austria and (Weimar) Germany, allowed for an enhanced rationalization between policy needs and a rational legal construction. A method he sought to replicate in Portugal. His main critique was, again, the excessive power devoted to parliaments and the consequent subordination of the executive in matters of legislation, the inoperativeness of multi-party systems, the constitutional insignificance of most Heads of State and the weakness (and dependence) of governmental agencies vis-à-vis the parliament. Salazar considered these constitutional features as the root of the political and institutional instability of the 1920's, and as a solution he proposed governmentalizing the Constitution, providing extensive executive powers to the Government and / or Heads of State, legally constitutionalizing the rights of corporations (as in the Austrian case), promote parliamentary authoritarian governments (as in the case of Poland, Yugoslavia or Germany), or even support fascist revolutions. In this comparative analysis, Salazar acknowledged that his main juridical references came from the Weimar Constitution, not in what it meant its democratic and liberal content but rather in its form and organization.[21]

Salazar also displayed his awareness of contemporary European affairs, asserting that the main political (and ideological) conflict in Europe in the early 1930s was between individual liberalism, Socialism and Bolshevism on the one hand, and the ideals of order, tradition, authority and property on the other. Furthermore, he believed the Portuguese constitutional process, although inserted in this broad debate, should not take the European constitutional dynamics as an example, but instead create a political model of

---

21 IANTT/AOS/CO/PC – 1.

exclusively national characteristics afar from imported legal constructions, an idea of nationalist constitutional exceptionalism often inspirational for right-wing European authoritarian (semi) peripheral leaders and that will become one of the main points of interest in the Portuguese case.[22] For these leaders, the Portuguese example demonstrated the possibility to keep transitional political processes impervious to any international pressure or excessive influence, presenting itself as a third way to both Fascism and Nazism.[23]

Furthermore, Salazar will also be clear about his intentions to replace the liberal experiment of the nineteenth century and their individual and autonomous democratic features, as they had been the basis for the existing demo-plutocratic climate of political anarchy that prevented the existence of strong enough executives able to implement articulated and coherent set of policies. He further claimed that the new constitution should enshrine the Nation as its fundamental principle, as it represented its political and societal ethos, soul and spirit, individuals and groups, combating therefore the excessive doctrinal influence of economic liberalism and the exacerbated anti-clerical spirit of the 1911 text. From this basis, Salazar concluded that the future constitution should be nationalist, recognizing the Nation as a legal reality (and not the individual, as defined by liberalism) in order to take advantage of its historical tradition, incorporating all its vital elements in the "the nation as a whole".[24]

The new constitution should also manage a balanced relationship between the individual and the State (a relationship that if balanced towards the side of the individual could degenerate into excessive individualism) and between the State and the Individual (which could degenerate into statism, Bolshevism or Socialism). An intermediate and balanced solution should, in Salazar's opinion, take from individualism and liberalism their Fundamental Rights and from counter-individualism the essential interests of the nation and its vital groups. Within this mind-set, Salazar identified that the new constitutional system should provide a deeply realistic body of text, questioning however whether

22 We dealt with these aspects in another body of work, cf. Reis Santos, "Retóricas do Fascismo".

23 It helps to explain the Portuguese capacity to keep its distance and autonomy from the areas of influence of fascism and Nazism its geographical position in Europe, its Colonial Empire and not having any disputed borders nor revisionist stance with its only neighbouring country, Spain, a reality rarely shared by most of the New Europe. See also Reis Santos, "Retóricas do Fascismo"; António Oliveira Salazar, *Como se reerge um Estado* (*Comment on releve un État*) (Lisbon: Esfera do Caos, 2007 [1937]); and *Idem*, António Oliveira Salazar, *Une Révolution dans la paix* (Paris: Flammarion, 1937).

24 IANTT/AOS/CO/PC – 1; also Araújo, *ob. cit.*

it should be soaked in a "conservative and retrograde? [or a] Revolutionary spirit?".[25]

4 The First Draft

These first notes would serve as the basis for Salazar's first public proposal, published to fill in the political space occupied by Carmona' National Political Council and take the lead of the constitutional debate. It will be a beardless proposal, as it will undergo significant changes until its plebiscitary approval in March 1933, but it is noteworthy to appreciate not only the detailed work systematized by Salazar and his limited entourage, and in tracking its main genetic influences, but also to access the form in which the Portuguese Finance wizard would choose to present, publicly, *his* proposal, knowing beforehand it would be strongly scrutinized.

This first draft was announced in January 1932, and disclosed a bicameral system with a parliamentary assembly and a Senate 50% directly elected by Heads of Family, and the President, with a single term limit, elected through organic voting (local, municipal and provincial administrations, economic, moral and colonial corporations). Materializing the concern to present a constitutional solution that could articulate and please the ambitions of the different and influential political families in the right, this first proposal specified that "the state is Liberal, Social and Corporative", a lack of political coherence justified by Salazar's attempt (and need) to build an implicit (and somehow contradictory) compromise between a corporate and liberal model.

Due to the obvious influences of the 1911 Constitution and the failure to provide an ideologically sound proposal, this draft was promptly criticized by all ranges of political families within the Dictatorship. Thus, for example, if the electoral model for the Presidency could please the corporatist, it strongly displeased Carmona and his supporters, who enjoyed the *sidonista* legitimacy enshrined in the direct election of the President. As such, the proposal to keep active the single mandate for the Head of State from the 1928 electoral law has to be seen as a manoeuvre to condition the symbolism of the President in the regime's future constitutional architecture, and a distractive matter to Carmona.[26] In this sense, Salazar hoped that the President, in the envisioned

25 IANTT/AOS/CO/PC – 1; also, Araújo, *ob. cit.*

26 According to the 1928 electoral law, the mandate of the President was fixed in single 7 years term. Accordingly, Carmona would not be able to present himself for re-election in 1935. Law-Decree 15 063, February 25th, 1928.

negotiating process, would concentrate itself more on the defining role of the Presidency then in other institutional settings, allowing those to be directly determined by Salazar. In other words, Salazar, aware of what could condition Carmona, set the constitutional battleground around the institutional figure of the Presidency in order to lure Carmona into this turf, hopping he would relinquish the leadership of the transitional process, drop the National Political Council, and concentrate instead on fine-tuning his role on the future constitutional frame, abandoning further institutional claims, and leave Salazar as the uncontested leader of the constitutional transition.

The nuances around the Presidency, although important in the constitutional definition of the Portuguese New State, should also be understood in the light of the political balance between different actors and sectors within the Dictatorship. There were those from the radical right and corporatist sectors that wanted a complete rupture with the 1st Republic and desired a strong ideological text sharply embodying the underlying promises made by Salazar during his 1928/1930 radical speeches, when he was setting the ideological foundations of the Estado Novo and presenting himself as a radical duly aligned and ready to (re)present the new times.[27] For this sector, a hybrid first proposal raised an aggressive chorus of criticism, especially as the promised corporate and authoritarian regime that would embed the spirit of the "National Revolution" in the Era of Fascisms had been lost in Salazar's constitutional emptiness proposal.

These purists of the New Order repeatedly criticized this lack of revolutionary nerve, both nationally and internationally.[28] José Pequito Rebelo, for example, an influential integralist of strong monarchical convictions in a personal letter to Salazar, pointed out the «excessively democratic» features observed in the electoral systems and the «inadequate and indeterminate corporatist dimension of the Constitution». In his opinion this would only mean the quick restoration of a multi-party regime and an obvious denial of the principles laid out in Salazar's pivotal speech of July 30th, 1930. Another integralist, Afonso Lucas, likewise confessed to Salazar his perplexity in trying to conciliate his revolutionary speeches with the direct suffrage of his proposal, or the role

27 Namely the speeches of April 27th,1928, "Condições da reforma financeira"; of October 21st, 1929, "Política de verdade. Política de sacrifício. Política nacional"; May 28th, 1930, "Ditadura administrativa e revolução política"; and finally his intervention in July 30th, 1930, "Princípios fundamentais da revolução política": Salazar, *Discursos, 1928–1934*. See also Reis Santos, "Self-fashioning of a conservative revolutionary".

28 Reis Santos, "Retóricas do Fascismo".

assigned to Parliament, as "if the parties-or factions of public opinion- have no place in the new state, why then a place for them in the National Assembly?".[29]

These criticisms are hardly surprising, given the distance between Salazar's speeches and the proposal given to consultation. Between 1928 and 1930 Salazar had indeed promised a constitutional national revolution to break with the liberal legacy and build an unequivocally Corporative State. And this first draft represented a clear break with these statements as it displayed a surprising lack of ideological coherence and reflected a politician-like behaviour on the part of a self-proclaimed non-politician. If Salazar wanted to be truthful to his public interventions he would never, for instance, keep any liberal institutions or procedures, as a Parliament, nor would present for debate a text so close to the *old order*. He did that in order to gain support from the conservative right and Carmona. Moreover, the inconsistent and carefree mode in which Salazar dealt with some fundamental theoretical concepts (such the dichotomy citizen-elector / Head of Family), when he insisted in removing any liberal abstractionisms, clearly demonstrates that Salazar did not hold any pre-defined and ready-to-apply political model, as claimed by some fascist and integralist intellectuals, such as Baldi-Papini, Gil Robles, Biagi, among others.[30] It also exposes the methodological shortcomings of Salazar' journey to power, further demonstrating his political consensus skills and the distance between his publicly declared intentions and the legal and constitutional outcomes of his actions. For someone who presented himself as an anti-plutocrat and a new type of politician, Salazar stood evidently closer to those he criticised.

In any case, the harsh criticism stemming from the corporative and extreme right was not isolated. The liberal right will also criticize the draft and even the Portuguese Church will express its concerns, as the proposal failed to underscore the country's Catholic tradition, upholding the separation between State and Church and the laicism of the State. On behalf of the Church the critique was headed by the Patriarch Cardinal of Lisbon, Manuel Cerejeira, personal friend of Salazar since Coimbra university. On a personal letter to Carmona (February 27th 1933), the Cardinal identified as his main critiques (1) the absence of any references to the Divine in the constitutional project, something that other more democratic and modern republics have done; (2) the lack of recognition of the freedom and independence of the Catholic Church in the

---

29 Araújo, *ob. cit.*

30 U. Baldi-Papini, *Portogallo Nuovo: Lineamenti critice della riforma politico-costituzionale del Portogallo* (Florence: Poligrafica Universitaria, 1936); Bruno Biaggi, *Il Portogallo d'oggi* (Florence: Felice Le Monnier, 1939); José M. Gil Robles, "Prefacio" in António Oliveria Salazar, *El pensamiento de la Revolución Nacional* (Buenos Aires: Poblet, 1938).

sphere of education; and (3) not assuming the "moral ideas of Catholic origin" as the "root of the foundational institutions of our European civilization".[31]

From the Republican-liberal camp came some of the fiercest attacks, namely through Cunha Leal, who, after the initial support to the May Revolution, drifted from the path of the dictatorship on the same rhythm that Salazar gained preponderance in the corridors of power. From his exile in Spain, Leal announced his solution to the ongoing constitutional process by publishing in the summer of 1931 a small book entitled *Ditadura, democracia ou comunismo: O problema português* (*Dictatorship, Democracy or Communism: The Portuguese problem*).[32] In this concise text, Leal suggested that the new Portuguese political system should evolve from the 1911 Constitution, keeping direct election with proportional representation for the legislative chamber and a semi–elected Senate with a quarter of its representatives coming from several professional sectors. Leal also kept in his proposal the strong parliamentary dominance of the First Republic, as well as the Government's dependency on the Assembly.[33]

5 The Second Draft

Some of these criticisms and counterproposals produced immediate effects. On February 22nd, 1932, during a meeting of the Council of Ministers, several changes to the proposal were to occur. The indirect election of the president was dropped, as well as any notion of organic suffrage, which also removed the heads of family from the new electoral architecture. Salazar was thus willing to forsake a fully corporate electoral system, keeping instead the liberal concept of citizen-elector. Beside these, other amendments in the institutional architecture underwent major changes as the Senate disappeared, replaced by a professional camera, and the idea of a "Congress" abandoned.

According to Araújo, after Salazar decided to abandon the bicameral system inherited from the Republic, restructuring the parliament was one of the more complex problems found in the genesis of the system of government attached to the New State Constitution. In the end Salazar will support a parliamentary structure that should "translate the spirit of unity to a national level", as the parliamentarians should be a "group of people no longer prepared to act

31 Cf. IANTT/AOS/CO/PC – 5 A; and Rita Almeida Carvalho, *A concordata de Salazar* (Lisbon: Temas e Debates / Círculo de Leitores, 2013).

32 Cunha Leal, *Ditadura, democracia ou comunismo. O problema português* (La Curuña: Moret, 1931).

33 Cunha Leal, *ibidem*.

separately but to carry out work together in all policy moments". Furthermore, in his famous interviews with António Ferro in 1933, Salazar would try to justify the liberal features of the National Assembly, as a necessary concession, a temporary experience to be abandoned once the country's cultural conditions could permit the establishment of a fully corporative State.[34]

This second proposal, while leaving some liberal traits, already meant a clear departure from the 1911 text. However, it maintained the liberal concept of citizen-elector at the expense of the corporative principle of Heads of Family. These changes expressed Salazar's concerns to find a suitable formula that could bring together the different right-wing families around his "Frankenstein model", knitted accordingly to the weights and relative scale of the different (political) sensibilities, knowing that the personal ambitions of Carmona must always be consider firstly. In this context, acting more like a veteran politician than as a purist ideologue, Salazar was well aware that he could more easily antagonize the radical right then the liberals gathered around the President. And he would act accordingly.

In light of this, after being appointed President of the Council in June 1932, Salazar immediately curbed his revolutionary interventions, no longer focusing on the imperative to break with the Portuguese liberal constitutional tradition or on replacing it with an authoritarian modern fascist or corporatist state. Rather, he focused on the need to publicly clarify the roadmap of integration that all political forces supporting the Dictatorship should follow into the ultimate absorption in the nascent institutional framework, leaving few doubts about where the limits were and where their boundaries were drawn.[35] Simultaneously, this visible adjustment of narrative proves that in the genesis of the New State, Salazar's ability to combine his personal dynamics and negotiating skills was instrumental in building a balanced proposal that could give everyone a place, be they integralists, corporatists, fascists, monarchists, liberals, militaries and civilians. Salazar hence masterfully articulated this complex

34 These interviews, immediately translated and disseminated through Europe, served to introduce Salazar to a wider audience and to campaign for the 1933 Plebiscite. Araújo, *ob. cit.*; António Ferro, *Salazar. O homem e a sua obra* (Lisbon: Empresa Nacional de Publicidade, 1933).

35 These speeches were delivered in 1932 and 1933, and addressed consecutively the military, the different political families and finally the national-syndicalists (Portuguese fascists), presenting to each the conditions of political participation: see "O exército e a revolução Nacional" (28 May 1932); "As diferentes forças políticas em face da Revolução Nacional" (23 November 1932); "É esta a revolução porque esperávamos?" (27 April 1933): Salazar, *Discursos*.

network of converging and conflicting interests, skilfully channelling them at the service of his personal ambitions.

This second draft of the Constitution, dully adapted to the wishes of the conservative right, was published on the occasion of the sixth anniversary of the May revolution (1932). But it still kept the Sidonist presidential electoral mandate of a single term, thus not allowing the possibility of an incumbent President to run for re-election, a detail that will be the last act of this intricate and dynamic constitutional waltz between Salazar and Carmona. But before these last accords, this dance would be abruptly interrupted by the intrusion of Vicente de Freitas, former President of the Council and at the time Mayor of Lisbon, who will lead a final liberal charge from the balconies of the capital's City Hall.

As we mentioned, soon after the publication of a second version of the Constitution, Salazar will be invited to head the government (June 28th, 1932), replacing General Domingues de Oliveira. This appointment meant that the dictatorship had extinguished their military solutions and entrusted the government leadership to a civilian.[36] In addition, an historical coincidence of significant political impact occurred on July 2nd, 1932: D. Manuel II, Portugal's last King, deposed in 1910, died in his British exile without any heir, nullifying any direct monarchic restoration claims. This would release the royalist elite to support the *situation* and indirectly pressure the top echelons of the Dictatorship to finally resolve the constitutional interlude lived since 1926.[37]

Within this crescendo, Vicente de Freitas saw his (final) opportunity to take advantage of Carmona's institutional exposure to the single-term rules and requested a visit to the President to present him with an alternative proposal. The President, also a seasoned politician, cited health reasons to refuse a meeting, but gave the capital's mayor access to the liberal newspaper *O Século* that on February 12th, 1933, published this alternative proposal. In it, Freitas claimed that the country was not ready for a new constitutional regime, offering instead the election of a constituent Assembly with extended space for plural political participation, a clearly challenge to the monopoly of participation around Salazar's *União Nacional* (National Union), Portugal's single party presented in 1930. In addition, Freitas proposed a presidential system with

36 According to Leal Marques's diary (Salazar's chief of staff between 1928–1940), these were moments of high political intensity, as Salazar still had strong adversaries within the *situation*, namely in the former head of government, and now Mayor of Lisbon, José Vicente de Freitas.

37 D. Manuel II's body arrived in Lisbon on August 2nd, 1932, receiving a state honour funeral organized by Salazar.

two chambers elected directly, a Parliament with openly liberal features and a Corporate Chamber of professional nature, with wider powers than the one promised by Salazar, namely legislative ones.

Duly informed about Vicente de Freitas's request to visit Carmona, Salazar immediately reacted and visited the President in Cascais the next day. Contrary to the mayor of Lisbon, Carmona didn't refuse this call, as it suited his plans to pressure the President of the Council to abandon the single presidential term. Carmona's move had produced its effects and his strategy played out perfectly, as Salazar immediately summoned the Council of Ministers to work on a new solution to solve the presidential question. And in order to definitely win the good side of the President, and clinch him definitively to the constitutional process, any limits for presidential re-elections were promptly abandoned,

6 The Final Version

After this last episode, the new constitutional text finally found the necessary balance between the conservative Republicanism of Carmona and the corporate authoritarianism of Salazar. The epilogue of this long process would be a constitutional plebiscite; a formula of electoral legitimation quite popular in the Age of Fascisms that sought to solve through direct popular consultation the traditional dependence of political parties to act as intermediaries and representatives of factions or citizens. Instead, plebiscites will directly connect the nation with the political institutions, establishing a mechanism to truly ascertain the feeling of the nation, free and independent from the traditional parties.

Inserted in the general lineage of the *Ventennio Fascista*, the Portuguese constitutional text was then submitted to a «referendum restricted to citizens who could read and write», which excluded more than half of the population (*The Times*, February 1935), and where abstentions counted as positive votes. The 1933 Constitution confirmed the lengthy negotiation process navigated by Salazar: direct election by citizens-electors for the Presidency and the National Assembly, indirect and organic vote for Local Government and the Corporate Chamber. The new electoral code was not constitutionalized, but rather subject to specific legislation. In 1934 the first general elections to the National Assembly were held. In 1935 Carmona was (re)elected, completing the circle of legitimacy of the *Estado Novo* representative institutions. By 1936 the Portuguese model was widely admired throughout Europe. And in 1937, responding to a challenge from a French publisher, a small booklet entitled *Comment on relève un État*, presented in a propagandistic manner the

Portuguese constitutional process as a transitional blueprint to those who in the New European Order sought for an alternative to fascist or national socialist influences.[38]

7 Conclusions

The negotiations around the Portuguese New State 1933 Constitution were long and reflected the difficulties Carmona and Salazar had to overcome in order to build a political model that could, at least, drawn minimum support and consensus from the different political forces supporting the Military Dictatorship and the personal ambitions of each protagonist. These tensions were visible in the multiple versions of the Constitution, as each of these political forces and movements represented, desired and expected different outcomes from the constitutionalization process, an antagonism that spammed from those closer to the liberal First Republic to a full-fledged corporative fascist model. During this process, it was evident that Salazar never favoured a model that would enshrine the constitutional architecture he had promised during his purist revolutionary speeches of 1930, during his ascension to power. His constitutional notes also confirmed an open path towards the constitutionalization of the dictatorship, confirming that soon to be Portuguese Dictator never had a fully defined model, but a set of guidelines to manage through a complex process of constitutional deliberation and a willingness to negotiate most of its fundamentals in order to keep the stewardship of the constitutional process and ultimately to preserve his position in the top echelon of power.

The 1933 text reflected then the technical draw between Salazar and Carmona, as both players understood the need of each other to operate a peaceful constitutional transition for a lasting regime grounded on their charismatic dual leadership. Finally, the Constitution of 1933 also reflects a pragmatic balance between the different right-wing political forces within the military dictatorship, a feature that had the advantage of simultaneously not leaving anyone fully satisfied nor dissatisfied. The old liberals could be pleased with the direct election of the National Assembly and the Presidency of the Republic, and the corporatist with the institutionalization of a Corporate Chamber elected by organic vote, procedure replicated in the local Administrative Bodies. Only the purists and fanatics were displeased, positioning themselves as opponents to

38 Reis Santos, "Self-fashioning of a conservative revolutionary" and "Retóricas do Fascismo".

the constitutional solution and outside the borders of the *situation*. The vast majority came to terms with the new reality.

Bibliopgraphy

Main Sources

Constituição política de la República Portuguesa, 1933.

Leo XIII, Papal Encyclical *Rerum* Novarum, 1891.

Pius XI, Papal Encyclical *Quadragesimo Anno*, 1931.

Salazar, António Oliveira, *Discursos, 1928–1934* (Coimbra: Coimbra Editora, 1935)

Torre do Tombo National Archives, Lisbon, IANTT/AOS/CO/PC – 1.

Main Bibliographical References

Araújo, António, *A Lei de Salazar: Estudos sobre a Constituição política de 1933* (Coimbra: Tenacitas, 2007).

Ferro, António, *Salazar: O homem e a sua obra* (Lisbon: Empresa Nacional de Publicidade, 1933).

Manoilescu, Mihael, *Le Siècle du Corporatisme: Doctrine du corporatisme intégral et pur* (Paris: Librairie Félix Alcan, 1934).

Pinto, António Costa; and Aristotle Kallis, *Rethinking the Nature of Fascism* (London: Palgrave Macmillan, 2014).

Reis Santos, José, "Self-fashioning of a Conservative Revolutionary: Salazar's Integral Corporatism and the International Networks of the 1930s", in António Costa Pinto and Federico Finchelstein, eds., *Authoritarianism and Corporatism in Europe and Latin America: Crossing Borders* (London and New York: Routledge, 2018), ch. 4.

CHAPTER 20

The Framing of a Liberal Democratic Constitution in Post-War Western Germany

Niall Bond

The "constitutional moment" of the adoption of the *Grundgesetz* or Basic Law on May 23th, 1949, founding the Federal Republic of Germany four years to the month after the capitulation of the Third Reich, was marked by Germany's position as a not fully sovereign state whose destiny was determined by outside forces, by discussions of the collapse of the Weimar Republic and the Third Reich, and by the onset of the Cold War. The *Grundgesetz* is paradoxically notable for both its provisional intent and design for eternity: it initially applied to only a part of the German nation and was destined to be replaced by a *Verfassung* upon reunification, and yet a "clause for eternity" ensures that its vital parts may never be rescinded. The term, *Grundgesetz* was a translation of the Latin expression, *lex fundamentalis*. It was elaborated after instructions from the occupying powers, the United States, the United Kingdom and France and adopted by the *Landtage*, notwithstanding non-ratification by Bavaria, without recourse to a referendum. Recently archived documents related to the Basic Law, including the discussions of the Parliamentary Council, the Länder and the Allies, amount to roughly 30,000 pages. While the Basic Law drew from German constitutional traditions, Germany's constitutional moment was fraught with the awareness that the previous German constitutional moment of liberal democracy – that of the Weimar Republic – had been brought down among other things by a widespread belief that the prevailing constitution had been imposed by foreign powers in foreign interests and was at odds with the genius of Germany. The success of Germany's post-war constitution has laid this fear to rest. Another notable constraint was competition between the two Germanies: the adoption of the Basic Law competed with the adoption of the constitution of the German Democratic Republic: the earliest complete draft constitution in post-war Germany had been elaborated by Karl Polak on behalf of Wilhelm Pieck, the first president of the Sozialistische Einheitspartei Deutchlands, Otto Grotewohl, Walter Ulbricht and Max Fechner, after the Soviet military administration had requested that the SED present its concept for post-war governance in Germany as early as July, 1946. On October 3, 1990,

 | DOI:10.1163/9789004549159_022

the Basic Law became the constitution for "the entire German people". Here, we propose to consider endogenous and exogenous origins of the Basic Law, the models of democracy under consideration, the importance of basic rights, the organization of federal democracy and the preclusion of direct democracy, concluding with some reflections on the double provisional and permanent nature of the document.

1 From the Potsdam Conference to the Grundgesetz

At the end of the Potsdam Conference, convened from July 17th to August 2nd, 1945, to debate the treatment of the Axis powers, the Allies announced that one of their objectives was to establish democracy in Germany. The United States were represented by Harry Truman and Secretary of State James Byrnes, the U.S.S.R by Joseph Stalin and his foreign minister, Viatcheslav Molotov, and the United Kingdom first by Winston Churchill and his minister Anthony Eden, and then by Clement Atlee, assisted by Ernest Bevin. According to the protocol following a meeting of heads of government of the Soviet Union, the United States and the United Kingdom at the Berlin conference of August 1st, 1945, the supreme authority over Germany would reside with the military commandments of the United States, the United Kingdom, the Soviet Union and France so as to ensure the uniform treatment of the German population throughout Germany and attain the objectives of the occupation, i.e. the total disarmament and demilitarization of Germany, the control of all German industry that could serve military production, the abolition of militarism and National Socialism, the destruction and confiscation of instruments of war and their production sites, the persuasion of the Germans that the total military defeat and ensuing suffering was of their own responsibility, the destruction of the National Socialist party and all military propaganda, the abolition of Nazi laws, the arrest and persecution of war criminals and eminent members of the Nazi party, and the reconstruction of German democracy and peaceful international cooperation by Germany. This included controlling German education to promote democracy, the organization of the judiciary along democratic lines, the equality of all citizens irrespective of race, nationality or religion, decentralization, rights for democratic parties, principles of representation throughout regional, provincial and Länder administrations, the setting up of central administrative departments under the control of secretaries of state, and the guaranteeing of freedoms of speech, press and religion within limits imposed by military security.[1] The Third Reich was dismantled, and Germany was separated from Austria; each territory was divided into four occupation zones. Germany lost East Prussia and Konigsberg, accounting for roughly a fourth of its territory, with the ensuing displacement of German populations from eastern Europe: more than eleven million Germans left their homes, while 2.6 million remained in the former German territories. The "four Ds" of Potsdam were disarmament or demilitarization, denazification, decartelization and democratization.[2]

The role of this agreement in democratizing Germany has been controversial; the historian of the U.S. occupation of Germany, Harold Zink, claims that preparing Germany for democracy had never been taken very seriously by the U.S. Joint Chiefs of Staff and had been included in the Potsdam Agreement because it "sounded good",[3] arguing that the revanchist program accentuating denazification, the reduction of the standards of living of the Germans, the ban on fraternizing with the Germans, the destruction of German industry, etc. made the project of democracy seem insignificant.[4] Democratization was ultimately undertaken in competing programs between the western and Soviet zones: the Soviets were first to authorize political parties, and the first to hold a referendum.

2 Competing Models of Democracy

The competition between the Soviet Union and the English-speaking allies had been foreseen by Winston Churchill when he wrote to Stalin on April 29th, 1945 that he was disturbed by the division of the world into the English-speaking countries and those dominated by communist parties, leading the world to ruin, or when he wrote to Truman on May 12th, 1945 that he feared the advancement of Soviet forces to the Atlantic, or in his famous Fulton address on Soviet expansion on March 5th, 1946. Churchill regretted that the western allies had withdrawn their armies from the territories conquered

1 Cf. the Protocol of the Proceedings of the Berlin (Potsdam) Conference in: A Decade of American Foreign Policy: Basic Documents, 1941–49 Prepared at the request of the Senate Committee on Foreign Relations by the Staff of the Committee and the Department of State. Washington, DC: Government Printing Office, 1950, consultable at: http://avalon.law.yale.edu/20th_century/decade17.asp.

2 Alfons Klafkowski, *L'Accord de Potsdam du 2 août 1945: Umowa Poczdamska*. Traduit par Jadwiga Filipowska (Varsovie: Instytut Wydawniczy Pax Warszawa, 1964).

3 Harold Zink, *The United States in Germany 1944–1955* (Princeton: D. Van Nostrand, 1957), 326.

4 Zink, *ibid.*, 327.

in eastern Germany and feared that the Germans would support the better offer between the Soviets and western democracies. In Fulton, Churchill came out in favour of the premises of liberty and democracy in Germany and first applied the term “iron curtain” to the mine and mirador ridden border running from Stettin on the Baltic to Trieste on the Adriatic.[5] The term, “the Cold War” was coined by Bernard Baruch, the U.S. representative to the U.N. Atomic Energy Commission in 1947 to describe tensions between the United States and the Soviet Unions, and was manifest in Truman’s “containment policy” and George Kennan’s article in the July 1949 issue of *Foreign Affairs*, questioned by the liberal conservative, Walter Lipmann, who doubted that the U.S. had the economic or military power to contain Soviet influence and that the capitalist system would be as effective as a centralized planned economy.[6] The hemorrhaging of east Germany was to lead the Soviet Union to set up a five-kilometer demarcation area on May 26th, 1952. A further aspect of competition was the fraternal aid offered by Secretary of State George Marshall in a speech held in June 1947, inauguring the European Recovery Program with its 13 billion dollars of funds, rejected by Stalin and thereafter Poland and Czechoslovakia, and accepted by France, the United Kingdom, Austria, Belgium, the Netherlands, Luxemburg, Greece, Ireland, Iceland, Italy, Norway, Sweden, Denmark, Finland, Portugal, Switzerland and Turkey. The Soviet response was the creation of the Cominform in October 1947 based on Andrei Jdanov’s assertion that the world was divided between and “imperialist, antidemocratic camp” directed by the United States and an “anti-imperialist and democratic camp” protected by the Soviet Union. The Soviet’s Berlin blockade from June 24th, 1948 to May 12th, 1949 was countered by the “air bridge” set up by the United States to transport necessities to West Berlin.[7]

3 The London Conferences and the Frankfurt Documents

The London Conferences, which started on November 25th, 1947, bringing together the foreign ministers of the U.S. (George Marshall), the U.K. (Ernest Bevin), France (Georges Bidault) and the Soviet Union (Molotov) bore witness

5 Martin Gilbert, *Winston S. Churchill*, VIII: *Never Despair, 1945–1965*, Churchill Biography, book 8 (3 vols., 1988) (London: Minerva, 1990).

6 Walter Lippmann. *The Cold War. A Study in U.S. Foreign Policy* (London: Hamish Hamilton, 1947), 13.

7 Melvyn P. Leffler, Odd Arne Westad, eds., *The Cambridge History of the Cold War*, volume 1: *Origins* (Cambridge: Cambridge University Press, 2010).

to the deterioration of relations between the two camps, leading Marshall to abandon hopes for reunifying Germany in the immediate future and the U.S. and the U.K. to create the bi-zone. While the issue of whether Germany should be a centralized power (favoured by the Soviet Union) or federal has led to controversy over whether federalism was imposed upon the Federal Republic by the western, and most importantly French allies. Division was latent within Germany, as the Social Democrats in the British Zone favoured a centralized state, while the Länder of the south, Bavaria, Wurttemberg and Baden preferred renewing with the federalist tradition. The expression, "federal republic" was first used by the French occupiers in Wurttemberg-Hohenzollern in May 1947. From February 23th to March 6th, 1948, the U.S., the U.K. and France held a conference to discuss the future political order of their respective zones, thwarted by France's intention to retain control of the Saarland. In a further conference from April 20th to June 1st, the U.K. came out in favour of German unity, with no preference for a central or federal structure, however the U.S. were in favour of a federal state consisting of the three western zones. The French were in favour of the lasting weakening of Germany and the integration of the Saarland into France. Given the inevitability of the creation of a German state, the French accepted a federal state with the Ruhr Authority in control over coal and steel mining in Europe's most industrialized region, inducing Germany to cooperate with France in setting up the European Coal and Steel Community in 1951. The final communiqué enjoined the German Länder to create a federal state which would not pose an obstacle to future German unification and led the military governors to elaborate the Frankfurt documents, guidelines for the elaboration of a German constitution, presented to the Minister Presidents on July 1st, 1948. They included Germany's continued status as an occupied country and permission to convoke an assembly to adopt a German constitution guaranteeing basic rights and a federal structure under the control of the military governors. Wishing to avoid the impression that they were dictating the principles of the German constitution, the military governors primarily set the date of the Constitutional Assembly, September 1st, 1948, while stipulating that the new German state for the three zones would be a federal, democratic state, that the constitution had to be ratified by an absolute majority in a referendum in each Land and would enter effect following ratification by two-thirds of the eleven Länder, i.e. eight Länder, that each constitutional amendment would have to be approved by the allied military governments, and that the military governors were to be consulted in issues concerning foreign policy, the Ruhr, the reparations, industry and the rights of the occupying troops.[8]

These documents were presented by Lucius D. Clay for the United States, Marie-Pierre Koenig for France and Sir Brian Robertson for the U.K. at I.G. Farben in Frankfurt to the representatives of the Länder. The Minister Presidents in their meeting from July 8th to 10th in Koblenz were confronted with the creation of a partial state in western Germany without a solution for Germany as a whole, however they declared they would accept the Frankfurt documents, while observing that measures should be taken to avoid deepening the rift between the east and the west. They also observed they would rather not hold a referendum, given the provisional nature of the solution, and rejected the status of occupation. On July 20th, 1948, the Minister Presidents finally accepted the governors' demands, but maintained that it would be an error to call the provisional document a *Verfassung*, a constitution, instead opting for the term, *Grundgesetz*, the basic law. The election of the members of the Parliamentary Council by the *Landtage*, the parliaments of each Land, which were to ratify the basic law, was also specified, avoiding recourse to a referendum, as requested by the governors.

4 Herrenchiemsee

The constitutional convention at Herrenchiemsee took place from August 10th to 23rd, with a commission of experts consisting principally of representatives of the administration rather than politicians in charge of drafting a constitution. Points included a strong and effective federal government, a powerless and neutral head of state, the preclusion of referenda and a clause stating that the Basic Law would be permanent, a precursor to the *Ewigkeitsklausel*. As the parties had not yet been established beyond the zones, *Länder* representatives participated in the debate, however differences in the emerging parties soon became clear. Konrad Adenauer's conservative party's Principles for a German Federal Constitution of April 1948 showed a clear preference for powers to the *Länder*, while the SPD's Nuremberg directives of 1947 sought to maintain the unity of the Reich, corresponding to the conviction that the left had more influence in the east.

8 Büro der Ministerpräsidenten des amerikanischen, britischen und französischen Besatzungssgebietes, ed., *Dokumente betreffend die Begründung einer neuen staatlichen Ordnung in den amerikanischen, britischen und französischen Besatzungszonen* (Wiesbaden: 1948), 14–7.

The principles adopted in Herrenchiemsee were 1) a bicameral legislative including a parliament and representation of the Länder, 2) dependency of the government on a parliamentary majority allowing for a government to be formed, 3) the avoidance of presidential government by making sure that a majority that was not capable of governing might not overturn the existing government, 4) a federal president as a neutral head of state alongside the head of government, the chancellor, 5) the adoption of emergency law allowing the President to pass decrees in a transitional state of emergency, and a stipulation for the head of the federal government to implement federal law in the Länder. Furthermore, 6) the federal system of justice would be of aid in federal supervision of the Länder, 7) in cases not provided for by the Basic Law, legislation, administration, justice and financial responsibilities and duties lay within the remit of the Länder, 8) the finances of the federation and Länder were to be separate, 9) popular initiatives were not authorized at the federal level, and popular referenda could only be carried out at a federal level for amending the Basic Law, and finally, 10) no amendment to the Basic Law could put an end to the basic order of liberal democracy (*freiheitlich-demokratische Grundordnung*).

The Parliamentary Council was set up by the eleven Minister Presidents of the U.S., British and French zones in 1948 to draft the Basic Law of the Federal Republic of Germany and convened between September 1st, 1948, and August 14th, 1949. Konrad Adenauer was elected as president of the Parliamentary Council on September 1. The draft Basic Law was adopted on May 8th, 1949, accepted by the three western military governors on May 12nd, and became effective as of May 23rd; the first Bundestag was elected on August 14th, effectively triggering the dissolution of the Parliamentary Council. The Bavarian Landtag alone did not ratify the text as it appeared insufficiently federalist, however acknowledging that it would accept the Basic Law if the two-third majority of the Länder was obtained

The future main parties of the Federal Republic already existed: the Christlich Demokratische Union, the Christlich-Soziale Union (Bavaria), the Sozialdemokratische Partei Deutschlands and the Frei Demokratische Partei, (Theodor Heuss), the Kommunistische Partei Deutschlands and the Deutsche Zentrumspartei. The republic was both a "chancellor democracy" and "party democracy", with stable government with a strong role for political parties. While during the Reich ministers were merely neutral officials under a weak chancellor, the Basic Law anchored ministerial responsibilities in party democracy. While the Herrenchiemsee draft provided that each minister would be voted by the Bundestag, the Grundgesetz provided that the Chancellor be voted by the Bundestag and could appoint ministers. The chancellor laid down the guidelines of government policy but ministers prepared draft legislation without directions from the chancellor, though the chancellor guided negotiations on differences within the cabinet.[9] Hugo Preuss was the first to have given the primacy of the head of government in establishing guidelines a theoretical foundation.[10] While Max Weber felt that the position of chancellor had to be largely superior to that of the other ministries because of his responsibility for the whole,[11]*Richtlinienkompetenz* in the political culture of the Federal Republic falls short of Weber's ideal of democracy through charismatic leaders inasmuch as the chancellor remains primus inter pares in a process of collaboration. The ascendancy of the chancellor has varied in the history of the Federal Republic depending on majorities, coalition government, the personality of the chancellor and public opinion; under Konrad Adenauer, "chancellor democracy" was long dominated by a single man, which has retroactively been interpreted as a period of transition from a culture of authoritarianism to the pluralist and more libertarian democracy that emerged during the 1960s.

If no majority can be formed in the Bundestag, the Federal President can dissolve the parliament. The chancellor has greater democratic legitimacy than the ministers as the chancellor alone is elected by the parliament. The chancellor decides on the distribution of competencies among the ministers without being influenced by the Bundestag.[12] The chancellor and ministers are subject to parliamentary responsibility. If a chancellor is overturned, the entire government is dissolved, thereby reducing crises and limiting the parliament's margin of manoeuvre so as to stabilize government.[13] The Bundestag was designed less as a counter-power to control the government than as a forum for the formation of a majority capable of governing.

9 Karlheinz Niclauss, *"Restauration" oder Renaissance der Demokratie. Die Entstehung der Bundesrepublik Deutschland 1945–1949* (Berlin: Colloquium Verl., 1982), 87ff.

10 Evelyn Schmidtke, *Der Bundeskanzler im Spannungsfeld zwischen Kanzlerdemokratie und Parteiendemokratie. Ein Vergleich der Regierungsstile Konrad Adenauers und Helmut Kohls* (Marburg: Tectum Verlag, 2001), 47. Cf. Ernst Ulrich Junker, *Die Richtlinienkompetenz des Bundeskanzlers* (Tübingen, 1965), 5.

11 Max Weber, "Parlament und Regierung im neugeordneten Deutschland", *Politische Schriften* (Tübingen, 1984), 585ff.

12 Ernst-Wolfgang Böckenförde, *Die Organisationsgewalt im Bereich der Regierung. Eine Untersuchung zum Staatsrecht der Bundesrepublik Deutschland* (Berlin: Duncker und Humblot, 1964), 151ff.

13 Jürgen Domes, "Regierungskrisen in Bund und Ländern 1949 und die Funktion des konstruktiven Misstrauensvotums", in Peter Haungs, ed., *Res publica. Studien zum Verfassungswesen. Dolf Sternberger zum 70. Geburtstag* (Munich, 1977), 54.

The founding fathers and (four) mothers of the Basic Law recalled the dangers of a strong executive,[14] but also the risks of Germany's culture of political parties.[15] The German State was considered as being neutral enough to ensure the general good or above the parties. Article 130 of the Weimar Constitution had specified that officials were at the service of the whole and not a party, but the occupying forces saw the need for strong political parties and the parties had used their position in the Parliamentary Council to perpetuate their role in the organization of the republic; Carlo Schmidt had declared on August 12nd, 1948, that "whether one likes it or not", the forces that were to have a political and social effect would be the political parties.[16] However, Germany has remained ambivalent regarding political parties; while article 21 of the Basic Law calls upon the German legislator to establish the parliamentary tasks of parties, the 1967 law on the parties remained silent on the parties' role in articulating political will.

Given the intended provisional nature of the Basic Law and the express aim of article 23 to replace the Basic Law with a new constitution following unification, no referendum took place – neither in 1949 when the Basic Law was adopted, nor in 1989, following reunification, when the territory of the former German Democratic Republic was subsumed in the Federal Republic. The historian Hermann-Josef saw the purpose of the Frankfurt papers as lying in reinforcing federalism and opposing centralism and avoiding an excessively strong and authoritarian state without democratic legitimacy, however the Allies' ideological objective was occasionally overshadowed by technical discussions of the financial and fiscal competencies of the federal and Länder governments.[17]

In many other respects, the Parliamentary Council updated the German constitutional tradition from that of the 1848 to that of the Weimar Republic, while the authoritarian Bismarck constitution of 1871 was shrouded in a taboo.[18] While the Nazi takeover and the fall of the Weimar Republic were

---

14 Nikolas Dörr, *Die Sozialdemokratische Partei Deutschlands im Parlamentarischen Rat 1948/1949. Eine Betrachtung der SPD in den Grundgesetzberatungen vor dem Hintergrund der ersten Bundestagswahl 1949* (Berlin: Wissenschaftliche Verlag Berlin, 2007), 138 p. Cf. Hans Christian Meiser, *Die Väter der Republik. Ausgewählte Texte* (Munich: Goldmann-Verlag, 1989).

15 Ilona K. Klein, *Die Bundesrepublik als Parteienstaat. Zur Mitwirkung der politischen Parteien an der Willensbildung des Volkes 1945–1949* (Frankfurt am Main: Lang, 1990).

16 Carlo Schmidt, quoted in Michael F. Feldmann, *Der Parlamentarische Rat, 1948–1949; die Entstehung des Grundgesetzes* (Göttingen, Vandenhoeck und Ruprecht, 1998), 167.

17 Cf. Hermann Josef Rupieper, *Die Wurzeln der westdeutschen Nachkriegsdemokratie. Der amerikanische Beitrag 1945–1952* (Opladen: Westdeutscher Verlag, 1993), 54.

18 *Ibid.*, 55.

understood by the military governors as being part and parcel of Germany's authoritarian culture, the Parliamentary Council saw the lessons of Weimar as mainly technical issues to be hammered out while maintaining valued German traditions such as that of a solid civil service and the social welfare institutions introduced by Bismarck. While the importance of the Frankfurt documents in drafting a constitution has been emphasized, the U.S. military officer during the occupation Zink maintained it was "definitely a German product",[19] while the historian Eugene Davidson wrote that it was "mainly a German document".[20] A certain German resistance towards the process has been noted in the very name the Council gave the Basic Law: *Grundgesetz für die Bundesrepublik Deutschland* indicates that it is not a definitive constitution and it was adopted *for* the new republic without fully belonging to it or being entirely German.

5 The Weimar Heritage

The specter of Weimar presided at the cradle of the Basic Law, as the German journalist, Friedrich Karl Fromme noted.[21] Although the importance of the U.S. constitution, notably the position of the judiciary is often alluded to, the main reference to experienced democracy is the Weimar constitution, whose legacy is to be found both in the Basic Law and the first constitution of the GDR. The Weimar constitution broke with the Bismarck constitution of 1871, with its strong monarchy and weak parliament and no mention of basic rights. The Weimar Republic combined a presidential and parliamentary democracy inspired by the thwarted 1948 constitution of the Paulskirche and included basic rights. The author of the Weimar constitution, Hugo Preuss, had been deeply influenced by the parliamentary theoretician Robert Redslob. The national assembly was elected by universal suffrage of men and women with a distribution of seats proportionate to votes for the party. The SPD was the strongest party, forming the "Weimar coalition" with the *Zentrum* and the *Deutsche Demokratische Partei*. The republicans, opposed to the monarchists, adopted the Weimar constitution on July 31st, 1919, and it was ratified and signed by the Social Democratic president Friedrich Ebert on August 11th, 1919. The constitution was merely suspended during the Third Reich and only became

19 Zink, *The United States in Germany*, 186.

20 Eugene Davidson, *The Death and Life of Germany* (New York: Knopf, 1959), 237.

21 Friedrich Karl Fromme, *Von der Weimarer Verfassung zum Bonner Grundgesetz* (Tübingen, 1962).

officially obsolete on June 5th, 1945, when abolished by Allied Control. The Weimar constitution included three parts: the first governed relations between the Reich and the Länder, the second between the organs of the Reich, and the third was a catalogue of citizens' basic rights and duties. The Weimar republic was a federal republic, however with a more pronounced federal power than under Bismarck, e.g., in education and universities. Importantly, the Weimar republic provided for direct democracy through plebiscitary initiatives and referenda. Referenda were held if 10 percent of the electorate were obtained by a plebiscitary initiative, and only overruled parliamentary resolutions if a majority of qualified electors participated. According to article 73 of the Weimar constitution, the president could stipulate that a law be confirmed by referendum before taking effect. These plebiscitary provisions were to be regarded with suspicion by the framers of the Basic Law. The Reichstag was elected proportionately every four years with the possibility of a vote of no confidence, accounting for the notorious instability of the Weimar republic with its twenty-one governments. The president had the power to dissolve the parliament. The legislators were free to carry out fundamental amendments such as the distribution of power or federalism by simply adopting laws, allowing the Reichstag to turn over all powers to the chancellor Adolf Hitler through the 1933 Enabling Act.

The Weimar constitution is a mixture of both parliamentary and presidential democracy; the president was elected directly by the "entire German people" for a seven-year term of office, with vast powers to represent the Reich in international law and as commander in chief of the armed forces or to suspend basic rights to ensure safety and public order inter alia through states of emergency. Sometimes the President was referred to as the *Ersatzkaiser*. The Länder were represented through the *Reichsrat*, whose members had either imperative or free mandates from the *Länder* governments. The *Reichsrat* could veto *Reichstag* resolutions. Constitutional controversies and differences between Länder or the Reich and a Land were decided by the State Court for the German Empire.

Shortcomings in the Weimar constitution were broadly discussed after 1945. The Weimar constitution had a catalogue of rights and duties for Germans, not for all humans; the Basic Law laid down human rights. The Weimar constitution declared all Germans equal before the law, with the abolition of class differences, the guaranteed freedom of expression and assembly, vote and religion and economic activities. While it was argued that extremist parties gained ground in the Weimar republic due to the absence of a barrier clause such as that requiring five percent in a federal election for admission to the Bundestag, it has also been argued that moderate parties would have been excluded from

1930 onwards, given the excellent scores of the communists and Nazis. The post-war prohibition of anti-constitutional parties is a further consequence of the failure of the Weimar republic. The fact political parties were not mentioned in the Weimar constitution was seen as a shortcoming, although most constitutions do not mention parties. The excessive power of the President was also seen as one of the reasons for the fall of Weimar, since Hindenburg appointed Hitler. The presidential role in Weimar can in part be ascribed to Max Weber's influence and his desire that charismatic leaders independent of parliament and directly accountable to the people may achieve political leadership, as in the U.S. federal presidency, an example of charismatic authority for Weber. The President under Weimar appointed or dismissed the chancellor or dissolved parliament or mobilized the army to establish public order. The Weimar constitution did not protect its own institutions from hostile legislation and could be overturned with a two-thirds majority of the Reichstag, making Hitler's obtaining full powers possible. In the Basic Law, this lack of decision (in the sense of decisionism) on behalf of liberal democracy was taken into account in two instances: on the one hand, it is impossible to adopt a law conflicting with the constitution without a constitutional amendment, and on the other hand, an "eternal clause" stipulated aspects of the Basic Law which were an inalienable part of German law: democracy, federalism and basic rights. The basic rights of the Weimar constitution only applied in dealings with the administration, and not for the legislator; article 1, paragraph 3 of the Basic Law insists that basic rights are part of the law that governs the entirety of the State, while article 19, paragraph 2 states that their essence may not be affected. As a response to the violation of human rights by the Nazi regime, the inviolability of human dignity was placed at the very beginning of the Basic Law in article 1.

The position of the president in the Basic Law was reduced to the representative function of signing laws adopted by the Bundestag. The government depends only on the parliament, while in the Weimar republic, it could also be overturned by the *Reichspräsident*. The Bundestag can only overturn a government if capable of forming a new one. The Reichstag could withdraw confidence from a single minister, whereas the Bundestag is only able to withdraw confidence from an entire government. While it was possible under Weimar to adopt laws contrary to the constitution with a two-thirds Reichstag majority, this is impossible in the Bundestag. The Federal Constitutional Court nullifies unconstitutional legislation.

The Basic Law marked the continuing weakening of the executive in German constitutional history. The constitutional monarchy of 1870 was replaced by parliamentary monarchy in October 1918 with the Emperor as head of state, still able to appoint the chancellor and the civil service who remained under his control, replaced in August 1919 by the Weimar parliamentary democracy, yet with a *Reichspräsident* who appointed the government and chancellor, could dissolve the Reichstag, could adopt laws in states of emergency, command the *Reichswehr*, and appoint judges. Carl Schmitt's obsession with power laying in the hands of the person disposing of power in a state of emergency is understandable against the backdrop of the Weimar constitution. The excessive power of the executive was dealt with in the Basic Law by according the Bundestag alone the legitimacy of democratic representation. States of emergency or *Notverordnung* occupied a prominent place in the Weimar constitution but not the Basic Law. The president is no longer the commander in chief of the armed forces; under the Basic Law, this is the role of the defense minister at peace and the chancellor at war. The power of the Länder is also enhanced in the Basic Law. Finally, the framers of the Basic Law in their distrust of extremist populist politics took care to avoid any plebiscitary elements apart from amendments to the federal territory or the constitution.

6 Aspects of the Basic Law

The Basic Law consists of a preamble committing Germany to serve peace as an equal partner and pursue reunification, a first part listing normative basic rights, a second part organizing the federal state and determining the relationship between federation and Länder. In that section, the most important principles are laid down: western Germany is to be a democratic welfare state, a federal republic, with the separation of powers and the rule of law. The intended restoration of full German sovereignty and the definition of Germany's role in the post-war order are explicit. Legal entities may have basic rights. The aim is to protect legal goods and since 1951, citizens have the right of direct appeal to the Court with a constitutional complaint, which now accounts for the vast majority of the Court's cases.

The first article, written under the impression of National Socialist tyranny, announces "Human dignity shall be inviolable. To respect and protect it shall be the duty of all state authority". The second article declares that "every person shall have the right to free development of his personality insofar as he does not violate the rights of others or offend against the constitutional order or the moral law". "Freedom of the person shall be inviolable. These rights may be interfered with only pursuant to a law". Article 3 states the equality of all people before the law and the illegality of discrimination on the basis of "sex, parentage, race, language, homeland and origin, faith, or religious or political opinions" or "disability". Freedoms of belief, conscience and faith are guaranteed in article 4, while article 5 lays down freedoms of expression and prohibits censorship. Article 8 guarantees rights of assembly, but such rights cannot be abused to subvert the state. Article 15 allows for the "socialization" of resources or property providing that such socialization leads to compensation. Article 16 states that German nationality cannot be withdrawn from any German and provides for asylum rights. Article 17 provides for the right of petition. Basic rights are applicable law, and the Constitutional Court is their guarantor.

7 Amendments

Amendments to the Basic Law are possible with a two-thirds majority in both the Bundestag and the Bundesrat excepting the eternity clause, which lays down limits to the sovereignty of the German people, and material values in the German constitutional order. Paragraph 3 states that "amendments to this Basic Law affecting the division of the Federation into Länder, their participation on principle in the legislative process, or the principles laid down in Articles 1 and 20 shall be inadmissible". These principles are so basic as to bound the constituent power itself, as corroborated by the Federal Constitutional Court in its ruling of October 23rd, 1951, stating that the constituent power is bound by "fundamental legal principles prior to and higher than all written law". On December 18th, 1953, it declared natural law superior to the Basic Law and asserted its own competence to establish this compliance, including the principle of basic human dignity and the free development of the personality.

8 The Volk or People in the Basic Law and Limits to the Constituent People

The term people or *Volk* occupies a difficult terrain in Germany due to the abuse of the term under the racist doctrine of National Socialism. In the FRG, the people retain sovereignty within the State.[22] Nationality is governed by the constitution and citizenship by the laws. The concept of "people", so central to constitutional law, refers to the source of power, conferring legitimacy and expressing sovereignty within the State. The people have the political status of

22 Cf. Thierry Rambaud, 'DasVolk' en droit constitutionnel allemande, du 2 février 2007 @ http://archive.sens-public.org/IMG/SensPublic_Peuple_TRambaud.pdf, consulted on October 6, 2023.

a community superior to the sum of the individuals or groups which constitute it. For the constitutionalist Georg Jellinek, it is "an element of the group of the State", "belongs to the State as a subject of political power" and is the subject of political power and the object of state activity.[23] Article 20, paragraph 2 of the Basic Law stipulates "All state authority is derived from the people". Hans Kelsen commented that those who govern are accountable to the people.[24] The people exercise their power indirectly through the Bundestag. The sovereign people consist of German nationals. Further references to Germans or the German people are to be found in articles 33, establishing equality of rights and duties of Germans, and article 56, committing the President to the well-being of the German people. Article 116 states that "a German within the meaning of this Basic Law is a person who possesses German citizenship or who has been admitted to the territory of the German Reich within the boundaries of 31st December 1937 as a refugee or expellee of German ethnic origin or as the spouse or descendant of such person".

9 Organs and Legislative Procedure

Of the organs of the Federal Republic, the *Bundestag*, the Federal Council or Bundesrat, the Common Commission, the Federal Presidency, the government, the negotiations committee and the Federal Constitutional Court, the Bundestag is the sole organ to derive its democratic legitimacy directly from universal, direct, equal and secret suffrage: "They shall be representatives of the whole people, not bound by orders or instructions, and responsible only to their conscience". Any citizen of at least eighteen years of age is eligible to be elected to a term of four years. The Bundesrat is not deemed to be an organ of the Länder, but the federal representation of the Länder, allowing the Länder to participate in legislation concerning and the administration of the Federation and consists of members of the governments of the Länder who appoint and revoke them. The Federal Assembly consists of members of the Bundestag and an equal number of members elected according to proportional representation by the representatives in the Länder; its primary mission is to elect the President, who has a five-year term of office. Any citizen with the right to vote having attained the age of forty can be elected President.

23 Georg Jellinek, *Allgemeine Staatslehre* (= *Recht des modernen Staates*, Bd. 1) (Berlin: Häring, 1913, third edition).

24 Hans Kelsen, "Vom Wesen und Wert der Demokratie", *Archiv für Sozialwissenschaft und Sozialpolitik*, 47 (1920) S. 50 ff.

Legislative procedures are stipulated in article 77 of the Basic Law: "Federal laws shall be adopted by the Bundestag. After their adoption, the President of the Bundestag shall submit them to the Bundesrat without delay". Constitutionality is verified by the Federal Constitutional Court, which also checks compatibility between federal and Länder law, and constitutional complaints from citizens or companies. "The Länder shall have the right to legislate insofar as this Basic Law does not confer legislative power on the Federation", leaving them broad jurisdiction outside fields of federal jurisdiction.

The government of the Federal Republic consists of the chancellor, elected by the Bundestag upon the proposal of the President with the majority of the votes of members of the Bundestag, and ministers. If the candidate is not elected, the Bundestag can elect a chancellor with an absolute majority of its members within fifteen days. Failing an absolute majority, a new vote is carried out; without a majority the President dissolves the Bundestag. While the chancellor "shall determine and be responsible for the general guidelines of policy", the federal ministers run their ministries autonomously and responsibly. A no-confidence vote is only possible if the the Bundestag has another majority; then the Bundestag members can request that the Federal President revoke the chancellor and appoint q new chancellor. If not approved, the President can dissolve the Bundestag, terminating the entire government; though the President may request the chancellor to manage affairs until the appointment of a successor.

The Federal Constitutional Court is composed of federal judges and other members, half of whom are elected by the Bundestag and half by the Bundesrat and rules on the interpretation of the Basic Law or differences in opinion on the formal and material compatibility of federal or Länder law with the Basic Law or between the laws of the Länder and those of the federation.

10 The Basic Law and Direct Democracy

While the Weimar constitution provided for various measures of direct democracy, the framers of the Basic Law were suspicious of referenda. In 1994, shortly before the renewal of interest in "participatory democracy" throughout Europe, the political scientist Jung wrote a work on the basis of the founders' decision to dispense with direct democracy at a federal level.[25] The German founders

25 Otmar Jung, *Grundgesetz und Volksentscheid. Gründe und Reichweite der Entscheidungen des Parlamentarischen Rats gegen Formen direkter Demokratie* (Berlin: Westdeutscher Verlag, 1994).

were more suspicious of direct democracy than the military governors in the western zones; the latter had been in favour of a constitutional referendum, which the Parliamentary Council rejected on the grounds that the Basic Law was merely provisional, but may have also mirrored the concern that the population might vote in protest against the occupation. The readiness of the government of the Soviet zone to resort to participatory democracy before the Basic Law was elaborated led political forces in the western zones to reject it.

Jung observes that historians and notably jurists have worked on the assumption that the Basic Law's founders were a group with a single rational, normative will, the "will of the constitution".[26] Jurists have gone so far as to suggest that plebiscitary elements to be found in the constitutions of the Länder deviated from the Basic Law, although those constitutions had been adopted before the Basic Law. For instance, Scheuner celebrated "belief in the representative principle".[27] Jung demonstrates that there was not a collective intention but a debate among opposed currents, direct democracy had been part of constitutional projects of exiled Germans, Länder constitutions of 1946 and 1947 had accepted it, and experts in Herrenchiemsee were not opposed. Between 1948 and 1949, there was a radical swing in opinion following the 1946 referendum in Saxony to adopt the Socialist Unity Party of Germany (SED) constitution and other SED referenda prior to 1949. Jung sees the move towards purely representative democracy as a result of the Cold War.

For various forms of democratic participation had been envisaged prior to the adoption of the Basic Law: a founding plebiscite, a constitutional referendum, popular legislation and other plebiscites. Within the German resistance, Carl Goerdeler and Ludwig Beck had been in favour of popular referenda on specific subjects.[28] The Bavarian Social Democrat Wilhelm Hoegner, exiled in Switzerland, argued that proportional representation rather than direct democracy had been the downfall of the Weimar Republic, and that attempts to apply direct democracy to disenfranchise German princes in 1926 and a project against the Young Plan had not succeeded; the President had not called upon the German people to avoid offending the Reichstag.[29] He also argued that representative democracy did not suffer a loss in Länder with direct

26 Jung, 15–6.

27 Ulrich Scheuner, "Das Bekenntnis des Grundgesetzes zum repräsentativen Prinzip und zum Föderalismus als verfassungsrechtliches Problem", in Alexander Höllerbach, Ulrich Scheuner, and Walter Strauss, eds., *Totalrevision des Grundgetzes?* (Karlruhe: Katholische Akademie der Erzdiözese Freiburg), Nr. 24, 25–42, at 25.

28 Jung, 23.

29 *Ibidem*, 29.

democracy.[30] In 1941, Franz L. Neumann, saw direct legislation as a corrector to parliamentary rule.[31]

In their *Principles for a New Order* of 1942 and 1943, the Kreisau Circle concluded that referenda should not be used against the elected parliament, but that the parliament could turn to the people for their opinion, or in those instances in which the legislature disagreed with the government, the government might be obliged to appeal to the people as arbitrator.[32] The political scientist Theodor Eschenburg expressed reserves on direct democracy, writing in 1945 that democracy should be constructed progressively, avoiding direct elections to the Bundestag and referenda and plebiscites for the same reason. Once the most elementary material needs had been filled, the German administration functioned, and the people had psychologically recovered its intellectual autonomy and political judgement,[33]more democracy could be phased in. In western Länder, various constitutions of 1946 and 1947 provided for direct democracy. Hoegner felt that constitutional issues were among those issues for which direct democracy was inappropriate, inasmuch as a constitution should be longer lasting than popular moods. Hoegner put the question of popular legislation to the Bavarian assembly in 1946, warning the assembly not to put financial questions to the people, while Nawiasky argued it was a disservice to the state for the disorganized masses to be a decisive factor. The CSU defined limits to plebiscites.[34] For Hoegner, referenda were a means to educate people to democracy. Ultimately, the Bavarian constitution included the principle of referenda for various points, including its own adoption and amendments. In Württemberg-Baden, Carlo Schmid had suggested that parliamentarians could submit questions to referenda prior to their debate in parliament. Although the parliamentary solution was adopted, Theodor Heuss argued that under certain circumstances, the people might express themselves directly.[35]

Jung observes a pronounced turn against direct democracy; for instance, in Lower Saxony, initial debates on the constitution were in favour of plebiscites, whereas the constitution of the Land as adopted in 1950 precluded them. The Cold War plaid a major role: plebiscites had been used by the SED

---

30 *Ibidem*, 30–1.

31 *Ibidem*, 27.

32 Hans Mommsen, "Die künftige Neuordnung Deutschlands und Europas aus der Sicht des Kreisauer Kreises", in Tuchel Steinbach, ed., *Widerstand gegen den Nationalsozialismus.* Schriftenreihe der Bundeszentrale für politische Bildung, volume 323 (Bonn, 1994).

33 Jung, 27.

34 *Ibidem*, 30.

35 *Ibidem*, 68.

for revolutionary objectives, when the property of former Nazis was confiscated by the state following a plebiscite on June 30th, 1946. Jung observes in passing that the U.S. military government had confiscated the Krupp fortune after the Nuremberg trials.[36] The use of the referendum in eastern Germany led many to conclude that while it was celebrated as an "anti-fascist and democratic mass action", it left no place for discussion and alternatives.[37] In the western zone, attempts by left-wing assemblies to reform industries through plebiscites were struck down, as in North-Rhine Westphalia for confiscating the coal industry or a proposed land reform in Schleswig-Holstein prohibited by the British occupying forces.

The reaction against the SED's manipulation of referenda was felt throughout the political spectrum in the western zones, and leading the SPD to abandon its democratic radical, Jacobine traditions.[38] In mid-1946, Molotov suggested a plebiscite throughout Germany to see whether the Germans were in favour of centralism or federalism. The SED appeared to be the party for German unity, creating a united front from below. The SED organized a plebiscite on German unity between May 23rd and June 13th, 1948, asking the citizenry to vote in favour of the proposition that "Germany is an indivisible democratic republic", showing that there was not a disagreement between the people and its representatives, but one between politicians in a German party and the occupying powers; the initiative was top down.[39] This reinforced the impression in the western zones that the very idea of a plebiscite was an SED manipulation. The SPD adopted the position that general parliamentary elections were the true plebiscite. These uses of plebiscites between 1947 and 1948 illuminate the distrust of the Basic Law's founders. The main political parties of the western zones opted for purely representative democracy.

11 The Double Provisional and Eternal Nature of the Basic Law

The final article, article 146 of the Basic Law of 1949 sets the duration for the Basic Law, which shall "cease to apply on the day on which a constitution freely adopted by the German people takes effect". Its provisional nature was a reason for not submitting the document to a referendum in the hopes that German unity would soon be achieved. Yet differences between the western

36 *Ibidem*, 144.
37 *Ibidem*, 148–50.
38 *Ibidem*, 158–60.
39 *Ibidem*, 160–200.

and Soviet zones regarding the centralized or federal structure of Germany or the use of plebiscites or most importantly the economic constitution of the two Germanies ensured that this division was to last a full four decades. Article 146 provides for the adoption of a new constitution but does not articulate a norm for its necessary organization. The purely representative nature of the democracy of the Federal Republic of Germany legitimized not framing a new German constitution. The *Grundgesetz* is accepted as the German *Verfassung*.

Apart from the desire in 1949 that the *Grundgesetz* remain a provisional affair, one of the concerns issuing from National Socialism was ensuring the permanency of the arrangement of liberal, representative and federal democracy. The terms, "militant" and "defensive" democracy inspired by the exiled German political scientist, Löwenstein,[40] included the eternal clause, but also applied to other constitutional measures to defend the liberal democratic order, for instance allowing groups or parties to be labelled hostile to the constitution and prohibited by the government, or allowing for limiting basic rights of individuals combatting the constitution, or granting all German citizens the right to resist anyone wishing to abolish the constitutional order, or excluding enemies of the constitution from the civil service.

The success of the Basic Law is remarkable given its provisional intent and the historic tensions behind its adoption. The Federal Constitutional Court has played a major role in its success and is regarded as one of those features of the Basic Law worthy of exportation. The negotiation of laws between the Bundestag and the Bundesrat has created a climate of a democracy of consensus rather than one of competition. If the success of democracy in the Federal Republic is often attributed as much to the prosperity of the post-war years as to the conception of the Basic Law, it was in Germany that the term, *Verfassungspatriotismus* or constitutional patriotism was adopted by such diverse political thinkers as Sternberger and Habermas, a norm in favour of political attachment to the norms of pluralistic democracy rather than national culture or cosmopolitan society.[41] Despite fears of the founders regarding forces hostile to the constitution, there have been no serious movements to supplant it.

---

40 Karl Loewenstein, "Militant Democracy and Fundamental Rights", *American Political Science Review*, 31 (1937), 417–33 and 638–58.

41 Cf. Dolf Sternberger, *Verfassungspatriotismus*, (Frankfurt a.M.: Insel, 1990), Jürgen Habermas, *Staatsbürgerschaft und nationale Identität*, in Habermas, *Faktizität und Geltung* (Frankfurt a M.: Suhrkamp, 1992). Cf. also Jan-Werner Müller, *Verfassungspatriotismus*. (Berlin: Suhrkamp, 2010).

Bibliography

Main Sources

Der Parlamentarische Rat 1948–1949, Akten und Protokolle, Band 9: Plenum, bearbeitet von Wolfram Weber (Munich: Harold Boldt Verlag, 1996).

Frankfurter Dokumente: https://www.1000dokumente.de/index.html?c=dokument_de&dokument=0012_fra&object=translation&st=&l=de

Germany's Fundamental Law or Grundgesetz: https://www.gesetze-im-internet.de/gg/index.html.

Weimar Constitution: http://www.verfassungen.de/de19-33/verf19-i.htm.

Main Bibliographical References

Habermas, Jürgen, *Staatsbürgerschaft und nationale Identität*, in Habermas, *Faktizität und Geltung* (Frankfurt a M.: Suhrkamp, 1992).

Jung, Otmar, *Grundgesetz und Volksentscheid. Gründe und Reichweite der Entscheidungen des Parlamentarischen Rats gegen Formen direkter Demokratie* (Berlin: Westdeutscher Verlag, 1994).

Loewenstein, Karl, "Militant Democracy and Fundamental Rights", *American Political Science Review*, 31 (1937).

Sternberger, Dolf, *Verfassungspatriotismus* (Frankfurt a.M.: Insel, 1990).

CHAPTER 21

From 1989 to 2010

Founding Myths and Moments of the Liberal and the Illiberal Constitutional Revolutions in Hungary

Nóra Chronowski and András L. Pap

1 Introduction*

The paper provides a comparative overview of the foundational narratives and historical ontogenesis of the two constitutional transitions that took place in Hungary within the 21 years between 1989, the transition from communism to a liberal democracy, and 2010, the inauguration of prime minister Viktor Orbán's self-proclaimed illiberal democracy.

The first part of the paper provides an overview of the two constitutional moments of the "negotiated revolution", based on legal continuity, of 1989/90. One of these moments was the comprehensive revision, in practice full-scale reconfiguration, of the preexisting constitution by parliament. The constitutional amendment, which instituted a de facto new (and only technically and symbolically revised) constitution, was based on another (stream of) constitutional moment(s), the "National Round Table Talks", a unique process of negotiation, which included leaders of the Communist regime, as well as representatives of dissident political groups. These "founding fathers", many of whom were not members of the parliament elected in the ancient (socialist) regime, agreed on the terms of the peaceful orchestration of the political transition and the creation of a pluralist democratic republic, a liberal democracy.

The second part of the paper investigates how the self-proclaimed revolutionary regime of the government under Orbán claimed to have reconstituted and re-conceptualized the relationship between the state and its citizens,

---

* Nóra Chronowski's research was supported by NKFI No. K-128796, 'Normative Content of Democracy'. András L. Pap's research has received funding from the People Programme (Marie Curie Actions) European Union's Seventh Framework Programme under REA grant agreement No. 609427; the research has been further co-funded by the Slovak Academy of Sciences SASPRO-Programme, and also supported by the DEMOS – Democratic efficacy and the varieties of populism in Europe' H2020 RIA project, as well as the 129018, 129245 and 134962 Hungarian National Research and Innovation Grants.

 | DOI:10.1163/9789004549159_023

both in institutional and normative terms. Here, the new constitution does not actually take up the task of declaring a new political community. This is done by another, formally non-binding, unique pre-constitutional document, Political Declaration 1 of 2010 (16th June) of the Hungarian Parliament on national cooperation. The authors argue that this document foresees and legitimizes the unmitigated break with the preexisting political community and declares the emergence of a new regime, the System of National Cooperation (henceforth SNC), the system which originates retroactively from a "voting booth revolution", a term used by Orbán to describe the election which created the parliamentary supermajority of the governing coalition (Fidesz and the Hungarian Christian Democratic Party, the two parties that ran jointly). Under retroactivity, we refer to the fact that the idea of the creation of a new political community (or even the adoption of a new constitution) was not even mentioned during electoral campaign and, needless to say, the contours and fundamentals of this new regime were not subject to political deliberation either. Nevertheless, the overwhelming political victory, where the two parties actually received only 52,7 percent of the votes, which number earned them 67,8 percent of the parliamentary mandates, was claimed by Orbán to be the sole and unique founding constitutional moment to ingrain and establish a new constitutional identity according to the Hungarian model of illiberal democracy.

2 The 1989 Liberal Constitution

The first Hungarian constitutional moment discussed in this study ended in a liberal but transitory constitution in 1989–1990 (hereinafter: the 1989 constitution). The peaceful "rule of law turn" was spectacular in those two years, however the Hungarian transition from state-socialist regime to the rule of democratic constitutionalism was a longer process.

It is worth to mention that Hungary does not have too much experience with written constitutions. Before the second world war, for more than one thousand years the Hungarian Kingdom and later as a not totally sovereign part of the Austro-Hungarian Monarchy the country followed the tradition of unwritten – so-called historic – constitution consisting of conventions and acts of national assemblies, bills and proclamations of the monarchs and fundamental laws usually enacting deviations from the conventions.[1] The acts on

1 See more in Miklós Lojkó, ed., *Hungary's Long Nineteenth Century: Constitutional and Democratic Traditions in a European Perspective. Collected studies of László Péter* (Leiden-Boston: Brill, 2012).

the Kingdom were repealed by the Act I of 1946 on the Republic, however this was not a "full" constitution as it described only the form of state and instruments of the governance.[2] Under the state-socialist or communist rule, the Act XX of 1949 was adopted as the constitution of the People's Republic of Hungary, and it was largely influenced by the 1936 Soviet constitution produced by Stalin and Buharin. Thus, the first written and effective constitution[3] was not the result of an independent constitutional moment, and it did not outline the normative basic law of a sovereign nation. It reflected the characteristics of the state-socialist constitutions of the time: one-party system with the leading role of the Hungarian Socialist Worker's Party, centralized and undivided state power, periodical-but-formal elections, no enforceable rights and freedoms for the citizens, limited private property, communist ideological state, no constitutional review etc. The declarations in the constitution outlined the constitutional architecture of a totalitarian dictatorship. During the four decades of the state-socialist rule some constitutional amendments took place giving a kind of national character to the original document, but it remained a rather symbolic instrument without any effect on the effective exercise of state power.[4]

The changes in the world politics and the sinking economy of the soviet bloc brought favorable circumstances for social and political changes in the Eastern-European socialist countries, among others in Hungary as well in the mid-1980's. The civil society started to organize itself on political basis, in the parliament some MPs quitted the ruling party and continued their activity as independents,[5] and a new act on legislation was adopted in 1987, preserving the competences of the Parliament to enact laws (instead of the formerly common law decrees of the Presidential Council of the People's Republic, which was a collective head of state enforcing the will of the ruling party). Even a Constitutional Council was established with a very limited power to signal the unconstitutionality of governmental orders and ministerial decrees (although

2 The Act I of 1946 on the form of state was an important source in the course of constitution making during the 1989 roundtable talks. The Hungarian legal history identifies it as a 'small constitution'. See I. Kukorelli, "Az 1946. évi I. törvény közjogtörténeti jelentősége és az alkotmányos jogfolytonosság", *Acta Humana,* 5.1 (2017), 25.

3 More precisely, the very first codified constitution in Hungary was enacted on 23 June 1919 by the Hungarian Soviet Republic though this constitution had no significant effect on constitutional development as the soviet regime was fallen on 1 August 1919.

4 József Petrétei, *Magyar alkotmányjog I.* (Budapest-Pécs: Dialóg Campus, 2002), 25–7.

5 In 1989 there were 91 independent MPs out of 386. István Kukorelli, "Adalékok az alkotmányos rendszerváltásban közreműködő, 1985/90-es Országgyűlés történetéhez", in István Kukorelli and Károly Tóth, eds., *A rendszerváltozás államszervezeti kompromisszuma* (Lakitelek: Antológia Kiadó, 2016), 42.

this body had no competence to establish the unconstitutionality of acts of parliament and law decrees of Presidential Council, and was not authorized to annul any legislative acts).[6] In the late 1980's the democratic opposition established the Opposition Round Table (in Hungarian the *Ellenzéki Kerekasztal*, the so-called EKA), the members of which were those political organizations that played a significant role in the later constitution-making and set up candidates on the first free elections of 1990 (e.g. Hungarian Democrats' Forum, Independent Smallholders Party, Young Democrats, Alliance of Free Democrats, Independent Lawyers Forum – most of them were originally not "parties" in their name as the act on freedom of forming political parties was adopted in the autumn of 1989). In 1988 the Ministry of Justice started to elaborate the draft of a potential new constitution, and several academic studies and discussion papers were revealed about a new constitutional design.[7] Against this background a "three-sided" National Round Table was established in the summer of 1989, the members of which were the so-called reform-socialist (the non-very-orthodox members of the Hungarian Socialist Worker's Party, MSZMP), the Opposition Round Table (EKA) and the Third Side (or Third Negotiating Party composed of civil unions). Gábor Halmai explains, why and how this irregular constitutionalizing process started in 1989:

> The immediate reason for the formation of the EKA was the fact that in March 1989 the regulatory principles of the new Constitution drawn up by the MSZMP were set before the Parliament. It was therefore feared that those previously in power would themselves frame the "new" constitutional order. At first it was only the prevention of this that the EKA wanted to achieve at the National Roundtable talks that began in mid-June: it regarded the establishment of the constitutional order as the task of the new Parliament that would assemble after the election.[8]

The National Round Table, having its meetings in the house of Parliament, elaborated the most important bills – amongst them the bill on amendment to the constitution – for the peaceful transition ensuring the legality of the regime change. The Parliament, which was elected in 1985, adopted these bills and the amendment to the existing constitution without any changes.

6 András Holló, *Az alkotmányjognak asztalánál* (Budapest: HVG-ORAC, 2015), 18–9.

7 G. Kilényi, ed., *Egy alkotmány-előkészítés dokumentumai. Kísérlet Magyarország új Alkotmányának megalkotására, 1988–1990* (Budapest: Államtudományi Kutatóközpont, 1991).

8 Gábor Halmai, "The Making of the Hungarian Constitution", in András Sajó, ed., *Out of and into Authoritarian Law* (The Hague: Kluwer Law International, 2002), 111.

This meant that the substantive constitution-making power was vested in the Round Table, but the formal constitution maker under the public law was the National Assembly. Later, especially during the 2010/11 constitution-drafting process, this procedure of 1989 Round Table Talk was harshly criticized and labelled with "elite constitutionalisation".

The 1989 constitution consisted of a vast amendment (involving over 100 provisions) of the state-socialist constitution of 1949. This amendment, Act XXXI of 1989, promulgated on the thirty-third anniversary of the 1956 revolution and just two weeks before the fall of the Berlin Wall, practically created a new constitution with essentially only one provision remaining from the original state-socialist document: the provision that declared Budapest as the state capitol. Formerly defined as a people's republic based on a one-party system, the state became a republic on 23rd October 1989, with a parliamentary democracy based on a multi-party system and respecting the separation of powers.[9]

However, despite it was a vast amendment, the 1989 constitution-making remained an unfinished project, at some points it contained strange compromises, and the then-adopted text declared itself as 'transitory', leaving the duty of adopting a new constitution to the freely elected parliament.

The parliamentary elections held on 25th March and 8th April 1990 resulted in the establishment of a freely elected parliament which now realized a real political representation embodying the multi-party system. The democratic opposition won the elections, however, the government coalition led by the Hungarian Democrats' Forum (MDF), in cooperation with the Independent Smallholders Party (FKGP) and the Christian Democratic People's Party (KDNP), did not obtain qualified majority, that is, two-thirds of the number of all members of parliament which were necessary for the amendment of the constitution. But for the stability of democratic institutions and for the governing ability, the constitution had to be amended. For its sake, MDF, as the leading party of the governmental majority, and the major opposition party, the Alliance of Free Democrats (SZDSZ), concluded an agreement, a result of which the Act XXIX of 1990 and the Act XL of 1990 on the amendment of the constitution were adopted. These led to the formation of a stable and responsible government which meant basically the establishment of a parliamentary governmental system of the chancellery type.[10] These background political

9 Nora Chronowski, Tímea Drinóczi, and József Petrétei, "The Governmental System of Hungary", in Nora Chronowski, Tímea Drinóczi, and Tamara Takács, eds., *Governmental Systems of Central and Eastern European States* (Warsaw: Oficyna, 2011), 299.

10 Chronowski, Drinóczi, and Petrétei, "The Governmental System of Hungary", 299.

pacts, however, characterized the Hungarian constitutional amendments in the next two decades.

It was already mentioned that formally the Republic of Hungary adopted no new constitution, but this did not mean that the amended one could not fulfil its functions as a basic law – the Act XX of 1949 after the 1989/90 amendments was regarded as a substantially new constitution by the Constitutional Court, other constitutional institutions, jurisprudence and also by the wider public. However, this constitutional balance and arrangement was fragile, and it has turned out during the 2010/11 constitution-drafting.

In Art. 2(1), the Constitution declared that the Republic of Hungary is an independent, democratic state founded on the rule of law. This definition introduced a new quality of state, the legal and political system of which was radically different from the former one. The qualification of Hungary as a state founded on the rule of law was a statement of a fact and a programme at the same time. Rule of law was realized by the actual and unconditional coming into force of the "new" constitution, and the Constitutional Court was the guardian of this "rule of law-turn". The Constitutional Court clarified in the upcoming years the most important achievements of the old-new constitution:

> The realization of the rule of law is a process and it is a constitutional obligation for public bodies to make efforts to this end.[11] This general provision of the Constitution declares basic values of the Republic, that is, independence, democracy and rule of law.[12] The constitutional declaration of the rule of law refers further to other specific principles and rights in content issues, that is, the principles of the rule of law are detailed in further provisions of the basic law but these rules do not constitute the whole content of this basic value. So, it is an important task of the Constitutional Court to interpret the concept of the rule of law.[13]

In sum, the old-new document, alongside a correction passed instantly by the first democratically elected parliament in 1990, met most of the criteria liberal constitutional democracies require: a representative government, a parliamentary system, an elaborate system of checks and balances, an independent judiciary, an ombudsman to guard fundamental rights, and probably

11 Decision 11/1992. (III. 5.) of the Constitutional Court. ABH 1992. 77 (80).

12 Decision 9/1992. (I. 30.) of the Constitutional Court. ABH 1992. 59 (64).

13 Principles of the basic value of the rule of law were expressed gradually with regard to specific cases. ABH 1992. 59 (65).

the world's most powerful Constitutional Court.[14] The unique feature of the Hungarian "velvet revolution" thus lies in the fact that as the amended constitution was suitable for liberal democracy and a capitalist market economy, there was no political and legal-technical, or constitutional pressure to write a new constitution, and the constitutional moment has passed.

We referred already, that the 1989/90 Constitution had inherent fragilities. As János Kis[15] points out back from the perspective of the illiberal 2010/11 constitution making, the symbolic defect – that the Constitution was old and new at the same time – had a price to pay. He claims that the very weakness of the substantially workable constitution lies in the fact that while it was democratic in nature, the 1989 amendment lacked democratic confirmation, and the unfulfilled (and substantially moot) reference in the preamble of the 1989 amendment, which stated that a new constitution will be adopted after the first free elections, created the impression that the new Hungarian post-communist society is still unfit for constituting a political community. The old-new constitution, thus, could not serve as the symbolic glue for the Hungarian Republic, and subsequently, it was too weak to withstand most of the shocks of the political transition. Kis identifies the shocks of the dark side of the fundamental rights (i.e., hate speech, due process provided for even the guilty, and claims by minority communities – such as the LGBTQ community, which is seen as controversial by the conservative majority); the shocks brought by the market economy; the shock of weak institutions, which were unable to sustain corruption; and the shock of globalization. The constitution could not stop the erosion of social solidarity, it could not build trust in the political class, it was incapable of combating skepticism towards market economy and democracy, it could not sustain anti-establishment sentiments, and most of all, although being built to foster a constitutional partnership, could not withstand a polarizing and obstructive powerful political party. In sum, the constitution became an easy target and a useful scapegoat.[16]

It is noteworthy that despite the fact that Orbán's Young Democrats Party (Fidesz) played a crucial role in the 1989 negotiations, his rhetoric in 2010 played on the lack of constitutional-making mandate of the Round Table talks

14 K. Kovács and G.A. Tóth, "Hungary's Constitutional Transformation", *European Constitutional Law Review*, 7.2 (2011), 184.

15 János Kis, "Introduction: From the 1989 Constitution to the 2011 Fundamental Law", in Gábor Attila Tóth, ed., *Constitution for a Disunited Nation on Hungary's 2011 Fundamental Law* (Budapest, New York: Central European University Press, 2012), 6–8.

16 Kis, "Introduction". 13. See also Andrew Arato, "Regime Change, Revolution and Legitimacy", in the same volume, Tóth, ed., *Constitution for a Disunited Nation*, 45.

in 1989. At the end of the day, instead of completing its mission, Orbán created a construct that builds on its negation.

3 The 2011 Illiberal Constitution[17]

The starting point of the 2010–2011 constitutional moment is the 2010 spring elections, where a coalition of the Fidesz and the Christian Democratic Party, two self-identified right wing, conservative parties led by Fidesz-president Viktor Orbán, received the support of 41,5% of all the people entitled to vote and 53,1% of all the votes, which was translated to 68% of all the parliamentary mandates,[18] giving the winners a two-third majority, which allowed them to amend the old constitution.

A Parliamentary Ad Hoc Committee Preparing the Constitution was established[19] on 28th June 2010. 30 out of its 45 members were the MPs of the governing coalition. The committee prepared a Concept Paper, which in the end was only considered to be a working document, and a Draft was prepared by Fidesz/Christian Democrat MPs and introduced to Parliament on 14th March 2011. The new constitution, the so-called Fundamental Law was adopted with only the votes of the Fidesz/Christian Democrats coalition on 18th April and entered into force on 1st January 2012. It has been the sole product of the governing political party and has been adopted by the governing majority without the support of any other political force. The text of the Bill, widely criticized by national, European and international NGOs and organizations,[20] was adopted after an only 35 day-long debate.

---

17 More details on the 2010/11 constitution-making in András L. Pap, *Democratic Decline in Hungary: Law and Society in an Illiberal Democracy* (New York, Abingdon: Routledge, 2018), 11–43; and Nora Chronowski, *Human Rights in a Multilevel Constitutional Area: Global, European and Hungarian* Challenges, (Paris: L'Harmattan, 2018), 105–14.

18 János Kornai, "Hungary's U-Turn", *Capitalism and Society,* 10.1 (2015), 12.

19 Parliamentary Resolution 47/2010. (VI. 29.).

20 Opinions Nos CDL(2011)016, and CDL(2011)001 of the European Commission for Democracy through Law (Venice Commission) on the new Hungarian constitution and the three legal questions arising out of the process of drafting the new Hungarian constitution. European Parliament resolution of 5 July 2011 on the Revised Hungarian Constitution. See also the motion for resolution No 12490 on serious setbacks in the fields of the rule of law and human rights in Hungary tabled on 25 January 2011 in the Parliamentary Assembly of the Council of Europe, oral questions tabled in the European Parliament on the new Hungarian Constitution and to the Council and Commission statements on the revised Hungarian constitution and following the debate held on 8 June 2011.

To create the delusion of popular support, a so called "national consultation" was launched. The National Consultation Committee sent questionnaires to all the eight million Hungarian citizens entitled to vote, asking them to answer 13 questions concerning the draft. According to the government (as there were no transparent means to verify this), 12% of voters returned it.[21]

Although it was never a part of the 2010 electoral campaign, the cornerstone of the rhetoric of Orbán's regime is that the new constitution finally finishes the political transition and completes the de-communization process that was suspended in 1990.[22] In Jenne and Mudde's words,[23] Fidesz has argued that their proposed transformations represent the realization of the promises of 1989, which went unfulfilled by the communists and dissidents who signed the "pacted" transitions. Hungary followed a unique path in post-communist transitions: unlike in other states, the first wave of democratization of the pacted or "post-sovereign" constitution making, the adoption of an interim constitution, which was designed as the first of a two-step process, was never followed by the adoption of a final constitution after the first democratic elections.[24]

The remainder part of this paper consists of a thought-experiment: modeling and conceptually positioning the new political community and the political (theoretical) and constitutional construct Prime Minister Orbán claims to have created and institutionalized through a new constitution. The methodology is to follow statements and declarations by legal, most of all constitutional documents, and the grand architect Mr. Orbán: thus, the self-assessment of the "design" and the designers. Two concepts will be in the center of the analysis: the contours, organizational foundations and defining features of the self-proclaimed new political community, and the morphology and consequences of the illiberal nature of the newly established regime. In most cases constitutional and political regimes do not self-identify themselves as illiberal (or even as liberal), analysts and academics do this job. In our case, in a quite unique declaration, Prime Minister Orbán has done us the favor of actually

---

21 See for example K. Osvát and Sz. Osvát, "Hungary's 2011 Constitution: Key Features and Political Background", *ANU Centre for European Studies Briefing Paper Series,* 2.2 (2011), 1–17, http://politicsir.cass.anu.edu.au/sites/default/files/docs/2011-2_Hungarian-Constitution-Osvat-and-Osvat.pdf, (accessed 6 March 2018).

22 See for example Foreign Policy Research Institute, "Can the EU Rescue Democracy in Hungary?", *E-Notes,* Wiktorek Sarlo, A. and Otarashvili, M., 9 July 2013, https://www.fpri.org/article/2013/07/can-the-eu-rescue-democracy-in-hungary/, (accessed 6 March 2018).

23 Erin K. Jenne and Cas Mudde, "Can outsiders help?", *Journal of Democracy,* 23. 3 (2012), 8.

24 See Gábor Halmai, "The Rise and Fall of Hungarian Constitutionalism", in *The Democratic Disconnect: Citizenship and Accountability in the Transatlantic Community* (Washington: Transatlantic Academy, 2013), 75.

doing so. We will, on the other hand, find no authentic, first-hand definitions for the details and precise circumstances of what the specificities of the newly emerged political community and source of legitimacy are, or what nature and role of illiberalism is. These are the questions that this thought experiment will try to answer.

As it will be shown, both core concepts scrutinized within this chapter, "illiberal democracy", and the emergence of a new political community (labeled as the "System of National Cooperation") appear to be marketing products. As an analysis of official government and Fidesz-communications shows, the concept of illiberal democracy as a new path for Hungary, introduced in a seminal speech by Prime Minister Orbán, and which placed him on the headlines of international media, was completely abandoned and never mentioned again after the first wave of publicity and media discourse-setting subdued. The concept of the System of National Cooperation had a similar fate. It was identified as the epiphany of the new political community legitimizing a new constitutional regime, it was solemnly declared in the form of a parliamentary resolution, it was the rhetorical centre of the government program, and a government order even made it mandatory to be displayed in all government facilities in Hungary. However, after October 2012 not a single reference has been made to it in government sources, the politicians' speeches, or documents. This makes one skeptical in regards of intellectual endeavors involving grand theoretical designs.

4 Illiberalism and the Emergence of a New Political Community: the System of National Cooperation

Orbán's regime claims no less than having created a new a political community. This is reflected for example in the changing of the official name of the state from *Magyar Köztársaság* (the Republic of Hungary) to *Magyarország* (Hungarian Country). Signs at the borders, cover pages of passports and identity cards have been changed, and even courts deliver judgments in the name of the new subject.

The new political community was officially declared in a formally non-binding, unique pre-constitutional document, Political Declaration 1 of 2010 (16 June) of the Hungarian Parliament on national cooperation. This document foresees and legitimizes a total break with the preexisting political community and declares the emergence of SNC as a new political community, originating retroactively from the aforementioned "voting booth revolution".

The Declaration, adopted shortly after the new government had taken office, was to be displayed in all government facilities in Hungary per a government order, which even specified the size, color, fonts, and the details of framing.[25] The President, the Speaker of the Parliament, the Presidents of the Constitutional Court and the Supreme Court, the President of the Central Bank, mayors, the ombudspersons, chief prosecutors and judges were requested in forming a Government Resolution to follow suit. Most state institutions, such as hospitals or universities also complied. Opposition parties and human rights NGOs considered this duty to display an oath of allegiance an intrusion to the separation of powers and the independence of crucial institutions.

The political credo of the new regime and the new political community reads as follows:

> At the end of the first decade of the 21st century, after forty-six years of occupation and dictatorship and two turbulent decades of transition Hungary has regained the right and ability of self-determination. [...] In the spring of 2010 the Hungarian nation once again summoned its vitality and brought about another revolution in the voting booths. [...] The National Assembly declares that a new social contract was laid down in the April general elections through which the Hungarians decided to create a new system: the National Cooperation System. [...] We, members of the National Assembly declare that we shall elevate the new political and economic system emerging on the basis of the popular democratic will.[26]

The term and concept of the SNC was used as a central theme in the government program, submitted to Parliament on May 22nd, 2010.[27] In fact, the 80-page-long program, which contains a subchapter on the "New Social Contract", and where the government consistently refers to itself as "The Government of National Affairs", is titled "The Programme of National Cooperation", and has three chapters: The Declaration of National Cooperation, the (description of) the System of National Cooperation, and Issues of National Importance, and a joint declaration with the Hungarian Chamber of Commerce and Industry. Let us see some of the highlights of the government program:

---

25 Government Decree 1140/2010. (VII. 2.).

26 Official government translation.

27 *"The Programme of National Cooperation"*, Office of the National Assembly, Document Number: H/47, Received 22 May 2010, http://www.parlament.hu/irom39/00047/00047_e.pdf (accessed 7 March 2018).

> Hungarians want deep-seated and fundamental change in every area of life. […] [T] hey have authorized us, through the strength of national cooperation, to establish a new political, economic, and social system built on new rules in every area of life.

The government program contains important statements and points of references for constitutional identity:

> In April 2010 the long period of transition rife with struggles, divisiveness, and crises came to an end. The era was brought to an end by the act of the revolution which took place in the polling booths. In spring 2010 for the first time in Hungary since the system change a single political force was granted democratic authority of constituent import. This act imposes historical responsibility on the newly formed parliament. […] The new Assembly is in fact a constituent national assembly and system-founding parliament. With the two-thirds mandate voters entrusted the new Assembly and the new government […] to carry out revolutionary changes.

The idea that the new government program is actually a new social contract is made explicit:

> For lack of a social contract Hungary during the era of transition was controlled by elite agreements and invisible pacts; fruitless debates hampered the country's progress […] our common national causes were obscured. The current Constitution […] is a temporary, transitional constitution. Its authors intended it as temporary precisely because there was no underlying and valid social contract. The new social contract has now been concluded in the 2010 parliamentary elections. Legislators have been entrusted over the next four years with the creation of the country's new constitution. […] [I] n April 2010 Hungarian voters […] gave their […] to a new system founded on national cooperation. […] The responsibility of the first government of the new era is to enforce the new social contract, namely, to erect the System of National Cooperation. The System of National Cooperation will be the foundation of the country's reconstruction and of the creation of a strong Hungary.

Having identified the agents of the new constitutional identity, the government program sets forth the framework of the modus operandi and administration of the new political community:

> The new social contract calls for cooperation instead of divisiveness, service of the public good instead of the advocacy of private interests, and the strong and effective representation of common national causes. A government for whom the sole benchmark is the nation and the advancement of its members. [...] The System of National Cooperation is built instead of ostracism on unity, instead of political irresponsibility on political responsibility, instead of tolerance of extremes on the rejection and elimination of such, instead of the limitation of citizens' self-determination on the proliferation of such, and on the restoration of balance between rights and obligations. [...] A government and governance is needed which once again turns towards people and their everyday problems, and which is based on the representation of our common national causes.

The government program, thus, both declares a supreme source of political legitimacy, which actually created a new constitutional community, embodied by the government (majority in parliament), and expresses a messianic determination for transformative changes in political and spiritual life. It is illuminating to look at the how the concept and the very term had been used in subsequent government communication. We carried a comprehensive survey of press releases and other entries in the archives of the national news agency, Magyar Távirati Iroda (MTI), which supposedly contains all relevant entries. The SNC was mentioned for the first time on the night of the elections in Orbán's speech announcing victory. The next time it was mentioned, again by Orbán, during the first meeting of Fidesz's parliamentary group, and a few days later in the opening session of the parliament. He, again, talked about that SNC at two campaign rallies in May, and later in June 2010, when signing an agreement with a leader of Hungarians living in Serbia (where he declared that the System of National Cooperation includes Hungarians living outside Hungary). In parliament, on the 56th (!) day of his office (reflecting on the revolution of 1956), the prime minister stated that the new political community, the "national center" is a community of rationality, and his efforts are focused on transforming the two-third parliamentary majority into a political community of a "central force field", the system of national cooperation. In a somewhat contradictory fashion, he also said that the reason to govern is the creation of this "political center", and the way to achieve it is the SNC. In September 2011, on the 100th day of his government in office, Orbán reported to parliament on the development of the four distinct "national cooperations of politics, economy, administration and morality – the latter to be elaborated within and by the new constitution". According to my research, the last time he ever mentioned the SNC, was on October 23rd, 2012, when giving out awards on the national holiday. Besides in Orbán speeches, only for other times was the term mentioned by other politicians: once by the spokesman for the Prime Minister, the deputy spokesman for Fidesz in political rebuttals, and by an under-secretary, and an MP in connection with the new law on churches, expressing the importance of including traditional churches in the SNC. That is all. After October 2012 not once was this term and concept, so corollary to the new political community that it was ordered to be displayed in state buildings, mentioned by government sources. After the adoption of the new constitution, the displayed copies of the Declaration of National Cooperation in government offices were mostly replaced by the Preamble of the new constitution, the National Avowal of Faith.[28]

5 Illiberalism and the System of National Cooperation

Another term and concept that is corollary to understanding Orbán's Hungary, is self-proclaimed illiberalism, and identifying his regime as an illiberal democracy. No normative legal document, formal political manifesto or official government communication ever provided a coherent description of the nature, design or constitutional philosophy of the Hungarian illiberal democracy model. It is therefore the task and challenge of academic analyses to decipher its normative and analytic content. We will argue that Hungarian illiberal democracy manifests itself in the SNC – a vaguely defined, yet even normatively presented political construct in which majority rule may operate unbounded by the rule of law, separation of powers, and other constraints of liberal democracies. The SNC, which was never actually defined or explained in a normative document or even a political manifesto, is arguably both the conceptualization and a metaphor of the political community. And although it is not a formalized set of political institutions, it is the conceptualization of the illiberal democratic decision-making process, which makes traditional constitutionalism obsolete.

It needs to be added that illiberalism was not part of the first marketing package of the SNC. On the contrary, the aforementioned 2010 government

28 Curiously, while the initial display was ordered by law, in the form of a government order, we could not locate a source of law for the replacement, only a communiqué on the Fidesz website. A Nemzeti Hitvallás Szövege, 18 May 2011, http://www.fidesz.hu/hirek/2011-04-18/a-nemzeti-hitvallas-szovege/, (accessed 7 March 2018).

program of "National Cooperation" contained several commitments to liberal democracy, and even a quote from Abraham Lincoln:

> The Government of National Affairs intends to pursue a policy that ensures everyone the greatest possible freedom, [...] Overall, given our aims, we can avow the words of Abraham Lincoln as applicable to us: "It is rather for us to [ensure] [...] that this nation, under God, shall have a new birth of freedom – and that government of the people, by the people, for the people, shall not perish from the earth".[29]

Part 5.1 contains important references the Fidesz's self-proclaimed identity. It starts by stating that: "We will remain loyal to the ideas of democracy and the rule of law" as "Fidesz was formed in 1988 [...] so that Hungarians can live in real democracy enjoying the same freedom and wealth as Western-European states". It continues by holding that "Fidesz – Hungarian Civic Union has for 20 years consistently represented politics which rests on unconditional respect for solidarity, freedom, civil rights and human dignity, as well as legal certainty".

6 Illiberal Democracy as Constitutional Identity

Illiberalism as a chosen feature of the new regime was introduced by Orbán, at a speech delivered at the Summer Open University of Bálványos in July 2014,[30] which immediately went viral and was reported widely in international media. Here Orbán identified his regime as illiberal in the following manner:

> [W]hile breaking with the dogmas and ideologies that have been adopted by the West and keeping ourselves independent from them, we are trying to find the form of community organisation, the new Hungarian state, which is capable of making our community competitive in the great global race for decades to come. [...] [A] democracy does not necessarily have

29 "*The Programme of National Cooperation*", Office of the National Assembly, Document Number: H/47, Received 22 May 2010, p. 16, http://www.parlament.hu/irom39/00047/00047_e.pdf (accessed 7 March 2018).

30 "*A munkaalapú állam korszaka következik*", Orbán Viktor beszéde a XXV. Bálványosi Nyári Szabadegyetem és Diáktáborban 2014. július 26. Tusnádfürdő (Băile Tuşnad), 28 July 2014, https://2015-2019.kormany.hu/hu/a-miniszterelnok/beszedek-publikaciok-interjuk/a-munkaalapu-allam-korszaka-kovetkezik (accessed 2 October 2023).

> to be liberal. Just because a state is not liberal, it can still be a democracy. [...] [U]ntil now we have known three forms of state organisation: the nation state, the liberal state and the welfare state. And the question is, what's next? The Hungarian answer to this question is that the era of the work-based state is approaching. We want to organise a work-based society that [...] undertakes the odium of stating that it is not liberal in character. [...] [W]e must break with liberal principles and methods of social organisation, and in general with the liberal understanding of society. [...] [A]nd forge a new method of Hungarian state organisation [...], following [in the sense of bypassing ..., NC-ALP] the liberal state and the era of liberal democracy. [...] [W]e suggest and are attempting to construct Hungarian state life around this idea, that (liberalism) should not be the principle on which society is built. [...] And [...] the new state that we are constructing in Hungary is an illiberal state, a non-liberal state. [...] [W]e want to organise our national state to replace the liberal state, construct a new state built on illiberal and national foundations within the European Union. [...] [T]he Government has come to a decision according to which within this new state concept, this illiberal state concept, the reorganisation of the Hungarian state is underway, in contrast to the liberal state organisation logic of the previous twenty years.[31]

As Csillag and Szelényi argue, "liberalism" for Orbán means the excessive emphasis of individual interest over the "national" interest.[32] Orbán envisions that in the next 15–20 years Hungary should be dominated by a single, massive right-wing political party that would rule the whole political field without "unnecessary" debates.[33] Although the populist rhetoric (of the SNC) aims at targeting and attracting both moderate and far-right voters, the SNC is not

---

31 Speaking in interview with Bloomberg, Orbán said the following: "Hungarians welcomed illiberal democracy. The fact that in English it means something else is not my problem. In the Hungarian context, the word liberal has become negative. Liberal democracy has no or very little support in Hungary. What I want to say is that it's not true that a democracy can only be liberal", Z. Simon, "Hungary on Path to Shed Junk Grade and Shield Forint, Orbán Says", *Bloomberg*, 14 December, http://www.bloomberg.com/news/articles/2014-12-15/hungary-on-path-to-shed-junk-grade-and-shield-forint-Orbán-says (accessed 6 March 2018).

32 Tamás Csillag and Iván Szelényi, "Drifting from liberal democracy: Traditionalist/neo-conservative ideology of managed illiberal democratic capitalism in post-communist Europe", *Intersections: East European Journal of Society and Politics*, 1.1 (2015), 23.

33 András Rácz, "Multi-vectorialism failing? The Russia-policy of the Orbán-government", *Russkii vopros*, 15.1 (2015), http://www.russkiivopros.com/?pag=one&id=619&kat=7&csl=69 (accessed 6 March 2018).

inherently and intrinsically racist, misogynist, anti-Semitic, or homophobic. It does, however, neglect and deny the discursive recognition, and questions the importance, relevance, and legitimacy of liberal values, and fails to adopt an individual freedom and human rights-oriented approach that would, for example endorse Roma inclusion, feminism and multiculturalism, post-nationalism, individualism, or a particular vision of modernism – ideals and commitments Hungarian liberal public intellectuals would advocate. In other words, the discourse is not inherently anti-liberal, only "a-liberal".

We need to note here that Orbán, the omnipotent charismatic leader, and his party before its sharp turn to the right in 1993, which a former mentor and political ally Miklós Haraszti calls a purely political maneuver, was "the ultimate anarcho-liberal, a pupil and an embodiment of the Democratic Opposition's underground culture. [...] He has led himself and his Fidesz party from radical anti-authoritarians to radical Christian-Conservatives. He took pride in 1990 in making Fidesz a member of the Liberal International one step earlier than SZDSZ (the Alliance of Free Democrats)", the leading opposition party in 1990–94 and Fidesz's political and ideological role model before and during the Round Table talks and the transition.[34] Michael Shafir calls the crowning of the party's "transfiguration" when it left the Liberal International and joined the conservative European People's Party in 2010.[35]

Thus, allegiance to illiberalism is also a quasi-Freudian reiteration of Orbán's conservative turn in 1993. Illiberal democracy as per Orbán is a manifesto against the now mostly imagined, but habitually demonized archenemy, a once envied powerful and popular father-party advocating the above liberal values and commitment.

Again, let us return to the seminal Orbán-speech:

> [T]he Hungarian nation is not simply a group of individuals but a community that must be organised, reinforced and in fact constructed. And [...] the new state that we are constructing in Hungary is an illiberal state, a non-liberal state. It does not reject the fundamental principles of liberalism such as freedom, and I could list a few more, but it does not make this ideology the central element of state organisation, but instead includes a different, special, national approach.

34 Miklós Haraszti, "The 'real' Viktor Orbán", *Open Democracy,* 2 May 2002, https://www.opendemocracy.net/democracy-newright/article_358.jsp (accessed 6 March 2018).

35 Michael Shafir, "The politics of public space and the legacy of the holocaust in post-communist Hungary, Part 3. Viktor Orbán's 'Transfiguration' or the Making of a Radical Conservative", *East European Perspectives,* 6.12 (2004).

As he points out, "this cannot be entered into law, we are talking about an intellectual starting point now". Thus, illiberalism in Hungary goes beyond political and legal action. It is a form of ideology and a discursive construct. Even though self-identified "unorthodox" legal and political institutions are instrumental for the establishment, solidification and cementing of the Orbán-regime, they are only by-products. The real product is the (conceptual framework of the) newly established political community. Illiberal democracy and the SNC serve as tools for constitutional identity and an ideological framework for institutionalizing the well-documented process of anti-democratic backlash in Hungary.

It would, therefore, be a mistake to identify the Hungarian illiberal democracy model with these constitutional and legal developments. Instead, an alternative, not institution-focused analysis is offered. "Hungarian illiberal democracy" is neither a construct of constitutional philosophy, nor is it a principle for constitutional design. It cannot be properly described by the evisceration of classic democratic institutions, and it is also not characteristically illiberal within the interpretative framework of political theory. It would equally not qualify as a *sui generis* un-republican,[36] un-participatory,[37] un-agonistic,[38] or un-deliberative model.[39] Despite the political mantra used by Orbán's party of the legitimating force of a parliamentary supermajority being based on a single event of popular vote, the Hungarian model of illiberal democracy cannot be equated with the unfettered freedom of a parliamentary majority to do as it pleases. Rather, it is a tool to channel, define and dominate general political discourse and to provide a discursive framework for political identification and ideologically biased yet divergent and ad hoc legislation.

We argue that "illiberal democracy" and "illiberalism" in Hungary are actually forms of constitutional identity guiding the discursive framework of this new political community. Viktor Orbán's regime instrumentalizes a special form of nationalism that is built on the uniqueness of the Hungarian "people", where illiberalism is a form of ethnosymbolism. Here, the myth of election of

36 See for example Andreas Niederberger and Philipp Schink, eds., *Republican Democracy: Liberty, Law and Politics* (Edinburgh: Edinburgh University Press, 2013); Philip Pettit, *On the People's Terms: A Republican Theory and Model of Democracy* (Cambridge: Cambridge University Press, 2013).

37 See for example Luis Bouza Garcia, *Participatory Democracy and Civil Society in the EU: Agenda-Setting and Institutionalisation* (Basingstoke: Palgrave Macmillan, 2015).

38 See for example Mark Wenman, *Agonistic Democracy: Constituent Power in the Era of Globalisation* (Cambridge: Cambridge University Press, 2013).

39 See for example J. Mansbridge *et al.*, *Why Deliberative Democracy?* (Princeton: Princeton University Press, 2012).

the new political community via the SNC is constituted through independence from modernist universalist values, which only brought failure and frustration.

As argued briefly above, the morphosis of this Hungarian model for illiberal democracy manifests itself normatively through value preferences expressed in the new constitution, the Fundamental Law, as well as in a quasi-normative political declaration that serves as a manifesto for not only Orbán's new political regime, but also the new political community he and his regime envisages. It is important to highlight that, contrary to what it claims to be, the SNC is not an actual institutionalized modus operandi for the Hungarian illiberal democracy, nor is it a form of political institutional design. It is rather the manifesto of illiberal democracy: the political and quasi-normative declaration of the Orbán-regime's discursive framework.

In sum, the quintessential feature of the Hungarian illiberal democracy is that it is the discursive framework through which the Orbán-government constructed a new national and constitutional identity. It is a form of a constitutional commoditization aimed at selling a political regime, where a significant emphasis is put on authenticity and difference. Thus, illiberalism is not so much a constitutional term describing and legitimizing an overall backlash in democratic control mechanisms and the protection of human rights as it is a discursive framework constructed to describe and market[40] the new imagined community of the SNC-Hungarian nation and to narrate its shared common belonging.[41] "Illiberalism" is a mobilizing tactic utilized to question the validity and sustainability of the post WWII (liberal) consensus on human rights centered political language, disenchantment, certain sacred democratic institutions, and neoliberal policies. The term (which is not a coherent concept) can be operationalized by neoconservative movements as an anti-modernist and fundamentalist[42] answer to the neoliberal consensus, similarly, for example, to the ways in which "(anti-)gender ideology" is used. As Kováts et. al argue, "gender" has been identified as the common ground, a label amidst diverse political cultures, different party structures and a variety of mobilizing tactics,

40 John L. Comaroff and Jean Comaroff, *Ethnicity, Inc.* (Chicago: University of Chicago Press, 2009).

41 For scholarly assessments on the role of discursive action in the process of identity formation, see J. E. Fox and C. Miller-Idriss, "Everyday Nationhood", *Ethnicities*, 8.4 (2008), 536–63; Anthony P. Cohen, *Symbolic Construction of Community* (London, New York: Routledge, 1985–1995).

42 Zsuzsa Vidra, Aniko Horváth and Jon Fox, "Tolerance and Cultural Diversity Discourses in Hungary", in Ricard Zapata-Barrero and Anna Triandafyllidou, eds., *Addressing Tolerance and Diversity Discourse in Europe Comparative Overview of 16 European Countries* (Barcelona: Barcelona Centre for International Affairs, 2012), 317–43.

compressing different fears and values and used against diverse causes.[43] Orbán's illiberalism is also very similar to how Hobsbawm[44] sees nationalism in the 21st century – as a substitute, a placebo for disorientation, and a surrogate for integration in a disintegrating society; when society fails, the nation appears as an ultimate guarantee (and in post-communist societies, also as a device to distinguish between the innocent and the guilty). In the Hungarian case, the strategy worked. As Pető and Vasali point out,[45] the government successfully built a state-funded (pseudo) NGO sector and this, alongside racist and nationalist movements,[46] convincingly offered anti-modernism, and anti-cosmopolitanism/Europeanism[47] as a viable alternative to neo-liberal democracy and the market economy.

It also needs to be added that, similarly to the grand vision of the national system of cooperation, the concept of (announcing and defining) Hungary as an illiberal democracy, in contrast to its corollary status, does not appear to be something that government communication would utilize for a long term, in fact, it creates the impression of a mere short-term marketing slogan, a tool to control public discussion and media attention. According to the media analysis we carried out, using the database of the national news agency, which is mandated to document all relevant government and public communication, the term and the concept was used only seven times. Five times by Orbán: following the seminal speech, once in a debate in the Hungarian, once in the European Parliament, and once during a press conference following a meeting with German Chancellor Angela Merkel (who specifically mentioned her

43 Foundation for European Progressive Studies, "Beyond gender? Anti-gender mobilization and the lessons for progressives", *FEPS-FES Policy Brief,* E. Kováts, M. Põim, and J. Tánczos, 11 June 2015, 4–5, http://www.fesbp.hu/common/pdf/FEPS_FES_Policy_Brief_2015.pdf (accessed 8 March 2018).

44 E. J. Hobsbawm, *Nations and Nationalism since 1780: Programme, Myth, Reality* (Cambridge: Cambridge University Press, 1992), 163–92.

45 Andrea Pető and Zoltán Vasali, "The 'laboratory' called Hungary: a challenge for understanding protest movements", *Open Democracy,* 20 January 2014, https://www.opendemocracy.net/can-europe-make-it/andrea-pet%C5%91-zolt%C3%A1n-vasali/%E2%80%98laboratory%E2%80%99-called-hungary-challenge-for-understanding (accessed 6 March 2018).

46 Margit Feischmidt and Peter Hervik, "Mainstreaming the Extreme: Intersecting Challenges from the Far Right in Europe", *Intersections: East European Journal of Socety and Politics,* 1.1 (2015), 3–15; Zsusza. Vidra and Jon Fox, "Mainstreaming of Racist Anti-Roma Discourses in the Media in Hungary", *Journal of Immigrant and Refugee Studies,* 12.4 (2014), 437–55.

47 Fore more to this, see Attila Melegh, *On the East/West Slope: Globalization, Nationalism, Racism and Discources on Eastern Europe* (New York: Central European University Press, 2006).

concerns in regards of this statement), as well as in an interview in the German economic weekly, Wirtschaftswoche. The two other substantive references were made by Orbán's spokesperson, and by one of his cabinet members.[48]

To sum up the findings of the thought experiment, which built on the presumption that there is a substantive theoretical construction behind legislative and political developments, and it can and is worthy of being deciphered, this chapter made the following arguments: First, the Orbán-government's self-proclaimed revolutionary regime claims to have reconstituted and reconceptualized the relationship between the state and its citizens, both in institutional and normative terms. For example, the Republic of Hungary was renamed Hungary. Second, the new regime in several fields of life made a significant departure from the constitutional standards generally held in liberal democracies. However, neither its creators argued convincingly, nor could any academic analysis support the claim that this would indeed constitute a new, coherent, sui generis illiberal democracy model from the constitutional legal or the political theoretical point of view. Third, this self-identified illiberal regime, however, sets forth a political discourse and a discursive framework that also materializes in the form of legal, constitutional documents, which reject ideological and policy commitments towards human rights and an autonomy centered (and in this sense liberal) concept of personhood.

7 Concluding Thoughts

The chapter does not offer an answer to the lingering question of why these constitutional moments happened to and in Hungary. A possible reply would be Hungary's relative good fortune; moderate economic and political freedom in the last years of communism and a peaceful negotiated transition caused its bad fate. The two constitutional moments took place under very different circumstances, which makes the comparison difficult. The first, in 1989–90 raised a real claim for and necessity for constitution-making and was an integral element within an international and regional stream of political events. In 2011 there was no pressing need for constitution-writing, and the 'moment' was created retroactively by the communications team of the Orbán-government. The 1989–90 constitutional moments amounted to a constitutional revolution

48 For more on the anti-moderninst discourse and values, see András Kovács, Anikó Horváth, and Zsuzsanna Vidra, "The Ferry-Country between East and West: Debates on Modernity and Europe in Hungary", in Atsuko Ichijo, ed., *Europe, Nations and Modernity* (London: Palgrave Macmillan, 2011), 158–82.

(i.e., a fundamental shift in constitutional thought). As for the illiberal 2011 moment, the new Fundamental Law originally did not bring groundbreaking changes to the constitutional landscape. The (counter-)revolutionary transition of emptying constitutional institutions and building a hybrid, illiberal regime was orchestrated by more subtle, fragmented legislation and extra-legal instruments, like court-packing.

As for the discursive connection of the two, by the founding fathers of 2011 Fundamental Law, the 1989 constitution, and liberal democracy was portrayed as an elite project, bringing only legalism and not justice, wealth and prosperity for former communist elites, but no economic miracle for the ordinary people. And the constitutional partnership, designed by the 1989 constitution, which required a broad consensus was unfit to withstand the deliberate and lethal combat by a super charismatic leader, who successfully built on the dark side of Hungarians' values and orientation: populism, pessimism, and conspiracy theories that blame all of the nation's problems on the hostile cooperation of foreign interests and a general disenchantment from democracy and the free market. Thus, a new promise to complete the political transition in the "right way" led to victory.

Bibliography

Main Sources

Act XX of 1949 as amended by Act XXXI of 1989 on the Constitution of Republic of Hungary.

Fundamental Law of Hungary published on 25th April 2011.

"Orbán's Proclamation of National Cooperation on Every", *Hungarian Spectrum* [web blog], Wall 3rd July 2010, https://hungarianspectrum.wordpress.com/2010/07/03/Orbans-proclamation-of-national-cooperation-on-every-wall/, (accessed 7 March 2018)

Political Declaration 1 of 2010 (16th June) of the Hungarian Parliament on national cooperation

"The Programme of National Cooperation", Office of the National Assembly, Document Number: H/47, Received 22nd May 2010, http://www.parlament.hu/irom39/00047/00047_e.pdf

Main Bibliographical References

Chronowski, Nora, *Human Rights in a Multilevel Constitutional Area: Global, European and Hungarian* Challenges (Paris: L'Harmattan, 2018).

Chronowski, Nora; Tímea Drinóczi, and József Petrétei, "The Governmental System of Hungary", in Nora Chronowski, Tímea Drinóczi, and Tamara Takács, eds., *Governmental Systems of Central and Eastern European States* (Warsaw: Oficyna, 2011).

Halmai, Gábor, "The Making of the Hungarian Constitution", in András Sajó, ed., *Out of and into Authoritarian Law* (The Hague: Kluwer Law International, 2002).

Kis, János, "Introduction: From the 1989 Constitution to the 2011 Fundamental Law", in Gábor Attila Tóth, ed., *Constitution for a Disunited Nation on Hungary's 2011 Fundamental Law* (Budapest, New York: Central European University Press, 2012).

Pap, András L., *Democratic Decline in Hungary: Law and Society in an Illiberal Democracy* (New York, Abingdon: Routledge, 2018).

PART 6

Theoretical Issues

CHAPTER 22

An Unbroken Continuity? Constitutional Crises and Historical Imagination

Javier Fernández-Sebastián

1 Paradoxes of Modernity*

Social theorists usually describe western modernity as the result of a process, or of several interwoven processes, with a more or less identifiable historical origin, call it Humanism, Renaissance, Reformation, Scientific Revolution, Enlightenment or Revolution. According to received wisdom, modernity would have arisen from an abrupt discontinuity, from a break with tradition which triggered a series of chain reactions that spread gradually to a diversity of spheres: philosophical and aesthetic, scientific and technical, economic and social, religious and political, legal and constitutional.

Yet, given that the concept of modernity is anything but consensual, univocal and unproblematic, the difficulties begin as soon as we try to identify the precise moment and to disentangle the ultimate "causes" of this rupture – or of this succession of ruptures – capable of engendering a new world and a new temporality. The same happens regarding the initial moment. There is indeed a rosary of conjectures, a not insignificant number of which incur in what Roger Chartier described years ago as the "chimera of origin".[1]

In any case, for the purpose of this essay we can safely assume that western political modernity arose from a cascade of constitutional crises that affected both sides of the Atlantic during the final quarter of the 18th and the first quarter of the 19th century. It is no coincidence that the meanings of a handful of fundamental terms such as "crisis", "revolution" or "history" underwent profound transformation during those decades. The very word "constitution" was

* This text arises from the work of the Research Group IT1663–22 and the Research Project HAR2017-84032-P, financed by the Basque Department of Education, Universities and Research, and by the Ministry of Science and Innovation, Government of Spain (plus ERDF, UE), respectively.

1 Roger Chartier, "La chimère de l'origine. Foucault, les Lumières et la Révolution française", in *Au bord de la falaise* (*L'histoire entre certitudes et inquiétude*) (Paris: Albin Michel, 1998), 132–60.

 | DOI:10.1163/9789004549159_024

radically redefined in that "age of revolutions and constitutions" (famously described thus by John Adams in a letter in 1815).[2] To such an extent that, from basically referring to a range of historical, evolutionary forms of government, particularly of limited government, it came to designate a supreme fundamental law, that is, a written document resulting from an exceptionally robust momentaneous will: constituent power.[3] The idea of a *pouvoir constituent*, however, turns out to be inescapably paradoxical, for, as has often been emphasised, the action of enacting a constitution presupposes the existence of an actor to perform this. However, the collective "pre-juridical" actor – the people, the nation – to whom is attributed the supreme power of *constituting* a system of government would itself be constituted at precisely the moment of the creation of a constitution and not before. But, in creating a constitution it acts as if that "we" already existed.[4] Furthermore, given that neither in politics, nor in the legal order, nor in any other sphere is it possible to conceive of a *creatio ex nihilo*, this constituent power, however innovative it is claimed to be, would ultimately rest on pre-existing, in other words, *constituted* subjects and powers.[5]

The circular nature of this aporetic reasoning is also applicable to other fundamental political concepts such as representation, independence or sovereignty. Thus, as Sièyes insightfully noticed, it is national representation which, in the act of assembly, actually *institutes* the nation represented here, as "the nation" would not exist politically – i.e., would be incapable of deliberating or taking any decisions – except via the national assembly that in theory represents it.[6] And something similar might be said a fortiori with regard to the

2 John Adams to James Lloyd, March 29th, 1815, in *The Works of John Adams*, ed. Charles Francis Adams, 10 vols. (Boston: Little, Brown and Co., 1850–1856), x, 149.

3 Luigi Corrias, "Populism in a Constitutional Key: Constituent Power, Popular Sovereignty and Constitutional Identity", *European Constitutional Law Review*, 12 (2016), 6–26, at 15–16; Christoph Möllers, "Pouvoir Constituant-Constitution-Constitutionalisation", in Armin von Bogdandy and Jürgen Bast, eds., *Principles of European Constitutional Law* (Oxford and Portland, Oregon: Hart Publishing, 2006), 183–226; Martin Loughlin and Neil Walker, eds., *The Paradox of Constitutionalism: Constituent Power and Constitutional Form* (Oxford: Oxford University Press, 2007).

4 Martin Loughlin, "The Concept of Constituent Power", *European Journal of Political Theory*, 13.2 (2014), 218–37; Lucien Jaume, "Constituent Power in France: The Revolution and its Consequences", in Loughlin and Walker, eds., *The Paradox of Constitutionalism*, 67–85; Lucia Rubinelli, *Constituent Power: A History* (Cambridge: Cambridge University Press, 2020).

5 Luigi Corrias, "Revolution, Authority and the Institution of Legal Order: Phenomenological Reflections", *Archiv für Rechts- und Sozialphilosophie*, 100.3 (2014), 295–307.

6 Emmanuel-Joseph Sieyès, *Dire de l'abbé Sieyès, sur la question du Veto royal, à la séance du 7 septembre 1789* (Paris: François-Jean Baudouin, 1789), 17; Paul Bastid, *Sieyès et sa pensée* (Geneva: Slatkine, 1978), 436.

people invoked in the Declaration of Independence of the thirteen colonies. As if by magic, thanks to a "sort of fabulous retroactivity", the signatories of that foundational act invented the people as signatory.[7] In this light, it is the representatives who establish the represented, and not the other way round. The Atlantic constitutional revolutions would thus be seen as a founding moment, performative and paradoxical, in which certain actors, speaking in the name of great abstractions – such as the nation or the people –, invented by their acts and words the collective subjects *in fieri* that supposedly prompted their actions.

Because, as Hannah Arendt noted, so singular an event as revolution – and the procession of concepts which accompany it – place us before the irresolvable enigma of new beginnings.[8] After all the act of birth, any birth, is by definition highly paradoxical: be it a meaning, an institution, or an individual, every new born entity inevitably arises from the transformation of other previous entities – people, words, ideas – and form part of a certain continuity, although the discontinuity and innovation inherent to the act of birth are at the same time beyond doubt.[9]

Such paradoxes hardly surprise us given that "modernity locates its legitimacy in its very lack of ultimate legitimation, in its contingency".[10] It might be said, then, that constituent power – and the concept of "constitutional moment" to which this volume is devoted –, in spite of appearances, is a perfect metaphor of modernity.

A further paradox has to do with the question of the continuity or discontinuity of the ideas or processes that constitute the focus of our study. This will be the first theme that will briefly occupy me in the first section, before moving on to discuss some examples, taken in particular from the Hispanic

---

7 Jacques Derrida, "Declarations of independence", *New Political Science*, 7.1 (1986), 7–15, at 10–1. Something similar might be said vis-à-vis "transubstantiation" and the argumentative loop implicit in the constitutent *fiat*: "A constitution constitutes The People who in turn constitute it": Duncan Ivison, "Pluralism and the Hobbesian Logic of Negative Constitutionalism", *Political Studies*, 47 (1999), 83–99, at 84. See also Mareike Gebhardt's chapter in this volume.

8 Hannah Arendt, *On Revolution* [1963] (London: Penguin Books, 1990), 21, 34. An enigma that recalls Carl Schmitt's oft-quoted passage in reference to the *creation* of a new order: "Looked at normatively, the decision emanates from nothingness", *Political Theology* (Chicago: The University of Chicago Press), 2005, 31–2.

9 Marcia Sá Cavalcante Schuback, "Hermeneutics of Tradition", in Hans Ruin and Andrus Ers, eds., *Rethinking Time: Essays on History, Memory and Representation*, (Stockholm: Södertörn Philosophical Studies, 2011), 63–74, at 64; I. Bernard Cohen, *The Newtonian Revolution* (Cambridge: Cambridge University Press, 1980), 280–9.

10 William Rasch, *Niklas Luhmann's Modernity: The Paradoxes of Differentiation* (Stanford: Stanford University Press, 2000), 23.

revolutions, which will afford us a glimpse of how the actors of that axial period experienced and interpreted the drastic constitutional changes they had to face in the early decades of the 19th century. I will focus my attention above all on how the protagonists of those epoch-making events resorted to historical imagination in order to legitimise the unusual courses of political action they recommended or undertook (or to delegitimize the actions or solutions advocated by their opponents). Finally, I shall return to the question of continuity to, via the cases considered, seek to extract some useful lessons in order to rethink change, a question that particularly concerns us as historians.

2 Continuity at All Costs

To begin with, I would like to recall the fact that history itself as an academic discipline is a child of the great historical rupture we are speaking about. Indeed, it is no secret that modern historical conscience emerged in the West from that "constitutional moment" par excellence represented by the Atlantic revolutions; and the new historical discipline – precisely when the word history began to embrace a range of meanings similar to today's – first appeared in part as a narration of that rupture or, in other words, marking the differences between the present and the recent past that has been left behind (a past reviled by such all-encompassing and denigrating labels as "despotism" or *ancien régime*).[11] It is curious, however, that having been born from that huge rift that we in Europe tend to identify with the French Revolution, both the philosophy of history and 19th-century historiography were almost unanimous in their determination to suture that caesura – and other earlier or later ones – placing them within the grand narrative of a single historical becoming which transcends them. In fact, 19th-century European historians, regardless of school or nationality, would become true experts in manufacturing continuity. This affirmation applies equally to Ranke and the German school, to English *whig* historiography and to the French historians of the Revolution (Guizot,

11 Michel de Certeau, *L'écriture de l'histoire* (Paris: Gallimard, 1975), 15; Aleida Assmann, "Transformations of the Modern Time Regime", in Chris Lorenz and Berber Bevernage, eds., *Breaking up Time. Negotiating the Borders between Present, Past and Future* (Göttingen: Vandenhoeck & Ruprecht, 2013), 39–56. See also my work "Historia, historiografía, historicidad. Conciencia histórica y cambio conceptual", in Manuel Suárez Cortina, ed., *Europa del sur y América latina: Perspectivas historiográficas* (Madrid: Biblioteca Nueva, 2014), 35–64.

Thiers, Michelet, Tocqueville). Also, of course, to liberal Spanish and Hispano-American historians of the 19th century.[12]

European historiography had accustomed readers to a representation of historical time via writings that articulated a long series of mutations and disruptions, lending to the whole a certain coherence.[13] And, in spite of its considerable interest in the critical moments of accelerated change and its insistence on the peculiar spirit of each age, the historicist cultural revolution of the 19th century remained essentially faithful to this basic pattern of continuity in discontinuity. The progressive philosophy of history, in any of its versions, provided the thread guide – History with a capital "H"– in which all the ages and histories of events and particular subjects were strung together like the beads on a necklace. Historical time was imagined fundamentally in the form of a *continuum*. The discreet segments into which it was usually divided – periodizations – were but stages during an uninterrupted metamorphosis in which, despite the evidence of the revolutions, there would be no real hiatuses.[14]

The need to ensure that a certain stability was granted to narrative subjects – in particular to nations – who were the protagonists of their histories and to provide their societies with a usable past to justify their present actions and future expectations might offer sufficient explanation of the continuist and teleological nature of the bulk of European historiography. Moreover, it is worth bearing in mind that throughout the 19th century there prevailed in the West an evolutionary vision which emphasized continuity in the most diverse fields. In fact, until philosophers like Cassirer and Bachelard (basing their views on

12 Thomas Gil, "Leopold Ranke", in Aviezer Tucker, ed., *A Companion to the Philosophy of History and Historiography* (Chichester, UK: John Wiley & Sons, 2009), 383–92; Ann Rigney, *The Rhetoric of Historical Representation: Three Narrative Histories of the French Revolution* (Cambridge: Cambridge University Press, 1990), 170 and *passim*; Stephan Collini, Donald Winch and John Burrow, *That Noble Science of Politics. A Study in Nineteenth-Century Intellectual History* (Cambridge: Cambridge University Press, 1983), 197–201, 203; P.M.B. Blaas, *Continuity and Anachronism: Parliamentary and Constitutional Development in Whig Historiography and in the Anti-Whig Reaction between 1890 and 1930* (The Hague: Martinus Nijhoff, 1978).

13 François Furet, *Faire de l'histoire* (Paris: Gallimard, 1976), 3 vols., I, 54.

14 Various works have emphasised the complexity of the concept of continuity and have even questioned its relevance for historical and social sciences: Alexander Gerschenkron, "On the Concept of Continuity in History", *Proceedings of the American Philosophical Society*, 106.3 (1962), 195–209; Herman Bausinger and Wolfgang Brueckner, eds., *Kontinuitaet? Geschichtlichkeit und Dauer als ein volkskundliches Problem* (Berlin: Erich Schmidt Verlag, 1969); Alexander Gerschenkron, "The Concept of Continuity in German Anthropology", *Comparative Studies in Society and History*, 13.3 (1971), 351–7; Hans Michael Baumgartner, *Kontinuität und Geschichte. Zur Kritik und Metakritik der historischen Vernunft* (Frankfurt am Main: Suhrkamp 1972).

Husserl and Bergson, respectively), or the Gestalt psychologists, began to challenge that incremental view of change, numerous authors strove to demonstrate the genetic logic and the underlying continuity of the world order.

Whatever the case, the emphasis upon the basic continuity of the national subject is certainly a typical trait of all national histories, very present too in 19th-century Spanish historiography. Not even the most abrupt ruptures, like the Moorish invasion of 711, deter historians, who generally affirm against all the odds the essential continuity of the national character above and beyond all kinds of catastrophes and traumas (and, albeit with a few qualifications, something similar could be said with regard to other smaller scale histories, provincial or regional). And on occasions authors draw upon historical parallelisms (some taken from the Old Testament) that come in aid of this continuism. Thus, for historian and jurist Manuel Colmeiro there is no doubt that, in the same way that Noah's family represent in the Bible the indispensable link between the generations before and after the Flood, the formation of the kingdom of Asturias at the beginning of the Reconquest against the Muslim invaders of the Peninsula was derived from the Visigothic monarchy that preceded it, from which it drew its legitimacy. The figure of Pelagius (Don Pelayo), first king of Asturias, would thus represent the *iuris continuatio* of that of the Goth king Roderic (Don Rodrigo).[15]

Of course, the affirmation that the leader of the Asturs, Don Pelayo, regarded by many for centuries as the true founder of the Spanish Monarchy, was of Gothic stock and continuator of the Visigothic kingdom of Toledo was at that time anything but a novelty. On this question, Colmeiro echoed a long tradition of over a thousand years. We already find these ideas mentioned in 9th-century chronicles, repeated throughout the Middle Ages and the Modern Age and flowing into the 18th and 19th centuries.[16] Gradually, however, the myth had been enriched and transformed with increasingly republicanising readings

15 Manuel Colmeiro, *De la constitución y del gobierno de los reinos de León y Castilla* (Madrid: Librería de Ángel Calleja, 1855), 2 vols., II, 302. There is more than one parallelism between this episode and what was represented by the Norman Conquest according to Whig historiography in relation to the history of England. Indeed, the great watershed of 1066 was described as continuity by various British authors until at the end of the 19th century some historians began to question that vision: C.W. Hollister and J.C. Holt, "Two Comments on the Problem of Continuity in Anglo-Norman Feudalism", *The Economic History Review*, 16 (1963), 104–18; J.O. Prestwich, "Anglo-Norman Feudalism and the Problem of Continuity", *Past and Present*, 26 (1963), 39–57; Blaas, *Continuity and Anachronism*.

16 Diego Catalán, "La invención de España en su historiografía: de objeto a sujeto de la historia", in Ramón Menéndez Pidal, *Los españoles en la historia* (Madrid: Espasa Calpe, 1982), 9–67, at 16ff.

referring to a more and more distant past. If the neo-Gothicist accounts of diplomat Diego de Saavedra Fajardo in the 17th century and jurist Pedro José Pérez Valiente a hundred years later credited the Goths with having retrieved the ancestral civil liberties of the original *hispani* (which made it possible to link Gothicism with indigenism),[17] in the latter author's case the first king of Asturias is presented not only as the legitimate monarch of all Spain (*Rex Hispaniae*), but as the restorer of a Gothic legislation with a republican touch even as the reviver of an ancient constitution typical of the *populus hispanus*.[18]

But if, by ending Roman rule, the Goths – regarded more as liberators than as conquerors – re-establish in the 5th century that supposed primitive Spanish constitution; if Don Pelayo, risen up in arms against the Muslim invaders, restores the Goths' constitution; if shortly afterwards the Kingdoms of León, Castile, Navarre and Aragon – albeit with some innovations and not in identical fashion – apply the essence of those laws and during the Middle Ages observe the practice of convoking national assemblies (*juntas nacionales*) or cortes just as the Goths had in the councils (*concilios*) of Toledo; if all this is so, it should be acknowledged that the picture painted by that narrative is eminently continuist. We would be contemplating a rosary of "constitutions" that, basically, seem to be always one and the same. Different only insofar as each of their political incarnations is separated from the next by a major disruption which collectively might be interpreted as a series of constitutional crises which every now and then make it necessary to recover and refound the old autochthonous libertarian laws, repeatedly damaged or annulled by the emergence of some despotic power of foreign origin: Romans in the 3rd century B.C., Muslims in the 8th century, the accession to the Spanish throne of the Habsburg dynasty in the 16th century, and of the Bourbons in the 18th

17 Pablo Fernández Albaladejo, "Entre 'godos' y 'montañeses'. Reflexiones sobre una primera identidad española", in his *Materia de España. Cultura política e identidad en la España moderna* (Madrid: Marcial Pons, 2007), 287–321, at 299.

18 Pablo Fernández Albaladejo, "*Gothica Civitas*. La lectura iusnaturalista de la historia de España en el *Apparatus Iuris Publici Hispanici* de Pedro José Pérez Valiente", in his *Materia de España*, 245–86. Pérez Valiente argued the popular origins of the *regia potestas*, thus following a number of authors in the 16th century (Francisco de Vitoria, Martín de Azpilicueta, Domingo de Soto, Diego de Covarrubias, Fernando Vázquez de Menchaca, Luis de Molina and Francisco Suárez) who can be grouped as the school of "Spanish Catholic Republicanism". Similar emphasis on the pre-eminence of the kingdom was famously claimed by Aragonese writers, quoted among others by François Hotman: Ralph E. Giesey, *If not, not. The Oath of the Aragonese and the Legendary Laws of Sobrarbe* (Princeton: Princeton University Press, 1968).

(curiously, according to this prevailing account, the only invaders not regarded as such would be the Goths).

This renewed neo-Gothicism seems to deeply impregnate the first Hispanic constitutionalism, in particularly the work of Francisco Martínez Marina, who underlines the fact that the Goths established a "new constitution" (in reference to the *Visigothic Code* or *Forum Iudicum*) and laid "the foundations of a new monarchy that successfully continued for generation after generation until the present day" (1813).[19] Later, as Rodrigo Jiménez de Rada and Alfonso x had suggested in the 8th century in his primitive histories of Spain, the victorious battle of Covadonga against an invading Muslim army had opened a new era, a new covenant in which Don Rodrigo appeared as both the protagonist of a successful *translatio imperii* and as a new Noah.[20] At the end of this process, Don Rodrigo would no longer be seen as simply the warrior hero who connects with the line of the Gothic kings, but as one of the main architects of the unity of the nation, the restorer of the old republican freedoms and the advocate of a new/old constitution, of which the constitutional code of 1812 might be considered to be the legitimate heir.[21] The Gothic myth – without ceasing occasionally to be present in the legendary origins of certain provinces and kingdoms –[22] thus serves above all to justify the essential continuity of an age-old political subject: the Spanish nation.[23]

---

19 Francisco Martínez Marina, *Discurso sobre el origen de la Monarquía y sobre la naturaleza del gobierno español*, ed. José Antonio Maravall (Madrid: CEPC, 1988), 28, 29, 125; *Idem*, *Teoría de las Cortes*, ed. José Antonio Escudero (Oviedo: Junta General del Principado de Asturias, 1996), 2 vols., I, CVI–CIX and 26ff.; Joaquín Varela, *Tradición y liberalismo en Martínez Marina* (Oviedo: Caja Rural Provincial de Asturias, 1983); Clara Álvarez Alonso, "Un Rey, una Ley, una Religión (Goticismo y constitución histórica en el debate constitucional gaditano)", *Historia Constitucional. Revista Electrónica de Historia Constitucional*, 1 (2000).

20 Alan Deyermond, "The Death and the Rebirth of Visigothic Spain in the *Estoria de España*", *Revista Canadiense de Estudios Hispánicos*, 9.3 (1985), 345–67; Fernández Albaladejo, "Entre 'godos' y 'montañeses'", 292.

21 Presenting the draft Constitution before the Cortes, their President, Agustín de Argüelles, declared that in reality the text contained nothing substantially new, since its fundamental principles regarding the nation, the citizens and the assemblies were already reflected in the old laws of Aragon, of Navarre and of Castile, and previously in "the Gothic code": *Discurso preliminar a la Constitución de 1812*, ed. Luis Sánchez-Agesta (Madrid, CEPC, 2011), 67–68, 71.

22 Such were the cases of Asturias, León, Castile, Biscay and Catalonia: Paul Freedman, "Cowardice, Heroism and the Legendary Origins of Catalonia", *Past and Present*, 121 (1988), 3–28; Jon Juaristi, *El bosque originario: Genealogías míticas de los pueblos de Europa* (Madrid: Taurus, 2000), 187–98, 201–3.

23 Argüelles: "The Spanish were in the times of the Goths a free and independent nation, forming one same and unique power", *Discurso preliminar*, 76.

Reinterpreted in this manner by the first Hispanic liberals, this tradition might have been imagined as a thread of gold connecting over the centuries two peninsular scenarios very far apart in both space and time: a secluded Asturian cave in the 8th century and an active and cosmopolitan Andalusian port early in the 19th century. The enormous differences between them notwithstanding, those rugged warriors of Covadonga and the peaceful and educated parliamentarians of Cadiz do indeed appear to be linked by historical imagination applied to that tradition of Hispanic freedoms of which the latter described themselves as loyal heirs.[24] At the end of that long process, the 1812 Constitution, methodically and coherently bringing together these disperse principles and freedoms, would finally have established "a system capable of triumphing over the vicissitudes of time and passion".[25]

3 Mutatio Constitutionis

The eagerness of historians to knit the fractures of time does not alter the fact, of course, that the historical trajectory of societies has been littered with turmoil and breaks, more or less sudden interruptions, accelerations and changes of direction. And it is interesting to note that the attitudes of those who experienced these changes vis-à-vis their own pasts are not far removed from the historiographic continuism I have been describing.

Without entering here and now into the well-trodden theme of the continuity or discontinuity between ancient and modern constitutionalism – to use the classic terms of McIlwain –,[26] a well-known example is the intensive use of the rhetoric of the *Ancient Constitution* by the actors of the English revolutions of the 17th century and of the American Revolution of the following century.[27] And not even the French revolutionaries, despite their determination to break with the past, renounced the use of more or less remote precedents and parallels in order to underpin the nascent republican institutions.[28] Everything

24 On this kind of chosen tradition, see my work "Tradiciones electivas: Cambio, continuidad y ruptura en historia intelectual", *Almanack*, 7 (2014), 5–26.

25 Argüelles, *Discurso preliminar*, 128.

26 Charles McIlwain, *Constitutionalism: Ancient and Modern* [1940] (Ithaca, NY: Cornell University Press, 1947).

27 Maurizio Fioravanti, *Los derechos fundamentales: Apuntes de historia de las constituciones* (Madrid: Trotta, 1996), 31.

28 François Furet, *Penser la Révolution Française* (Paris: Gallimard, 1978); Pasquale Pasquino, *Sieyès et l'invention de la constitution en France* (Paris: Odile Jacob, 1998), 115ff; Harold T. Parker, *The Cult of Antiquity and the French Revolutionaries* (Chicago: The University of

suggested that the radical innovators found it difficult, if not impossible, to fulfil their designs without appealing to some or other form of historical legitimation. And in this respect, neither can it be said that the situation was a novel one. Back in ancient Rome, the *mutatio morum* of the time of Augustus, which resulted in significant changes in the organisation of political power and, more profoundly, in fundamental cultural aspects such as the order of time and language, was presented by its advocates not as *res novae*, but as a return to old customs (*consuetudo*) and republican traditions.[29] And, what is more, as we know the apparently so "western" and "modern" idea that shared history confers identity actually originates in the Hebraic world.[30]

On the basis of these assumptions, it comes as no surprise that, as Sir John Elliott so masterfully demonstrated almost half a century ago, what we call "revolutions" of the Early Modern Age, from the point of view of the actors, were really restorative movements (or if you prefer "revolutionary", only in the original sense of the word revolution, of return to the starting point).[31] In fact, none of the movements that historians usually describe *lato sensu* as "revolutionary" – including the Protestant Reformation and the so-called Copernican revolution in astronomy – occurred in the name of a desire for drastic change, but rather to the contrary: precisely as resistance to innovation. In other words, these "revolutions" – be they in the sphere of religion, science, morals or politics – took place in defence of a traditional order considered to have been unfairly or maliciously disrupted.[32]

As far as the Hispanic revolutions are concerned, the appeal to history was also very present in the discourse of actors once the abdications of Bayonne and the captivity of Ferdinand VII prompted an unprecedented constitutional crisis in May 1808. And there can be no doubt that only a tiny minority of radicals sought, in Jacobin fashion, to make a clean break with the past. In the

---

Chicago Press, 1937); Wilfried Nippel, "The French Revolution and Antiquity", in Keith Tribe, ed., *Ancient and Modern Democracy: Two Concepts of Liberty?* (Cambridge: Cambridge University Press, 2016), 148–90.

29 Andrew Wallace-Hadrill, "*Mutatio morum*: The Idea of a Cultural Revolution", in Thomas Habinek and Alessandro Schiesaro, eds., *The Roman Cultural Revolution* (Cambridge: Cambridge University Press, 1997), 3–22.

30 Jan Assmann, *Historia y mito en el mundo antiguo: Los orígenes culturales de Egipto, Israel y Grecia* (Madrid: Gredos, 2011), 32, 266–8; Erich Auerbach, *Mimesis: The Representation of Reality in Western Literature* (New York: Princeton University Press, 2003), 3–23.

31 J.H. Elliott, "Revolution and Continuity in Early Modern Europe", *Past and Present*, 42 (1969), 35–56.

32 Rod Aya, "Theories of Revolution Reconsidered: Contrasting Models of Collective Violence", *Theory and Society*, 8.1 (1979), 39–99, at 64; Heiko Oberman, *The Reformation: Roots and Ramifications* (London: T&T Clark International, 1994), 206.

debates in the Cadiz Cortes the question of constituent power arose several times, especially when Parliament first met and, later, when there was discussion over future reforms of the Constitution and the technical difference between an ordinary and a constituent assembly. Whilst, before the promulgation of the 1812 Constitution, Jovellanos and the royalists argued that the nation had indeed power to reform and improve its fundamental laws, but certainly not to repeal the existing constitution and draft a new one, the more staunch liberals showed no hesitation in attributing constituent power to national sovereignty. Halfway between the two positions, one of the most influential theorists of the time, Martínez Marina, accepted society's power to give itself a new fundamental law, but did so with many nuances and caveats to avoid any hint of rupture à la française.[33]

The so-called "[Spanish] doctrine of historical constitution",[34] however, does not appear to me to be a political theory, strictly speaking, but rather an all-purpose ideological tool, used in the service of very diverse political objectives. The old imaginary of legitimacy based upon a pact between communities and the monarchy – and the recurrent invocation of the Code by Alfonso X of Castile, the *Siete Partidas* – made possible the formation of the juntas in 1808, while the so-called *liberal* MPs resorted to a mixed language of Catholic Republicanism – or "civic Christianity", as Fernández Albaladejo has termed it –[35] and second Scholasticism, rationalist contractualism and historicist constitutionalism. A language that derived from a multitude of heterogeneous sources, from the Greco-Roman classics and the Holy Scriptures to elements drawn from the modern law of nations, from political economy and public law. Wavering discourses, varying in their radicalism, particular to a hinge period, whose ideologues did not hesitate to assemble heterogeneous ideas of Montesquieu, Suárez and Filangieri, of Mably, Mariana and Saavedra Fajardo, of Rousseau, Cicero and Aquinas. A language which, beyond the not insignificant nuances between different authors, enabled those early liberals

33 Joaquín Varela, *La teoría del Estado en los orígenes del constitucionalismo hispánico (Las Cortes de Cádiz)* (Madrid: CEC, 1983), 147, 153, 161–2, 171, 326–32; *Idem*, *Política y Constitución en España (1808–1978)* (Madrid: CEPC, 2014), 268–72, 306–12; Carlos Garriga and Marta Lorente, *Cádiz, 1812: La Constitución jurisdiccional* (Madrid: CEPC, 2007), 392. The affirmation by these two authors that the liberals of Cádiz – unlike the French revolutionaries – in no way rejected the past should be qualified: it is true that it was not dismissed as a whole, but there is no doubt that there were quite a few aspects of the past – especially of the recent past – that they completely rejected.

34 Varela, *Política y Constitución*, 115–59.

35 Pablo Fernández Albaladejo, "El cristianismo cívico de Francisco Martínez Marina", in his *Materia de España*, 323–50.

to forge a tailor-made intellectual genealogy and insert the reformism of the Cadiz Cortes and their great expectations of the future into a long historical process, which had its roots in the Middle Ages.[36]

Along with these historical monuments, most liberals looked with sympathy upon a few vestiges of those old laws and institutions which, spanning centuries, had endured until their own age, such as the Basque-Navarran *fueros*. Between the old constitution and the new – in other words, between the ancient and the modern freedoms – stretched an immense wasteland of "three hundred years of despotism" under the yoke of two successive foreign dynasties (first the Habsburgs, then the Bourbons), a yoke which, taking advantage of the monarchic crisis of 1808, they were determined to shake off. The historical imagination of the liberals came to the aid of their constitutional imagination and allowed them to distinguish between a distant past, essentially indigenous, worthy of admiration and emulation, and another more recent, foreign in origin, despotic and abominable. Strangely enough this second past, flatly rejected by liberals and progressives, embraced most of the Hispanophobic clichés that had accumulated in various European countries over the previous three centuries, clichés that at the beginning of the 20th century would be grouped together by Julián Juderías within the colligatory concept "black legend".[37]

Given that the so-called "historicism" of the liberals did not consist so much in positing the existence of certain constitutional law inherited from the past, as in affirming the persistence of the sovereign nation since time immemorial, for their leaders and ideologues the historicist evocation made it possible at one and the same time to conceive of the continuity of the essential core of the collective political subject and the break with undesirable aspects of that recent past branded by all as despotic.[38] The question of continuity appeared

36 Clizia Magoni, *Fueros y libertades: El mito de la Constitución aragonesa en la Europa moderna*, trans. by Antonio Pérez Martín (Zaragoza: El Justicia de Aragón, 2012); José Manuel Nieto Soria, *Medievo constitucional: Historia y mito político en los orígenes de la España contemporánea (ca. 1750–1814)* (Madrid: Akal, 2007); Fernando Wulff, *Las esencias patrias: Historiografía e historia antigua en la construcción de la identidad española (siglos XVI-XX)* (Barcelona: Crítica, 2003), 84–124.

37 Javier Fernández-Sebastián, "'Los desaciertos de nuestros padres'. Los liberales y los orígenes del llamado 'problema español'", in María José Villaverde and Francisco Castilla, eds., *La sombra de la leyenda negra* (Madrid: Biblioteca Nueva, 2016), 483–510.

38 María Cruz Romeo Mateo, "'Nuestra antigua legislación constitucional', ¿modelo para los liberales de 1808–1814?", in Pedro Rújula and Jordi Canal, eds., *Guerra de ideas: Política y cultura en la España de la Guerra de la Independencia* (Madrid: Marcial Pons, 2012), 75–103, at 92 and 96.

in the foreground. And it is curious to note that, even today, two centuries on from those events, the debates between historians of constitutionalism continue to revolve to a large extent around the degree of continuity or discontinuity represented by the constitutional experiment of Cadiz vis-à-vis the *statu quo ante*.[39]

What is very clear, in any case, is that the Cadiz liberals fuelled their constitutional imagination – necessary in that delicate wartime scenario to breathe life into a peculiar Hispanic model of constitutionalism – with the products of a no less active historical imagination. That constitutionalism *sui generis*, which though it had some elements in common with other previous constitutional experiences – English, North American and French, fundamentally – was quite different from all of them, sought backing in a narrative that situated the origins of Spanish freedom back in the medieval roots of the nation. As would occur on other occasions in the new time, inherently perspectivist, of modernity, "with each new future [there began] to emerge new pasts".[40]

In Hispano-America too, new pasts were emerging. While a few reclaimed the American "ancient constitution" (equivalent to the Laws of the Indies), several proponents of the insurgent emancipation movements preferred to interpret Independence as the final moment of a cycle of "three centuries of despotism" – a *topos* shared with the peninsular liberals – that had begun with the conquest. For this reason, some Creole leaders – instead of going back to the Goths and to the Cortes of Castile and Aragon, like the liberals of the motherland –[41] did not hesitate to declare themselves the successors of the Aztecs and the Incas, presenting their secessionist action as the *recovery* of a pre-Hispanic independence lost at the hands of the conquistadores. Manuel Belgrano, for instance, went so far as to speculate with regard to the "restoration" of an Incan

39 Ignacio Fernández Sarasola, *La Constitución de Cádiz: Origen, contenido y proyección internacional* (Madrid: CEPC, 2011); Garriga and Lorente, *Cádiz, 1812*, 18–21. Collected short articles with a variety of interpretations: Manuel Aragón and Juan José Solozábal, eds., *Constitución de 1812: El nacimiento de la libertad*, in *Anthropos*, 236 (2013), 6–195.

40 Reinhart Koselleck, *historia/Historia* (Madrid: Trotta, 2004), 126.

41 Nonetheless, in some early texts in defence of Creole interests – for example, by the Peruvian Jesuit Juan Pablo Viscardo, or the Neo-granadian lawyer Camilo Torres – we can read very similar arguments to those of the peninsular writers. Torres, in his *Memorial de agravios* (1809) addressed to the Junta of Seville on behalf of the municipality of Santa Fe of Bogota insists with regard to the Americans of Hispanic origin: "we are as Spanish as the descendants of Don Pelayo, and as entitled for that reason to the distinctions, privileges and prerogatives of the rest of the nation, as those who, descending from the mountains [of the North of Spain], drove out the Moors and gradually populated the Peninsula; with this difference, if there is one: that our parents, as has been said, by dint of indescribable work and effort, conquered and populated for Spain this New World".

dynasty (an idea that, in reality, had already been suggested by Miranda and other political activists some years earlier).[42]

Years later, the independence of their countries having been consolidated, in spite of the efforts of most Hispano-American intellectuals to sever all ties with the motherland, they also persisted in the search for some kind of essential continuity for their respective nations, be it with the Creole founding fathers of their new nations, or with the pre-Hispanic past. After all, as the Argentine historian and politician Bartolomé Mitre wrote, the writing of history would always seek to "discover the common thread" underlying the events narrated.[43]

4 Creative Destruction

So, it seems that constituent periods are moments of intensive production of new pasts, in other words of emergence of founding myths and forging of alternative traditions competing with one another, each of them seeking to build a different future. This being the case, it is no less true that the concern with modalities of constitutional innovation, with transition periods and with the very nature of constituent power, obsessed many theorists in the age of revolutions. In the Spanish case, it would be above all in the thirties and the early forties of the 19th century, in the midst of the instability that accompanied the definitive establishment of the liberal institutions, when various publicists paid particular attention to these questions.

---

42 David A. Brading, *Mito y profecía en la historia de México* (México: FCE, 2004), 91; José Emilio Burucúa and Fabián Alejandro Campagne, "Mitos y simbologías nacionales en los países del Cono Sur", in Antonio Annino and François-Xavier Guerra, coords., *Inventando la nación: Iberoamérica, siglo XIX* (México: FCE, 2003), 433–74; José M. Portillo Valdés, *Crisis atlántica: Autonomía e independencia en la crisis de la monarquía hispana* (Madrid: Marcial Pons, 2006), 252; Rebecca Earle, *The Return of the Native: Indians and Myth-Making in Spanish America, 1810–1930* (Durham, NC, and London: Duke University Press, 2008); Enique Krauze, *La presencia del pasado* (México and Barcelona: Tusquets, 2005), 43–52; Hans-Joachim Köning, *En el camino hacia la nación: Nacionalismo en el proceso de formación del Estado y de la nación de la Nueva Granada, 1750 a 1856* (Bogotá: Banco de la República, 1994), 384–85. On Belgrano's project: Emilio Ravignani, "Sesión secreta del 6 de julio de 1816", *Actas Secretas del Soberano Congreso de las Provincias Unidas de Sud América*, en *Asambleas constituyentes argentinas* (Buenos Aires: Jacobo Peuser, 1937), I, 482.

43 Bartolomé Mitre, *Historia de Belgrano y de la independencia argentina* (Buenos Aires: Felix Lajouane Editor, 1887), I, 52. See José Luis Romero, *Crisis históricas e interpretaciones historiográficas*, ed. Julián Gallego (Madrid and Buenos Aires: Miño y Dávila, 2009), 95; and Fabio Wasserman, *Entre Clío y la Polis: Conocimiento histórico y representaciones del pasado en el Río de la Plata (1830–1860)* (Buenos Aires: Teseo, 2008), 227–8.

If previously political change had been usually seen according to the image of a change in the course of the ship of the state's, that is, carried out gently and smoothly, with the advent of the revolutions political literature underwent a substantial change. Thus, the idea that the 19th was a "critical century", a "century of transition" "in which one regime ends and another begins", spread like wildfire through the press to become a commonplace. A liberal journalist like Mariano José de Larra, basing his views on a progressive philosophy of history, compared the crisis of Spanish society of his time, understood as regeneration and as a leap forward towards the triumph of liberalism, to an "apparent death" to be born again and with the "efforts of the chrysalis to shake off its previous casing and proceed to the next phase"; "Spain is at the critical moment of the transition and is going to take the great step", wrote Larra in 1835, "with one foot still in the past and another in the future;" but, unlike those who trusted in a smooth and bloodless transition, he warned that it was not possible "to build without first destroying (…), and for the day to begin the night must end".[44]

Comments and reflections like these conform to a characteristic trait of what Aleida Assmann has called "modern time regime". I refer to "creative destruction", to borrow Schumpeter's expression, that is, modern society's penchant for that kind of incessant innovation which, in order to be successful, needs periodically to demolish previous standards.[45] In fact, the historical imagination of the moderns, especially in revolutionary times, tends to follow a bifacial pattern, with one negative and another positive side: whilst its *pars destruens* is responsible for undermining the legitimacy of the establishment and therefore acts as a de-constituent of that which is beginning to be regarded as obsolete, its *pars construens* campaigns in favour of constituent power. Thus, in order that the North American colonists, the French revolutionaries or the Spanish liberals could build their respective new constitutions upon more or less solid historical imaginaries – English liberties, the republics of Antiquity, medieval Castilian and Aragonese freedoms –, they first had to paint a picture of that hateful past with which they wished to break, be it the arbitrary government of the mother country, the old regime, or three centuries of despotism. The glorious past that in some cases one sought to emulate or recover was built upon another (generally more recent) past branded as abominable, which had to be broken with at all costs. While the first past imagined by historical actors is associated with attitudes usually described as "historicist", the second has been largely ignored by historiography, which normally limits itself to underlining

44 Doris Ruiz Otín, *Política y sociedad en el vocabulario de Larra* (Madrid: CEC, 1983), 344, 484.
45 Assmann, "Transformations of the Modern Time Regime", 41–7.

the desire to break with history (iusrationalism vs. iushistoricism). In any case, various authors have suggested a clear opposition between those revolutions that, like the Glorious Revolution or the American Revolution, employed the rhetoric of the *Ancient Constitution*, and those others which, with the French Revolution as epitome, invented the *Ancien Régime*. From this point of view, the rhetoric of the *Ancient Constitution* would in principle be totally incompatible with that of the *Ancien Régime*.

Rather than the pattern of French-style "creative destruction", which accumulates a long series of constitutions each displacing its predecessor, the continuist Liberal-Conservative pattern, essentially Burkean and typically represented by England – also after a fashion by the United States –, we could synthesise it in the historian Macaulay's statement in favour of a moderately reformist politics encapsulated in "the historical message that constitutional innovation was actually renovation for the purposes of preservation".[46] The Spanish case, often assimilated into the French one, is original and does not exactly correspond to either of these models. Instead, as we have seen, it would constitute a middle way between both, a way that could be summarised in this mixed formula: old medieval freedoms + three hundred years of despotism = Ancient Constitution-*cum*-Ancien Régime.

A formula in which the two adjectives of the second part of the equation, the English ancient and the French *ancien*, as J. G. A. Pocock once noted, do not have the same meaning: two apt synonyms for each of these adjectives would be *old* and *former*, respectively.[47] The expression Ancient Constitution refers, indeed, to old freedoms, while *Ancien* Régime alludes in pejorative fashion to the socio-political system prior to the revolution, despised as despotic. Hence, in the Spanish case, and bearing in mind the liberals' view of national history, they would find it perfectly possible to combine praise of an old constitution of freedoms, which they longed to recover, with the rejection of an arbitrary and despotic system, much more recent, which they sought to abolish forever.[48] For this reason perhaps, influential politician and intellectual Joaquín Costa observed in one of his writings that the originality of a "historical-national"

46 Collini, Winch and Burrow, *That Noble Science of Politics*, 119.

47 Jonathan C.D. Clark, *The Language of Liberty, 1660–1832: Political Discourse and Social Dynamics in the Anglo-American World* (Cambridge: Cambridge University Press, 1994) 142.

48 This ambiguity of the word *antiguo* would explain why the syntagm *antiguo régimen* enjoyed such limited success in Spanish political language of the 19th century: Juan Francisco Fuentes, "Antiguo Régimen", in Javier Fernández-Sebastián and Juan Francisco Fuentes, eds., *Diccionario político y social del siglo XIX español* (Madrid: Alianza, 2002), 92–4.

revolution like Spain's lay in the fact that it was neither as traditional as the English one, nor as idealistic as the French version.[49]

5 Like Lightning that Tears Open the Sky

The theme of constitutional crises and constituent power would be systematically addressed in the lessons in Public Law imparted by Juan Donoso Cortés and Joaquín Pacheco in the Athenæum of Madrid, against the background of the turmoil in Spanish politics at the time.[50] Since his youth, Donoso had been particularly concerned with the question of ruptures and continuities in history. In his first speech, in 1829, he characterised the "revolution" that destroyed the Roman Empire as a "moment of (deep) crisis" in which "past ages conclude and new ones are born", and at the same time as "the great link (…) between the ancient civilisation that is dying and the modern civilisation that is being born". Seven years later the same author turned to constituent power, which he described as "a terrible exception" to which mankind is condemned when "in the midst of a social crisis" they put all the power in the hands of one (or several) exceptional men "who might save them from the shipwreck". In these exceptional situations, dictatorship – be it of a monarch or of the people – is legitimate because it is necessary. Donoso compared that extraordinary and ephemeral power with "the lightning that tears asunder the cloud, ignites the atmosphere, wounds the victim and is extinguished".[51] Other liberal authors do not stray far from this vision. In the following decade, Joaquín F. Pacheco would say something very similar, also confining the activation of that formidable constituent power to "genuinely extreme cases". Slightly to his left, the writer Nicomedes Pastor Díaz demanded respect for legally constituted powers, and regretted the endless string of revolutions that, like Penelope's shroud, shook the nation. The state of permanent crisis that gripped modern societies, he said, prevented anything stable from coming into existence. And constituent

49 Joaquín Costa, *Historia crítica de la Revolución española* [1875], ed. Alberto Gil Novales (Madrid: CEPC, 1992), 48, 165.

50 Ángel Garrorena Morales, *El Ateneo de Madrid y la teoría de la monarquía liberal, 1836–1847* (Madrid: IEP, 1974). See also my work "Politique et droit chez les doctrinaires espagnols", in *Droit et pensée politique* (Aix-en-Provence: Presses Universitaires d'Aix-Marseille, 1998), 231–48.

51 Juan Donoso Cortés, "Discurso de apertura del Colegio de Humanidades de Cáceres" [1829], *Obras*, ed. Gavino Tejado (Madrid: Imprenta de Tejado, 1854), I, 4; *Idem*, *Lecciones de derecho político* [1836–1837], 199–201.

power was in his opinion part of the problem, since "in history we never see it born of theories, but of facts".[52]

As far as *constitutional crises* are concerned, the 19th-century writers who addressed the subject can be divided into two main blocks, depending on the author's perspective. We have, firstly, those texts in which the agents celebrate the opportunity and the expectations presented by the crisis, or to the contrary, complain about the political uncertainty generated by the collapse of a regime and the absence of a stable framework of coexistence. These are, then, crises *lived*, experienced at first-hand by their interpreters. These texts often transmit an impression of drama, disquiet and transience. Also, on occasions, they urge that advantage be taken of certain opportunities regarded as exceptional and decisive. In a manifesto which the *Junta Central* organised by the insurgents addressed to the nation in the autumn of 1809 the situation was described as a "terrible crisis" in which the future of the Spanish was being decided on two fronts. What was at stake, they insisted, was not only their external independence from the French enemy against whom they had taken up arms, but also their internal freedom against any kind of domestic despotism.[53] In this, as in other similar cases, the concept of crisis was deployed by actors above all in order to accentuate the drama of a crucial, potentially revolutionary time. In this sense, the concept of constitutional crisis is close to the notion of Kairos or right moment, supreme moment of truth when an individual or a nation has to handle matters with dexterity in order to emerge unscathed from difficult circumstances. Other texts, however, transmit feelings of fragility and consternation. For instance, not long after the independence of Guatemala, politician and journalist José Cecilio del Valle wrote that the country was going through "the most critical period of the States. We are going to establish new institutions, new laws, we are going to create everything anew". Less than four years later, the feeling of uncertainty is even greater: "Any movement that revokes the existing social bond, and replaces it with another, leaves in the middle of the operation a space of empty time in which society exists courtesy of moral

52 Joaquín Francisco Pacheco, *Lecciones de derecho político* [1844–1845], ed. Francisco Tomás y Valiente (Madrid: CEC, 1984), 66–9; Nicomedes Pastor Díaz, article in *El Conservador*, 1841, in *Obras políticas*, ed. José Luis Prieto Benavent (Barcelona: Fundación Caja Madrid, 1996), 95.

53 "Manifiesto fijando los días en que se han de convocar y celebrar las Cortes generales de la Monarquía española", Seville, 28th October, 1809, in *Leyes electorales y proyectos de ley* (Madrid: Imprenta Hijos de J. A. García, 1906), 1–10, at 1.

bonds rather than political ones. It abolishes the old law, but the new one is not yet in place".[54]

We have another set of texts that refer the concept of crisis to crucial moments situated in the recent or distant past. In this case one is really dealing with *historical* crises, even when their effects may occasionally last until the present time. Thus, Francisco Martínez de la Rosa wrote in his work *El espíritu del siglo* [*Spirit of the Age*] (1835) that the French Revolution, far from being a strictly French phenomenon, was in fact "the announcement of a social *crisis* common to all European nations". Martínez de la Rosa himself, who as a professional politician frequently employed the phrase "political crisis" referring to transitory ministerial difficulties, in his role as historian retrospectively applies this same expression, in a far more emphatic tone, to the Revolt of the Comuneros of Castile, 1520–21. Given that that war, he insisted, initiated a major historical shift which marked the future of the nation for several centuries and represented a true change of era, in one of his writings (1838) he did not hesitate to label it as the "political crisis of Spain in the 16th century". Subsequent historiography would prove him right in this respect: from Joaquín Costa to José Antonio Maravall, many authors since then have described that Castilian war as a "political crisis", and have even interpreted it as a sign of the first great crisis of Hispanic modernity.[55]

The theoretical interest in historical crises and major constitutional changes has not ceased to grow since the mid-19th century. Shortly after Jacob Burckhardt wrote the first essay of any length on the topic of crises in history, the Spanish philosopher Nicolás Salmerón advocated in an article published in 1877 the need to "examine the principles that determine human development and the law obeyed by moments of crisis [...] like the present".[56] The first more or less developed theory on crisis in history was presented by José Ortega y Gasset in 1933. According to Ortega, genuinely decisive social and cultural changes are characterised more by the eruption of a feeling of contempt for what begins to be perceived as obsolete than by the emergence of a political and intellectual alternative that might be proclaimed as new. The essence of

54 *El Amigo de la Patria*, November 1821; *Gaceta del Supremo Gobierno de Guatemala*, 35 (February 1825), 277; José Cecilio del Valle, *Obra escogida* (Caracas: Ayacucho, 1982), 54, 220.

55 Francisco Martínez de la Rosa, *El espíritu del siglo* (Madrid: Tomás Jordán, 1835–1851), 10 vols., I, 109; *Idem*, "Crisis política de España en el siglo XVI", *Revista de Madrid*, 1 (1838), 182–90; José Antonio Maravall, *Las Comunidades de Castilla* (Madrid: Alianza, 1994), 16.

56 Jacob Burckhardt, "The Crises of History", in *Reflections on History* (London: George Allen & Unwin, 1943), 135–71; Nicolás Salmerón's article, in *Boletín de la Institución Libre de Enseñanza*, 1 (Madrid, 7thth March, 1877).

crisis would then lie principally in the collapse of a world – or, perhaps more accurately, in the decline of a world-view –, not so much in the construction of a new alternative reality, that slowly and laboriously was taking shape.[57]

6 Closing Thoughts

The notion of constitutional crisis has often been paired with the concept of crisis of regime, an expression that historians frequently employed during the second half of the 20th century to refer above all to the so-called "crisis of the Old Regime".

One must acknowledge, nevertheless, the considerable service that the word crisis – be it as a heuristic tool, be it merely as a rhetorical resource – has provided to historians for a century and a half at least.[58] Historians of thought have also often turned to this term in order to combine in their writings, in more or less harmonious fashion, rupture and continuity. As a convenient and flexible solution of continuity, the concept of historical crisis has enabled us to refer to both crucial moments, short and decisive, and – in the opposite sense – to prolonged periods of indecision and deadlock. But the concept has served above all as an irreplaceable rhetorical device to bridge the chasms that separate one era from another.

Current historiography is caught between two partly opposing demands. On the one hand, it is reasonable for history, as Herbert Butterfield wished, to concern itself above all with transitions, with the mediations between the old and the new. But it also, on the other hand, seems correct to expect the historical discipline to pay preferential attention to those kinds of "hinges of historical time" that are turning points.[59] In any case, I have little doubt that cutting-edge historiography has recently tended to favour caesuras rather than inertias, ruptures rather than continuations, in short, discontinuity rather than continuity.

57 José Ortega y Gasset, *En torno a Galileo. Esquema de las crisis* [1933], in *Obras Completas* (Madrid: Revista de Occidente, 1964), 8 vols., V, 55–106.

58 I elaborated upon and discussed this theme in my (unpublished) paper: "Crucial Times: Crisis as a Solution of Continuity", Keynote for the 19th International Conference on Conceptual History: *Key Concepts in Times of Crisis*, Institute for Advanced Studies, Aarhus University, Denmark, 16th September 2016.

59 Herbert Butterfield, *The Whig Interpretation of History* [1931] (London: Penguin Books, 1973), 40, 47; Alicia García Ruiz, "The Concept of the Present and Historical Experience", in F. Thomas Burke, Krzysztof Skowronski, eds., *George Herbert Mead in the Twenty-First Century* (Lanham, MD: Lexington Books, 2013), 37–47, at 43–4.

Let me add that in my view neither can we as historians of thought ignore this methodological dilemma. The study of crises or constituent moments may be an excellent testing ground in order to evaluate the viability of new discontinuist approach. It is no surprise that a *constituent moment* refers us to a disruptive event par excellence that may be observed on various levels. Firstly, as a crisis *lived* by numerous actors of the past who have left valuable first-hand accounts of their impressions (especially in the modern revolutions). Secondly, as an ideal-typical situation of profound transformation; and these kinds of situations have been *thought*, theorised by a handful of more or less crucial writers on western political thought (Machiavelli, Hobbes, Spinoza, Rousseau, Madison, Sieyès, Hegel, Donoso, Ortega, Schmitt, Gramsci, Negri and *tutti quanti*). Thirdly, as a collection of historical texts that refer to specific circumstances and revolutionary events that have been *historised* in the last two centuries.

François Furet, an author who identified the essential strategy of continuity in the discontinuity that characterised historiography since its 19th-century origins, himself later favoured continuism in his interpretation of that genuine paradigm of historical rupture that was the French Revolution. Indeed, following Tocqueville, Furet wrote that the French revolutionaries, in spite of their clear desire to break with the past, were really continuing, without knowing it, a long trajectory discernible in the history of France: "The Revolution ... did not represent a break but, on the contrary, a continuity, contrary to its own idea of itself".[60]

Some celebrated historians of thought of very different leanings, from Arthur Lovejoy to John G. A. Pocock, have suggested that the historian's essential task is to track continuities in ideas and in discourse.[61] The implementation of these programmes, however, has often led their practitioners to retroject on the past their own categories and concepts, thus creating a tangle of historiographical illusions. The challenge facing us now is whether we will be capable of abandoning that old urge to point out influences and trace genealogies of thinkers, works and languages, in order to proceed to practise

60 François Furet, "The French Revolution Revisited", in Gary Kates, ed., *The French Revolution: Recent Debates and New Controversies* (London: Routledge, 1998), 71–90, at 81–2.

61 J.G.A. Pocock, *Political Thought and History: Essays on Theory and Method* (Cambridge: Cambridge University Press, 2009), 113. See, however, by the same author, "The Origins of the Study of the Past: A Comparative Approach", *Comparative Studies in Society and History*, 4 (1961–1962), 237; Maurice Mandelbaum, "The History of Ideas, Intellectual History, and the History of Philosophy", *History and Theory*, 5 (1965), 33–66, at 44, 53–4.

our craft in a different way. In my opinion we need a different approach. A new intellectual history that, taking advantage of the interesting methodological debates in the field over almost half a century, definitively takes seriously the ruptures and the abrupt caesuras in concepts and discourses, as well as systemic shifts in political theories and ideologies.

Bibliography

Main Sources

Adams, John, *The Works of John Adams*, ed. Charles Francis Adams, 10 vols. (Boston: Little, Brown and Co., 1850–1856).

Argüelles, Agustín de, *Discurso preliminar a la Constitución de 1812*, ed. Luis Sánchez-Agesta (Madrid, CEPC, 2011).

Colmeiro, Manuel, *De la constitución y del gobierno de los reinos de León y Castilla* (Madrid: Librería de Ángel Calleja, 1855), 2 vols.

Martínez Marina, Francisco, *Discurso sobre el origen de la Monarquía y sobre la naturaleza del gobierno español*, ed. José Antonio Maravall (Madrid: CEPC, 1988).

Sièyes, Emmanuel-Joseph, *Dire de l'abbé Sieyès, sur la question du Veto royal, à la séance du 7 septembre 1789* (Paris: François-Jean Baudouin, 1789).

Main Bibliographical References

Elliott, J.H., "Revolution and Continuity in Early Modern Europe", *Past and Present*, 42 (1969), 35–56.

Fernández Albaladejo, Pablo, *Materia de España: Cultura política e identidad en la España moderna* (Madrid: Marcial Pons, 2007).

Martin Loughlin, *"The Concept of Constituent Power", European Journal of Political Theory*, 13.2 (2014), 218–37.

Martin Loughlin and Neil Walker, eds., *The Paradox of Constitutionalism: Constituent Power and Constitutional Form* (Oxford: Oxford University Press, 2007).

Varela, Joaquín, *La teoría del Estado en los orígenes del constitucionalismo hispánico* (*Las Cortes de Cádiz*) (Madrid: CEC, 1983).

CHAPTER 23

The Dirty Secret of New Beginnings

Founding a Democracy between Nothing and Narration

Mareike Gebhardt

To answer the classical question of how democratic orders should be founded, we can turn to rational concepts economizing the relation between state and citizenship or draw attention to the "non-rational" dimensions of founding. We can investigate the argumentative structure of contracts and treatises or analyze the affects of founding and the stories revolving around beginnings. In the following, I will concentrate on the latter, thereby exploring the constitutional moment's narrative regime and affective atmosphere. My argumentation is guided by the thesis that founding is always violent. Beginnings of political orders are shaped by (illegitimate and illegal) appropriation, occupation, and oppression. Hence, founding is power-laden. To counter the intricate yet tacit power structures of founding, the introduction of checks and balances helps legitimize the violent beginning. However, legitimization does not only work by rationalization—understood here as effectiveness, rationality, and reason. It is also based on establishing a narrative regime that comprises stories, myths, and legends. The narrative regime affectively unites the many in a community. It renders them "one" and legitimates the founding's violence.[1] Founding produces a *dirty secret* by and through which the violent beginning is narratively legitimized as a necessary means to end violence.

The chapter proceeds in four steps: I elaborate a theoretical framework drawing from Birgit Sauer's, Sara Ahmed's, and Arlie Russel Hochschild's works on affects and emotion. I combine those approaches with Hannah Arendt's political-theoretical narratology to introduce the concept of *narrative regime* (1). Afterwards, I scrutinize the phantasmagoric structures of the founding's narrative regime showing how a paradoxical entanglement of absence and presence works through the *dirty secret* of founding. In reference to Jacques Derrida's deconstruction, I discuss the Declaration of Independence, both the constitutional text from 1776 and John Trumbull's painting from 1819, located in

1 Benedict Anderson, *Imagined Communities: Reflections on the Origin and Spread of Nationalism* [1983] (London and New York: Verso, 2006).

 | DOI:10.1163/9789004549159_025

the Capitol's Rotunda in Washington D.C. (2).[2] Besides the paradox of absence/presence, the power-laden mechanism of in- and exclusion works within the *dirty* secret as well. I analyze it through a critical reading of Emma Lazarus's sonnet, *The New Colossus* (1883), engraved on the Statue of Liberty's pedestal.[3] I understand the poem as a *melting pot* story of immigration and arrival in which different "ingredients" come together to build a new, homogeneous mass. The poem, thus, entails an assimilationist vision of how to become *one* (3). I close the paper by arguing that storytelling can be both a regressive form of hegemony and a political act of emancipation that scrutinizes how hi/stories are told, depicted, and commemorated (4–5).

1 Narrative Regimes and Democratic Un-/Reasoning

The founding of a democratic community is violent. It is driven by narcissistic and egocentric affective forces such as vanity and ignorance. It works through an (illegitimate) submission of the "feeble", the appropriation of land, and socio-political marginalization. Therefore, founding needs to be checked regularly for a power play at work. Plausibility checks confirm the necessity of foundational violence in retrospect because a democratic community sprang from it. The retrospective legitimization does not only work by rationalization understood as effectiveness and reasoning. Instead, it needs to be reinforced by a "good" story; a good story tells about the triumphant glory of founding. A narration, thus, checks and validates the violence of the first founding rationally and affectively.

Retrospective narrative legitimization works and operates through affects understood as "political and cultural, i.e., symbolically coded and socially constructed patterns of perception and action". Moreover, "the specific order of affect and politics [...] within the political realm can be considered the result

---

2 Jacques Derrida, "Declarations of Independence", *New Political Science*, 15 (1986), 7–15; John Trumbull, "Declaration of Independence" (1818), *Architect of the Capitol*. Accessed May 5, 2018. https://www.aoc.gov/art/historic-rotunda-paintings/declaration-independence. See also Javier Fernández Sebastián's chapter in this volume.

3 "Statue of Liberty", Encyclopædia Britannica Online. Accessed May 5, 2018. https://www.britannica.com/topic/Statue-of-Liberty. Statue Of Liberty, National Monument New York, National Park Service. Accessed May 7, 2018. https://www.nps.gov/media/photo/gallery.htm?id=FB826465-155D-451F-6719C52FE2FAC2FE. The Colonial Williamsburg Foundation. Accessed May 5, 2018. https://www.history.org/foundation/journal/Winter11/painting/.

of a historically formed 'politics of feeling'".[4] By interrelating different stories, a supposedly coherent history is woven, whose tropes, images, and representations circulate through decades, centuries, and generations. This web of narrations affectively forms a unity and creates a sense of belonging.

Ahmed's concept of "affective economy" captures the dissemination of affects through discourse. In affective economies, "emotions *do things*, and [...] align individuals with communities—or bodily space with social space [...]". Ahmed understands affects not as "psychological dispositions" possessed by individuals but as products of discursive operation. Ahmed outlines an "economic model" of affects that "works to bind subjects together [...]".[5] Ahmed combines a Marxian model of economic exchange with a Foucauldian understanding of discourse to show how affects are produced, disseminated, and amplified in trans-generational discursive operations to which the telling of stories belongs.[6] Much like Sauer's, Ahmed's model of affects shows that feelings are politically, socially, and culturally produced and therefore determine how individuals perceive and evaluate feelings.

While both Sauer and Ahmed concentrate on the analysis of gender formation and affect production towards "the Other", I focus on the affective formation of stories; however, I argue that it works similarly: Stories are discursively produced and exchanged, and thus constitute a circulatory narrative economy. Stories are shaped, coded, and reproduced in tropes and imaginations by society, politics, and culture; they are inherited and passed on from one generation to another. They circulate over time and space, reinforcing, consolidating, and reiterating their social meaning and political relevance. I refer to these sociopolitical processes and structures as a *narrative regime* in which (tacit) knowledges about the "right", proper, and acceptable use of feelings are generated, passed on, and put into practice, such as storytelling and "feeling rules".[7]

4 Birgit Sauer, "'Bringing emotions back in': Gefühle als Regierungstechnik: Geschlechter- und demokratietheoretische Überlegungen", in Claudia Jarzebowski and Anne Kwaschik, eds., *Performing Emotions: Interdisziplinäre Perspektiven auf das Verhältnis von Politik und Emotion in der Frühen Neuzeit und in der Moderne*, edited (Göttingen: V&R unipress, 2013), 264; Brigitte Bargetz and Birgit Sauer, "Der affective turn: Das Gefühlsdispositiv und die Trennung von öffentlich und privat", *Femina Politica*, 24.1 (2015), 93–102. All translations from German to English by the author. I use the term affect for feelings and sentiments produced via discursive operations. I avoid the notion of emotionality as it is inscribed in a gender asymmetry where masculinity equals rationality/ reason/ politics, while femininity equals emotion/ irrationality/ privacy.

5 Sara Ahmed, "Affective Economy", *Social Text*, 79, 22.2 (Summer 2004), 119, original italics.

6 Ahmed, *ibidem*, 120ff.

7 Mareike Gebhardt, "The Populist Moment: Affective Orders, Protest, and Politics of Belonging", *Distinktion* 22.2 (2019): DOI: 10.1080/1600910X.2019.1653346, 3.

To scrutinize the inner workings of a narrative regime, I refer to Arlie Russel Hochschild's sociological works on emotions and feelings. In her study of the US-American far-right, Hochschild introduces the concept of "deep stories" that are re-/told to create social cohesion within a narrowly, often racist, and racially defined community. Hochschild outlines how deep stories imagine a threatening "Outside" or "Other" to guarantee social cohesion. As in Ahmed's economic model of affect, the deep story and its adjacent affects stick people together: social coherence is gained by affective adherence. Othering builds on and further develops the narrative regime to strengthen a community by establishing and reaffirming a (narrative-affective) bulwark of "own-ness" and belonging. Social boundaries and cultural borders are neatly drawn by sealing the community off from a threatening Other/Outside.

To work as a "coherent" deep story—at least from the community's perspective—the constitutional moment's narrative regime weaves an intricate fabric of sociopolitical cohesion that, paranoidly, dwells on phantasies of unity and purity. Many convincing stories transform into an intra- and intergenerational persuasive narrative regime that allows the community to sustain and thrive. "Proper" stories tell coherent, simplistic tales of fortitude, victory, and liberation that ooze through the collective memory to stabilize a narrative regime. Affectively and narratively, the deep story binds together that which beforehand did not stick together. Hochschild captures the character of a narrative regime as a "feels-as-if story": Within a narrative regime, society focuses on "the story feelings tell, in the language of symbols. It removes judgment. It removes fact. It tells us how things feel [...]".[8]

The more consistent the story about the new beginning is told and affirmed through scriptures, documents, monuments, and tales, the "deeper" it is inscribed into the collective memory that tells the new beginning as glorious. And the more glorious the beginning is perceived, the more legitimate the founding's violence seems. After the violence is putatively legitimized in such a way, it is thus forgotten as violence. Instead, it transforms and becomes re-inscribed into the community's collective memory as triumph and victory. Within this transformative procedure, a dirty secret is produced working within the founding moment. Its dirtiness stems from the discrepancy between what happened—which nobody can know after the narrative regime has been established—and what is told. While without a narrative regime, a plurality of different, sometimes contradictory, sometimes complementary, stories can be

8 Arlie Russel Hochschild, *Strangers in their Own Land: Anger and Mourning on the American Right* (New York / London: The New Press, 2016), 221ff, 135.

equitably told. Once the narrative regime is set into motion, there can only be one "true" storyline. Consequently, the narrative regime becomes a "regime of truth".[9] Different stories still might exist, but they need to "make sense": and align with the hegemonic storyline.

The narrative regime camouflages the founding moment's violence. It is legitimized *after* it has been transformed into a *public* story that interprets the usage of violence as a necessary means to end the violence once and for all. Bonnie Honig describes this transformative procedure in her critique of Arendt's depiction of the American Revolution as truly political and, therefore, emancipatory. Her critique can be applied to the broader framework of the narrative regime woven around the violent beginning of a community:

> Arendt's fable [...] is meant to define and enable new horizons of possibility. It presents itself as a recovery of the origins and heroes of the republic, as an act of memory and dereification meant to recapture and thereby reenable the revolutionary spirit that is the vitality of republican politics. [...] Arendt claims that this fable is the product of her commitment to memory, to the recovery of the American revolutionary spirit; but it *invents* that spirit. It claims to be a dereification, a recovery of the origins; but *it erases the violence and the ambiguity that marked the original act of founding*. And the effect of Arendt's fable is the same as that of all legitimating fables: to *prohibit further inquiry into the origins of the system* and to protect its center of illegitimacy from the scrutiny of prying eyes.[10]

According to Honig, narrative legitimation renders the founding's violence ethically plausible. It invents a particular "spirit"—an affective atmosphere—that transforms the a-democratic violence of the new beginning to a comprehensive and intelligible (hi-)story of democratic beginnings. Since the founding is accompanied by a good story, a "fable", as Honig puts it, the violent acts of founding turn into narratives of liberation: liberation from oppression and evil by the revolutionary "spirit" and liberating "heroes" fighting the "barbaric" and "uncivilized" communities of othered populations. Therefore, hegemonic storytelling revolves around a philosophy of ethical violence that dwells on

9 Stuart Hall, "The West and the Rest: Discourse and Power", in David Morley, ed., *Essential Essays*, vol. 2 (Durham: Duke University Press, 2018), 163.

10 Bonnie Honig, "Declarations of Independence: Arendt and Derrida on the Problem of Founding a Republic", *The American Political Science Review*, 85.1 (1991), 107, my italics. Accessed December, 13 2017. http://www.jstor.org/stable/1962880.

the idea that the founding's violence will have been legitimate because it will have ended all other forms of violence *once and for all*. Rational reasoning shall persuade the community with a better argument. However, feelings and sentiments about the founding's glory, a particular "spirit", must be added to affectively support and reinforce the "rationality" of the first beginning's violence. Accordingly, the violent first act is narratively modified into a story of good and right that tells about a heroic moment in which the dark, desperate, improper, and unorderly days have been defeated.

2 The Paradoxical Entanglement of Absence and Presence

Once a community is established, two processes become crucial to its unification: First, convincing and consistent stories about the necessity of violence must be created and passed on from one generation to another. The narrative regime weaves those stories together to render them convincing and sacrosanct. It becomes impenetrable and immune to critique or scrutiny. Second, the narrative regime needs material underpinning to let the story become more tangible and thus "true". Not only does someone need to tell the story about the victorious first founding, but scripts, statues, and scriptures must historiographically document the first founding. To render the founding and its triumph "real", constitutions, declarations, paintings, and things build a material political culture where hopes, dreams, and aspirations become tangible. The material culture not only represents or symbolizes the first founding but *is* the first founding. Hence, it adds to the truthfulness and trustworthiness of the narrative regime. It stabilizes the stories told and renders them thus less precarious. In turn, the narrative regime's stability and material representations counterbalance feelings of contingency, uncertainty, and insecurity polities face.

Material representations of the narrative regime's commemorative cultural production are drawings, reliefs, and sculptures depicting the founding and the foundational myths invented around it. Among the U.S. material landscapes of memory are eight large oil paintings telling the story of becoming "America": *The Baptism of Pocahontas* by John Chapman (1837), for instance, tells the hegemonic, sentimental, and patriarchal story of "transatlantic love".[11] It shows how the Europeans bring "peace" and "civilization" to the

11 Heike Paul, *The Myths that Made America: An Introduction to American Studies* (Bielefeld: transcript, 2014), 89–126, 43–78.

"barbaric" and "primitive" tribes of the indigenous population. *The Landing of Columbus* by John Vanderlyn (1836/1837) shows the "discovery" of "America" by Christopher Columbus in 1492. The picture breathes the romantic yet violent Eurocentrism neatly captured in John Locke's phrase, "In the Beginning, All the World Was America".[12] Here, we can witness how "Europe" transfers its hegemonic power over the Atlantic, where "Europe" begins anew: seemingly pure and improved. The stories of the "old" and the "new world" merge, claiming the Global North as the normative center for centuries. Accordingly, these paintings echo[13] a hegemonic discourse on "the West and the Rest" about the glorious becoming of a white, male, Christian "America" as opposed to the strange, unholy rituals of those "savage" tribes populating the continent before it became "America".[14] The narrative regime provides the stories of the "American" nation-building with central motifs, tropes, and protagonists that join in to tell tales of overcoming one's demons, fighting barbarism and savagery, and eventually winning the (Euro-Christian) battle against the forces of (unholy) evil. However, the other sides of these storylines entail fantasies of "white" supremacy, misogyny, patriarchy, and racism, of Christian prevalence over "uncivilized" and "unholy" tribes and rituals. They are rarely told as blatantly and boldly as the hegemonic stories.

Consequently, they became (almost) forgotten while being buried deep down by the epistemic violence of the U.S.'s narrative archives. The othered side of the archive, the stories of refusal and the repertoire of protest, only slowly and recently become told and unearthed by othered populations, de-, and postcolonial scholars, and research in Indigenous Studies.[15] However, it is essential to emphasize that othered populations always tell their own stories.

---

12 Hall "The West and the Rest", 172.

13 Besides the *Declaration of Independence* there are another three "revolutionary period scenes" that were commissioned by Congress from John Trumbull in 1817 and placed between 1819 and 1824: *Surrender of General Burgoyne, Surrender of Lord Cornwallis* and *General George Washington Resigning his Commission.* Another four scenes of "early exploration"—including *Baptism of Pocahontas* and *Landing of Columbus* —were added between 1840 and 1855: *Discovery of the Mississippi* by William Powell and *Embarkation of the Pilgrims* by Robert Weir; see: https://www.aoc.gov/capitol-buildings/capitol-rotunda.

14 Hall "The West and the Rest".

15 The post- and/or de-colonial thinking and the research of African-American and Indigenous Studies resonates in recent protests against the unchallenged material culture and celebrations of Civil War Heroes and Memorials, the institutionalized racism in the U.S., but also in the U.K. or South Africa, as well as in the movement *#blacklivesmatter*.

They never ceased telling their stories. Instead, while they kept telling their stories, the hegemonic places, subjects, and realms (almost) never listened.[16]

With the epistemic violence of non- or misrepresentation in mind, I want to turn to the painting *Declaration of Independence* by John Trumbull. In it, John Adams, Roger Sherman, Robert R. Livingston, Thomas Jefferson, and Benjamin Franklin—the so-called Committee of Five—present the *Declaration of Independence* to President John Hancock.[17] The Declaration was introduced in front of the Second Continental Congress in July 1776 at the Independence Hall in Philadelphia.

However, the painting is not historically correct: only 42 of the 56 undersigned are depicted, while 14 are missing. Trumbull also added four men to the painting who did not sign the Declaration: George Clinton, Robert R. Livingston, Thomas Willing, and John Dickinson.[18] The painting invisibilizes the violence and darkness of the first act of founding. Moreover, another issue is kept hidden: before the community, there is no community. At the very moment of the first act, *the* people do not exist (yet). Nowhere in the painting nor the written document does the sociopolitical entity that, according to the text, signed the declaration, is visualized or (re-)present(ed)—the "good people" are missing. The missing of "the people" is paradoxically rendered visible by their absence. Their absence is still very present once you realize that 'the people' do not exist in the very moment of founding. The people's in/existence becomes even more startling when we ask who founded the community, if not "the people". The community is founded by a (privileged, white, and male) group who acts, in Arendt's words, in the spirit of the people. To render visible the people's present absence and thus the violence prevailing within their invisibility, Derrida

16 On the epistemic violence of not-listening and the cruel misinterpretation of othered populations and cultures cf. Bonnie Honig, *A Feminst Theory of Refusal* (Cambridge/London: Harvard University Press, 2021); Linda Zerilli, "Fact-Checking and Truth-Telling in an Age of Alternative Facts", *Le Foucaldien,* 6.1 (2020), 1–22, 15f.; Gayatri Chakravorty Spivak, "Can the Subaltern Speak?", in Cary Nelson and Lawrence Grosberg, eds., *Marxism and the Interpretation of Culture* (Basingstoke: Macmillian Education, 1988).

17 John Adams acted as representative of Massachusetts and became the second US President; Roger Sherman represented Connecticut and was the only person to sign all four of the US state papers: The Continental Association, the Declaration, the Articles of Confederation, and the Constitution; Robert R. Livingston represented the state of New York; Thomas Jefferson, representative of Virginia, became the third US President and Benjamin Franklin, representative of Pennsylvania, is known as one of the most famous of the Founding Fathers and acted as first US Minister to France.

18 For more information: https://www.aoc.gov/art/historic-rotunda-paintings/declaration-independence and https://www.history.org/foundation/journal/Winter11/painting/.

FIGURE 23.1 John Trumbull, *Declaration of Independence* (1819)
SOURCE: HTTPS://WWW.AOC.GOV/ART/HISTORIC-ROTUNDA-PAINTINGS/DECLARATION-INDEPENDENCE

deconstructs the Declaration of Independence written by Thomas Jefferson. Derrida shows, in the words of Honig,

> that in every system (even in practice), whether linguistic, cultural, or political, there is a moment or place that the system cannot account for. Every system is secured by placeholders that are irrevocably, structurally arbitrary and *prelegitimate*. They enable the system but are *illegitimate* from its vantage point.[19]

The paradox of founding consists of foundational illegitimacy that marks the beginning of a process of legitimation. In the constitutional moment of illegitimacy, legitimacy must be *performed* to legitimize illegitimacy by declaring a legitimizing entity present which, however, is not yet existing. Hence, "the people". Neither temporally nor spatially do "the people" exist, even though they "are" the political subjectivity in whose name the community is founded. Representation is put to work as a "placeholder", as Honig writes, to

19 Honig, "Declarations of Independence", 106, my italics.

legitimize the absent presence of the people. In the case of the Declaration of Independence, a group of (privileged white) men meets in a room. They create a space where exclusion and marginalization are already at work. Neither women, children, the poor, people (!) of color, nor the native populations can be seen or even partake in the founding moment.

Consequently, the first act of founding is not only violent and forceful—which one cannot see in the painting at all—but also a hollow and empty yet important ritual telling of a political community that is not yet. The ritual's only goal and meaning are to create an illusion of unity and belonging that is about to be developed. The moment of founding invents the subject in whose name the polity is founded. Only when the polity is declared as existing will the founding event become meaningful.

The establishment of a people alone is not secure enough, however. Since it keeps being exposed to precarity, injury, and vulnerability, the Declaration of Independence adds a compelling justification—the grace of God. As Jacques de Ville has argued in his analysis of Derrida's deconstruction of the Declaration of Independence:

> The invocation of the people and of God must be understood in the context of the political onto-theology of sovereignty, of the metaphysical desire for presence. By pointing out to the people (of the United States) and ultimately to God, the Declaration seeks to invoke a presence and a ground in order to halt the play of signification. It attempts to ground the Declaration in proper names (with a fixed meaning and referent) outside of the act of language and writing which the Declaration is, unsoiled by the common.[20]

To de Ville, the declaration and its signatories become different versions of placeholders of the not yet existing community, but it calls for a higher authority. Divine sovereignty is located beyond legitimation and satisfies the necessity for someone or something to be *there* to justify the founding ("the metaphysical desire for presence"). It serves a democratic state's need for robust sovereignty and unchallenged authority and starts to breathe legitimacy accordingly. Besides scrutinizing the exclusionary mechanism of the Declaration's Gentlemen's Club, which will go on to be reproduced in different versions and historical stages of the U.S. repeatedly, we can conclude that

---

20 Jacques de Ville, "Sovereignty without sovereignty: Derrida's Declarations of Independence", *Law and Critique*, 19 (2008), 87–114.

before a community is founded by and in the act of declaration, "the people" are nowhere to be found. However, they are invented as the declaring subject of the constitution. The founding will always be burdened with this paradox. As this paradox is rendered invisible by the founding's cultural productions, the othered population's exposure to injury and suffering is camouflaged by the narrative regime—among other regimes such as the law—creating the illusion of protection, safety, and security.

Derrida has shown this paradox in his deconstruction of the Declaration of Independence—not the painting but the written document itself. I want to summarize Derrida's thought shortly since it trenchantly illustrates the paradox of present absence in the act of signing a declaration. Derrida asks: "[*W*]*ho signs, and with what so-called proper name, the declarative act which founds an institution?*".[21] Derrida considers a few options to answer the question and analyzes them one by one: First, he asks if Thomas Jefferson, as the "draftsman" of the Declaration of Independence, could be considered the (legitimate) signatory of the document. Jefferson represents the representatives delegated to him—and the Committee of Five—the task of drawing up what they knew *they* wanted to say. However, like a secretary, Jefferson was not responsible for "*writing*" but only for "*drawing up*" the document, Derrida argues. He concludes that Jefferson cannot be considered the ("proper") signatory of the Declaration of Independence. Second, Derrida asks whether the representatives are the legitimate signatories of the Declaration but negates this. He proposes that they might be those who signed it "by right", but as in law, this right was only established after the founding. It was still invalid at the very moment of signing. Moreover, the representatives did not sign in their name but in another one's name. Thus, they cannot be considered the proper signatories. Derrida, third, asks about the group of people in whose name the representatives sign the declaration. It follows that by right, the signatory is *the people*; more precisely, the "good people". Derrida draws our attention to this "decisive detail because it guarantees the value of the intention and of the signature" and concludes:

> But this people does not exist. They do *not* exist as an entity, it does *not* exist, *before* this declaration, not *as such*. It gives birth to itself, as free and independent subject, as possible signer, this can hold only in the act of

21 Derrida,"Declarations of Independence", 8, original italics. Speaking in 1976 at the University of Virginia in Charlottesville, Derrida prefaced a lecture on Nietzsche with some remarks on the American Declaration of Independence at its bicentennial celebrations. In the face of far-right protests against the de-installation of the equestrian statue of Robert E. Lee in Charlottesville, Derrida's lecture is even more worth re-reading.

> signature. The signature events the signer. This signer can only authorize him- or herself to sign once he or she has come to the end […], if one can say this, of his or her own signature, in a sort of fabulous retroactivity.[22]

The retroactivity is "fabulous" because it invents and imagines an entity that does not yet exist. However, the ones who declare independence need to pretend the existence of this same entity. Without it, there is no proper signatory and, hence, no legitimate first act of founding. Therefore, it is always only in retrospect that "the people" signed the declaration. We can already witness the rendering present of someone absent and a mechanism in and through which inclusion, exclusion, and dis/closure interlock.

Fourth and last, Derrida outlines that when the "good people" of 'America' "sign" the declaration, they invent a signing identity for themselves. They sign in the name of the "laws of nature" and "in the name of God". They pose their institutional laws on the foundation of natural law, and since God is deemed the creator of nature, it is in God's name that the declaration is signed. Derrida ends his four-fold deconstruction on the question of who signed the Declaration of Independence:

> One can understand this Declaration as a vibrant act of faith, as a hypocrisy indispensable to a politico-military-economic, etc. coup of force, or, more simply, more economically, as the analytic and consequential deployment of a tautology: for this Declaration to have a meaning *and* an effect, there must be a last instance. God is the name, the best one, for this last instance and this ultimate signature. Not only the best one in a determined context (such and such a nation, such and such a religion, etc.), but the name of the best name in general. Now, this (best) name also *ought to be* a proper name. God is the best proper name, the proper name best […]. One could not replace 'God' by 'the best proper name' […]. Jefferson knew it.[23]

At the end of Derrida's deconstruction, "God" is the "proper" signatory of the Declaration of Independence, which makes it, paradoxically, a declaration of dependence. It denotes a dependence upon a higher authority, a "last instance", as Derrida said, to legitimize the founding of a (supposedly secular) state.

---

22 Derrida, *ibidem*.

23 Derrida, *ibidem*, 8–12, original italics.

We can even radicalize Derrida's conclusion when focusing on the relationship between founding and belonging. To become a member of a particular polity rests on the will of this higher authority because "the people" do not exist in the constitutional moment. However, a polity can only come into being if its existence is declared and witnessed. Consequently, only in retrospect, the constitutional moment produces *the people*. Their absence in the founding moment is compensated by the presence of a higher authority, such as the "noble men" (!), a god, or the end of tyranny. Only by performing and uttering a supposedly democratic entity are "the people"—the constitutional moment and its "people"—produced. Hence, the constitutional moment is always structured by a paradox of presence and absence. "Someone" needs to symbolically step in the people's place to legitimize the first act of founding. And this legitimizing democratic entity is most commonly the figurative and narrative construction of "the people".

In sum: To legitimize the founding's violence, it is not only necessary to refer to the putative democratic unity established within the constitutional moment ("the people"). Rather, an a-democratic element, God's irrevocable, unbreakable, and unchallengeable authority, secures the founding and assures its legitimacy. Founding thus oscillates between a-democratic and democratic moments. The shifting, however, does not necessarily denote flaws in the texture of democracy but demarcates the foundational necessity in the praxis of democracy. However, the deconstruction of the a-democratic foundational moment guarantees the democratic reiteration of the polity founded on the grounds of a-democracy. Only the inscription of "the other" within a system of signification prevents polities from falling into the abyss of totalitarianism and metaphysics.[24] Derrida does not legitimatize the violence of the constitutional moment. Instead, he discloses the violence inherent in a democracy's founding in a brutal gesture of openness. He drags the violence into the light where everyone can see the dark side of democracy: its dirty secret. Only by facing it, in permanently deconstructing the dirty secret, a democratic polity can hope to become more democratic.

24 Like, for instance, Rousseau did. As de Ville puts it in his reading of Derrida: "Representation is viewed by Rousseau and the whole of metaphysics [...] as the loss of an original presence, the loss of the self-presence of sovereignty. Representation is in other words evil, an accident, a catastrophe that occurs to what is good, to a pure and self-sufficient origin. Rousseau consequently desires the disappearance of representation [...]". For more information on Rousseau's political philosophy and Derrida's reading of Rousseau, see Magdalena Scherl, *Ersehnte Einheit, unheilbare Spaltung: Geschlechterordnung und Republik bei Rousseau* (Bielefeld: transcript, 2016).

3 The Mechanism of In-and Exclusion

To become a body politic, both in- and exclusion are necessary. This mechanism determines the criteria of belonging to unify the many to an "us" and specifies the terms, conditions, and criteria of (non-)belonging. In the Declaration, peoples and populations are unified not only as "a people" but as "one nation"—additionally, "under God". The foundational moment adheres to nationalistic identity politics that work on and by racist, heteronormative, and sexist mechanisms of in- and exclusion: While persons meeting the criteria are included and become "one", all those considered others, alien or strange, are excluded. This in- and exclusion materialize in gates, fences, and walls—especially in times of crisis and waning (national) sovereignty.[25]

Thinking in- and exclusion not as a binary distinction but as a transgressive threshold, I emphasize the exclusionary character of borders and boundaries of belonging *and* its inclusionary character. Consequently, I do not consider in- and exclusion as two separate mechanisms. Instead, both work as one (unifying) mechanism where one cannot be set in motion without the other and vice versa. In (liberal-)democratic contexts, the intricate and often tacit mechanism of in- and exclusion is overwritten by narrations of (societal) openness, (individual) freedom, and (legal, civic) equality. However, this rhetoric camouflages power play within the mechanism fortified and stabilized by a hegemonic narrative regime.

To illustrate the mechanism of in- and exclusion's intertwinement, I turn to the *melting pot* narrative. This narrative is prevalent, even though challenged by recent politics, especially in the U.S., but has been told in European countries as well (e.g., U.K. and Germany).[26] Western liberal democracies' memorial cultures, sociopolitical landscapes, and legal texts tell stories about the virtues of individual freedom and civic equality that are open "to all". One can witness the narrative's impact and potency when reading the sonnet *The New Colossus* by Emma Lazarus from 1883, engraved on a bronze plaque and mounted inside the Statue of Liberty's pedestal in 1903:[27]

---

25 Wendy Brown, *Walled States, Waning Sovereignty* (New York: Zone Books, 2010), 23ff.

26 I would want to add France as well even though the notion of republicanism is rhetorically much stronger. However, the ideal of republican equality—that erases all differences to the degree of the prohibition of religiously based veiling—is organized quite similarly to the melting pot-narrative.

27 US-American poet Emma Lazarus (1849–1887) wrote the poem to raise money for the Statue of Liberty's pedestal. The poem was a donation to an auction of art and literary works conducted by the Art Loan Fund Exhibition in Aid of the Bartholdi Pedestal Fund for the Statue of Liberty. Lazarus's contribution was solicited by fundraiser William

Not like the brazen giant of Greek fame,
With conquering limbs astride from land to land;
Here at our sea-washed, sunset gates shall stand
A mighty woman with a torch, whose flame.

Is the imprisoned lightning, and her name
Mother of Exiles. From her beacon-hand
Glows world-wide welcome; her mild eyes command
The air-bridged harbor that twin cities frame.

"Keep, ancient lands, your storied pomp!" cries she
With silent lips. "Give me your tired, your poor,
Your huddled masses yearning to breathe free,
The wretched refuse of your teeming shore.

Send these, the homeless, tempest-tost to me,
I lift my lamp beside the golden door!"

The title of the poem and the first two lines refer to the *Colossus of Rhodes*, which was one of the Seven Wonders of antiquity, sometimes described as standing astride the harbor of Rhodes.[28] The "sea-washed, sunset gates" are the

---

Maxwell Evarts. Though Lazarus initially refused to contribute, she was later convinced by Constance Cary Harrison that the statue would be of great significance to immigrants sailing into the harbor. However, the poem was forgotten and played no role at the opening of the statue in 1886. In 1901, Lazarus's friend Georgina Schuyler began an effort to memorialize Lazarus and her poem, which succeeded in 1903 when a plaque bearing the text of the poem was put on the inner wall of the pedestal of the Statue of Liberty. For more information see https://www.britannica.com/topic/Statue-of-Liberty. The poem is still influential in contemporary culture: Paul Auster wrote that *The New Colossus* reinvented the "statue's purpose, turning Liberty into a welcoming mother, a symbol of hope to the outcasts and downtrodden of the world". John T. Cunningham concluded that "the Statue of Liberty was not conceived and sculpted as a symbol of immigration, but it quickly became so as immigrant ships passed under the torch and the shining face, heading toward Ellis Island. However, it was [Lazarus's poem] that permanently stamped on Miss Liberty the role of unofficial greeter of incoming immigrants". Finally, the poem entered politics when it was quoted in John F. Kennedy's book *A Nation of Immigrants* (1958) as well as in 2010 by President Obama advocating immigration policy reforms.

28 The ancient Colossus of Rhodes represented Helios, the sun god, was made by Chares of Lyndus in 305 bce. The Colossus was said to stood beside Mandrákion harbor, even though it is technically impossible that the statue could have straddled the harbor entrance. This popular belief dates back from the Middle Ages. The statue was toppled by an earthquake about 225/226 bce. Hi/story tells us that the fallen Colossus was left in place until 654

mouths of the Hudson and East River west of Brooklyn, and the "imprisoned lightning" refers to the electric light in the torch, which was then a novelty. Moreover, the "air-bridged harbor that twin cities frame" refers to New York Harbor between New York City and Brooklyn consolidated into one urban unit in 1898, 15 years after the poem was written.

Against the interpretation of the Statue of Liberty as welcoming the newly arrived, one could also conclude that the "mighty woman" symbolizes a mechanism of in- and exclusion: She stands at the entrance to a "free land", not indifferent to those arriving, watching, protocolling (controlling?), and selecting those who arrive and those who might enter. The Statue of Liberty might even symbolize the dark side of liberty, while it also represents the hope that even in darkness, there is light. However, it also reminds us that liberty can be used to justify exclusion and privileged entry. Yet, liberty is narratively constructed, at least in "Western" contexts referring to Enlightenment as a universal right. However, those who (want to) come to the U.S. go through an intricate legal procedure conducted by the *United States Citizenship and Immigration Services*.

Moreover, those to arrive at the harbor have already endured pain and were exposed to bodily and psychological injury. A legal and social precarity is added to the physical, mental, emotional, and socioeconomic vulnerability when the "tempest-tost" arrive: They never know if they will truly belong. The "downtrodden" immigrants are asked to adapt to the new society, its rites, rituals, and procedures. At the same time, they do not yet know whether they will be (legally) acknowledged as "rightfully", or in Derrida's words, "properly", belong. Therefore, the Statue of Liberty also works as a symbol for the narrative regime of liberal democracy in which the stories of individual freedom, societal openness, and legal/civic equality often hide the power-laden textures of its narrations. Eventually, the Statue of Liberty decides who meets the criteria of belonging and is, thus, allowed to enter the "harbor" that "the twin cities frame". Hence, the Statue can be viewed as a materialization of liberal democracy's narrative regime.

The poem's voice continues stating that the Statue of Liberty welcomes "world-wide" all exiled, persecuted, and those who had to leave their home country. However, recent migration movements show that those entering New York City, or the U.S. more generally, are no longer the "huddled masses"—referring to the miserable and many immigrants that came to the United States in the late 19th and early 20th century. Instead, current migration flows entail

---

ce, when "Arabian" forces raided Rhodes, had the statue broken up and the bronze sold for scrap.

FIGURES 23.2A AND 23.2B The Colossus of Rhodes and the Statue of Liberty
"COLOSSUS OF RHODES", WOOD ENGRAVING RECONSTRUCTION BY SIDNEY BARCLAY (1875), SOURCE: ENCYCLOPÆDIA BRITANNICA, HTTPS://WWW.BRITANNICA.COM/TOPIC/COLOSSUS-OF-RHODES#/MEDIA/1/501620/32052 [11/7, 2022]
BRITANNICA, T. EDITORS OF ENCYCLOPAEDIA. "STATUE OF LIBERTY". ENCYCLOPEDIA BRITANNICA. HTTPS://WWW.BRITANNICA.COM/TOPIC/STATUE-OF-LIBERTY [11/17 2022]

highly-skilled and well-educated elites who enter with work permits or have been headhunted by the U.S.'s vast corporate industries. In contrast, the contemporary versions of the migratory "huddled masses" no longer arrive—and by no means safely—at the harbor in NYC. Instead, illegalized immigrants starve or die of thirst in the U.S.'s southern borderlands. U.S. immigration patterns have shifted dramatically both geographically and demographically: The precarious immigrants, the undocumented and illegalized, do enter the U.S. mostly at its Southern borders and have endured hunger, thirst, pain, and desperation on their gruesome journeys through (border) wastelands and deserts. When the contemporary *huddled masses*—often Latin American women in search of employment, mainly in the low-wage industries, such as cleaning or care, to support their families at home—finally arrive in what they consider a secure country, they do no longer "breathe free" at the "teeming shore". Instead, they are exhausted and traumatized. After their arrival, they are forced into invisible spaces and (no) contact zones, such as refugee camps and detention centers. They are processed, often several times, through the U.S. deportation machinery.

Moreover, they are exposed to poor housing conditions, low-wage labor so that only several full-time jobs can roughly provide enough money, and a precarious, illegalized legal state that renders them deportable. Contemporary immigrants are illegalized, rendered invisible, and unheard. The grand U.S. narrative of an open and free society where diverse ethnic and cultural communities come and live together is no longer told. The melting pot no longer, if it ever did, holds its promises of wealth and happiness—instead, new (or old) stories about walls (re-)surface.

The poem by Emma Lazarus is not to blame for the U.S. migration politics, of course. However, it stabilizes the narrative regime. With Derrida, I read it as a "fabulous" story: a phantasy that materializes in the pedestal's engravings or constitutions. It is also part of the material landscapes, the symbolic political cultures, the juridico-political orders, and the collective memory of the U.S. and most Western democracies. The paradoxical entanglement of absence and presence prevails, while an arbitrary mechanism of in- and exclusion is tacitly and invisibly reproduced. Both—absent presence and inclusion/exclusion—demarcate hermetic and violent processes of closure and contingent standards of entry. Consequently, Lazarus' poem tells the story of the *melting pot* as a celebration of an assimilationist paradigm where the many become one under suspicious "democratic" conditions: *e pluribus unum*?!

4 Hegemonic Storytelling and Pearl-Diving

In my reading—and there are, of course, other readings—Lazarus's poem illustrates the power-laden mechanisms of the narrative regime of liberal democracy while leaving it unchallenged. In contrast, Derrida reveals the "dirty secret" of founding in his deconstruction of the Declaration of Independence. The secret, as well as the poem, deploy affects of security and narratives of safety: the Declaration for "the people" and the poem for those who want to become part of "the people". By telling a great story about the constitutional moment, both help to forget the founding's violence—like in Nietzsche's story of the "clever animal" in *On Truth and Lie in an Extra-Moral Sense*. Nietzsche shows how humanity invented and constructed a world and words around it but forgot about their own powerful creative and imaginative act. In the end, humans, Nietzsche calls them clever animals, praise and worship a fabulated higher authority, God, for their creation. The pattern of hidden or forgotten knowledge and the power structures working within the production of knowledge, as well as the people's ignorance, are demonstrated in Nietzsche's fable, which manifests in the constitutional moment: in its retrospective depictions, representations, and symbols, as well as in its narrations, poems, and imaginaries.[29]

Referring to Derrida's deconstruction, I identified two mechanisms that work within the constitutional moment: a mechanism of presence/absence accompanied by a mechanism of in-/exclusion. Both render a people present that did not exist before the constitutional moment. They push the violent character of the founding to a latent status where it is invisible, if not vanished. Instead, the glorious constitutional moment is visualized and materialized by cartas, declarations, and constitutions, as well as by paintings, statues, memorials, and buildings that celebrate the constitutional moment since it (putatively) ended all violence. All these artifacts, speech acts, and discourse operations contribute to a memorial culture that attests to and commemorates how the polity became itself—how "nothing" became "we, the people". The inclusion is celebrated, while the exclusion is forgotten. The memorial culture develops ignorance and fosters forgetfulness towards those *already there* before the constitutional moment—*as if* there was nothing and nobody. However, other communities have been denigrated and discriminated against because they are interpreted as "tribal", "primitive", "barbaric" and thus (worth) "nothing". Within this normative process of colonial-imperialist and orientalist oppression, a pattern of hegemonic storytelling becomes apparent: The transformation of the first act of violence into a glorious and triumphant moment of founding not only renders the structures that existed beforehand invisible but demotes them. In its degradation, the "before" becomes nothing and can be forgotten and lost. Still, "the before" somehow prevails and haunts the archive of hegemonic storytelling.[30]

Like Arendt's narratology, in counter-hegemonic storytelling, the "before" is not lost (forever) but sinks to the bottom of the sea where the storyteller can salvage, rescue, and recover long-lost stories. Therefore, Arendt calls storytelling an act of "pearl-diving", which she valued as a profoundly political act. She dedicated it to her friend Walter Benjamin whom she considered one of the most virtuoso pearl divers. Arendt's oceanic storytelling finds forgotten, maybe

29 Friedrich Nietzsche, "On Truth and Lie in an Extra-Moral Sense" (1896). Accessed April, 28 2018. https://www.kth.se/social/files/5804ca7ff276547f5c83a592/On%20truth%20and%20lie%20in%20an%20extra-moral%20sense.pdf.

30 Honig, *A Feminst Theory of Refusal*, 97f.

sedimented, stories to (re-)tell them. It is the task of the storyteller to politicize the archive: to contest its archival tactics and knowledge orders. *Political* storytellers dive into the narrative sediments at the bottom of the sea to retrieve the "treasures" lost in narrative regimes.[31]

Following Arendt, it becomes clear that storytellers can be the critics who uncomfortably burst into the public realm telling stories nobody has heard before, often exposed to ridicule or worse. In contrast to Arendt, they can also be the apologists telling hegemonic storylines and thereby consolidating dominant narrative regimes—a version of hegemonic storytelling, one must add, that Arendt herself often clung to in her work.[32] Those two versions of storytelling echo Derrida's deconstruction of the archive as a place of power, while he thoroughly unearths the power play within archival practices. Nevertheless, both authors believe that storytelling must be considered a political act. If done from a *critical* position, storytelling is a fragile, challenging, even risky, and sometimes life-threatening political endeavor that renders narrators vulnerable. Those concerned with the implicit, the absent, forgotten, invisible, and unheard in the narrative regime are prone to violence and oppressive mechanisms. Storytelling, therefore, can be a critical intervention in systems of power or the forerunner of hegemonic knowledge production and circulation.

5 Never Only Listen to One Single Story[33]—Concluding Remarks

As we have seen, the mechanism of absence and presence is twofold paradoxical: First, it renders visible a community that is not yet existing and thus absent; second, it renders othered communities and their stories invisible, even though they are present and told. When integrated into a coherent narrative regime, these paradoxes stabilize nationalist and racialized politics of

31 Hannah Arendt, "Walter Benjamin" [1968], in Ursula Ludz, ed., *Menschen in finstern Zeiten* (Munich: Piper, 2012), 244–58 (my translation). Arendt's essay was published in English in *The New Yorker*, October 19, 1968, as well as in *Men in Dark Times* (1968, Harcourt Brace); since the essay was translated, modified, and updated several times I refer to the German version. More on Arendt's storytelling cf. Mareike Gebhardt, "Politische Pluralität und philosophischer Wahrheitsanspruch. Hannah Arendt, Jürgen Habermas und Richard Rorty zwischen Kommunikation und Narrativität", in Wilhelm Hofmann, Judith Renner, and Katja Teich, eds., *Narrative Formen der Politik* (Wiesbaden: VS, 2014), 236ff.

32 Honig, *A Feminst Theory of Refusal*, 72–100.

33 Chimamanda Ngozi Adichie, "The Danger of a Single Story" (2009, TED Global). Accessed November 26, 2021. https://www.ted.com/talks/chimamanda_ngozi_adichie_the_danger_of_a_single_story/transcript.

belonging that help forget the constitutional moment's violence. A narrative principle is at work that, reversing Arendt's concept, can be described as anti-pearl diving: Whereas Arendt outlines how storytelling salvages the lost (counter-hegemonic) narrative treasures that plunged to the bottom of the archival ocean, the 'dirty secret' of the *deep story*—that it is built on violence and a phantasmagoric notion of community—must not be recovered by storytelling. Instead, it must be buried within a (hegemonic) narrative regime that decides which stories are being told and heard.

Moreover, the fantasies about the founding's triumphant moment are constantly retold to make the founding's glorious story "true" and "real". The multitude of stories about the first founding is thus transformed into a narrative regime. It serves as a basis for forming identity and belonging. Over time, the narration about the nation's first founding becomes a myth and is commemorated in specific rituals, symbols, and material cultures. Those symbolic representations make for a powerful and robust regime of hegemonic storytelling stabilizing political systems and societal formations. In contemporary sociopolitical landscapes, decreasing feelings of belonging and affective states of loss resurface: eroding voting loyalties, changing political and social adherences, the diversification of ethnicity and genders, or the individualizing effects of late capitalism erode the power of co- and adherence of the narrative regime.

Consequently, it needs to deepen the already deep story of the founding and, thus, its dark side of exclusion. When a narrative regime's strength and power wane in times of change, persons, populations, and systems hold even more firmly on to it, defending what they believe to be "true". As Hochschild has shown, a *deep story* becomes even more critical to the social cohesion of communities when they are challenged or under change. Since democratic systems cannot refer to the bodies of kings and queens, nor to a higher divine authority, to symbolize and celebrate unity and belonging, the symbolic and narrative representations become crucial to the system's preservation. Instead of a royal body, democracy needs symbols and stories building up and stabilizing the community's identity —as you can see in the Rotunda of the Capitol in Washington D.C., in poems like *The New Colossus* or scriptures such as the Declaration of Independence.

Despite its stories of individual freedom, legal equality, and societal openness, liberal democracies develop mechanisms of closure and power-laden standards of entry. Consequently, from the historiographical deconstruction of a declaration of independence and the critical reading of a sonnet, one can point to the pitfalls of contemporary anti-pearl diving politics regarding migration, borders, and citizenship. In times of change and overwhelming complexities, the narrative construction of "own-ness"—as phantasmagoric it may be—shall fight putative threats from the Outside and the Othered. Those affective atmospheres of mistrust and menace shall stabilize the narrative regime. They unleash hatred, anger, and fear towards "foreigners", "strangers", and "aliens" to foster the polity's persistence and perseverance. The narrative regime's role in understanding voting behavior, political partisanship, and social adherences that overwhelm democratic storytelling cannot be underestimated. What is even more critical, thus, is the radical democratization of storytelling by the multiplication of stories not just told but listened to.

Bibliography

Main Sources

Ahmed, Sara, "Affective Economy", *Social Text* 79, 22.2 (Summer 2004), 117–139.

Arendt, Hannah, "Walter Benjamin" [1968], in Ursula Ludz, ed., *Menschen in finsteren Zeiten* (Munich: Piper, 2012), 244–58.

Derrida, Jacques, "Declarations of Independence", *New Political Science*, 15 (1986), 7–15.

Honig, Bonnie, "Declarations of Independence: Arendt and Derrida on the Problem of Founding a Republic", *The American Political Science Review*, 85.1 (1991), 97–113.

Ville, Jacques de, "Sovereignty without sovereignty: Derrida's Declarations of Independence", *Law and Critique*, 19 (2008), 87–114.

Main Bibliographical References

Gebhardt, Mareike, "The Populist Moment: Affective Orders, Protest, and Politics of Belonging", *Distinktion*, 22.2 (2019): DOI: 10.1080/1600910X.2019.1653346.

Hall, Stuart, "The West and the Rest: Discourse and Power [1992]", in David Morley, ed., *Essential Essays*, vol. 2: *Identity and Diaspora* (Durham: Duke University Press, 2018), 141–184.

Hochschild, Arlie Russel, *Strangers in their Own Land: Anger and Mourning on the American Right* (New York/London: The New Press, 2016).

Honig, Bonnie, *A Feminist Theory of Refusal* (Cambridge/London: Harvard University Press, 2021).

Paul, Heike, *The Myths that Made America: An Introduction to American Studies* (Bielefeld: transcript, 2014).

Index

Printed in the United States
by Baker & Taylor Publisher Services